EXPORT/IMPORT PROCEDURES AND DOCUMENTATION

FOURTH EDITION

EXPORT/IMPORT PROCEDURES AND DOCUMENTATION

FOURTH EDITION

THOMAS E. JOHNSON

AMACOM
American Management Association
New York • Atlanta • Brussels • Buenos Aires • Chicago • London • Mexico City
San Francisco • Shanghai • Tokyo • Toronto • Washington, D.C.

Special discounts on bulk quantities of AMACOM books are available to corporations, professional associations, and other organizations. For details, contact Special Sales Department, AMACOM, a division of American Management Association, 1601 Broadway, New York, NY 10019.
Tel.: 212-903-8316. Fax: 212-903-8083.
Web site: www.amacombooks.org

Library of Congress Cataloging-in-Publication Data

Johnson, Thomas E., 1948–
Export/import procedures and documentation / Thomas E. Johnson. — 4th ed.
p. cm.
Includes index.
ISBN 0-8144-0734-X (hardbound)
1. Export marketing—United States. 2. Exports—United States—Forms. 3. Imports—United States—Forms. 4. Foreign trade regulation. 5. International trade. I. Title.

HF1416.5.J64 2002
658.8′48—dc21 2002023610

Printing number

10 9 8 7 6 5 4

Contents

List of Figures xiii

Foreword by Eugene J. Schreiber xvii

Preface xix

Acknowledgments xxi

Part I
Organizing for Export and Import Operations 1

Chapter 1. Organizing for Export and Import Operations 3

- *A. Export Department* 3
- *B. Import Department* 4
- *C. Combined Export and Import Departments* 4
- *D. Manuals of Procedures and Documentation* 8
- *E. Record-Keeping Compliance* 9
- *F. Software* 13
- *G. Federal, State, International, and Foreign Law* 14

Part II
Exporting: Procedures and Documentation 15

Chapter 2. Exporting: Preliminary Considerations 17

- *A. Products* 17
- *B. Volume* 18
- *C. Country Market and Product Competitiveness Research* 18
- *D. Identification of Customers: End Users, Distributors, and Sales Agents* 18
- *E. Compliance With Foreign Law* 19
  - *1. Industry Standards* 20
  - *2. Foreign Customs Laws* 20
  - *3. Government Contracting* 21
  - *4. Buy American Equivalent Laws* 21
  - *5. Exchange Controls and Import Licenses* 22

6. Value-Added Taxes 22
7. Specialized Laws 22

F. Export Controls and Licenses 22
G. Patent, Trademark, and Copyright Registrations and Infringements 23
H. Confidentiality and Non-Disclosures Agreements 23
I. Antiboycott Compliance 24
J. Employee Sales Visits to Foreign Countries—Immigration and Customs Compliance 24
K. Utilization of Freight Forwarders and Foreign Customs Brokers 28
L. Export Packing and Labeling (Hazardous Materials) 30
M. Terms of Sale 32
N. Consignments 36
O. Leases 36
P. Marine and Air Casualty Insurance 37
Q. Methods of Transportation; Booking Transportation 38
R. Country of Origin Marking 45
S. Foreign Warehousing and Free Trade Zones 45
T. Export Financing and Payment Insurance 45
U. Tax Incentives 46
V. Export Trading Companies, Export Trade Certificates of Review, and Export Management Companies 46
W. Translation 57
X. Foreign Branch Operations, Subsidiaries, Joint Ventures, and Licensing 57
Y. Electronic Commerce 57

Chapter 3. Exporting: Sales Documentation 60

A. Isolated Sales Transactions 60

1. Importance of Written Agreements 60
2. Telex or Facsimile Orders 61
3. The Formation of Sales Agreements 61
4. Common Forms for the Formation of Sales Agreements 63

a. Price Lists 63
b. Requests for Quotations 63
c. Quotations and Costing Sheets 65
d. Purchase Orders 65
e. Purchase Order Acknowledgments, Acceptances, and Sales Confirmations 70
f. Pro Forma Invoices 73
g. Commercial Invoices 81
h. Conflicting Provisions in Seller and Buyer Sales Documentation 81
i. Side Agreements 84

B. Ongoing Sales Transactions 84

1. Correlation With Documentation for Isolated Sales Transactions 85
2. Important Provisions in International Sales Agreements 86

a. Selling and Purchasing Entities 86
b. Quantity 87

c. *Pricing* 87
d. *Currency Fluctuations* 90
e. *Payment Methods* 90
f. *Export Financing* 92
g. *Security Interest* 95
h. *Passage of Title, Delivery, and Risk of Loss* 95
i. *Warranties and Product Defects* 95
j. *Preshipment Inspections* 96
k. *Export Licenses* 97
l. *Import Licenses and Foreign Government Filings* 97
m. *Governing Law* 97
n. *Dispute Resolution* 99
o. *Termination* 101

C. *Export Distributor and Sales Agent Agreements* 101

1. *Distinction Between Distributor and Sales Agent* 101
2. *Export Distributor Agreements* 103

a. *Territory and Exclusivity* 103
b. *Pricing* 106
c. *Minimum Purchase Quantities* 107
d. *Handling Competing Products* 107
e. *Effective Date and Government Review* 107
f. *Appointment of Subdistributors* 107
g. *Use of Trade Names, Trademarks, and Copyrights* 108
h. *Warranties and Product Liability* 108

3. *Export Sales Agent Agreements* 109

a. *Commissions* 109
b. *Pricing* 109
c. *Shipment* 112
d. *Warranties* 112
e. *Relationship of the Parties* 112

D. *Foreign Corrupt Practices Act Compliance* 112

Chapter 4. Exporting: Other Export Documentation 114

A. *Freight Forwarder's Powers of Attorney* 114
B. *Shipper's Letters of Instructions* 114
C. *Commercial Invoices* 116
D. *Bills of Lading* 118
E. *Packing Lists* 120
F. *Inspection Certificates* 120
G. *Marine and Air Casualty Insurance Policies and Certificates* 120
H. *Dock and Warehouse Receipts* 133
I. *Consular Invoices* 133
J. *Certificates of Origin* 133
K. *Certificates of Free Sale* 162
L. *Delivery Instructions and Delivery Orders* 162
M. *Special Customs Invoices* 162

N.	*Shipper's Declarations for Dangerous Goods*	169
O.	*Precursor and Essential Chemical Exports*	169
P.	*Animal, Plant, and Food Export Certificates*	169
Q.	*Drafts for Payment*	175
R.	*Letters of Credit*	175
S.	*Shipper's Export Declarations*	181
T.	*Freight Forwarder's Invoices*	195

Chapter 5. Export Controls and Licenses 197

A.	*Introduction*	197
B.	*Scope of the EAR*	198
C.	*Commerce Control List*	198
D.	*Export Destinations*	203
E.	*Customers, End Users, and End Uses*	210
F.	*Ten General Prohibitions*	210
G.	*License Exemptions and Exceptions*	212
H.	*License Applications and Procedures*	213
	1. *Documentation From Buyer*	213
	2. *License Application Form*	215
	3. *Procedures*	223
I.	*Re-Exports*	223
J.	*Export Documentation and Record-Keeping*	223
K.	*Special Comprehensive Licenses*	225
L.	*Technology, Software, and Technical Assistance Exports*	230
M.	*Violations and Penalties*	232
N.	*Munitions and Arms Exports*	232

Part III
Importing: Procedures and Documentation 237

Chapter 6. Importing: Preliminary Considerations 239

A.	*Products*	239
B.	*Volume*	240
C.	*Country Sourcing*	240
D.	*Identification of Suppliers*	241
E.	*Compliance With Foreign Law*	242
	1. *Foreign Export Controls*	242
	2. *Exchange Control Licenses*	242
	3. *Export Quotas*	243
F.	*U.S. Customs Considerations*	243
	1. *Utilization of Customs Brokers*	243
	2. *Importation Bonds*	244
	3. *Importer's Liability and Reasonable Care*	250
	4. *Application for Importer's Number*	250
	5. *Ports of Entry*	250
	6. *Import Quotas*	254

7. *Antidumping, Countervailing, and Other Special Duties* 255
8. *Classification* 256
9. *Valuation* 256
10. *Duty-Free and Reduced Duty Programs* 257
11. *Column 2 Imports* 258
12. *Deferred Duty Programs (Bonded Warehousing and Foreign Trade Zones)* 258
13. *Temporary Importations* 259
14. *Country of Origin* 260
15. *Assists* 260
16. *Specialized Products* 262
17. *Record-Keeping Requirements* 262
18. *Customs Rulings* 262

G. *Import Packing and Labeling* 262
H. *U.S. Commercial Considerations* 263

1. *Prevailing Market Price* 263
2. *Buy American Policies* 264
3. *U.S. Industry Standards* 264

I. *Terms of Purchase* 264
J. *Consignments* 266
K. *Leases* 267
L. *Marine and Air Casualty Insurance* 267
M. *Method of Transportation; Booking Transportation* 268
N. *Import Financing* 268
O. *Patent, Trademark, and Copyright Registrations and Infringements* 268
P. *Confidentiality and Non-Disclosure Agreements* 269
Q. *Payment* 269
R. *Translation* 270
S. *Foreign Branch Operations, Subsidiaries, Joint Ventures, and Licensing* 270
T. *Electronic Commerce* 276

Chapter 7. Importing: Purchase Documentation 280

A. *Isolated Purchase Transactions* 280

1. *Importance of Written Agreements* 280
2. *Telex or Facsimile Orders* 281
3. *The Formation of Purchase Agreements* 281
4. *Common Forms for the Formation of Purchase Agreements* 282

a. *Price Lists* 283
b. *Requests for Quotations and Offers to Purchase* 283
c. *Quotations* 283
d. *Purchase Orders* 284
e. *Purchase Order Acknowledgments, Acceptances, and Sales Confirmations* 284
f. *Commercial Invoices* 285
g. *Conflicting Provisions in Seller and Buyer Sales Documentation* 285
h. *Side Agreements* 286

B. *Ongoing Purchase Transactions*	286
1. *Correlation With Documentation for Isolated Purchase Transactions*	287
2. *Important Provisions in International Purchase Agreements*	288
a. *Purchasing and Selling Entities*	288
b. *Quantity*	288
c. *Pricing*	289
d. *Currency Fluctuations*	291
e. *Payment Methods*	292
f. *Import Financing*	294
g. *Security Interest*	294
h. *Passage of Title, Delivery, and Risk of Loss*	294
i. *Warranties and Product Defects*	295
j. *Preshipment Inspections*	295
k. *Export Licenses*	296
l. *Governing Law*	296
m. *Dispute Resolution*	298
n. *Termination*	299
C. *Import Distributor and Sales Agent Agreements*	299
1. *Distinction Between Distributor and Sales Agent*	300
2. *Import Distributor Agreements*	300
a. *Territory and Exclusivity*	300
b. *Pricing*	301
c. *Minimum Purchase Quantities*	301
d. *Handling Competing Products*	301
e. *Appointment of Subdistributors*	302
f. *Use of Trade Names, Trademarks, and Copyrights*	302
g. *Warranties and Product Liability*	302
3. *Import Sales Agent Agreements*	303
a. *Commissions*	303
b. *Pricing*	303
c. *Shipment*	303
Chapter 8. Import Process and Documentation	305
A. *Bills of Lading*	305
B. *Commercial Invoices*	307
C. *Pro Forma Invoices*	307
D. *Packing Lists*	307
E. *Inspection Certificates*	309
F. *Drafts for Payment*	309
G. *Arrival Notices*	309
H. *Pick-Up and Delivery Orders*	309
I. *Entry/Immediate Delivery*	311
J. *Entry Summary*	311
K. *Other Entries*	317
L. *Reconciliation*	322

M. GSP, CBI, ATPA, AGOA—Special Programs 322
N. NAFTA Certificate of Origin 322
O. Specialized Products Customs Entry Forms 324
P. Examination and Detention 324
Q. Liquidation Notices 334
R. Notices of Redelivery 334
S. Requests for Reliquidation 334
T. Requests for Information 339
U. Notices of Action 339
V. Protests, Supplemental Information Letters, and Post-Entry Amendments 339
W. Administrative Summons 345
X. Search Warrants 345
Y. Grand Jury Subpoenas 350
Z. Seizure Notices 350
AA. Prepenalty Notices 353
BB. Penalty Notices 353
CC. Customs Audits 353
DD. Prior Disclosure 362
EE. Court of International Trade 365
FF. Appeals 365
GG. Offers of Compromise 365
HH. ITC and Commerce Questionnaires 372

Part IV
Specialized Exporting and Importing 373

Chapter 9. Specialized Exporting and Importing 375

A. Drawback 375
B. Foreign Processing and Assembly Operations 382
C. Plant Construction Contracts 385
D. Barter and Countertrade Transactions 387

Appendices 389

Appendix A. Government Agencies and Export Assistance 391
Appendix B. International Sales Agreement (Export) 409
Appendix C. Correct Way to Complete the Shipper's Export Declaration 417
Appendix D. Automated Export System (AES) and AES Direct 437
Appendix E. U.S. Customs Reasonable Care Checklists 455
Appendix F. Harmonized Tariff Schedules (Excerpts) 465
Appendix G. International Purchase Agreement (Import) 483
Appendix H. Rules for Completing an Entry Summary 491
Appendix I. Rules for Constructing Manufacturer/Shipper Identification Code 525
Appendix J. Customs Audit Questionnaires 533

Appendix K. List of Export/Import-Related Web Sites 541

Glossary of International Trade Terms 547

Index 571

About the Author 583

List of Figures

1–1.	Export organization chart.	5
1–2.	Export order processing—quotation.	6
1–3.	Export order processing—order entry.	7
1–4.	Export order processing—shipment.	8
1–5.	Export order processing—collection.	9
1–6.	Interrelationships with outside service providers.	10
1–7.	Export manual table of contents.	11
1–8.	Import manual table of contents.	12
2–1.	Report of request for restrictive trade practice or boycott—single transaction.	25
2–2.	Report of request for restrictive trade practice or boycott—multiple transactions (and continuation sheet).	26
2–3.	Application for carnet.	29
2–4.	Examples of Incoterm usage.	33
2–5.	Diagram of the Incoterms.	34
2–6.	Ocean marine insurance coverage.	39
2–7.	Sample steamship tariff.	40
2–8.	Booking confirmation.	44
2–9.	Application for Export-Import Bank insurance.	47
2–10.	Application for export trade certificate of review.	50
2–11.	Export trade certificate of review.	54
3–1.	Formation of sales agreements.	62
3–2.	Quotation request.	64
3–3.	Export quotation worksheet.	66
3–4.	Quotation.	67
3–5.	Quotation.	68
3–6.	Quotation.	71
3–7.	Purchase order.	74
3–8.	Purchase order.	75
3–9.	Purchase order acceptance.	77
3–10.	Pro forma invoice.	82
3–11.	Commercial invoice.	83
3–12.	International credit terms/payment methods.	93
3–13.	Legal comparison of distributors and agents.	102

3–14. Financial comparison of using distributors and sales agents. 103
3–15. Foreign distributorship appointment checklist. 104
3–16. Foreign sales representative appointment checklist. 110
4–1. Power of attorney. 115
4–2. Shipper's letter of instructions. 117
4–3. Contents of a commercial invoice. 118
4–4. Inland bill of lading. 121
4–5. Ocean bill of lading. 124
4–6. International air waybill. 126
4–7. "House" air waybill. 128
4–8. Packing list. 130
4–9. Preshipment inspection worksheet. 131
4–10. Preshipment inspection certificate. 132
4–11. Marine insurance policy. 134
4–12. Marine insurance certificate. 153
4–13. Standard form for presentation of loss or damage claim. 155
4–14. Request for information for insurance claim. 157
4–15. Dock receipt. 158
4–16. Consular invoice. 160
4–17. Certificate of origin. 161
4–18. NAFTA certificate of origin and instructions. 163
4–19. Certificate of free sale. 165
4–20. Delivery instructions. 166
4–21. Delivery order. 167
4–22. Special customs invoice (Canada). 168
4–23. Shipper's declaration for dangerous goods. 170
4–24. Shipper's certification of articles not restricted. 171
4–25. DEA import/export declaration. 172
4–26. Export certificate—animal products. 174
4–27. Meat and poultry export certificate. 176
4–28. Instructions for documentary collection. 177
4–29. Sight draft. 178
4–30. Time draft. 178
4–31. Letter of credit instructions. 179
4–32. Common discrepancies in letters of credit. 181
4–33. Checklist for a letter of credit beneficiary. 182
4–34. Letter of indemnity. 186
4–35. Advice of irrevocable letter of credit (confirmed). 187
4–36. Advice of irrevocable letter of credit (unconfirmed). 188
4–37. Letter of credit. 189
4–38. SWIFT letter of credit codes. 191
4–39. Shipper's export declaration. 192
4–40. Shipper's export declaration (in-transit). 193
4–41. Freight forwarder's invoice. 196
5–1. Sample pages from the Commerce Control List (ECCN 2B001). 201
5–2. Country group A. 204

5–3.	Country group B.	205
5–4.	Country group D.	206
5–5.	Country group E.	208
5–6.	Excerpts from Commerce Country Chart.	209
5–7.	Red flags.	211
5–8.	Decision tree for exporters.	214
5–9.	Import certificate (U.S.).	216
5–10.	Statement by ultimate consignee and purchaser.	217
5–11.	Multipurpose application.	218
5–12.	Item appendix.	221
5–13.	End user appendix.	222
5–14.	Sample export license.	224
5–15.	Delivery verification certificate.	226
5–16.	Statement by consignee in support of special comprehensive license.	228
5–17.	Reexport territories.	229
5–18.	Customs export enforcement subpoena.	233
6–1.	Power of attorney for customs broker.	245
6–2.	Importer's letter of instruction.	246
6–3.	Application for customs bond.	247
6–4.	Customs bond.	248
6–5.	Owner's declaration.	251
6–6.	Application for importer's number and instructions.	252
6–7.	Exportation of articles under special bond.	261
6–8.	Application for letter of credit.	271
6–9.	Applicant's checklist for letter of credit.	275
6–10.	Instructions by importer's bank to correspondent bank in seller's country regarding opening of letter of credit.	277
8–1.	Import process.	306
8–2.	Pro forma invoice.	308
8–3.	Arrival notice.	310
8–4.	Pick-up order.	312
8–5.	Entry/Immediate Delivery form.	313
8–6.	Order for public sale.	314
8–7.	Entry summary and continuation sheet.	315
8–8.	Transportation entry.	318
8–9.	Application for foreign trade zone admission.	320
8–10.	Application for foreign trade zone activity permit.	321
8–11.	GSP declaration.	323
8–12.	FDA Form 2877.	325
8–13.	FCC Form 740.	327
8–14.	U.S. Department of Agriculture Form 368 Notice of Arrival.	329
8–15.	U.S. Fish and Wildlife Service Form 3-177.	330
8–16.	Textile declaration form—single country.	331
8–17.	Textile declaration form—multiple countries.	332
8–18.	Notice of detention.	333
8–19.	Bulletin notice of liquidation.	335

8–20. Courtesy notice of liquidation. 336
8–21. Notice of redelivery. 337
8–22. Request for information. 340
8–23. Notice of action. 342
8–24. Protest and instructions. 343
8–25. Administrative summons. 346
8–26. Summons notice to importer of record. 347
8–27. Affidavit. 348
8–28. Search warrant. 349
8–29. Grand jury subpoena. 351
8–30. Notice of seizure. 354
8–31. Consent to forfeiture. 359
8–32. Petition for remission or mitigation. 360
8–33. Prepenalty notice. 361
8–34. Notice of penalty. 363
8–35. Court of International Trade summons. 366
8–36. Information statement. 369
8–37. Transmittal to the Court of International Trade. 371
9–1. Drawback entry. 377
9–2. Delivery certificate. 379
9–3. Notice of intent to export. 381
9–4. Declaration by foreign shipper and importer's endorsement. 383
9–5. Foreign repairer's declaration and importer's endorsement. 384
9–6. Foreign assembler's declaration. 386

Foreword

Engaging in international trade is a never-ending challenge for a host of reasons: political turmoil in one or another country, protectionist regulations, market uncertainties, exchange rate fluctuations, trade organization edicts, compliance requirements, payment problems, shipping delays, cultural differences, and an awful lot of changing procedures and documentation to contend with in every country, including our own. While there is a favorable trend toward harmonization, we're not there yet.

As most experienced international traders will confirm, however, the rewards overall are well worth the risks and the difficulties. The United States' volume of international trade now exceeds $2.5 trillion a year in total exports and imports of goods and services.

While the economic competition in the global marketplace is greater than ever, so are the potential benefits. Practical knowledge, training, and persistence by the members of America's business community are vital to our future success in the international arena. We need to maintain our efforts to produce high-quality products and services and to market them aggressively and competitively abroad.

At the same time, U.S. companies more than ever recognize that to be globally competitive in their exports, they also have to look to other countries for needed raw materials, components, and final products and compare them with those that are produced in this country. That is what the global economy is all about—breaking down international barriers and encouraging the free flow of goods, services, technology, and capital.

It is essentially for these reasons that Tom Johnson originally decided to write this book. It has been my pleasure to have worked with Tom around the country for many years conducting training seminars and counseling companies on international trade. We are continually heartened by the ever-expanding interest we see expressed by companies in exporting and importing.

The special value of this book is that it takes a myriad of increasingly complex foreign trade rules, regulations, procedures, and practices and integrates them into a useful "how-to" volume explaining the export and import process in great detail.

While the book covers all the basic export/import procedures and documentation, experienced foreign traders also are likely to find many new nuggets of practical, cost-saving information and advice. The learning process never stops. Tom and I meet many exporters and importers each year who are motivated to attend seminars and workshops because of problems that suddenly surfaced in their trading operations: a shipment delayed, a payment not promptly made, or a penalty imposed because of incorrect documentation. To their chagrin, these exporters and importers quickly discover that they were not as knowledgeable or up-to-date as they thought. Advance preparation and planning invariably would have prevented these problems.

Export/Import Procedures and Documentation serves as a valuable guide to international trade operations and contains a sample of virtually every relevant document used in foreign trade. Equally important, the reasons for government-imposed documentary and procedural requirements are clearly explained.

As in most endeavors, the basic ingredients of enthusiasm, interest, and hard work are important to achieving success in exporting and importing, but they alone are not sufficient. The critical additional factors needed are technical knowledge and training, which will lead to success for those who carefully apply what they learn. This all-encompassing book makes that learning process orderly and understandable.

We hope you enjoy competing in the global market and achieving all the rewards it can offer you and your business.

Eugene J. Schreiber
Managing Director
World Trade Center of New Orleans

Preface

For the past twenty years, I have been teaching American Management Association seminars on international business. About thirteen years ago, I began teaching a course entitled Export/Import Procedures and Documentation. There has been a very strong interest in this seminar and excellent attendance wherever it has been given in various cities throughout the United States.

Since the last edition of this book, we have experienced the Asian economic crisis and a strong U.S. dollar. This has made exporting more difficult but has increased the opportunities for U.S. importers. Lower prices for imported raw materials and finished goods have helped the U.S. economy, but increased imports have spawned dumping cases and import restraints.

We have also experienced recession exacerbated by the September 11, 2001 tragedies in New York and Washington, D.C. While these are having a temporary dampening effect on world trade, more recently the countries of the world approved a new round of World Trade Organization negotiations. This will further stimulate trade.

As an attorney who has concentrated on international business transactions for many years, I have seen firsthand the increasing globalization of markets and international competition. Those U.S. companies that do not export, establish name recognition in other markets, import to reduce costs, and learn to compete on a global basis cannot survive long. My years living in Japan also convinced me that greater familiarity with international trade is essential for U.S. businesses to compete on a worldwide basis.

This book focuses on the procedures for exporting and importing and the relevant documentation. Although the procedures and documents generally arise from legal requirements in the United States or foreign countries, I have tried to present the information in a practical, non-technical manner. This book may be of help to freight forwarders, customs brokers, transportation carriers, and others, but it is primarily intended for manufacturers who are exporting their own products or importing raw materials or components or for importers of finished goods. Since readers of this book will have varying levels of expertise, I have tried to discuss the subject at an intermediate level. Hopefully, this book will be not only a useful training tool for beginners but also a reference work for more experienced exporters and importers as new situations arise.

This book tries to answer the questions: What procedures should be followed, and what documentation is utilized in exporting and importing? It is often said that international sales move on the documents. This book attempts to describe the roles that various documents play in export and import transactions and to show how well-prepared documents can eliminate problems; it attempts to present alternatives so that the reader can make his or her own decisions regarding exporting and importing strategies. The actual samples of documents shown should be helpful in understanding export and import transactions in general, but they may require modification for particular transactions.

Both exporting and importing are discussed in this book, and for those engaged in only one or the other, an attempt has been made to discuss all of the relevant considerations in each section, although this has created some redundancy. Furthermore, to shorten the book, the forms used in both export and import transactions are included only once with a cross-reference.

I wish to acknowledge and express my appreciation for the assistance provided by Donna Bade at Sandler, Travis & Rosenberg, P.A.; Ric Frantz at LR International, Inc.; and Nadia Khalil at Bank One and for the patience of my wife, Norma, and my children. I also wish to thank my editors, Ray O'Connell and Erika Spelman.

The information contained herein is accurate as far as I am aware and is based on sources available to me. Nevertheless, it is not legal advice, and specific legal advice based upon the facts and circumstances of the reader's own situation should be sought in making export or import decisions.

Any comments or suggestions for the improvement of this book will be gratefully accepted.

Thomas E. Johnson
Sandler, Travis & Rosenberg, P.A.
Chicago, Illinois

Acknowledgments

The author gratefully acknowledges the courtesy of the following in authorizing inclusion of their forms in this book:

Apperson Business Forms, Inc.
1200 Arlington Heights Road
Itasca, Illinois 60143

The First National Bank of Chicago
One North Dearborn
Chicago, Illinois 60670

Matthew Bender & Company, Inc.
11 Penn Plaza
New York, New York 10001

Roanoke Trade Services, Inc.
1501 East Woodfield Road
Schaumburg, Illinois 60173

Sea-Land Service, Inc.
3501 West Algonquin Road
Rolling Meadows, Illinois 60008

SGS Control Services, Inc.
42 Broadway
New York, New York 10004

Tops Business Forms
111 Marquardt Drive
Wheeling, Illinois 60090

United States Council for International Business, Inc.
1212 Avenue of the Americas
New York, New York 10036

Unz & Co.
190 Baldwin Avenue
Jersey City, New Jersey 07306

Washington International Insurance Company
1930 Thoreau Drive
Schaumburg, Illinois 60173

West Publishing Company
50 West Kellogg Boulevard
St. Paul, Minnesota 55164

Part I

Organizing for Export and Import Operations

Chapter 1

Organizing for Export and Import Operations

Smooth and efficient (and, therefore, profitable) exporting or importing requires certain personnel who have specialized knowledge. The personnel involved and their organization vary from company to company, and sometimes the same personnel have roles in both exporting and importing. In small companies, one person may perform all of the relevant functions, and in large companies or companies with a large amount of exports or imports, the number of personnel may be large. In addition, as a company decides to perform in-house the work that it previously contracted with outside companies (such as customs brokers, freight forwarders, packing companies, and others) to perform, the export/import department may grow. As business increases, specialties may develop within the department, and the duties performed by any one person may become narrower.

A. Export Department

For many companies, the exporting department begins in the sales or marketing department. As that department develops leads or identifies a customer located in another country, an order may come in and the salespeople may have to determine what additional steps that are different from domestic sales procedures need to be taken in order to fill that export order. Often the exporter's first foreign sales are to Canada or Mexico. Because the export order may require special procedures in manufacturing, credit checking, insuring, packing, shipping, and collection, it is likely that a number of people within the company will have input on the appropriate way to fill the order. As export orders increase (for example, as a result of an overseas distributor having been appointed), the handling of such orders should become more routine and the assignment of the special procedures related to an export sale should be given to specific personnel. It will be necessary to interface with freight forwarders, banks, packing companies, steamship lines, airlines, translators, government agencies, domestic transportation companies, and attorneys. Because most manufacturers have personnel who must interface with domestic transportation companies (traffic department), often additional personnel will be assigned to that department to manage export shipments and interface with other outside services. Some of this interface, such as with packing companies and steamship lines, and possibly governmental agencies and banks, may be handled by a freight forwarder. The number of personnel needed and the assignment of responsibilities depends upon the size of the company and the volume of exports involved. A chart for a company with a large export department is shown in Figure 1–1. The way in which an export order is processed at the time of quotation, order entry, shipment, and collection is shown in Figures 1–2, 1–3, 1–4, and 1–5, respectively. Smaller companies will combine some of these functions into tasks for one or more persons.

B. Import Department

A manufacturer's import department often grows out of the purchasing department, whose personnel have been assigned the responsibility of procuring raw materials or components for the manufacturing process. For importers or trading companies that deal in finished goods, the import department may begin as the result of being appointed as the U.S. distributor for a foreign manufacturer or from purchasing a product produced by a foreign manufacturer that has U.S. sales potential. Because foreign manufacturers often sell their products Ex-Factory or FOB plant, a U.S. company intending to import such products must familiarize itself with ocean shipping, insurance, U.S. customs clearance, and other procedural matters. Increasingly, a number of U.S. manufacturers are moving their manufacturing operations overseas to cheaper labor regions and importing products they formerly manufactured in the United States. That activity will also put them in contact with foreign freight forwarders, U.S. customs brokers, banks, the U.S. Customs Service, marine insurance companies, and other service companies.

C. Combined Export and Import Departments

In many companies, some or all of the functions of the export and import departments are combined in some way. In smaller companies, where the volume of exports or imports does not justify more personnel, one or two persons may have responsibility for both export and import procedures and documentation. As companies grow larger or the volume of export/import business increases, these functions tend to be separated more into export departments and import departments. However, because both departments may end up being in contact with some of the same outside parties (such as banks, those freight forwarders that are also customs brokers, or domestic transportation companies), some of these activities may be consolidated in specific persons for both export and import while other personnel will work exclusively on exports or on imports. A diagram of the interrelationships between the export and import personnel in the company and outside service providers is shown in Figure 1–6.

(*Text continues on page 8.*)

Figure 1–1. Export organization chart.

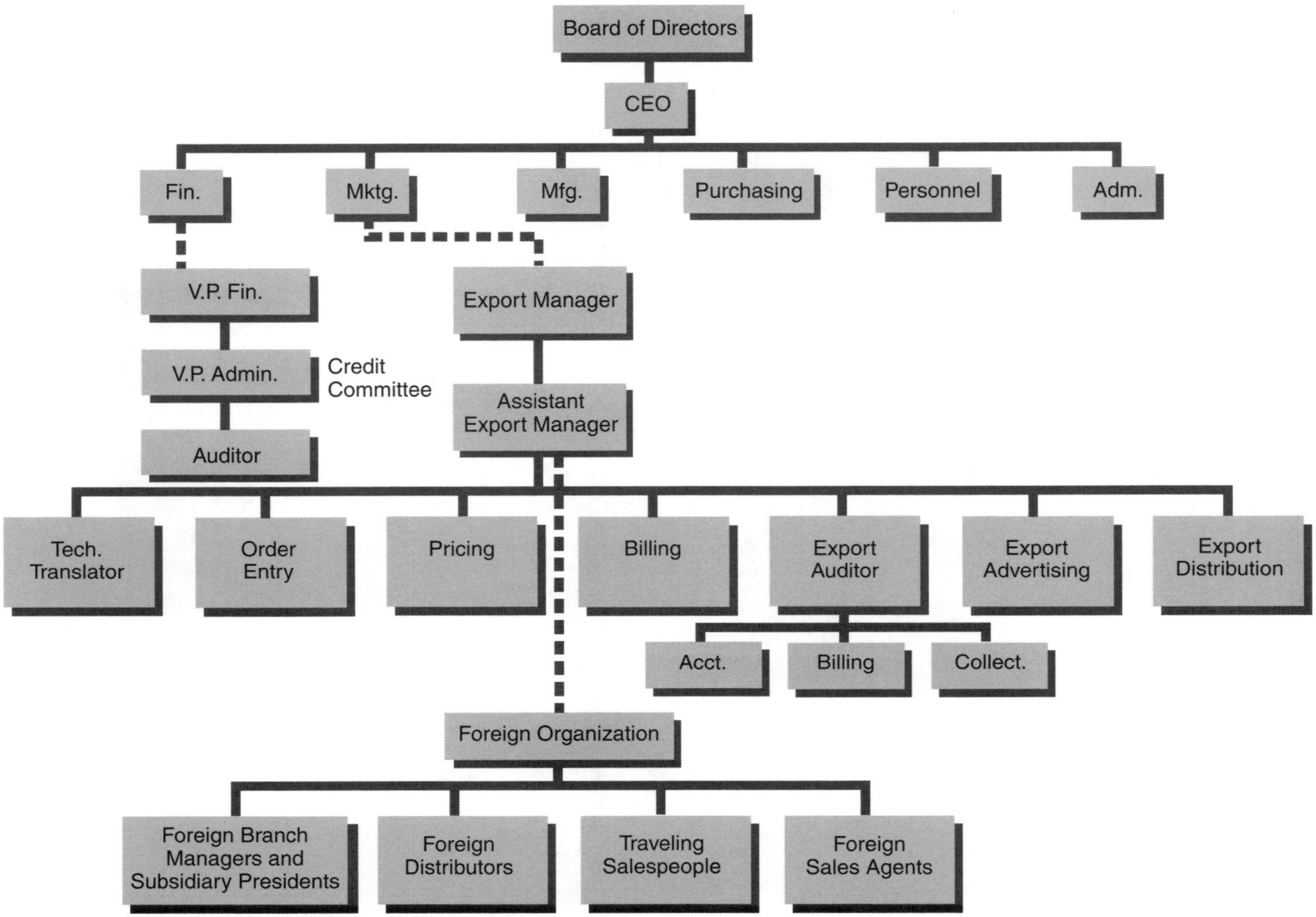

Figure 1–2. Export order processing—quotation.

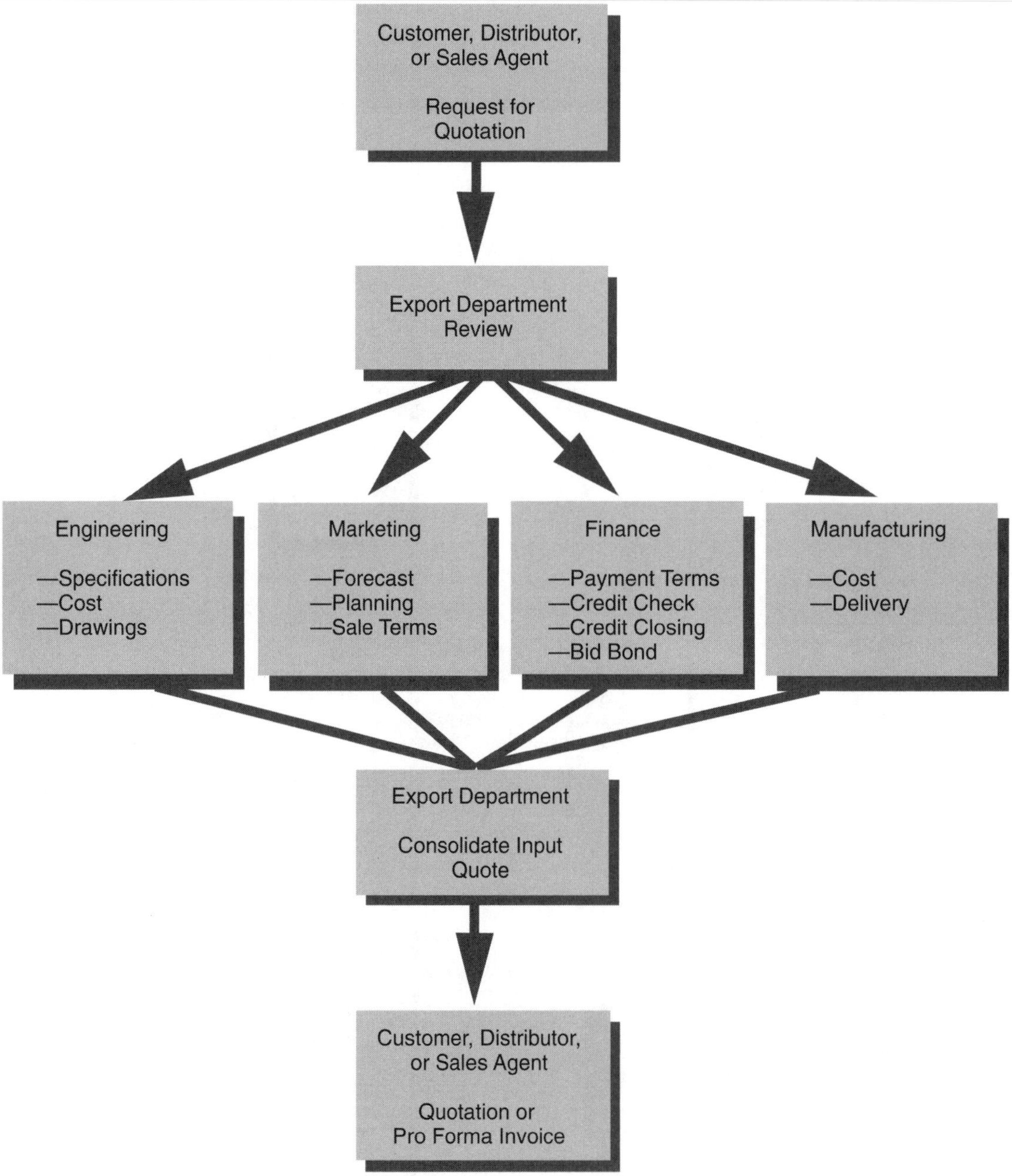

Figure 1–3. Export order processing—order entry.

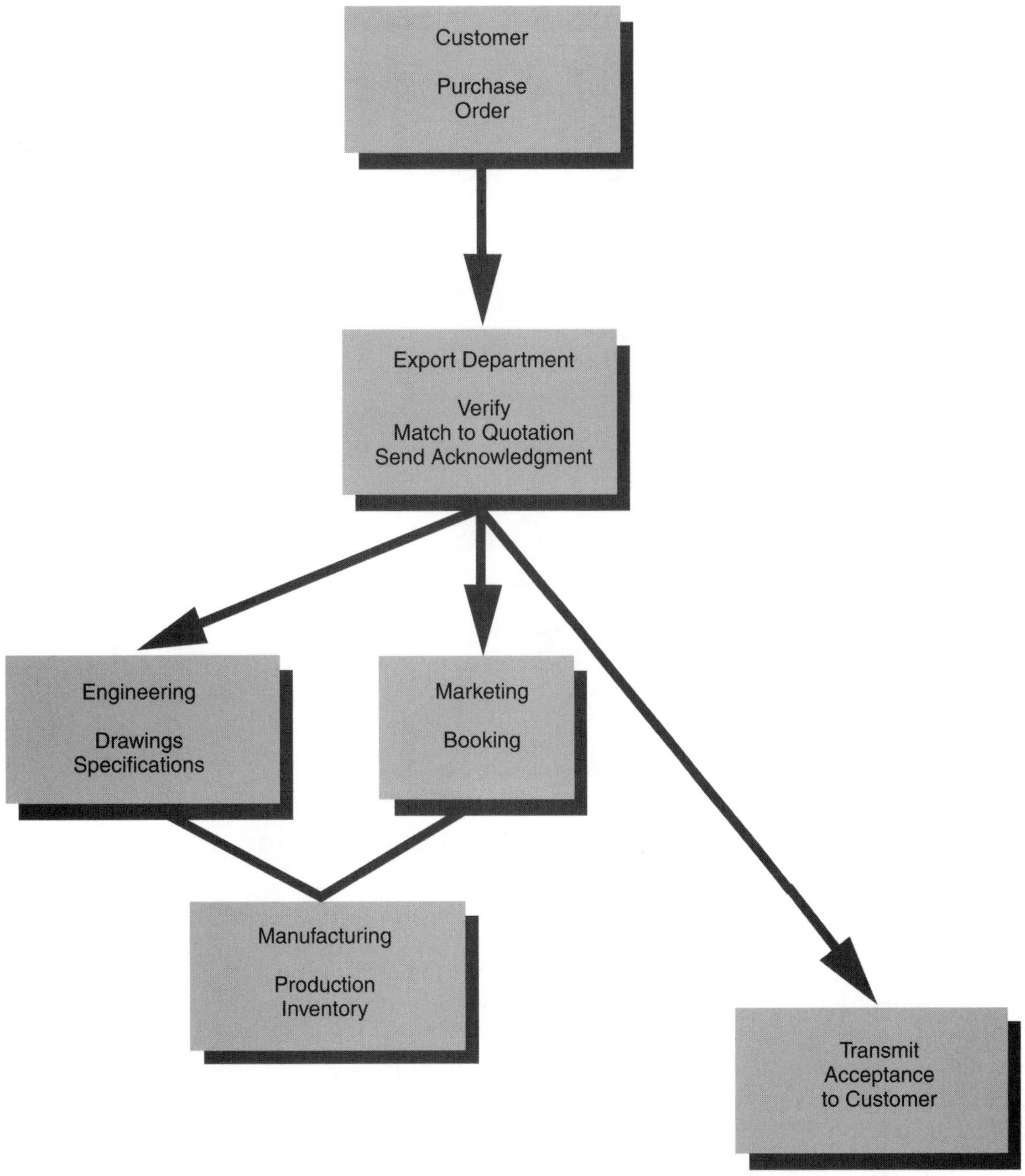

Figure 1–4. Export order processing—shipment.

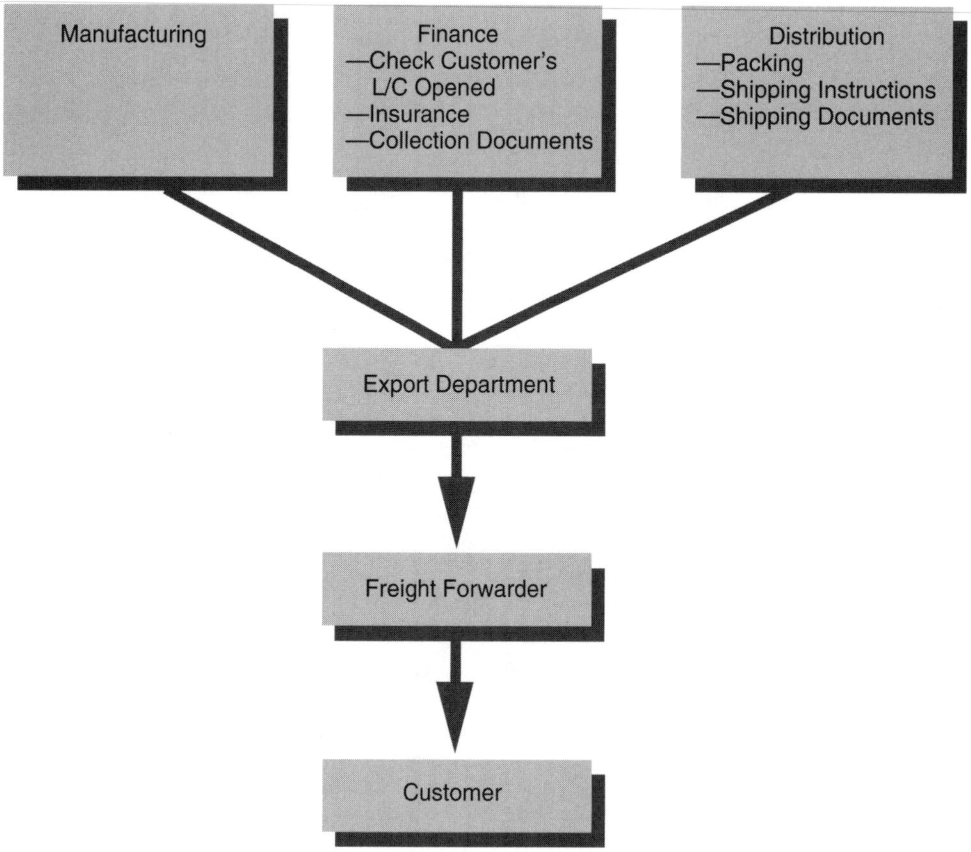

D. Manuals of Procedures and Documentation

It is often very helpful for companies to have a manual of procedures and documentation for their export and import departments. Such manuals serve as a reference tool for smooth operation and as a training tool for new employees. Moreover, since the Customs Modernization Act, such manuals are required to establish that the importer is using "reasonable care" in its importing operations and they are recommended by the Bureau of Export Administration for export operations. Such manuals should be customized to the particular company. They should describe the company's export process and import process. They should contain names, telephone numbers, and contact persons of the freight forwarders and customs brokers, steamship companies, packing companies, and other services that the company has chosen to utilize as well as government agencies. They should contain copies of the forms that the company has developed or chosen to use in export sales and import purchases and transportation, identify the internal routing of forms and documentation within the company for proper review and authorization, and contain job descriptions for the various personnel who are engaged in export/import operations. The manuals should be kept on a word processor and updated from time to time as changes in contact

Figure 1–5. Export order processing—collection.

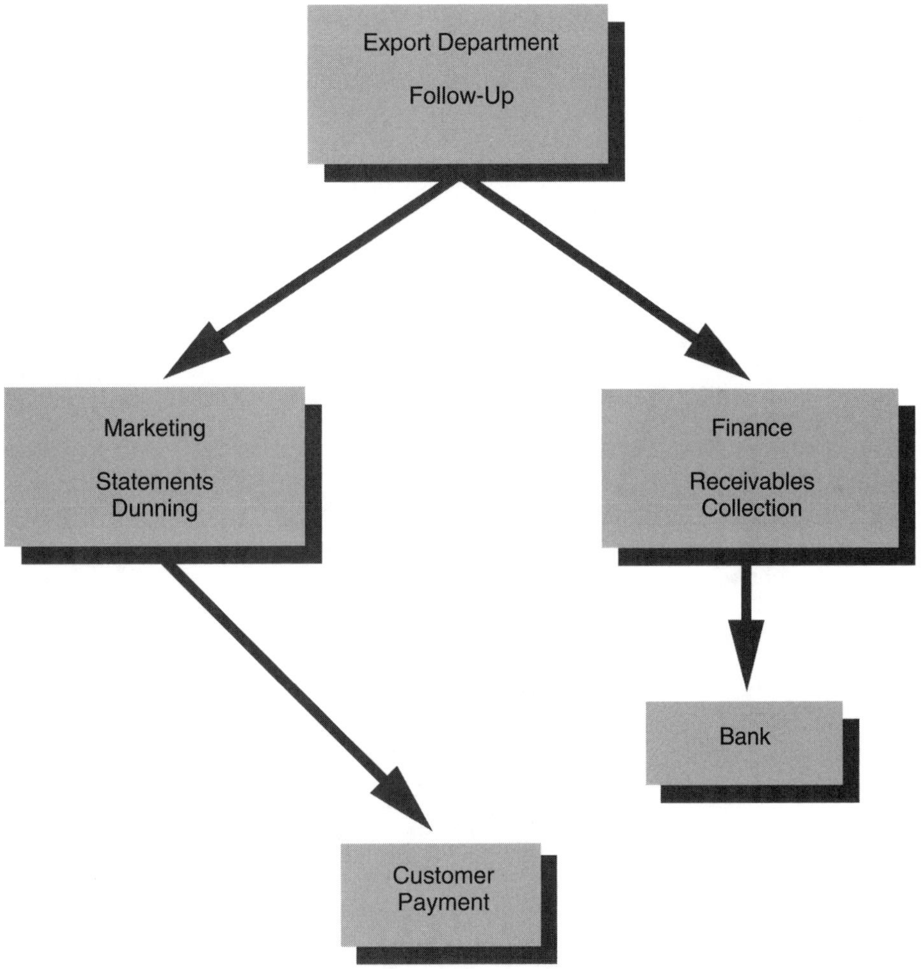

persons, telephone numbers, forms, or governmental regulations occur. Sample tables of contents for export and import manuals are shown in Figures 1–7 and 1–8, respectively.

E. Record-Keeping Compliance

Exporters and importers have always had an obligation to maintain records relating to their international trade transactions. Recently, however, these obligations have assumed a place of central importance due to technological advances and related changes in the law. As the volume of export and import commerce has increased, it has become necessary to automate such transactions. The use of electronic purchase orders, acceptances, and invoices, and the related need of the governmental agencies to reduce their own paperwork burden has spurred some governmental initiatives. Under the Customs Modernization Act, the U.S. Customs Service agreed to allow electronic filing

(*Text continues on page 13.*)

Figure 1–6. Interrelationships with outside service providers.

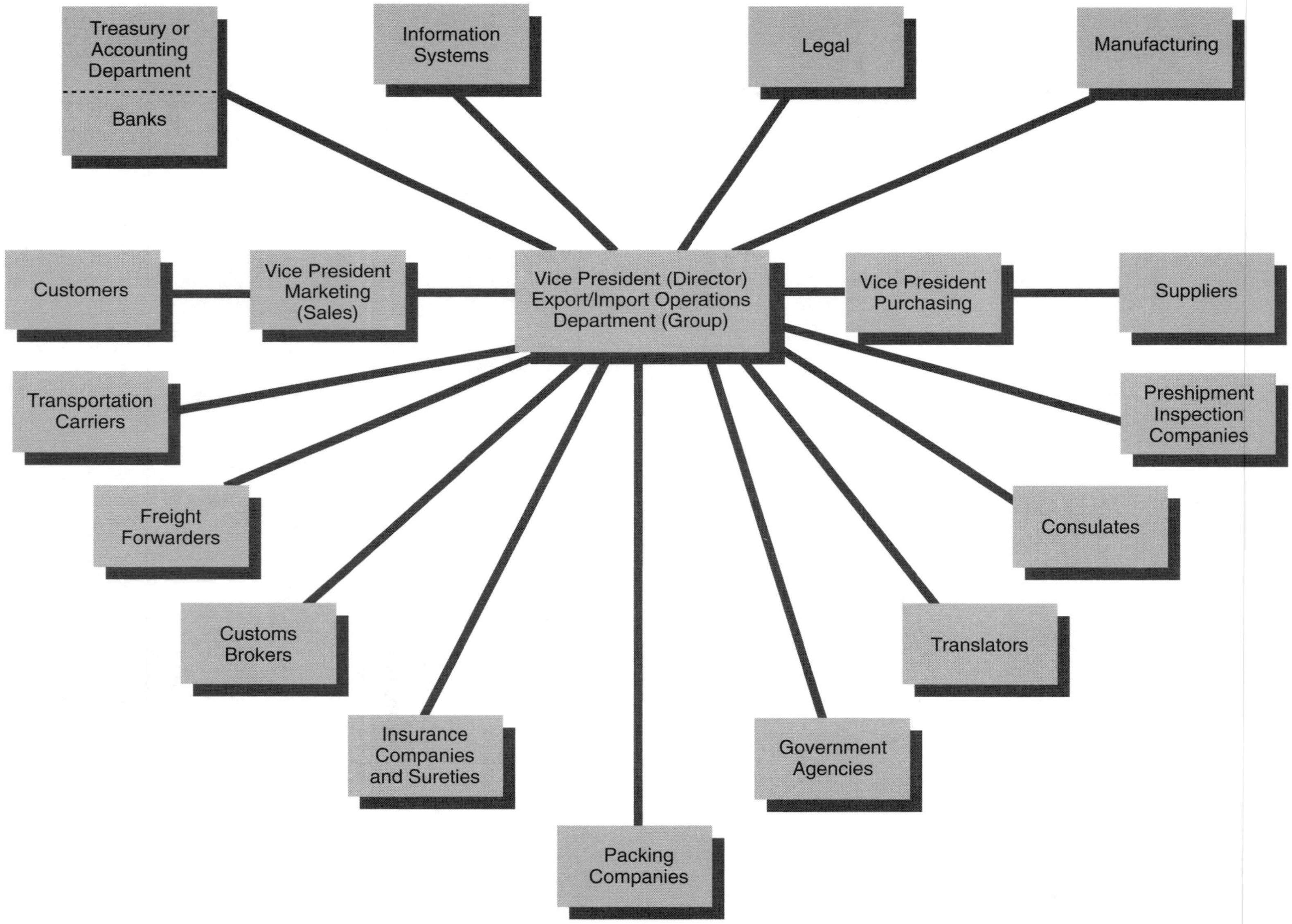

Figure 1–7. Export manual table of contents.

I. Statement of Manual's Purpose
- Company Policies Relating to Exporting

II. The Export Department
- Role
- Function/Operation Statement
- Organization Chart—Personnel; Export Compliance Manager
- Job Descriptions and Responsibilities
- Initial and Periodic Training Requirements
- Procedures for Disseminating Current Regulatory Developments Information

III. Export Procedures
- Preliminary Considerations
- Formation of Sales Agreement
- List of Existing Agents and Distributors
- List of Freight Forwarders, Steamship Companies, Insurance Brokers, Packing Companies, Attorneys
- Collections and Banking Procedures (Drafts, Letters of Credit)
- Record-Keeping Compliance

IV. Export Documents (Samples of Company-Approved Standard Forms)
- Quotations, Costing Sheets
- Purchase Order Acknowledgments
- Purchase Order Acceptances
- Invoices (Commercial, Pro Forma, and Special Customs)
- Shipper's Export Declaration
- Powers of Attorney
- Shipper's Letter of Instructions
- Bills of Lading
- Packing Lists
- Inspection Certificates
- Insurance Certificates
- Dock and Warehouse Receipts
- Consular Invoice
- Certificates of Origin
- Delivery Instructions
- Declarations for Dangerous Goods [if applicable]

V. Export Licenses
- Procedures for Determining Applicability of Regulations, Including Exemptions
- Procedures for Monitoring Changes in Products
- Procedures for Monitoring Changes to Denied Persons and Specially Designated Nationals Lists and Customers and Embargoed Countries
- Procedures for Applying for Export Licenses

Figure 1–8. Import manual table of contents.

I. Statement of Manual's Purpose
- Company Policies Relating to Importing

II. The Import Department
- Role
- Function/Operation Statement
- Organization Chart—Personnel; Import Compliance Manager
- Job Descriptions and Responsibilities
- Initial and Periodic Training Requirements
- Procedures for Disseminating Current Regulatory Developments Information

III. Import Procedures
- Preliminary Considerations
- Formation of Purchase Agreement
- List of Existing Suppliers
- List of Customs Brokers, Foreign Freight Forwarders, Steamship Companies, Insurance Brokers, Inland Carriers, Attorneys
- Payment and Banking Procedures (Drafts, Letters of Credit)
- Record-Keeping Compliance

IV. Import Documents (Samples of Company-Approved Standard Forms)
- Requests for Quotations
- Purchase Orders
- Invoices (Commercial, Pro Forma)
- Bills of Lading
- Packing Lists
- Inspection Certificates
- Customs Broker's Letter of Instructions
- Customs Entries
- Certificates of Origin
- Special Product Entry Forms
- Liquidation Notices
- Notices of Redelivery, Requests for Information, and Notices of Action
- Requests for Reliquidation
- Protests
- Summons, Warrants, Subpoenas, Seizure Notices
- Prepenalty and Penalty Notices
- ITC Questionnaires

of customs entries, and under the Automated Export System the Department of Commerce and Customs have established a program for the electronic filing of export documentation. Under these scenarios, export and import trade will be facilitated; however, the potential for exporters/importers to avoid their legal responsibilities, including filing fraudulent entries with improper values or classifications or evading their responsibilities to obtain export licenses is substantially increased. As a result, in the Customs Modernization Act, new penalties were imposed upon importers and exporters who fail to keep proper documentation, which the Customs Service intends to audit from time to time to verify that the electronic filings are accurate. Now, even if the electronic filing was accurate, if an importer/exporter fails to provide documents requested by Customs, it can be fined up to $100,000 (or 75 percent of the appraised value, whichever is less) if the failure to produce a document is intentional, or $10,000 (or 40 percent of the appraised value, whichever is less) if it is negligent or accidental.

Other laws, such as the Export Administration Act, the Foreign Trade Statistics Regulations, and the North American Free Trade Agreement, also impose record-keeping requirements on exporters. For most companies that engage in both exporting and importing, it is important to establish a record-keeping compliance program that maintains the documents required by all the laws regulating international trade. In general, U.S. export and import laws require that the records be kept for a period of five years (or three years from date of payment on drawback entries). However, other laws, for example state income tax laws or foreign laws (Canada under NAFTA), may require longer periods.

The U.S. Customs Service has issued a *Recordkeeping Compliance Handbook* describing in detail its interpretation of the proper record-keeping responsibilities for importers. This *Handbook* states that the Customs Service expects each importer to designate a manager of record-keeping compliance who can act as the point of contact for all document requests from Customs and who is responsible for managing and administering the record-keeping compliance within the company. The manager, as well as all employees involved in importing (and exporting), is expected to receive regular training on compliance with the customs laws and on documentation and record-keeping requirements. Each company is expected to maintain a procedures manual to ensure compliance with all customs laws and record-keeping requirements. In addition, Customs offers a program for voluntary certified record-keepers who register with the U.S. Customs Service and demonstrate their capabilities of compliance. In return for participating in the voluntary record-keeping compliance program, the record-keeper will not be fined for its first violation of the regulations. In return, the record-keeper has to agree to a number of responsibilities.

F. Software

Many companies offer software programs for managing the export process, including order-taking, generation of export documentation, compliance with export control regulations, calculation of transportation charges and duties, and identification of trade leads. The Department of Commerce, Trade Information Center maintains a list of software producers and a description of their products and prices on its Web site at *www.ita.doc.gov/td/tic* (select "Export Resources," then "Publications and Software," and then "Export Software").

On the import side, a substantial number of companies offer "supply chain management" (SCM) software. A good collection can be accessed on the Web at *http://directory.google.com / Top / Business / Business_Services / Distribution_and_Logistics/Logistics/Software*).

G. Federal, State, International, and Foreign Law

The Constitution of the United States specifically provides that the U.S. Congress shall have power to regulate exports and imports (Art. 1, §8). This means that exporting or importing will be governed primarily by federal law rather than state law. On the other hand, the law of contracts, which governs the formation of international sales and purchase agreements and distributor and sales agent agreements, is almost exclusively governed by state law, which varies from state to state. As discussed in Chapter 3, Section B.2.m, and Chapter 7, Section B.2.l, a number of countries, including the United States, have entered into an international treaty that governs the sale of goods and will supersede the state law of contracts in certain circumstances. Finally, in many circumstances, the laws of the foreign country will govern at least as to that portion of the transaction occurring within its borders, and in certain situations, it may govern the international sales and purchase agreements as well. Most of the procedures and forms that are used in exporting and importing have been developed to fulfill specific legal requirements, so that an exporter or importer should disregard such procedures and forms only after confirming that doing so will not subject the company to legal risks or penalties.

Part II

Exporting: Procedures and Documentation

Chapter 2

Exporting: Preliminary Considerations

This chapter will discuss the preliminary considerations that anyone intending to export should consider. Before beginning to export and on each export sale thereafter, a number of considerations should be addressed to avoid costly mistakes and difficulties. Those companies that begin exporting or continue to export without having addressed the following issues will run into problems sooner or later.

A. Products

Initially, the exporter should think about certain considerations relating to the product it intends to export. For example, is the product normally utilized as a component in a customer's manufacturing process? Is it sold separately as a spare part? Is the product a raw material, commodity, or finished product? Is it sold singly or as part of a set or system? Does the product need to be modified—such as the size, weight, or color—to be saleable in the foreign market? Is the product new or used? (If the product is used, some countries prohibit importation or require independent appraisals of value, which can delay the sale.) Often the appropriate method of manufacturing, marketing, the appropriate documentation, the appropriate procedures for exportation, and the treatment under foreign law, including foreign customs laws, will depend upon these considerations.

Some products are subject to special export limitations and procedures. In addition to the general export procedures discussed in this Part, exporters of munitions; narcotics and controlled substances; nuclear equipment, materials, and waste; watercraft; natural gas; electric power; hazardous substances; biological products; consumer products not conforming to applicable product safety standards, adulterated or misbranded food, drugs, medical devices, and cosmetics; endangered species; ozone-depleting chemicals; flammable fabrics; precursor chemicals; tobacco seeds and plants; fish and wildlife; crude oil; certain petroleum-based chemicals and products; and pharmaceuticals intended for human or animal use must give notices or apply for special licenses, permits, or approvals from the appropriate U.S. government agency before exporting such products.

B. Volume

What is the expected volume of export of the product? Will this be an isolated sale of a small quantity or an ongoing series of transactions amounting to substantial quantities? Small quantities may be exported under purchase orders and purchase order acceptances. Large quantities may require more formal international sales agreements; more secure methods of payment; special shipping, packing, and handling procedures; the appointment of sales agents and/or distributors in the foreign country; or after-sales service (see the discussion in Chapter 3).

C. Country Market and Product Competitiveness Research

On many occasions, a company's sole export sales business consists of responding to orders from customers located in foreign countries without any active sales efforts by the company. However, as a matter of successful exporting, it is imperative that the company adequately evaluate the various world markets where its product is likely to be marketable. This will include review of macro-economic factors such as the size of the population and the economic development level and buying power of the country, and more specific factors, such as the existence of competitive products in that country. The United Nations publishes its *International Trade Statistics Yearbook* and the International Monetary Fund (IMF) publishes its *Direction of Trade Statistics Yearbook* showing what countries are buying and importing all types of products. The U.S. Department of Commerce, Bureau of Census gathers and publishes data to assist those who are interested in evaluating various country markets, including their International Data Base and Export and Import Trade Data Base. It has also compiled detailed assessments of the international competitiveness of many U.S. products and information on foreign trade fairs to identify sales opportunities for such products. Another useful tool for evaluating the political and commercial risk of doing business in a particular country is the Country Limitation Schedule published periodically by the Export-Import Bank of the United States. An excerpt from the Web site of the Trade Information Center listing governmental agencies that provide general export and marketing information for exporters is included in Appendix A. See also Appendix K listing Web sites for marketing information and trade leads. Of course, other private companies also publish data, such as those contained in the Dun & Bradstreet *Exporters Encyclopedia* or BNA's *Export Reference Manual.* With limited personnel and resources, all companies must make strategic decisions about which countries they will target for export sales and how much profit they are likely to obtain by their efforts in various countries.

D. Identification of Customers: End Users, Distributors, and Sales Agents

Once the countries with the best market potential and the international competitiveness of your company's products have been evaluated, the specific purchasers, such as end users of the products, sales agents who can solicit sales in that country for the products, or distributors who are willing to buy and resell the products in that country, must be identified. This is a highly important decision, and some of the worst experiences in exporting result from not having done adequate homework in selecting customers, sales agents, and distributors. It is far more efficient and profitable to spend significant amounts of time evaluating potential customers, sales agents, and distributors than having to start over again because such customers, sales agents, or distributors turn out to be unable to pay, unable to perform, or difficult to work with. The U.S. Department of Commerce International Trade Administration offers a number of services and publications, such as overseas trade missions and fairs, "matchmaker" events, the National Trade Data Bank, Export Contact List Service, Customized Sales Survey, Trade Opportunities Program, the International Partner Search, Gold Key Service, International Company Profiles, *Commerce Business Daily,* and *Commercial News U.S.A.,* all designed to assist U.S. companies in identifying possible customers.

Once potential customers have been identified, if an ongoing relationship is contemplated, a personal visit to evaluate the customer is essential. One efficient way that the author has used is to arrange a schedule of interviews at its foreign offices where representatives of the U.S. company could meet with numerous potential customers, sales agents, and distributors in that country in the course of a two- or three-day period. Based on such meetings, one or more distributors or sales agents can be selected, or the needs of a customer can be clearly understood.

In evaluating potential customers, sales agents, and distributors it is important to obtain a credit report. Credit reports are available from Dun & Bradstreet, Parsippany, New Jersey, telephone number (973) 605-6000; Graydon America, New York, New York, telephone number (212) 385-9580; Justitia International, Bristol, Connecticut, telephone number (860) 283-5714; Teikoku Data Bank America, Inc. [Japan], New York, New York, telephone number (212) 421-9805; Owens Online, Tampa, Florida, telephone number (813) 877-2008; and local offices of the U.S. Department of Commerce (International Company Profiles).

E. Compliance With Foreign Law

Prior to exporting to a foreign country or even agreeing to sell to a customer in a foreign country, a U.S. company should be aware of any foreign laws which might affect the sale. Information about foreign law often can be obtained from the customer or distributor to which the U.S. company intends to sell. However, if the customer or distributor is incorrect in the information that it gives to the exporter, the exporter may pay dearly for having relied solely upon the advice of the customer. Incorrect information about foreign law may result in the prohibition of importation of the exporter's product; or it may mean that the customer cannot resell the product as profitably as expected. Unfortunately, customers often overlook those things that may be of the greatest concern to the exporter. As a result, it may be necessary for the U.S. exporter to confirm its customer's advice with third parties, including attorneys, banks, or government agencies, to feel confident that it properly understands the foreign law requirements. Some specific examples are as follows:

1. Industry Standards

Foreign manufacturers and trade associations often promulgate industry standards that are enacted into law or that require compliance in order to sell successfully there. It may be necessary to identify such standards even prior to manufacture of the product that the company intends to sell for export or to modify the product prior to shipment. Or, it may be necessary to arrange for the importing customer to make such modifications. Sometimes compliance with such standards is evidenced by certain marks on the product, such as "JIS" (Japan), "CSA" (Canada), and "UL" (Underwriters Laboratories-U.S.).

One type of foreign safety standard that is becoming important is the "CE" mark required for the importation of certain products to the European Community. The European Community has issued directives relating to safety standards for the following important products: toys, simple pressure vessels and telecommunications terminal equipment, machinery, gas appliances, electromagnetic compatibility, low-voltage products, and medical devices (see www.newapproach.org). Products not conforming to these directives are subject to seizure and the assessment of fines. The manufacturer may conduct its own conformity assessment and self-declare compliance in most cases. For some products, however, the manufacturer is required (and in all cases may elect) to hire an authorized independent certifying service company to conduct the conformity assessment. The manufacturer must maintain a Technical Construction File to support the declaration and must have an authorized representative located within the European Community to respond to enforcement actions.

The ISO 9000 quality standards are becoming increasingly important for European sales. One helpful source of information in the United States is the National Center for Standards and Certification Information, a part of the Department of Commerce National Institute of Standards and Technology, located in Gaithersburg, Maryland, telephone number (301) 975-4040, which maintains collections of foreign government standards by product. The National Technical Information Service in Springfield, Virginia, telephone number (703) 605-6000, the Foreign Agricultural Service of the Department of Agriculture in Washington, D.C., telephone number (202) 408-5386, and the American National Standards Institute in New York City, telephone number (212) 642-4900, which maintains over 100,000 worldwide product standards on its NSSN network, also collect such information. Canada has the Standards Council, telephone number (613) 238-3222, and Germany has the Deutshes Institut for Normung (DIN).

2. Foreign Customs Laws

The countries of export destination may have absolute quotas on the quantity of products that can be imported. Importation of products in excess of the quota will be prohibited. Similarly, it is important to identify the amount of customs duties that will be assessed on the product, which will involve determining the correct tariff classification for the product under foreign law in order to determine whether the tariff rate will be so high that it is unlikely that sales of the product will be successful in that country, and to evaluate whether a distributor will be able to make a reasonable profit if it resells at the current market price in that country. It would be especially important to confirm that there are no antidumping, countervailing, or other special customs duties imposed on the products. These duties are often much higher than regular *ad valorem* duties, and may be applied to products imported to the country even if the seller was not subject to the original antidumping investigation.

Some countries, such as Ethiopia, Belarus, Cambodia, Yugoslavia, Kazakhstan, Lebanon, Liberia, Saudi Arabia and Ukraine do not fully adhere to the GATT Valuation Code and may assess duties on fair market value rather than invoice price.

Another problem is "assists." If the buyer will be furnishing items used in the production of merchandise, such as tools, dies, molds, raw materials, or engineering or development services to the seller, the importer of record (whether that is the buyer or the seller through an agent) may be required to pay customs duties on such items, and the seller may be required to identify such items in its commercial invoices.

Many countries have severe penalties for import violations; for example, France assesses a penalty of two times the value of the merchandise, India a penalty of five times the value of the merchandise, and China confiscates the merchandise.

One source for foreign customs service contact information is the *World Trade and Customs Directory* published by Arrowhead World Regulatory Directories, telephone number (202) 833-0089. See also Appendix K listing Web sites for foreign customs agencies and tariff information.

In any case, where there is doubt as to the correct classification or valuation of the merchandise, duty rate, or existence of assists, the importer (whether buyer or seller) may wish to seek an administrative ruling from the foreign customs agency. This will usually take some period of time, and the seller and buyer may have to adjust their production and delivery plans accordingly. (A more thorough understanding of the types of considerations that the buyer may have to take into account under its customs laws can be gained by reviewing the similar considerations for a U.S. importer discussed in Chapter 6, Section F).

3. Government Contracting

Sales to foreign governments, government agencies, or partially government-owned private businesses often involve specialized procedures and documentation. Public competitive bidding and compliance with invitations to bid and acquisition regulations, and providing bid bonds, performance bonds, guarantees, standby letters of credit, and numerous certifications may be required. Commissions may be prohibited, or the disclosure of commissions paid may be required. Government purchases may qualify for customs duty, quota, or import license exemptions. Barter or countertrade may be necessary.

4. Buy American Equivalent Laws

Foreign governmental agencies often promulgate regulations which are designed to give preferential treatment to products supplied by manufacturers in their own country. This may consist of an absolute preference, or it may be a certain price differential preference. Determining whether such laws or agency regulations exist for your company's products is mandatory if government sales are expected to be important.

5. *Exchange Controls and Import Licenses*

Unlike the United States, many nations of the world have exchange control systems designed to limit the amount of their currency that can be used to buy foreign products. These require that an import license from a central bank or the government be obtained in order for customers in that country to pay for imported products. For a U.S. exporter who wishes to get paid, it is extremely important to determine (1) whether an exchange control system exists and an import license is necessary in the foreign country, (2) what time periods are necessary to obtain such licenses, and (3) the conditions that must be fulfilled and documentation that must be provided in order for the importer to obtain such license. (See *www.imf.org.*)

6. *Value-Added Taxes*

Many countries impose a value-added tax on the stages of production and distribution. Such taxes usually apply to imported goods so that the importer, in addition to paying customs duties, must pay a value-added tax based, usually, on the customs value plus duties. When the importer marks up and resells the goods, it will collect the tax from the purchaser, which it must remit to the tax authorities after taking a credit for the taxes due on importation. (Exporters are often exempt from the value-added tax.) The amount of value-added tax can be significant as it is usually higher than traditional sales taxes and, therefore, whether the product can be priced competitively in the foreign market is a matter of analysis.

7. *Specialized Laws*

Foreign countries often enact specialized laws prohibiting the importation of certain products except in compliance with such laws. In the United States, there are many special laws regulating the domestic sale and importation of a wide variety of products (see Chapter 6, Section A). Some U.S. laws regulate all products manufactured in the United States; others do not apply to products being manufactured for export. In any case, like the United States, foreign countries often have special laws affecting certain products or classes of products, and the existence of such regulation should be ascertained prior to manufacture, prior to entering into an agreement to sell, and even prior to quoting prices or delivery dates to a customer.

F. Export Controls and Licenses

This subject is treated in detail in Chapter 5. However, it is a very important preliminary consideration because if an export license is required from the U.S. Department of Commerce, Bureau of Export Administration, and such license is not obtained by the exporter, the U.S. Customs Service will detain the shipment, and the sale cannot be completed. Even if the exporter sells ex-factory and the buyer is technically responsible for U.S. inland transportation, export, and ocean shipment, the buyer may file a lawsuit if the exporter does not inform the customer that an export license is necessary and the shipment is detained. The method for determining whether an export license is required for a particular product is discussed in Chapter 5.

G. Patent, Trademark, and Copyright Registrations and Infringements

These rights are sometimes called intellectuals or industrial property rights. This topic includes two common problems. First, a U.S. company that invents and manufactures a product may secure a patent, trademark, or copyright in the United States, but might not apply for any registration of its rights in a foreign country. In many countries, if the U.S. rights are not filed there within a specific period such as one year after filing in the United States, they are forever lost and are part of the public domain in the foreign country. This means that without registering its rights in that country, an exporter cannot prevent copying, pirating, and the marketing of imitation products.

Second, without conducting a patent, trademark, or copyright search, a U.S. company cannot know whether the product that it is exporting will infringe a patent, trademark, or copyright that has been filed in a foreign country. Unfortunately, in many foreign countries, the first person to file a patent, trademark, or copyright will be the legal owner, even if it was previously invented and used by someone in another country. Consequently, it is not uncommon for foreign competitors, distributors, or customers to register a U.S. company's patents, trademarks, or copyrights, so that if the U.S. company exports to the foreign country, it would result in an infringement of the intellectual property rights that the foreign entity now owns in that country. Thus, in order for the U.S. company to export its products to that country, it may have to negotiate to obtain a license and pay a royalty to the foreign company or to purchase back the intellectual property rights that have been registered there. In sales documentation commonly used in the United States, the U.S. manufacturer will give a warranty, or it will automatically be implied under the Uniform Commercial Code, that the product does not infringe any person's intellectual property rights. A U.S. exporter may be using the same type of documentation for export sales. If the U.S. exporter has not searched the foreign intellectual property registrations, and the product does infringe a foreign registration, the U.S. exporter will be in breach of warranty and may be unable to perform its sales agreement with its customer.

H. Confidentiality and Non-Disclosure Agreements

As a preliminary consideration, before exporting products to foreign countries or providing samples to potential customers, it is important to ask the foreign company to sign a confidentiality and non-disclosure agreement. In many countries, especially if the U.S. company has no patent registration there, the ability of the U.S. company to prohibit copying and piracy by reverse engineering is virtually nil. Some measure of protection can be obtained by requiring the foreign company to sign a confidentiality and non-disclosure agreement which commits it to not reverse engineer the product or engage in its manufacture itself or through third parties. Such agreements are not unusual, and any potential customer who refuses to sign such an agreement should be suspect.

I. Antiboycott Compliance

Especially if you plan to make sales in the Middle East or you receive an order from a customer located there, before proceeding to accept and ship the order, you should be aware of the U.S. antiboycott regulations. Certain countries in the Middle East maintain international boycotts, usually of Israel. Currently those countries include Bahrain, Iraq, Kuwait, Lebanon, Libya, Oman, Qatar, Saudi Arabia, Syria, United Arab Emirates, and Republic of Yemen. Other, less extensive boycotts exist by Pakistan, the People's Republic of China, and Nigeria. U.S. law prohibits any U.S. company from refusing or agreeing to refuse to do business pursuant to an agreement or request from a boycotting country or to discriminate on the basis of race, religion, sex, or national origin. Perhaps more importantly, the law requires that if a U.S. company receives a request for information about its business relationships with black-listed companies or boycotted countries, it must promptly report the request to the U.S. Department of Commerce. Failure to do so can result in penalties including civil penalties of $12,000 per violation, criminal penalties for intentional violations, and denial of export privileges altogether. The forms for reporting single and multiple transactions are shown in Figures 2–1 and 2–2, respectively.

J. Employee Sales Visits to Foreign Countries—Immigration and Customs Compliance

In the course of developing export sales, it is likely that sales employees of the U.S. company will visit foreign countries to identify customers and evaluate markets. Another common export sales activity is exhibiting products in trade fairs sponsored by U.S. or foreign governmental agencies or trade associations. It is important that the U.S. company satisfy itself that its sales employees traveling to foreign countries comply with the immigration and customs laws of those countries. In particular, many countries require that individuals entering their country to engage in business activities obtain a different type of visa (which is stamped in the U.S. passport) to enter the country. Entering the country on a visitor's visa or engaging in activities inconsistent with the visa which has been issued can subject an employee to serous penalties and delay. In regard to the U.S. company's employees bringing samples of its products into a foreign country for display or sale, it is necessary that the regular customs duties be paid on the samples or that salesmen arrange for compliance with the local temporary importation procedures. Most countries have a temporary importation procedure whereby a bond must be posted to guarantee that the product which is being imported

(*Text continues on page 28.*)

Figure 2–1. Report of request for restrictive trade practice or boycott—single transaction.

Form **BXA-621P**
(REV 1-94)

U.S. DEPARTMENT OF COMMERCE
Bureau of Export Administration

REPORT OF REQUEST FOR RESTRICTIVE TRADE PRACTICE OR BOYCOTT
SINGLE TRANSACTION

(For reporting requests described in Part 769 of the Export Administration Regulations)

NOTICE OF RIGHT TO PROTECT CERTAIN INFORMATION FROM DISCLOSURE

The Export Administration Act permits you to protect from public disclosure information regarding the quantity, description, and value of commodities or technical data supplied in Item 11 of this report and in any accompanying documents. *If you do not claim this protection, all of the information in your report and in accompanying documents will be made available for public inspection and copying.*

You can obtain this protection by certifying, in Item 10 of the report, that disclosure of the information referred to above would place a United States company or individual involved in the report at a competitive disadvantage. If you make such a certification in Item 10, you may remove information regarding the quantity, description, and value of the commodities or technical data supplied by you from Item 11 of the inspection copy of the report form and from the public inspection copies of the accompanying documents.

The withholding of this information will be honored by the Department unless the Secretary determines that disclosure of the information would not place a United States company or individual at a competitive disadvantage or that it would be contrary to the national interest to withhold the information.

THIS SPACE FOR BXA USE 9 5 4 4 5 7

A BATCH 2 5

MONTH/YEAR 6 9

RSN 10 15 SUBSET 16 17

RTP 18 27

CLASS 28 FILING 55 TAG 70 80

This report required by law (50 U.S.C. App. §2407 (b)(2) P.L. 103-10; 15 C.F.R. Part 769. Failure to report can result both in criminal penalties, including fines or imprisonment, and administrative sanctions.

Instructions: 1. Complete all items that apply. 2. Assemble original report form and accompanying documents as a unit, and submit intact and unaltered. 3. Assemble and submit the duplicate copy of report form (marked Duplicate (Public Inspection Copy)) and additional copies of accompanying documents (marked with the legend "Public Inspection Copy.") 4. *If you certify, in item 10,* that the disclosure of the information specified there would cause competitive disadvantage, edit the "Public Inspection Copy" of the documents submitted to exclude the specified information and remove the bottom of the Duplicate "Public Inspection Copy" of the report form relating to Item 11.

Public reporting for this collection of information is estimated to average one hour per request, including the time for reviewing instructions, searching existing data sources, gathering and maintaining the data needed, and completing and reviewing the collection of information. Send comments regarding this burden estimate or any other aspect of this collection of information, including suggestions for reducing this burden, to Office of Security and Management Support, Bureau of Export Administration, U.S. Department of Commerce, Washington, D.C. 20230; and to the Office of Management and Budget, Paperwork Reduction Project (0694-0012), Washington, D.C. 20503.

1a. Identify firm submitting this report:
Name: ______
Address: ______
City, State, and ZIP: ______
Country *(if other than USA)*: ______
Telephone: ______
Firm Identification No. *(If known)*: ______ 29-34

Specify firm type:
☐ Exporter
☐ Bank
☐ Forwarder
☐ Carrier
☐ Insurer
☐ Other 35

1b. Check any applicable box:
☐ Revision of a previous report (attach two copies of the previously submitted report)
☐ Resubmission of a deficient report returned by BXA (attach form letter that was returned with deficient report)
☐ Report on behalf of the person identified in Item 2
☐ Dual report on behalf of self and the person identified in Item 2

2. If you are authorized to report and are reporting on behalf of another U.S. person, identify that person (e.g., domestic subsidiary, controlled Foreign subsidiary, exporter, beneficiary);
Name: ______
Address: ______
City, State, and ZIP: ______
Country *(if other than USA)*: ______
Type of firm: ***(see list in Item 1a)***
Firm Identification No. *(If known)*: ______

3. Identify exporting firm, unless same as item 1a or 2:
Name: ______
Address: ______
City, State, and ZIP: ______
Country *(if other than USA)*: ______
Firm Identification No. *(If known)*: ______ 36-41 42

4. (a) Name of boycotting country from which request originated: ______
(b) Name of country directing inclusion of request, if different from (a) above: ______ 43-44

5. Name of country or countries against which request is directed: ______ 45-46

6. Reporting firm's reference number *(e.g., letter of credit, customer order, invoice)*: ______ 71-77

7. Date firm received request: ***(use digits for month/day/year)*** ______ 47-52

8. Specify type(s) of document conveying the request:
☐ Request to carrier for blacklist certificate *(submit two copies of blacklist certificate or transcript of request)*
☐ Unwritten, not otherwise provided for *(make transcript of request and submit copies)* 53-54
☐ Letter of credit
☐ Requisition/purchase order/accepted contract/shipping instruction
☐ Bid invitation/tender/proposal/trade opportunity
☐ Questionnaire *(not related to a particular dollar value transaction)*
☐ Other written *(specify)* ______

Submit two copies of each document or relevant page in which the request appears

9. Decision on request: *(Check one)*
☐ Have not taken and will not take the action requested.
☐ Have taken or will take the action requested.
☐ Have taken or will take the action requested and claim it is subject to a grace period ***(attach detailed explanation).*** 56-57
☐ Have taken or will take the action requested but in a modified form ***(attach detailed explanation).***
☐ Unable to report ultimate decision on the request at this time and will inform the Bureau of Export Administration of the decision within ten days after decision is made.

Additional Information: The firm submitting this report may, if it so desires, state on a separate sheet any additional information relating to the request reported or the response to that request. This statement will constitute a part of the report and will be made available for public inspection and copying, subject to the right to protect certain confidential information from disclosure described in Item 10.

10. Protection of Certain Information from Disclosure: (Check appropriate boxes and sign below)
1. ☐ I (We) certify that disclosure to the public of the information regarding quantity, description, and value of the commodities or technical data contained in:
☐ Item 11 below *(If you check this box,* be sure to remove the bottom of the Duplicate (Public Inspection Copy) of the report form relating to Item 11.)
☐ Attached documents *(If you check this box,* be sure to edit the "Public Inspection Copy" of the documents submitted to exclude the specified information) would place a United States person involved at a competitive disadvantage, and I (We) request that it be kept confidential.
2. ☐ I (We) authorize public release of all information contained in the report and in any attached documents. I (We) certify that all statements and information contained in this report are true and correct to the best of my (our) knowledge and belief.

Sign here in ink ______ Type or print ______ Date ______

11. Describe the commodities or technical data involved, and specify quantity and value:
Description
Quantity:
Value to the nearest whole dollar $

ORIGINAL Submit to Office of Antiboycott Compliance BXA, U.S. Department of Commerce, Room 6099-C, Washington, D.C. 20230

Figure 2–2. Report of request for restrictive trade practice or boycott—multiple transactions (and continuation sheet).

FORM BXA-6051P
(REV 10-89)

U.S. DEPARTMENT OF COMMERCE
BUREAU OF EXPORT ADMINISTRATION

THIS SPACE FOR BXA USE

772602

A

BATCH

MONTH/YEAR

REPORT OF REQUEST FOR RESTRICTIVE TRADE PRACTICE OR BOYCOTT MULTIPLE TRANSACTIONS (Sheet No. 1)

(For reporting requests described in 769 of the Export Administration Regulations)

NOTICE OF RIGHT TO PROTECT CERTAIN INFORMATION FROM DISCLOSURE
The Export Administration Act permits you to protect from public disclosure information regarding the quantity, description, and value of the commodities or technical data supplied in Item 9 of this report and in any accompanying documents. ***If you do not claim this protection, all of the information in your report and in accompanying documents will be made available for public inspection and copying.*** You can obtain this protection by certifying, in Item 5 of the report, that disclosure of the information regarding the quantity, description and value of the commodities or technical data referred to above would place a United States company or individual involved in the report at a competitive disadvantage. If you make such a certification in Item 5, you may remove information regarding the quantity, description, and value of the commodities or technical data supplied by you from Item 9 of the public inspection copy of the report form and from the public inspection copies of the accompanying documents. The withholding of this information will be honored by the Department unless the Secretary determines that disclosure of the information would not place a United States company or individual at a competitive disadvantage or that it would be contrary to the national interest to withhold the information.

This report is required by law (50 U.S.C. App. §2403-1a(b), P.L. 95-52, E.O. 12002, 15 CFR Part 769). Failure to report can result both in criminal penalties, including fines or imprisonment, and administrative sanctions.

INSTRUCTIONS: 1. This form may not include a transaction report that is filed late, nor indicate a decision on request other than those coded in Item 4 below. 2. This form may be used to report on behalf of another United States person if all transactions apply to the person identified in Item 2, but may not be considered as a dual report on behalf of both persons identified in Item 1a and Item 2. 3. Limit each report to 75 transactions or less. 4. Attach as many continuation sheets as needed. Enter sheet number and name of reporting firm on each continuation sheet (starting with Sheet No 2). 5. List each transaction across the continuation sheet, completing all items that apply. Use as many lines as necessary but separate transactions with a blank space or line. 6. Assemble original report form and accompanying documents as a unit, and submit intact and unaltered. 7. Assemble and submit the duplicate copy of report form (marked Duplicate (Public Inspection Copy)) and additional copies of accompanying documents (marked with the legend "Public Inspection Copy.") *4. If you certify, in Item 5, that the disclosure of the information specified there would cause competitive disadvantage, edit the "Public Inspection Copy" of the documents submitted to exclude the specified information and remove the right hand portion of the Duplicate (Public Inspection Copy) of the continuation sheet(s) relating to Column 9.* **MULTIPLE TRANSACTIONS:** Public reporting for this collection of information is estimated to average one hour per reported request, including the time for reviewing instructions, searching existing data sources, gathering and maintaining the data needed, and completing and reviewing the collection of information. Send comments regarding this burden estimate or any other aspect of this collection of information, including suggestions for reducing this burden to Office of Security and Management Support, Bureau of Export Administration, U.S. Department of Commerce, Washington, D.C. 20230; and to the Office of Management and Budget, Paperwork Reduction Project (0694-0012), Washington, D.C. 20503.

1a. Identify firm submitting this report:

Name:
Address:
City, State and ZIP:
Country *(if other than USA)*
Telephone:
Firm Identification No. *(if known)*

Specify firm type:

Exporter
Bank
Forwarder
Carrier
Insurer
Other

1b. Check any applicable box:

Revision of a previous report (attach two copies of the previously submitted report)
Resubmission of a deficient report returned by BTR (attach form letter that was returned with deficient report)
Report on behalf of the person identified in item 2

2. If you are authorized to report and are reporting on behalf of another U.S. person, identify that person (e.g., domestic subsidiary, controlled foreign subsidiary, exporter, beneficiary):

Name
Address
City, State and ZIP
Country *(if other than USA)*
Type of firm *(see list in item 1a)*

3. REQUESTING DOCUMENT CODES ***(use to code Column 6 of continuation sheet)***

C Request to carrier for blacklist certificate (submit two copies of blacklist certificate or transcript of request)
U Unwritten, not otherwise provided for (make transcript of request and submit two copies)
L Letter of credit
R Requisition/purchase order/accepted contract/ shipping instruction
B Bid invitation/tender/proposal/trade opportunity
Q Questionaire (not related to a particular dollar value transaction)
9 Other written

} Submit two copies of each document or relevant page in which the request appears

4. DECISION ON REQUEST CODES ***(use to code Column 7 of continuation sheet)***

R Have not taken and will not take the action requested
T Have taken or will take the action requested

5. Protection of Certain Information from Disclosure: ***(Check appropriate boxes and sign Below)***

☐ I (we) certify that disclosure to the public of the information regarding quantity, description, and value of the commodities or technical data contained in

☐ Column 9 of the attached continuation sheets (If you check this box, be sure to remove column 9 from the Duplicate (Public Inspection Copy)) of the continuation sheets

☐ Attached documents *(If you check this box* be sure to edit the "Public Inspection Copy" of the documents submitted to exclude the specified information.) would place a United States person involved at a competitive disadvantage, and I (we) request that it be kept confidential

☐ I (we) authorize public release of all information contained in the report and in any attached documents

I (we) certify that all statements and information contained in this report are true and correct to the best of my (our) knowledge and belief

Sign here in ink ______ Type or print ______ Date ______

ORIGINAL - Submit to Office of Antiboycott Compliance, BXA, Room 6099C, U.S. Department of Commerce, Washington, D.C. 20230

Figure 2–2. *(continued)*

Column (2) Also enter firm identification number assigned to exporting firm, if known.
(6) Use codes found on Sheet No. 1 to specify type(s) of document conveying the request.
(7) Use codes found on Sheet No.1 to indicate whether action taken or not taken.
(8) Enter reporting firm's reference number (e.g., letter of credit, customer order, invoice). This number must appear on corresponding copy of document or relevant page. Attach copies in same order as listed on continuation sheet(s).

SHEET NO.

REPORTING FIRM *(Name)*

FORM **BXA-6051P-a**
(Rev. 10-89)

U.S. DEPARTMENT OF COMMERCE
Bureau of Export Administration

REPORT OF REQUEST FOR RESTRICTIVE TRADE PRACTICE OR BOYCOTT
MULTIPLE TRANSACTIONS (Continuation Sheet)

RSN SUBSET RTP/CLASS OTHER PARTY FIN (1)	NAME AND ADDRESS OF EXPORTING FIRM INVOLVED *(unless same as item 1a or item 2 on Sheet No 1)* (2)	BOYCOTTING COUNTRY (3)	BOYCOTTED COUNTRY OR COUNTRIES (4)	DATE REQUEST RECEIVED BY FIRM (month/day/year) (5)	REQUEST-ING DOCUMENT CODE (6)	DECISION ON REQUEST CODE (7)	YOUR REFERENCE NUMBER (8)	COMMODITIES OR TECHNICAL DATA *(description, quality, and value to the nearest whole dollar)* (9)
THIS SPACE FOR BXA USE								

(Remove stub from public inspection copy at perforation if confidentiality is requested in Sheet No. 1)

ORIGINAL - Attach to and submit with the original of Sheet No. 1 (BXA-6051P)

will be exported at a later time. For employees visiting a number of countries on sales visits, posting temporary importation bonds in a number of countries can be burdensome and must be arranged significantly in advance. One solution to this problem is the ATA carnet developed by the Customs Cooperation Council and administered by the International Chamber of Commerce. In effect, the carnet is both a customs entry and a temporary importation bond which is honored by sixty countries and which permits temporary entry of samples for order solicitation, display, and exhibition. Products entered by carnet must be exported and not sold. The carnet is obtained by applying to the International Chamber of Commerce and posting cash or a bond for 40 percent of the value with them. Additional information about carnets can be obtained from the U.S. Council of International Business in New York City, telephone number (212) 354-4480. An application for a carnet is shown in Figure 2–3. In order to avoid having to pay U.S. customs duties on the sample when the salesperson returns to the United States, the carnet should be signed by the U.S. Customs Service.

K. Utilization of Freight Forwarders and Foreign Customs Brokers

A competent freight forwarder can handle routing, inland and international transportation, containerization, scheduling of carriers, transshipments, bills of lading, consular certifications, legalizations, inspections, export licenses, marine and air insurance, warehousing, and export packing, either itself or through its agents. Unless the U.S. company is large enough to have a number of personnel who can perform the services in-house that are offered by freight forwarders, it is likely that the U.S. company will have to select and interface with a freight forwarder on export sales (and possibly a foreign customs broker on landed, duty-paid sales) in exporting its products to foreign countries. Transportation carriers are allowed to pay compensation (commissions) only to licensed freight forwarders for booking shipments. Freight forwarders have inherent conflicts of interest because they receive compensation from carriers and also receive freight-forwarding fees from shippers. Selection of the right freight forwarder is no small task, as freight forwarders have various levels of expertise, particularly in regard to different types of products and different country destinations. Some of the things that should be considered include reputation, size, financial strength, insurance coverage, fees, and automation. References should be checked. A list of freight forwarders can be obtained from the local commercial Yellow Pages or from the National Customs Brokers and Freight Forwarders Association of America in Washington, D.C., telephone number (202) 466-0222. Before selecting a freight forwarder, a face-to-face meeting with alternative candidates is recommended. At the outset of the relationship, the U.S. exporter will be asked to sign an agreement appointing the freight forwarder as its agent and giving it a power of attorney. It is important that the U.S. exporter ask its attorney to review such an agreement and make appropriate changes. (A simple sample power of attorney is shown in Figure 4–1.) Some exporters prefer to quote terms of sale where the exporter is responsible for the transportation and to control delivery by selection of and payment to their own freight forwarder. In other cases the buyer selects the freight forwarder, known as a "routed"

Figure 2–3. Application for carnet.

ATA Carnet Application

A. Holder Information:

1. Carnet Holder (Corporation or Individual):
Street Address (No P.O. Box):
City: **State:** **Zip:** **Phone:** **Fax:**
2. IRS/SS No.: **E-mail:**
3. Parent Company: **IRS No. of Parent Company:**
4. Person Duly Authorized & Title:
5. Authorized Representatives (individuals or agents) who will be shipping or hand-carrying the merchandise on the Carnet:

B. Carnet Preparation/Country Information:

6. Goods to be exported as: (mark more than one if applicable)
☐ **Professional Equipment (PE)**
☐ **Commercial Samples (CS)**
☐ **Exhibitions and Fairs (EF)**

7. Approximate Date of Departure from U.S.: (enter date as "MM/DD/YY")

8. Type the NUMBER of visits in the space provided beside each country you expect to visit:

__ Algeria (DZ)	__ Gibraltar (GI)	__ Macedonia (MK)	__ South Africa (ZA)
__ Andorra (AD)	__ Greece (GR)	__ Malaysia (MY)	__ Spain (ES)
__ Australia (AU)	__ Hong Kong (HK)	__ Malta (MT)	__ Sri Lanka (LK)
__ Austria (AT)	__ Hungary (HU)	__ Mauritius (MU)	__ Sweden (SE)
__ Belgium (BE)	__ Iceland (IS)	__ Morocco (MA)[2]	__ Switzerland (CH)
__ Bulgaria (BE)	__ India (IN)[2]	__ Netherlands (NL)	__ Taiwan (TW) – Call First
__ Canada (CA)[1]	__ Ireland (IE)	__ New Zealand (NZ)	__ Thailand (TH)
__ China (CN)[2] – Call First	__ Israel (IL)[3]	__ Norway (NO)	__ Tunisia (TN)[4]
__ Croatia (HR)	__ Italy (IT)	__ Poland (PL)	__ Turkey (TR)
__ Cyprus (CY)	__ Ivory Coast (CI)	__ Portugal (PT)	__ United Kingdom (GB)
__ Czech Republic (CZ)	__ Japan (JP)	__ Romania (RO)	__ Other
__ Denmark (DK)	__ Korea (KR)[3]	__ Russia (RU)	
__ Estonia (EE)	__ Latvia (LV)	__ Senegal (SN)	
__ Finland (FI)	__ Lebanon (LB)[4]	__ Singapore (SG)	
__ France (FR)	__ Lithuania (LT)	__ Slovakia (SK)	
__ Germany (DE)	__ Luxembourg (LU)	__ Slovenia (SI)	

[1] certain PE items are admitted [2] only EF items for certain events [3] 100% security required [4] CS items are not admitted

9. Number of times your merchandise will be leaving and re-entering the U.S.:__________

10. Number of countries transiting(s): **List Countries to be transited:**

C. Delivery Instructions:

11. Courier Service (Include completed airway bill with your account number OR to use our courier service, include $20.00 for Shipping & Handling)
12. Messenger Pick-up
13. Regular Mail

D. Processing Fees:

14. Basic Processing Fee: **Ship to:**
15. Expedited Service:
16. Additional Certificate Sets Fee: ($5 each add'l set after 8)
17. Continuation Sheet Fee: ($0 first sheet, $5 each add'l)
18. Shipper's Export Declaration Fee: ($5 each)
19. Refundable Claim Deposit:
(for government agencies only; waiver must be download and submitted)
20. Shipping and Handling:
21. Country Surcharge:
Total:

Continue to next page for Security and Obligation.

Figure 2–3. *(continued)*

E. Security:

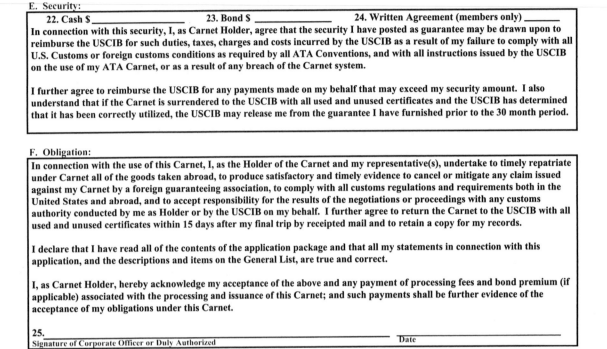

22. Cash $____________ 23. Bond $____________ 24. Written Agreement (members only) ______

In connection with this security, I, as Carnet Holder, agree that the security I have posted as guarantee may be drawn upon to reimburse the USCIB for such duties, taxes, charges and costs incurred by the USCIB as a result of my failure to comply with all U.S. Customs or foreign customs conditions as required by all ATA Conventions, and with all instructions issued by the USCIB on the use of my ATA Carnet, or as a result of any breach of the Carnet system.

I further agree to reimburse the USCIB for any payments made on my behalf that may exceed my security amount. I also understand that if the Carnet is surrendered to the USCIB with all used and unused certificates and the USCIB has determined that it has been correctly utilized, the USCIB may release me from the guarantee I have furnished prior to the 30 month period.

F. Obligation:

In connection with the use of this Carnet, I, as the Holder of the Carnet and my representative(s), undertake to timely repatriate under Carnet all of the goods taken abroad, to produce satisfactory and timely evidence to cancel or mitigate any claim issued against my Carnet by a foreign guaranteeing association, to comply with all customs regulations and requirements both in the United States and abroad, and to accept responsibility for the results of the negotiations or proceedings with any customs authority conducted by me as Holder or by the USCIB on my behalf. I further agree to return the Carnet to the USCIB with all used and unused certificates within 15 days after my final trip by receipted mail and to retain a copy for my records.

I declare that I have read all of the contents of the application package and that all my statements in connection with this application, and the descriptions and items on the General List, are true and correct.

I, as Carnet Holder, hereby acknowledge my acceptance of the above and any payment of processing fees and bond premium (if applicable) associated with the processing and issuance of this Carnet; and such payments shall be further evidence of the acceptance of my obligations under this Carnet.

25. ________________________ ____________
Signature of Corporate Officer or Duly Authorized Date

USCIB May, 2001

forwarder. The U.S. exporter should be aware that a freight forwarder and any foreign customs broker selected by it or by the freight forwarder are the exporter's agents, and any mistakes that they make will be the exporter's responsibility as far as third parties and governmental agencies are concerned. This is not always understood by companies that pay significant amounts of money to hire such persons. Where a freight forwarder is responsible for some loss or damage and refuses to make a reasonable settlement, the exporter may be able to proceed against the surety bond or even seek cancellation of the forwarder's Federal Maritime Commission license. Where the forwarder is bankrupt and has failed to pay transportation carriers amounts paid by the exporter, the exporter may be required to pay twice.

L. Export Packing and Labeling (Hazardous Materials)

It may be necessary for the U.S. company to have special packing for its products for long-distance ocean shipments. The packing used for domestic shipments may be totally inadequate for such shipping. Identification marks on the packages should be put in the packing list. Containers may be various lengths (20′, 40′, 45′, 48′, or 53′), widths (8′ or 8′6″), and heights (8′6″ or 9′6″). Special types of containers may be needed such as insulated, ventilated, open top, refrigerated ("reefers"), flat, and/or high-cube. Containerized shipments may be eligible for lower insurance rates com-

Figure 2–3. *(continued)*

INTERNATIONAL GUARANTEE CHAIN .... / *CHAINE DE GARANTIE INTERNATIONALE*

B.I.C.C.

.... INTERNATIONAL GUARANTEE CHAIN / *CHAINE DE GARANTIE INTERNATIONALE*

GENERAL LIST / *LISTE GENERALE*

(May be used for Continuation Sheets / *Feuille Supplementaire*

X..**X**

Signature of Holder / *Signature du titulaire*

....

Signature of authorized official and stamp of the issuing Association / *Signature du delegué et timbre L'association emettrice*

VOUCHER No. .... *VOLET DE No.*

Continuation Sheet No. .... *FEUILLE SUPPLEMENTAIRE No.*

A.T. A. Carnet No. *Carnet A.T.A. No.*

Item No./ *No. d'ordre*	**Trade description of goods and marks and numbers, if any**/ *Désignation commerciale des marchandises et, le cas échéant, marques et numéros*	**Number of Pieces**/ *Nombre de Pièces*	**Weight or Volume**/ *Poids ou Volume*	**Value**/* *Valeur*	****Country of origin**/ *Pays d'origine*	**For Customs Use**/ *Réservé à la douane*
1	2	3	4	5	6	7
TOTAL CARRIED OVER/REPORT						
General List includes ________ *(number) "Continuation Sheets".*						
TOTAL or CARRIED OVER/*TOTAL ou A REPORTER*						

***Commercial value in country of issue and in its currency, unless stated differently.**/ * *Valeur commerciale dans le pays d'émission et dans sa monnaie, sauf indication contraire.*
**** Show country of origin if different from country of issue of the Carnet, using ISO country codes.**/ ** *Indiquer le pays d'origine s'il est différent du pays d'émmission du carnet, en utilisant le code international des pays ISO.*

F13 (6/00)

pared with breakbulk or palletized cargo. Specialized export packing companies exist and can often do the packing or can act as consultants in assisting the U.S. company with formulating packing that would be suitable for such shipments. Under the U.S. Uniform Commercial Code and the Convention on the International Sale of Goods (discussed in Chapter 3, Section B.2m), unless expressly excluded, a seller makes a warranty that its products have been properly packaged. Under the Carriage of Goods by Sea Act, a steamship line is not responsible for damage to cargo due to insufficient packing. Improper packing can lead to disputes and claims for breach of warranty.

Under the Intermodal Safe Container Transportation Act as amended, a shipper arranging for intermodal transportation of a container or trailer carrying more than 29,000 pounds and traveling in any part by truck over the road must provide the initial carrier with a certificate of gross weight including a description of contents, which certificate must be transferred to each subsequent carrier.

As of January 1, 1991, all hazardous materials must be packed in accordance with the United Nations' Performance Oriented Packaging Standards. Shippers of hazardous materials must be registered with the Department of Transportation. "Hazmat employees," including those who handle, package, or transport hazardous materials and those who fill out shipping papers must have training at least every three years (see discussion in Chapter 4, Section N).

Passenger air carriers and air freight forwarders are required to obtain a "Shippers Security Endorsement" from the shipper certifying that the shipment does not contain any unauthorized, explosive, destructive devices or hazardous materials and including a consent to search the shipment. Personal identification is required from the person tendering the shipment.

Labeling is equally important. If the product is a hazardous substance, special labeling is required. Furthermore, any product labeling may require printing in the foreign country's language. The types of information and disclosures required on such labeling may be prescribed by foreign law in the country of destination and should be confirmed as part of the pre-export planning. A European Union Directive that would have required that products sold in the European Union be labeled with only metric measurements after January 1, 2000, has been postponed indefinitely.

M. Terms of Sale

Although there are ordinarily many terms and conditions which the seller will include in its export sales agreements, one of the terms of sale upon which seller and buyer must agree is that relating to passage of title, risk of loss, price, and payment. Although a seller can sell on different terms of sale to different buyers in accordance with whatever terms are expressed in each buyer's purchase order, it is ordinarily much better for the seller to think about and formulate policies relating to its terms of sale in advance of receipt of orders. There are a number of considerations, the first of which relates to the use of abbreviations.

In order to standardize the understanding of the seller and buyer relating to their obligations in international sales agreements, various nomenclatures have been developed which use abbreviations, such as *ex-factory, ex-works, FOB plant, CIF, landed,* and so on. While these shorthand abbreviations can be useful, they can also be sources of confusion. The International Chamber of Commerce (INCO) has developed the "Incoterms," which were revised in 2000 (see Figure 2–4). There are also the Revised American Foreign Trade Definitions, the Warsaw Terms, and the abbreviations in the United States Uniform Commercial Code. Although these abbreviated terms of sale are similar, they also differ from nomenclature to nomenclature, and it is important to specify in the sales agreement which nomenclature is being used when an abbreviation is utilized. For example, on a CIF sale under the Uniform Commercial Code the seller is required to furnish war risk along with the other coverage. Under the Incoterms, however, the seller need provide war risk coverage only if requested by the buyer. Furthermore, even though it is assumed that sellers and buyers know the responsibilities and obligations that flow from utilizing specific terms such as *FOB plant,* the parties in fact may not always understand all of their rights and responsibilities in the same way, and disputes and problems may arise. For example, even though on an FOB seller's plant sale the buyer is responsible for obtaining and paying for ocean insurance, often the buyer will expect the seller to obtain such insurance, which the buyer will reimburse the seller for paying. It is also possible that the seller will arrange for such insurance at the same time that the buyer does so, resulting in expensive duplication. Or, even though the buyer may be responsible for paying freight, the buyer may

Figure 2–4. Examples of Incoterm usage.

	Terms for Any Mode of Transport (including Intermodal)	
EXW	ex-works	South Bend, Indiana
FCA	free carrier	South Bend, Indiana
CPT	carriage paid to	Munich, Germany
CIP	carriage and insurance paid to	Munich, Germany
DAF	delivered at frontier	Amhof, Holland
DDU	delivered duty unpaid	Tubingen, Germany
DDP	delivered duty paid	Tubingen, Germany
	Terms Limited to Sea and Inland Waterway Transport	
FAS	free alongside ship	Port of New Orleans
FOB	free on board	Port of New Orleans
CFR	cost and freight	Port of Rotterdam
CIF	cost, insurance & freight	Port of Rotterdam
DES	delivered ex-ship	Port of Rotterdam
DEQ	delivered ex-quay	Port of Rotterdam

Courtesy of Eugene J. Schreiber.

expect the seller to arrange for shipment "freight collect." Finally, under the new Incoterms, certain traditional terms such as "C&F," "FOR," "FOT," and "FOB airport" have been abolished, and certain new terms such as "CFR," "DES," "DEQ," and "DDU" have been created. A diagram of the Incoterms is shown in Figure 2–5. In the author's experience, even if the parties choose to use an abbreviation to specify the way in which title will pass and delivery will be made, the author strongly recommends that the "who does what" be stated in detail in the sales agreement to avoid the possibility of a misunderstanding.

It is also important for the seller to realize that the price term may differ from the place of passage of title and risk of loss or time of payment. For example, under an INCO CFR, or CIF term, the seller will be quoting a price to the buyer that includes the seller's cost of shipping the merchandise to the destination, but, in actuality, title and risk of loss will pass to the buyer when the merchandise is loaded on the ship at the time of export. Similarly, in a sales quotation CIF means only that the price quoted by the seller will include all expenses to the point of destination—it does not mean payment will be made upon arrival. Payment may be made earlier or later depending upon the agreement of the parties. Sellers should be sure that their export sales documentation distinguishes between price terms, title and risk of loss terms, and payment terms.

Under the Convention on the International Sale of Goods (discussed in Chapter 3,

Figure 2–5. Diagram of the Incoterms.

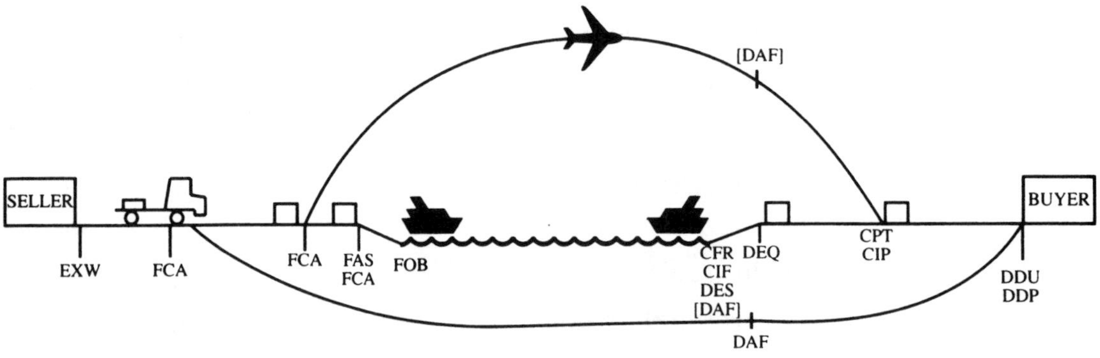

NOTES

1. On CFR, CIF, CPT, and CIP shipments delivery and risk of loss transfer to buyer at port of *shipment*, although seller is responsible for paying for costs of freight (CFR, CPT) and insurance (CIF, CIP).
2. Except for CIP and CIF sales (where insurance is part of the contract price), the seller is not required to purchase insurance but may do so up to the place of delivery, which becomes a cost to be factored into the seller's profitability and sales quotation.
3. Under CIF and CIP, seller must only provide minimum coverage (110% of contract price) but no war risk or strike, riot, and civil commotion coverage unless buyer agrees to bear expense.
4. Packing costs for shipment to known ultimate destination are an expense of the seller (even on EXW sales).
5. Cost of pre-shipment inspections is always the expense of the buyer unless inspections are required by country of exportation or otherwise agreed in the sales contract.

Section B.2.m), if the parties do not agree upon a place for the transfer of title and delivery in their sale agreement, title and delivery will transfer when the merchandise is delivered to the first transportation carrier.

Another consideration relates to tax planning. Under U.S. law, if title on the sale of inventory passes outside the United States, foreign source income is created and in some situations, depending upon the seller's tax situation, the seller can reduce its U.S. income taxes by making sales in such manner. It is usually advisable to ensure that title passes prior to customs clearance in the foreign country, however, to make sure that the seller is not responsible for payment of customs duties, which could include expensive antidumping or other special duties.

In most international transactions, the buyer will be responsible for importing the products to its own country, clearing customs, and paying any applicable customs duties. This is because the importer is liable for all customs duties, even antidumping duties. However, if the seller agrees to sell landed, duty paid, or delivered to the buyer's place of business (so-called "free domicile" or "free house" delivery), the seller will be responsible for such customs duties. Ordinarily, the seller cannot act as the importer of record in a foreign country unless it obtains a bond from a foreign bonding company and appoints an agent in that country for all claims for customs duties. Generally, a seller would not want to sell delivered, duty paid, but sometimes the buyer's bargaining leverage is such or competition is such that the seller cannot get the business unless it is willing to do so. If the buyer is wary of paying dumping duties, it may refuse to act as the importer of record. Similarly, when the seller is selling to a related buyer, such as a majority or wholly owned subsidiary, the parent company may want to sell landed, duty paid, and assume such expenses.

In general, if the seller sells ex-factory (ex-works), it will have the least responsibility and risk. The buyer will then be responsible for arranging and paying for inland transportation to the port of export, ocean transportation, and foreign importation. In many cases an ex-factory sale can result in the buyer being able to avoid customs duties on the inland freight from the seller's factory to the port of export. In such instances, even though the buyer will have the responsibility for complying with all U.S. export laws, such as export control licenses, filing Shipper's Export Declarations, arranging insurance, and complying with foreign laws, it is a short-sighted seller who does not thoroughly discuss with the buyer all of these items during the formation of the sales agreement. If the buyer is unable to complete export or effect import, the fact that the seller is not legally responsible will be of little consolation and will lead to lawsuits, nonpayment, and loss of future business.

Even though selling ex-factory may be attractive to a seller, there are many reasons why the seller may not want or need to sell on other terms. For example, the buyer may be inexperienced in arranging international shipments; the seller's competitors may be offering delivered terms; the seller may be selling to an affiliated company; the seller may need to control diversion back into the United States or other countries; the seller may be trying to assure delivery of goods subject to U.S. export controls; the seller may want to control the shipment until loaded on board the ship for letter of credit sales; the seller may want to control title and ownership until payment; or the seller may have warehouse-to-warehouse marine insurance under an open-cargo policy and, therefore, by agreeing to pay the insurance costs can save the buyer some money; and sometimes the seller is in a better position to obtain lower ocean transportation or insurance rates. As already indicated, sometimes sales effected outside of the United States can lower the U.S. seller's income tax liability. For all of these reasons, a thorough discussion of the terms and conditions of sale between the seller and buyer, rather than simply following a set policy, may be advantageous.

N. Consignments

In addition to sales transactions where title to the merchandise transfers to the foreign buyer in the United States or sometime up to delivery in the foreign country in accordance with the terms of sale between the parties, in consignment transactions the exporter/seller maintains ownership of the goods, and the consignee in the foreign country takes possession of the goods. The consignee then offers the goods for sale, and when a customer purchases the goods, title transfers from the exporter/seller to the importer/buyer and to the customer simultaneously. Such transactions have various procedural and documentary considerations. As the owner, the exporter/seller will be responsible for all transportation costs, insurance, filing of Shipper's Export Declarations, and obtaining export control licenses. While foreign customs regulations may permit the consignee to effect customs clearance, legally the goods are owned by the exporter/seller, and the exporter/seller will be liable for the foreign customs duties. Additional taxes may be assessed, such as personal property taxes assessed on the goods while they are awaiting sale and income taxes because title will pass to the importer/buyer at the buyer's place of business in the foreign country. In addition, to avoid the inability to take possession of the goods in case of bankruptcy of the importer-buyer or other claims by the importer's creditors, special arrangements under the buyer's law such as chattel mortgages, conditional sale agreements, public notices, or security interests may be required. Because the export/import transaction is not a sale at the time of entry, transaction value cannot be used—the customs authorities will assess customs duties based upon an alternative valuation method.

O. Leases

In export transactions which are leases, no sales documentation should be used. The ability of the exporter/lessor to retain title and ownership, repossess the goods at the end of the lease, and obtain income tax benefits depends upon using lease documentation rather than sales agreements. As with the consignment, the exporter/seller is legally responsible for all exporting and importing obligations, although those obligations can be delegated to the importer in the lease agreement. For customs valuation purposes, a lease is not a sale; therefore, transaction value will not be used and the customs duties payable will depend upon an alternative valuation method. Whether the transaction will be subject to value-added taxes or other exactions depends upon the law of the destination country.

P. Marine and Air Casualty Insurance

Marine (or ocean) and air insurance is important on export shipments. Under the Carriage of Goods by Sea Act, ocean carriers are responsible for the seaworthiness of the vessel, properly manning the vessel, and making the vessel safe for carriage of the cargo. The ocean carrier is not responsible for negligence of the master in navigating the vessel, fires, perils, dangers, accidents of the sea, acts of God, acts of war, acts of public enemies, detention or seizures, acts or omissions of shippers, strikes or lock-outs, riots and civil commotions, saving or attempting to save a life or property at sea, inherent defect, quality or vice of the goods, insufficiency of packing, quarantine restrictions, insufficiency or inadequacy of marks, latent defects not discoverable by due diligence, and any other causes arising without the actual fault and privity of the ocean carrier.

Without insurance, even when the carrier can be proven liable, responsibility is limited to $500 per "package" on ocean shipments and $20 per kilogram on air shipments unless a higher value is declared in advance and a higher transportation charge paid. The seller may be responsible for (1) obtaining and paying for such insurance with no reimbursement by the buyer, or (2) obtaining and paying for such insurance with reimbursement by the buyer. Or, the buyer may be responsible for (1) obtaining and paying for such insurance with no reimbursement by the seller, or (2) obtaining and paying for such insurance with reimbursement by the seller. Although abbreviated trade terms, such as FOB port of shipment, are supposedly designed to clarify which parties are responsible for arranging and paying for various aspects of an export shipment, often confusion and misunderstandings occur. It is extremely important to clearly determine who will pay for such insurance and who will arrange for it. It is necessary for a seller or buyer to have an "insurable interest" in the merchandise in order to obtain insurance coverage. Depending on the terms of sale, the seller may have an ownership interest up to a particular point or a financial interest in the safe arrival of the shipment up until the time it is paid.

A U.S. company can buy an open or blanket cargo marine or air insurance policy that is in continuous effect for its shipments, or a special onetime cargo policy that insures a single shipment. Alternatively, it can utilize its freight forwarder's blanket policy. There are many advantages for a company to have its own open cargo policy, but the quantity of exports must justify it; otherwise, it is probably more appropriate to utilize the freight forwarder's blanket policy. Some insurance brokers recommend that a company have its own policy when exports and/or imports reach $500,000 to $1 million. When a blanket policy is used, a separate certificate is issued by the insurance company or the holder of the policy to evidence coverage for each shipment. (A sample marine insurance policy and certificate are shown in Chapter 4, Figures 4–11 and 4–12, respectively.)

Familiarizing oneself with such insurance policies is also important in the event that a casualty occurs and a claim needs to be filed. Generally, it is best to obtain "all risks" (rather than "named peril") and "warehouse-to-warehouse" (or "marine extension") coverage. Even "all risks" coverage does not include war risk or "strike, riot and civil commotion" coverage, and the seller should specifically determine whether these risks and others, such as delay in arrival and change in customs duties, should be covered by a rider and payment of an additional premium (see Figure 2–6). Under the Incoterms it is necessary to insure the shipment at 110 percent of the invoice value; in the case of some letter of credit sales, payment cannot be obtained unless insurance in that amount has been obtained. The filing of claims is discussed in Chapter 4, Section G.

In order to get paid under letters of credit or documentary collections through banking channels, it may be necessary for the seller to furnish a certificate to the bank evidencing that insurance coverage exists.

Marine insurance companies and insurance brokers can advise on the different types of coverage available and comparative premiums. The premium will depend on the type of merchandise, its value (risk of pilferage), its packing, the type of coverage (including riders), the method of transportation, the country of destination and routing, the loss history of the insured, the carriers used, whether transshipment will occur, etc.

Q. Methods of Transportation; Booking Transportation

In determining the general method by which the U.S. company will export, or in filling a specific shipment to a particular customer, marine transportation and air transportation must be evaluated. Obviously, air transportation is much quicker but is more expensive. Large shipments cannot be shipped by air. The exporter may choose to charter a vessel to obtain lower rates for bulk commodities. Inland transportation by truck, rail, or air must be selected. The booking of steamship lines, shipping schedules, any delays necessary to load a full container, and any intermediate stops for the ship must all be considered by the U.S. company or its freight forwarder before selecting the appropriate transportation method and carrier. The transportation companies maintain lists of service charges based upon commodity classifications called "tariffs" (not to be confused with the customs duties paid to governments on imported merchandise). These tariffs are subject to change and often contain numerous exceptions and surcharges (a sample tariff is shown in Figure 2–7). Independent lines, not members of a shipping conference, may offer lower rates but more limited service. The exporter should be careful in recording quotations, dates, tariff classification numbers, rates, and the person making the quotation in order to avoid disputes. A sample Confirmation of Booking from a steamship line is shown in Figure 2–8. Airfreight rates are based on actual weight or dimensional weight, whichever is more. The size of the shipment (height × width × length in inches) divided by 166 equals the dimensional weight. Ocean freight rates will also be based on weight or measure, whichever is greater. Measure is calculated by multiplying the height by width by length in inches and dividing by 1,728 to get cubic feet. Sometimes the carrier's tariff will be expressed in tons (short ton = 2,000 pounds, long ton = 2,240 pounds, or metric ton = 1,000 kilograms = 2,200 pounds) or in units of 40 cubic feet of volume. Miscellaneous freight shipped together is classified as "Freight All Kinds," which pays a higher rate than specific commodities. It is a violation of the Shipping Act of 1984 for a shipper

(*Text continues on page 44.*)

Figure 2–6. Ocean marine insurance coverage.

OCEAN MARINE COVERAGE SURVEY - IMPORTERS / EXPORTERS

DATE:

NAMED INSURED:	
PRODUCER:	

INSURED	UNINSURED	COVERAGES	INSURED	UNINSURED	COVERAGES
		POLICY FORM:			**SPECIAL COVERAGES**
		100% CERTAIN UNDERWRITERS AT GROUPE CHEGARAY			Airfreight Replacement
		- AMERICAN INSTITUTE CLAUSES - MARINE/WAR			Atmospheric Conditions
		- LONDON INSTITUTE CLAUSES - MARINE/ WAR			Brands
		All Risk			Concealed Damage # of Days:
		FPA /Limited Conditions			Consequential Damage
					Contingency Insurance Unpaid Vendor (SELLERS INTRST)
		Geographic Scope :			Contingency Insurance for Assured as Consignee (BUYERS INTRST)
					Control of Damaged Goods
					Debris Removal
					Duty (ADD'L FREIGHT/DUTY)
		Location Risks:			Extension of Coverage After Arrival (INS MUST CALL)
		Warehousing - Storage (Processing Location)			FOB/FAS Sales
		Consolidation / Deconsolidation			FOB/FAS Purchases with Insured as Consignee
		Processing of Goods			Household Goods / Personal Effects
		Exhibition / Trade Shows			Automobiles
					Interruption of Transit within control of the Insured (INS MUST CALL)
		Barge Shipments (TMT OR LASH)			Labels
		Domestic Transit - U.S.			Pairs & Sets
		Inland Transit within another country:			Refrigeration Breakdown (AKA "Reefer Clause")
					Rejection
		Accumulation Clause			Return Shipment
		Duration of Risk Clause / Warehouse to Warehouse Clause			Shortage From Container
		Fumigation Clause			Used Machinery (SECOND HAND REPLACEMENT)
		Difference In Conditions Clause			Valuation Clause:

Conveyance Limits:

Underdeck: **$** Ondeck: **$** Air Limit: **$**

Truck/Rail Limit: **$** Parcel Post Limit: **$**

Other Limits:

Storage Locations: **Location limits for Storage**

Deductible:

Cancellation Clause: 30 Days - Marine Policy War Policy / SR&CC Endt: 48 Hours or 7 Days (circle one)

THE COVERAGES INDICATED ON THIS SURVEY WERE DEVELOPED FROM INFORMATION PROVIDED BY THE INSURED AND ARE THOUGHT TO BE ACCURATE AS OF THE DATE THEY WERE DEVELOPED. THIS SURVEY DOES NOT REPRESENT A DETAILED ANALYSIS OF YOUR INSURANCE POLICY(IES). PLEASE REFER TO YOUR ACTUAL POLICY(IES) FOR EXCLUSIONS, LIMITATIONS ND CONDITIONS.

PLEASE CALL US WITH ANY CHANGES

ROANOKE BROKERAGE SERVICES, INC.

A COPY OF THIS SURVEY HAS BEEN GIVEN TO THE INSURED. SIGNED:

ed. 2/1/95

DATE 07/16/96

Figure 2–7. Sample steamship tariff.

SEA-LAND SERVICE, INC. Tariff No.353 SEAU ICC No. 353 (Between US/Guam & Marianas)	Orig/Rev 2nd	Page Section 2 2,720,001
FROM: TARIFF ORIGIN SCOPE TO: TARIFF DESTINATION SCOPE	Cancels 1st	Cancels Page Section 2 2,720,001
SECTION 2 - RULES	CORR: 1930	Issued: 26Apr1994 Eff: 27Apr1994EAN
Items with effective dates prior to page Issue Date are brought forward without change.		

RULE 720
PAYMENT OF CHARGES
Effective: 27Apr1994 (R)

PAYMENT OF FREIGHT AND RELATED CHARGES

Rates, Charges and Monies due are in U.S. Currency. Terms of payment may be prepaid or collect in accordance with Paragraph (B). The following Rules will apply for the payment of all charges:

(A) Freight Monies and Charges shall be prepaid not later than the time of release of any Original Ocean Bill of lading by the Carrier to the Shipper or his Duly Authorized Licensed Freight Forwarder or Agent acting in his behalf.

(B) In accordance with the Carrier's current policies, credit is available to qualifying Commercial or Government Shipper/Consignee upon notification.

(1) To be so qualified, a Shipper/Consignee must be able to demonstrate his credit worthiness to the satisfaction of the Carrier.

(2) At the Carrier's option, credit will be extended on prepaid shipments for a period not to exceed 28 calendar days from the date of vessel sailing from the port of origin. On Collect Shipments, all charges are due 14 calendar days from vessel arrival.

(3) All credit provisions are subject to suspension or cancellation for failure to keep accounts with carrier paid as required. Upon suspension or cancellation of credit privileges, all prepaid shipments must be fully paid in cash upon receipt of the Bill of Lading. All collect shipments must be fully paid in cash upon delivery of cargo at destination. The cash requirements shall continue until (1) above is satisfied.

(C) All Wharfage and Terminal Charges as described in Rule 974 and 974 may be paid at origin or destination and within the same time as outlined for the freight charges. Any supplemental billings, including Demurrage/Detention Charges and Ocean Freight Adjustments, shall be billed within two (2) working days of the return of the container or Carrier's awareness of the need for issuing supplemental billings. All supplemental charges are due fourteen (14) calendar days from the date of the invoice.

(D) Dangerous or Hazardous Cargo requiring special handling or disposition in accordance with the Code of Federal Regulations (Title 46 Part 164.29 and Title 49 Parts 100 and 199, as Revised), CFR 46 and 49 will be accepted under PREPAID terms only.

(E) Shipper and Consignee are absolutely liable for the payment of the freight, even if the freight has been advanced to a defaulting forwarder. Carrier may require that freight charges be prepaid or guaranteed on any shipment which, in the judgement of the carrier, would not bring at forced sale the amount of the freight charges at destination.

Figure 2–7. *(continued)*

8900 LINES RATE AGREEMENT, THE 8900 BB/OOG RATES TARIFF TO MIDDLE-EAST	Orig/Rev 2nd	Page Section 4 8900-00-2000.001
FROM: TARIFF ORIGIN SCOPE TO: TARIFF DESTINATION SCOPE	Cancels 1st	Cancels Page Section 4 8900-00-2000.001
C O D E — SECTION 4 - COMMODITIES AND RATES	CORR: 294	Issued: 26Jan1996 Eff: 26Jan1996EAN

Except as otherwise provided, rates apply per 1000 KGS or 1.000 CBM. Effective Dates (Eff:) shown below. Items with effective dates prior to page Issue Date are brought forward without change.

```
(R)          Effective: 26Jan1996                                    COMMODITY: 8900-00-2000

Boats, including Boat moulds, viz:
 Cruisers, Launchers,
 Motor, Row, Yacht, Sail,
 Including Bridges and Spoilers, N.E.C.

NOTES:
 XX15a  Item Note  xx15
 XX15a  ================
 XX15a
 XX15a  1. Rates apply per boat only when there is
 XX15a  reference in the TLI to this note.
 XX15a
 XX15a  2. Rates are subject to all tariff additionals
 XX15a  in effect at time of receipt of cargo by
 XX15a  the Carrier.
 XX15a
 XX15a  3. Shipper must supply cradle or road trailer
 XX15a  with unboxed boats.  Measurement and weight
 XX15a  of cradle or road trailer are to be included
 XX15a  in calculating freight.
 XX15a
 XX15a  4. Lump sum rates apply per Carriers container.
 XX15a
 XX15a  5. When two or more boats are loaded per
 XX15a  Carrier's container, the beam of the largest
 XX15a  size boat will be used in determining the
 XX15a  applicable rate.
 XX15a
 XX15a  6. Rates do not apply on boats exceeding 45'L
 XX15a  and/or 21'H.
 XX15a
 XX15a  7. Pier/House or House/Pier cargo (that which
 XX15a  is not source loaded by the shipper) will be
 XX15a  subject to an additional charge of $25 per
 XX15a  linear foot, or fraction thereof, per boat;
 XX15a  maximum $1000 per container in addition to
 XX15a  the applicable ocean rate.  Pier/Pier cargo
 XX15a  will be subject to $50 per linear foot, or
 XX15a  fraction thereof, per boat; maximum $2000
 XX15a  per container.  Terminal tariff charges will
 XX15a  not apply.  The charges named in this note
 XX15a  cover the cost for transferring between
 XX15a  Carrier's equipment and other than Carrier's
(Continued in next column)

                 (Continued from preceding column)
XX15a  equipment, and includes all blocking and
XX15a  bracing charges at origin terminal.
XX15a  Provisions of this note not applicable on
XX15a  boats exceeding 180 inches in beam (width).
XX15a
XX15a  ( xx15  continued next page)
XX15a
XX15b  Item Note  xx15  (continued)
XX15b  ================
XX15b
XX15b  8. Cargo exceeding 14'H will be subject to
XX15b  the following additional charges:
XX15b
XX15b  exceeding 14'H but less 16'H - $450/FR
XX15b  exceeding 16'H               - $700/FR
XX15b
XX15b  Charge is subject to CAF in effect at time
XX15b  of shipment.
XX15b
XX15b  9. Bridges and spoilers will be assessed the
XX15b  rates applicable on the beam width of the
XX15b  accompanying boat when they are moved on
XX15b  separate equipment.
XX15b
XX15b  10. If a mast is loaded with the boat, then it
XX15b  must be attached/secured to the boat by the
XX15b  shipper or supplier prior to delivery to
XX15b  the Carriers pier.  If ocean carier secures
XX15b  or attaches the mast to the boat, then all
XX15b  lashing and secureing charges will be billed
XX15b  per ocean Carriers applicable termninal
XX15b  tariff.  Any mast exceeding 45' will be
XX15b  lifted sepearately from accompanying
XX15b  boat at the following additional charges:
XX15b
XX15b  EXCEEDING 45' BUT NOT EXCEEDING 50' - 2500
XX15b  EXCEEDING 50' BUT NOT EXCEEDING 55' - 3000
XX15b  EXCEEDING 55' BUT NOT EXCEEDING 60' - 3500
XX15b
XX15b  MAST RATES HEREIN ARE NOT SUBJECT TO
XX15b  TARIFF ADDITIONALS.
XX15b
```

(continues)

Figure 2–7. *(continued)*

```
            8900 LINES RATE AGREEMENT, THE                 | Orig/Rev  |                Page
      8900 BB/OOG RATES TARIFF TO MIDDLE-EAST              |   1st     |  Section 4  8900-00-2000.005
-----------------------------------------------------------+-----------+-----------------------------------
 FROM: TARIFF ORIGIN SCOPE                                 | Cancels   |            Cancels Page
   TO: TARIFF DESTINATION SCOPE                            | Original  |  Section 4  8900-00-2000.005
-----------------------------------------------------------+-----------+-----------------------------------
 C |         SECTION 4 - COMMODITIES AND RATES             | CORR: 197 |  Issued: 24Jan1996   Eff: 24Jan1996EAN
 O |--------------------------------------------------------------------------------------------------------
 D |      Except as otherwise provided, rates apply per 1000 KGS or 1.000 CBM. Effective Dates (Eff:) shown below.
 E |            Items with effective dates prior to page Issue Date are brought forward without change.
-----------------------------------------------------------------------------------------------------------
   (R)        (Continuation of item Eff: 24Jan1996)                                 COMMODITY: 8900-00-2000

   Boats, including Boat moulds, viz: Cruisers, Launchers,
----
    | From: BALTIMORE (port), MD, USA, 21201-99                        |Svc| Basis |   Rate    | Minimum |TLI#|
(+) |   To: JEDDAH (port), SAUDI ARABIA                                |---+-------+-----------+---------+----|
(+) |                                                                  |   |       | In USD    |         |    |
(+) | (I)(R)(E)Effective: 24Jan1996      Expires: 30Jul1996            | YY| EA    |  6,089.00 |         |0002|
(+) |          INDEPENDENT RATE BY:                                    | YS|       |           |         |    |
(+) |            SEAU  -SEA-LAND SERVICE, INC.                         | HP|       |           |         |    |
(+) |          QUALIFIERS: Ctr type: N/A(Not Applicable), Ctr temp: N/A(Not | PH|  |           |         |    |
(+) |                      Applicable)                                 | PP|       |           |         |    |
(+) |          NOTES: (d53)    Exceeding 90" W but                     |   |       |           |         |    |
(+) |                 (d53)    not exceeding 96" W                     |   |       |           |         |    |
(+) |                 (sv995)  Services: PH, HP, PP, YS, YY.           |   |       |           |         |    |
(+) |                                                                  |   |       | In USD    |         |    |
(+) | (I)(R)(E)Effective: 24Jan1996      Expires: 30Jul1996            | YY| EA    |  8,071.00 |         |0008|
(+) |          INDEPENDENT RATE BY:                                    | YS|       |           |         |    |
(+) |            SEAU  -SEA-LAND SERVICE, INC.                         | HP|       |           |         |    |
(+) |          QUALIFIERS: Ctr type: N/A(Not Applicable), Ctr temp: N/A(Not | PH|  |           |         |    |
(+) |                      Applicable)                                 | PP|       |           |         |    |
(+) |          NOTES: (d115)   Exceeding 96" W but                     |   |       |           |         |    |
(+) |                 (d115)   not exceeding 103" W                    |   |       |           |         |    |
(+) |                 (sv995)  Services: PH, HP, PP, YS, YY.           |   |       |           |         |    |
(+) |                                                                  |   |       | In USD    |         |    |
(+) | (I)(R)(E)Effective: 24Jan1996      Expires: 30Jul1996            | YY| EA    |  8,250.00 |         |0014|
(+) |          INDEPENDENT RATE BY:                                    | YS|       |           |         |    |
(+) |            SEAU  -SEA-LAND SERVICE, INC.                         | HP|       |           |         |    |
(+) |          QUALIFIERS: Ctr type: N/A(Not Applicable), Ctr temp: N/A(Not | PH|  |           |         |    |
(+) |                      Applicable)                                 | PP|       |           |         |    |
(+) |          NOTES: (d109)   Exceeding 103" W but                    |   |       |           |         |    |
(+) |                 (d109)   not exceeding 112" W                    |   |       |           |         |    |
(+) |                 (sv995)  Services: PH, HP, PP, YS, YY.           |   |       |           |         |    |
(+) |                                                                  |   |       | In USD    |         |    |
(+) | (I)(R)(E)Effective: 24Jan1996      Expires: 30Jul1996            | YY| EA    |  8,443.00 |         |0020|
(+) |          INDEPENDENT RATE BY:                                    | YS|       |           |         |    |
(+) |            SEAU  -SEA-LAND SERVICE, INC.                         | HP|       |           |         |    |
(+) |          QUALIFIERS: Ctr type: N/A(Not Applicable), Ctr temp: N/A(Not | PH|  |           |         |    |
(+) |                      Applicable)                                 | PP|       |           |         |    |
(+) |          NOTES: (d108)   Exceeding 112" W but                    |   |       |           |         |    |
(+) |                 (d108)   not exceeding 128" W                    |   |       |           |         |    |
(+) |                 (sv995)  Services: PH, HP, PP, YS, YY.           |   |       |           |         |    |
(+) |                                                                  |   |       | In USD    |         |    |
(+) | (I)(R)(E)Effective: 24Jan1996      Expires: 30Jul1996            | YY| EA    |  9,187.00 |         |0026|
(+) |          INDEPENDENT RATE BY:                                    | YS|       |           |         |    |
(+) |            SEAU  -SEA-LAND SERVICE, INC.                         | HP|       |           |         |    |
(+) |          QUALIFIERS: Ctr type: N/A(Not Applicable), Ctr temp: N/A(Not | PH|  |           |         |    |
(+) |                      Applicable)                                 | PP|       |           |         |    |
```

Figure 2–7. *(continued)*

```
-----------------------------------------------------------------------------------------------------------------------
|              8900 LINES RATE AGREEMENT, THE                  |  Orig/Rev   |                      Page                  |
|        8900 BB/OOG RATES TARIFF TO MIDDLE-EAST               |    1st      |         Section 4    8900-00-2000.006      |
|--------------------------------------------------------------+-------------+--------------------------------------------|
| FROM: TARIFF ORIGIN SCOPE                                    |  Cancels    |                 Cancels Page               |
|   TO: TARIFF DESTINATION SCOPE                               |  Original   |         Section 4    8900-00-2000.006      |
|--------------------------------------------------------------+-------------+--------------------------------------------|
| C |            SECTION 4 - COMMODITIES AND RATES             |  CORR: 198  |   Issued: 24Jan1996     Eff: 24Jan1996EAN  |
| O |-------------------------------------------------------------------------------------------------------------------|
| D |          Except as otherwise provided, rates apply per 1000 KGS or 1.000 CBM. Effective Dates (Eff:) shown below.  |
| E |                  Items with effective dates prior to page Issue Date are brought forward without change.            |
|-----------------------------------------------------------------------------------------------------------------------|
|   (R)          (Continuation of item Eff: 24Jan1996)                                          COMMODITY: 8900-00-2000  |
|                                                                                                                       |
|   Boats, including Boat moulds, viz: Cruisers, Launchers,                                                             |
|----                                                                    -----------------------------------------------|
|    | From: BALTIMORE (port), MD, USA, 21201-99                         |Svc|  Basis  |      Rate     |  Minimum  |TLI#|
|    |   To: JEDDAH (port), SAUDI ARABIA                                 |---+---------+---------------+-----------+----|
|(+) |                                                                   |   |         |     In USD    |           |    |
|(+) | (I)(R)(E)Effective: 24Jan1996        Expires: 30Jul1996           | YY| EA      |   10,894.00   |           |0032|
|(+) |              INDEPENDENT RATE BY:                                 | YS|         |               |           |    |
|(+) |                SEAU  -SEA-LAND SERVICE, INC.                      | HP|         |               |           |    |
|(+) |              QUALIFIERS: Ctr type: N/A(Not Applicable), Ctr temp: N/A(Not | PH|  |               |           |    |
|(+) |                          Applicable)                              | PP|         |               |           |    |
|(+) |              NOTES: (d104)  Exceeding 140" W but                  |   |         |               |           |    |
|(+) |                     (d104)  not exceeding 150" W                  |   |         |               |           |    |
|(+) |                     (sv995) Services: PH, HP, PP, YS, YY.         |   |         |               |           |    |
|(+) |                                                                   |   |         |     In USD    |           |    |
|(+) | (I)(R)(E)Effective: 24Jan1996        Expires: 30Jul1996           | YY| EA      |   11,885.00   |           |0038|
|(+) |              INDEPENDENT RATE BY:                                 | YS|         |               |           |    |
|(+) |                SEAU  -SEA-LAND SERVICE, INC.                      | HP|         |               |           |    |
|(+) |              QUALIFIERS: Ctr type: N/A(Not Applicable), Ctr temp: N/A(Not | PH|  |               |           |    |
|(+) |                          Applicable)                              | PP|         |               |           |    |
|(+) |              NOTES: (d101)  Exceeding 150" but not                |   |         |               |           |    |
|(+) |                     (d101)  exceeding 155" W                      |   |         |               |           |    |
|(+) |                     (sv995) Services: PH, HP, PP, YS, YY.         |   |         |               |           |    |
|----+-------------------------------------------------------------------|   |         |               |           |    |
|(+) | From: CHARLESTON (port), SC, USA, 29401-25                        |   |         |               |           |    |
|(+) |   To: AD DAWHAH (port), QATAR                                     |   |         |               |           |    |
|(+) |                                                                   |   |         |     In USD    |           |    |
|(+) | (I)(R)(E)Effective: 24Jan1996        Expires: 30Jul1996           | YY| EA      |    7,314.00   |           |0044|
|(+) |              INDEPENDENT RATE BY:                                 | YS|         |               |           |    |
|(+) |                SEAU  -SEA-LAND SERVICE, INC.                      | HP|         |               |           |    |
|(+) |              QUALIFIERS: Ctr type: N/A(Not Applicable), Ctr temp: N/A(Not | PH|  |               |           |    |
|(+) |                          Applicable)                              | PP|         |               |           |    |
|(+) |              NOTES: (d53)   Exceeding 90" W but                   |   |         |               |           |    |
|(+) |                     (d53)   not exceeding 96" W                   |   |         |               |           |    |
|(+) |                     (sv995) Services: PH, HP, PP, YS, YY.         |   |         |               |           |    |
|(+) |                                                                   |   |         |     In USD    |           |    |
|(+) | (I)(R)(E)Effective: 24Jan1996        Expires: 30Jul1996           | YY| EA      |    9,296.00   |           |0047|
|(+) |              INDEPENDENT RATE BY:                                 | YS|         |               |           |    |
|(+) |                SEAU  -SEA-LAND SERVICE, INC.                      | HP|         |               |           |    |
|(+) |              QUALIFIERS: Ctr type: N/A(Not Applicable), Ctr temp: N/A(Not | PH|  |               |           |    |
|(+) |                          Applicable)                              | PP|         |               |           |    |
|(+) |              NOTES: (d115)  Exceeding 96" W but                   |   |         |               |           |    |
|(+) |                     (d115)  not exceeding 103" W                  |   |         |               |           |    |
|(+) |                     (sv995) Services: PH, HP, PP, YS, YY.         |   |         |               |           |    |
|(+) |                                                                   |   |         |     In USD    |           |    |
|(+) | (I)(R)(E)Effective: 24Jan1996        Expires: 30Jul1996           | YY| EA      |    9,475.00   |           |0050|
|(+) |              INDEPENDENT RATE BY:                                 | YS|         |               |           |    |
```

Figure 2–8. Booking confirmation.

```
*****************************************************************************
*                                                                           *
* DELIVER TO:                                                               *
*                                                                           *
*                                                                           *
* FORM                                                                      *
* FROM:           CHICAGO GMA                                               *
* SUBJECT:        BOOKING CONFIRMATION                                      *
* PRINT DATE:     04/25/96   TIME: 16:01                                    *
*                                                                           *
*****************************************************************************
```

ATTENTION: ______________________

COMPANY NAME: ______________________

CONFIRMATION OF BOOKING

BOOKING -- ______________________

SHIPPER -- ______________________

FORWARDER-- ______________________

VESSEL/VOYAGE -- ______________________

PORT OF LOAD -- ______________________

DESTINATION -- ______________________

COMMODITY -- ______________________

EQUIPMENT TYPE -- ______________________

ETD -- ______________________

ETA -- ______________________

COMMENTS -- ______________________

HERE IS YOUR BOOKING CONFIRMATION. FOR FURTHER INFORMATION OR ASSISTANCE, PLEASE FEEL FREE TO CONTACT ME AT 1-800-732-5263.
*****FROM CANADA, PLEASE CONTACT ME AT 1-800 759-9000.*****
THANK YOU FOR YOUR BUSINESS

____

CHICAGO CUSTOMER SERVICE

to seek to obtain a lower shipping rate by misclassifying merchandise or stating false weights or measurements. Likewise, it is a violation for a steamship line to charge more or less than its publicly filed tariff rate (except under a service contract) or pay rebates to shippers. If a shipper (exporter or importer) has satisfactory credit arrangements with a steamship line it can ship "freight collect."

If the exporter is shipping significant quantities, it may be able to negotiate a service contract with the carrier for transportation service at a lower rate. Smaller shippers can join a shippers' association and obtain similar benefits. For more information on shippers' associations, contact the American Institute for Shippers' Associations, a trade association, at (202) 628-0933.

R. Country of Origin Marking

As in the United States, many foreign countries require that the product and the product packaging be marked with the country of manufacture or production before the product can enter the foreign country. The regulations may be quite specific, for example, requiring that the country of origin be die-stamped, cast-in-the-mold, etched, or engraved in the product at the time of production or otherwise permanently marked. The size and location of the marking may be specified and exemptions from marking certain types of products may be available. Since the shipment cannot enter the country unless such marking has been done properly, it is important to check the foreign regulations prior to manufacture and shipment.

S. Foreign Warehousing and Free Trade Zones

Many companies use a regional distribution center (for example, in Rotterdam or Hong Kong) for re-export to various countries in the region. Shipments to such regional distribution centers can be entered into that country temporarily for repackaging, relabeling, manipulation, modification, and sometimes further manufacturing without the payment of any customs duties if the product is going to be re-exported. Foreign countries often have certain bonded warehousing and free trade zone systems which permit such activities. If the U.S. exporter wishes to avail itself of those benefits, it must carefully check and comply with those procedures in order to obtain the duty-free treatment.

T. Export Financing and Payment Insurance

A number of governmental agencies, U.S. and foreign, provide financing for U.S. exporters. The U.S. Export-Import (EXIM) Bank has financing available for large exporters as well as a new program for smaller exporters. The Agency for International Development under its tied aid program, the Department of Agriculture, the International Development Cooperation Agency, the International Bank for Reconstruction and Development (World Bank), the Inter-American Development Bank, the Asian Development Bank, the African Development Bank, and the Small Business Administration all have programs designed to finance exports. Some foreign countries even finance the importation of products that they are seeking to obtain. Most recently, in the United States, the federal government has encouraged states to develop export financing programs. At last count, twenty-three states, including California and Illinois, have established successful programs, and a U.S. exporter should check with its state agencies or the National Association of State Development Agencies to determine the availability and terms and conditions of financing prior to manufacture and export of its products. This is an important preliminary consideration because the buyer may have to provide documentation before the exporter can apply for such financing, and there may be longer lead times in completing the sale.

Related to this subject is insurance issued by the Foreign Credit Insurance Association and marketed by the U.S. Export-Import Bank, which has offices in major U.S. cities. This association of U.S. insurance companies offers a policy that can protect an exporter against default in payment due to expropriation, foreign government political risks, and customer nonpayment due to commercial reasons. Several different types of policies are available covering 90 to 95 percent of the risk. Such insurance may be required in order to obtain certain export financing. A sample application is shown in Figure 2–9.

U. Tax Incentives

Up until September 2000 the United States had in place tax reduction programs for export profits called the Foreign Sales Corporation and Domestic International Sales Corporation programs. However, based on findings by the World Trade Organization that these programs violated the world trading rules, the United States developed a replacement program. However, the WTO also found that the replacement program violated the same rules. Benefits under the old Foreign Sales Corporation program ended on December 31, 2001.

V. Export Trading Companies, Export Trade Certificates of Review, and Export Management Companies

In 1982, Congress enacted the Export Trading Company Act which established two benefits: (1) banks are permitted to own all or part of exporting companies, and (2) exporting companies can obtain exemptions from the U.S. antitrust laws on their export activities. The latter benefit is of most interest to the individual exporter and can be useful in avoiding costly treble damage liability and expensive attorney's fees and court costs if the exporter obtains such a certificate. Certified activities often include the appointment of exclusive distributors and agents, and the imposition of restrictions on distributors, such as territories, prices, the handling of competitive products, and the termination of such distributors, all of which might normally violate U.S. antitrust laws. Furthermore, if a U.S. company wishes to cooperate with other companies in exporting, even with competitors, such activities can be protected under the certificate. Those certificates are issued by the U.S. Department of Commerce with the concurrence of the Department of Justice and are not difficult to apply for. However, the U.S. exporter should also check foreign law in the country of destination, as such certificates do not exempt the U.S. exporter from foreign law. A sample application and a certificate are shown in Figures 2–10 and 2–11, respectively.

An export management company, or EMC, is usually an export intermediary located in the United States that acts as a sales agent or representative for the manufacturer for exports to certain foreign markets. Typically, EMCs are paid a commission and may be helpful where the manufacturer is new to exporting or does not have its own distributor or sales agent in that foreign country. Theoretically, the difference

(*Text continues on page 57.*)

Figure 2–9. Application for Export-Import Bank insurance.

OMB No. 3048-0009
Expires 05/31/02

EXPORT IMPORT BANK OF THE UNITED STATES
SHORT-TERM MULTI-BUYER EXPORT CREDIT INSURANCE POLICY APPLICATION

Applicant: ______________________ dba: ______________________
Contact: ______________________ Title: ______________________ Website: ______________
Address: ____
Phone: ______________ Fax: ______________ E-Mail: ______________
Bank credit line (if any) with: ______________________ Broker: ______________

1. How did you learn about Ex-Im Bank? ☐ Ex-Im Bank regional office ☐ Broker ☐ Bank ☐ US Export Assistance Center
☐ Ex-Im Bank City/State Partner ______________________ ☐ Other______________________

2. Have you ever applied for a U.S. Small Business Administration or Ex-Im Bank program? ☐Yes or ☐ No
If so, please name the agency, program, outcome and status: ______________________

If you wish to insure sales made by your affiliates, please see Question 17 (Additional Named Insureds) prior to continuing.

3. Primary reason for application: ☐ risk mitigation ☐ financing ☐ extend more competitive terms

4. Policy Aggregate Limit Requested: $______________ (maximum export credit receivables outstanding at any one time)

5. Product and/or services to be exported: ______________________

6. Are the products to be covered under the policy:
   - Manufactured in the U.S. with a minimum of 51% U.S. content (excluding mark-up)? ☐ Yes or ☐ No
   - Manufactured by the applicant? (If no, provide a list of suppliers with addresses.) ☐ Yes or ☐ No
   - Shipped from the United States to your buyers? ☐ Yes or ☐ No
   - Listed on the U.S. Munitions List (part 121 of title 22 of the Code of Federal Reg.)? ☐ No or ☐ Yes
   - Used? (If yes, please attach Used Equipment Questionnaire EBD-M-25) ☐ No or ☐ Yes

7. # of years exporting: _______ # of years exporting on terms other than cash in advance (CIA) or confirmed L/C (CILC):_______

8. Total export sales for the prior 2 years: Year: _____ $ ______________ Year: _____ $ ______________
Total export *credit* sales (exclude CIA, CILC) for the prior 2 years: $ ______________ $ ______________

9. Buyer Types: ____% Manufacturers ____% Wholesalers/ Distributors ____% Retailers ____% End-users

10. Export Credit Portfolio - attach additional pages if necessary.

	PREVIOUS YEAR			PROJECTIONS FOR NEXT YEAR		
Country	**# of Buyers**	**Sales**	**Payment Terms**	**# of Buyers**	**Sales**	**Payment Terms**
EXAMPLE: Mexico	10	$2,500,000	50% CILC 50% 60 day OA	12	$3,000,000	100% 60 day OA

EIB92-50 (7/01) Page 1 of 3

Figure 2–9. *(continued)*

OMB No. 3048-0009
Expires 05/31/02

11. Please list your 5 largest export buyers:

Buyer Name	City/Country	Last 12 Months Sales	Payment Terms	Credit Limit Needed
		$		$
		$		$
		$		$
		$		$
		$		$

12. Name(s) of export credit decision maker(s): ________ Title(s): ________ Years of Credit Experience ________ Years of Foreign Credit Exp. ________

13. At what point do you stop shipping to a past due account? ____________ days past due

14. Total export receivables outstanding: $____________ at ___/___/___ (date should be within 60 days of the application)

$__________ Current $__________ 1-60 days past due $__________ 61-90 days past due $__________ 91-180 days past due $__________ 181+ days past due

For each buyer over 60 days past due, attach an explanation including: name of buyer, country, amount past due, due date, and collection efforts made.

15. Export credit losses per year or rescheduled debts during each of last three years - attach additional pages if necessary.

YEAR	AMOUNT (US$)	EXPLANATION OF LOSS OR RESCHEDULING (SPECIFY REASON, COUNTRY, AND BUYER)
	$	
	$	
	$	

16. **Please submit the following as Attachments:**
- Credit Report on your company dated within 6 months of the application or attach a check for $35 payable to Ex-Im Bank.
- Your financial statements for the two most recent completed fiscal years (with notes if available).
- Resume(s) on each credit decision maker identified in question 12.
- Descriptive product brochures (if available).

17. **Special Coverages Required:** If "none" check ☐ N/A

☐ **Add Additional Named Insureds (ANI's).** Credit decisions of each affiliate listed must be centralized with the Applicant and each affiliate must invoice export credit sales in their own name (or tradestyle); if either is not applicable, please attach an explanation. Questions 3-15 should include export sales of prospective ANI's.

Affiliate Company / Trade style	City / State / Country	Relationship to Applicant

☐ **Services (Please attach a copy of your sample services contract)** Services must be: performed by U.S. based personnel or those temporarily domiciled overseas, and billed (invoiced) separately fromany product sales.

☐ **Enhanced Assignment** of small business insurance policy proceeds. This is exporter performance risk protection that may be offered to lenders willing to finance Ex-Im Bank insured receivables. **Applicant Please Attach:**
- Written bank reference describing your relationship to date and size of existing credit line.
- 2 written trade references from principal commercial suppliers.
- For applications with policy limits over $500,000, financial statements must be audited or CPA reviewed with notes.

☐ **Other** (please specify):____________________________________

EIB92-50 (7/01)   Page 2 of 3

Figure 2–9. *(continued)*

OMB No. 3048-0009
Expires 05/31/02

The Applicant (it) CERTIFIES and ACKNOWLEDGES to the Export-Import Bank of the United States (the Bank) that:

a) it is either organized, or registered to do **business, in the United States**.

b) it and each additional named insured applicant **has not entered into any contract of insurance** or indemnity in respect of any case of loss covered by the Export Credit Insurance Policy or Loss chargeable to a deductible under such Policy, and the applicant will not enter into any such contract of insurance or indemnity without the Bank's consent in writing.

c) neither it nor any of its principals is currently, nor has been within the preceding three years:
- debarred, suspended or declared ineligible from participating in any Covered Transaction or
- formally proposed for debarment, with a final determination still pending;
- voluntarily excluded from participation in a Covered Transaction; or
- indicted, convicted or had a civil judgment rendered against it

for any of the offenses listed in the Regulations governing Debarment and Suspension as defined in the Government Wide Nonprocurement Debarment and Suspension Regulations; Common Rule 53 Fed. Reg. 19204 (1988). It further certifies that it has not nor will it knowingly enter into any agreement in connection with this Policy with any individual or entity that has been subject to any of the above.

d) it is not delinquent on any amount due and owing to the U.S. Government, its agencies, or instrumentalities as of the date of this application.

e) it shall complete and submit standard form-LLL, "Disclosure Form to Report Lobbying" to the Bank (31 USC 1352), if any funds have been paid or will be paid to any person for influencing or attempting to influence i) an officer or employee of any agency, ii) a Member of Congress or a Member's employee, or iii) an officer or employee of Congress in connection with this Policy. This does not apply to insurance broker commissions paid by the Bank.

f) the Bank shall have a right to transfer to another Government authority any financial records included in the application or Policy, as necessary to process, service, foreclose or collect on an insured debt. This is notice to you as required under the **Right of Financial Privacy Act of 1978 (12 USC 3401)** that the Bank will not permit any other transfer of records to private parties or another U.S. Government authority except as required or permitted by law.

g) the information is being requested under the authority of the **Export-Import Bank Act of 1945** (12 USC 635 et. seq.); disclosure of this information is mandatory **and failure to provide the requested information may** result in the Bank being unable to determine eligibility for the Policy. The information collected will be analyzed to determine the ability of the participants to perform and pay under the Policy. The Bank may not require the information, and applicants are not required to respond, unless a currently valid OMB control number is displayed on this form. The information collected will be held confidential subject to the **Freedom of Information Act** (5 USC 552) and the **Privacy Act of 1974** (5 USC 552a), except as required to be disclosed pursuant to applicable law. The **public burden** reporting for this collection of information is estimated to average 1 hour per response, including time for reviewing instructions, searching existing data sources, gathering the data needed, and completing and reviewing the collection of information. Send **comments** regarding the burden estimate or any other aspect of the collection of information, including suggestions for reducing this burden, to Office of Management and Budget, Paperwork Reduction Project OMB# 3048-0009, Washington, D.C. 20503.

h) the representations made and the facts stated in the application for said Policy are true, to the best of it's knowledge and belief, and it has not misrepresented or omitted any material facts relevant to said representations. It agrees that this application shall form a part of the Policy, if issued, and the truth of the representations and facts, and performance of every undertaking in this application shall be a condition precedent to any coverage under such Policy. It further understands that this certification is subject to the penalties for fraud against The U.S. Government (18 USC 1001).

(Signature) (Print Name and Title) (Date)

SMALL BUSINESS POLICIES APPLICANT CERTIFICATION

"We are an entity which **together with our affiliates** had **average annual export credit sales** during our preceding two fiscal years not exceeding **$5,000,000**, excluding sales made on terms of confirmed irrevocable letters of credit (CILC) or cash in advance (CIA)."

(Signature)

Send, or ask your insurance broker or city/state participant to review and send this application to the Ex-Im Bank Regional Office nearest you. Please refer to Ex-Im Bank's website at http://www.exim.gov for Regional Office addresses.

Ex-Im Bank reserves the right to request additional information upon review of the application. Please refer to Ex-Im Bank's Short Term Credit Standards (EIB 99-09) to determine the likelihood of approval of a policy.

EIB92-50 (7/01) Page 3 of 3

Figure 2–10. Application for export trade certificate of review.

OMB Approved 0625-0120
Expires 03/31/2002

Form **ITA-4093P** LF
(5-94)

U.S. DEPARTMENT OF COMMERCE
International Trade Administration

APPLICATION FOR AN EXPORT TRADE CERTIFICATE OF REVIEW

No export trade certificate may be issued unless a completed application form has been received (15 USC 4011-4021).

Special Action

☐ Application for Amendment

☐ Request for Expedited Review

See instructions below

DEPARTMENT OF COMMERCE USE ONLY

NAME OF APPLICANT	DATE RECEIVED	DATE DEEMED SUBMITTED

TRACKING SYSTEM NUMBER	MONITOR

CONFIDENTIALITY OF APPLICATION

Information submitted by any person in connection with the issuance, amendment, or revocation of a certificate of review is exempt from disclosure under the Freedom of Information Act, Section 552, Title 5, United States Code.

Except as provided under Section 309(b)(2) of the Export Trading Company Act ("ACT") and 15 CFR 325.16(b)(3), no officer or employee of the United States shall disclose commercial or financial information submitted pursuant to the Act if the information is privileged or confidential and if disclosure of the information would cause harm to the person who submitted the information.

OTHER CONSIDERATIONS

NOTE: The exchange among competitors of competitively sensitive information may, in some circumstances, create risks that competition among the firms will be lessened and antitrust questions raised. The exchange of information about recent or future prices, production, sales or confidential business plans is especially sensitive. As a general matter, the danger that such exchanges will have anticompetitive effects is less when the firms involved have a small share of the market and greater if they have a substantial share.

Applicant may consider seeking the advice of legal counsel on whether any steps would be advisable in the applicant's particular circumstances to avoid issues of this nature. One possible step that the applicant may consider in preparing the application is to compile and submit these types of information through an unrelated third party, such as an attorney or consultant.

INSTRUCTIONS

The Department of Commerce urges applicants to read Title III of the Export Trading Company Act (P.L. 97-290, Section 4011-4021, Title 15, United States Code) and the accompanying regulations (Volume 15, Code of Federal Regulations, Part 325) and the guidelines (50 FR 1786) before completing this application form. These documents and additional information and guidance on the certification program are available free from the Office of Export Trading Company Affairs, Telephone (202) 482-5131.

Space is provided on the attached form for some of the information requested. In most cases you are being asked to supply additional information on supplemental sheets or attachments. Please include the name of the applicant on each supplement or attachment, and specifically identify the item number to which the attachment refers. The two certifying statements on the last page of this form MUST be completed before your application will be deemed submitted.

Designate the documents or information which you consider privileged or confidential and disclosure of which would cause you harm.

File an original and two copies of the completed application either by first class mail, or registered mail to: Office of Export Trading Company Affairs, International Trade Administration, Room 1104, U.S. Department of Commerce, Washington, DC 20230; or by personal courier service during business hours to: U.S. Department of Commerce Courier Center, Room 1874.

In response to the questions in this application the applicant is requested to be as specific as possible, including, where applicable, a discussion of the antitrust concerns which caused the applicant to seek a certificate.

Some information, in particular the identification of goods or services that the applicant exports or proposes to export, is requested in a certain form (standard industrial classification (SIC) numbers) if reasonably available. Where information does not exist in this form, an applicant is not required to create it, and may satisfy the request for information by providing it in some other convenient form.

NOTE: If an applicant is unable to provide any of the information requested or if the applicant believes that any of the information requested would be burdensome to obtain and unnecessary for a determination on the application, the applicant should state that the information is not being provided or is being provided in lesser detail, and explain why. It may not be necessary for every applicannt to respond to every question on this form. If an applicant believes that certain information requested is not necessary for a determination on the application, the applicant may request a waiver prior to submitting the application. The applicant should contract the Office of Export Trading Company Affairs on (202) 482-5131.

If the applicant has a special need for a quick decision on its application, it should set forth the facts and circumstances that warrant expedited processing in the space provided in item 17. The justification should explain why expedited action is needed, such as bidding deadliness or other circumstances beyond the control of the applicant that require the applicant to act in less than 90 days and that have significant impact on the applicant's export trade.

AGENCY DISCLOSURE OF ESTIMATED BURDEN

Public reporting for this collection of information is estimated to be 32 hours per response, including the time for reviewing instructions, and completing and reviewing the collection of information. All responses to this collection are voluntary. Notwithstanding any other provision of law, no person is

Figure 2–10. *(continued)*

required to respond to nor shall a person be subject to a penalty for failure to comply with a collection of information subject to the requirements of the Paperwork Reduction Act unless that collection of information displays a current valid OMB Control Number. Send comments regarding the burden estimate or any other aspect of this collection of information, including suggestions for reducing this burden, to the Reports Clearance Officer, International Trade Administration, Department of Commerce, Room 4001, 14th and Constitution Avenue, N.W. Washington, DC 20230.

ITEM 1: Applicant/Organizer Information

Name of Applicant:____________________________

Principal Address: ____________________________
Street Room or Suite

____
City State Zip

Name if Applicant's Controlling Entity, if any (if none enter "none"):____________________________

Principal Address:____________________________
Street Room or Suite

____
City State Zip

Individual(s) authorized by the applicant to submit application and to whom all correspondence should be addressed:

Name:____________________________

Title:____________________________

Address:____________________________
Street Room or Suite

____
City State Zip

Telephone:____________________________

Relationship to Applicant:____________________________

ITEM 2: Name and principal address of each member, and of each member's controlling entity, if any:
(Attach to this application, clearly identifying attachment as response to ITEM 2.)

ITEM 3: Copy of any legal instrument under which the applicant is organized or will operate. Include copies, as appropriate, of its corporate charter, bylaws, partnership, joint venture, membership, or other agreements or contracts under which the applicant is organized.
(Attach to this application, clearly identifying attachment as response to ITEM 3.)

ITEM 4: A copy of the applicant's most recent annual report, if any, and that of its controlling entity, if any.
(Attach to this application, clearly identifying attachment as response to ITEM 4.)

To the extent the information is not included in the annual report, or in other document submitted in connection with this application, attach a brief description of the applicant's domestic (including import) and export operations, including:
(a) The nature of its business;
(b) The types of products or services in which it deals;
(c) The places where it does business

(This description may be supplemented by a chart or table.)

Figure 2–10. *(continued)*

ITEM 5: A copy of each member's most recent annual report, if any, and that of its controlling entity, if any.
(Attach to this application, clearly identifying attachment as response to ITEM 5.)

To the extent the information is not included in the annual report, or in other documents submitted in connection with this application, attach a brief description of each member's domestic (including import) and export operations, including:
(a) The nature of its business;
(b) The types of products or services in which it deals;
(c) The places where it does business.

(This description may be supplemented by a chart or table.)

ITEM 6: Names, titles, and responsibilities of the applicant's directors, officers, partners, and managing officials, and their business affiliations with other members or other businesses that produce or sell any of the types of goods or services described in ITEM 7, (below).
(Attach this information to this application, clearly identifying attachment as response to ITEM 6.)

ITEM 7(A): A description of the goods or services which the applicant exports or proposes to export under the certificate of review. This description should reflect the industry's customary definitions of product and services.
(Attach this information to this application clearly identifying attachment as response to ITEM 7(A).)

ITEM 7(B): If the information is reasonably available, please identify the goods or services according to the Standard Industrial Classification (SIC) number. Goods should normally be identified at the 7-digit level. Services should be identified at the most detailed SIC level possible.
(Attach this information to this application, clearly identifying attachment as response to ITEM 7(B).)

ITEM 7(C): Identify the foreign geographic areas to which the applicant and each member export or intend to export their goods and services
(Attach this information to this application, clearly identifying attachment as response to ITEM 7(C).)

For each class of the goods, wares, merchandise, or services set forth in ITEM 7, please provide the following information:

ITEM 8(A): The principal geographic areas or areas in the United States in which the applicant and each member sell their goods and services.
(Attach this information to this application, clearly identifying attachment as response to ITEM 8 (A).)

ITEM 8(B): For each of the previous two fiscal years the dollar value of the applicant's and each member's (i) total domestic sales, if any, and (ii) total export sales, if any. Include the value of sales of any controlling entities and all entities under their control.
(Attach this information to this application, clearly identifying attachment as response to ITEM 8(B).)

ITEM 9: For *each* product or service to be covered by the certificate, indicate the best information or estimate accessible to the applicant of the total value of sales in the United States by all companies (whether or not members of the proposed certificate) for each of the last two (2) years. Identify the source of the information or the basis of the estimate.
(Attach this information to this application, clearly identifying attachment as response to ITEM 9.)

ITEM 10: Describe the specific export conduct which the applicant seeks to have certified. Only the specific export conduct described in the application will be eligible for certification. For each item, the applicant should state the antitrust concern, if any, raised by that export conduct.

Examples of export conduct which applicants may seek to have certified include the manner in which goods and services will be obtained or provided; the manner in which prices or quantities will be set; exclusive agreements with U.S. suppliers or export intermediaries; territorial, quantity, or price agreements with U.S. suppliers or export intermediaries; and restrictions on membership or membership withdrawal.
(These examples are given only to illustrate the type of export conduct which might be of concern. The specific activities which the applicant may wish to have certified will depend on its particular circumstances or business plans.)
(Attach this information to this application, clearly identifying attachment as response to ITEM 10.)

ITEM 11: If the export trade, export trade activities, or methods of operation for which certification is sought will involve any agreement or any exchange of information among suppliers of the same or similar products or services with respect to domestic prices, production, sales, or other competitively sensitive business information, specify the nature of the agreement or exchange of information.
(Attach this information to this application, clearly identifying attachment as response to ITEM 11.)

ITEM 12: A statement whether the applicant intends or reasonably expects that any exported goods or services covered by the proposed certificate will re-enter the United States, either in its original or modified form. If so, identify the goods or services and the manner in which they may re-enter the United States.
(Attach this information to this application, clearly identifying attachment as response to ITEM 12)

Figure 2–10. *(continued)*

ITEM 13: The names and addresses of the suppliers of the goods and services to be exported (and the goods and services to be supplied by each) unless the goods and services to be exported are to be supplied by the applicant and/or its members.
(Attach this information to this application, clearly identifying attachment as response to ITEM 13.)

ITEM 14: For *each* product to be covered by the certificate provide the following background information:
(a) detailed description of the product and its purpose or use;
(b) the estimated number of competitors (both foreign and domestic) in the particular U.S. market;
(c) a list of the top five competitors who are *not* proposed members of this certificate, in terms of sales in the U.S. market, and an estimate of their respective (%) share in the market;
(d) the ranking of the applicant and each proposed member in terms of their sales in the U.S. market.

Please provide any other background information that the applicant believes will be necessary or helpful to a determination of whether to issue a certificate under the standards of the Export Trading Company Act.
(Attach this information to this application, clearly identifying attachment as response to ITEM 14.)

ITEM 15: (Optional) A proposed draft certificate
(Attach this information to this application, clearly identifying attachment as response to ITEM 15.)

ITEM 16: If the applicant is requesting expedited review, specify the facts and circumstances which warrant it in the space below
(If additional space is necessary, attach the information to this application, clearly identifying attachment as response to ITEM 16.)

CERTIFICATIONS

I certify that the applicant named in ITEM 1 above and each of the members listed in ITEM 2 above has authorized me to submit this application and the attachments, and to represent the applicant and members, if any, in seeking an export trade certificate of review.

TYPED OR PRINTED NAME **SIGNATURE (SIGN IN INK)** **DATE**

I certify that to the best of my knowledge and belief the information submitted in this application and the attachments, and to represent the applicant and members, if any, in seeking an export trade certificate of review.

TYPED OR PRINTED NAME **SIGNATURE (SIGN IN INK)** **DATE**

FORM ITA 4093-P (REV. 10-98) USCOMM-DC 85-2 1655

Figure 2–11. Export trade certificate of review.

EXPORT TRADE
CERTIFICATE OF REVIEW
for
Universal Trading Group Ltd.
Application No. 83-00005

Universal Trading Group, Ltd. ("UTG"), a Missouri corporation, has applied to the Department of Commerce for a certificate of review under Title III of Pub. L. No. 97-290 (96 Stat. 1240–45 (to be codified at 15 U.S.C. §§4011–21) ("the Act")) and its implementing regulations (48 Fed. Reg. 10595-604, March 11, 1983) (to be codified at 15 CFR pt. 325 (1983)) ("the Regulations").

The application was deemed submitted on June 15, 1983 and a summary of the application was published in the Federal Register on June 29, 1983 (48 Fed. Reg. 29934–35 (1983)).

The Department of Commerce and the Department of Justice have reviewed the information contained in the application and the response to supplementary questions, and other information in their possession.

Based upon analysis of this information, the Department of Commerce has determined, and the Department of Justice concurs, that the export trade, export trade activities and methods of operation set forth below meet the four standards set forth in section 303(a) of the Act.

Accordingly, under the authority of the Act and the Regulations, the conduct of UTG is certified for the following Export Trade in the following Export Markets when UTG is engaged in the Export Trade Activities and Methods of Operation described below:

Export Trade

1. Health care goods and services, in the following categories:
   a. The design and construction of hospitals, clinics, and other health care facilities,
   b. The staffing, management and operation of health care facilities (including the training of health care facilities personnel to perform these functions),
   c. The sale and/or leasing of health care products, equipment and supplies related to the design, construction, equipment and management of health care facilities,
   d. The provision of data processing and general consultation services related to health care facilities, and
   e. The provision of hospital and medical insurance plans in conjunction with health care facilities.
2. Foodstuffs of all types.
3. Passenger and commercial vehicle tires and tubes.

Export Markets

Worldwide, including the Mid-East, Africa, Far East, Latin America and Europe, but not including the United States (the fifty States of the United States, the District of Columbia, the Commonwealth of Puerto Rico, the Virgin Islands, American Samoa, Guam, the Commonwealth of the Northern Mariana Islands, and the Trust Territory of the Pacific Islands).

Figure 2–11. *(continued)*

Export Trade Activities and Methods of Operation

1. UTG may enter into any number of nonexclusive agreements with individual buyers in the Export Markets to act as a purchasing agent in Export Trade, or with individual U.S. suppliers to act as a sales representative or broker in Export Trade. UTG may enter into such agreements with U.S. suppliers regardless of whether the suppliers produce or sell similar or substitutable goods and services in Export Trade.
2. With respect to dental, medical, hospital or other health care products or services, UTG may enter into exclusive agreements with individual U.S. suppliers of the products or services whereby UTG would act as the exclusive sales representative or broker for the products or services in the Export Markets and/or the supplier would agree not to export through any other export intermediary. UTG may enter into such agreements with U.S. suppliers regardless of whether the suppliers produce or sell similar or substitutable goods and services in Export Trade.
3. UTG may enter into exclusive agreements with individual U.S. suppliers of foodstuffs and tires in which UTG would act as the exclusive sales representative or broker for the products or services in the Export Markets and/or the supplier would agree not to export through any other export intermediary. The term of such agreements will not exceed three years and will be renewable by mutual consent of the supplier and UTG. UTG may enter into such agreements with U.S. suppliers regardless of whether the suppliers produce or sell similar or substitutable goods and services in Export Trade.
4. UTG may enter into nonexclusive agreements appointing distributors or sales agents in the Export Markets.
5. UTG may enter into, refuse to enter into, and from time to time terminate, exclusive or nonexclusive agreements with individual distributors, sales agents, and/or customers in the Export Markets in which UTG would deal in the Export Market only through its representative and/or the representative would not represent UTG's competitors in the Export Market, unless authorized by UTG. With respect to these agreements UTG may do any or all of the following:
   (a) designate the price at which goods or services in Export Trade will be sold or resold in the Export Markets;
   (b) restrict the quantities of goods or services in Export Trade to be sold in the Export Markets;
   (c) limit the territories in the Export Markets in which the distributors or sales agents may sell;
   (d) limit the customers to which a distributor or sales agent can sell, or allocate customers among UTG's distributors, sales agents, or UTG itself.
6. As UTG becomes aware of invitations to bid or sales opportunities in the Export Markets, UTG may contact individual U.S. suppliers of the various or similar products and services specified in the invitation to bid or the purchase specifications, invite the suppliers to provide independent quotations to UTG for the products or services, and enter into agreements with the individual suppliers whereby UTG will submit a response to the bid invitation or request for quotation.

(*continues*)

Figure 2–11. *(continued)*

Terms and Conditions of Certificate

UTG and its members will not intentionally disclose, directly or indirectly, to any supplier or prospective supplier any business information obtained from any other supplier of similar or substitutable goods and services. For purposes of this certificate, business information means any information about costs, production, capacity, inventories, domestic prices, domestic sales, domestic orders, terms of domestic marketing or sale, U.S. business plans, strategies or methods, or any other business information that is not materially related to the conduct of the export business of the supplier through UTG, unless such business information already has been made generally available to the trade or public.

UTG and its members will comply with requests made by the Department of Commerce on behalf of itself or the Department of Justice for information or documents relevant to conduct under the certificate. The Department of Commerce will request such information or documents when either the Department of Justice or the Department of Commerce believes it requires the information or documents to determine that the Export Trade, Export Trade Activities or Methods of Operation of a person protected by this certificate of review continues to comply with the standards of section 303(a) of the Act.

Protection Provided by Certificate

The protections afforded by this certificate shall apply only to UTG and the following members: [names deleted], and to the directors, officers, and employees of the foregoing acting on their behalf. The certificate provides protection to UTG, its directors, officers and employees acting on its behalf, and to the above identified members, from private treble damage actions and government criminal and civil suits under U.S. federal and state antitrust laws for the export conduct specified in the certificate and carried out during its effective period in compliance with its terms and conditions.

Other Conduct

Nothing in this certificate prohibits UTG from engaging in conduct not specified in this certificate, but such conduct is subject to the normal application of the antitrust laws.

Disclaimer

The issuance of this certificate of review to UTG by the U.S. Government under the provisions of the Act does not constitute, explicitly or implicitly, an endorsement or opinion of the U.S. Government concerning either (a) the viability or quality of the business plans or products of UTG, or (b) the legality of such business plans or products of UTG under the laws of the U.S. (other than as provided by the Act) or under the laws of any foreign country. This certificate does not apply to sales to the United States government or to any sale more than half the cost of which is borne by the United States government.

In accordance with the authority accorded under the Act and Regulations, this certificate of review is hereby issued to UTG.

/s/ Malcolm Baldrige
Secretary of Commerce

Effective Date:
Nov 28 1983

between the EMC and the ETC is that ETCs are supposed to have sufficient capital to purchase from the manufacturer, paying in advance and making its compensation on a resale markup rather than a commission. In actuality, some EMCs and ETCs do both.

W. Translation

An exporter should give sufficient forethought to the necessity of translating its advertising materials, instructions, warranties, and labeling into the language of the destination country. Not only will this be necessary in order to achieve sales, but failure to do so can lead to legal liabilities. For example, if a patent application is not properly translated, the rights may be lost. Some countries require that certain labeling be in their language. The location of a competent translator and completion of the translation may require significant lead time and, depending on the quantity of material, involve a significant expense.

X. Foreign Branch Operations, Subsidiaries, Joint Ventures, and Licensing

Sometimes the exporter will be exporting to its or its parent company's existing branch of subsidiary company in a foreign country. Or, rather than selling to an independent distributor, utilizing a sales agent or selling directly to the end user, the exporter may decide to establish such a branch operation or subsidiary company. If personnel are available to staff the foreign branch or company, this step may increase the exporter's marketing penetration and may smooth export and import operations. Similarly, the exporter may form a joint venture with a foreign company to manufacture or market the exporter's products in one or more foreign countries. Where laws prohibit the importation of the exporter's products or where transportation costs or delays are unreasonable, the exporter may need to license a foreign company to manufacture the product and sell it in that market in return for payment of a royalty. All of these methods of doing business will require some modifications to the sales and other export and import documentation and procedures. For example, sales to affiliated companies often raise income tax issues of transfer pricing and the related issue of proper customs valuation. License royalties may in certain circumstances be dutiable, and licensed technology may require export control approvals. A big, recent problem is the inadequacy of sales and purchase documentation for export audits due to simplified electronic ordering procedures between affiliated companies.

Y. Electronic Commerce

The development of the Internet and e-mail and the proliferation of Web sites have created a revolution in electronic commerce. Because of the essentially worldwide availability of the Internet and access to Web sites, new issues for cross-border exporting and importing have arisen. This has opened a new channel of direct marketing using electronic catalogs and has created conflict with the seller's traditional foreign distribution channels, such as distributors and sales agents. Sellers are more interested in marketing internationally and are forced to cope with the logistical issues that arise from purchase orders from abroad. Some of the more important issues that must be considered and managed include the following:

- *Validity and enforceability of electronic sales contracts.* This concern has required the consideration and development of legal terms of sale on the Web site that are modified and appropriate for foreign as well as domestic customers. It has also forced the use of "click-wrap" agreements to record the purchaser's agreement to the sales terms and authentication procedures to confirm that the person purporting to place the order is actually that person. For low-price items, sellers may be willing to accept the risk of lack of enforceability of the sales contract, but for expensive items or ongoing business this is not feasible. Many sellers have required their distributors and customers who are making ongoing purchases to sign hard-copy "umbrella" agreements at the outset of the relationship before undertaking electronic sales. This is a less satisfactory solution for onetime purchasers.
- *Delivery and logistics.* At least with direct sales to consumers, and for consumer goods, the customer wants and expects the convenience of direct delivery to his or her door. These "delivered duty paid" terms of sale are almost a necessity for this type of business. Customers also want prompt delivery, which is difficult to achieve if there is no stock of inventory in the buyer's country. For smaller products, delivery by international courier services such as UPS, Federal Express, and DHL has become more practical. In such cases, the transportation carrier is also able to act as the customs broker in the foreign country, paying customs duties and value-added taxes and billing them back to the seller. For large capital goods, however—such as in business-to-business (B2B) transactions, the issues of containerized or other packaging, transportation booking, export licenses or permits, foreign customs clearance, and lack of skilled in-house personnel, thereby requiring the use of a freight forwarder—have limited the expansion of Internet sales. Challenges continue to exist relating to establishing in-country inventory for immediate delivery without the expenses of establishing branch offices or subsidiary companies.
- *Price.* Since many customers want to have delivery to their door, when they see a price quotation on a Web site, they expect to see an "all-in" (delivered duty paid) price. The difficulty of maintaining up-to-date quotations online, including freight charges, insurance, duties, quotas, and value-added taxes for multiple countries of the world, has forced many sellers to hire software companies that offer such services.
- *Payment.* For low-price consumer goods, payment by credit card has enabled sellers to increase Internet sales. However, the fact that credit card purchases are not guaranteed payments and the virtual impossibility of pursuing a collection lawsuit overseas because of prohibitive cost has limited expansion. For expensive purchases or ongoing accounts, the seller may need the security of a letter of credit or documents against payment. On the other side, buyers dislike having to pay for purchases in advance without inspection of the goods. Where the seller has done business in the past on open account, or is willing to do so in the future, Internet sales can be practical.

- *Taxation.* Although one of the great spurs to the growth of electronic commerce in the past has been the ability to avoid certain taxes in certain countries, such as sales, value-added, corporate franchise, or personal property taxes, there is an increasing demand by governments to recover those tax revenues that are being lost. It is likely that some forms of taxation will increase and sellers may have to comply with foreign tax claims.
- *Information security.* Although there has been significant progress in maintaining the confidentiality of information transmitted over the Internet, the sophistication of "hackers" has also increased. For information from credit card numbers to purchase order numbers and customer lists, confidentiality, particularly from competitors and fraud artists, is crucial. The most secure current technologies using "key" systems are cumbersome, especially for small orders and onetime sales. Furthermore, exporting such software may require an export license.

Despite the foregoing difficulties, the outlook is good that more creative ways of dealing with these problems will evolve and that Internet sales will continue to expand.

Chapter 3

Exporting: Sales Documentation

The single most important document in the export sale is the sales agreement. Repeat: The single most important document in the export sale is the sales agreement! Most of the problems that occur in exporting can be eliminated or greatly reduced by using a suitable sales agreement. Generally, different types of sales agreements are used for isolated sales transactions as opposed to ongoing sales transactions. I will discuss these as well as look at the important provisions in international sales agreements, distribution agreements, and sales agent agreements.

A. Isolated Sales Transactions

For the purposes of discussion in this chapter, isolated sales transactions are defined as situations where, for example, the customer purchases infrequently, or sales are made on a trial basis in the anticipation of establishing an ongoing sales relationship, or when a customer is not being granted any credit until a satisfactory history of payment has been established. Sales agreements for such transactions should be in writing, and the seller and buyer may use a variety of common, preprinted forms. The seller should check carefully to try to eliminate as much as possible any conflicting provisions between the seller's forms and the forms received from the buyer.

1. Importance of Written Agreements

In some industries, for example, the commodities industry, it is common to conduct purchases and sales orally through telephone orders and acceptances. Sometimes oral agreements occur in international sales when the seller receives an order at a trade show, by long-distance telephone, or in a meeting. (Under the new Convention on the International Sale of Goods discussed in Section B.2.m, a sales agreement may be formed or modified orally.) It is highly advisable to formalize the purchase and sale agreement in a written document, even for domestic sales, and there are many additional reasons why export sales should be embodied in a written agreement. Under the Uniform Commercial Code applicable in the United States, if the sale exceeds $500 in value, an agreement to sell, and therefore to get paid for the sale, is enforceable by the seller only if the agreement is in writing. While there are some exceptions to this law, and sometimes even informal notes will be sufficient to create an enforceable sales agreement, by far the safest practice is to formalize the sales agreement in a written document signed by the parties.

In addition to legal issues, an old Chinese proverb states: "The lightest ink is better than the brightest memory." This is one way of saying that often disputes arise in international sales transactions because the parties did not record their agreement or failed to discuss an issue and reach agreement. A written sales agreement acts both as a checklist to remind the buyer and seller what they should discuss and agree upon and as a written record of their agreement. All modifications of the agreement should also be in writing.

2. *Telex or Facsimile Orders*

While a telex or facsimile order and acceptance can satisfy the legal requirements of written evidence of an agreement, such sales agreements commonly contain only the specification of the quantity, usually a price, and sometimes a shipment date. There are many other terms and conditions of sale that should be inserted in a good sales agreement, and a simple acceptance by the seller to such telex or facsimile orders will fall far short of adequately protecting the seller in case of problems in the transaction. Consequently, acceptances of orders by telex or facsimile should specifically and expressly state that the sale incorporates the seller's other standard terms and conditions of sale. Those additional terms and conditions of sale should be included in the seller's telex or facsimile response to the buyer so that there can be no argument that the buyer was not aware of such terms and conditions of sale before proceeding with the transaction.

3. *The Formation of Sales Agreements*

The sales agreement is a formal contract governed by law. In general, a sales agreement is formed by agreement between the seller and the buyer and is the passing of title and ownership to goods for a price. An agreement is a mutual manifestation of assent to the same terms. Agreements are ordinarily reached by a process of offer and acceptance. This process of offer and acceptance can proceed by the seller and the buyer preparing a sales agreement contained in a single document that is signed by both parties; by the exchange of documents such as purchase orders and purchase order acceptances; or by conduct, such as when the buyer offers to purchase and the seller ships the goods.

From the point of view of clarity and reducing risks, preparation of a sales agreement contained in a single document is best. Both parties negotiate the agreement by exchanges of letters, faxes, or in person. Before proceeding with performance of any part of the transaction, both parties reach agreement and sign the same sales agreement. This gives both the seller and the buyer the best opportunity to understand the terms and conditions under which the other intends to transact business, and to negotiate and resolve any differences or conflicts. This type of sales agreement is often used if the size of the transaction is large; if the seller is concerned about payment or the buyer is concerned about manufacture and shipment; or if there are particular risks involved, such as government regulations or exchange controls, or differences in culture, language, or business customs that might create misunderstandings.

Quite often, however, the process of formation of the sales agreement is an exchange of documents that the seller and buyer have independently prepared and that, in the aggregate, constitute the sales agreement. These documents may contain differences and conflicts. Figure 3–1 shows the chronology of exchange and common documents used in many sales transactions. Although all documents will not be used in all sales transactions, these documents are in common use.

Several questions arise when a sales transaction is formed by such an exchange of documents. The first relates to the time of formation of the sales agreement. For example, a seller or buyer may send certain preliminary inquiries or information such as a price list, not intending to actually offer to sell or place an order, but may find that the other party's understanding (or the applicable law) has created a binding sales agreement prior to that party's intention. This can arise because under some countries' laws, an offer to sell or buy is accepted when the acceptance is dispatched, rather than when it is received. It can also arise because silence can be considered as acceptance if the parties are merchants.

The second issue that arises relates to the governing law. Contracts are often governed by the law of the country where the contract is negotiated and performed or

Figure 3–1. Formation of sales agreements.

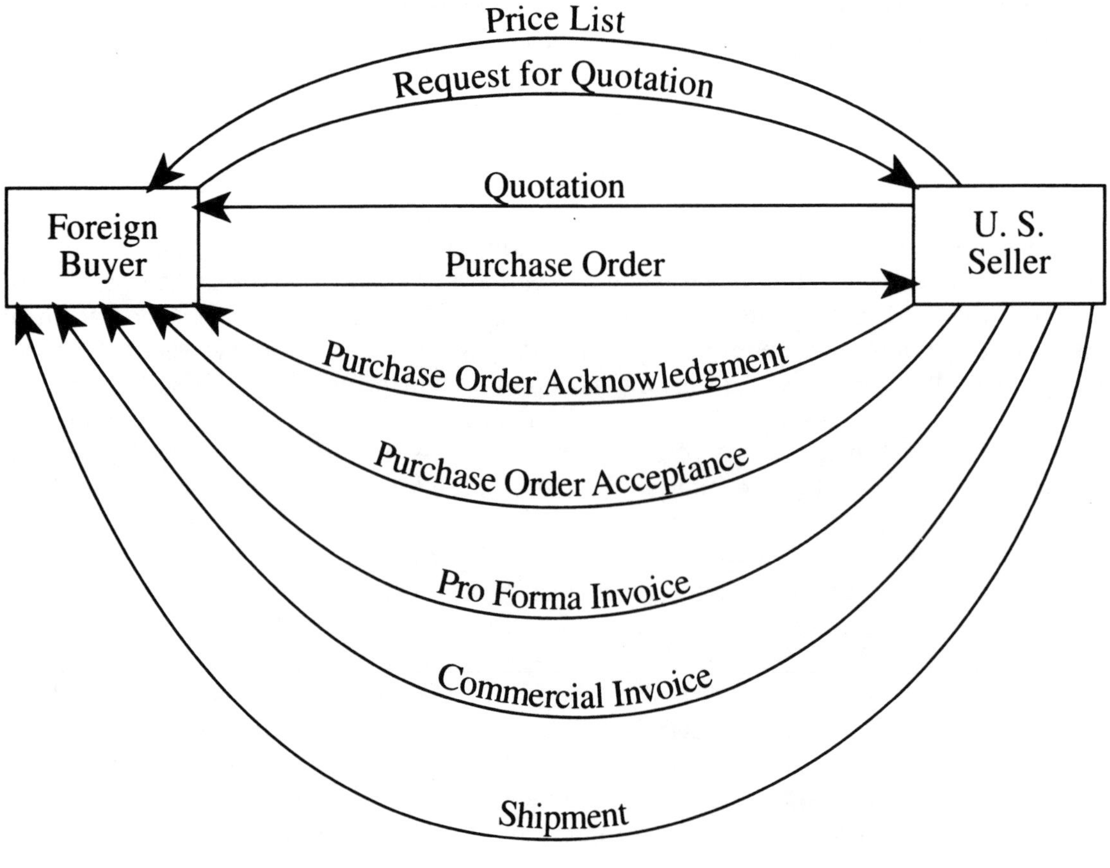

where the offer to sell or buy was accepted. Since an international agreement may be partly negotiated and partly performed in both countries, and since there may be a question as to whether the buyer accepted the offer to sell or the seller accepted the offer to purchase, situations can arise where the sales agreement is governed by the law of the buyer's country. Since foreign law may be quite different from U.S. law, the seller's rights and responsibilities may differ greatly from what he or she anticipated. Customary local ways of doing business, called trade usages, may unknowingly become a part of the sales agreement under the sales laws of some countries. Sellers and buyers sometimes try to resolve this problem by including a governing law term in their documents, but again, these may conflict.

A final method of formation of a sales agreement involves conduct. A simple example is where a buyer sends a purchase order and the seller, without communicating, simply ships the goods; or if the seller offers to sell the goods and the buyer simply sends payment. In such cases, the conduct in accepting the offer will include all of the terms and conditions of the offer. If the seller is not satisfied with the buyer's terms and conditions of purchase, he should send some communication to negotiate those terms before simply shipping the goods.

4. *Common Forms for the Formation of Sales Agreements*

There are a number of forms customarily used in the formation of sales agreements. In order to save time (and discourage changes by the other party), both buyers and sellers often purchase preprinted forms from commercial stationers or develop and preprint their own forms. Not all of the same documents are used by the seller or the buyer in all sales transactions. For example, a seller may submit a quotation to a potential buyer without receiving any request for quotation, or the first communication the seller receives may be a purchase order from the buyer. However, it is important to be familiar with the various forms and the role they play in bringing the negotiations to agreement.

a. *Price Lists*

Sometimes a seller will send a price list to a prospective buyer as its first communication. Ordinarily, such price lists would not be considered as an offer to sell, entitling the buyer to immediately accept. However, in order to prevent the unexpected formation of a sales agreement, such price lists should specify that it is not an offer to sell and no agreement will arise until a purchase order has been received and accepted. Such price lists should also specify their expiration date and that they are subject to change.

b. *Requests for Quotations*

Sometimes the first document involved in the formation of a sales agreement is a request from the buyer to the seller for a quotation (RFQ). Ordinarily, such a request—whether it be informal in a telex, facsimile, or letter, or formal in a printed form—will ask for a price quotation from the seller for a specific quantity and often a shipping date. (A sample printed form is shown in Figure 3–2). When receiving such a request

Figure 3–2. Quotation request.

QUOTATION REQUEST

From ______

Street Address ______

City and State ______

To

Inquiry No. ______

Date ______

Classification ______

PLEASE NOTE CAREFULLY

This inquiry implies no obligation on the part of the buyer.

Unless otherwise specified, there is no restriction on the number of items, that may be ordered.

In quoting, use duplicate copy of this form provided. Fill in complete information before returning.

Do not quote on articles you cannot supply. If substitutes are offered, make full explanation.

THIS IS AN INQUIRY—NOT AN ORDER

Delivery Point | By ☐ Parcel Post ☐ Rail Freight Line ______ ☐ Express ☐ Motor Freight Line ______ | If not indicated, suggest most practical way.

Prices Quoted F.O.B. ______ Freight Allowance ______

Shipping Point ______

Terms: ______ % Discount ______ Days Net Cash ______ Days — No charge to be made for packing, boxing crating or delivery to Transportation Co.

ITEM NO.	QUANTITY	ITEM AND SPECIFICATIONS	*	UNIT	LIST PRICE OF UNIT	DISCOUNT OFFERED	NET UNIT PRICE	ESTIMATED GROSS WT.

* Check-mark in this column indicates shipment can be made from stock.

Delivery of other items as follows: ______

Subject to withdrawal ______ Date returned ______

For Seller ______ For Buyer ______

CASCADE® L1-C2451 PRINTED IN U.S.A.

for quotation, the seller should be particularly careful to ascertain whether the request contains other terms and conditions of purchase that are incorporated by reference to another document or are contained in the fine print "boiler plate" on the front or back of the request for quotation. If other terms are referenced, the best precaution is to ask the buyer to send such terms and conditions for the seller's review before replying. If additional terms of purchase are provided, they should be reviewed to determine if they conflict with the seller's usual terms and conditions of sale.

c. Quotations and Costing Sheets

In response to a request for a quotation, the seller ordinarily prepares and forwards a quotation. Before quoting a price for any specific quantity or a shipment date, it is extremely important that the seller accurately calculate its additional costs relating to an export sale and shipment before providing the quotation. The use of a costing sheet is highly recommended. (A sample costing sheet is shown in Figure 3–3.) By accurately completing the costing sheet, the seller can avoid quoting prices that will result in sales commitments with too little or no profit. In making quotations, the seller can use a printed form or prepare them on a case-by-case basis. (Three samples are shown in Figures 3–4, 3–5, and 3–6.) If this is the first communication from the seller to the buyer, the seller should be careful to ensure that it contains all of the seller's terms and conditions of sale in addition to the price, quantity, and shipment date, or the quotation should specify that the seller will not be bound until he has received a written purchase order and has issued a written purchase order acceptance. Otherwise, when the buyer receives the quotation, he may find the price, quantity, and shipment date acceptable and accept that quotation when he receives it. This means that the sales agreement is formed at that time in the buyer's country, or it may be formed when the buyer issues his purchase order (but before the purchase order is received by the seller). This may be so whether or not the seller designates his quotation as firm, because under the laws of some countries, quotations by merchants are deemed irrevocable for a certain period of time. When the sales agreement is formed under the law of the country of the buyer, the seller's rights and responsibilities under the sales agreement may be quite different from those of U.S. law. Sometimes it is necessary or acceptable to have a sales agreement governed by foreign law, but only after the seller has investigated the differences and has made an informed choice—not a mistaken one. Moreover, unless the seller has forwarded all of his terms and conditions of sale with his first communication (the quotation), the terms and conditions included in subsequent communications from the seller may not be binding on the buyer.

d. Purchase Orders

The next document that may occur in a sales transaction is a purchase order (PO) issued by the buyer. Again, the purchase order may be informal, such as in a telex, facsimile, or letter, or it may be on a printed form. Purchase orders are likely to contain many additional terms and conditions that the buyer wants to be a part of the sales agreement when the purchase order is accepted by the seller. (Samples are shown in Figures 3–7 and 3–8.) Even though the seller may expect that no sales agreement will

(*Text continues on page 70.*)

Figure 3–3. Export quotation worksheet.

EXPORT QUOTATION WORKSHEET

DATE ____________________ REF/PRO FORMA INVOICE NO. ____________________
COMMODITY ____________________ EXPECTED SHIP DATE ____________________
CUSTOMER ____________________ PACKED DIMENSIONS ____________________
COUNTRY ____________________ PACKED WEIGHT ____________________
PAYMENT TERMS ____________________ PACKED CUBE ____________________

PRODUCTS TO BE SHIPPED FROM ____________________
TO ____________________

SELLING PRICE OF GOODS: $ ________

SPECIAL EXPORT PACKING:
$ ________ quoted by ____________________
$ ________ quoted by ____________________
$ ________ quoted by ____________________ $ ________

INLAND FREIGHT:
$ ________ quoted by ____________________
$ ________ quoted by ____________________
$ ________ quoted by ____________________ $ ________
Inland freight includes the following charges:
☐ unloading ☐ pier delivery ☐ terminal ☐ ____________

OCEAN FREIGHT

	quoted by	tariff item
$ ______	____________	# ______
$ ______	____________	# ______
$ ______	____________	# ______

Ocean freight includes the following surcharges:
☐ Port congestion ☐ Heavy lift
☐ Currency adjustment ☐ Bunker
☐ Container rental ☐ Wharfage
☐ ____________ ☐ ____________

☐ INSURANCE ☐ includes war risk
rate: ____________ per $100 or $ ______

TOTAL OCEAN CHARGES $ ______
notes:

AIR FREIGHT

	quoted by	spec code
$ ______	____________	# ______
$ ______	____________	# ______
$ ______	____________	# ______

Air freight includes the following surcharges:
☐ Fuel adjustment
☐ Container stuffing
☐ ____________

☐ INSURANCE ☐ includes war risk
rate: ____________ per $100 or $ ______

TOTAL AIR CHARGES $ ______ $ ________
notes:

FORWARDING FEES: $ ________
Includes: ☐ Courier Fees ☐ Certification Fees ☐ Banking Fees ☐ ____________

CONSULAR LEGALIZATION FEES: $ ________

INSPECTION FEES: $ ________

DIRECT BANK CHARGES: $ ________

OTHER CHARGES: ____________________ $ ________
____________________ $ ________

TOTAL: ☐ FOB ____________ ☐ C & F ____________
☐ FAS ____________ ☐ CIF ____________ $ ________

Form 10-020 Printed and Sold by UNZCO 190 Baldwin Ave., Jersey City, NJ 07306 • (800) 631-3098 • (201) 795-5400

Figure 3–4. Quotation.

QUOTATION

From

To

We are pleased to quote as follows. Your inquiry

Inquiry No.__________

Date__________

Terms__________

Prices quoted are
F.O.B.__________

Delivery__________

Quantity	Description	Price	Amount
	SPECIMEN		

By__________

TOPS FORM 3448 LITHO IN U. S. A.

Courtesy of Tops Business Forms.

Figure 3–5. Quotation.

§2.4—Form 5

Quotation

[*Face side*]

SELLER COMPANY

____

____

Date: ______

BUYER COMPANY

____

____

We are pleased to quote as follows on your recent inquiry:

Quantity	Description	Price

Very truly yours,
SELLER COMPANY

By ____________________

THIS QUOTATION INCLUDES ALL OF THE PROVISIONS ON THE REVERSE SIDE HEREOF.

[*Reverse side*]

PROVISIONS

1. ANY PURCHASE ORDER PURSUANT TO THE ACCOMPANYING QUOTATION SHALL NOT RESULT IN A CONTRACT UNTIL IT IS ACCEPTED AND ACKNOWLEDGED BY SELLER AT SELLER'S OFFICE IN ____, ____.[1]

2. Payment terms are net ten (10) days after the rendering of seller's invoice.[2]

3. Delivery terms are f.o.b. cars at seller's

§ 2.4—Form 5

1. See § 2.5.

2. See § 9.6.

Figure 3–5. *(continued)*

plant in ____. Dates of delivery are determined from the date of seller's acceptance of any order or orders by buyer and are estimates of approximate dates of delivery, not a guaranty of a particular day of delivery.[3] Seller shall not be liable for failure or delay in shipping goods hereunder if such failure or delay is due to an act of God, war, labor difficulties, accident, inability to obtain containers or raw materials, or any other causes of any kind whatever beyond the control of seller.[4]

4. Any tax imposed by federal, state or other governmental authority on the sale of the merchandise and service referred to in this quotation shall be paid by buyer in addition to the quoted purchase price.

5. Buyer shall in respect of goods packaged by seller in accordance with designs, processes or formulas supplied, determined or requested by buyer, defend seller at buyer's expense and pay costs and damages awarded in any suit brought against seller for infringement of any letters patent by reason of use of such designs, processes or formulas, provided seller promptly notifies buyer in writing of any claim of or suit for infringement and tenders defense thereof to buyer. Seller is entitled to be represented in any suit at its own expense.[5]

6. Except for the warranty that the goods are made in a workmanlike manner and in accordance with the specifications therefor supplied or agreed to by buyer and are made or packaged pursuant to seller's customary manufacturing procedures, SELLER MAKES NO WARRANTY EXPRESS OR IMPLIED; AND ANY IMPLIED WARRANTY OF MERCHANTABILITY OR FITNESS FOR A PARTICULAR PURPOSE WHICH EXCEEDS THE FOREGOING WARRANTY IS HEREBY DISCLAIMED BY SELLER AND EXCLUDED FROM ANY AGREEMENT MADE BY ACCEPTANCE ANY ORDER PURSUANT TO THIS QUOTATION.[6] Seller will not be liable for any consequential damages, loss or expense arising in connection with the use of or the inability to use its goods for any purpose whatever. Seller's maximum liabil-

3. See § 9.4.

4. See § 9.19.

5. See §§ 8.1, 8.9.

6. See §§ 8.2 et seq.

(continues)

Figure 3–5. *(continued)*

ity shall not in any case exceed the contract price for the goods claimed to be defective or unsuitable.[7]

8. Buyer shall notify seller within ten days of receipt of merchandise of any complaint whatsoever buyer may have concerning such merchandise.[8]

9. There are no provisions with respect to this quotation which are not specified herein.[9] IF BUYER PLACES AN ORDER WITH SELLER BASED ON THIS QUOTATION, WHETHER IN WRITING OR ORALLY, THEN THIS QUOTATION AND BUYER'S ORDER AND SELLER'S ACCEPTANCE OR CONFIRMATION WILL CONSTITUTE THE ENTIRE CONTRACT BETWEEN BUYER AND SELLER WITH RESPECT TO THE SUBJECT MATTER OF THIS QUOTATION.[10] Any agreement so made shall be governed by the law of [*state*].[11]

SELLER COMPANY

COMMENT

This is a quotation, as distinguished from a firm offer. Since a quotation is only an invitation to submit an offer or to place an order, no power of acceptance is created in the addressee or recipient. See UCC § 2-205.

7. See §§ 8.12, 15.2.

8. See §§ 8.8, 9.9, 9.14, 9.15, 14.1.

9. See § 5.2.

10. See § 2.7.

11. See § 1.2.

be formed until he has received the buyer's purchase order, if he has previously sent a quotation to the buyer, the terms and conditions stated in the buyer's purchase order may govern the sales agreement. Of course, the terms and conditions contained in the buyer's purchase order are always written to be most favorable to the buyer. Another way in which the seller can try to guard against such a result is to expressly state in her quotation that the quotation is not an offer to sell and that no sales agreement will exist until such time as the seller has received a purchase order from the buyer and has issued its purchase order acceptance.

e. Purchase Order Acknowledgments, Acceptances, and Sales Confirmations

When a purchase order is received, some sellers prepare a purchase order acknowledgment form. A purchase order acknowledgment may state that the seller has received the purchase order from the buyer and is in the process of evaluating it, such as checking on the credit of the buyer or determining the availability of raw materials for manufacture, but that the seller has not yet accepted the purchase order and will issue a purchase order acceptance at a later date. In other cases, the language of the

(*Text continues on page 73.*)

Figure 3–6. Quotation.

§ 2.4–Form 1

Firm Offer by Merchant

[*Face side*]

SELLER COMPANY

[*Address*]

____

Date: ______

BUYER COMPANY
[*Address*]

____

We are pleased to make the following offer which is firm for ______ days from the above date:[1]

Quantity	Description	Price

THIS OFFER INCLUDES ALL OF THE PROVISIONS ON THE REVERSE SIDE HEREOF.

Very truly yours,
SELLER COMPANY

By ______________________
[*Title*] ______________

[*Reverse side*]

PROVISIONS

1. This offer expires in ______ days from the date appearing at the top of the face side hereof. This offer may be accepted ONLY by signing and returning to the seller's office in ______ the attached duplicate acceptance copy of this offer. Acceptance is limited to the provisions contained herein only.[2]

2. Payment terms are net ten (10) days after the rendering of seller's invoice.[3]

§ 2.4–Form 1

1. UCC § 2–205. See § 3.2.

2. Ucc § 2–207. See § 2.7.

3. UCC § 2–310. See § 9.6.

(*continues*)

Figure 3–6. *(continued)*

3. Delivery terms are f.o.b. cars at seller's plant in ______. Dates of delivery are determined from the date of seller's acceptance of any order or orders by buyer and are estimates of approximate dates of delivery, not a guaranty of a particular day of delivery.[4] Seller shall not be liable for failure or delay in shipping goods hereunder if such failure or delay is due to an act of God, war, labor difficulties, accident, inability to obtain containers or raw materials, or any other causes of any kind whatever beyond the control of seller.[5]

4. Any tax imposed by federal, state or other governmental authority on the sale of the merchandise and service referred to in this quotation shall be paid by buyer in addition to the quoted purchase price.

5. Buyer shall, in respect of goods packaged by seller in accordance with designs, processes or formulas supplied, determined or requested by buyer, defend seller at buyer's expense and pay costs and damages awarded in any suit brought against seller for infringement of any letters patent by reason of use of such designs, processes, or formulas, provided seller promptly notifies buyer in writing of any claim of or suit for infringement and tenders defense thereof to buyer.[6] Seller is entitled to be represented in any suit at its own expense.

6. Except for the warranty that the goods are made in a workmanlike manner and in accordance with the specifications therefor supplied by or agreed to by buyer and are made or packaged pursuant to seller's customary manufacturing procedures, SELLER MAKES NO WARRANTY EXPRESS OR IMPLIED; AND ANY IMPLIED WARRANTY OF MERCHANTABILITY OR FITNESS FOR A PARTICULAR PURPOSE WHICH EXCEEDS THE FOREGOING WARRANTY IS HEREBY DISCLAIMED BY SELLER AND EXCLUDED FROM ANY AGREEMENT MADE BY ACCEPTANCE OF THIS OFFER.[7]

7. Seller will not be liable for any consequential damages, loss or expense arising in connection with the use of the goods or the inability to use its goods for any purpose whatever. Seller's maximum li-

4. UCC §§ 2-319, 2-503. See § 9.4.

5. UCC § 2-615. See § 9.19.

6. UCC § 2-312(3). See §§ 8.1, 8.9.

7. UCC §§ 2-313, 2-316. See §§ 8.2 et seq.

Figure 3–6. *(continued)*

ability shall not in any case exceed the contract price for the goods claimed to be defective or unsuitable.[8]

8. Buyer shall notify seller within twenty (20) days of receipt of merchandise of any complaint whatsoever buyer may have concerning such merchandise.[9]

9. Any contract made by acceptance of this offer shall be governed by the law of [*state*].[10]

SELLER COMPANY

Library References:
C.J.S. Sales §§ 57, 59, 62.
West's Key No. Digests, Sales ⚷ 28.

8. UCC §§ 2-714, 2-715, 2-719. See §§ 8.12, 15.2.

9. UCC §§ 2-602(1), 2-607(3), 2-608(3). See §§ 8.8, 9.14, 14.1.

10. UCC § 1-105. See § 1.2.

purchase order acknowledgment indicates that it is also an acceptance of the order and no further communication is issued. Sales confirmations usually perform the same role as purchase order acceptances. The seller will normally include its detailed terms and conditions of sale in its purchase order acknowledgment or purchase order acceptance. If the seller's request for a quotation or purchase order does not contain detailed terms and conditions of purchase, the seller can feel reasonably comfortable that its terms and conditions of sale will control if included in the purchase order acknowledgment or acceptance form. If the buyer has previously sent detailed terms and conditions of purchase, however, the seller is at risk that those terms and conditions will control unless it expressly states that the order is accepted and the sale is made *only* on the seller's terms and conditions of sale *and* thereafter (prior to production and shipment) the buyer confirms its acceptance of the seller's terms. (A sample purchase order acceptance is shown in Figure 3–9.) The purchase order acceptance should specify that the agreement cannot be modified except in writing signed by the seller.

f. Pro Forma Invoices

If the buyer is in a country that has foreign exchange controls, he may need to receive a pro forma invoice from the seller in order to get government approval to make payment, and the seller may want to receive such approval before commencing production. This is an invoice that the buyer will submit to the central bank to obtain permission and clearance to convert foreign currency into U.S. dollars in order to

(*Text continues on page 81.*)

Figure 3–7. Purchase order.

PURCHASE ORDER

UNITRAK™

VENDOR	PURCHASER
PRO FORMA INVOICE NO. DATE	PURCHASE ORDER NO. DATE
CONSIGNEE	NOTIFY/INTERMEDIATE CONSIGNEE

MFR. ITEM NO., SYMBOL, OR BRAND	QUANTITIES, FULL DESCRIPTION OF MERCHANDISE, AND PACKAGING INSTRUCTIONS	UNIT PURCHASE PRICE CURRENCY	TOTAL PURCHASE PRICE CURRENCY

SPECIAL PACKAGING REQUIREMENTS		OCEAN/AIR FREIGHT
	INCLUDED	
	COSTS	
		TOTAL

RELEASE NO.	ITEM AND QUANTITY	DELIVERY DATE	PORT OF ENTRY	CARRIER

DOCUMENT REQUIREMENTS	TERMS OF PAYMENT

Form 16-310 Printed and Sold by UNZCO 190 Baldwin Ave., Jersey City, NJ 07306 • (800) 631-3098 • (201) 795-5400

VENDOR

Reprinted with permission from Bradford Stone's *West's Legal Forms,* Second Edition, copyright © 1985 by West Publishing Co.

Figure 3–8. Purchase order.

§ 2.6—Form 2

Buyer's Purchase Order—Another Form

Purchase Order No. ____________
Purchase Order Number Must Appear on Invoices, n/l. Packages and Packing Slips.

BUYER COMPANY

P.O. Date

IMPORTANT
READ ALL INSTRUCTIONS, TERMS AND CONDITIONS ON FACE AND REVERSE SIDES.
ONLY SUCH INSTRUCTIONS, TERMS AND CONDITIONS SHALL CONSTITUTE THE AGREEMENT BETWEEN THE PARTIES.

TO:

SELLER COMPANY

Ship via	f.o.b.	terms	ship to

as per your quotation	promised delivery date at destination

Please Enter Our Purchase Order of Above No. Subject to All Instructions, Terms and Conditions on Face and Reverse Side Hereof.

QUANTITY	DESCRIPTION	Price Per	AMOUNT
		TOTAL	

ADDITIONAL INSTRUCTIONS, TERMS AND CONDITIONS ON REVERSE SIDE

INSTRUCTIONS, TERMS AND CONDITIONS:

BUYER COMPANY

By ____________

1. **Acceptance Copy** must be signed and returned immediately.
2. **Packing Slips** must be included in all shipments and last copy must state "ORDER COMPLETED."
3. **Order Number** must be shown on each package, packing slip and invoice.
4. **Invoices** must be rendered in duplicate not later than the day following shipment. Attach bill of lading or express receipt to each invoice.[1]
5. **Deliveries** must be made to Buyer's receiving room, not to individuals or departments.[2]
6. **Extra Charges.** No additional charges of any kind, including charges for boxing, packing, cartage, or other extras will be allowed unless specifically agreed to in writing in advance by Buyer.
7. **Payment.** It is understood that the cash discount period will date from the receipt of

§2.6—Form 2

1. UCC §§ 2-503, 2-504(b) and (c). See § 9.4. 2. UCC §§ 2-308, 2-309(1), 2-503. See § 9.4.

(*continues*)

Figure 3–8. *(continued)*

the goods or from the date of the invoice, whichever is later. C.O.D. shipments will not be accepted. Drafts will not be honored.[3]

8. **Quantities.** The specific quantity ordered must be delivered in full and not be changed without Buyer's consent in writing. Any unauthorized quantity is subject to our rejection and return at Seller's expense.[4]
9. **Price.** If price is not stated in this order, it is agreed that the goods shall be billed at the price last quoted, or billed at the prevailing market price, whichever is lower. This order must not be filled at a higher price than last quoted or charged without Buyer's specific authorization.[5]
10. **Applicable Laws.** Seller represents that the merchandise covered by this order was not manufactured and is not being sold or priced in violation of any federal, state or local law.
11. **Fair Labor Standards Act.** Seller agrees that goods shipped to Buyer under this order will be produced in compliance with the Fair Labor Standards Act.[6]
12. **Warranty Specifications.** Seller expressly warrants that all the materials and articles covered by this order or other description or specification furnished by Buyer will be in exact accordance with such order, description or specification and free from defects in material and/or workmanship, and merchantable. Such warranty shall survive delivery, and shall not be deemed waived either by reason of Buyer's acceptance of said materials or articles or by payment for them. Any deviations from this order or specifications furnished hereunder, or any other exceptions or alterations must be approved in writing by Buyer's Purchasing Department.[7]
13. **Cancellation.** Buyer reserves the right to cancel all or any part of the undelivered portion of this order if Seller does not make deliveries as specified, time being of the essence of this Contract, or if Seller breaches any of the terms hereof including, without limitation, the warranties of Seller.[8]
14. **Inspection and Acceptance.** All goods shall be received subject to Buyer's right of inspection and rejection. Defective goods or goods not in accordance with Buyer's specifications will be held for Seller's instruction at Seller's risk and if Seller so directs, will be returned at Seller's expense. If inspection discloses that part of the goods received are not in accordance with Buyer's specifications, Buyer shall have the right to cancel any unshipped portion of the order. Payment for goods on this order prior to inspection shall not constitute acceptance thereof and is without prejudice to any and all claims that Buyer may have against Seller.[9]
15. **Patents.** Seller warrants the material purchased hereunder does not infringe any letters patent granted by the United States and covenants and agrees to save harmless and protect Buyer, its successors, assigns, customers and users of its product, against any claim or demand based upon such infringement, and after notice, to appear and defend at its own expense any suits at law or in equity arising therefrom.[10]
16. **Interpretation of Contract and Assignments.** This contract shall be construed according to the laws of the State of [*state*]. This contract may not be assigned by Seller without Buyer's written consent.[11]

3. UCC §§ 2-310, 2-511. See § 9.6.
4. UCC §§ 2-307, 2-601, 2-602. See §§ 9.4, 9.8 et seq.
5. UCC § 2-305. See § 2.3.
6. 29 U.S.C.A. § 215.
7. UCC §§ 2-313, 2-316. See §§ 8.2, 8.10.
8. UCC § 2-703(f); see UCC §§ 2-612, 2-719, 2-720. See §§ 9.16, 13.2, 15.2.
9. UCC §§ 2-512, 2-513, 2-601 through 2-607. See §§ 9.5, 9.7, 9.8 et seq.
10. UCC § 2-312(3). See §§ 8.1, 8.9.
11. UCC §§ 1-105, 2-210. See §§ 1.2, 6.1 et seq.

Figure 3–9. Purchase order acceptance.

§ 2.6—Form 8

Seller's Sales Order—Another Form

[*Face side*]

SELLER COMPANY

PRODUCT

TO: [*Buyer Company*]

GENTLEMEN:

We thank you for the order listed below which we are pleased to have accepted subject to only those terms and conditions of sale which are set forth below and on the reverse side hereof.[1]

Trusting that we have your assent to these terms and conditions we accordingly have entered your order in our mill schedules.

DATE

YOUR ORDER:

TERMS OF DELIVERY:[2]

§ 2.6—Form 8

1. UCC § 2-207(1). These terms probably will not ribbon match those on buyer's purchase order form. See discussion and forms at § 2.7 below.

2. UCC §§ 2-307, 2-308, 2-309(1), 2-319 et seq., 2-503. See § 9.4.

(*continues*)

Figure 3–9. *(continued)*

TERMS OF PAYMENT:[3]

PLEASE ADDRESS CORRESPONDENCE RELATING TO THIS ORDER TO OUR DISTRICT SALES OFFICE AT

VERY TRULY YOURS,
SELLER COMPANY

By ____________________
[*Manager of Sales*]

[*Reverse side*]

TERMS AND CONDITIONS OF SALE

In accordance with the usage of trade, your assent to the terms and conditions of sale set forth below and on the reverse side hereof shall be conclusively presumed from your failure seasonably to object in writing and from your acceptance of all or any part of the material ordered.[4]

All proposals, negotiations, and representations, if any, regarding this transaction and made prior to the date of this acknowledgment are merged herein.[5]

PRICES—All prices, whether herein named or heretofore quoted or proposed, shall be adjusted to the Seller's prices in effect at the time of shipment.[6]

If transportation charges from point of origin of the shipment to a designated point are included in the prices herein named or heretofore quoted—

(a) any changes in such transportation charges shall be for the account of the Buyer;

3. UCC § 2-310; see UCC § 2-511. See § 9.6.

4. See § 2.6—Form 7 and Comment. See also § 2.7.

5. UCC § 2-202. See § 5.2.

6. UCC § 2-305. See § 2.3.

Figure 3–9. *(continued)*

(b) except as otherwise stated in the Seller's quotation, the Seller shall not be responsible for switching, spotting, handling, storage, demurrage or any other transportation or accessorial service, nor for any charges incurred therefor, unless such charges are included in the applicable tariff freight rate from shipping point to the designated point.

TAXES—Any taxes which the Seller may be required to pay or collect, under any existing or future law, upon or with respect to the sale, purchase, delivery, storage, processing, use or consumption of any of the material covered hereby, including taxes upon or measured by the receipts from the sale thereof, shall be for the account of the Buyer, who shall promptly pay the amount thereof to the Seller upon demand.

DELAY—The Seller shall be excused for any delay in performance due to acts of God, war, riot, embargoes, acts of civil or military authorities, fires, floods, accidents, quarantine restrictions, mill conditions, strikes, differences with workmen, delays in transportation, shortage of cars, fuel, labor or materials, or any circumstance or cause beyond the control of the Seller in the reasonable conduct of its business.[7]

INSPECTION—The Buyer may inspect, or provide for inspection, at the place of manufacture. Such inspection shall be so conducted as not to interfere unreasonably with the manufacturer's operations, and consequent approval or rejection shall be made before shipment of the material. Notwithstanding the foregoing, if, upon receipt of such material by the Buyer, the same shall appear not to conform to the contract between the Buyer and the Seller, the Buyer shall immediately notify the Seller of such condition and afford the Seller a reasonable opportunity to inspect the material. No material shall be returned without the Seller's consent.[8]

EXCLUSION OF WARRANTIES—The Implied Warranties of Merchantability and Fitness for Purpose Are Excluded From This Contract.[9]

BUYER'S REMEDIES—If the material furnished to the Buyer shall fail to conform to this contract or to any express or implied warranty, the Seller shall replace such non-conforming material at the original point of delivery and shall furnish instructions for its disposition. Any transportation charges involved in such disposition shall be for the Seller's account.

The Buyer's exclusive and sole remedy on account or in respect of the furnishing of material that does not conform to this contract, or to any express or implied warranty, shall be to secure replacement thereof as aforesaid. The Seller shall not in any event be liable for the cost of any labor expended on any such material or for any special, direct,

7. UCC § 2-615. See § 9.19.
8. UCC §§ 2-512, 2-513. See § 9.7.
9. UCC §§ 2-314, 2-315, 2-316. See §§ 8.4, 8.5, 8.6, 8.11.

(continues)

Figure 3–9. *(continued)*

indirect, incidental or consequential damages to anyone by reason of the fact that such material does not conform to this contract or to any express or implied warranty.[10]

PERMISSIBLE VARIATIONS, STANDARDS AND TOLERANCES—Except in the particulars specified by Buyer and expressly agreed to in writing by Seller, all material shall be produced in accordance with Seller's standard practices. All material, including that produced to meet an exact specification, shall be subject to tolerances and variations consistent with usages of the trade and regular mill practices concerning: dimension, weight, straightness, section, composition and mechanical properties; normal variations in surface, internal conditions and quality; deviations from tolerances and variations consistent with practical testing and inspection methods; and regular mill practices concerning over and under shipments.[11]

PATENTS—The Seller shall indemnify the Buyer against any judgment for damages and costs which may be rendered against the Buyer in any suit brought on account of the alleged infringement of any United States patent by any product supplied by the Seller hereunder, unless made in accordance with materials, designs or specifications furnished or designated by the Buyer, in which case the Buyer shall indemnify the Seller against any judgment for damages and costs which may be rendered against the Seller in any suit brought on account of the alleged infringement of any United States patent by such product or by such materials, designs or specifications; provided that prompt written notice be given to the party from whom indemnity is sought of the bringing of the suit and that an opportunity be given such party to settle or defend it as that party may see fit and that every reasonable assistance in settling or defending it shall be rendered. Neither the Seller nor the Buyer shall in any event be liable to the other for special, indirect, incidental or consequential damages arising out of or resulting from infringement of patents.[12]

CREDIT APPROVAL—Shipments, deliveries and performance of work shall at all times be subject to the approval of the Seller's Credit Department. The Seller may at any time decline to make any shipment or delivery or perform any work except upon receipt of payment or security or upon terms and conditions satisfactory to such Department.

TERMS OF PAYMENT—Subject to the provisions of CREDIT APPROVAL above, terms of payment are as shown on the reverse side hereof and shall be effective from date of invoice. A cash discount shall not be allowed on any transportation charges included in delivered prices.[13]

10. UCC §§ 2-508, 2-714, 2-715, 2-719. See §§ 9.17, 14.1, 14.2, 15.2.

11. UCC §§ 1-205, 2-208, 2-313, 2-314(2)(d). See §§ 5.1, 8.2, 8.4.

12. UCC § 2-312(3). See §§ 8.1, 8.9.

13. UCC §§ 2-310, 2-511. See § 9.6.

Figure 3–9. *(continued)*

COMPLIANCE WITH LAWS—The Seller intends to comply with all laws applicable to its performance of this order.[14]

RENEGOTIATION—The Seller assumes only such liability with respect to renegotiation of contracts or subcontracts to which it is a party as may be lawfully imposed upon the Seller under the provisions of any Renegotiation Act applicable to this order.[15]

NON-WAIVER BY SELLER—Waiver by the Seller of a breach of any of the terms and conditions of this contract shall not be construed as a waiver of any other breach.[16]

14. UCC § 1-103. See § 1.1.

15. See, e.g., Renegotiation Act (Renegotiation of Contracts), 50 U.S.C.A.App. §§ 1211 et seq.

16. UCC § 1-107; see UCC §§ 2-209, 1-207. See §§ 3.3, 10.2.

make payment to the seller. The seller should exert some care in preparing this invoice, because it may be extremely difficult to change the price in the final invoice due to changes in costs or specifications. Sometimes, a pro forma invoice is used as the first document sent by the seller in response to a buyer's request for quotation. (A sample pro forma invoice is shown in Figure 3–10.) It should contain the complete terms and conditions of sale. This type of pro forma invoice should not be confused with that used by an importer when the seller has not provided a commercial invoice (see Figure 8–2).

g. Commercial Invoices

Later, when manufacture is complete and the product is ready for shipment, ordinarily the seller will prepare a commercial invoice, which is the formal statement for payment to be sent directly to the buyer or submitted through banking channels for payment by the buyer. Such invoices may also contain the detailed terms or conditions of sale on the front or back of the form. (A sample is shown in Figure 3–11.) However, if this is the first time that the seller has brought such terms to the attention of the buyer, it is likely that they will not be binding on the buyer because the seller has already accepted the buyer's order by the seller's conduct in manufacturing and/or shipping the products. (See also the discussion of commercial invoices in Chapter 4, Section C.)

h. Conflicting Provisions in Seller and Buyer Sales Documentation

It is common in international trade for sellers and buyers to use preprinted forms designed to reduce the amount of negotiation and discussion required for each sales agreement. Undoubtedly, such forms have been drafted by attorneys for each side and contain terms and conditions of purchase or terms and conditions of sale which are favorable to the buyer and seller, respectively. Consequently, it is not unusual for sellers and buyers intent on entering into a sales transaction to routinely issue such documentation with little or no thought regarding the consistency of those provisions.

(*Text continues on page 84.*)

Figure 3–10. Pro forma invoice.

PROFORMA INVOICE/EXPORT ORDER **UNITRAK™**

CUSTOMER:

SHIP TO (Consignee):

NOTIFY (Intermediate Consignee):

IN-HOUSE ORDER NO.	DATE
PRO FORMA INVOICE NO.	DATE
COMMERCIAL INVOICE NO.	DATE
CUSTOMER PURCHASE ORDER NO.	DATE
CUSTOMER ACCOUNT NO.	
PURCHASER'S NAME	TITLE
SHIP VIA	EST. SHIP DATE
TELEPHONE NO.	
TELEX/FAX/CABLE NO.	

PART NUMBER	UNIT OF MEASURE	QUANTITY	DESCRIPTION	UNIT PRICE	TOTAL PRICE

SPECIAL INSTRUCTIONS:

ADDITIONAL CHARGES		TERMS OF PAYMENT	
FREIGHT ☐ Ocean ☐ Air		☐ LETTER OF CREDIT	Bank
CONSULAR/LEGALIZATION		☐ DRAFT	Terms
INSPECTION/CERTIFICATION		☐ OPEN ACCOUNT	Terms
SPECIAL PACKING		☐ OTHER	
		CURRENCY OF PAYMENT	

Form 15-330 Printed and Sold by UNZCO 190 Baldwin Ave., Jersey City, NJ 07306 • (800) 631-3098 • (201) 795-5400

PROFORMA INVOICE

Reprinted with permission of Unz & Co., 190 Baldwin Ave., Jersey City, NJ 07306, USA.

Figure 3–11. Commercial invoice.

COMMERCIAL INVOICE

SHIPPER/EXPORTER

CONSIGNEE

NOTIFY: INTERMEDIATE CONSIGNEE

FORWARDING AGENT

COMMERCIAL INVOICE NO. | DATE

CUSTOMER PURCHASE ORDER NO. | B/L, AWB NO.

COUNTRY OF ORIGIN | DATE OF EXPORT

TERMS OF PAYMENT

EXPORT REFERENCES

AIR/OCEAN PORT OF EMBARKATION

EXPORTING CARRIER/ROUTE

Terms of Sale and Terms of Payment under this offer are governed by Incoterms # 322, "Uniform Rules For The Collection Of Commercial Paper" and # 400 "Uniform Customs And Practice For Documentary Credits"

PKGS.	QUANTITY	NET WT. *(Kilos)*	GROSS WT. *(Kilos)*	DESCRIPTION OF MERCHANDISE	UNIT PRICE	TOTAL VALUE

PACKAGE MARKS:

MISC. CHARGES *(Packing, Insurance, etc.)*

INVOICE TOTAL

CERTIFICATIONS

AUTHORIZED SIGNATURE

Form 15-320 Printed and Sold by UNZ&CO 190 Baldwin Ave., Jersey City, NJ 07306 • (800) 631-3098 • (201) 795-5400

Reprinted with permission of Unz & Co., 190 Baldwin Ave., Jersey City, NJ 07306, USA.

Afterward, if the sales transaction breaks down and either the buyer or seller consults its attorney regarding its legal rights and obligations, the rights of the parties may be very unclear. In the worst case, the seller may find that a sales agreement has been validly formed on all of the terms and conditions of the buyer's purchase order and is governed by the law of the buyer's country. In order to reduce or eliminate this problem, often the seller's attorney drafts requests for quotations, purchase order acknowledgments, and acceptances and invoices with language stating that, notwithstanding any terms or conditions that might be contained in the buyer's request for quotation or purchase order, the seller agrees to make the sale only on its own terms and conditions. While this can be of some help, sometimes the buyer's requests for quotation and purchase orders also contain such language, and consequently, the buyer's terms and conditions may win out. If the buyer was the last to send its terms and conditions of purchase, and the seller did not object, the seller's conduct in shipping the goods can result in an agreement under the buyer's terms and conditions. In fact, the only way to be comfortable regarding the terms and conditions of sale that will govern a sales agreement is to actually review the terms and conditions contained in the buyer's forms and compare them with the terms and conditions that the seller desires to utilize. Where specific conflicts exist or where the buyer's terms and conditions of purchase differ from the seller's terms and conditions of sale, the seller should expressly bring that to the attention of the buyer, the difference should be negotiated to the satisfaction of the seller, and appropriate changes should be made in the form of a rider to the standard form or a letter to clarify the agreement that has been reached between the parties (which should be signed by both parties).

In some isolated sales transactions where the quantities are small, the seller may simply choose to forgo this effort and accept the risk that the transaction will be controlled by the buyer's terms and conditions of sale. However, the seller should establish some dollar limit over which a review is to be made and should not continue a practice that might be appropriate for small sales but would be very dangerous for large sales.

i. Side Agreements

Occasionally, the buyer may suggest that the seller and buyer enter into a side or letter agreement. In some cases, the suggestion may be innocent enough, for example, where the parties wish to clarify how they will interpret or carry out a particular provision of their sales agreement. Even then, however, it is better practice to incorporate all of the agreements of the parties in a single document. Unfortunately, more often the buyer's proposal of a side agreement is designed to evade the buyer's foreign exchange control, tax, customs, or antitrust laws. Sellers should be wary of entering into such agreements unless they fully understand the consequences. Such agreements may be unenforceable, the seller may not be able to get paid on its export sale, and/or the seller may be prosecuted as a co-conspirator for violating such laws.

B. Ongoing Sales Transactions

When a customer begins to purchase on a regular basis, or when the seller desires to make regular sales to a particular end user or reseller, the seller and the buyer should enter into a more comprehensive agreement to govern their relationship. Often these types of agreements are a result of the buyer being willing to commit to regular purchases, and, therefore, to purchase a larger quantity of the goods, in return for obtaining a lower price. Or, they may result from the buyer's desire to "tie-up," that is, to obtain more assurance from the seller to commit to supply the buyer's requirements, or from the seller's desire to plan its production. The three major types of agreements used in ongoing sales transactions are: (1) international sales agreements, that is, supply agreements where the seller sells directly to an end-user customer who either incorporates the seller's product as a component into a product the buyer manufactures, or who consumes the product and does not resell the product; (2) distributor agreements, where the seller sells the product to a purchaser, usually located in the destination country, who resells the product in that country, usually in the same form but sometimes with modifications; and (3) sales agent or sales representative agreements, where a person, usually located in the destination country, is appointed to solicit orders from potential customers in that country. In the last case, the sale is not made to the sales agent, but is made directly to the customer, with payment of a commission or other compensation to the sales agent.

In any of the three foregoing agreements, there is a correlation between the documentation used in isolated sales transactions and the documentation used in ongoing sales transactions. Furthermore, there are a number of important provisions which are not relevant to domestic sales which should be included in international sales, distributor, and sales agent agreements.

1. Correlation With Documentation for Isolated Sales Transactions

As discussed in Section A.4 above, it is common for sellers and buyers to use forms such as requests for quotation, purchase orders, purchase order acknowledgments, purchase order acceptances, sales confirmations, pro forma invoices, and invoices during the course of ordering and selling products. When an ongoing sales relationship is being established with a particular customer, it is usual to enter into an umbrella or blanket agreement which is intended to govern the relationship between the parties over a longer period of time, for example, one year, five years, or longer. Sometimes the parties will enter into a trial marketing agreement which will last for a short period of time, such as one year, before deciding to enter into a longer-term agreement. In any event, the international sales (supply) agreement, the distributor agreement, and the sales agent (representative) agreement define the rights and obligations of the parties over a fairly long period of time and commit the seller and the buyer to doing business with each other so that both sides can make production, marketing, and advertising plans and expenditures. Special price discounts in return for commitments to purchase specific quantities are common in such agreements. Such agreements may contain a commitment to purchase a specific quantity over the life of the agreement and may designate a specific price or a formula by which the price will be adjusted over the life of the agreement. To this extent, these agreements serve as an umbrella over the parties' relationship with certain specific acts to be accomplished as agreed by the parties from time to time. For example, it is usually necessary during the term of such agreements for the buyer to advise the seller from time to time of the specific quantity that it wishes to order at that time to be applied against the buyer's overall purchase commitment. This will be done by the issuance of a purchase order.

If the price of the product is likely to fluctuate, no price may be specified in the umbrella agreement. Instead, the price may be changed from time to time by the seller depending on the seller's price at the time the buyer submits a purchase order, perhaps with a special discount from such price because the buyer has committed to buy a substantial quantity over the life of the agreement. In such cases, depending upon whether or not a specific price has been set in the umbrella agreement, the buyer will send a request for a quotation and the seller will provide a quotation, or a purchase order will be sent describing the specific quantity the buyer wishes to order at that time, a suggested shipment date, and the price. The seller will still use a purchase order acknowledgment and/or a purchase order acceptance form to agree to ship the specific quantity on the specific shipment date at the specific price. The seller will continue to provide pro forma invoices if they are necessary for the buyer to obtain a foreign exchange license to make payment, as well as a commercial invoice against which the buyer must make payment.

In summary, where the seller and buyer wish to enter into a longer-term agreement, they will define their overall relationship in an umbrella agreement, but the usual documentation utilized in isolated sales transactions will also be utilized to set specific quantities, prices, and shipment dates. Sometimes conflicts can arise between the terms and conditions in the umbrella agreement and the specific documentation. Usually the parties provide that in such cases, the umbrella agreement will control, but this can also lead to problems in situations where the parties wish to vary the terms of their umbrella agreement for a specific transaction.

2. *Important Provisions in International Sales Agreements*

There are numerous terms and conditions in an international sales agreement which require special consideration different from the usual terms and conditions in a domestic sales agreement. Unfortunately, sometimes sellers simply utilize sales documentation which was developed for U.S. domestic sales, only to discover that it is woefully inadequate for international sales. A simple sample international sales agreement (export) is included as Appendix B.

a. *Selling and Purchasing Entities*

In entering into an international sales agreement, it is important to think about who the seller and buyer will be. For example, rather than the U.S. company acting as the seller in the international sales agreement, it may wish to structure another company as the seller, primarily for possible U.S. tax savings. Two tax incentives which are available to U.S. exporters were discussed in Chapter 2, Section U. There are two main structures available to take advantage of such tax savings: the commission agent structure or the buy-sell structure. In the commission agent structure, the exporter will incorporate another company (in the United States or abroad, depending upon the tax incentive being utilized) and pay that company a commission on its export sales (which is, of course, a payment to a related company). In the buy-sell structure, an exporter would sell and transfer title to a related company that it sets up (in the United

States or abroad), and the related company would act as the seller for export sales in the international sales agreement. If the exporter is not manufacturing products but is instead buying from an unrelated manufacturing company and reselling to unrelated companies, such activities sometimes can be more profitably conducted if the company incorporates a subsidiary in a low-tax jurisdiction, such as the Cayman Islands or Hong Kong.

If the seller and the buyer are related entities, such as a parent and subsidiary corporation, the foreign customs treatment may be different, for example, in the valuation of the merchandise or assessment of dumping duties. Some transactions may be structured to involve the use of a trading company, either on the exporting side, the importing side, or both. Depending upon whether the trading company takes title or is appointed as the agent (of either the buyer or the seller), or whether the trading company is related to the seller or the buyer, the foreign customs treatment may be different. For example, commissions paid to the seller's agent are ordinarily subject to customs duties in the foreign country, but commissions paid to the buyer's agent are not.

b. Quantity

The quantity term is even more important than the price. Under U.S. law, if the parties have agreed on the quantity, the sales agreement is enforceable even if the parties have not agreed on price—a current, or market, price will be implied. When no quantity has been agreed upon, however, the sales agreement will not be enforceable.

One reason for forming a formal sales agreement is for the buyer to obtain a lower price by committing to purchase a large quantity, usually over a year or more. The seller may be willing to grant a lower price in return for the ability to plan ahead, schedule production and inventory, develop economies of sale, and reduce shipping and administrative costs. The seller should be aware that price discounts for quantity purchases may violate some countries' price discrimination laws, unless the amount of the discount can be directly related to the cost savings of the seller for that particular quantity.

Quantity agreements can be for a specific quantity or a target quantity. Generally, if the commitment is a target only, failure to actually purchase such amount will not justify the seller in claiming damages or terminating the agreement (although sometimes the buyer will agree to a retroactive price increase). Failure to purchase a minimum purchase quantity, however, will justify termination and a claim for breach.

Sometimes the buyer may wish to buy the seller's entire output or the seller may seek a commitment that the buyer will purchase all of its requirements for the merchandise from the seller. Usually such agreements are lawful, but in certain circumstances they can violate the antitrust laws, such as when the seller is the only supplier or represents a large amount of the supply, or the buyer is the only buyer or represents a large segment of the market.

c. Pricing

There are a number of considerations in formulating the seller's pricing policy for international sales agreements. In addition to the importance of using a costing sheet to identify all additional costs of exporting to make sure that the price quoted to a customer results in a net profit acceptable to the seller (see Section A.4.c), the seller has to be aware of several constraints in formulating its pricing policy.

The first constraint relates to dumping. Many countries of the world are parties to the GATT Antidumping Code or have domestic legislation that prohibits dumping of foreign products in their country. This generally means that the price at which products are sold for export to their country cannot be lower than the price at which such products are sold in the United States. The mere fact that sales are made at lower prices for export does not automatically mean that a dumping investigation will be initiated or that a dumping finding will occur. Under the laws of most countries, no dumping will occur if the price to that market is above that country's current market price, even if the seller's price to that country is lower than its sales price in its own country.

On the other hand, there are essentially no U.S. legal constraints on the extent to which a price quoted for export can exceed the price for sale in the United States. The antitrust laws in the United States (in particular the price discrimination provisions of the Robinson-Patman Act) apply only when sales are being made in the United States. Consequently, a seller may charge a higher or lower price for export without violating U.S. law. However, if the seller is selling to two or more customers in the same foreign country at different prices, such sales may violate the price discrimination provisions of the destination country's law.

If the price is below the seller's total cost of production, there is always a risk that such sales will be attacked as predatory pricing in violation of the foreign country's antitrust laws. The accounting calculation of cost is always a subject of dispute, particularly where the seller may feel that the costs of domestic advertising or other costs should not be allocated to export sales. However, in general, any sales below total, fully allocated costs are at risk.

Another very important pricing area relates to rebates, discounts, allowances, and price escalation clauses. Sometimes the buyer will ask for and the seller will be willing to grant some form of rebate, discount, or allowance under certain circumstances, such as the purchase of large quantities of merchandise. Such price concessions generally do not, in and of themselves, violate U.S. or foreign law, but if such payments are not disclosed to the proper governmental authorities, both the U.S. exporter and the foreign buyer can violate various laws, and the U.S. exporter also may be charged with conspiracy to violate, or aiding and abetting the buyer's violation of those laws. For example, the U.S. exporter must file a Shipper's Export Declaration on each shipment (see discussion in Chapter 4, Section Q), and must declare the price at which the goods are being sold. If, in fact, this price is false (because the exporter has agreed to grant some rebate, discount, or allowance, or, in fact, does so), the U.S. exporter will violate U.S. law and be subject to civil and criminal penalties. Similarly, when the buyer imports the goods to the destination country, the buyer will be required to state a value for customs and foreign exchange control purposes in its country and will receive U.S. dollars through the central bank to pay for the goods and must pay customs duties on the value declared. In addition, the buyer will probably use that value to show a deduction from its sales or revenues as a cost of goods sold, that is, as a tax deduction. Consequently, the true prices must be used. If the buyer requests the seller to provide two invoices for different amounts or if the buyer asks the seller to pay the rebate, discount, or allowance outside of its own country (for example, by deposit in a bank account in the United States, Switzerland, or some other country), there is considerable risk that the intended action of the buyer will violate the buyer's foreign exchange control laws, tax laws, and/or customs laws. If the seller cooperates by providing any such documentation or is aware of the scheme, the seller can also be charged with conspiracy to violate those foreign laws and can risk fines, arrest, and imprisonment in those countries. Similarly, retroactive price increases (for example, due to currency fluctuations) or price increases or decreases under escalation clauses may cause a change in the final price which may have to be reported to the customs, foreign exchange, or tax authorities. Before agreeing to grant any price rebate, discount, or allowance, or before agreeing to use a price escalation clause, or to implement a retroactive price increase or decrease, or to make any payment to the buyer in any place except the buyer's own country, the seller should satisfy itself that its actions will not result in the violation of any U.S. or foreign law.

If the sale is to an affiliated company, such as a foreign distribution or manufacturing subsidiary, additional pricing considerations arise. Because the buyer and seller are related, pricing can be artificially manipulated. For example, a U.S. exporter that is taxable on its U.S. manufacturing and sales profits at a rate of 35 percent when selling to an affiliated purchaser in a country that has a higher tax rate may attempt to minimize taxes in the foreign country by charging a high price to its foreign affiliate. Then, when the foreign affiliate resells the product, its profit will be small. Or, if the foreign affiliate uses the product in its manufacturing operation, the deduction for cost of materials will be high, thereby reducing the profits taxable in that country. When the sale is to a country where the tax rate is lower than in the United States, the considerations are reversed and the transfer price is set at a low rate, in which case the U.S. profits will be low. These strategies are well known to the tax authorities in foreign countries and to the Internal Revenue Service in the United States. Consequently, sales between affiliated companies are always susceptible to attack by the tax authorities. In general, the tax authorities in both countries will require that the seller sell to its affiliated buyer at an arm's length price, as if it were selling to an unaffiliated buyer. Often, preserving evidence that the seller was selling to its unaffiliated customers at the same price as its affiliated customers will be very important in defending a tax audit. When the U.S. seller is selling to an affiliated buyer in a country with a lower tax rate, the customs authorities in the foreign country will also be suspicious that the transfer price is undervalued, and, therefore, customs duties may be underpaid.

Another consideration in the pricing of goods for export concerns parallel imports or gray market goods. If buyers in one country (including the United States) are able to purchase at a lower price than in another country, an economic incentive will exist for customers in the lower-price country to divert such goods to the higher-price country in hopes of making a profit. Obviously, the seller's distributor in the higher-price country will complain about such unauthorized imports and loss of sales. The laws of many countries, however, such as the European Economic Community (EEC) and Japan, encourage such parallel imports as a means of encouraging competition and forcing the authorized distributor to reduce its price. In the EEC, attempts to prohibit a distributor from selling outside of its country (but within the EEC) can violate the law. Unfortunately, maintaining pricing parity is not always easy because of floating exchange rates, not only between the United States and other countries, but among those other countries.

d. Currency Fluctuations

Related to the issue of pricing are the currency fluctuations which occur between the markets of the seller and the buyer. If the U.S. exporter quotes and sells only in U.S. dollars, the fluctuation of the foreign currency will not affect the final U.S. dollar amount that the exporter receives as payment. However, if the buyer is a much larger company than the seller and has more negotiating and bargaining leverage, or if the seller is anxious to make the sale, it may be necessary to agree to a sale denominated in foreign currency, such as Japanese yen or German marks. In such a case, if the foreign currency weakens between the time of the price agreement and the time of payment, the U.S. exporter will receive fewer U.S. dollars than it had anticipated when it quoted the price and calculated the expected profit. In such a case, the exporter is assuming the foreign exchange fluctuation risk. Sometimes, when the term of the agreement is long, or when major currency fluctuations are anticipated, neither the seller nor the buyer is comfortable in entirely assuming such risk. Consequently, they may agree to some sharing of the risk as a 50/50 price adjustment due to any exchange fluctuations which occur during the life of the agreement, or some other formula which attempts to protect both sides against such fluctuations.

e. Payment Methods

In a domestic sales transaction, the seller may be used to selling on open account, extending credit, or asking for cash on delivery. In international agreements, it is more customary to utilize certain methods of payment which are designed to give the seller a greater level of protection. The idea is that if the buyer fails to pay, it is much more difficult for a seller to go to a foreign country, institute a lawsuit, attempt to attach the buyer's assets, or otherwise obtain payment. When sellers are dealing with buyers who are essentially unknown to them, with whom they have no prior payment experience, or who are small or located in countries where there is significant political upheaval or changing economic circumstances, the seller may insist that the buyer pay by cash in advance. This is particularly important if the sale is of specially manufactured goods. Where a seller wants to give the buyer some credit but also to have security of payment the seller often requires the buyer to obtain a documentary letter of credit from a bank in the buyer's country. The seller may also require that the letter of credit be confirmed by a bank in the seller's country which guarantees payment by the buyer's bank. The seller may still sell on terms with payment to be made at the time of shipment or the seller may give the buyer some period of time (for example, from 30 days to 180 days) to make payment, but the letter of credit acts as an umbrella obligation of the bank guaranteeing the buyer's payment. In some cases, however, the buyer will be unable to obtain a letter of credit, for example, because the buyer's bank will not feel comfortable with the buyer's financial solvency. Furthermore, issuance of letters of credit involves the payment of bank fees which are normally paid for by the buyer, and the buyer usually does not wish to incur such expenses in addition to the cost of purchasing the goods. In such cases, particularly if the seller is anxious to make the sale or if other competitors are willing to offer more liberal payment terms, the seller may be forced to give up a letter of credit and agree to make the sale on some other, less secure, method of payment.

The next best method of payment is by sight draft documentary collection, commonly known as documents against payment or D/P transactions. In this case, the exporter uses the services of a bank to effect collection, but neither the buyer's bank nor a U.S. bank guarantees payment by the buyer. The seller will ship the goods, and the bill of lading and a draft (that is, a document like a check in the amount of the sale drawn on the buyer—rather than a bank—and payable to the seller) will be forwarded to the seller's bank. The seller's bank will forward such documents to a correspondent bank in the foreign country (sometimes the seller or its freight forwarder sends the documents directly to the foreign bank—this is known as direct collection), and the foreign bank will collect payment from the buyer prior to the time that the goods arrive. If payment is not made by the buyer, the correspondent bank does not release the bill of lading to the buyer, and the buyer will be unable to take possession of the goods or clear customs. Although it can still be a significant problem for the seller if the buyer does not make payment and the shipment has already gone, the seller should still be able to control the goods upon arrival, for example, by asking the bank to place them in a warehouse or by requesting that they be shipped to a third country or back to the United States at the seller's expense. Direct collections are often used for air shipments to avoid delays through the seller's bank and, also, because air waybills are non-negotiable.

The next least secure payment method is to utilize a time draft, commonly known as documents against acceptance or D/A transactions. Like the sight draft transaction, the bill of lading and time draft are forwarded through banking channels, but the buyer agrees to make payment within a certain number of days (for example, 30 to 180) after he receives and accepts the draft. Normally, this permits the buyer to obtain possession of the goods and may give the buyer enough time to resell them before his obligation to pay comes due. However, documents against acceptance transactions are a significantly greater risk for the seller because, if the buyer does not pay at the promised time, the seller's only recourse is to file a lawsuit—the goods have already been released to the buyer. Where the buyer is financially strong, sometimes such acceptances can be discounted by the seller, however, permitting the seller to get immediate payment but giving the buyer additional time to pay. This discounting may be done with recourse or without recourse depending upon the size of the discount the seller is willing to accept. There may also be an interest charge to the buyer for the delay in payment, which the seller may decide to waive in order to make the sale. The buyer's bank may also agree to add its "aval." This then becomes a bank guaranty of payment equivalent to a letter of credit.

The least secure payment method is sale on open account, where the seller makes the sale and the shipment by forwarding the bill of lading and a commercial invoice directly to the buyer for payment. Because the bill of lading is sent directly to the buyer, once it leaves the possession of the seller, the seller will be unable to control what happens to the goods and the buyer will be able to obtain the goods whether or not payment is made. When a seller agrees to sell on open account, it must look to an alternative method, for example, a security interest under foreign law (see subsection g, below), to protect its right to payment in case the buyer fails to pay at the agreed time. For this method of payment and for documents against acceptance, the seller should definitely consider obtaining commercial risk insurance through the Foreign Credit Insurance Association (see Chapter 2, Section T).

Another type of letter of credit transaction which adds security is the standby letter of credit. If a buyer opens a standby letter of credit in favor of the seller, invoices, bills of lading, and similar documentation are forwarded directly to the buyer without using a bank for collection, but the issuing bank's guaranty is there in case of default by the buyer.

Sometimes a seller will begin selling to a particular customer under letters of credit, and as the seller becomes more familiar with the customer (the customer honors its obligations, increases its purchases, or enters into an ongoing sales agreement), the seller will be willing to liberalize its payment terms.

In addition, in international transactions the seller will have to consider alternative payment methods, such as wire transfers via banking channels, since payment by check will often involve an inordinate length of time if the check is first sent to the seller in the United States and then sent back to the foreign country to be collected from the buyer's bank. Direct telegraphic transfer from bank account to bank account is a highly efficient and useful way to deal with international payments. However, buyers may be unwilling to wire the money to the seller until they are satisfied that the goods have been sent or until after arrival and inspection. Other methods of payment, such as cash payments made by employees traveling from the buyer to the seller or vice versa, or payments made in third countries, all carry the risk of violating the buyer's foreign exchange control, tax and/or customs laws, and should only be agreed to after detailed investigation of the possible risks. A chart comparing these various methods of payment is shown in Figure 3–12.

Another method of payment which may arise in international sales is countertrade. Countertrade describes a variety of practices, such as barter (an exchange of goods), counterpurchase (where the seller must agree to purchase a certain amount from the buyer or from another seller in the buyer's country), or offset (where the seller must reinvest some of the sales profits in the buyer's country). The risks and complications of such sales are higher. Sometimes, of course, the seller may have to agree to such arrangements in order to get the business, but specialized sales agreements adequately addressing many additional concerns must be utilized. Countertrade is further discussed in Part IV, Chapter 9.

Finally, an additional method of obtaining payment is the factoring of export accounts receivable. While many banks and some factors are reluctant to accept receivables on foreign sales due to the greater risks and uncertainties of collection, other factors are willing to do so. This may represent an opportunity for an exporter to obtain its money immediately in return for accepting a lesser amount, some discounted from the sales price. If the factor buys the accounts receivable with recourse, that is, the right to charge back or get back the money paid to the exporter in case of default in payment by the customer, the factor's charge or discount should be correspondingly lower.

f. Export Financing

The substantive aspects of export financing were discussed in Chapter 2, Section R. If export financing is going to be utilized, it should be discussed in the international

(*Text continues on page 95.*)

Figure 3–12. International credit terms/payment methods.

FIRST CHICAGO

INTERNATIONAL CREDIT TERMS/PAYMENT METHODS

TERM	DEFINITION	APPLICATION	ADVANTAGES	DISADVANTAGES
Open Account	Exporter makes shipment and awaits payment direct from importer. Any documents needed by importer sent when sale is invoiced.	1. Importer has excellent credit rating. 2. Importer is long-time, well-known customer. 3. Importer is subsidiary of exporter or vice-versa. 4. Small shipments to good customers. 5. Low-risk country.	1. Simple bookkeeping for exporter. 2. Easy documentation. 3. Competitive. 4. Low cost. 5. May be insured.	1. Full brunt of financing falls on exporter. 2. In matters of dispute, no interested third party involved. 3. Problems of availability of foreign exchange. 4. Exporter assumes credit risk of importer and risk of importer's country's political condition.
Consignment or Extended Terms	Exporter makes shipment and receives payment as goods are sold or used by importer.	1. Normally used only between subsidiaries of the same company. 2. Promissory notes may be used along with trust receipts and other legal agreements.	1. Exporter may retain title until goods are sold and/or paid for. 2. Competitive.	1. Same as Open Account. 2. Subject to local laws and customs. 3. Requires periodic inventorying of goods.
Time or Date Draft, Documents against Acceptance (D/A)	Exporter makes shipment and presents draft and documents to bank with instructions that documents are to be released to importer upon importer's acceptance of the draft (importer's acknowkedgement of his debt and promise to pay at a future date).	1. Importer has excellent and/or good credit rating. 2. Low-risk country. 3. Extended terms necessary to make sale.	1. Draft is evidence of indebtedness. 2. Receivable may be discountable by exporter's bank with or without recourse. 3. Gives importer time to sell goods before having to pay for them. 4. Interested third party involved in case of dispute (bank). 5. Low cost. 6. May be insured.	1. Exporter is financing shipment until maturity of draft. 2. Problems of availability of foreign exchange. 3. Exporter assumes credit risk of importer and risk of importer's country's political condition. 4. Exporter assumes risk of refused shipment.

(continues)

Figure 3–12. *(continued)*

[reverse]

TERM	DEFINITION	APPLICATION	ADVANTAGES	DISADVANTAGES
Sight Draft, Documents against Payment (D/P), Cash against Documents	Exporter makes shipment and presents documents to bank with instructions that documents be released to importer only upon payment of draft.	1. Importer has excellent and/or good credit rating. 2. Small shipments. 3. Medium volume. 4. Low-risk country. 5. May be used in countries having foreign exchange restrictions not allowing open account purchases or sales.	1. Evidence of indebtedness. 2. Documents not released to importer before payment. (Exporter may retain title to merchandise until paid.) 3. Interested third party involved (bank). 4. Low cost. 5. May be insured.	1. Exporter must wait until draft has been received and paid. 2. Exporter assumes credit risk of importer and risk of importer's country's political condition. 3. Exporter assumes risk of refused shipment.
C.O.D.	Cash on delivery, collected by the carrier.	1. Importer's credit is excellent or good. 2. Small shipments. 3. Carrier accepts such shipments.	1. Exporter assured of payment before delivery of goods to importer by carrier.	1. Importer must have cash available. 2. Someone must pay C.O.D. charges. 3. Service not available to all countries. 4. Discourages repeat sales. 5. Exporter assumes risk of refused shipment.
Irrevocable L/C	Instrument issued by importer's bank in favor of exporter, payable against presentation to the issuing bank of specified documents.	1. Importer's credit rating may be excellent, good, fair, or unknown. 2. First-time sale. 3. Large sale. 4. Sale to country which requires L/Cs. 5. Low-risk country.	1. Exporter looks to bank for payment if documents are proper and in order. 2. Credit is irrevocable and may be amended only upon concurrence of all parties. 3. May be insured at preferred rate. 4. Banks may be willing to offer engagements to negotiate.	1. Cost of L/C. 2. Documents must be carefully prepared by exporter. 3. Exporter's credit risk is the foreign bank: foreign exchange and political risk still exist. 4. Importer exposed to possibilities of fraud.
Confirmed Irrevocable Letter of Credit	Same as above, except importer's bank asks advising bank to add its confirmation. Payable upon presentation of documents to the advising/ confirming bank.	1. Importer's credit rating may be excellent, good, fair, or unknown. 2. First-time sale. 3. Large sale. 4. Country which requires L/Cs. 5. High-risk country.	1. Exporter looks to confirming bank for payment immediately upon shipment if documents are proper. 2. Credit is irrevocable and may be amended only upon concurrence of all parties. 3. Exporter's credit risk is confirming bank; confirming bank takes credit of issuing bank.	1. Cost of L/C. 2. Documents must be carefully prepared by exporter. 3. Importer exposed to possibility of fraud.
Cash in Advance	Importer sends good funds before exporter ships.	1. Importer is good, fair or unknown credit risk. 2. One-time sale. 3. Small shipment. 4. High-risk country.	1. Exporter may use funds to prepare shipment. 2. No risk to exporter. 3. Low cost.	1. Importer bears costs of financing as well as risk of never receiving goods. 2. Uncompetitive; may preclude repeat business. 3. Some countries prohibit payment in advance.

sales agreement. The buyer will thus be clearly aware that the seller intends to use such export financing. The documentation which the buyer is required to provide in order for the seller to obtain such financing should be specified in the agreement and the seller's obligation to sell and make shipment at specific dates should be subject to obtaining such export financing in a timely manner.

g. Security Interest

If the seller intends to sell on open account or on documents against acceptance, the seller should carefully investigate obtaining a security interest under the law of the buyer's country to protect its rights to payment. Under the laws of most countries, unless the seller has registered its lien or security interest with a public agency, if the buyer goes into bankruptcy or falls into financial difficulties, the seller will be unable to repossess the merchandise which it sold, even if the merchandise is still in the possession of the buyer. Also, the seller may be unable to obtain priority over other creditors, and after such creditors are paid, nothing may remain for the seller. For example, through an attorney the seller should investigate the availability of a security interest in the buyer's country and the requirements for establishing a security interest. The seller may need to retain title or a chattel mortgage or make a conditional sale. Then, in the international sales agreement, the fact that the buyer is granting a security interest to the seller and the documents which will be furnished by the buyer for public registration should be discussed and specified. The security interest normally should be established, including public registration, prior to delivery to the buyer, whether such transfer occurs in the United States (for example, ex-factory sales) or in the foreign country (for example, landed sales). The attorney would conduct a search of the public records in the buyer's country, and if other security interests have been granted, the seller should require the buyer to obtain a written subordination agreement from the other creditors before going forward.

h. Passage of Title, Delivery, and Risk of Loss

Ownership is transferred from the seller to the buyer by the passage of title. Under U.S. law, title will pass at the time and place agreed to by the parties to the international sales agreement. It can pass at the seller's plant; at the port of export; upon arrival in the foreign country; after clearance of customs in the foreign country; upon arrival at the buyer's place of business; or at any other place, time, or manner agreed to by the parties. Under the new Convention on the International Sale of Goods (discussed in subsection m), if the parties do not agree on the time and place for transfer of title and delivery, title will pass when the merchandise is transferred to the first transportation carrier. Usually the risk of loss for any subsequent casualty or damage to the products will pass to the buyer at the same time the title passes. However, it is possible in the sales agreement to specify that it will pass at a different time. Up to the point where the risk of loss passes to the buyer, the seller should be sure that the shipment is insured against casualty loss.

i. Warranties and Product Defects

From the seller's point of view, next to the payment provision, perhaps the most important single provision in an international sales agreement is the one that specifies the warranty terms. Under the laws of most countries and the Convention on the International Sale of Goods (discussed in subsection m), unless the seller limits its warranty expressly in writing in its international sales agreement, the seller will be responsible and liable for foreseeable consequential damages which result to the buyer from defective products. Since such consequential damages can far exceed the profits which the seller has made on such sales, unless the seller expressly limits its liabilities, the risk of engaging in the sales transaction can be too great. The sales agreement should specify exactly what warranty the seller is giving for the products, whether the products are being sold "as is" with no warranty, whether there is a limited warranty such as repair or replacement, whether there is a dollar limit on the warranty, whether there is a time period within which the warranty claim must be made, and/or whether there is any limitation on consequential damages. In many countries as a matter of public policy, the law prohibits certain types of warranty disclaimers or exclusions. Consequently, in drafting the warranty limitation, the seller may need to consult with an attorney to make sure that the warranty will be effective in the destination country. In addition, of course, the buyer will be seeking the strongest warranty possible, so this is an area in which the seller must be particularly careful. If the sales agreement is formed by a mere exchange of preprinted forms, as discussed in Section A.4 above, the seller may find that the buyer's terms or conditions control the sale and that no limitation of warranty has been achieved. In such cases, the seller must negotiate a warranty acceptable to both sides before going ahead with the sale. One related point is that the Magnuson-Moss Warranty Act, which prescribes certain warranties and is applicable to merchandise sold in the United States, including imported merchandise, is not applicable to export sales. Laws in the foreign country may be applicable, however.

j. Preshipment Inspections

A number of countries, particularly in South America and Africa (see list in Chapter 4, Section F), require that before companies located in their country purchase products from a foreign seller, the foreign seller submit to a preshipment inspection. The ostensible purpose of such inspections is to eliminate a situation where a dishonest seller ships defective products or even crates of sawdust, but obtains payment through a letter of credit or banking channels because the seller has provided a fraudulent bill of lading and draft to the bank, and the buyer has not yet been able to inspect the goods. Even if the buyer has not paid in advance, if the products arrive in the foreign country and are defective, the buyer may be faced with substantial losses or the necessity of re-exporting the merchandise to the seller. Consequently, it is not unreasonable for a buyer to request and for a seller to agree to a preshipment inspection, but the terms and conditions of such an inspection should be specified in the international sales agreement. In particular, in recent years, some of the inspection agencies have been reviewing more than the quality of the goods and have been requiring sellers to produce documentation relating to sales of the same product to other customers to ascertain the prices at which sales were made. If the particular customer that is getting the preshipment inspection determines that the price that it is paying is higher than the prices that the seller has charged other customers, the customer may refuse to go forward with the transaction or attempt to renegotiate the price. Consequently, in an international sales agreement, if the seller simply agrees to a preshipment inspection satisfactory to the buyer, the inspection company's report may be an unfavorable one based upon price, and the buyer would be excused from going forward with the purchase. In summary, the type of preshipment inspection which will be permitted, its scope, terms, and the consequences if the inspection is unfavorable should be specified in the international sales agreement.

The seller (and buyer) should also realize that providing for a preshipment inspection will usually delay the shipment anywhere from twenty to forty days.

k. Export Licenses

The importance of an export license was touched upon in Chapter 2, Section F, and is discussed in detail in Chapter 5. If an export license will be required in an international sales agreement, the exporter should state that it is required and should require the buyer to provide the necessary documentation to apply for the license. If the buyer fails to provide such documentation, the seller would be excused from making the export sale and could claim damages. Furthermore, in order to protect the seller from a violation of U.S. export control laws, the international sales agreement and the provisions therein relating to any export license would be evidence that the seller had fulfilled its responsibilities to inform the buyer that the products cannot be re-exported from the buyer's own country without obtaining a re-export license from the U.S. authorities. Finally, the sales agreement should provide that if the seller cannot obtain the export license, the seller's performance of the sales agreement will be excused without the payment of damages to the buyer. (Under the Incoterms, the buyer is responsible for obtaining the export license on "ex-works" sales, but recent changes to U.S. law make the seller responsible unless the buyer has specifically agreed to such responsibility and has appointed a U.S. agent.)

l. Import Licenses and Foreign Government Filings

An international sales agreement should specify that the buyer will be responsible for obtaining all necessary import licenses and making any foreign governmental filings. The buyer should state exactly what licenses must be obtained and what filings must be made. The sales agreement should specify that the buyer will obtain such licenses sufficiently in advance, for example, prior to manufacture or shipment, so that the seller can be comfortable that payment will be forthcoming. In regard to the applications for such licenses or any foreign government filings, the exporter should insist upon and should obligate the buyer in the international sales agreement to provide copies of those applications prior to their filing. In this way, the seller can confirm that the information in the application is correct; for example, that the prices being stated to the governmental agencies are the same as those which the seller is quoting to the buyer, or if there is any reference to the seller in the applications, that the seller will know what is being said about it. This will also permit the seller to know the exact time when such applications are being made and, therefore, whether the approval will delay or interfere with the anticipated sales shipment and payment schedule.

m. Governing Law

In any international sales agreement, whether the agreement is formed by a written agreement between the parties or whether it is an oral agreement, the rights and obligations of the parties will be governed either by the law of the country of the seller or the law of the country of the buyer. The laws of most countries permit the seller and buyer to specifically agree on which law will apply, and that choice will be binding upon both parties whether or not a lawsuit is brought in either the buyer's or the seller's country. Of course, whenever the subject is raised, the seller will prefer the agreement to be governed by the laws of the seller's country, and the buyer will prefer it to be governed by the laws of the buyer's country. If the bargaining leverage of the parties is approximately equal, it is fair to say that it is more customary for the buyer to agree that the seller's law will govern the agreement. However, if the buyer has more bargaining leverage, the seller may have to agree that the buyer's foreign law applies. Before doing so, however, the seller should check on what differences exist between the foreign law and U.S. law so that the seller can fully appreciate the risks it is assuming by agreeing to the application of foreign law. The seller can also determine whether or not the risk is serious enough to negotiate a specific solution to that particular problem with the buyer. Frequently, however, the parties do not raise, negotiate, or expressly agree upon the governing law. This may occur as a result of an exchange of preprinted forms wherein the buyer and seller each have specified that their own law governs, which results in a clear conflict between these two provisions. It may also occur when the parties have not agreed upon the governing law, as in a situation where an oral agreement of sale has occurred, or when the facsimile, telex, or other purchase or sale documentation does not contain any express specification of the governing law. In such cases, if a dispute arises between the parties, it will be extremely difficult to determine with any confidence which law governs the sales agreement. Often the seller believes that the law of the country where the offer is accepted will govern. However, the laws of the two countries may be in conflict on this point, and it may be unclear whether this means an offer to sell or an offer to buy and whether or not the acceptance must be received by the offeror before the formation of the sales agreement.

An additional development relating to this issue is the relatively new Convention on Contracts for the International Sale of Goods (the Convention). On January 1, 1988, this multinational treaty went into effect among the countries that signed it, including the United States. The following list includes the parties to the Convention as of August 2000.

Parties to the Convention on Contracts for the International Sale of Goods (as of August 2000)

Argentina	China	Germany
Australia	Croatia	Greece
Austria	Czech Republic	Guinea
Belarus	Denmark	Hungary
Belgium	Ecuador	Iraq
Bosnia-Herzegovina	Egypt	Italy
Bulgaria	Estonia	Kyrgyzstan
Burundi	Finland	Latvia
Canada	France	Lesotho
Chile	Georgia	Lithuania

Luxembourg	Romania	Uganda
Mexico	Russian Federation	Ukraine
Moldova	Singapore	United States
Mongolia	Slovak Republic	Uruguay
Netherlands	Slovenia	Uzbekistan
New Zealand	Spain	Venezuela
Norway	Sweden	Yugoslavia
Peru	Switzerland	Zambia
Poland	Syria	

Because the Convention is relatively new, and because the United States has signed it, it is expected that many more countries will sign it hereafter and it will become a major force in international trade. The Convention is a detailed listing of over one hundred articles dealing with the rights and responsibilities of the buyer and the seller in international sales agreements. It is similar in some respects to Article 2 of the Uniform Commercial Code in the United States. Nevertheless, there are many concepts, such as fundamental breach, avoidance, impediment, and nonconformity, that are not identical to U.S. law.

The Convention permits buyers and sellers located in countries that are parties to the Convention to exclude the application of the Convention (by expressly referring to it) and to choose the law of either the seller or the buyer to apply to the international sales agreement. However, for companies located in any of the countries that are parties to the convention (including U.S. companies), if the seller and buyer cannot or do not agree on which law will apply, the provisions of the Convention will automatically apply. In general, this may be disadvantageous for the U.S. seller because the Convention strengthens the rights of buyers in various ways.

In summary, the seller should include provisions on governing law in its international sales agreement, and if the buyer disagrees, the seller should negotiate this provision. The seller should also determine what differences exist between the Convention and U.S. law in case the parties cannot agree and the Convention thereby becomes applicable.

n. Dispute Resolution

One method of resolving disputes which may arise between the parties is litigation in the courts. For a U.S. exporter, the most likely dispute to arise is the failure of the buyer to make payment. In such a case, the exporter may be limited to going to the courts of the buyer's country in order to institute litigation and seek a judgment to obtain assets of the buyer. Even if the parties have agreed that U.S. law will govern the sales agreement, there is a risk that a foreign court may misapply U.S. law, disregard U.S. law, or otherwise favor and protect the company located in its own country. Furthermore, there can be significant delays in legal proceedings (from two to five years), court and legal expenses can be high, and the outcome may be unsatisfactory. In order to reduce such risks, the exporter can specify in the international sales agreement that all disputes must be resolved in the courts of the seller's country, that the buyer consents to jurisdiction there, and to the commencement of any such lawsuit by the simple forwarding of any form of written notice by the seller. Of course, buyers may resist such provisions and whether or not the seller will be able to finally obtain this agreement will depend upon the negotiating and bargaining strength of the parties. The seller does need to realize that even if it obtains a judgment in the United States, if the buyer has no assets in the United States, its judgment may be of limited value.

Another form of dispute resolution which is common in international sales agreements is arbitration. In many foreign countries, buyers take a less adversarial approach to the resolution of contractual disputes and they feel more comfortable with a less formal proceeding, such as arbitration. While arbitration can be included in an international sales agreement, an exporter should thoroughly understand the advantages and disadvantages of agreeing to resolve disputes by arbitration.

First, arbitration is unlikely to save much in expenses, and quite often may not involve a significantly shorter time period to resolve the dispute. In fact, from the point of view of expense, in some cases, if the buyer refuses to go forward with the arbitration, the seller will have to advance the buyer's portion of the arbitration fees to the arbitration tribunal; otherwise, the arbitrators will not proceed with the dispute. Furthermore, in litigation, of course, the judges or juries involved are paid at the public expense, whereas in arbitration, the parties must pay the expenses of the arbitrators, which can be very substantial.

Second, the administering authority must be selected. The International Chamber of Commerce is commonly designated as the administering authority in arbitration clauses, but the fees they charge are very high. The American Arbitration Association also handles international disputes, but the foreign buyer may be unwilling to agree to arbitration by a U.S. administering authority. Other administering authorities, such as the Inter-American Commercial Arbitration Commission, the London Court of International Arbitration, the Stockholm Chamber of Commerce Arbitration Institute, the British Columbia International Arbitration Centre, or an arbitration authority in the buyer's country, may be acceptable.

Third, the number of arbitrators should be specified. Since the parties will be paying for them, I recommend that one arbitrator be utilized and specified in the agreement to resolve disputes of a smaller amount (a specified dollar figure) and that three arbitrators be utilized for larger disputes.

Fourth, the place of arbitration must be specified. Again, the seller and buyer will have a natural conflict on this point, so some third country or intermediate location is probably most likely to be mutually agreeable. Another variation which has developed, although its legal validity has been questioned, is an agreement that if the exporter commences the arbitration, arbitration will be conducted in the buyer's country, and if the buyer commences the arbitration, the arbitration will be conducted in the exporter's country. This has the effect of discouraging either party from bringing arbitration and forcing the parties to reach amicable solutions to their disputes.

Finally, the seller should ascertain beforehand whether an arbitral award would be enforced in the courts of the buyer's country. Some fifty-five countries have become parties to a multinational treaty known as the New York Convention, which commits them to enforcing the arbitral awards of other member countries. Without this assurance, the entire dispute may have to be relitigated in the buyer's country.

o. Termination

Termination of an international sales agreement or distributor or sales agent agreement may prove to be much more difficult than termination of a domestic agreement. Presently, approximately sixty-five countries have enacted laws which as a matter of public policy are designed to protect buyers, distributors, and sales agents located in their country against unfair terminations. The rationale for these laws is generally that the U.S. seller has significant economic leverage by virtue of its position, and after a buyer has invested a great deal of time in purchasing products or building up a market for resale of such products, the sellers should not be permitted to terminate the agreement on short notice or without payment of some compensation. Of course, such rationale may be totally inconsistent with the facts, such as when the seller is a small company or when the buyer is breaching the agreement. In any event, before engaging in an ongoing sales relationship with any customer in a foreign country or appointing a distributor or sales agent there, the seller should get specific legal advice and determine what protective legislation exists. Often, avoidance of such legislation or reduction in the amount of compensation which must be paid at the time of termination is highly dependent upon inserting in the international sales agreement at the outset certain specific provisions (which will vary from country to country) limiting the seller's termination liability. For example, the seller's right to terminate without any payment of compensation when the buyer is in breach should be specified. The right of the seller to appoint another distributor in the country and to require the former distributor to cooperate in transferring inventory to the new distributor and the right to terminate for change in control, bankruptcy, or insolvency of the buyer should be specified.

Related thereto is the term of the agreement. Often agreements will be set up for a one-year term with automatic renewal provisions. Such agreements are treated as long-term agreements or indefinite or perpetual agreements under some laws and can result in the payment of maximum termination compensation. The term of the agreement which will best protect the seller's flexibility and reduce the compensation payable should be inserted after review of the buyer's law.

C. Export Distributor and Sales Agent Agreements

In addition to the foregoing provisions which arise in all international sales agreements, there are other, specific provisions which arise in export distributor agreements and sales agent agreements.

1. Distinction Between Distributor and Sales Agent

A distributor is a company which buys products from a seller, takes title thereto, and assumes the risk of resale. A distributor will purchase at a specific price and will be compensated by reselling the product at a higher price. Under the antitrust laws of most countries, the seller cannot restrict or require a distributor to resell the product at any specific price, although it may be able to restrict the customers or territories to which the buyer resells.

A sales agent does not purchase from the seller. The sales agent or representative locates customers and solicits offers to purchase the product from them. In order to avoid tax liability for the seller in a foreign country, the sales agent normally will not have any authority to accept offers to purchase from potential customers in that country. Instead, the offers from the customer are forwarded to the seller for final acceptance, and shipment and billing is direct between the seller and the customer. For such services, the sales agent is paid a commission or some other type of compensation. Because no sale occurs between the seller and the sales agent, the seller can specify the price at which it will sell to customers, and the sales agent can be restricted to quoting only that price to a potential customer. Likewise, the sales agent can be restricted as to its territory or the types of customers from which it can solicit orders. Sometimes the sales agent will guarantee payment by the customers or perform other services, such as after-sales service or invoicing of the customers. A chart summarizing these differences is shown in Figure 3–13.

The financial returns and accounting will differ when using a distributor versus a

Figure 3–13. Legal comparison of distributors and agents.

COMPARISON OF DISTRIBUTORS AND AGENTS

		Distributor	Agent
1.	Compensation	Mark-up	Commission
2.	Title	Owner	Not owner
3.	Risk of loss	On distributor	On seller
4.	Price control	Cannot control	Can control
5.	Credit risk	On distributor	On seller
6.	Tax liability in foreign country	On distributor	Potentially on seller if agent given authority to accept orders or if distributor maintains inventory for local delivery

Figure 3–14. Financial comparison of using distributors and sales agents.

Seller's Profit and Loss	*Distributor*	*Sales Agent*
Net sales	$2,000,000	$4,000,000
Gross profit	$1,000,000	$3,000,000
Commission (10%)		$ 400,000
Possible need to warehouse inventory in foreign country		$ 400,000
Advertising		$ 400,000
Customer service, after sales service		$ 300,000
General, selling and administrative	$ 200,000	$ 200,000
Operating income	$ 800,000	$ 900,000
Operating income/net sales	40%	22.5%

sales agent. The main reason is that the sales price will be direct to the customer, which will be higher than the sale price to a distributor. A comparison of these revenues and expenses is shown in Figure 3-14.

2. *Export Distributor Agreements*

As previously indicated, when a distributor agreement is utilized, such agreement will act as an umbrella agreement, and specific orders for specific quantities, shipment dates, and, possibly, prices will be stated in purchase orders, purchase order acceptances, and similar documentation. A checklist for negotiation issues for the appointment of a distributor is shown in Figure 3-15.

The important provisions in an international distributor agreement include the following:

a. Territory and Exclusivity

The distributor will normally want to be the exclusive distributor in a territory, whereas the seller would generally prefer to make a nonexclusive appointment so that if the distributor fails to perform, it can appoint other distributors. Also, the seller may simply wish from the outset to appoint a number of distributors in that country to

(*Text continues on page 106.*)

Figure 3–15. Foreign distributorship appointment checklist.

1 Appointment

- (a) Appointment
- (b) Acceptance
- (c) Exclusivity
- (d) Sub-Distributors

2 Territory

3 Products

4 Sales Activities

- (a) Advertising [optional]
- (b) Initial purchases [optional]
- (c) Minimum purchases [optional]
- (d) Sales increases [optional]
- (e) Purchase orders
- (f) Distributor's resale prices
- (g) Direct shipment to customers
- (h) Product specialists [optional]
- (i) Installation and service
- (j) Distributor facilities [optional]
- (k) Visits to distributor premises
- (l) Reports
- (m) Financial condition

5 Prices

- (a) Initial
- (b) Changes
- (c) Taxes

6 Acceptance of Orders and Shipment

- (a) Acceptance
- (b) Inconsistent terms in distributor's order
- (c) Shipments
- (d) No violation of U.S. laws
- (e) Passage of title, risk of loss

7 Payments

- (a) Terms
- (b) Letter of credit
- (c) Deposits
- (d) Payments in dollars
- (e) No setoff by distributor
- (f) Security interest

Figure 3–15. *(continued)*

8 Confidential Information

9 Sales Literature
- (a) Advertising literature
- (b) Quantities
- (c) Mailing lists

10 Patents, Trademarks and Copyrights; Agency Registrations

11 No Warranty Against Infringement

12 No Consequential Damages – Indemnity

13 Product Warranty, Defects, Claims, Returns

14 Relationship Between Parties

15 Effective Date and Duration
- (a) Effective date and term
- (b) Early termination
    - (i) Breach
    - (ii) Insolvency
    - (ill) Prospective breach
    - (iv) Change in ownership or management
    - (v) Foreign protective law
    - (vi) Unilateral (reciprocal) on agreed notice (without cause)

16 Rights and Obligations upon Termination
- (a) No liability for seller
- (b) Return of promotional materials
- (c) Re-purchase of stock
- (d) Accrued rights and obligations

17 Non-Competition

18 No Assignment

19 Government Regulation
- (a) Foreign law
- (b) U.S. law
- (c) Foreign Corrupt Practices Act compliance

20 Force Majeure

21 Separability

22 Waiver

23 Notices
- (a) Written notice
- (b) Oral notice

Figure 3–15. *(continued)*

24. Governing Law
25. Dispute Resolution
26. Entire Agreement and Modifications
    (a) Entire agreement
    (b) Modifications

adequately serve the market. A possible compromise is that the appointment will be exclusive unless certain minimum purchase obligations are not met, in which case the seller has the right to convert the agreement to a nonexclusive agreement.

Usually the country or part of the country which is granted to the distributor is specified. The distributor agrees not to solicit sales from outside the territory, although under the laws of some countries, it may not be possible to prohibit the distributor from reselling outside the territory. In such cases, the distributor may be prohibited from establishing any warehouse or sales outlet outside the territory.

b. Pricing

As previously indicated, normally it will be illegal to specify the price at which the foreign distributor can resell the merchandise. This may present some problems because the distributor may mark the product up very substantially, gouging end users and resulting in less sales and market penetration for the seller's products. Consequently, in some countries it is possible to restrict the maximum resale price but not the minimum resale price. In addition, because of the gray market problem, the price at which the seller sells to the distributor must be set very carefully. Depending on the price at which the distributor buys or whether or not the distributor can be legally prohibited from exporting, the distributor may resell products which will create a gray market in competition with the seller's other distributors or even the seller in its own markets. This can occur especially as a result of exchange rate fluctuations, where the distributor is able to obtain a product at a lower price in its own currency than is available in other markets where the product is being sold.

The seller must monitor currency fluctuations and retain the right to make price adjustments in the distributor agreement to make sure that the seller is fairly participating in the profits being created along the line of distribution. For example, if the U.S. seller sells a product for $1 at a time when the Japanese exchange rate is ¥250 to $1, the buyer will be paying ¥250 for the $1 product and perhaps marking it up to ¥400. However, if the yen strengthens and the buyer can purchase a $1 product by paying only ¥150, and if the buyer continues to resell at ¥400, the buyer will make inordinate profits. Sometimes the buyer will continue to ask for price reductions from the seller even though the buyer has had a very favorable exchange rate movement. Normally the seller's interest is that the buyer reduce the resale price (for example, to ¥250) in order to make more sales, increase volume, increase market penetration, and capture the long-term market. When the distributor will not agree to reduce its resale price, the price from the seller should be raised to make sure that part of the profits, which the distributor is making on resales in its own country, are recovered by the seller.

c. Minimum Purchase Quantities

In most long-term sales agreements or distributor agreements, one of the reasons for entering into such agreements is that the seller expects a commitment for a significant quantity to be purchased and the buyer is requesting some price discount for such a commitment. Consequently, before a seller agrees to give a distributor an exclusive appointment in a territory or to grant any price reductions, a provision relating to the minimum purchase quantities (which may be adjusted from time to time according to some objective formula or by agreement of the parties) should be inserted in the distributor agreement. Distributors will ordinarily be required to commit to using their best efforts to promote the sale of the merchandise in the territory, but since best efforts is a somewhat vague commitment, minimum purchase quantities (or dollar amounts) are important supplements to that commitment.

d. Handling Competing Products

Normally a seller will want a provision wherein the distributor agrees not to handle competing products. If the distributor is handling any competing products (either manufacturing them or purchasing them from alternative sources), it is likely that the distributor will not always promote the seller's products, especially if the buyer is getting larger markups or margins on the other products. In addition, if the seller grants an exclusive distribution right to the distributor, the seller has given up the opportunity to increase its sales by appointing more distributors in the territory. Under such circumstances, the distributor should definitely agree not to handle any competing products. In some countries, the distributor can be restricted from handling competing products only if an exclusive appointment is given by the seller.

e. Effective Date and Government Review

In some countries it is necessary to file distributor or long-term sales agreements with governmental authorities. Sometimes there is a specific waiting period before the agreement can become effective or government review will be completed. In any event, the distributor agreement should provide that it does not become effective until government review is completed. If the distributor's government suggests changes to the agreement, for example, the elimination of minimum purchase quantities, the seller should have the opportunity to renegotiate the agreement or withdraw from the agreement without being bound to proceed. In that respect, the seller must be careful not to ship a large amount of inventory or accept a large initial order while government review is pending.

f. Appointment of Subdistributors

Whether or not a distributor has the right to appoint subdistributors should be expressly stated in the distributor agreement. If this right is not discussed, the distributor may have the right under its own law to appoint subdistributors. This can cause various problems for the seller. Not only will the seller have no immediate direct contact with the subdistributors, but it may not even be aware of who such subdistributors are, their location, or the territories into which they are shipping. Soon the seller's products may show up in territories granted to other distributors, be imported back into the United States, or significant gray market sales or counterfeits may develop. If the right to appoint subdistributors is granted, the distributor should remain responsible for its activities, including payment for any goods sold to such subdistributors, and for providing the names of such distributors to the seller in advance so that the seller will have the opportunity to investigate the financial strength, creditworthiness, and business reputation of all persons who will be distributing its products.

g. Use of Trade Names, Trademarks, and Copyrights

As discussed in Chapter 2, Section G, there are risks that the seller's intellectual property rights will be lost. Sometimes distributors are the biggest offenders. In an effort to protect their market position, they use the seller's name or trademark in their own business or corporate name or register the seller's intellectual property in their own country. This is a particular disadvantage for the seller, because if the distributor does not perform properly and the seller wishes to terminate the distributor and to appoint a new distributor, the past distributor may own the intellectual property rights or have a registered exclusive license to distribute the products in that country. Until the distributor consents to the assignment of the intellectual property rights to the seller or the new distributor or de-registers its exclusive license, any sales by the seller into the territory or by the new distributor will be an infringement of the intellectual property rights owned by the former distributor and cannot proceed. This puts the former distributor in a very strong bargaining position to negotiate a substantial termination compensation payment. Even when the distributor is granted an exclusive territory, the distributor agreement should provide that the distributor is granted a nonexclusive patent, trademark, and/or copyright license to sell the products (but not to manufacture or cause others to manufacture the products), and should obligate the distributor to recognize the validity of the intellectual property rights and to take no steps to register them or to otherwise interfere with the ownership rights of the seller. Of course, the seller should register its intellectual property rights directly in the foreign country in its own name and not permit the distributor to do so on the seller's behalf or in the distributor's name.

h. Warranties and Product Liability

In addition to the considerations discussed in Section B.2.i above, the seller should require the distributor to maintain product liability insurance in its own name and to name the seller as an additional insured in amounts which are deemed satisfactory by the seller. Although product liability claims are not as common overseas as they are in the United States, they are increasing substantially, and under most product liability laws, even though the distributor sold the product to the customer, the customer will have a right to sue the manufacturer (or supplier) directly. Furthermore, the fact that the manufacturer was aware that its product was being sold in that country will make it foreseeable that a defective product will be sold there and the U.S. manufacturer may be subject to the jurisdiction of the courts in that country. The seller should also make sure that the distributor does not modify or add any additional warranties in the resale of the product beyond those that the manufacturer or U.S. seller has given. Practically, this means that the distributor should be obligated to provide a copy of its warranty in advance of resale for approval by the seller. The distributor may also be authorized or required to perform after-sales service, but the seller will need an opportunity to audit the books and service records from time to time to prevent abuses and warranty compensation reimbursement claims by the distributor for service that has not actually been performed.

3. Export Sales Agent Agreements

Like distributor agreements, sales agent agreements often contain many of the same provisions included in an international sales agreement, but there are certain provisions which are peculiar to the sales agent agreement that must be considered. A checklist for negotiation issues for the appointment of a sales agent is shown in Figure 3–16.

a. Commissions

The sales agent is compensated for its activities by payment of a commission by the seller. The sales agent is appointed to solicit orders, and when such orders are accepted by the seller, the agent may be paid a commission. Sometimes payment of the commission is deferred until such time as the customer actually makes payment to the seller. Generally, the seller should not bill the agent for the price of the product (less commission) because such practice could result in characterizing the relationship as a distributorship rather than a sales agency. Generally, any commissions payable should be made by wire transfer directly to the sales agent's bank account in the foreign country. Payments in cash, checks delivered in the United States, or payments in third countries may facilitate violation of the foreign exchange control or tax laws of the foreign country, and the seller may be liable as an aider and abettor of the violation.

b. Pricing

Because there is no sale between the seller and the sales agent, the seller can lawfully require the sales agent to quote only prices that the seller has authorized. For sellers who wish to establish uniform pricing on a worldwide basis, eliminate gray market, and control markups, use of the sales agent appointment can be highly beneficial. However, the trade-off is that the seller will ordinarily assume the credit risk and will have to satisfy itself in regard to the ability of the customer to pay. This sometimes presents difficulties in obtaining sufficient information, although the sales agent can be given the responsibility of gathering and forwarding such information to the seller prior to acceptance of any orders. In addition, some sales agents are willing to be appointed as del credere agents, whereby the sales agent guarantees payment by any customer from whom it solicits an order. Obviously, sales agents will require higher commissions for guaranteeing payment, but it can reduce the seller's risks in having to investigate the customer's credit while permitting the seller to specify the price that the sales agent quotes.

(*Text continues on page 112.*)

Figure 3–16. Foreign sales representative appointment checklist.

1 Appointment – Acceptance
   (a) Exclusivity
   (b) Sub-Representatives

2 Territory

3 Product

4 Responsibilities
   (a) Promotional efforts
   (b) Price quotations
   (c) Minimum orders [optional]
   (d) Increase in orders (optional]
   (e) Representative's facilities

5 Confidential Information

6 Reports
   (a) Operations report
   (b) Credit information

7 Visits to Representative's Premises by Supplier

8 Promotional Literature

9 Trademarks and Copyrights

10 Acceptance of Orders and Shipments
   (a) Acceptance only by supplier
   (b) No violation of U.S. laws
   (c) Direct shipments to customers

11 Commissions
   (a) Commission percentage or fee
   (b) Accrual
   (c) Refund

12 Discontinuation of Products

13 Repair and Rework

14 Relationship Between Parties

15 No Warranty Against Infringement

Figure 3–16. *(continued)*

16 Product Warranty (to customers)

17 Effective Date and Duration
- (a) Effective date and term
- (b) Early termination
  - (i) Breach
  - (ii) Insolvency
  - (iii) Prospective breach
  - (iv) Change in ownership or management
  - (v) Foreign protective law
  - (vi) Unilateral (reciprocal) on agreed notice

18 Rights and Obligations upon Termination
- (a) No liability of supplier
- (b) Commissions
- (c) Return of promotional materials
- (d) Accrued rights and obligations

19 Non - Competition

20 Indemnity

21 No Assignment

22 Government Regulation
- (a) Foreign laws
- (b) U.S. laws
- (c) Foreign Corrupt Practices Act compliance

23 Force Majeure

24 Separability

25 Waiver

26 Notices
- (a) Written notice
- (b) Oral notice

27 Governing Law

28 Dispute Resolution

29 Entire Agreement and Modifications
- (a) Entire Agreement
- (b) Modifications

c. Shipment

Shipment is not made to the sales agent; it is made directly to the customer from whom the sales agent has solicited the order. Generally there will be problems associated with trying to maintain an inventory at the agent's place of business in the foreign country. Under the laws of many countries, if the seller maintains an inventory abroad in its own name or through an agent, the seller can become taxable on its own sales profits to customers in that country. If the customer cannot wait for shipment from the United States, or if it is important to maintain an inventory in the country, the appropriate way to do so while using sales agents must be investigated with an attorney knowledgeable in foreign law.

d. Warranties

It is important to keep in mind that product warranties should be made only to customers (purchasers). Since sales agents are not purchasers, the inclusion of warranty provisions in a sales agency agreement can cause confusion unless it is made clear that the warranty in the agreement with the sales agent is for the purpose of informing the sales agent as to what warranty it is authorized to communicate to prospective purchasers.

e. Relationship of the Parties

Although businesspersons frequently refer to intermediaries as distributors and "agents," legally, it is dangerous for a seller to enter into a principal-agent relationship. In such cases, the seller may become legally responsible for the acts and omissions of the agent. Generally, the "agent" should be an independent contractor and that should be clearly expressed in the agreement. For this reason, it is usually better to designate the intermediary as a sales "representative." Furthermore, the seller should make clear that it does not control the day-to-day activities of the agent; otherwise, he or she may be deemed an agent or even an employee (if he or she is an individual) with corresponding liability risks and potential tax obligations.

D. Foreign Corrupt Practices Act Compliance

Another provision which should be included in the agreement relates to the Foreign Corrupt Practices Act (FCPA). In the United States, the FCPA makes it a violation of U.S. law for an agent of a U.S. exporter to pay any money or compensation to a foreign government agency, official, or political party for the purpose of obtaining or retaining business. If this occurs, the U.S. exporter will have violated the law if it knew that the foreign agent was engaged in such activities. Obviously, whether the exporter "knew" can be a matter of dispute, but if unusual circumstances occur, for instance, a distributor or agent asks for a special discount, allowance, or commission, or that payment be made to someone other than the distributor or agent, the exporter can be charged with knowledge of unusual circumstances that should have caused it to realize that something improper was occurring. One way to help avoid such liability is to specify expressly in the agreement that the agent recognizes the existence of the FCPA and commits and agrees not to make any payments to foreign government officials or political parties for the purpose of gaining business, or at least not to do so without consultation with the seller and receiving confirmation that such activity will not violate the FCPA. Distributors and agents should also be informed and agree not to make such payments to the buyer's employees, even if the buyer is not a government agency, as such payments will usually violate foreign commercial bribery laws.

In 1997, thirty-four countries signed the Organization of Economic Cooperation and Development Anti-Bribery Convention, which has now been ratified and is in effect.

Chapter 4

Exporting: Other Export Documentation

Although the sales agreement is by far the most important single document in an export sales transaction, there are numerous other documents with which the exporter must be familiar. In some cases, the exporter may not actually prepare such documents, especially if the exporter utilizes the services of a freight forwarder. Nevertheless, as discussed in Chapter 2, Section K, relating to the utilization of freight forwarders, the exporter is responsible for the content of the documents prepared and filed by its agent, the freight forwarder. Since the exporter has legal responsibility for any mistakes of the freight forwarder, it is very important for the exporter to understand what documents the freight forwarder is preparing and for the exporter to review and be totally comfortable with the contents of such documents. Furthermore, the documents prepared by the freight forwarder are usually prepared based on information supplied by the exporter. If the exporter does not understand the documents or the information that is being requested and a mistake occurs, the freight forwarder will claim that the mistake was due to improper information provided by the exporter.

A. Freight Forwarder's Powers of Attorney

A freight forwarder will ordinarily provide a form contract that specifies the services it will perform and the terms and conditions of the relationship. Among other things, the contract will contain a provision appointing the freight forwarder as an agent to prepare documentation and granting a power of attorney for that purpose. (A simple form of power of attorney is shown in Figure 4–1. (Under new regulations, if the freight forwarder will have the authority to prepare Shipper's Export Declarations that must be expressly stated in the power of attorney.) Usually, however, the freight forwarder will have a more elaborate contract which includes other specific terms of, or provisions relating to, the services which it will provide.

B. Shipper's Letters of Instructions

On each individual export transaction, the freight forwarder will want to receive instructions from the exporter on how the export is to be processed. The terms or

Figure 4–1. Power of attorney.

POWER-OF-ATTORNEY FORMS

POWER OF ATTORNEY—DESIGNATION OF FORWARDING AGENT

Know all men by these presents, That ....,
(Name of exporter)
organized and doing business under the laws of the State of ....,
and having an office and place of business at ....,
hereby authorizes ....,
(Forwarding agent)
of ....,
from this day forward to act as its forwarding agent for export control and customs purposes.
IN WITNESS WHEREOF, the said exporter has caused these presents to be sealed and signed by its ....
(Owner, partner, or, if corp., Pres., Vice-Pres., Sec'y, Treas. or other duly authorized officer or employee)
City of .... State of .... this ..... day of .... 19 ......

....
(Exporter)

[SEAL] By .... Title ....

Sample form showing text of acceptable power-of-attorney form designating forwarding agent

POWER OF ATTORNEY TO EXECUTE SHIPPER'S EXPORT DECLARATIONS

Know all men by these presents, That ....,
(Name of exporter or forwarding agent)
organized and doing business under the laws of the State of ....,
and having an office and place of business at ....,
hereby designates the following officers or employees of the exporter or forwarding agent named above
....
....
as true and lawful agents of the exporter or forwarding agent named above for and in the name, place and stead of said exporter or forwarding agent from this day forward and in no other name, to make, endorse, sign, declare, or swear to any shipper's export declaration required by law or regulation in connection with the exportation of any commodity shipped, consigned or forwarded by said exporter or forwarding agent and to perform any act or condition which may be required or authorized by any law or regulation relating to export control and customs purposes.
IN WITNESS WHEREOF, the said exporter or forwarding agent has caused these presents to be sealed and signed by its ....
(Owner, partner, or if corp., Pres., Vice-Pres., Sec'y, Treas. or other duly authorized officer or employee)
City of .... State of .... this ..... day of .... 19 ......

☐ Exporter or
....☐ Forwarding agent

[SEAL] By .... Title ....

Sample form showing text of acceptable power-of-attorney form authorizing execution of Shippers Export Declaration

Export Administration Regulations October 1989
U.S.G.P.O. 1989-242-181-20035

conditions of sale agreed between the seller and the buyer may vary from sale to sale. Consequently, in order for the freight forwarder to process the physical export of the goods and prepare the proper documentation, it is necessary for the exporter to advise the freight forwarder as to the specific agreement between the seller and buyer for that sale. Freight forwarders often provide standard forms containing spaces to be filled in by the exporter for the information that it needs. Commercial stationers also sell forms that are designed to fit most transactions. (An example of such a form is shown in Figure 4–2.) As previously noted, the exporter should take special care in filling out this form, since any mistakes will be the basis on which the freight forwarder avoids responsibility.

C. Commercial Invoices

When the export is shipped, the exporter must prepare a commercial invoice, which is a statement to the buyer for payment. Usually English is sufficient but some countries require the seller's invoice to be in their language. Multiple copies are usually required, some of which are sent with the bill of lading and other transportation documents. The original is forwarded through banking channels for payment (except on open account sales, where it is sent directly to the buyer). On letter of credit transactions, the invoice must be issued by the beneficiary of the letter of credit and addressed to the applicant for the letter of credit. Putting the commercial invoice number on the other shipping documents helps to tie the documents together. The customs laws of most foreign countries require that a commercial invoice be presented by the buyer (or the seller if the seller is responsible for clearing customs), and the price listed on it is used as the value for the assessment of customs duties where the customs duties are based upon a percentage of the value (ad valorem rates). (Brazil, Egypt, Colombia, Guatemala, Senegal, Côte d'Ivoire, Bahrain, Sri Lanka, Dominican Republic, Myanmar, and other countries may assess duties on fair market value rather than invoice price.) Perhaps the most important thing to note here is that many countries, like the United States, have special requirements for the information that, depending upon the product involved, must be contained in a commercial invoice. It is extremely important that, before shipping the product and preparing the commercial invoice, the exporter check either through an attorney, the buyer, or the freight forwarder to determine exactly what information must be included in the commercial invoice in order to clear foreign customs. In addition, often certain items, such as inland shipping expenses, packing, installation and service charges, financing charges, international transportation charges, insurance, assists, royalties, or license fees, may have to be shown separately because some of these items may be deducted from or added to the price in calculating the customs value and the payment of duties. Many countries in the Middle East and Latin America require that commercial invoices covering shipments to their countries be "legalized." This means the country's U.S. embassy or consulate must stamp the invoice. When a U.S. export control license is needed for the shipment (and on some other types of shipments), a destination control statement must be put on the commercial invoice. (See discussion in Chapter 5, Section J.) (Commercial invoices are also discussed in Chapter 3, Section A.4.g, and a sample is shown in Figure

Figure 4–2. Shipper's letter of instructions.

SHIPPER *(Name and address including ZIP code)*

ZIP CODE

INLAND CARRIER *(See note #2 below)* | SHIP DATE | PRO NO.

EXPORTER EIN NO.

PARTIES TO TRANSACTION ☐ Related ☐ Non-related

ULTIMATE CONSIGNEE

INTERMEDIATE CONSIGNEE

FORWARDING AGENT

POINT (STATE) OF ORIGIN OR FTZ NO. | COUNTRY OF ULTIMATE DESTINATION

SHIPPER'S LETTER OF INSTRUCTIONS

NOTE:
1. IF YOU ARE UNCERTAIN OF THE SCHEDULE B COMMODITY NO.—DO NOT TYPE IT IN—WE WILL COMPLETE WHEN PROCESSING THE 7525-V.
2. IF YOU HAVE SHIPPED THIS MATERIAL TO US VIA AN INLAND CARRIER—PLEASE GIVE US THE INLAND CARRIER'S NAME, SHIPPING DATE, AND RECEIPT OR PRO. NO. (IF AVAILABLE). THIS WILL HELP US EXPEDITE YOUR SHIPMENT WITH THE INLAND CARRIER.
3. BE SURE TO PICK UP TOP SHEET AND SIGN THE FIRST BUFF EXPORT DECLARATION WITH PEN AND INK.

SHIPPER'S REF. NO. | DATE | SHIP VIA ☐ AIR ☐ OCEAN | ☐ CONSOLIDATE ☐ DIRECT

SCHEDULE B DESCRIPTION OF COMMODITIES

D/F	MARKS, NOS., AND KIND OF PKGS. SCHEDULE B NUMBER	QUANTITY— SCHEDULE B UNIT(S)	SHIPPING WEIGHT *(Kilos)*	SHIPPING WEIGHT *(Pounds)*	CUBIC METERS	VALUE (U.S. dollars, omit cents) *(Selling price or cost if not sold)*

VALIDATED LICENSE NO./GENERAL LICENSE SYMBOL | ECCN *(When required)* | SHIPPER MUST CHECK ➧ ☐ PREPAID OR ☐ COLLECT

Duly authorized officer or employee | The exporter authorizes the forwarder named above to act as forwarding agent for export control and customs purposes. | C.O.D. AMOUNT $

SPECIAL INSTRUCTIONS

BE SURE TO PICK UP TOP SHEET AND SIGN THE FIRST BUFF EXPORT DECLARATION WITH PEN & INK.

SHIPPER'S INSTRUCTIONS IN CASE OF INABILITY TO DELIVER CONSIGNMENT AS CONSIGNED: ☐ ABANDON ☐ RETURN TO SHIPPER ☐ DELIVER TO

SHIPPER REQUESTS INSURANCE ☐ NO ☐ YES $

If Shipper has requested insurance as provided for at the left hereof, shipment is insured in the amount indicated (recovery is limited to actual loss) in accordance with the provisions as specified in the Carrier's Tariffs. Insurance is payable to Shipper unless payee is designated in writing by the shipper.

NOTE The Shipper or his Authorized Agent hereby authorizes the above named Company, in his name and on his behalf, to prepare any export documents, to sign and accept any documents relating to said shipment and forward this shipment in accordance with the conditions of carriage and the tariffs of the carriers employed. The shipper guarantees payment of all collect charges in the event the consignee refuses payment. Hereunder the sole responsibility of the Company is to use reasonable care in the selection of carriers, forwarders, agents and others to whom it may entrust the shipment.

Form 15-305 Printed and Sold by UNZ&CO 190 Baldwin Ave., Jersey City, NJ 07306 • (800) 631-3098 • (201) 795-5400

Reprinted with permission of Unz & Co., 190 Baldwin Ave., Jersey City, NJ 07306, USA.

Figure 4–3. Contents of a commercial invoice.

1. Full name of seller, including address and telephone number, on letterhead or printed form.
2. Full name of buyer and buyer's address (or, if not a sale, the consignee).
3. The place of delivery (for example, Ex Works, FOB port of export, CIF).
4. The sale price and grand total for each item, which includes all charges to the place of delivery. "Assists," royalties, proceeds of subsequent resale or use of the products, and indirect payments, if any, must also be included in the sale price. If it is not a sale, list the fair market value, a statement that it is not a sale, and that the value stated is "For Customs Purposes Only."
5. A description of the product(s) sufficiently detailed for the foreign Customs authorities to be able to confirm the correct Harmonized Tariff classification, including the quality or grade.
6. The quantities (and/or weights) of each product.
7. A date for the invoice (on or around the date of export).
8. The currency of the sale price (or value) (U.S.$ or foreign).
9. The marks, numbers, and symbols on the packages.
10. The cost of packaging, cases, packing, and containers, if paid for by the seller, which is not included in the sales price and being billed to the buyer.
11. All charges paid by the seller, separately identified and itemized, including freight (inland and international), insurance, and commissions, etc., which is not included in the price and being billed to the buyer.
12. The country of origin (manufacture).
13. CHECK WITH THE BUYER OR IMPORTER BEFORE FINALIZING THE INVOICE TO CONFIRM THAT NO OTHER INFORMATION IS REQUIRED.

3–11.) While there is no international standard for the contents of invoices, Figure 4–3 summarizes typical requirements.

D. Bills of Lading

Bills of lading are best understood if considered as bills of loading. These documents are issued by transportation carriers as evidence that they have received the shipment and have agreed to transport it to the destination in accordance with their usual tariffs (rate schedule). Separate bills of lading may be issued for the inland or domestic portion of the transportation and the ocean (marine) or air transportation, or a through bill of lading covering all transportation to the destination may be issued. The domestic portion of the route will usually be handled by the trucking company or railroad transporting the product to the port of export. Such transportation companies have their own forms of bills of lading and, again, commercial stationers make available forms that can be utilized by exporters, which generally say that the exporter agrees to all of the specific terms or conditions of transport normally contained in the carrier's usual bill of lading and tariff. The inland bill of lading should be prepared in accordance with the freight forwarder's or transportation carrier's instructions.

The ocean transportation will be covered by a marine bill of lading prepared by the exporter or freight forwarder and issued by the steamship company. Information in bills of lading (except apparent condition at the time of loading) such as marks, numbers, quantity, weight, and hazardous nature is based on information provided to the carrier by the shipper, and the shipper warrants its accuracy. Making, altering, negotiating, or transferring a bill of lading with intent to defraud is a criminal offense. If the transportation is by air, the airline carrier will prepare and issue an air waybill. A freight consolidator will issue house air waybills which are not binding on the carrier but are given to each shipper to evidence inclusion of its shipment as part of the consolidated shipment. In such cases the freight consolidator becomes the "shipper" on the master bill of lading.

Bills of lading, whether inland or ocean, can be issued in either non-negotiable (straight) form or in negotiable form. (Air waybills are issued only in a non-negotiable form.) (The Uniform Commercial Code requires bills of lading to be negotiable unless the seller and buyer expressly agree otherwise.) If the bill of lading is specified as non-negotiable, the transportation carrier must deliver it only to the consignee named in the bill of lading, and the bill of lading serves more as a record of the receipt of the goods and the agreement to transport them to a specific destination and consignee in return for payment of the transportation charges. If the bill of lading is a negotiable bill of lading, however, the right to receive delivery and the right to re-route the shipment are with the person who has ownership of the bill of lading properly issued or negotiated to it. Such bills of lading are issued to the shipper's order, rather than to a specific, named consignee. Where collection and payment is through banking channels, such as under a letter of credit or documentary collection governed by the Uniform Customs and Practices, negotiable bills of lading are required (except for air shipments). The exporter must endorse the bill of lading and deliver it to the bank in order to receive payment. Ocean bills of lading are usually issued in three originals, any of which may be used by the buyer to obtain possession. Inland bills and air waybills are issued in only one original. Where a negotiable bill of lading cannot be produced at the time of delivery, the steamship line may agree to make delivery if it receives a "letter of indemnity" from the exporter or importer (or both). Letters of credit require that before payment can be made the exporter must furnish evidence to the bank that the goods have been loaded "on board" a steamship and the bill of lading must be "clean." This latter term means that the steamship company has inspected the goods and found no damage to them at the time they were loaded on board. Steamship companies also issue "received for shipment" bills of lading. Steamship companies will hold such shipments in storage for some time until one of their steamships is going to the designated destination but, until such bill of lading is stamped "on board," it is not clear when the shipment will actually depart and when it will arrive in the country of destination. When a U.S. export control license is needed for the shipment (and on some other types of shipments), a destination control statement must be put on the bill of lading. (See discussion in Chapter 5, Section J.) (Samples of an inland bill of lading, an ocean bill of lading, an international air waybill, and a house air waybill are shown in Figures 4–4, 4–5, 4–6, and 4–7, respectively.)

E. Packing Lists

Packing lists are utilized to describe the way in which the goods are packed for shipment, such as how many packages the shipment is broken into, the types of packaging used, the weight of each package, the size of each package, and any markings that may be on the packages. Forms for packing lists are available through commercial stationers or are provided by packing companies who prepare export shipments. Sometimes packing lists are required by the customs laws of foreign countries, but even if they are not, an important use of the packing list is for filing insurance claims if there is some damage or casualty to the shipment during transportation (see Figure 4–8).

F. Inspection Certificates

In some situations, the buyer may request and the seller may agree to a preshipment inspection; in other cases, preshipment inspection may be required by the buyer's government (see discussion in Chapter 3, Section B.2.j). If there will be preshipment inspection, one of the documents provided as part of the export documentation is the certificate issued by the inspection company. Sometimes the inspection certificate will be furnished directly to the buyer (or the buyer's government) by the inspection company, but other times the seller must provide the inspection certificate to the bank, as for example in a letter of credit transaction specifying that an inspection certificate is required in order to obtain payment. (A worksheet for completing preshipment inspections is shown in Figure 4–9, and a sample certificate issued by an inspection company is shown in Figure 4–10.)

Although the list tends to change frequently, countries requiring preshipment inspection include Angola, Argentina, Bolivia, Burkina Faso, Burundi, Cambodia, Cameroon, Central African Republic, Democratic Republic of Congo, Ecuador, Ethiopia, Guinea, Iran, Malawi, Mali, Mauritania, Mexico (certain goods), Moldova, Nigeria, Peru, Rwanda, Uzbekistan, and Zanzibar. (See *www.sgsgroup.com.*)

G. Marine and Air Casualty Insurance Policies and Certificates

As discussed in Chapter 2, Section P, it is extremely important to identify both who is arranging for the transportation insurance (to guard against casualty and loss) and who is going to pay for it. Even when the buyer is responsible for paying for such

(*Text continues on page 129.*)

Figure 4–4. Inland bill of lading.

STRAIGHT BILL OF LADING — SHORT FORM — ORIGINAL — NOT NEGOTIABLE

RECEIVED subject to the classifications and tariffs in effect on the date of the issue of this Bill of Lading the property described above in apparent good order except as noted (contents and condition of contents of packages unknown) marked consigned and destined as indicated above which said carrier (the word carrier being understood throughout this contract as meaning any person or corporation in possession of the property under the contract) agrees to carry to its usual place of delivery at said destination if on its route otherwise to deliver to another carrier on the route to said destination It is mutually agreed as to each carrier of all or any of said property over all or any portion of said route to destination and as to each party at any time interested in all or any said property, that every service to be performed hereunder shall be subject to all the bill of lading terms and conditions in the governing classification on the date of shipment

Shipper hereby certifies that he is familiar with all the bill of lading terms and conditions in the governing classification and the said terms and conditions are hereby agreed to by the shipper and accepted for himself and his assigns

From ____________________

DESIGNATE WITH AN (X)

At ____________________ 19____ BY TRUCK ☐ FREIGHT ☐ Shipper's No. ____________

Carrier ____________________ Agent's No. ____________

(Mail or street address of consignee— For purposes of notification only.)

Consigned to ____________________

Destination ____________________ State of ____________ County of ____________

Route ____________________

Delivering Carrier ____________________ Vehicle or Car Initial ____________ No. ____________

No Packages	Kind of Package, Description of Articles, Special Marks and Exceptions	*Weight (Sub. to Cor.)	Class or Rate	Check Column
TOTAL PIECES				

† The fibre containers used for this shipment conform to the specifications set forth in the box maker's certificate thereon and all other requirements of Rule 41 of the Uniform Freight Classification and Rule 5 of the National Motor Freight Classification †Shipper's imprint in lieu of stamp not a part of bill of lading approved by the Interstate Commerce Commission

____________________ Shipper, Per

____________________ Agent, Per ____________________

Permanent post-office address of shipper

Subject to Section 7 of conditions of applicable bill of lading, if this shipment is to be delivered to the consignee without recourse on the consignor, the consignor shall sign the following statement:

The carrier shall not make delivery of this shipment without payment of freight and all other lawful charges.

Per ____________________

(Signature of Consignor.)

If charges are to be prepaid, write or stamp here, "To be Prepaid."

Received $ ____________
to apply in prepayment of the charges on the property described hereon.

____
Agent or Cashier.

Per ____________________
(The signature here acknowledges only the amount prepaid.)

Charges Advanced.

____

C.O.D. SHIPMENT

Prepaid ☐
Collect ☐ $ ____________

Collection Fee ____________

Total Charges ____________

*If the shipment moves between two ports by a carrier by water, the law requires that the bill of lading shall state whether it is "Carrier's or Shipper's weight."

†Shipper's imprint in lieu of stamp; not a part of bill of lading approved by the Department of Transportation.

NOTE—Where the rate is dependent on value, shippers are required to state specifically in writing the agreed or declared value of the property.

THIS SHIPMENT IS CORRECTLY DESCRIBED CORRECT WEIGHT IS

____________________ LBS.

Subject to verification by the Respective Weighing and Inspection Bureau According to Agreement

Per ____________________

If lower charges result, the agreed or declared value of the within described containers is hereby specifically stated to be not exceeding 50 cents per pound per article

This is to certify that the above-named materials are properly classified, described, packaged, marked and labeled and are in proper condition for transportation according to the applicable regulations of the Department of Transportation

____________________ SIGNATURE

Form No. 35-643 ©, 1986 UNZCO 190 Baldwin Ave., Jersey City, NJ 07306 - (800) 631-3098 - (201) 795-5400

1

Reprinted with permission of Unz & Co., 190 Baldwin Ave., Jersey City, NJ 07306, USA.

(*continues*)

Figure 4–4. *(continued)*

THIS SHIPPING ORDER must be legibly filled in, in Ink, in Indelible Pencil, or in Carbon, and retained by the Agent.

RECEIVED subject to the classifications and tariffs in effect on the date of the issue of this Bill of Lading the property described above in apparent good order except as noted (contents and condition of contents of packages unknown) marked consigned and destined as indicated above which said carrier (the word carrier being understood throughout this contract as meaning any person or corporation in possession of the property under the contract) agrees to carry to its usual place of delivery at said destination if on its route otherwise to deliver to another carrier on the route to said destination It is mutually agreed as to each carrier of all or any of said property over all or any portion of said route to destination and as to each party at any time interested in all or any said property that every service to be performed hereunder shall be subject to all the bill of lading terms and conditions in the governing classification on the date of shipment

Shipper hereby certifies that he is familiar with all the bill of lading terms and conditions in the governing classification and the said terms and conditions are hereby agreed to by the shipper and accepted for himself and his assigns

From ______

DESIGNATE WITH AN (X)

At ______ 19 ____ BY TRUCK ☐ FREIGHT ☐ Shipper's No. ______

Carrier ______ Agent's No. ______

(Mail or street address of consignee— For purposes of notification only.)

Consigned to ______

Destination ______ State of ______ County of ______

Route ______

Delivering Carrier ______ Vehicle or Car Initial ______ No. ______

No Packages	Kind of Package, Description of Articles, Special Marks and Exceptions	*Weight (Sub. to Cor.)	Class or Rate	Check Column
TOTAL PIECES				

† The fibre containers used for this shipment conform to the specifications set forth in the box maker's certificate thereon and all other requirements of Rule 41 of the Uniform Freight Classification and Rule 5 of the National Motor Freight Classification †Shipper's imprint in lieu of stamp, not a part of bill of lading approved by the Interstate Commerce Commission

______ Shipper, Per

______ Agent, Per ______

Permanent post-office address of shipper

Subject to Section 7 of conditions of applicable bill of lading, if this shipment is to be delivered to the consignee without recourse on the consignor, the consignor shall sign the following statement:

The carrier shall not make delivery of this shipment without payment of freight and all other lawful charges.

Per ______

(Signature of Consignor.)

If charges are to be prepaid, write or stamp here, "To be Prepaid."

Received $ ______ to apply in prepayment of the charges on the property described hereon.

______
Agent or Cashier.

Per ______
(The signature here acknowledges only the amount prepaid.)

Charges Advanced:

______

C.O.D. SHIPMENT

Prepaid ☐
Collect ☐ $ ______

Collection Fee ______

Total Charges ______

*If the shipment moves between two ports by a carrier by water, the law requires that the bill of lading shall state whether it is "Carrier's or Shipper's weight."

†Shipper's imprint in lieu of stamp; not a part of bill of lading approved by the Department of Transportation.

NOTE—Where the rate is dependent on value, shippers are required to state specifically in writing the agreed or declared value of the property.

THIS SHIPMENT IS CORRECTLY DESCRIBED CORRECT WEIGHT IS

______ LBS.

Subject to verification by the Respective Weighing and Inspection Bureau According to Agreement

Per ______

If lower charges result, the agreed or declared value of the within described containers is hereby specifically stated to be not exceeding 50 cents per pound per article

This is to certify that the above-named materials are properly classified, described, packaged, marked and labeled and are in proper condition for transportation according to the applicable regulations of the Department of Transportation

______ SIGNATURE

Form No. 35-643 ©, 1986 UNZCO 190 Baldwin Ave., Jersey City, NJ 07306 - (800) 631-3098 - (201) 795-5400

2

Figure 4–4. *(continued)*

THIS MEMORANDUM is an acknowledgment that a Bill of Lading has been issued and is not the Original Bill of Lading, nor a copy or duplicate, covering the property named herein, and is intended solely for filing or record.

RECEIVED, subject to the classifications and tariffs in effect on the date of the issue of this Bill of Lading, the property described above in apparent good order, except as noted (contents and condition of contents of packages unknown), marked, consigned, and destined as indicated above which said carrier (the word carrier being understood throughout this contract as meaning any person or corporation in possession of the property under the contract) agrees to carry to its usual place of delivery at said destination, if on its route, otherwise to deliver to another carrier on the route to said destination. It is mutually agreed as to each carrier of all or any of, said property over all or any portion of said route to destination and as to each party at any time interested in all or any said property, that every service to be performed hereunder shall be subject to all the bill of lading terms and conditions in the governing classification on the date of shipment.

Shipper hereby certifies that he is familiar with all the bill of lading terms and conditions in the governing classification and the said terms and conditions are hereby agreed to by the shipper and accepted for himself and his assigns.

From ______

DESIGNATE WITH AN (X)

At ______ 19____ BY TRUCK ☐ FREIGHT ☐ Shipper's No. ______

Carrier ______ Agent's No. ______

(Mail or street address of consignee— For purposes of notification only.)

Consigned to ______

Destination ______ State of ______ County of ______

Route ______

Delivering Carrier ______ Vehicle or Car Initial ______ No. ______

No. Packages	Kind of Package, Description of Articles, Special Marks, and Exceptions	*Weight (Sub. to Cor.)	Class or Rate	Check Column
TOTAL PIECES				

Subject to Section 7 of conditions of applicable bill of lading, if this shipment is to be delivered to the consignee without recourse on the consignor, the consignor shall sign the following statement:
The carrier shall not make delivery of this shipment without payment of freight and all other lawful charges.

Per ______
(Signature of Consignor.)

If charges are to be prepaid, write or stamp here, "To be Prepaid."

Received $ ______
to apply in prepayment of the charges on the property described hereon.

______
Agent or Cashier.

Per ______
(The signature here acknowledges only the amount prepaid.)

Charges Advanced:

______

C.O.D. SHIPMENT

Prepaid ☐
Collect ☐ $ ______

Collection Fee ______

Total Charges ______

*If the shipment moves between two ports by a carrier by water, the law requires that the bill of lading shall state whether it is "Carrier's or Shipper's weight."

†Shipper's imprint in lieu of stamp; not a part of bill of lading approved by the Department of Transportation.

NOTE—Where the rate is dependent on value, shippers are required to state specifically in writing the agreed or declared value of the property.

THIS SHIPMENT IS CORRECTLY DESCRIBED. CORRECT WEIGHT IS

______ LBS.

Subject to verification by the Respective Weighing and Inspection Bureau According to Agreement

Per ______

† The fibre containers used for this shipment conform to the specifications set forth in the box maker's certificate thereon, and all other requirements of Rule 41 of the Uniform Freight Classification and Rule 5 of the National Motor Freight Classification. †Shipper's imprint in lieu of stamp, not a part of bill of lading approved by the Interstate Commerce Commission.

If lower charges result, the agreed or declared value of the within described containers is hereby specifically stated to be not exceeding 50 cents per pound per article.

______ Shipper, Per

______ Agent, Per ______

Permanent post-office address of shipper

This is to certify that the above-named materials are properly classified, described, packaged, marked and labeled and are in proper condition for transportation according to the applicable regulations of the Department of Transportation.

______ SIGNATURE

Form No. 35-643 ©, 1986 UNZCO 190 Baldwin Ave., Jersey City, NJ 07306 - (800) 631-3098 - (201) 795-5400

3

Figure 4–5. Ocean bill of lading.

SEA-LAND SERVICE, INC.

INTERNATIONAL BILL OF LADING
NOT NEGOTIABLE UNLESS CONSIGNED "TO ORDER"
(SPACES IMMEDIATELY BELOW FOR SHIPPERS' MEMORANDA)

(2) SHIPPER/EXPORTER (COMPLETE NAME AND ADDRESS)	(5) BOOKING NO. / (5A) BILL OF LADING NO.
	(6) EXPORT REFERENCES
(3) CONSIGNEE (COMPLETE NAME AND ADDRESS)	(7) FORWARDING AGENT/F M C NO.
	(8) POINT AND COUNTRY OF ORIGIN
(4) NOTIFY PARTY (COMPLETE NAME AND ADDRESS)	(9) ALSO NOTIFY - ROUTING & INSTRUCTIONS
(12) INITIAL CARRIAGE BY (MODE) * / (13) PLACE OF INITIAL RECEIPT *	(9A) FINAL DESTINATION (OF THE GOODS NOT THE SHIP)
(14) VESSEL VOY FLAG / (15) PORT OF LOADING	(10) LOADING PIER/TERMINAL / (10A) ORIGINAL(S) TO BE RELEASED AT
(16) PORT OF DISCHARGE / (17) PLACE OF DELIVERY BY ON-CARRIER *	(11) TYPE OF MOVE (IF MIXED, USE BLOCK 20 AS APPROPRIATE)

PARTICULARS FURNISHED BY SHIPPER

MKS. & NOS./CONT. NOS.	NO. OF PKGS.	HM**	DESCRIPTION OF PACKAGES AND GOODS	GROSS WEIGHT	MEASUREMENT
(18)	(19)		(20)	(21)	(22)

(23) DECLARED VALUE $ — IF SHIPPER ENTERS A VALUE, CARRIERS "PACKAGE" LIMITATIONS OF LIABILITY DOES NOT APPLY AND THE AD VALOREM RATE WILL BE CHARGED. | (24) FREIGHT PAYABLE AT/BY

FREIGHT CHARGES	RATED AS	PER	RATE	PREPAID	COLLECT	CURRENCY/RATE OF EXCHANGE
THE RECEIPT, CUSTODY, CARRIAGE AND DELIVERY OF THE GOODS ARE SUBJECT TO THE TERMS APPEARING ON THE FACE AND BACK HEREOF AND TO CARRIER'S APPLICABLE TARIFF			TOTALS►			

In witness whereof original bills of lading all the same tenor and date one of which being accomplished the others to stand void, have been issued by Sea-Land Service, Inc. or its designated agent on behalf of itself, other participating carriers, the vessel, her master and owners or charterers.

* APPLICABLE ONLY WHEN USED FOR MULTIMODAL OR THROUGH TRANSPORTATION
** INDICATE WHETHER ANY OF THE CARGO IS HAZARDOUS MATERIAL UNDER DOT IMCO OR OTHER REGULATIONS AND INDICATE CORRECT COMMODITY NUMBER IN BOX 20

AT ....

BY ....
FOR SEA-LAND SERVICE, INC. (As Carrier)

SL-2855 (6/94) **BILL OF LADING NO.** **DATE**

Courtesy of Sea-Land Service, Inc.

Figure 4–5. *(continued)*

[reverse]

RECEIVED in apparent good order and condition from the shipper, or shipper's agent, the number of containers or other packages or units said by shipper to contain the goods described in the "Particulars Furnished By Shipper," to be transported from the Port of Loading (Box 15) or, if applicable, the Place of Initial Receipt (Box 13) to the Port of Discharge (Box 16) or, if applicable, the Place of Delivery by On-carrier (Box 17), there to be delivered to consignee or on-carrier on payment of all charges due thereon. Carrier makes no representation as to the correctness of the particulars furnished by the shipper.

In accepting this bill of lading, the shipper, consignee, holder hereof and the owners of the goods (each of whom is sometimes referred to herein as "Merchant") agree, the same as if signed by each of them, that the receipt, custody, carriage, relay, delivery and any transshipping of the goods are subject to the terms appearing on the face and back hereof, which shall govern the relations, whatsoever they may be, between shipper, consignee, the owners of the goods and any holder hereof and Carrier, its agents, contractors, employees, master and vessel in every contingency occurring and whether Carrier be acting as such or bailee. Carrier shall have the right to stow containers, vans or trailers on deck and without notice as per Clause 9. The terms hereof shall not be deemed waived by Carrier except by written waiver signed by Carrier or its duly authorized agent.

1. **CLAUSE PARAMOUNT.** This bill of lading shall have effect subject to all the provisions of the Carriage of Goods by Sea Act of the United States of America, approved April 16, 1936, as if set forth herein. However, insofar as it may provide greater rights to the holder hereof, the provisions of the International Convention for the Unification of Certain Rules of Law Relating to Bills of Lading signed at Brussels, August 25, 1924 as amended by the 'Protocol', signed at Brussels, February 23, 1968 (VISBY RULES) and at Brussels, December 21, 1979 (S.D.R. Protocol) shall apply to goods whether carried on or under deck, to carriage of goods between U.S. ports, or between non-U.S. ports, before the goods are loaded on and after they are discharged from the vessel, and throughout the entire time the goods are in the actual custody of Carrier, whether acting as carrier, bailee or stevedore.

If this bill of lading is issued in or the goods are delivered to a locality where there is in force a compulsorily applicable Carriage of Goods by Sea Act, ordinance or statute similar to the International Convention for the Unification of Certain Rules Relating to Bills of Lading dated at Brussels, August 25, 1924, then it is subject to such Act, ordinance or statute before the goods are loaded on and after they are discharged from the vessel and thoughout the entire time the goods are in the actual custody of Carrier, whether acting as carrier, bailee or stevedore.

Carrier shall be entitled to the full benefit of all rights and immunity under, and all limitations of or exemptions from liability contained in any law of the United States or any other place whose law shall be compulsorily applicable. If any term of this bill of lading be repugnant to the Carriage of Goods by Sea Act of the United States or any other law compulsorily applicable, such term only shall be void to that extent but no further.

This bill of lading shall be construed and the rights of the parties hereunder determined according to the laws of the United States.

2. **PARTIES COVERED.** If the vessel or other craft in use is not owned by or chartered by demise to Carrier Sea-Land Service, Inc., this bill of lading shall take effect for purposes of limitation of liability only, as a contract with the owner or demise charterer, as the case may be. If it shall be adjudged that any person other than the owner or demise charterer (including the master, time charterer, agents, stevedores, lashers, watchmen and other independent contractors) is the carrier or bailee of the goods, or is otherwise liable in contract or in tort, all rights, exemptions, and limitations of liability provided by law and by the terms of this bill of lading shall be available to such other persons. In contracting for the foregoing rights, exemptions, and limitations of liability, Carrier is acting as agent and trustee for the persons above mentioned. Particulars of the ownership of the vessel or other craft used may be obtained from Carrier or its agents.

3. **SCOPE OF VOYAGE.** The voyage herein contracted for shall include ports in or out of the advertised, geographical, usual or ordinary route or order. The vessel may omit calling at any port or ports whether scheduled or not, and may call at the same port more than once; may before or after proceeding toward the port of discharge, make trial trips or tests, take fuel or stores at any port in or out of the regular course of the voyage, sail with or without pilots, tow and be towed, and save or attempt to save life, vessels in distress or other property, and all of the foregoing are included in the contract voyage.

Carrier shall have the right, without notice, to substitute or employ a vessel, watercraft, or other means rather than the vessel named herein to perform all or part of the carriage. When the port of destination or discharge is not served by Carrier's containership, Carrier may, at any intermediate port, break bulk of cargo shipped in containers.

4. **RISKS AND LIBERTIES.** In any situation which in the judgment of Carrier or the master is likely to give rise to risk of seizure, arrest, detention, damage, delay to, or loss of any goods or the vessel, or to make it imprudent for any other reason to receive, keep or load the goods, or continue the voyage, or discharge the goods, Carrier or the master shall have the right (a) to decline to receive, keep or load the goods or to discharge or devan them at any convenient port or place and to require the shipper or person entitled thereto to take delivery and if he fails to do so, to store them at the risk and expense of the goods; or (b) to discharge or devan the goods into any lighter, craft, depot or other place; or (c) to retain the goods on board until the return trip or until such time as Carrier or the master deems advisable; or (d) to substitute another vessel or to transship or forward the goods, or any part thereof, by any means, but always at the risk and expense of the goods. Any disposition of the goods pursuant to this clause shall constitute complete performance of this contract by Carrier who shall be free of further responsibility. For any and all service rendered as herein provided, Carrier shall be entitled to reasonable extra compensation and shall have a lien on the goods.

Goods shut out or not loaded on a vessel for any reason can be forwarded on a subsequent vessel or by feederships, lighters, aircraft, trucks, trains or other means in addition to the ocean vessel, or its substitute, to accomplish the carriage herein.

5. **GOVERNMENTAL ORDERS.** Carrier or the master shall have liberty to comply with any orders, directions, regulations, requests or suggestions given by or received from the government of any nation or by any person purporting to act with the authority of such government. Any disposition of the goods pursuant to this clause shall constitute completion of the contract of carriage by Carrier, and the goods thereafter shall be solely at their own risk and expense.

6. **PACKING OF CONTAINERS - SHIPPER'S GUARANTY - INDEMNITY.** Carrier shall not be responsible for the safe and proper stowing of cargo in containers if such containers are packed by the shipper or shipper's agent and no responsibility shall attach to Carrier for any loss or damage caused to contents by shifting, overloading, or failure to label or properly chock, lash or pack the goods in the container or within their individual packages. The shipper or shipper's agent shall properly seal containers loaded by them. The shipper, or its agent shall carefully inspect and clean containers, if necessary, before packing them. Acceptance and packing of the containers shall be prima facie evidence that the containers were sound, clean and suitable for use and shall relieve Carrier of responsibility for any damage to goods carried resulting from the condition of the container used. "Containers" as used herein include all types of containers for dry, liquid, and perishable cargo, as well as vans and trailers.

The shipper, consignee, holder hereof and owner of the goods agree to be liable for and shall hold harmless and indemnify Carrier for any injury, loss or damage, including fines, penalties, and reasonable attorney's fees arising from the shipper's failure to properly describe, label, stow or secure the goods in containers or to clean containers and also for damage or expense caused by the goods to the containers, other property, or for injury or death to persons.

7. **PERISHABLE GOODS.** Goods of a perishable nature are carried in dry containers without environmental or atmospheric control or other special services unless the face of this bill of lading notes that the goods are to be carried in a refrigerated, heated, specially ventilated or otherwise specially equipped container. This carriage is subject to the special services and charges offered in the Carrier's tariff.

The Merchant is responsible for bringing the goods to the proper temperature before loading the goods into the containers, for the proper stowage of the goods within the container, for setting the temperature (including maintenance and repair), during all times before containers are delivered to the Carrier and after they are delivered by the Carrier. The Carrier is not responsible for product deterioration caused by inherent vice, defects in the merchandise or transit times in excess of the product's shelf life. Refrigerated, heated, specially ventilated or otherwise specially equipped containers are not equipped to change the temperature of goods. (They are equipped only to maintain temperature.) Merchant will give written notice of requested temperature setting of the thermostatic controls before receipt of the goods by the Carrier. When a loaded container is received, the Carrier will verify that the thermostatic controls are set to maintain container temperature as requested. The Carrier is unable to determine whether the goods were at the proper temperature when they were loaded into the container or when the container is delivered to the Carrier. Air temperature at the unit sensor will be maintained within a range of plus or minus 5 degrees Fahrenheit of the temperature requested by the shipper on the face of this bill of lading, if the goods were at that temperature when loaded into the container and if the temperature controls were properly set when the container was loaded. The Carrier is not responsible for temperature fluctuations that do not exceed 4 hours duration.

8. **LIVE ANIMALS.** Live animals, birds, and fish are received, kept and carried solely at shipper's risk of accident, disease or mortality and without warranty or undertaking whatsoever by Carrier.

9. **STOWAGE ON DECK.** Goods may be stowed in any covered-in space or loaded in or on a container, van or trailer and carried on deck and such shall be deemed to be stowed under deck for all purposes, including General Average and the Carriage of Goods by Sea Act, the Hague Rules or other compulsorily applicable legislation.

If the goods are shipped on deck not in containers, they will be carried solely at the risk of the goods and without any liability, but, in any event, the Carrier shall have the benefits, defenses and limitations of liability available under the Carriage of Goods by Sea Act, the Hague/Visby Rules or as contained herein.

10. **TRANSSHIPMENT.** If the goods are destined for a port or destination not served by Sea-Land Service, Inc., or other carriers serving through routes with Sea-Land, then upon the request and at the risk of the shipper, the goods will be delivered for transshipment or forwarding at the Port of Discharge or Place of Delivery by On-carrier served by Carrier's(') vessel(s) or other mode of transport. In such case, Sea-Land Service, Inc. or participating carriers will have no further duty or responsibility whatsoever as Carrier, this bill of lading operating only as a document of title thereafter.

11. **DELIVERY AND STORAGE.** Except at ports where Carrier delivers goods directly to the consignee, delivery shall take place and Carrier shall have no further responsibility when the goods are landed upon a safe dock, lighter, or other craft and custody is taken by port or government authorities, terminal operator or lighterman. At ports where Carrier delivers goods to consignee, if the consignee does not take delivery as soon as the goods are ready, the goods shall thereafter be at their own risk and expense. Carrier shall have the right, but not the duty, to store containers in the open before loading or after discharge.

12. **EXPENSES, FINES.** The shipper and consignee shall be liable for, and shall indemnify Carrier and vessel and hold them harmless against, and Carrier shall have a lien on the goods for all expenses and charges of mending, coopering, repairing, fumigating, devanning, restowing, storing or reconditioning, and all expenses incurred for the benefit or protection of the goods, also for any payment, duty, fine or other expenses including but not limited to court costs, expenses, and reasonable attorney's fees incurred or levied upon Carrier or the vessel in connection with the goods because of shipper's failure to comply with any laws or regulations.

13. **FREIGHT, LIENS, QUANTITY.** Freight shall be payable, at Carrier's option, on gross weight, measurement ton, or on value as set forth in Carrier's tariff. Carrier shall have the right, but not the duty to open packages or containers and, if shipper's particulars are found to be erroneous, the shipper, consignee and the goods shall be liable for the correct freight charge and any expenses incurred in examining, weighing, measuring or valuing the goods.

Full freight to the port of discharge named on the face of this document and all advance charges against the goods shall be considered completely earned on receipt of the goods by Carrier, even though the vessel or goods are damaged or lost or the voyage is frustrated or abandoned.

All sums payable to Carrier are due when incurred and shall be paid in full, in United States currency, or, at Carrier's option, in its equivalent in the currency of the port of loading or the port of discharge, or as specified in tariffs or conference agreement.

The shipper, consignee, holder hereof, and owner of the goods shall be jointly and severally liable to Carrier for the payment of all freight, demurrage, General Average and other charges, including but not limited to court costs, expenses and reasonable attorney's fees incurred in collecting sums due Carrier. Payment of ocean freight and charges to a freight forwarder, broker or anyone other than Sea-Land Service, Inc. or its authorized agent, shall not be deemed payment to the Carrier and shall be made at payor's sole risk.

Carrier shall have a lien on the goods, which shall survive delivery, for all charges due and may, without notice, enforce this lien by public or private sale of the goods and other property belonging to the shipper, consignee, holder hereof or owner of the goods, which may be in Carrier's possession.

14. **BOTH TO BLAME COLLISIONS.** If the vessel comes into collision with another ship as a result of the negligence of the other ship and any act, neglect or default of the master, mariner, pilot or of the servants of Carrier in the navigation or in the management of the vessel, the owners of the goods carried hereunder will indemnify Carrier against all loss or liability to the other or non-carrying ship or her owners insofar as such loss or liability represents loss of, or damage to, or any claim whatsoever of the owners of said goods, paid or payable by the other or non-carrying ship or her owners to the owners of said goods and set-off, recouped or recovered by the other or non-carrying ship or her owners as part of their claim against the carrying vessel or Carrier. The foregoing provisions shall also apply where the owners, operators or those in charge of any ship or ships or objects other than, or in addition to, the colliding ships or objects are at fault in respect of a collision, contact, stranding or other accident.

15. **GENERAL AVERAGE.** General Average shall be adjusted, stated and settled according to York Antwerp Rules 1974, except Rule XXII thereof, at the place selected by Carrier, and as to matters not provided for by these Rules, according to the laws and usage at the port of New York. Average agreement or bond and such additional security as may be required by Carrier, must be furnished before delivery of the goods.

In the event of accident, danger, damage, or disaster, before or after commencement of the voyage resulting from any cause whatsoever, whether due to negligence or not, for which, or for the consequence of which, Carrier is not responsible, by statute, contract or otherwise, the goods, the shipper and the consignee shall contribute with Carrier in General Average to the payment of any sacrifices, losses or expenses of a General Average nature that may be made or incurred, and shall pay salvage and special charges incurred in respect of goods. If a salvaging ship is owned or operated by Carrier, salvage shall be paid for as fully and in the same manner as if the salvaging ship belonged to strangers. Cargo shall pay its contribution to General Average even when such average is the result of fault, neglect or error of the master, pilot or crew. The shippers and consignees expressly renounce all codes, statutes, laws or regulations which might otherwise apply.

16. **FIRE.** Carrier shall not be liable for any loss or damage to goods occurring at any time, even though before loading on or after discharge from the vessel, by reasons or by means of any fire whatsoever, unless such fire shall be caused by the actual fault or privity of Carrier.

17. **VALUATION.** In the event of loss, damage or delay to or in connection with goods exceeding in actual value the equivalent of $1,000 lawful money of the United States, per package, or in case of goods not shipped in packages, per shipping unit, the value of the goods shall be deemed to be $1,000 per package or unit, unless the nature and higher value of goods have been declared by the shipper herein and extra charges paid as provided in Carrier's tariff. However, Carrier's liability shall not exceed the invoice value of the goods. The word "package" shall include a skid, cradle, pallet or unitized load, group or assemblage. When the U.S. Carriage of Goods by Sea Act does not apply of its own force, the $1,000 limitation shall apply to each shipping or customary freight unit or piece, provided always that any compulsorily applicable limitation which is greater than the $1,000 limitation shall apply in place of the $1,000 limitation.

18. **NOTICE OF CLAIM–TIME FOR SUIT–JURISDICTION.** Unless notice of loss or damage and the general nature of such loss or damage be given in writing to the Carrier or his agent at the port of discharge before or at the time of the removal of the goods into the custody of the person entitled to delivery thereof under the contract of carriage, such removal shall be prima facie evidence of the delivery by Carrier of the goods as described in the bill of lading. If the loss or damage is not apparent the notice must be given within three days after delivery.

Carrier and the vessel shall be discharged from all liability in respect of loss or damage unless a claim in writing has been made within one year after delivery of the goods or the date when the goods should have been delivered, or, if a claim has been timely made, but declined, suit is not brought within two years from date of declination of the claim in whole or in part. Suit shall not be deemed brought against Carrier or vessel until jurisdiction shall have been obtained over Carrier or the vessel, or both, by service of process thereon.

Carrier may, at its sole discretion, and on the basis that it has not been prejudiced by the passage of time, waive notice requirements or other time limits. Nevertheless, Carrier will not entertain claims which are filed later than three years from the date of delivery of the goods, or the date when the goods should have been delivered.

19. **FINAL AGREEMENT.** All prior agreements, dock receipts or freight engagements for the shipment of the goods and all other arrangements are superseded by this bill of lading and Freight Tariff Rules and Regulations on file with the Federal Maritime Commission, and Interstate Commerce Commission in the case of through transportation, which are incorporated herein by reference and form part of this bill of lading as if set forth herein at length. Copies of the Freight Tariff Rules and Regulations are available upon request.

20. **SHIPPER'S WARRANTIES.** The shipper warrants that he is the owner of and entitled to possession of the goods or has the authority of the owner and all persons entitled to possession of the goods to agree to the terms hereof.

21. **THROUGH AND ON BOARD BILLS OF LADING.** When used in or endorsed on this bill of lading the words "ON BOARD" shall mean on board the exporting vessel or on board another mode of transportation operated by or on behalf of the originating carrier and enroute to the port of loading for loading aboard the participating carrier's vessel.

The participating land carrier's bill of lading lawfully in effect on the date of issue of this bill of lading shall, together with the rules, tariffs and classifications of such participating carrier and applicable rules and regulations of government agencies with jurisdiction over such land carriage govern and control the possession and carriage of the goods by such participating carrier. Copies of said bill of lading form are available from such participating carrier or its agents on request. However, insofar as Clauses 1, 9, 17, 18 and 22 shall give greater rights to the holder hereof, they shall be applied.

22. **CLAIMS.** Claims for loss of or damage to the goods agreed to be carried under the terms of this bill of lading may be filed against Sea-Land Service, Inc., which agrees to be solely responsible for processing said claims to conclusion. It is agreed that in the event of payment of any such claims by Sea-Land Service, Inc. it shall automatically be subrogated to all the rights of the shipper or consignee against all others, including participating carriers, on account of such loss or damage. Claims must be filed and suit commenced within the time limits provided by law and the terms of the bill of lading and tariff. When loss or damage occurs at any time from the time the cargo has been delivered to Carrier at the Port of Loading or, if applicable, Place of Initial Receipt until it has been delivered to the Consignee or its agent at the Port of Discharge or, if applicable, the Place of Delivery by On-carrier, it shall be deemed, as between the shipper, consignee or holder hereof and Sea-Land Service, Inc. that the loss or damage occurred aboard the vessel while in the custody or control of Sea-Land Service, Inc. All adjustments of such loss or damage shall be made in accordance with Clause 1, "CLAUSE PARAMOUNT" of this bill of lading. However, should Sea-Land Service, Inc. recover an amount greater than such adjustment from the actual person which was responsible for the loss or damage, such amounts shall be forwarded to the claimant upon receipt.

Except as otherwise provided herein, Carrier will not be liable for indirect, special or consequential damages.

Figure 4–6. International air waybill.

131 | 7369 5473 — 131-7369 5473

Shipper's Name and Address | Shipper's account Number

Not negotiable
Air Waybill*
Issued by
Japan Airlines
TOKYO, JAPAN

JAL CARGO

Copies 1, 2 and 3 of this Air Waybill are originals and have the same validity

Consignee's Name and Address | Consignee's account Number

It is agreed that the goods described herein are accepted in apparent good order and condition (except as noted) for carriage SUBJECT TO THE CONDITIONS OF CONTRACT ON THE REVERSE HEREOF. THE SHIPPER'S ATTENTION IS DRAWN TO THE NOTICE CONCERNING CARRIERS' LIMITATION OF LIABILITY. Shipper may increase such limitation of liability by declaring a higher value for carriage and paying a supplemental charge if required.

☎ Telephone

Issuing Carrier's Agent, Name and City | Accounting Information

Agent's IATA Code | Account No.

Airport of Departure (Addr. of first Carrier) and requested Routing

to	By first Carrier (Routing and Destination)	to	by	to	by	Currency	CHGS Code	WT/VAL PPD	WT/VAL COLL	Other PPD	Other COLL	Declared Value for Carriage	Declared Value for Customs

Airport of Destination | Flight/Date (For Carrier Use only) Flight/Date | Amount of Insurance | INSURANCE - If Carrier offers insurance, and such insurance is requested in accordance with conditions on reverse hereof, indicate amount to be insured in figures in box marked 'amount of insurance'.

Handling Information

No. of Pieces RCP	Gross Weight	kg lb	Rate Class (Commodity Item No.)	Chargeable Weight	Rate / Charge	Total	Nature and Quantity of Goods (incl. Dimensions or Volume)

THESE COMMODITIES LICENCED BY U.S. FOR ULTIMATE DESTINATION ——— DIVERSION CONTRARY TO U.S. LAW PROHIBITED

prepaid | Weight Charge | Collect | Other Charges

Valuation Charge

Tax

Total other Charges Due Agent

Total other Charges Due Carrier

Shipper certifies that the particulars on the face hereof are correct and that insofar as any part of the consignment contains dangerous goods, such part is properly described by name and is in proper condition for carriage by air according to the applicable Dangerous Goods Regulations.

Signature of Shipper or his Agent

Total prepaid | Total collect

Currency Conversion Rates | cc charges in Dest. Currency

Executed on (Date) at (Place) Signature of Issuing Carrier or its Agent

For Carriers Use only at Destination | Charges at Destination | Total collect Charges

131-7369 5473

COPY 5 (FOR AIRPORT OF DESTINATION)

FORM AC-12501A

PRINTED IN JAPAN

Figure 4–6. *(continued)*

[reverse]

NOTICE CONCERNING CARRIERS' LIMITATION OF LIABILITY

IF THE CARRIAGE INVOLVES AN ULTIMATE DESTINATION OR STOP IN A COUNTRY OTHER THAN THE COUNTRY OF DEPARTURE, THE WARSAW CONVENTION MAY BE APPLICABLE AND THE CONVENTION GOVERNS AND IN MOST CASES LIMITS THE LIABILITY OF THE CARRIER IN RESPECT OF LOSS, DAMAGE OR DELAY TO CARGO TO 250 FRENCH GOLD FRANCS PER KILOGRAMME, UNLESS A HIGHER VALUE IS DECLARED IN ADVANCE BY THE SHIPPER AND A SUPPLEMENTARY CHARGE PAID IF REQUIRED

THE LIABILITY LIMIT OF 250 FRENCH GOLD FRANCS PER KILOGRAMME IS APPROXIMATELY US$ 20 PER KILOGRAMME ON THE BASIS OF US$ 42 22 PER OUNCE OF GOLD

CONDITIONS OF CONTRACT

1 As used in this contract "Carrier" means all air carriers that carry or undertake to carry the goods hereunder or perform any other services incidental to such air carriage. "Warsaw Convention" means the Convention for the Unification of certain Rules relating to International Carriage by Air signed at Warsaw 12 October 1929, or that Convention as amended at The Hague 28 September 1955, whichever may be applicable, and "French gold francs" means francs consisting of 65½ milligrams of gold with a fineness of nine hundred thousandths

2 (a) Carriage hereunder is subject to the rules relating to liability established by the Warsaw Convention unless such carriage is not "international carriage" as defined by that Convention

(b) To the extent not in conflict with the foregoing, carriage hereunder and other services performed by each Carrier are subject to

(i) applicable laws (including national laws implementing the Convention), government regulations, orders and requirements,

(ii) provisions herein set forth, and

(iii) applicable tariffs, rules, conditions of carriage, regulations and timetables (but not the times of departure and arrival therein) of such carrier, which are made part hereof and which may be inspected at any of its offices and at airports from which it operates regular services In transportation between a place in the United States or Canada and any place outside thereof the applicable tariffs are the tariffs in force in those countries

3 The first Carrier's name may be abbreviated on the face hereof, the full name and its abbreviation being set forth in such Carrier's tariffs, conditions of carriage, regulations and timetables The first Carrier's address is the airport of departure shown on the face hereof The agreed stopping places (which may be altered by Carrier in case of necessity) are those places, except the place of departure and the place of destination, set forth on the face hereof or shown in Carrier's timetables as scheduled stopping places for the route Carriage to be performed hereunder by several successive carriers is regarded as a single operation

4 Except as otherwise provided in Carrier's tariffs or conditions of carriage, in carriage to which the Warsaw Convention does not apply Carrier's liability shall not exceed US$ 20 00 or the equivalent per kilogramme of goods lost, damaged or delayed, unless a higher value is declared by the shipper and a supplementary charge paid

5 If the sum entered on the face of the Air Waybill as "Declared Value for Carriage" represents an amount in excess of the applicable limits of liability referred to in the above Notice and in these Conditions and if the shipper has paid any supplementary charge that may be required by the Carrier's tariffs conditions of carriage or regulations this shall constitute a special declaration of value and in this case Carrier's limit of liability shall be the sum so declared Payment of claims shall be subject to proof of actual damages suffered

6 In cases of loss damage or delay of part of the consignment the weight to be taken into account in determining Carrier's limit of liability shall be only the weight of the package or packages concerned

Note

Notwithstanding any other provision, for foreign air transportation as defined in the U S Federal Aviation Act, as amended, in case of loss or damage or delay of a shipment or part thereof, the weight to be used in determining the carrier's limit of liability shall be the weight which is used (or a pro rata share in the case of a part shipment loss, damage or delay) to determine the transportation charge for such shipment

7 Any exclusion or limitation of liability applicable to Carrier shall apply to and be for the benefit of Carrier's agents, servants and representatives and any person whose aircraft is used by Carrier for carriage and its agents, servants and representatives For purposes of this provision Carrier acts herein as agent for all such persons

8 (a) Carrier undertakes to complete the carriage hereunder with reasonable dispatch Carrier may substitute alternate carriers or aircraft and may without notice and with due regard to the interests of the shipper substitute other means of transportation Carrier is authorized to select the routing or to change or deviate from the routing shown on the face hereof This Subparagraph is not applicable to from USA,

(b) Carrier undertakes to complete the carriage hereunder with reasonable dispatch Except within USA where carrier tariffs will apply Carrier may substitute alternate carriers or aircraft and may without notice and with due regard to the interests of the shipper substitute other means of transportation Carrier is authorized to select the routing or to change or deviate from the routing shown on the face hereof This Subparagraph is applicable only to from USA

9 Subject to the conditions herein, the Carrier shall be liable for the goods during the period they are in its charge or the charge of its agent

10 (a) Except when the Carrier has extended credit to the consignee without the written consent of the shipper, the shipper guarantees payment of all charges for carriage due in accordance with Carrier's tariffs, conditions of carriage and related regulations, applicable laws (including national laws implementing the Convention), government regulations, orders and requirements,

(b) When no part of the consignment is delivered, a claim with respect to such consignment will be entertained even though transportation charges thereon are unpaid

11 Notice of arrival of goods will be given promptly to the consignee or to the person indicated on the face hereof as the person to be notified On arrival of the goods at the place of destination, subject to the acceptance of other instructions from the shipper prior to arrival of the goods at the place of destination, delivery will be made to, or in accordance with the instructions of the consignee If the consignee declines to accept the goods or cannot be communicated with, disposition will be in accordance with instructions of the shipper

12 (a) The person entitled to delivery must make a complaint to the Carrier in writing in the case

(i) of visible damage to the goods, immediately after discovery of the damage and at the latest within 14 days from receipt of the goods,

(ii) of other damage to the goods, within 14 days from the date of receipt of the goods,

(iii) of delay, within 21 days of the date the goods are placed at his disposal, and

(iv) of non-delivery of the goods, within 120 days from the date of the issue of the Air Waybill

(b) For the purpose of Subparagraph (a) above complaint in writing may be made to the Carrier whose Air Waybill was used or to the first Carrier or to the last Carrier or to the Carrier who performed the transportation during which the loss, damage or delay took place

(c) Any rights to damages against Carrier shall be extinguished unless an action is brought within two years from the date of arrival at the destination or from the date on which the aircraft ought to have arrived, or from the date on which the transportation stopped

13 The shipper shall comply with all applicable laws and government regulations of any country to, from, through or over which the goods may be carried, including those relating to the packing, carriage or delivery of the goods and shall furnish such information and attach such documents to this Air Waybill as may be necessary to comply with such laws and regulations Carrier is not liable to the shipper for loss or expense due to the shipper's failure to comply with this provision

14 No agent, servant or representative of Carrier has authority to alter, modify or waive any provisions of this contract

15 If Carrier offers insurance and such insurance is requested and if the appropriate premium is paid and the fact recorded on the face hereof the goods covered by this Air Waybill are insured under an open policy for the amount requested as set out on the face hereof (recovery being limited to the actual value of goods lost or damaged provided that such amount does not exceed the insured value) The insurance is subject to the terms, conditions and coverage (from which certain risks are excluded) of the open policy, which is available for inspection at an office of the issuing Carrier by the interested party Claims under such policy must be reported immediately to an office of Carrier

16 Claims for overcharges must be made in writing within 180 days from the date of issue of the Air Waybill

Figure 4–7. "House" air waybill.

House Air Waybill Number

Shippers Name and Address

Shippers account Number

Not negotiable

Air Waybill

(Air Consignment note)
Issued by

Copies 1, 2 and 3 of this Air Waybill are originals and have the same validity

Consignee's Name and Address

Consignee's account Number

It is agreed that the goods described herein are accepted in apparent good order and condition (except as noted) for carriage SUBJECT TO THE CONDITIONS OF CONTRACT ON THE REVERSE HEREOF. THE SHIPPER'S ATTENTION IS DRAWN TO THE NOTICE CONCERNING CARRIERS' LIMITATION OF LIABILITY. Shipper may increase such limitation of liability by declaring a higher value for carriage and paying a supplemental charge if required.

These commodities licensed by the United States for ultimate destination

Diversion contrary to

United States law prohibited.

Airport of Departure (Addr. of first Carrier) and requested Routing

to	By first Carrier	Routing and Destination	Air Waybill Number	Currency	CHGS Code	WT/VAL PPD	WT/VAL COLL	Other PPD	Other COLL	Declared Value for Carriage	Declared Value for Customs

Airport of Destination	Flight/Date	For Carrier Use only	Flight/Date	Amount of Insurance	INSURANCE If Carrier offers insurance and such insurance is requested in accordance with conditions on reverse hereof, indicate amount to be insured in figures in box marked "amount of insurance".

Handling Information

No. of Pieces RCP	Gross Weight	kg lb	Rate Class / Commodity Item No.	Chargeable Weight	Rate / Charge	Total	Nature and Quantity of Goods (incl. Dimensions or Volume)

Prepaid	Weight Charge	Collect	Other Charges
	Valuation Charge		
	Tax		
	Total other Charges Due Agent		**Shipper certifies that the particulars on the face hereof are correct and that insofar as any part of the consignment contains dangerous goods, such part is properly described by name and is in proper condition for carriage by air according to the applicable Dangerous Goods Regulations.**
	Total other Charges Due Carrier		
			Signature of Shipper or his Agent
Total prepaid		Total collect	
Currency Conversion Rates		cc charges in Dest. Currency	Executed on (Date) at (Place) Signature of Issuing Carrier or its Agent

Form 16 810 © 1986 UNZ&CO 190 Baldwin Ave., Jersey City, NJ 07306 • (800) 631-3098 • (201) 795-5400

House Air Waybill Number

ORIGINAL 3 - FOR SHIPPER

Reprinted with permission of Unz & Co., 190 Baldwin Ave., Jersey City, NJ 07306, USA.

Figure 4–7. *(continued)*

[reverse]

NOTICE CONCERNING CARRIERS' LIMITATION OF LIABILITY

IF THE CARRIAGE INVOLVES AN ULTIMATE DESTINATION OR STOP IN A COUNTRY OTHER THAN THE COUNTRY OF DEPARTURE, THE WARSAW CONVENTION MAY BE APPLICABLE AND THE CONVENTION GOVERNS AND IN MOST CASES LIMITS THE LIABILITY OF THE CARRIER IN RESPECT OF LOSS DAMAGE OR DELAY TO CARGO TO 250 FRENCH GOLD FRANCS PER KILOGRAMME, UNLESS A HIGHER VALUE IS DECLARED IN ADVANCE BY THE SHIPPER AND A SUPPLEMENTARY CHARGE PAID IF REQUIRED.
THE LIABILITY LIMIT OF 250 FRENCH GOLD FRANCS PER KILOGRAMME IS APPROXIMATELY US $20.00 PER KILOGRAMME ON THE BASIS OF US $42.22 PER OUNCE OF GOLD.

CONDITIONS OF CONTRACT

1. As used in this contract "Carrier" means all air carriers that carry or undertake to carry the goods hereunder or perform any other services incidental to such air carriage. "Warsaw Convention" means the Convention for the Unification of certain Rules relating to International Carriage by Air, signed at Warsaw, 12 October 1929, or that Convention as amended at The Hague, 28 September 1955, which ever may be applicable and "French gold francs" means francs consisting of 65½ milligrams of gold with a fineness of nine hundred thousandths.

2. (a) Carriage hereunder is subject to the rules relating to liability established by the Warsaw Convention unless such carriage is not "international carriage" as defined by that Convention.
   (b) to the extent not in conflict with the foregoing, carriage hereunder and other services performed by each Carrier are subject to:
      (i) applicable laws (including national laws implementing the Convention), government regulations, orders and requirements.
      (ii) provisions herein set forth, and
      (iii) applicable tariffs, rules, conditions of carriage, regulations and timetables (but not the times of departure and arrival therein) of such carrier which are made part hereof and which may be inspected at any of its offices and at airports from which it operates regular services. In transportation between a place in the United States or Canada and any place outside thereof the applicable tariffs are the tariffs in force in those countries.

3. The first Carrier's name may be abbreviated on the face hereof, the full name and its abbreviation being set forth in such Carrier's tariffs, conditions of carriage, regulations and timetables. The first Carrier's address is the airport of departure shown on the face hereof. The agreed stopping places (which may be altered by Carrier in case of necessity) are those places, except the place of departure and the place of destination, set forth on the face hereof or shown in Carrier's timetables as scheduled stopping places for the route. Carriage to be performed hereunder by several successive carriers is regarded as a single operation.

4. Except as otherwise provided in Carrier's tariffs or conditions of carriage, in carriage to which the Warsaw Convention does not apply Carrier's liability shall not exceed US $20.00 or the equivalent per kilogramme of goods lost, damaged or delayed, unless a higher value is declared by the shipper and a supplemenetary charge paid.

5. If the sum entered on the face of the Air Waybill as "Declared Value for Carriage" represents an amount in excess of the applicable limits of liability referred to in the above Notice and in these Conditions and if the shipper has paid any supplementary charge that may be required by the Carrier's tariffs, conditions of carriage or regulations, this shall constitute a special declaration of value and in this case Carrier's limit of liability shall be the sum so declared. Payment of claims shall be subject to proof of actual damages suffered.

6. In cases of loss, damage or delay of part of the consignment, the weight to be taken into account in determining Carrier's limit of liability shall be only the weight of the package or packages concerned.
   NOTE
   Notwithstanding any other provision for foreign air transportation as defined in the U.S. Federal Aviation Act, as amended, in case of loss or damage or delay of a shipment or part thereof, the weight to be used in determining the carrier's limit of liability shall be the weight which is used (or a pro rata share in the case of a part shipment loss, damage or delay) to determine the transportation charge for such shipment.

7. Any exclusion or limitation of liability applicable to Carrier shall apply to and be for the benefit of Carrier's agents, servants and representatives and any person whose aircraft is used by Carrier for carriage and its agents, servants and representatives. For purposes of this provision Carrier acts herein as agent for all such persons.

8. (a) Carrier undertakes to complete the carriage hereunder with reasonable dispatch. Carrier may substitute alternate carriers or aircraft and may without notice and with due regard to the interests of the shipper substitute other means of transportation. Carrier is authorized to select the routing or to change or deviate from the routing shown on the face hereof. This Subparagraph is not applicable to/from USA.
   (b) Carrier undertakes to complete the carriage hereunder with reasonable dispatch. Except within USA where carrier tariffs will apply. Carrier may substitute alternate carriers or aircraft and may without notice and with due regard to the interests of the shipper substitute other means of transportation. Carrier is authorized to select the routing or to change or deviate from the routing shown on the face hereof. This Subparagraph is applicable only to/from USA.

9. Subject to the conditions herein, the Carrier shall be liable for the goods during the period they are in its charge or the charge of its age.

10. (a) Except when the Carrier has extended credit to the consignee without the written consent of the shipper, the shipper guarantees payment of all charges for carriage due in accordance with Carrier's tariffs, conditions of carriage and related regulations, applicable laws (including national laws implementing the Convention), government regulations, orders, and requirements.
    (b) when no part of the consignment is delivered, a claim with respect to such consignment will be entertained even though transportation charges thereon are unpaid.

11. Notice of arrival of goods will be given promptly to the consignee or to the person indicates on the face thereof as the person to be notified. On arrival of the goods at the place of destination, subject to the acceptance of other instructions from the consignor prior to arrival of the goods at the place of destination, delivery will be made to, or in accordance withi the instructions of the consignee. If the consignee declines to accept the goods or cannot be communicated with, disposition will be in accordance with instructions of the consignor.

12. (a) The person entitled to delivery must make a complaint to the Carrier in writing in the case.
       (i) of visible damage to the goods, immediately after discovery of the damage and at the latest within 14 days from the date of receipt of the goods.
       (ii) of other damage to the goods within 14 days from the date of receipt of the goods,
       (iii) of delay within 21 days of the date the goods are placed at his disposal, and
       (iv) of non-delivery of the goods, within 120 days from the date of the issue of the Air Waybill.
    (b) for the purpose of Subparagraph (a) above complaint in writing may be made to the Carrier whose Air Waybill was used, or to the first Carrier or to the last Carrier or to the Carrier who performed the transportation during which the loss, damage or delay took place.
    (c) any rights to damages against Carrier shall be extinguished unless an action is brought within two years from the date of arrival at the destination, or from the date on which the aircraft ought to have arrived, or from the date or which the transportation stopped.

13. The shipper shall comply with all applicable laws, and government regulations of any country to, from, through or over which the goods may be carried, including those relating to the packing, carriage or delivery of the goods, and shall furnish such information and attach such documents to this Air Waybill as may be necessary to comply with such laws and regulations. Carrier is not liable to the shipper for loss or expense due to the shipper's failure to comply with this provision.

14. No agent, servant or representative of Carrier has authority to alter, modify or waive any provisions of this contract.

15. On request and if the appropriate premium is paid and the fact recorded on the face hereof, the goods covered by this Air Waybill are insured under an open policy for the amount requested as set out on the face hereof (recovery being limited to the actual value of goods lost or damaged provided that such amount does not exceed the insured value). The insurance is subject to the terms, conditions and coverage (from which certain risks are excluded) of the open policy, which is available for inspection of an office of the issuing Carrier by the interested party. Claim under such policy must be reported immediately to an office of Carrier.

insurance, the buyer may be expecting the seller to arrange for it and to provide an insurance policy or certificate at the time of shipment as evidence that the shipment is properly covered. The usual practice is to insure for 110 percent of the CIF or invoice value of the goods (in order to cover loss, as well as any incidental surveying, inspection, or other expenses) and to obtain a policy or certificate in negotiable form and covering "all risks." "Warehouse-to-warehouse" coverage is best. Large exporters usually issue their own certificates under their open-cargo policy. Others may obtain insurance certificates issued by the freight forwarder under its open-cargo policy or individual policies from insurance agents for individual shipments. Letters of credit

(*Text continues on page 133.*)

Figure 4–8. Packing list.

PACKING LIST

____________________ 19 _______

Place and Date of Shipment

To

Gentlemen:

Under your Order No. ____________________ the material listed below was shipped via

To

Shipment consists of:	Marks
_____ Cases _____ Packages _____ Crates _____ Cartons _____ Bbls. _____ Drums _____ Reels __________	

*LEGAL WEIGHT IS WEIGHT OF ARTICLE PLUS PAPER, BOX, BOTTLE, ETC., CONTAINING THE ARTICLE AS USUALLY CARRIED IN STOCK.

PACKAGE NUMBER	WEIGHTS IN LBS. or KILOS			DIMENSIONS			QUANTITY	CLEARLY STATE CONTENTS OF EACH PACKAGE
	GROSS WEIGHT EACH	*LEGAL WEIGHT EACH	NET WEIGHT EACH	HEIGHT	WIDTH	LENGTH		

Reprinted with permission of Unz & Co., 190 Baldwin Ave., Jersey City, NJ 07306, USA.

Figure 4–9. Preshipment inspection worksheet.

INSPECTION/CERTIFICATION WORKSHEET

SEE REVERSE SIDE FOR INSTRUCTIONS

INSPECTIONS:

INSPECTION AGENCY	INSPECTION REQUIREMENTS	DATE	NOTES

CERTIFICATION/NOTARIZATION:

DOCUMENT (TYPE)	ISSUING PARTY	WORDING/OTHER REQUIREMENTS	DATE DOCUMENT REC'D

Form 18-400 Printed and Sold by UNZCO 190 Baldwin Ave., Jersey City, NJ 07306 • (800) 631-3098 • (201) 795-5400

UNITRAK™

Reprinted with permission of Unz & Co., 190 Baldwin Ave., Jersey City, NJ 07306, USA.

Figure 4–10. Preshipment inspection certificate.

SGS SGS Control Services Inc.

CERTIFICATE OF INSPECTION

42 Broadway
New York, N.Y. 10004
Tel. (212) 482-8700
Telex: 426974
426975
426976
Cables: Supervise

January 29, 1990

John Doe Co., Inc.
P.O. Box 789
Chicago, IL 60601

REF: 12345/CONTRACT I.K. 678

Inspection, Testweighing and Sampling were carried out at Warehouse 2D, Municipal Docks, Houston, Texas on January 26, 1990 on a shipment of 10,000 bags of Wheat Flour marked

ABC Flour Mills
Wheat Flour
Product of U.S.A.
100 lbs. net

PACKING: In polypropylene bags in good condition

WEIGHT: Testweighing of 500 bags (or 5%) selected at random, and test-taring of 5 empty bags, indicated:

SPECIMEN

Average per bag 100.5 lbs. gross
0.5 lbs. tare
100.0 lbs. net

On this basis 10,000 bags would weigh
1,005,000 lbs. gross
5,000 lbs. tare
1,000,000 lbs. or 453.597 tonnes net

SAMPLING & ANALYSIS: Representative sampling of 500 bags (or 5%) selected at random yielded 10 samples, a composite of which was analyzed by our Houston Laboratory with these results, which meet contract specifications:

(14% Moisture Basis)	
Protein	11.27
Ash	0.46%
Moisture	13.30%

LOADING: Shipment loaded aboard MV "MARY LOU," Lower Hold and Tweendeck No. 1, January 28, 1990 under our supervision.

SPECIMEN

SGS CONTROL SERVICES INC.

Member of the **SGS** Group (Société Générale de Surveillance)

ALL INSPECTIONS ARE CARRIED OUT TO THE BEST OF OUR KNOWLEDGE AND ABILITY AND OUR RESPONSIBILITY IS LIMITED TO THE EXERCISE OF REASONABLE CARE

Courtesy of SGS Government Programs Inc.

may require that an insurance policy or certificate be provided by the exporter in order to obtain payment. The exporter may receive the actual policy (see Figure 4–11) or a separate certificate (see Figure 4–12) certifying that the insurance has been issued. A sample form for presentation of loss or damage claims is shown in Figure 4–13 and a request for information from the insurance company to process a claim is shown in Figure 4–14. Under the Carriage of Goods by Sea Act shortages must be notified to the steamship line at the time of delivery and concealed damage within three days after delivery. Any lawsuit against the steamship line for loss or damage must be made within one year of delivery of the goods.

H. Dock and Warehouse Receipts

Upon completion of the inland transportation to the port of export, the inland carrier may deliver the goods to a warehouse company or to a warehouse operated by the steamship company as arranged by the freight forwarder. A dock receipt (see Figure 4–15) is often prepared by the freight forwarder on the steamship company's form and is signed by the warehouseman or agent of the steamship company upon receipt of the goods as evidence of the receipt. The inland carrier then provides a signed copy of the dock receipt to the freight forwarder as evidence that it has completed the delivery.

I. Consular Invoices

In addition to a commercial invoice, some countries, including Panama, Bolivia, Haiti, the Dominican Republic, and Honduras, also require that a consular invoice be prepared. A consular invoice is usually prepared from the information in the commercial invoice, but it must be signed by a representative of the country of destination stationed at that country's embassy or consulate located in the United States nearest the exporter. One reason for requiring such invoices is that the country of destination may deduct certain charges from the price of the goods in order to determine the value for customs duties. If the commercial invoice does not contain all of the information necessary, the foreign customs service would be unable to complete the duty assessment. The consular invoice (see Figure 4–16) lists the specific items about which that country requires information. The consul charges a fee for this service.

J. Certificates of Origin

Some countries require that goods shipped to the country be accompanied by a certificate of origin designating the place of manufacture or production of the goods. This is signed by the exporter, and, usually, a local chamber of commerce that is used to performing this service (again, for a fee) certifies to the best of its knowledge that the products are products of the country specified by the exporter. The exporter may

(Text continues on page 152.)

Figure 4–11. Marine insurance policy.

MARINE DEPARTMENT ***POLICY NO. [Policy #]***

MARINE OPEN CARGO POLICY

WASHINGTON INTERNATIONAL INSURANCE COMPANY

A CAPITAL STOCK COMPANY
1930 THOREAU DRIVE, SCHAUMBURG, IL 60173
Hereinafter called the Assurer

1. **ASSURED**

This policy does insure **[Assured]**
[Address]
[City, State, Zip]

2. **ACCOUNT**

For account of whom it may concern

3. **PAYEE**

Loss, if any, payable to Assured or order

4. **GOODS COVERED**

To cover all lawful goods and/or merchandise of every description (Under and/or On Deck) but consisting principally of **[Commodity]** and other merchandise incidental to the business of the Assured consigned and/or shipped by or to the Assured or by or to others for the Assured's account or control or in which the Assured may have an interest but excluding shipments sold on F.O.B., F.A.S., C. & F. or similar terms whereby the Assured is not obliged to furnish marine insurance and excluding shipments purchased on terms which include insurance to destination, also to cover all shipments for the account of others on which the Assured may receive instructions to insure, such instructions being given in writing prior to sailing of vessel and prior to any known or reported loss or accident. **This policy does not and is not intended to provide any legal liability coverage, except as explicitly agreed, absent a specific** endorsement to the contrary.

5. **ATTACHMENT / LIMIT OF LIABILITY**

To attach and cover for 100 per cent interest on goods and/or merchandise of every description shipped on and after **[Effective Date].**

In respect of the above stated interest, however, this policy shall not be liable for more than:

A.	**[Steamer Limit]**	by any one vessel or conveyance or in any one place at any one time;
B.	**[On Deck Limit]**	at any one time on Deck of any one vessel subject on Deck bill(s) of lading;
C.	**[Barge Limit]**	by any one barge, except as a connecting conveyance, but not exceeding
D.	**[Barge Limit]**	by any one tow;
E.	**[Air Limit]**	by any one aircraft or connecting conveyance at any one time;
F.	**[Mail Limit]**	in any one package by mail or parcel post.

Courtesy of Washington International Insurance Company.

(continues)

Figure 4–11. *(continued)*

6. **ACCUMULATION**

Should there be an accumulation of interests beyond the limits expressed in this policy by reason of any interruption of transit and/or occurrence beyond the control of the Assured, or by reason of any casualty and/or at a transshipping point and/or on a connecting steamer or conveyance, the Assurer shall hold covered such excess interest and shall be liable for the full amount at risk, (but in no event for more than twice the Policy limit which would be applicable to any one Vessel) provided notice be given to the Assurer as soon as known to the Assured.

7. **VALUATION**

Valued at amount of invoice, including all charges therein, plus any prepaid and/or advanced and/or guaranteed freight, if any, plus 10%. Goods not under invoice are valued at Sound Market Value at destination on date of shipment. Foreign currency to be converted into U.S. Dollars at rate of exchange in New York on date of invoice (shipment).

8. **CONVEYANCES**

Per iron or steel steamers, iron or steel motor vessels (but excluding all sailing vessels with or without auxiliary power), aircraft and/or air mail and/or parcel post and including connecting conveyances.
<u>NOTE:</u> *Wherever the words "ship, vessels, seaworthiness or vessel owner" appear in the policy, they are deemed to also include the words "aircraft, airworthiness and aircraft owner."*

9. **GEOGRAPHICAL LIMITS**

To be insured, lost or not lost, at and from ports and/or places in the World to ports and/or places elsewhere in the World, however, excluding domestic shipments originating and terminating within the Continental United States (meaning thereby the forty-eight (48) contiguous states and the District of Columbia) and/or Canada but including intercoastal and coastwise shipments via water, via any route, direct or via port or ports in any order, including risks of transhipment and lighterage, whether customary or otherwise.

10. **WAREHOUSE TO WAREHOUSE**

This insurance attaches from the time the goods leave the Warehouse and/or Store at the place named in the policy for the commencement of the transit and continues during the ordinary course of transit, including customary transshipment if any, until the goods are discharged overside from the overseas vessel at the final port. Thereafter the insurance continues whilst the goods are in transit and/or awaiting transit until delivered to final warehouse at the destination named in the policy or until the expiry of 15 days (or 30 days if the destination to which the goods are insured is outside the limits of the port) whichever shall first occur. The time limits referred to above to be reckoned from midnight of the day on which the discharge overside of the goods hereby insured from the overseas vessel is completed. Held covered at a premium to be arranged in the event of transhipment, if any, other than as above and/or in the event of delay in excess of the above time limits arising from circumstances beyond the control of the Assured.
<u>NOTE:</u> - *It is necessary for the Assured to give prompt notice to Assurer when they become aware of an event for which they are "held covered" and the right to such cover is dependent on compliance with this obligation.*

Figure 4–11. *(continued)*

11. MARINE EXTENSION CLAUSES

This Policy is extended to cover all shipments which become at risk hereunder in accordance with the following clauses, which supersede and override clauses #Ten (Warehouse to Warehouse) and #Thirty-One (Deviation) wherever they be contradictory or at variance.

I. This insurance attaches from the time the goods leave the warehouse at the place named in this Policy for the commencement of the transit and continues until the goods are delivered to the final warehouse at the original destination named in this Policy, or a substituted destination as provided in Clause III hereunder.

II. This insurance specially to cover the goods during
  a. deviation, delay, forced discharge, re-shipment and transshipment.
  b. any other variation of the adventure arising from the exercise of a liberty granted to the shipowner or charterer under the contract of affreightment.

III. In the event of the exercise of any liberty granted to the shipowner or charterer under the contract of affreightment whereby such contract is terminated at a port or place other than the originally insured destination, the insurance continues until the goods are sold and delivered at such port or place; or, if the goods be not sold but are forwarded to the originally insured destination or to any other destination this insurance continues until the goods have arrived at final warehouse as provided in Clause I.

IV. If while this insurance is still in force and before the expiry of 15 days from midnight of the day on which the discharge overside of the goods hereby insured from the overseas vessel at the final port of discharge is completed, the goods are re-sold (not being a sale within the terms of Clause III) and are to be forwarded to a destination other than that covered by this insurance, the goods are covered hereunder while deposited at such port of discharge until again in transit or until the expiry of the aforementioned 15 days whichever shall first occur. If a sale is effected after the expiry of the aforementioned 15 days while this insurance is still in force the protection afforded hereunder shall cease as from the time of sale.

V. Held covered at a premium to be arranged in case of change of voyage or of any omission or error in the description of the interest, vessel or voyage.

VI. This insurance shall in no case be deemed to extend to cover loss, damage or expense proximately caused by delay or inherent vice or nature of the subject matter insured.

VII. It is a condition of this insurance that there shall be no interruption or suspension of transit unless due to circumstances beyond the control of the Assured.

Nothing in the foregoing shall be construed as overruling the F.C. & S. Clause or as extending this insurance to cover any risks of war or consequences of hostilities.

12. SOUTH AMERICAN CLAUSE

With respect to shipments insured in U.S. Currency and shipped to South America, notwithstanding anything contained elsewhere herein to the contrary (particularly the Warehouse to Warehouse and Marine Extension Clauses), the insurance provided hereunder shall continue to cover for sixty (60) days

(continues)

Figure 4–11. *(continued)*

(ninety (90) days on shipments via the Magdalena River) after completion of discharge of the overseas vessel at port of destination or until the goods are delivered to the final warehouse at destination, whichever may first occur, and shall then terminate.

The time limit referred to above to be reckoned from midnight of the day on which the discharge of the overseas vessel is completed.

13. AVERAGE TERMS AND CONDITIONS

A. UNDER DECK SHIPMENTS

All goods and/or merchandise shipped except while On Deck of ocean vessel subject to an On Deck bill of lading and except as may be hereinafter especially provided, are insured:

Warranted free from Particular Average unless the vessel or craft be stranded, sunk or burnt, but notwithstanding this warranty this Assurer is to pay any loss of or damage to the interest insured which may reasonably be attributed to fire, collision or contact of the vessel and/or craft and/or conveyance with any external substance (ice included) other than water, or to discharge of cargo at port of distress. The foregoing warranty, however, shall not apply where broader terms of Average are provided for hereinafter.

Broader Terms:

Against all risks of physical loss or damage from any external cause, irrespective of percentage, but excepting those risks as are excluded by Clause Number 26 (F.C. & S., Nuclear Exclusion and S.R.& CC.), of this Policy.

B. ON DECK SHIPMENTS

All goods and/or merchandise shipped while On Deck of ocean vessel subject to an On Deck bill of lading are insured:

Free of Particular Average unless caused by the vessel and/or interest insured being stranded, sunk, burnt, on fire or in collision with another ship or vessel or with ice or with any substance other than water, but liable for jettison and/or washing overboard, irrespective of percentage. The foregoing clause however, shall not apply where broader terms of Average are provided for herein.

C. All goods and/or merchandise shipped on board the ocean vessel in containers and/or vans and/or lighters are insured subject to the provisions of this Policy applying to Under Deck shipments, provided such goods are subject to an Under Deck or an optional Under Deck/On Deck bill of lading.

Figure 4–11. *(continued)*

14. SHORE COVERAGE

Including while on docks, wharves or elsewhere on shore and/or during land transportation, risks of collision, derailment, fire, lightning, sprinkler leakage, wind, hail, flood, earthquake, landslide, volcanic eruption, aircraft, objects falling from aircraft, the rising of navigable waters, or any accident to the conveyance and/or collapse and/or subsidence of docks and/or structures, and to pay loss or damage caused thereby, even though the insurance be otherwise F.P.A.

15. CRAFT

Including risks of craft to and from the vessel; each lighter, craft or conveyance to be considered as if separately insured. Also to cover any special or supplementary lighterage at an additional premium if required. The Assured is not to be prejudiced by any agreement exempting lightermen from liability.

16. MACHINERY

On shipments of machinery or other manufactured products, consisting when complete for sale or use of several parts, the liability of the Assurer shall be only for the proportion of the insured value of the part or parts lost or damaged, or, at Assured's option, the cost and expense of replacing or duplicating the lost or damaged part or parts, and/or the repairing of the machine or product; but in no event shall the Assurer be liable for more than the insured value of the complete machine or product.

17. FULL VALUE REPORTING

If the full value at risk exceeds the limit of liability provided by this Policy or any endorsement attached hereto, the Assured shall nevertheless report the full amount at risk to the Assurer and shall pay full premium thereon. Acceptance of such reports and premiums by the Assurer shall not alter or increase the limit of liability of the Assurer, but the Assurer shall be liable for the full amount of covered loss up to but not exceeding the applicable limit of liability.

SPECIMEN

18. ILLICIT TRADE

Warranted free from any charge, expense, damage or loss which may arise in consequence of a seizure or detention for or on account of any illicit or prohibited trade or any trade in articles contraband of war or in violation of any port rules or regulations.

19. DUTY

This insurance also covers, subject to Policy terms of average, the risk of partial loss by reason of perils insured against on the duties imposed on goods imported into the United States and insured hereunder, it being understood and agreed, however, that when the risk upon the goods continues beyond the time of landing from the overseas vessel, the increased value, consequent upon the payment of such duties, shall attach as an additional insurance upon the goods from the time such duty is paid or becomes due, to the extent of the amounts thereof actually paid or payable.

Any limit of insurance expressed in this Policy shall be applied separately to such increased value.

The Assured warrants that on all risks insured hereunder a separate amount shall be reported sufficient to cover the said duty, upon which the rate of premium shall be an agreed percentage of the merchandise rate.

(continues)

Figure 4–11. *(continued)*

The Assured will, in all cases, use reasonable efforts to obtain abatement or refund of duties paid or claimed in respect of goods lost, damaged or destroyed. The Assured consents to permit Assurer or its representatives at Assurer's expense to file any claims in the name of the Assured with U.S. Customs which Assurer deems necessary for the recovery of duties reimbursed by the Assurer to the Assured. All recoveries based on such claims shall accrue to the benefit of the Assurer and shall be remitted to the Assurer promptly upon receipt from Customs by the Assured. It is further agreed that the Assured shall, when the Assurer so elects, surrender the merchandise to the customs authorities and recover duties thereon as provided by law, in which event the claim under this Policy shall be only for a total loss of the merchandise so surrendered and expenses.

This insurance on duty and/or increased value shall terminate at the end of the import movement covered under this Policy (including the Warehouse to Warehouse and/or Marine Extension Clauses incorporated therein), but nothing contained in these clauses shall alter or affect any coverage granted elsewhere in the Policy during the storage or transit subsequent thereto.

20. RETURNED / REFUSED SHIPMENTS

This Policy is extended to cover, at Policy terms and conditions, shipments of return goods which may have been refused at time of delivery and returned by the consignee and/or consignees and which have been continuously covered hereunder. Shipments returned to the Assured by consignee shall be subject to the same terms, conditions and rate under which such shipments were insured under this Policy while in transit to such consignees.

21. FUMIGATION

In the event that any vessel, conveyance, wharf, warehouse or premises are fumigated by order of properly consitituted authority and loss or damage to goods and/or merchandise insured hereunder results therefrom, this Assurer will indemnify the Assured for such loss or damage and the Assured hereby agrees to subrogate to underwriters any recourse that they have for recovery of such loss or damage from others.

22. LABELS

In case of damage from perils insured against affecting labels, the loss to be limited to an amount sufficient to pay the cost of new labels and the cost of relabeling and reconditioning the goods, provided same amounts to a claim under the terms of the Policy.

23. BRANDS

In case of damage to property bearing a Brand or Trade Mark, or sale of which carries or implies a guarantee of the supplier or Assured, the salvage value of such damaged property shall be determined after the removal of all Brands or Trade Marks.

24. EXPLOSION

The risks covered by this Policy are to include loss, damage or expense resulting from explosion, howsoever and wheresoever occurring, irrespective of percentage, whether the insurance be F.P.A. or otherwise, but excluding the risks excepted by the F.C. & S., Nuclear Exclusion and Strikes, Riots and Civil Commotions clauses of this Policy and further excluding explosion caused by inherent vice or nature of the subject matter insured or by the personal negligence or act of the Assured.

Figure 4–11. *(continued)*

25. LANDING / WAREHOUSING

Notwithstanding any average warranty contained herein, the Assurer agrees to pay landing, warehousing, forwarding or other expenses and/or particular charges should same be incurred, as well as any partial loss arising from transshipment. Also to pay the insured value of any package, piece or unit totally lost in loading, transshipment and/or discharge.

THE FOLLOWING WARRANTIES SET FORTH IN CLAUSE 26, SHALL BE PARAMOUNT AND SHALL NOT BE MODIFIED OR SUPERSEDED BY ANY OTHER PROVISION INCLUDED HEREIN OR STAMPED OR ENDORSED HEREON UNLESS SUCH OTHER PROVISION REFERS TO RISKS EXCLUDED BY SUCH WARRANTIES AND EXPRESSLY ASSUMES THE SAID RISKS.

26. I. F.C. & S.

Notwithstanding anything herein contained to the contrary, this insurance is warranted free from capture, seizure, arrest, restraint, detainment, confiscation, preemption, requisition or nationalization, and the consequences thereof or any attempt thereat, whether in time of peace or war and whether lawful or otherwise; also warranted free, whether in time of peace or war, from all loss, damage or expense caused by any weapon of war employing atomic or nuclear fission and/or fusion or other reaction or radioactive force or matter or by any mine or torpedo, also warranted free from all consequences of hostilities or warlike operations (whether there be a declaration of war or not), but this warranty shall not exclude collision or contact with aircraft, rockets or similar missiles or with any fixed or floating object (other than a mine or torpedo), stranding, heavy weather, fire or explosion unless caused directly (and independently of the nature of the voyage or service which the vessel concerned or, in the case of a collision, any other vessel involved therein, is performing) by a hostile act by or against a belligerent power; and for the purposes of this warranty "power" includes any authority maintaining naval, military or air forces in association with a power.

Further warranted free from the consequences of civil war, revolution, rebellion, insurrection, or civil strife arising therefrom, or piracy.

II. NUCLEAR EXCLUSION

Notwithstanding anything to the contrary herein, it is hereby understood and agreed that this Policy shall not apply to any loss, damage or expense due to or arising out of, whether directly or indirectly, nuclear reaction, radiation, or radioactive contamination, regardless of how it was caused. However, subject to all provisions of this Policy, if this Policy insures against fire, then direct physical damage to the property insured located within the United States or Puerto Rico by fire directly caused by the above excluded perils, is insured, provided that the nuclear reaction, radiation, or radioactive contamination was not caused, whether directly or indirectly, by any of the perils excluded by the F.C. & S. Warranty of this Policy.

Nothing in this clause shall be construed to cover any loss, damage, liability or expense caused by nuclear reaction, radiation or radioactive contamination arising directly or indirectly from the fire mentioned above.

III. S.R. & C.C.

Notwithstanding anything herein to the contrary, this insurance is warranted free from loss, damage or expense caused by or resulting from:

(continues)

Figure 4–11. *(continued)*

(a) strikes, lockouts, labor disturbances, riots, civil commotions, or the acts of any person or persons taking part in any such occurrences or disorders,

(b) vandalism, sabotage or malicious act, which shall be deemed also to encompass the act or acts of one or more persons, whether or not agents of a sovereign power, carried out for political, terroristic or ideological purposes and whether any loss, damage or expenses resulting therefrom is accidental or intentional.

27. S.R. & C.C. (FORM NO. TEN)

This insurance also covers:

(1) Physical loss of or damage to the property insured directly caused by strikers, locked-out workmen, or persons taking part in labor disturbances or riots or civil commotions; and,

(2) Physical loss of or damage to the property insured directly caused by vandalism, sabotage or malicious acts, which shall be deemed also to encompass the act or acts of one or more person, whether or not agents of a sovereign power, carried out for political, terroristic or ideological purposes, and whether any loss, damage or expense resulting therefrom is accidental or intentional; PROVIDED that any claim to be recoverable under this sub-section (2) be not excluded by the F.C. & S. Warranty in this Policy.

While the property insured is at risk under the terms and conditions of this insurance within the United States of America, the Commonwealth of Puerto Rico, the U.S. Virgin Islands and Canada, this insurance is extended to cover physical loss of or damage to the property insured directly caused by acts committed by an agent of any government, party or faction engaged in war, hostilities or other warlike operations, provided such agent is acting secretly and not in connection with any operation of military or naval armed forces in the country where the described property is situated.

Nothing in this clause shall be construed to cover any loss, damage or expense directly or indirectly arising from, contributed to or caused by any of the following, whether due to a peril insured against or otherwise:

(a) Change in temperature or humidity;
(b) The absence, shortage, or withholding of power, fuel, or labor of any description whatsoever during any strike, lockout, labor disturbance, riot or civil commotion;
(c) Loss of market or loss, damage or deterioration arising from delay;
(d) Hostilities, warlike operations, civil war, revolution, rebellion or insurrection, or civil strife arising therefrom, except to the limited extent that the acts of certain agents acting secretly have been expressly covered above; or,
(e) Nuclear reaction, radiation or radioactive contamination.

The Assured agrees to report all shipments attaching under this cover and to pay premiums therefore at the rates established by the Assurer from time to time.

This clause may be canceled by either party upon forty-eight hours written, telegraphic or telefaxed notice to the other party, but such cancellation shall not affect any risks which have already attached hereunder.

Figure 4–11. *(continued)*

28. DELAY

Warranted free of claim for loss of market or for loss, damage or deterioration arising from delay, whether such delay be caused by a peril insured against or otherwise, unless the risk of delay is expressly assumed in writing hereon.

29. BOTH TO BLAME

Where goods are shipped under a bill of lading containing the so-called "Both to Blame Collision" clause the Assurer agrees, as to all losses covered by this insurance, to indemnify the Assured for any amount (up to the amount insured) which the Assured may be legally bound to pay to the shipowners under such clause. In the event that such liability is asserted the Assured agrees to notify the Assurer who shall have the right, at its own cost and expense, to defend the Assured against such claim.

30. INCHMAREE

This insurance is also specially to cover any loss of or damage to the interest insured hereunder, through the bursting of boilers, breakage of shafts or through any latent defect in the machinery hull or appurtenances, or from faults or errors in the navigation and/or management of the vessel by the Master, Mariners, Mates, Engineers or Pilots; provided, however, that this clause shall not be construed as covering loss arising out of delay, deterioration or loss of market, unless otherwise provided elsewhere herein.

31. DEVIATION

In case of short shipment in whole or in part by the vessel reported for insurance hereunder, or if the goods be transshipped by another vessel or vessels, or be carried beyond or discharged short of destination, or in the event of deviation, or change of voyage, or any interruption or other variation of the voyage or risk beyond the control of the Assured or by reason of the exercise of any liberty granted the shipowner or charterer under the contract of affreightment, this insurance shall nevertheless cover the goods until arrival at the final destination named in the declaration or certificate of insurance or until the subject matter insured is no longer at the risk of the Assured, whichever may first occur, provided prompt notice be given the Assurer when such facts are known to the Assured and additional premium be paid if required. No additional risks (whether of delay or of any other description) are insured under this clause, which is intended merely to continue the insurance in force against the same risks named elsewhere in the Policy, and if the risks of war, strikes, riots or civil commotions, or any of these risks, are insured against, the insurance against such risks shall not be extended by this clause to cover contrary to any express provision of such insurance.

32. BILL OF LADING, ETC.

The Assured is not to be prejudiced by the presence of the negligence clause and/or latent defect clause in the bills of lading and/or charter party and/or contract of affreightment. The seaworthiness of the vessel and/or craft as between the Assured and Assurer is hereby admitted, and the Assurer agrees that in the event unseaworthiness or a wrongful act or misconduct of shipowner, charterer, their agents or servants, shall directly or indirectly, cause loss or damage to the cargo insured by sinking, stranding, fire, explosion, contact with seawater, or by any other cause of the nature of any of the risks assumed

(continues)

Figure 4–11. *(continued)*

in the Policy, the Assurer will (subject to the terms of average and other conditions of the Policy) pay to an innocent Assured the resulting loss. With leave to sail with or without pilots, and to tow and assist vessels or craft in all situations and to be towed.

Note: - *Wherever the terms seaworthiness, vessel and/or craft, and shipowner, are used in this Policy, they shall be construed also to include airworthiness, aircraft, and aircraft owner.*

33. INSOLVENCY

In no case shall this insurance cover loss, damage or expense arising from insolvency or financial default of the owners, managers, charterers or operators of the carrying conveyance should the Assured be aware that such insolvency or financial default could prevent the normal execution of the voyage.

34. GENERAL AVERAGE

General Average, Salvage and Special Charges as per foreign custom, payable according to foreign statement, and/or per York-Antwerp Rules and/or in accordance with the contract of affreightment, if and as required; or failing any provision in or thereby no contract of affreightment, payable in accordance with the Laws and Usages of the Port of New York.

35. PERILS

Touching the adventures and perils which the Assurer is contented to bear and takes upon itself, they are of the seas, fires, assailing thieves, jettisons, barratry of the master and mariners, and all other like perils, losses and misfortunes that have or shall come to the hurt, detriment or damage of the said goods and merchandise, or any part thereof except as may be otherwise provided for herein or endorsed hereon.

36. SUE & LABOR

In case of any loss or misfortune, it shall be lawful and necessary to and for the Assured, his or their factors, servants and assigns, to sue, labor and travel for in and about the defense, safeguard and recovery of the said goods and merchandise, or any part thereof without prejudice to this insurance, to the charges whereof the said Assurer will contribute according to the rate and quantity of the sum herein insured; nor shall the acts of the Assured or Assurers, in recovering, saving and preserving the property insured, in case of disaster, be considered a waiver or an acceptance of abandonment.

37. CARRIER CLAUSE

Warranted that this insurance shall not inure, directly or indirectly, to the benefit of any carrier or bailee.

38. CONSTRUCTIVE TOTAL LOSS

No recovery for a Constructive Total Loss shall be had hereunder unless the property insured is reasonably abandoned on account of its actual total loss appearing to be unavoidable, or because it cannot be preserved from actual total loss without an expenditure which would exceed its value when the expenditure has been incurred.

Figure 4–11. *(continued)*

39. PARTIAL LOSS

In all cases of damage caused by perils insured against, the loss shall as far as practicable, be ascertained by a separation and a sale or appraisement of the damaged portion only of the contents of the packages so damaged and not otherwise.

40. ASSIGNMENT VOID

Warranted by the Assured that the assignment of this Policy or any insurable interest therein or the subrogation of any right thereunder to any party without the prior written consent of the Assurer shall render the insurance affected by such assignment or subrogation void.

41. REPORT OF LOSS

Any loss or damage to the property hereby insured must be promptly reported to the Assurer or to the nearest Agent of the Assurer and such Agent must be represented on all surveys and must approve proofs of loss and bills of expense. If there be no such Agent at or near the port or place where the loss is discovered or the expenses incurred, then such report must be made to the nearest representative of the American Institute of Marine Underwriters or to Lloyds Agents, and his approval obtained as above. Failure to report loss or damage promptly and to file such proof of loss shall invalidate any claim under this Policy.

42. CLAIM AGAINST THIRD PARTIES

In the event of any loss of or damage to property insured hereunder, the Assured shall make claim immediately in writing against the carrier(s), bailee(s) or others involved.

43. PAYMENT OF LOSS

In case of loss, such loss to be paid within thirty days after interest in the property insured and loss thereto has been established (the amount of the premium if unpaid being first deducted). If settlement is required in a currency other than that of the United States, the rate of exchange will be that in effect on the date the claim is settled. The Assured and/or Certificate Holder agree to be examined under oath if so requested by the Assurer.

44. SUBROGATION AND IMPAIRMENT OF RECOVERY

It is a condition of this insurance that if the Assured or his or their assigns have entered or shall enter into any special agreement whereby any carrier or bailee is released from its common law or statutory liability for any loss, or have or shall have waived, compromised, settled or otherwise impaired any right of claim against a third party to which the Assurer would be subrogated upon payment of a loss without prior agreement of the Assurer and endorsement hereon, the Assurer shall be free from liability with respect to such loss but its right to retain or recover the premium shall not be affected.

It is a further condition of this insurance that upon payment of any loss the Assurer shall be subrogated to all rights and claims against third parties arising out of such loss. The Assured shall permit suit to be brought in its name but at the expense of this Assurer, and the Assured further agrees to render all reasonable assistance in the prosecution of said suit or suits. All recoveries effected from third parties, whether received in the first instance by the Assured or this Assurer, shall be the property of the insurance company up to the amount paid under this policy.

(continues)

Figure 4–11. *(continued)*

45. TIME FOR SUIT

No suit or action against this Assurer for the recovery of any claim by virtue of this insurance shall be sustained in any Court of Law or Equity unless commenced within one (1) year from the time the loss occurred or, if such limitation is not valid by the law of the place where the Policy is issued, within the shortest contractual period of limitation permitted by such law.

46. ATTACHMENT AND CONTINUANCE

This Policy and the coverage granted hereunder is to be deemed continuous and to attach and cover in respect of all merchandise and/or goods shipped on and after the attachment date named in Clause 5 hereof, and is to continue in force thereafter until canceled, as hereinafter provided in Clause 55, or otherwise voided by reason of breach of warranty, misrepresentation or concealment. Cancellation, however, shall not prejudice the insurance in effect in respect of shipments on which the risk hereunder attaches prior to the termination of this Policy by cancellation.

47. ISSUANCE OF CERTIFICATES

Privilege is hereby granted the Assured to countersign the Assurer's certificates or policies of insurance for any or all risks covered hereunder, and in consideration thereof the Assured warrants that no certificate or Policy will be issued with terms thereon varying from the conditions of this Policy and/or any written instructions that are or may be given by the Assurer and/or its agent from time to time. The Assured hereby agrees to furnish a copy of each such completed certificate or Policy to

[Broker]

for transmission to the Assurer as soon after completion as practicable.

The Original and Duplicate (and other negotiable copy, if any) of each spoiled or voided certificate or Policy are to be returned to the Assurer.

48. DECLARATIONS

The Assured by acceptance of this Policy warrants and agrees that all shipments coming within the terms hereof shall be reported to

[Broker]

as soon as known to the Assured and amounts declared as soon as ascertained, and failure to make such reports shall render this Policy null and void if this Assurer shall so elect. The Assurer and/or its agents shall be permitted to examine the books, accounts and records of the Assured for the purpose of tabulating and verifying all shipments in respect of which insurance is provided hereunder.

49. ERRORS AND OMISSIONS

This Policy shall not be prejudiced by any unintentional delay or omission in the reporting of shipments hereunder or any unintentional error in the amount or description of the interest, vessel or voyage, or if the subject matter of the insurance be shipped by any other vessel, if notice be given this Assurer as soon as practicable after said facts become known to the Assured and deficiency of premium, if any, made good.

Figure 4–11. *(continued)*

50. PREMIUM

Premium in consideration for this insurance is payable monthly or on demand, at rates as agreed, in funds current in the United States, on all shipments coming within the scope of this Policy, reported or not.

51. INSPECTION OF RECORDS

This Assurer shall have the privilege at any reasonable time either before or within one (1) year after cancellation of this Policy, to inspect the records of the Assured as respects shipments coming within the terms of this Policy.

52. MISREPRESENTATION AND FRAUD

This Policy shall be void if the Assured has concealed, failed to disclose or misrepresented any material fact or circumstance concerning this insurance or the subject thereof or in case of any fraud, attempted fraud or false swearing by the Assured touching any matter relating to this insurance or the subject thereof, whether before or after a loss.

53. DELIBERATE DAMAGE/POLLUTION HAZARD

This Policy also covers, but only while the property insured is on board a waterborne conveyance, loss of or damage to said property directly caused by governmental authorities acting for the public welfare to prevent or mitigate a pollution hazard or threat thereof, provided that the accident or occurrence creating the situation which required such governmental action would have resulted in a recoverable claim under the Policy (subject to all of its terms, conditions and warranties) if the property insured would have sustained physical loss or damage as a direct result of such accident or occurrence.

54. OTHER INSURANCE

In case the Assured or others shall have effected any other ocean marine insurance directly or indirectly upon the property insured, prior in day of date to the time of attachment of any specific risks hereunder, the Assurer shall be liable only for so much as the amount of such prior insurance may be deficient toward fully covering the property hereby insured, and in this event shall return the premium upon so much of the sum by them insured as they shall by such prior insurance, be exonerated. In case of any other Ocean Marine insurance upon the said property subsequent in day of date to the time of attachment of any specific risk hereunder, the Assurer shall nevertheless be liable for the full extent of the sum by them insured upon the said risk without right to claim contribution from such subsequent insurance.

Other Ocean Marine insurance upon the property insured hereunder, dated the same day as the time of attachment of any specific risk hereunder shall be deemed simultaneous herewith and the Assurer shall not be liable for more than a ratable contribution in the proportion that the sum insured by the Assurer bears to the aggregate of such simultaneous insurance.

This insurance shall in all cases be null and void as concerns loss or damage covered, or which would be covered in the absence of this Policy, by any fire, inland marine, sprinkler leakage, burglary, or any other form of insurance (except Ocean Marine insurance) whether prior, simultaneous, or subsequent in date hereto.

(continues)

Figure 4–11. *(continued)*

55. CANCELLATION

This Policy is to be deemed continuous and to cover all shipments as herein provided until canceled by either party giving the other thirty (30) days written notice to that effect, but such cancellation shall not affect any risk on which this insurance has attached prior to the effective date of such notice.

Notwithstanding the foregoing notice period, however, the Assurer may effect immediate cancellation by giving written notice thereof at any time when premiums have been due and unpaid for a period of sixty (60) days or more.

56. NOTICE OF CHANGE (BROKERS)

It is a condition of this Policy, and it is hereby agreed, that the Assured's brokers,

[Broker]

or any substituted brokers, shall be deemed to be exclusively the agents of the Assured and not of the Assurer. Any notice given or mailed by or on behalf of the Assurer to the said brokers in connection with or affecting this insurance, or its cancellation shall be deemed to have been delivered to the Assured.

In witness whereof, this Assurer has caused this Policy to be executed and attested, but this Policy shall not be valid unless countersigned below by a duly authorized representative of this Assurer.

Figure 4–11. *(continued)*

Effective Date: [Eff Date] **Endorsement No.** [End #]

CONSOLIDATION/DECONSOLIDATION

It is hereby understood and agreed that notwithstanding anything contained elsewhere herein to the contrary (particularly in the Warehouse to Warehouse and Marine Extension Clauses), this Policy is extended, subject to the terms and conditions contained elsewhere herein, to cover the property insured hereunder whenever said property is temporarily interrupted from due course of transit whether prior to loading and/or after discharge from carrying conveyance for the purpose of packing, repacking, consolidation, deconsolidation, containerization, decontainerization, distribution or redistribution on or at the premises of Freight Forwarders, Consolidators, Truckers, Warehousemen or others , anywhere in the world for a period of not exceeding thirty (30) days after receipt of the insured merchandise at such premises. Held covered in the event of delay in excess of the above time limit subject to approval of these Assurers at additional premium to be agreed.

These Assurers shall not be held liable under the terms of this endorsement for more than **[Limit]** at any one location, unless otherwise agreed upon.

Nothing contained in this endorsement shall be construed to alter any warranty contained elsewhere in this Policy, or modify or supersede any other endorsements contained in this Policy (particularly any endorsements pertaining to warehousing, processing or any storage risks).

All other terms and conditions remaining unchanged.

Endorsement is to be attached to and made a part of Open Policy No. **[Policy No.]**

of the **Washington International Insurance Company**

issued to: **[Assured]**

By ______________________________
Authorized Signature

Date July 16, 1996

(continues)

Figure 4–11. *(continued)*

MARINE DEPARTMENT ***POLICY NO. W[Policy #]***

WAR RISK ONLY OPEN POLICY
American Institute

WASHINGTON INTERNATIONAL INSURANCE COMPANY
A CAPITAL STOCK COMPANY
1930 THOREAU DRIVE, SCHAUMBURG, IL 60173
Hereinafter called the Assurer

[Effective Date]

THIS POLICY OF INSURANCE WITNESSETH, that in consideration of premiums as agreed to be paid, the Assurer does make insurance and cause

[Assured]

to be insured, lost or not lost, for account of whom it may concern, against Risks only, in accordance with the terms and conditions hereinafter set forth.

This Company shall not be liable hereunder for more than **[Limit]** by any one vessel.

In cases where the total value(s) at risk on any one vessel exceed(s) the limit of liability as set forth in this Policy the Assured agrees, nevertheless, to report to the Assurer full value(s) at risk and to pay premium thereon at the agreed rates. The Assured further agrees that acceptance of such reports and premium by the Assurer shall not serve to revoke or to overrule the limit of liability set forth in this Policy; however, subject to the limit of liability, the Assurer in accepting these reports does agree to pay partial losses covered by this Policy without reduction by reason of any coinsurance which otherwise may have existed in the absence of this special agreement.

Subject to the provisions of Clause 4 of this Policy, should there by an accumulation of interests exceeding the above limit of liability by reason of any interruption of transit beyond the control of the Assured or by reason of any casualty, and/or after the interest have been discharged from the incoming overseas Vessel at an intermediate port or place for on-carriage from that or any other port of place by another overseas Vessel, and/or on the on-carrying overseas Vessel, this Policy shall attach for the full amount at risk (but in no event for more than twice the Policy limit which would be applicable to any one Vessel) provided written notice be given to this Assurer as soon as known to the Assured.

This Policy shall cover only those shipments which are insurance against marine risks under Policy No. **[Policy #]** of this Company, it being agreed that the description of such shipment, the valuations thereof, the voyage, the designation of the overseas Vessel (which shall be construed to include aircraft if included under the marine policy) on which the goods are to be carried and the ports and/or places of loading and discharge, as reported under the said policy against marine risks, shall be deemed incorporated herein. Notwithstanding the foregoing, this policy shall not cover purely domestic shipments by air between points in the United States of America (excluding Alaska and Hawaii).

Any loss payable hereunder shall be payable in funds current in the United States to the order of Assured or Order thirty days after full proofs of loss and proofs of interest have been filed with the Assurer.

SPECIMEN

Figure 4–11. *(continued)*

1. (a) This insurance is only against the risks of capture, seizure, destruction or damage by men-of-war, piracy, takings at sea, arrests, restraints, detainments and other warlike operations and acts of kings, princes and peoples in prosecution of hostilities or in the application of sanctions under international agreements, whether before or after declaration of war and whether by a belligerent or otherwise, including factions engaged in civil war, revolution, rebellion or insurrection, or civil strife arising therefrom; the imposition of martial law, military or usurped power, and including the risks of aerial bombardment, floating or stationary mines and stray or derelict torpedoes. Warranted not to abandon (on any ground other than physical damage to ship or cargo) until after condemnation of the property insured.

(b) This insurance also covers, but only while the property insured is on board a waterborne conveyance, loss of or damage to said property directly caused by governmental authorities action for the public welfare to prevent or mitigate a pollution hazard or threat thereof, provided that the accident or occurrence creating the situation which required such governmental action would have resulted in a recoverable claim under this Policy (subject to all of its terms, conditions and warranties) if the property insured would have sustained physical loss or damage as a direct result of such accident or occurrence.

2. Warranted free from any claim based upon loss of, or frustration of, the insured voyage or adventure caused by arrests, restraints or detainments.

3. This insurance does not cover any loss, damage, or expense directly or indirectly arising from, contributed to, or caused by any of the following, whether due to a peril insured against or otherwise:

(a) commandeering, preemption, requisition or nationalization by the government (defacto or otherwise) of the country to or from which the goods are insured.
(b) Seizure or destruction under quarantine, environmental or customs regulations.
(c) Delay, deterioration and/or loss of market.
(d) Nuclear reaction, radiation or radioactive contamination, regardless of how it was caused.

4. (a) This insurance against the risks enumerated in clause 1, except the risks of floating or stationary mines and stray or derelict torpedoes, floating or submerged referred to in (b) below, shall not attach to the interest hereby insured or to any part thereof:

(I) prior to being on board an overseas Vessel (for the purpose of this Clause 4 an overseas Vessel shall be deemed to mean a Vessel carrying the interest from one port or place to another where such voyage involves a sea passage by that Vessel);
(ii) After being discharged overside from an overseas Vessel at the intended port or place of discharge,

or

after the expiry of 15 days from midnight of the day of arrival of the overseas Vessel at the intended port or place of discharge, whichever shall first occur;
(iii) after the expiry of 15 days from midnight of the day of arrival of the overseas Vessel at an intermediate port or place to discharge the interest for on-carriage from that or any other port or place by another overseas Vessel, but shall reattach as the interest is loaded on the on-carrying overseas Vessel. During the said period of 15 days the insurance remains in force whether the interest is awaiting transit or in transit between the overseas Vessels.
(iv) For the purpose of this Clause 4 arrival at the intended port or place of discharge shall be deemed to mean that time when the overseas Vessel first berths, anchors, moors or is secured in an area subject to regulation by the authorities of such port or place.

(continues)

SPECIMEN

Figure 4–11. *(continued)*

(b) The insurance against the risks of floating or stationary mines and stray or derelict torpedoes, floating or submerged, attaches as the interest hereby insured is first loaded on a lighter, craft or vessel after leaving the warehouse at point of shipment in transit for the destination declared hereunder and ceases to attach as the interest is finally landed from the vessel, craft or lighter prior to delivery to warehouse at such destination.

(c) If the contract of affreightment is terminated at a port or place other than the destination named therein such port or place shall be deemed the intended port or place of discharge for the purpose of this Clause 4.

(d) Shipments by mail, if covered by this Policy are insured continuously from the time of leaving the sender's premises until delivered to the place of address.

(e) Shipments by air (other than air mail) if covered by this Policy are insured subject to the same terms and conditions as shipments by overseas Vessel.

(f) It is a condition of this insurance that the Assured shall act with reasonable dispatch in all circumstances within their control.

(g) If anything contained in this Policy shall be inconsistent with this Clause 4 it shall to the extent of such inconsistency by null and void.

5. This insurance shall not be vitiated by deviation, over carriage, change of voyage, or by any error or unintentional omission in the description of interest, vessel or voyage provided the same be communicated to the Assurer as soon as known to the Assured and an additional premium paid if required.

6. And in case of any loss or misfortune, it shall be lawful and necessary to and for the Assured his or their factors, servants and assigns, to sue, labor and travel for, in and about the defense, safeguard and recovery of said goods, and merchandises, or any part thereof, without prejudice to this insurance; nor shall the acts of the Assured or Assurers, in recovering, saving and preserving the property insured, in case of disaster, be considered a waiver or an acceptance of an abandonment; and to the charges whereof, the said Assurers will contribute according to the rate and quantity of the sum hereby insured.

7. General Average and Salvage Charges payable according to United States laws and usage and/or as per Foreign Statement and/or York-Antwerp Rules (as prescribed in whole or in part) if in accordance with the Contract of Affreightment.

8. It is agreed that the reports of shipments made under the Policy against marine risks mentioned above shall be deemed to be reports under this Policy also, and the Assured agrees to pay premiums on all shipments under this Policy at the war risk rates of the Assurer as fixed from time to time.

9. No claim shall be payable hereunder which arises from collision, contact with any fixed or floating object (other than a mine or torpedo), stranding, heavy weather or fire unless caused directly (and independently of the nature of the voyage or service which the Vessel concerned or, in the case of collision, any other Vessel involved therein, is performing) by a hostile act by or against a belligerent power; and for the purpose of this paragraph "power" includes any authority maintaining naval, military or air forces in association with a power.

10. No recovery for a Constructive Total Loss shall be had hereunder unless the property insured is reasonably abandoned on account of its actual total loss appearing to be unavoidable, or because it cannot be preserved from actual total loss without an expenditure which would exceed its value if the expenditure had been incurred.

Figure 4–11. *(continued)*

11. It is agreed that this Policy is a separate and wholly independent contract and is not subject to any terms or conditions of the Policy against marine risks above mentioned (whether physically attached thereto or not) except as such terms or conditions shall have been expressly incorporated herein by reference.

12. This insurance may be canceled by either part upon forty-eight hours written, telegraphic or telefaxed notice to the other party, but such cancellation shall not affect any shipment on which this insurance has attached under the terms of Clause 4 hereof prior to the effective date of such notice. Shipments on which this insurance has not so attached but for which, prior to the effective date of such notice, bills of ladings have been issued and (in the case of exports) Certificates or special policies have been issued and negotiated, shall be covered from the time of loading on the overseas Vessel, as provided in Clause , at the rates of the Assurer, provided that, prior to said effective date, such shipments were at the risk of the Assured and were covered under the said Policy against marine risks.

In the event of loss which may give rise to a claim under this Policy, prompt notice shall be given to this Company.

In witness whereof, this Assurer has caused this policy to be executed and attested, but this policy shall not valid unless countersigned below by a duly authorized representative of this Assurer.

request the freight forwarder to ascertain and advise it whether a certificate of origin is required, but prior thereto, the exporter should check with the buyer for a list of all documents required to make customs entry in the country of destination. Certificates of origin must be distinguished from country of origin marking. Many countries require that the products themselves and the labels on the packages specify the country of origin (see discussion in Chapter 2, Section R). The country of origin certificate may be in addition to or in lieu of that requirement. (A generic sample, to be executed by a local chamber of commerce, is shown in Figure 4–17.)

An important certificate of origin is the one required under the recently concluded North American Free Trade Agreement (NAFTA). NAFTA contains product-specific country of origin criteria which must be met to qualify for reduced duty treatment on

(*Text continues on page 162.*)

Figure 4–12. Marine insurance certificate.

$______________
(sum insured)

CERTIFICATE OF MARINE INSURANCE

No. 97434

WASHINGTON INTERNATIONAL INSURANCE COMPANY

1930 THOREAU DRIVE, SCHAUMBURG, IL. 60173

This is to Certify, *That on the* *day of* *19* *this Company*

insured under Policy No. *made for*

for the sum of *Dollars,*

on

Valued at sum insured. Shipped on board the S/S or M/S *and/or following steamer or steamers*

at and from (Initial Point of Shipment) *via* (Port of Shipment)

to (Port of Places of Destination) *and it is understood and agreed, that in case of loss, the same*

is payable to the order of *on surrender of the Certificate which conveys the right of collecting any such loss as fully as if the property were covered by a special policy direct to the holder hereof, and free from any liability for unpaid premiums. This certificate is subject to all the terms of the open policy, provided however, that the rights of a bona fide holder of this certificate for value shall not be prejudiced by any terms of the open policy which are in conflict with the terms of this certificate.*

SPECIAL CONDITIONS

NEW MERCHANDISE shipped subject to an UNDER DECK bill of lading insured–

Against all risks of physical loss or damage from any external cause, irrespective of percentage, excepting those excluded by the F C & S and S R & C C Warranties, arising during transportation between the points of shipment and of destination named herein

USED MERCHANDISE AND/OR ON DECK SHIPMENTS (subject to an ON DECK bill of lading) insured–

Warranted free of particular average unless caused by the vessel being stranded, sunk, burnt, on fire or in collision but including risk of jettison and/or washing overboard, irrespective of percentage

MARKS & NUMBERS

COMMODITY CODE	COUNTRY CODE

TERMS AND CONDITIONS–SEE ALSO BACK HEREOF

WAREHOUSE TO WAREHOUSE This insurance attaches from the time the goods leave the Warehouse and/or Store at the place named in the Policy for the commencement of the transit and continues during the ordinary course of transit, including customary transhipment if any, until the goods are discharged overside from the overseas vessel at the final port. Thereafter the insurance continues whilst the goods are in transit and/or awaiting transit until delivered to final warehouse at the destination named in the Policy or until the expiry of 15 days (or 30 days if the destination to which the goods are insured is outside the limits of the port) whichever shall first occur. The time limits referred to above to be reckoned from midnight of the day on which the discharge overside of the goods hereby insured from the overseas vessel is completed. Held covered at a premium to be arranged in the event of transhipment, if any, other than as above and/or in the event of delay in excess of the above time limits arising from circumstances beyond the control of the Assured

NOTE–IT IS NECESSARY FOR THE ASSURED TO GIVE PROMPT NOTICE TO THESE ASSURERS WHEN THEY BECOME AWARE OF AN EVENT FOR WHICH THEY ARE "HELD COVERED" UNDER THIS POLICY AND THE RIGHT TO SUCH COVER IS DEPENDENT ON COMPLIANCE WITH THIS OBLIGATION.

PERILS CLAUSE Touching the adventures and perils which this Company is contented to bear and takes upon itself, they are of the seas, fires, assailing thieves, jettisons, barratry of the master and mariners, and all other like perils, losses and misfortunes (illicit or contraband trade excepted in all cases), that have or shall come to the hurt, detriment or damage of the said goods and merchandise, or any part thereof.

SHORE CLAUSE Where this insurance by its terms covers while on docks, wharves or elsewhere on shore, and/or during land transportation, it shall include the risks of collision, derailment, overturning or other accident to the conveyance, fire, lightning, sprinkler leakage, cyclones, hurricanes, earthquakes, floods (meaning the rising of navigable waters), and/or collapse or subsidence of docks or wharves, even though the insurance be otherwise F P A

BOTH TO BLAME CLAUSE Where goods are shipped under a Bill of Lading containing the so-called "Both to Blame Collision" Clause, these Assurers agree as to all losses covered by this insurance, to indemnify the Assured for this Policy's proportion of any amount (not exceeding the amount insured) which the Assured may be legally bound to pay to the shipowners under such clause. In the event that such liability is asserted the Assured agree to notify these Assurers who shall have the right at their own cost and expense to defend the Assured against such claim

MACHINERY CLAUSE When the property insured under this Policy includes a machine consisting when complete for sale or use of several parts, then in case of loss or damage covered by this insurance to any part of such machine, these Assurers shall be liable only for the proportion of the insured value of the part lost or damaged, or at the Assured's option, for the cost and expense, including labor and forwarding charges, of replacing or repairing the lost or damaged part, but in no event shall these Assurers be liable for more than the insured value of the complete machine.

LABELS CLAUSE In case of damage affecting labels, capsules or wrappers, these Assurers, if liable therefor under the terms of this policy, shall not be liable for more than an amount sufficient to pay the cost of new labels, capsules or wrappers, and the cost of reconditioning the goods, but in no event shall these Assurers be liable for more than the insured value of the damaged merchandise

DELAY CLAUSE Warranted free of claim for loss of market or for loss, damage or deterioration arising from delay, whether caused by a peril insured against or otherwise, unless expressly assumed in writing hereon.

AMERICAN INSTITUTE CLAUSES This insurance, in addition to the foregoing, is also subject to the following American Institute Cargo Clauses, current forms

1. MARINE EXTENSION CLAUSES
2. DEVIATION
3. CRAFT, ETC.
4. BILL OF LADING, ETC
5. CARRIER
6. BOTH TO BLAME
7. EXPLOSION
8. INCHMAREE
9. CONSTRUCTIVE TOTAL LOSS
10. GENERAL AVERAGE
11. SOUTH AMERICA 60 DAY CLAUSE
12. S R & C C ENDORSEMENT WAR RISK INSURANCE

PARAMOUNT WARRANTIES THE FOLLOWING WARRANTIES SHALL BE PARAMOUNT AND SHALL NOT BE MODIFIED OR SUPERSEDED BY ANY OTHER PROVISION INCLUDED HEREIN OR STAMPED OR ENDORSED HEREON UNLESS SUCH OTHER PROVISION REFERS SPECIFICALLY TO THE RISKS EXCLUDED BY THESE WARRANTIES AND EXPRESSLY ASSUMES THE SAID RISKS.

F C & S (a) Notwithstanding anything herein contained to the contrary, this insurance is warranted free from capture, seizure, arrest, restraint, detainment, confiscation, preemption, requisition or nationalization, and the consequences thereof or any attempt thereat, whether in time of peace or war and whether lawful or otherwise, also warranted free, whether in time of peace or war, from all loss, damage or expense caused by any weapon of war employing atomic or nuclear fission and/or fusion or other reaction or radioactive force or matter or by any mine or torpedo, also warranted free from all consequences of hostilities or warlike operations (whether there be a declaration of war or not), but this warranty shall not exclude collision or contact with aircraft, rockets or similar missiles or with any fixed or floating object (other than a mine or torpedo), stranding, heavy weather, fire or explosion unless caused directly (and independently of the nature of the voyage or service which the vessel concerned or, in the case of a collision, any other vessel involved therein, is performing) by a hostile act by or against a belligerent power; and for the purposes of this warranty 'power' includes any authority maintaining naval, military or air forces in association with a power.

Further warranted free from the consequences of civil war, revolution, rebellion, insurrection, or civil strife arising therefrom, or piracy.

S R & C C (b) Warranted free of loss or damage caused by or resulting from strikes, lockouts, labor disturbances, riots, civil commotions or the acts of any person or persons taking part in any such occurrence or disorder.

TIME FOR SUIT: No suit or action against this Company for the recovery of any claim by virtue of this insurance shall be sustained in any court of Law or Equity unless commenced within one year from the time loss occurred or within the shortest period of time, in excess of one year, permitted by the applicable law

This Certificate is issued in Original and Duplicate, one of which being accomplished the other to stand null and void

To support a claim local Revenue Laws may require this certificate to be stamped

Not transferable unless countersigned

Countersigned______________

President

Vice President

ORIGINAL

ADDITIONAL CONDITIONS AND INSTRUCTIONS TO CLAIMANTS ON REVERSE SIDE

Courtesy of Washington International Insurance Company.

Figure 4–12. *(continued)*

[reverse]

(SPACE FOR ENDORSEMENT)

(This policy conveys rights of claim collection to the payee named hereon at time of issue. Transfer and assignment of interest hereunder may only be accomplished through endorsement by the original payee)

ADDITIONAL CONDITIONS

PARTIAL LOSS In all cases of damage caused by perils insured against, the loss shall, as far as practicable be ascertained by a separation and a sale or appraisement of the damaged portion only of the contents of the packages so damaged, and not otherwise

SUE & LABOR In case of any loss or misfortune it shall be lawful and necessary for the Assured, his or their factors, servants and assigns, to sue, labor and travel for, in and about the defense, safeguard and recovery of the aforesaid subject matter of this insurance, or any part thereof, without prejudice to this insurance, the charges whereof the said Company shall bear in proportion to the sum hereby insured.

It is expressly declared and agreed that no acts of the Assurer or Assured in recovering, saving or preserving the property insured shall be considered as a waiver or acceptance of abandonment.

SUBROGATION It is agreed that upon the payment of any loss or damage, the Assurers are to be subrogated to all the rights of the Assured under their bills of lading or transportation receipts to the extent of such payments

IMPORTANT NOTICE—INSTRUCTIONS FOR FILING CLAIM

In case of loss, if covered by this insurance, the following IMPORTANT STEPS MUST BE TAKEN IMMEDIATELY

1 Report the details, as soon as goods are landed or you know loss has occurred or is expected, to the address below at port of discharge or disaster. If there is no one listed at or near such port, report the details to the nearest correspondent of the American Institute of Marine Underwriters or to Lloyd's agent. Produce this policy for examination and request that a survey be held

2 When cargo is received in a damaged condition, or in case of loss by theft, pilferage, non-delivery or negligence. IN ORDER TO SAVE FOR YOURSELF OR YOUR INSURER ALL RIGHTS AGAINST THE CARRIER, you must file a notice of claim in writing against such carrier before you take delivery of the goods. It is also necessary that carrier's reply be submitted when received

3 CONTAINER SHIPMENTS Seal numbers and condition of seals must be recorded on receipt given to delivering carrier. Also any external damage to container should be noted thereon

4 After compliance with the foregoing requirements, Complete Documents must be supplied for payment of your claim. Complete Documents normally consist of

A Survey Report
B Policy or Certificate of Insurance
C Invoice
D Bill of Lading
E Copy of letter making a claim upon carrier
F Carrier's reply to such claim
G Delivery receipts indicating exceptions

If all of the above documents are not available, do not delay in filing a claim. Forward the missing documents when they are received

Your full compliance will expedite the handling of your claim under this insurance which is payable at the office of the company at Chicago, (1930 Thoreau Drive, Schaumburg, IL 60173) at current rate of exchange on date of settlement

---

NORTH AMERICA
BALTIMORE, Maryland, Carman & Company
935 South Wolf Street
CHICAGO & MIDWEST, Washington International Insurance Company
1930 Throreau Drive
Schaumburg, IL 60173
HOUSTON, Texas, J R Bencal & Associates
4815 F M 2351, Friendswood, TX 77546
LOS ANGELES, California, Toplis & Harding, Inc
611 South Catalina Street
MIAMI Florida Donald J Mahoney & Company
8776 S W 8th Street Tamiami Mall
NEW YORK, New York Toplis & Harding, Inc
111 John Street
NEW ORLEANS, Louisiana Albert R Lee Co , Inc
610 Podydras Street
SEATTLE, Washington, Alexander Gow, Inc
221 First Avenue West
SAN FRANCISCO, California, Toplis & Harding, Inc
160 Pine Street

MEXICO AND CENTRAL AMERICA
BELIZE, Belize, The Belize Estate and Produce Co , Ltd
COSTA RICA, San Jose, Agencias Unidas, S A
EL SALVADOR, San Salvador, Gibson y Cia (Suc)
GUATEMALA, Guatemala City, Agencias Unitas De Guatamala
HONDURAS, San Pedro Sula, Adan Boza and Cia
MEXICO, Mexico City, Watson, Phillips & Cia Sucs S A
NICARAGUA, Managua, Adan Boza & Cia
PANAMA, Cristobal, Associated Steamship Agents S A
Panama City, Pacific Ford, S A

WEST INDIES
ARUBA, Oranjestad, Caribbean Mercantile Bank, N V
BAHAMAS, Nassau, Nassau Survey Agency, Ltd
BARBADOS, Bridgetown, Gardiner Austin & Co Ltd
BERMUDA, Hamilton, Hartnet & Richardson, Ltd
CURACAO, Maduro & Curiel's Bank, N V
HAITI, Port-au-Prince, J B Vital & Co Sucrs
JAMAICA, Kingston, Ins Co , of North America
PUERTO RICO, San Juan, San Miguel-Munch Inc
TRINIDAD, Port of Spain, Huggins Services, Ltd
VIRGIN ISLANDS, St Croix, Robert L Merwin & Co Inc

SOUTH AMERICA
ARGENTINA, Buenos Aires, James P Browne & Co
BOLIVIA, LaPaz, MacDonald & Co
BRAZIL, Rio De Janeiro, Sumare Processmento e Servicos S/A
CHILE, Santiago, AFIA Chilena Seguros Ltda
COLUMBIA, Bogota, Grancol, Asesoramiento y Services Ltda
ECUADOR, Guayaquil, S.A. Comercial Anglo Ecuatoriana
GUYANA, Georgetown, Guyana National Shipping Corp Ltd
PERU, Lima, International Inspection Services, Ltd
SURINAM, Paramaribo, Handelmij Van Romondt N.V
URUGUAY, Montevideo, John R. Ayling & Son
VENEZUELA, Caracas, Inversiones La Libertad C.A.

UNITED KINGDOM
LIVERPOOL, The Liverpool & Glasgow Salvage Association
LONDON, CIGNA Insurance Co , Maidstone-Kent

EUROPE
AUSTRIA, Vienna, Graham Miller Gesallschaft m b h
BELGIUM, Antwerp, Van Peborgh & Company
CZECHOSLOVAKIA, Prague, Ceska Statni Pojistouna
DENMARK, Copenhagen, Hecksher & Son Succsrs
FINLAND, Helsinki, O Y Lars Krogius, A B
FRANCE, Bordeaux, Andre Pierron
LeHavre, Jaques Durand-Viel
Marseilles, Gellatly, Hankey & Company
Paris, Toplis & Harding S A
GERMANY, Bremen, F Reck & Company
Hamburg, Gellatly, Hankey & Company, m b h
GREECE, Athens, CIGNA Insurance Co - Dept ESIS
HOLLAND, Amsterdam, DeVos & Zoon
Rotterdam, John Hudig & Son
HUNGARY, Budapest, Corporation of Average Adjusters and Agents
ITALY, Genova, ESIS International, Inc
Milan, ESIS International Inc
NORWAY, Oslo, Christen Thorbjornsen A/S
POLAND, Gdynia, Polish Chamber of Foreign Trade, Average Agents Office
PORTUGAL, Lisbon, James Rawes & Company Ltd
SPAIN, Barcelona, MacAndrews & Company, Ltd
Bilbao, Messrs Sucesor de J Innes
Madrid, MacAndrews & Company, Ltd
SWEDEN, Gothenburg, Lindahl & Collins A/B
Malmo, Frick & Frick, Ltd
Stockholm, Lindahl & Collins A/B
SWITZERLAND, Neuchatel, Commissariat d' Avaries
TURKEY, Istanbul, Vitsan Mumessillik ve Ticaret A.S
U.S.S.R., Moscow, U.S.S.R Foreign Ins Dept Ingosstrakh
YUGOSLAVIA, Rijeka Jadroagent

MIDDLE EAST AND NORTH AFRICA
BAHRAIN, Bahrain Maritime & Mercantile, International
EGYPT, Alexandria D.M & T.S Delany
Port Said, El Menia Shipping Agency
IRAN, Tehran, Irano - German Insurance Services (pvt Co Ltd)
JORDAN, Amman, Spinney's 1948 Ltd.
KUWAIT, Kuwait, Kuwait Maritime & Mercantile Co , K S C
LEBANON, Beirut, Catoni & Co., S.A.L
LIBYA, Benghazi, Shahat Shipping Co
MOROCCO, Casablanca, Marbar, S.A.
OMAN, Muscat, Oman United Agencies L.L.C
PEOPLES DEMOCRATIC REPUBLIC OF YEMEN, Aden, National Insurance & Reinsurance Co.
QATAR, Doha, Ace Qatar, Ltd.
SAUDI ARABIA, Jeddah, Arabian Establishment for Trade
Dammam, The Arabian Establishment for Trade
SYRIA, Lattakia, Syrian Maritime & Transport Agencies S.A.
TUNISIA, Tunis, Societe Commerciale Tunisienne
UNITED ARAB EMIRATES, Abu Dhabi, Abu Dhabi Maritime and Mercantile International
Dubai, Maritime & Mercantile Int'l (Private) Ltd
YEMEN ARAB REPUBLIC, Hodeidah, Hodeidah Shipping & Transport Co., Ltd

AFRICA
ETHIOPIA, Addis Ababa, Gellatly, Hankey & Co (Ethiopia)
GHANA, Accra, Ghana inspections Limited
KENYA, Nairobi, Toplis & Harding (Kenya) Ltd
LIBERIA, Monrovia, Denco Shipping Lines Inc
MAURITIUS, Port Louis, Scott & Company
MOZAMBIQUE, Beira, Rennies Freight Svcs Mocambique
NIGERIA, Lagos, Intercotra
SENEGAL, Dakar, La Compagnie Des Experts Maritimes
SOUTH AFRICA, Johannesburg, CIGNA Ins Co - ESIS
SUDAN, Khartoum, Gezira Trade & Services Co , Ltd
Port Sudan, Gezira Trade & Services Co , Ltd
TANZANIA, Dar-Es-Salaam, General Agricultural Products Export Corporation (GAPEX)
ZAIRE, Kinshasa, Zaire Containers S P R L
ZIMBABWE, Bulawayo, Gellatly, Hankey Marine Services

ASIA & FAR EAST
BANGLADESH, Chittagong, James Finlay & Company, Ltd
BURMA, Rangoon Burma Ports Corporation
CHINA, Beijing, The Peoples' Insurance Company of China
Shanghai, The Peoples' Insurance Company of China
HONG KONG, Hong Kong, ESIS International, Inc
INDONESIA, Jakarta, P T Asuransi CIGNA - ESIS
INDIA, Bombay, Global Insurance Claims & Allied Agencies Private, Ltd
Calcutta, Gladstone, Lyall & Co Ltd
JAPAN, Tokyo, Insurance Co of North America - Dept ESIS
MALASIA, Kuala Lumpur, Insurance Co of North America - Dept ESIS
PAKISTAN, Karachi, The Home Insurance Co - Dept ESIS
PHILIPPINES, Manila, Insurance Co of North America - Dept ESIS
SINGAPORE, Singapore, ESIS International, Inc
SOUTH KOREA, Busan, Hyposung Shipping Corporation
SRI LANKA, Colombo, Aitken, Spence & Co , Ltd
TAIWAN, Taipei, Jardine, Matheson & Co Ltd
THAILAND, Bangkok, The Borneo Co (Thailand), Ltd

AUSTRALIA, NEW ZEALAND AND PACIFIC ISLANDS
AUSTRALIA, Adelaide, ESIS International Inc
Brisbane, ESIS International, Inc
Perth, ESIS International, Inc
Sydney, ESIS International, Inc
NEW ZEALAND, Wellington, CIGNA Insurance - Dept ESIS
GUAM, Agana, AFIA
HAWAII, Honolulu, Theo H Davies & Co Ltd
OKINAWA, Naha, Connell Bros. Company, Ltd.

Figure 4–13. Standard form for presentation of loss or damage claim.

General Order No. 41 P. DF. D.G. D.G.

STANDARD FORM FOR PRESENTATION OF LOSS OR DAMAGE CLAIMS

Approved by
THE INTERSTATE COMMERCE COMMISSION
THE NATIONAL INDUSTRIAL TRAFFIC LEAGUE
THE FREIGHT CLAIM ASSOCIATION

(Address of Claimant)

------------------------------------ (Date) ------------------------ Claimant's Number §

(Name of person to whom claim is presented)

------------------------ (Carrier's Number

(Name of carrier) ------------------------------

(Address) ------------------------------

This claim for $------------is made against the carrier named above by (Name of claimant)------------------------------

------------------------------for (Loss or damage)------------------in connection with the following described shipment:

Description of shipment------------------------------
Name and address of consignor (shipper)------------------------------
Shipped from (City, town or station)------------------------------, To (City, town or station)------------------------------
Final destination (City, town or station)------------------------------Routed via------------------------------
Bill of Lading issued by------------------------------Co.; Date of Bill of Lading------------------------------
Paid Freight Bill (Pro) Number------------------------------ Original Car number and Initial------------------------------
Name and address of consignee (to whom shipped)------------------------------
If shipment reconsigned enroute, state particulars:------------------------------

DETAILED STATEMENT SHOWING HOW AMOUNT CLAIMED IS DETERMINED
(Number and description of articles, nature and extent of loss or damage, invoice price of articles, amount of claim, etc.)

Total Amount Claimed

IN ADDITION TO THE INFORMATION GIVEN ABOVE, THE FOLLOWING DOCUMENTS ARE SUBMITTED IN SUPPORT OF THIS CLAIM.*

( ) 1. Original bill of lading, if not previously surrendered to carrier.
( ) 2. Original paid freight ("Expense") bill.
( ) 3. Original invoice or certified copy.
4. Other particulars obtainable in proof of loss or damage claimed.

Remarks:--

The foregoing statement of facts is hereby certified to as correct.

(Signature of claimant)

§ Claimant should assign to each claim a number, inserting same in the space provided at the upper right hand corner of this form. Reference should be made thereto in all correspondence pertaining to this claim.

* Claimant will please check (x) before such of the documents mentioned as have been attached, and explain under "Remarks" the absence of any of the documents called for in connection with this claim. When for any reason it is impossible for claimant to produce original bill of lading, if required, or paid freight bill, claimant should indemnify† carrier or carriers against duplicate claim supported by original documents.

† Indemnity agreement for lost bill of lading. Form 71, Unz & Co.

Printed and Sold by Unz & Co., Division of Scott Printing Corp., 190 Baldwin
Form 30-048 Printed and Sold by UNZCO 190 Baldwin Ave., Jersey City, NJ 07306 • (800) 631-3098 • (201) 795-5400

Figure 4–13. *(continued)*

[reverse]

TO CLAIMANTS:

Persons presenting claims to a carrier will expedite settlement by furnishing the carrier with a complete and detailed statement of all pertinent facts tending to establish the validity of their claims. It is the desire of carriers to settle promptly all valid claims and the frank and hearty co-operation of the claimant is therefore solicited. Delayed settlement of claims is frequently due to the failure of the claimant to furnish carrier with the necessary information and documents with which to make investigation and establish liability promptly. It should be borne in mind that carriers under the terms of the Act to Regulate Commerce are required to thoroughly investigate each claim before payment. Claimants should, therefore, in every case furnish the carrier, as far as possible, with the information and documents called for on the other side of this form, even though there may be instances when it appears to the claimant that the information called for is more than necessary to establish the validity of the claim. There are claims, e. g., for concealed loss and damage, in connection with which it may be necessary to call for additional information from the claimant before making settlement.

Claimants are requested to make use of this form for filing claims with carriers. Claims may be filed with the carrier's agent either at the point of origin or destination of shipment, or direct with the Claim Department of the carrier, and will be considered properly presented only when the information and documents called for on the other side of this form have, as far as possible, been supplied. A duplicate copy thereof should be preserved by the claimant.

Claimants should read carefully the information appearing below.

IMPORTANT INFORMATION TO CLAIMANTS RESPECTING LOSS AND DAMAGE CLAIMS.

Before presenting a claim on account of loss and damage, the following important information respecting claims should be given careful consideration:

1. The terms under which property is accepted and transported by a carrier are stated on the bill of lading issued by the carrier; also in tariffs and classifications issued or subscribed to by the carrier. Persons intending to file claims should, before doing so, examine the terms and conditions under which property was accepted and transported. If any part of the shipment in question was subject to the Regulations for the Transportation of Explosives and Other Dangerous Articles, prescribed by the Interstate Commerce Commission, pursuant to Acts of Congress, the person filing the claim should know that all of these regulations applicable to the shipment had been complied with.

2. Carriers and their agents are bound by the provisions of law, and any deviation therefrom by the payment of claims before the facts and measure of legal liability are established will render them, as well as the claimant, liable to the fines and penalties by law. Attention is called to the following extract from Interstate Commerce Commission Conference Ruling No. 68:

> "It is not the proper practice for railroad companies to adjust claims immediately on presentation and without investigation. The fact that shippers may give bond to secure repayment in case, upon subsequent examination, the claims prove to have been improperly adjusted, does not justify the practice."

3. In order that the carrier may have an opportunity to inspect goods and thereby properly verify claims, any loss or damage discovered after delivery should be reported to the agent of the delivering line, as far as possible, immediately upon discovery, or within forty-eight hours after receipt of goods by consignee.

4. Pending the settlement of any dispute or disagreement between the consignee and the carrier as to questions of loss and damage in connection with property transported the consignee may avoid a possible accrual of demurrage or storage charges as well as other loss or damage, by promptly accepting the property from the carrier. Such action on his part in no way affects any valid claim which may exist against the carrier.

5. Under the provisions of the 6th section of the Act to Regulate Commerce, it is unlawful for a carrier to charge or demand or collect or receive, any greater or less or different compensation for the transportation of property than the rates and charges named in tariffs lawfully on file, nor to refund or remit in any manner or by any device any portion of the rates and charges so specified. The refund or remission of any portion of the rates and charges so specified through the payment of fraudulent, fictitious or excessive claims for loss of or damage to merchandise transported is as much a violation of the law as is a direct concession or departure from the published rates and charges.

In this connection, attention is also called to the following important quotation from section 10 of the Act to Regulate Commerce:

> "Any common carrier subject to the provisions of this Act, or, whenever such common carrier is a corporation, any officer or agent thereof, or any person acting for or employed by such corporation, who, by means of false billing, false classification, false weighing, or false report of weight, or by any other device or means, shall knowingly and willfully assist, or shall willingly suffer or permit, any person or persons to obtain transportation for property at less than the regular rates then established and in force on the line of transportation of such common carrier, shall be deemed guilty of a misdemeanor, and shall, upon conviction thereof in any court of the United States of competent jurisdiction within the district in which such offense was committed, be subject to a fine of not exceeding five thousand dollars, or imprisonment in the penitentiary for a term of not exceeding two years, or both, in the discretion of the court, for each offense."
>
> "Any person, corporation, or company, or any agent or officer thereof, who shall deliver property for transportation to any common carrier subject to the provisions of this Act, or for whom, as consignor or consignee, any such carrier shall transport property, who shall knowingly and willfully, directly or indirectly, himself or by employee, agent, officer, or otherwise, by false billing, false classification, false weighing, false representation of the contents of the package or the substance of the property, false report of weight, false statement, or by any other device or means, whether with or without the consent or connivance of the carrier, its agent, or officer, obtain or attempt to obtain transportation for such property at less than the regular rates then established and in force on the line of transportation; or who shall knowingly and willfully, directly or indirectly, himself or by employee, agent, officer, or otherwise, by false statement or representation as to cost, value, nature, or extent of injury, or by the use of any false bill, bill of lading, receipt, voucher, roll, account, claim, certificate, affidavit, or deposition, knowing the same to be false, fictitious, or fraudulent, or to contain any false, fictitious, or fradulent statement or entry, obtain or attempt to obtain any allowance, refund, or payment for damage or otherwise in connection with or growing out of the transportation of or agreement to transport such property, whether with or without the consent or connivance of the carrier, whereby the compensation of such carrier for such transportation, either before or after payment, shall in fact be made less than the regular rates then established and in force on the line of transportation, shall be deemed guilty of fraud, which is hereby declared to be a misdemeanor, and shall, upon conviction thereof in any court of the United States of competent jurisdiction, within the district in which such offense was wholly or in part committed, be subject for each offense to a fine of not exceeding five thousand dollars or imprisonment in the penitentiary for a term of not exceeding two years, or both, in the discretion of the court: Provided, That the penalty of imprisonment shall not apply to artificial persons."

Figure 4–14. Request for information for insurance claim.

WASHINGTON INTERNATIONAL INSURANCE CO.

1930 THOREAU DRIVE, SUITE 101 • SCHAUMBURG, ILLINOIS 60173
(312) 490-9540 • TELEX: 20-6830 • FAX: (312) 885-8710

Please return copy with your reply
Reverse fold for return mailing

To:

	DATE
OUR REFERENCE	
ASSURED/CLAIMANT	
CERTIFICATE #	YOUR REFERENCE #

☐ **DOCUMENTS REQUIRED:** To enable us to give this claim our consideration subject to the terms and conditions of the insurance, please submit the documents indicated below:

☐ Bill of Lading	☐ Estimate for Repairs	☐ Duty Letters as per attached samples
☐ Freight Bill	☐ Receipted Repair Bills	☐ Customs Consumption Entry
☐ Invoice	☐ Claim Against Carrier	☐ Survey Report
☐ Packing List	☐ Carrier's Reply	☐ Claim Statement
☐ Original & Duplicate Certificate of Insurance	☐ Carrier's Written Confirmation of Non-Delivery	☐
☐ Declaration Number and Date or Copy of Declaration	☐ Exception Report Issued by Carrier, Warehouse or Consignee, etc.	☐

☐ **REQUEST FOR SURVEY:** This file is referred to you for Survey. The documents indicated above are attached.

☐ **STATUS REQUEST:**

☐ What is the present Status of this case?
☐ What is the present estimate?
☐ Please reply to our communication of ____________________
☐ Please forward

OTHER REMARKS OR REPLY

____

____
ADJUSTER

Washington International Insurance Co.
1930 Thoreau Drive
Schaumburg, IL 60173

Courtesy of Washington International Insurance Company.

Figure 4–15. Dock receipt.

DOCK RECEIPT

2. EXPORTER (*Principal or seller-licensee and address including ZIP Code*)

ZIP CODE

5. DOCUMENT NUMBER

5a. B/L OR AWB NUMBER

6. EXPORT REFERENCES

3. CONSIGNED TO

7. FORWARDING AGENT (*Name and address - references*)

8. POINT (STATE) OF ORIGIN OR FTZ NUMBER

4. NOTIFY PARTY/INTERMEDIATE CONSIGNEE (*Name and address*)

9. DOMESTIC ROUTING/EXPORT INSTRUCTIONS

12. PRE-CARRIAGE BY

13. PLACE OF RECEIPT BY PRE-CARRIER

14. EXPORTING CARRIER

15. PORT OF LOADING/EXPORT

10. LOADING PIER/TERMINAL

16. FOREIGN PORT OF UNLOADING (*Vessel and air only*)

17. PLACE OF DELIVERY BY ON-CARRIER

11. TYPE OF MOVE

11.a CONTAINERIZED (*Vessel only*) ☐ Yes ☐ No

MARKS AND NUMBERS (18)	NUMBER OF PACKAGES (19)	DESCRIPTION OF COMMODITIES *in Schedule B detail* (20)	GROSS WEIGHT (*Kilos*) (21)	MEASUREMENT (22)

DELIVERED BY:

LIGHTER
TRUCK ______________________________

ARRIVED- DATE _________ TIME ________

UNLOADED-DATE _________ TIME ________

CHECKED BY _________________________

PLACED IN SHIP / ON DOCK LOCATION _____________

RECEIVED THE ABOVE DESCRIBED GOODS OR PACKAGES SUBJECT TO ALL THE TERMS OF THE UNDERSIGNED'S REGULAR FORM OF DOCK RECEIPT AND BILL OF LADING WHICH SHALL CONSTITUTE THE CONTRACT UNDER WHICH THE GOODS ARE RECEIVED, COPIES OF WHICH ARE AVAILABLE FROM THE CARRIER ON REQUEST AND MAY BE INSPECTED AT ANY OF ITS OFFICES.

FOR THE MASTER

BY ____________________________________
RECEIVING CLERK

DATE __________________________________

Courtesy of Apperson Business Forms, Inc.

FORM 502 (1-1-88)

ONLY CLEAN DOCK RECEIPT ACCEPTED.

Reprinted with permission of Unz & Co., 190 Baldwin Ave., Jersey City, NJ 07306, USA.

Figure 4–15. *(continued)*

Lighter / Car / Truck	No. ______	Started Date ______
		Finished Date ______
		Location ______

SHIPPERS ARE REQUIRED TO FILL OUT AS BELOW

MARKS	NO. of Pkge.	MEASUREMENTS						Total Cubic Ft.		Weight Gross
		Length		Breadth		Depth				
		Ft.	In.	Ft.	In.	Ft.	In.	Ft.	In.	
							Totals			

Figure 4–16. Consular invoice.

FACTURE CONSULAIRE **CONSULAR INVOICE**

CONSULAT DE LA REPUBLIQUE D'HAITI

B. L. No. ______

Marks (Marques) and Country of Origin

Merchandise Shipped on the S. S.: ______ on ______
Marchandises expédiées sur le SS. Nationality - Name (nom) le Date of Sailing
Sailing from the Port of ______ for ______, Haiti
Partant du port de Pour
Name and Address of Shipper ______
Nom et adresse de l'expéditeur
Consigned to order of ______ of ______
Consignées à l'ordre de
Notify ______ of ______, Haiti
Notifier de

Numbers Numéros	Number of pieces Nombre de colis	Nature of Packing Nature de l'emballage	Denomination and Details of Each Article (Quantity, Quality, Measure, Yardage, etc.) in Terms of the Haitian Tariff. Dénomination et détails de chaque article (quantité, qualité, mesure, yardage, etc.) dans les termes du Tarif Haïtien.	Weights in / Poids en: Gross Brut	Weights in / Poids en: Net Net	Values in U.S. Currency Valeur en Monnaie des E.U.

We affirm that this invoice is a correct and faithful expression of the truth, that it corresponds in every particular with our books, and that neither the usual designation, nor the weights, nor the quantity or quality, nor the value and origin named therein are in any way altered, and are thereof exactly the same than those appeared on our Export Declaration No. of (date) submitted to the U. S. Custom House.

J'affirme que cette facture est l'expression sincère et fidèle de la vérité, qu'elle est en tout conforme à mes livres, qu'aucune dénomination usuelle, ni le poids, ni la quantité ou la qualité, ni la valeur, ni l'origine des articles qui y sont portés, n'ont été altérés et sont, en conséquence, les mêmes que ceux accusés sur ma déclaration No. du soumise à la Douane des Etats-Unis.

______ Date ______ 19 ______

______ For Account of
Name of forwarding agent, broker or commissioner, etc.

Shippers ______
Expéditeurs

Per: ______
Signature

NOTE:—In all cases where the merchandise is taxed at net weight, the weight to be taxed of said merchandise will include all interior or immediate packing, including the paste board boxes or objects made of paste board, not subject to a higher tax. (Article 29, Law of July 26, 1926.)

Dans tous les cas où les marchandises sont taxées au poids net, le poids imposable des dites marchandises comprendra tous les emballages antérieurs ou immédiats, y compris les cartons ou objets en carton, non soumis à un droit plus élevé (Article 29, loi du 26 Juillet, 1926.)

ARRANGEMENT OF DOCUMENTS:

3 Consular Invoices and 3 Original Bills of lading clipped or stapled together, the invoice on top.

To each of the remaining Consular invoices a copy of signed B/L must be stapled and the whole set clipped together.

Value of merchandise Valeur des marchandises		
Packing (if not included in the value of the merchandise) Emballage (s'il n'est pas compris dans la valeur des marchandises)		
Inland Freight. Bill of Lading. Wharfage and Trucking Charges Frét et frais du connaissement, embarquement et camionnage.		
Total F. O. B. Value		
Brokerage fees Commission d'achat		
Interest Intérêts		
Export Duties paid at Port of Origin Droits d'exportation acquittés au port d'origine		
Ocean Freight and Bill of Lading Expenses (including embarking and disembarking) Frêt et frais du connaissement, embarquement et débarquement compris		
Insurance Assurance		
Consular fees: / Droits consulaires: *2% of F O B value $		
Stamp on Inv. ($1.20)		
B/L visa ($2.00)		
Stamp on B/L ($1.20)		
Other expenses Autres frais		
Total amount of invoice Montant total de la facture		

CONSULAR INVOICE FEES

*For any merchandise being shipped by boat to Haiti and whose value FOB is inferior to $200.00 — the fee is $3.00 plus B/L visa and Stamps — 7.40
Over $200.00 — the fee is 2% on the value FOB plus B/L visa and Stamps
Visa for Certificate of Origin $2.00 plus Stamps $1.20 — 3.20
Visa for Commercial Invoice if requested $2.00 plus Stamp $1.20 — 3.20

ADDITIONAL FEES:
Visa on Consular Invoice requested after 4 p. m. — 2.00*
Visa on Consular Invoice requested on holidays — 4.00*

Figure 4–17. Certificate of origin.

CERTIFICATE OF ORIGIN

The undersigned ______________________________
(Owner or Agent)

for ______________________________ declares
(Name and Address of Shipper)

that the following mentioned goods were shipped on S/S ______________________________

on the date of ______________ consigned to ______________________________

______________________________ are products of ______________________________ .
(Country of Origin of Goods)

Marks and Numbers	Number of Packages, Boxes or Cases	Weight in Kilos		Description of Merchandise, Material or Goods
		Gross	Net	

Sworn to before me

this _____ day of ______________ , ________
(Day) (Month) (Year)

____
(Signature)

Dated at ______________________________

this _____ day ______________ , ________
(Day) (Month) (Year)

____
(Signature of Owner or Agent

The ______________________________ , a recognized Chamber of Commerce under the laws of ______________________________ has examined the manufacturer's invoice or shipper's affidavit concerning the origin of the merchandise and, according to the best of its knowledge and belief, finds that the products named originated in the country shown above. This certification however, is solely based on the information provided by the shipper/exporter/manufacturer, and the chamber expresses no opinions regarding its accuracy and assumes no responsibility for inaccuracies or errors in the statements, affidavits or any other document.

Secretary: ______________________________

exports to or imports from Canada or Mexico. In general, in order to be eligible for the duty-free or reduced duty rates under NAFTA, all items imported from outside of North America must have undergone the "tariff shift" specified in Annex 401 during the manufacturing process for that product. In addition, some products must contain a specified "regional value content," usually 50 or 60 percent. Finished goods and sometimes raw materials purchased from others often must be traced backward to establish their country of origin. (A sample of the NAFTA Certificate of Origin and Instructions is shown in Figure 4–18.)

K. Certificates of Free Sale

Sometimes an importer will request that an exporter provide a certificate of free sale. Loosely speaking, this is a certification that a product being purchased by the importer complies with any U.S. government regulations for marketing the product and may be freely sold within the United States. Sometimes, depending upon the type of product involved, the importer will be able to accept a self-certification by the exporter. Frequently, however, the importer seeks the certificate of free sale because the importer's own government requires it. For example, these requests are common with regard to food, beverages, pharmaceuticals, and medical devices. The foreign government may or may not require the importer to conduct its own testing of the products for safety but may, either as a primary source or as backup for its own testing, seek confirmation that the products are in compliance with the U.S. Food, Drug and Cosmetics Act. The U.S. Food and Drug Administration has procedures for issuing a Certificate for Products for Export certifying that the product is registered with the FDA in the United States and is in compliance with U.S. law. (A sample is shown in Figure 4–19.)

L. Delivery Instructions and Delivery Orders

The Delivery Instructions (see Figure 4–20) form is usually issued by the freight forwarding company to the inland transportation carrier (the trucking or rail company), indicating to the inland carrier which pier or steamship company has been selected for the ocean transportation and giving specific instructions to the inland carrier as to where to deliver the goods at the port of export. This must be distinguished from the Delivery Order (see Figure 4–21), which is a document used to instruct the customs broker at the foreign port of destination what to do with the goods, in particular, the method of foreign inland transportation to the buyer's place of business.

M. Special Customs Invoices

In addition to the commercial invoice, some countries require a special customs invoice (see Figure 4–22) designed to facilitate clearance of the goods and the assess-

(*Text continues on page 169.*)

Figure 4–18. NAFTA certificate of origin and instructions.

DEPARTMENT OF THE TREASURY
UNITED STATES CUSTOMS SERVICE

Aproved through 12/31/96
OMB No. 1515-0204
See back of form for Paperwork Reduction Act Notice.

NORTH AMERICAN FREE TRADE AGREEMENT
CERTIFICATE OF ORIGIN

Please print or type 19 CFR 181.11, 181.22

1. EXPORTER NAME AND ADDRESS TAX IDENTIFICATION NUMBER:	2. BLANKET PERIOD *(DD/MM/YY)* FROM TO
3. PRODUCER NAME AND ADDRESS TAX IDENTIFICATION NUMBER:	4. IMPORTER NAME AND ADDRESS TAX IDENTIFICATION NUMBER:

5. DESCRIPTION OF GOOD(S)	6. HS TARIFF CLASSIFICATION NUMBER	7. PREFERENCE CRITERION	8. PRODUCER	9. NET COST	10. COUNTRY OF ORIGIN

I CERTIFY THAT:

• THE INFORMATION ON THIS DOCUMENT IS TRUE AND ACCURATE AND I ASSUME THE RESPONSIBILITY FOR PROVING SUCH REPRESENTATIONS. I UNDERSTAND THAT I AM LIABLE FOR ANY FALSE STATEMENTS OR MATERIAL OMISSIONS MADE ON OR IN CONNECTION WITH THIS DOCUMENT;

• I AGREE TO MAINTAIN, AND PRESENT UPON REQUEST, DOCUMENTATION NECESSARY TO SUPPORT THIS CERTIFICATE, AND TO INFORM, IN WRITING, ALL PERSONS TO WHOM THE CERTIFICATE WAS GIVEN OF ANY CHANGES THAT COULD AFFECT THE ACCURACY OR VALIDITY OF THIS CERTIFICATE;

• THE GOODS ORIGINATED IN THE TERRITORY OF ONE OR MORE OF THE PARTIES, AND COMPLY WITH THE ORIGIN REQUIREMENTS SPECIFIED FOR THOSE GOODS IN THE NORTH AMERICAN FREE TRADE AGREEMENT, AND UNLESS SPECIFICALLY EXEMPTED IN ARTICLE 411 OR ANNEX 401, THERE HAS BEEN NO FURTHER PRODUCTION OR ANY OTHER OPERATION OUTSIDE THE TERRITORIES OF THE PARTIES; AND

• THIS CERTIFICATE CONSISTS OF ______ PAGES, INCLUDING ALL ATTACHMENTS.

11.	11a. AUTHORIZED SIGNATURE		11b. COMPANY	
	11c. NAME *(Print or Type)*		11d. TITLE	
	11e. DATE *(DD/MM/YY)*	11f. TELEPHONE NUMBER ▷	*(Voice)*	*(Facsimile)*

Customs Form 434 (121793)

(continues)

Figure 4–18. *(continued)*

[*reverse*]

PAPERWORK REDUCTION ACT NOTICE: This information is needed to carry out the terms of the North American Free Trade Agreement (NAFTA). NAFTA requires that, upon request, an importer must provide Customs with proof of the exporter's written certification of the origin of the goods. The certification is essential to substantiate compliance with the rules of origin under the Agreement. You are required to give us this information to obtain a benefit.

Statement Required by 5 CFR 1320.21: The estimated average burden associated with this collection of information is 15 minutes per respondent or recordkeeper depending on individual circumstances. Comments concerning the accuracy of this burden estimate and suggestions for reducing this burden should be directed to U.S. Customs Service, Paperwork Management Branch, Washington DC 20229, and to the Office of Management and Budget, Paperwork Reduction Project (1515-0204), Washington DC 20503.

NORTH AMERICAN FREE TRADE AGREEMENT CERTIFICATE OF ORIGIN INSTRUCTIONS

For purposes of obtaining preferential tariff treatment, this document must be completed legibly and in full by the exporter and be in the possession of the importer at the time the declaration is made. This document may also be completed voluntarily by the producer for use by the exporter. Please print or type:

FIELD 1: State the full legal name, address (including country) and legal tax identification number of the exporter. Legal taxation number is: in Canada, employer number or importer/exporter number assigned by Revenue Canada; in Mexico, federal taxpayer's registry number (RFC); and in the United States, employer's identification number or Social Security Number.

FIELD 2: Complete field if the Certificate covers multiple shipments of identical goods as described in Field # 5 that are imported into a NAFTA country for a specified period of up to one year (the blanket period). "FROM" is the date upon which the Certificate becomes applicable to the good covered by the blanket Certificate (it may be prior to the date of signing this Certificate). "TO" is the date upon which the blanket period expires. The importation of a good for which preferential treatment is claimed based on this Certificate must occur between these dates.

FIELD 3: State the full legal name, address (including country) and legal tax identification number, as defined in Field #1, of the producer. If more than one producer's good is included on the Certificate, attach a list of additional producers, including the legal name, address (including country) and legal tax identification number, cross-referenced to the good described in Field #5. If you wish this information to be confidential, it is acceptable to state "Available to Customs upon request". If the producer and the exporter are the same, complete field with "SAME". If the producer is unknown, it is acceptable to state "UNKNOWN".

FIELD 4: State the full legal name, address (including country) and legal tax identification number, as defined in Field #1, of the importer. If the importer is not known, state "UNKNOWN"; if multiple importers, state "VARIOUS".

FIELD 5: Provide a full description of each good. The description should be sufficient to relate it to the invoice description and to the Harmonized System (H.S.) description of the good. If the Certificate covers a single shipment of a good, include the invoice number as shown on the commercial invoice. If not known, indicate another unique reference number, such as the shipping order number.

FIELD 6: For each good described in Field #5, identify the H.S. tariff classification to six digits. If the good is subject to a specific rule of origin in Annex 401 that requires eight digits, identify to eight digits, using the H.S. tariff classification of the country into whose territory the good is imported.

FIELD 7: For each good described in Field #5, state which criterion (A through F) is applicable. The rules of origin are contained in Chapter Four and Annex 401. Additional rules are described in Annex 703.2 (certain agricultural goods), Annex 300-B, Appendix 6 (certain textile goods) and Annex 308.1 (certain automatic data processing goods and their parts). **NOTE: In order to be entitled to preferential tariff treatment, each good must meet at least one of the criteria below.**

Preference Criteria

A The good is "wholly obtained or produced entirely" in the territory of one or more of the NAFTA countries as referenced in Article 415. **Note: The purchase of a good in the territory does not necessarily render it "wholly obtained or produced".** If the good is an agricultural good, see also criterion F and Annex 703.2. *(Reference: Article 401(a) and 415)*

B The good is produced entirely in the territory of one or more of the NAFTA countries and satisfies the specific rule of origin, set out in Annex 401, that applies to its tariff classification. The rule may include a tariff classification change, regional value-content requirement, or a combination thereof. The good must also satisfy all other applicable requirements of Chapter Four. If the good is an agricultural good, see also criterion F and Annex 703.2. *(Reference: Article 401(b))*

C The good is produced entirely in the territory of one or more of the NAFTA countries exclusively from originating materials. Under this criterion, one or more of the materials may not fall within the definition of "wholly produced or obtained", as set out in Article 415. All materials used in the production of the good must qualify as "originating" by meeting the rules of Article 401(a) through (d). If the good is an agricultural good, see also criterion F and Annex 703.2. *Reference: Article 401(c).*

D Goods are produced in the territory of one or more of the NAFTA countries but do not meet the applicable rule of origin, set out in Annex 401, because certain non-originating materials do not undergo the required change in tariff classification. The goods do nonetheless meet the regional value-content requirement specified in Article 401 (d). This criterion is limited to the following two circumstances:

1. The good was imported into the territory of a NAFTA country in an unassembled or disassembled form but was classified as an assembled good, pursuant to H.S. General Rule of Interpretation 2(a), or
2. The good incorporated one or more non-originating materials, provided for as parts under the H.S., which could not undergo a change in tariff classification because the heading provided for both the good and its parts and was not further subdivided into subheadings, or the subheading provided for both the good and its parts and was not further subdivided.

NOTE: This criterion does not apply to Chapters 61 through 63 of the H.S. *(Reference: Article 401(d))*

E Certain automatic data processing goods and their parts, specified in Annex 308.1, that do not originate in the territory are considered originating upon importation into the territory of a NAFTA country from the territory of another NAFTA country when the most-favored-nation tariff rate of the good conforms to the rate established in Annex 308.1 and is common to all NAFTA countries. *(Reference: Annex 308.1)*

F The good is an originating agricultural good under preference criterion A, B, or C above and is not subject to a quantitative restriction in the importing NAFTA country because it is a "qualifying good" as defined in Annex 703.2, Section A or B (please specify). A good listed in Appendix 703.2B.7 is also exempt from quantitative restrictions and is eligible for NAFTA preferential tariff treatment if it meets the definition of "qualifying good" in Section A of Annex 703.2. **NOTE 1: This criterion does not apply to goods that wholly originate in Canada or the United States and are imported into either country. NOTE 2: A tariff rate quota is not a quantitative restriction.**

FIELD 8: For each good described in Field #5, state "YES" if you are the producer of the good. If you are not the producer of the good, state "NO" followed by (1), (2), or (3), depending on whether this certificate was based upon: (1) your knowledge of whether the good qualifies as an originating good; (2) your reliance on the producer's written representation (other than a Certificate of Origin) that the good qualifies as an originating good; or (3) a completed and signed Certificate for the good, voluntarily provided to the exporter by the producer.

FIELD 9: For each good described in field #5, where the good is subject to a regional value content (RVC) requirement, indicate "NC" if the RVC is calculated according to the net cost method; otherwise, indicate "NO". If the RVC is calculated over a period of time, further identify the beginning and ending dates (DD/MM/YY) of that period. *(Reference: Articles 402.1, 402.5).*

FIELD 10: Identify the name of the country ("MX" or "US" for agricultural and textile goods exported to Canada; "US" or "CA" for all goods exported to Mexico; or "CA" or "MX" for all goods exported to the United States) to which the preferential rate of customs duty applies, as set out in Annox 302.2, in accordance with the Marking Rules or in each party's schedule of tariff elimination.

For all other originating goods exported to Canada, indicate appropriately "MX" or "US" if the goods originate in that NAFTA country, within the meaning of the NAFTA Rules of Origin Regulations, and any subsequent processing in the other NAFTA country does not increase the transaction value of the goods by more than seven percent; otherwise "JNT" for joint production. *(Reference: Annex 302.2)*

FIELD 11: This field must be completed, signed, and dated by the exporter. When the Certificate is completed by the producer for use by the exporter, it must be completed, signed, and dated by the producer. The date must be the date the Certificate was completed and signed.

*U.S. GPO: 1993-301-616/90743 **Customs Form 434 (121793)(Back)**

Figure 4–19. Certificate of free sale.

DEPARTMENT OF HEALTH & HUMAN SERVICES — Public Health Service

Food and Drug Administration
2098 Gaither Road
Rockville MD 20850

CERTIFICATE FOR PRODUCTS FOR EXPORT

The Food and Drug Administration certifies that the products as described below are subject to its jurisdiction. Products which are legally distributed in accordance with the Federal Food, Drug, and Cosmetic Act within the United States may be exported without restriction.

21 CFR 820 of the Food and Drug Administration regulations requires the manufacturer to follow Good Manufacturing Practices. The plant in the United States where these products are manufactured is subject to periodic inspections by the Food and Drug Administration.

This certificate is not valid unless the Foreign Country Certification Statement is completed by a responsible individual of the exporting firm.

PRODUCTS	MANUFACTURING PLANT LOCATION
See Attached List (one page)	

Marilyn K. Schoenfelder
Acting Branch Chief
Information Processing and
Office Automation Branch
Division of Program Operations
Office of Compliance

COUNTY OF MONTGOMERY
STATE OF MARYLAND

Subscribed and sworn to before me this 1st day of June, 1994.

MARY JO O'DONNELL
NOTARY [illegible] MARYLAND
My Commission [illegible] 19, 1997

Figure 4–20. Delivery instructions.

DELIVERING CARRIER TO STEAMER | DELIVERY DATE

1. Forwarding Agent—ADDRESS—REFERENCE NOS | EXPORT DEC No

2. Method of Transportation *(check one)*
☐ VESSEL ☐ AIR ☐ OTHER *(Specify)*

DELIVERY INSTRUCTIONS

SHIPPER ▶

Ship | Flag | Pier | Port of Landing

Port of Discharge from Ship | For Transshipment To

PARTICULARS FURNISHED BY SHIPPER OF GOODS				
MARKS AND NUMBERS	NO. OF PKGS	DESCRIPTION OF PACKAGES AND GOODS	CUBIC MEAS OR KILOS	GROSS WEIGHT IN POUNDS

SPECIAL INSTRUCTIONS: ISSUED .... 19.....

ATTACHED:

.....DELIVERY PERMIT, NO. .... DELIVERY DATE ....

.....DOCK RECEIPT

.....ARRIVAL NOTICE

.....INLAND BILL OF LADING

.....DELIVERY ORDER

..... CHECK FOR $ BY ....

Form No. 30-030 Printed and Sold by UNZCO 190 Baldwin Ave., Jersey City, NJ 07306 · (800) 631-3098 · (201) 795-5400

Reprinted with permission of Unz & Co., 190 Baldwin Ave., Jersey City, NJ 07306, USA.

Figure 4–21. Delivery order.

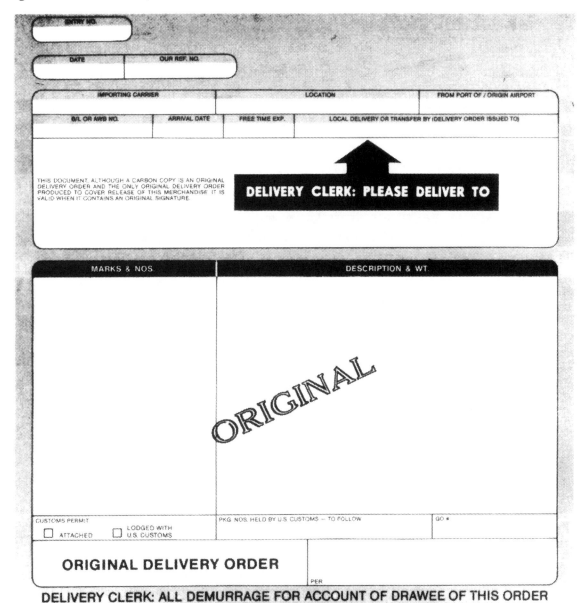

ENTRY NO.

DATE	OUR REF. NO.

IMPORTING CARRIER	LOCATION	FROM PORT OF / ORIGIN AIRPORT

B/L OR AWB NO.	ARRIVAL DATE	FREE TIME EXP.	LOCAL DELIVERY OR TRANSFER BY (DELIVERY ORDER ISSUED TO)

THIS DOCUMENT, ALTHOUGH A CARBON COPY IS AN ORIGINAL DELIVERY ORDER AND THE ONLY ORIGINAL DELIVERY ORDER PRODUCED TO COVER RELEASE OF THIS MERCHANDISE. IT IS VALID WHEN IT CONTAINS AN ORIGINAL SIGNATURE.

DELIVERY CLERK: PLEASE DELIVER TO

MARKS & NOS.	DESCRIPTION & WT.
	ORIGINAL

CUSTOMS PERMIT ☐ ATTACHED ☐ LODGED WITH U.S. CUSTOMS	PKG. NOS. HELD BY U.S. CUSTOMS — TO FOLLOW	GO #

ORIGINAL DELIVERY ORDER	PER

DELIVERY CLERK: ALL DEMURRAGE FOR ACCOUNT OF DRAWEE OF THIS ORDER

Figure 4–22. Special customs invoice (Canada).

Revenue Canada / Customs and Excise — Revenu Canada / Douanes et Accise

CANADA CUSTOMS INVOICE
FACTURE DES DOUANES CANADIENNES

Page of / de

1 Vendor (Name and Address)/Vendeur (Nom et adresse)

2 Date of Direct Shipment to Canada/Date d'expédition directe vers le Canada

3 Other References (Include Purchaser's Order No.)
Autres références (Inclure le n° de commande de l'acheteur)

4 Consignee (Name and Address)/Destinataire (Nom et adresse)

5 Purchaser's Name and Address (If other than Consignee)
Nom et adresse de l'acheteur (S'il diffère du destinataire)

6 Country of Transhipment/Pays de transbordement

7 Country of Origin of Goods
Pays d'origine des marchandises

IF SHIPMENT INCLUDES GOODS OF DIFFERENT ORIGINS ENTER ORIGINS AGAINST ITEMS IN 12
SI L'EXPÉDITION COMPREND DES MARCHANDISES D'ORIGINES DIFFÉRENTES PRÉCISER LEUR PROVENANCE EN 12

8 Transportation: Give Mode and Place of Direct Shipment to Canada
Transport: Préciser mode et point d'expédition directe vers le Canada

9 Conditions of Sale and Terms of Payment
(i.e. Sale, Consignment Shipment, Leased Goods, etc.)
Conditions de vente et modalités de paiement
(p. ex. vente, expédition en consignation, location de marchandises, etc.)

10 Currency of Settlement/Devises du paiement

11 No. of Pkgs / Nbre de colis	12 Specification of Commodities (Kind of Packages, Marks and Numbers, General Description and Characteristics, i.e. Grade, Quality) / Désignation des articles (Nature des colis, marques et numéros, description générale et caractéristiques, p. ex. classe, qualité)	13 Quantity (State Unit) / Quantité (Préciser l'unité)	Selling Price/Prix de vente: 14 Unit Price / Prix unitaire	Selling Price/Prix de vente: 15 Total

18 If any of fields 1 to 17 are included on an attached commercial invoice, check this box
Si tout renseignement relativement aux zones 1 à 17 figure sur une ou des factures commerciales ci-attachées, cocher cette case ☐

Commercial Invoice No./N° de la facture commerciale ____________

16 Total Weight/Poids Total — Net | Gross/Brut

17 Invoice Total
Total de la facture

19 Exporter's Name and Address (If other than Vendor)
Nom et adresse de l'exportateur (S'il diffère du vendeur)

20 Originator (Name and Address)/Expéditeur d'origine (Nom et adresse)

21 Departmental Ruling (If applicable)/Décision du Ministère (S'il y a lieu)

22 If fields 23 to 25 are not applicable, check this box
Si les zones 23 à 25 sont sans objet, cocher cette case ☐

23 If included in field 17 indicate amount
Si compris dans le total à la zone 17, préciser

(i) Transportation charges, expenses and insurance from the place of direct shipment to Canada
Les frais de transport, dépenses et assurances à partir du point d'expédition directe vers le Canada
____

(ii) Costs for construction, erection and assembly incurred after importation into Canada
Les coûts de construction, d'érection et d'assemblage après importation au Canada
____

(iii) Export packing
Le coût de l'emballage d'exportation
____

24 If not included in field 17 indicate amount
Si non compris dans le total à la zone 17, préciser

(i) Transportation charges, expenses and insurance to the place of direct shipment to Canada
Les frais de transport, dépenses et assurances jusqu'au point d'expédition directe vers le Canada
____

(ii) Amounts for commissions other than buying commissions
Les commissions autres que celles versées pour l'achat
____

(iii) Export packing
Le coût de l'emballage d'exportation
____

25 Check (If applicable)
Cocher (S'il y a lieu)

(i) Royalty payments or subsequent proceeds are paid or payable by the purchaser
Des redevances ou produits ont été ou seront versés par l'acheteur ☐

(ii) The purchaser has supplied goods or services for use in the production of these goods
L'acheteur a fourni des marchandises ou des services pour la production des marchandises ☐

DEPARTMENT OF NATIONAL REVENUE – CUSTOMS AND EXCISE — MINISTÈRE DU REVENU NATIONAL – DOUANES ET ACCISE ment of customs duties in that country. Such invoices list specific information required under the customs regulations of that country. It is similar in some ways to the consular invoice, except that it is prepared by the exporter and need not be signed or certified by the consulate.

N. Shipper's Declarations for Dangerous Goods

Under the U.S. Hazardous Materials Transportation Act, the International Air Transport Association Dangerous Goods Regulations, and the International Maritime Dangerous Goods Code, exporters are required to provide special declarations or notices to the inland and ocean transportation companies when the goods are hazardous. This includes explosives, radioactive materials, etiological agents, flammable liquids or solids, combustible liquids or solids, poisons, oxidizing or corrosive materials, and compressed gases. These include aerosols, dry ice, batteries, cotton, anti-freeze, cigarette lighters, motor vehicles, diesel fuel, disinfectants, cleaning liquids, fire extinguishers, pesticides, animal or vegetable fabrics or fibers, matches, paints, and many other products. The shipper must certify on the invoice that the goods are properly classed, described, packaged, marked and labeled, and are in proper condition for transportation in accordance with the regulations of the Department of Transportation (see Chapter 2, Section L). The Hazardous Materials regulations are extremely detailed and an exporter who has any doubt must check to determine whether its product is listed. If it is, the required declarations, invoicing, and labeling must be completed. (A sample declaration is shown in Figure 4–23.) Sometimes the exporter will be required to certify that the shipment is *not* a hazardous material (see Figure 4–24).

O. Precursor and Essential Chemical Exports

Those who export (or import) "precursor" chemicals and "essential" chemicals that can be used to manufacture illegal drugs are required to file Drug Enforcement Administration (DEA) Form 486 (see Figure 4–25). In some cases, this form must be filed fifteen days in advance of exportation (or importation).

P. Animal, Plant, and Food Export Certificates

The U.S. Department of Agriculture is supportive of companies that want to export livestock, animal products, and plants and plant products. Often, the destination country will have specific requirements in order to permit import to that country, but sometimes the foreign country will accept or require inspections performed and certificates issued in the United States. In general, the U.S. Department of Agriculture offers inspection services and a variety of certificates to enable exporters to satisfy foreign government requirements. One example is an "Export Certificate—Animal Products" issued by the Veterinary Services Division (see Figure 4–26). The Veterinary

(*Text continues on page 175.*)

Figure 4–23. Shipper's declaration for dangerous goods.

SHIPPER'S DECLARATION FOR DANGEROUS GOODS

Shipper

Air Waybill No.

Page of Pages

Shipper's Reference Number *(optional)*

Consignee

Two completed and signed copies of this Declaration must be handed to the operator.

TRANSPORT DETAILS

This shipment is within the limitations prescribed for: *(delete non-applicable)*

PASSENGER AND CARGO AIRCRAFT	CARGO AIRCRAFT ONLY

Airport of Departure:

Airport of Destination:

WARNING

Failure to comply in all respects with the applicable Dangerous Goods Regulations may be in breach of the applicable law, subject to legal penalties. This Declaration must not, in any circumstances, be completed and/or signed by a consolidator, a forwarder or an IATA cargo agent.

Shipment type: *(delete non-applicable)*

NON-RADIOACTIVE	RADIOACTIVE

NATURE AND QUANTITY OF DANGEROUS GOODS

Dangerous Goods Identification						
Proper Shipping Name	Class or Division	UN or ID No.	Subsidiary Risk	Quantity and type of packing	Packing Inst.	Authorization

Additional Handling Information

I hereby declare that the contents of this consignment are fully and accurately described above by proper shipping name and are classified, packed, marked and labelled, and are in all respects in the proper condition for transport by air according to the applicable International and National Government Regulations.

Name/Title of Signatory

Place and Date

Signature *(see warning above)*

Form 30 062 Printed and Sold by UNZCO 190 Baldwin Ave., Jersey City, NJ 07306 • (800) 631-3098 • (201) 795 5400

Reprinted with permission of Unz & Co., 190 Baldwin Ave., Jersey City, NJ 07306, USA.

Figure 4–24. Shipper's certification of articles not restricted.

SHIPPER'S CERTIFICATION OF ARTICLES NOT RESTRICTED

TYPE OR USE BLOCK LETTERS

WARNING: Failure to comply in all respects with Government and IATA restricted articles regulations may be a violation of the law, subject to fines, imprisonment, or both. This certification shall in no circumstance be signed by an employee of a forwarder, carrier or cargo agent.

NUMBER OF PACKAGES	ARTICLE AND DESCRIPTION Specify each article separately.	NET QUANTITY PER PACKAGE	FLASH POINT (for liquids)	
			°C.	°F.

I hereby certify that the contents of this consignment, in spite of product name or appearance, are not restricted for air transportation by the Air Transport Restricted Articles Tariff No. 6-D, Government Hazardous Material Regulations or IATA Restricted Articles regulations. I acknowledge that I may be liable for damages resulting from any misstatement or omission and I further agree that any air carrier involved in the shipment of this consignment may rely upon this Certification.

Name and full address of shipper	Name and title of person signing
Date	Signature of shipper. (See warning above.)

FOR CARRIER'S USE ONLY

Air Waybill No.	Airport of Departure	Airport of Destination

THIS CERTIFICATION IS NOT A REQUIREMENT OF U.S. DEPT. OF TRANS.

Form 30-090 Printed and Sold by UNZCO 190 Baldwin Ave., Jersey City, NJ 07306 • (800) 631-3098 • (201) 795-5400

Reprinted with permission of Unz & Co., 190 Baldwin Ave., Jersey City, NJ 07306, USA.

Figure 4–25. DEA import/export declaration.

U.S. Department of Justice
Drug Enforcement Administration

IMPORT/EXPORT DECLARATION
Precursor and Essential Chemicals

SEE REVERSE FOR INSTRUCTIONS AND PRIVACY ACT.

OMB Approval
No. 1117-0023

1. CHECK ONE: [ ] IMPORT DECLARATION [ ] EXPORT DECLARATION

1a. IMPORTER/EXPORTER (Name, Address, Telephone No. to include Area Code, Telex No. and where available FAX No.)	1b. BROKER OR FORWARDING AGENT, IF USED (Name, Address, Telephone No. to include Area Code, Telex No. and where available FAX No.)	U. S. CUSTOMS CERTIFICATION Date of Departure/Arrival Name of Carrier/Vessel Date of Certification Signature of Customs Official

1c. I CERTIFY THAT THE 15-DAY ADVANCE NOTICE REQUIREMENT HAS BEEN WAIVED. [ ] Check if applicable

2. LISTED CHEMICALS TO BE IMPORTED/EXPORTED

2a. Name and Description of Chemical appearing on label or container	2b. Name of Chemical as designated by Title 21 C.F.R. 1310.02	2c. Number of containers, size, net weight of each chemical (Kg.)	2d. Gross Weight of each item (Kg.)

3a. [ ] FOREIGN [ ] DOMESTIC PORT OF EXPORTATION (last U.S. Customs Port) AND APPROX. DEPARTURE DATE	3b. [ ] FOREIGN [ ] DOMESTIC PORT OF IMPORTATION (first U.S. Customs Port) AND APPROX. ARRIVAL DATE
4a. MODE OF TRANSPORT; NAME OF VESSEL, CARRIER	4b. NAME OF ALL INTERMEDIATE CARRIERS
5a. NAME, ADDRESS, TELEPHONE, TELEX, and where available FAX NO. OF FOREIGN CONSIGNEE/CONSIGNOR	5b. NAME, ADDRESS, TELEPHONE, TELEX, and where available FAX NO. OF ALL INTERMEDIATE CONSIGNEES

SIGNATURE OF AUTHORIZED INDIVIDUAL (Print or Type Name below Signature)	DATE	NAME OF FIRM

DEA Form – 486
(Jun 1989)

Copy 1

Figure 4–25. *(continued)*

INSTRUCTIONS FOR COMPLETING DEA Form 486

This form is to be used in notifying DEA of all imports or exports as required by the Chemical Diversion and Trafficking Act of 1988 (PL 100-690). The following instructions supplement the parts of the DEA Form 486 which are not completely self-explanatory. Detailed requirements are found in Title 21 C.F.R. Parts 1310 and 1313.

PART 1. The terms "Importer" and "Exporter" include the regulated person who, as the principal party in interest in the import or export transaction, has the power and responsibility for determining and controlling the bringing in or taking out of any chemical listed in 21 C.F.R. 1310.02 which meets or exceeds the threshold quantity found in 21 C.F.R. 1310.04. **If the 15-day advance notification requirement has been waived, the regulated person must check block 1c.**

"Precursor" means the following substances:

(1) Anthranilic acid and its salts (2) Benzyl cyanide (3) Ephedrine, its salts, optical isomers and salts of optical isomers
(4) Ergonovine, and its salts (5) Ergotamine, and its salts (6) 3,4-Methylenedioxyphenyl-2-propanone (7) Piperidine, and its salts
(8) N-acetylanthranilic acid, and its salts (9) Pseudoephedrine, its salts, optical isomers, and salts of optical isomers
(10) Phenylacetic acid, and its salts (11) Norpseudoephedrine, its salts, optical isomers, and salts of optical isomers
(12) Phenylpropanolamine, its salts, optical isomers, and salts of optical isomers

"Essential Chemical" means the following substances:

(1) Acetic anhydride (2) Acetone (3) Benzyl chloride (4) Hydriotic acid (5) Ethyl ether (6) Potassium permanganate
(7) Toluene (8) 2-Butanone (Methyl ethyl ketone, or MEK)

PART 2. Typical entries might read:

2a.	2b.	2c.	2d.
Butan-2-one	Methyl ethyl Ketone (MEK)	100 x 55 gal. drums 16,753 Kg. Net	18,571.200 Kg. Gr. Wt.

PART 5a. For imports this is the foreign source. For exports this is the foreign recipient of the chemicals; which has to be (a) the end user of the chemical, or (b) a distributor of chemicals.

PART 5b. This part applies to exports only and includes all entities between the exporter and foreign consignee who take possession of the shipment. It does not include common carriers.

INSTRUCTIONS FOR DISTRIBUTING DEA Form 486

If this form is prepared as an **IMPORT DECLARATION** distribute as follows:

Copy 1 shall be retained on file by the regulated person as the official record of import. Import declaration forms involving a listed precursor chemical must be retained for four years; declaration forms for listed essential chemicals must be retained for two years.

Copy 2 is the Drug Enforcement Administration copy used to fulfill the notification requirements of Section 6053 of the Chemical Diversion and Trafficking Act of 1988, through regulations required in 21 C.F.R. 1313.12. Notification must be received at P.O. Box 28346, Washington, D.C. 20038 at least 15 days prior to importation. Regulated persons who have satisfied the requirements for waiver of the 15-day advance notice described in 21 C.F.R. 1313.15 are required to provide notification on or before the day of importation.

Copy 3 must be presented to the U.S. Customs Service along with the customs entry. If the import is a regulated transaction for which the 15-day advance notice requirement has been waived, the regulated person must have declared this information to U.S. Customs by checking block 1c.

If this form is prepared as an **EXPORT DECLARATION** distribute as follows:

Copy 1 shall be retained on file by the regulated person as the official record of export. Export declaration forms involving a listed precursor chemical must be retained for four years; declaration forms for listed essential chemicals must be retained for two years.

Copy 2 is the Drug Enforcement Administration copy used to fulfill the notification requirements of Section 6053 of the Chemical Diversion and Trafficking Act of 1988, through regulations required in 21 C.F.R. 1313.21. This form must be received at P.O. Box 28346, Washington, D.C. 20038 at least 15-days prior to exportation. Regulated persons who have satisfied the requirements for waiver of the 15-day advance notice described in 21 C.F.R. 1313.24 are required to provide notification on or before the day of exportation.

Copy 3 must be presented to the U.S. Customs Service at the port of export along with the Shippers Export Declaration for each listed chemical or chemicals on or before the day of exportation. If the export is a regulated transaction for which the 15-day advance notice requirement has been waived, the regulated person must have declared this information to U.S. Customs by checking block 1c.

PRIVACY ACT INFORMATION

Authority: Chemical Diversion and Trafficking Act of 1988 (PL 100-690).

Purpose: To obtain information regarding the importation/exportation of certain chemicals in order to prevent the illicit manufacture of controlled substances.

Routine Uses: The Precursor and Essential Chemical Import/Export Declaration produces information required for law enforcement purposes. Disclosure of information is made to the following categories of users for the purposes stated:

a. Other Federal law enforcement and regulatory agencies for law enforcement and regulatory purposes.
b. State and local law enforcement and regulatory agencies for law enforcement and regulatory purposes.

Effect: Failure to complete this form will preclude importation/exportation of the listed chemicals.

Public reporting burden for this collection of information is estimated to average 12 minutes per response, including the time for reviewing instructions, searching existing data sources, gathering and maintaining the data needed, and completing and reviewing the collection of information. Send comments regarding this burden estimate or any other aspect of this collection of information, including suggestions for reducing this burden, to the Drug Enforcement Administration, Records Management Section, Washington, D.C. 20537; and to the Office of Management and Budget, Paperwork Reduction Project No. 1117-0023, Washington, D.C. 20503.

Figure 4–26. Export certificate—animal products.

UNITED STATES DEPARTMENT OF AGRICULTURE ANIMAL AND PLANT HEALTH INSPECTION SERVICE HEALTH CERTIFICATE **EXPORT CERTIFICATE** **Animal Products**	FOR OFFICIAL USE ONLY PORT DATE AND NO.

This is to certify that rinderpest, foot-and-mouth disease, hog cholera, swine vesicular disease, African swine fever, bovine spongiform encephalopathy, and contagious bovine pleuropneumonia do not exist in the United States of America.

ADDITIONAL DECLARATION

(SIGNATURE OF ENDORSING OFFICIAL) (TYPED NAME) (TITLE OF ENDORSING OFFICIAL)

DESCRIPTION OF THE CONSIGNMENT

NAME AND ADDRESS OF EXPORTER	NAME AND ADDRESS OF CONSIGNEE
PRODUCT (quantity, unit of measure, and kind)	
IDENTIFICATION	CONVEYANCE

No liability shall attach to the United States Department of Agriculture or to any officer or representative of the Department with respect to this certificate.

VS FORM 16-4 (MAR 99)

Services Division will also issue "U.S. Origin Health Certificates" (VS Form 17-140) to certify that animals and poultry are free from communicable disease and meet the requirements of the importing country. Another type of certification is a "Federal Phytosanitary Certificate" (PPQ Form 577) to certify that live plants are free from plant pests. An exporter may apply for an export certificate to the Food Safety Inspection Service on Form 9060-6 and a "Meat and Poultry Export Certificate of Wholesomeness" will be issued (see Figure 4–27).

Q. Drafts for Payment

If payment for the sale is going to be made under a letter of credit or by documentary collection, such as documents against payment ("DP" or sight draft) or documents against acceptance ("DA" or time draft), the exporter will draw a draft on the buyer's bank in a letter of credit transaction or the buyer in a documentary collection transaction payable to itself (sometimes it will be payable to the seller's bank on a confirmed letter of credit) in the amount of the sale. This draft will be sent to the seller's bank along with the instructions for collection, or sometimes the seller will send it directly to the buyer's bank (direct collection). (A sample set of instructions for direct collection is shown in Figure 4–28.) If the payment agreement between the seller and buyer is at sight, the buyer will pay the draft when it is received, or if issued under a letter of credit, the buyer's bank will pay the draft when it is received. If the agreement between the seller and the buyer is that the buyer will have some grace period before making payment, the amount of the delay, called the usance, will be written on the draft (time draft), and the buyer will usually be responsible for payment of interest to the seller during the usance period unless the parties agree otherwise. The time period may also be specified as some period after a fixed date, such as ninety days after the bill of lading or commercial invoice date, or payment simply may be due on a fixed date. (Samples of a sight draft and a time draft under a letter of credit are shown in Figures 4–29 and 4–30, respectively.)

R. Letters of Credit

When the buyer has agreed to provide a letter of credit as part of the payment terms, the buyer will apply to its local bank in its home country and a letter of credit will be issued. (A sample application is shown in Chapter 6, Figure 6–8.) The seller should send instructions to the buyer before the letter of credit is opened, advising the seller as to the terms and conditions it desires. (A sample set of instructions and documentation checklist is shown in Figure 4–31.) The seller should always specify that the letter of credit must be irrevocable. The bank in the buyer's country is called the issuing bank. The buyer's bank will contact a correspondent bank near the seller in the United States, and the U.S. bank will send a notice or advice to the exporter that the letter of credit has been opened. If the letter of credit is a confirmed letter of credit, the U.S. bank is called the confirming bank; otherwise, it is called the advising

(*Text continues on page 178.*)

Figure 4–27. Meat and poultry export certificate.

U.S. DEPARTMENT OF AGRICULTURE
FOOD SAFETY AND INSPECTION SERVICE
MEAT AND POULTRY INSPECTION OPERATIONS

MEAT AND POULTRY EXPORT CERTIFICATE OF WHOLESOMENESS

A knowingly false entry or false alteration of any entry on this certificate may result in a fine of not more than $10,000 or imprisonment for not more than five years or both (18 USC 1001). Additional penalties exist under the Federal Meat Inspection Act [21 USC 611 (b) (1), (2), and (5), 21 USC 676] and the Poultry Products Inspection Act [21 USC 458 (c) (1), (2), and (5), 21 USC 461] for an unauthorized or false alteration or misuse of this certificate.

AREA OFFICE	COUNTRY OF DESTINATION	DATE ISSUED	**MPD-** 003018

EXPORTED BY *(Applicant's name and address including ZIP Code)*

PRODUCT EXPORTED FROM:

EST. / PLANT NUMBER *(If applicable)*

CITY

CONSIGNED TO *(Name and address, including ZIP Code)*

SAMPLE

☐ @ SLAUGHTERING PLANT
☐ @ PROCESSING PLANT
☐ @ WAREHOUSE
☐ @ DOCKSIDE

TOTAL MARKED NET WEIGHT	TOTAL CONTAINERS

PRODUCT AS LABELED	MARKED WEIGHT OF LOT 1/	NUMBER OF PACKAGES IN LOT 1/	SHIPPING MARKS 1/	EST. / PLANT NUMBER ON PRODUCT
PRIORITY				

1/ As stated by applicant or contractor

REMARKS

☐ I CERTIFY that the meat or meat food product specified hereon is from animals that received both antemortem and postmortem inspection and were found sound and healthy and that it has been inspected and passed as provided by law and regulations of the Department and is sound and wholesome.

☐ I CERTIFY that the poultry and poultry products specified above came from birds that were officially given an antemortem and postmortem inspection and passed in accordance with applicable laws and regulations of the United States Department of Agriculture and are wholesome and fit for human consumption.

NOT VALID UNLESS SIGNED BY AN INSPECTOR OF MEAT AND POULTRY INSPECTION PROGRAM

By order of the Secretary of Agriculture	INSPECTOR AND CIRCUIT NUMBER

This certificate is receivable in all courts of the United States as prima facie evidence of the truth of the statements therein contained.
This certificate does not excuse failure to comply with any of the regulatory laws enforced by the United States Department of Agriculture.

FSIS FORM 9060-5 (9 / 92) REPLACES FSIS FORM 9060-5 (5/85), WHICH MAY BE USED UNTIL EXHAUSTED.

Figure 4–28. Instructions for documentary collection.

Telephone: (312) 407-3906
Fax: (312) 407-1065
Telex: ITT 4330253 FNBCUI
TRT 190201 FNBC UT
SWIFT: FNBCUS44

FIRST CHICAGO
The First National Bank of Chicago
Export Services
One North Dearborn, 9th Floor
Mail Suite 0812
Chicago, IL 60670-0812

ORIGINAL
MAIL DIRECTLY TO THE COLLECTING BANK WITH DOCUMENTS

4

We enclose the following for collection and remittance:

Date:

Collecting Bank	Drawee	Our Ref. 40542750
		Tenor
Principal (Exporter)	Goods	Draft Amount
Principal's Ref.		Collect our charges of

DOCUMENTS ENCLOSED (INDICATE NUMBER OF ORIGINALS "&" COPIES):

Draft	Commercial Invoice	Bill of Lading	Air Way Bill	Certificate of Origin	Packing List	Consular Invoice	Insurance Certificate	
&	&	&	&	&	&	&	&	

PLEASE COLLECT FOR ACCOUNT OF **THE FIRST NATIONAL BANK OF CHICAGO**, CHICAGO, ILLINOIS, FOLLOWING INSTRUCTIONS MARKED X BELOW. ALL CORRESPONDENCE, INCLUDING PAYMENT, IS TO BE SENT TO **THE FIRST NATIONAL BANK OF CHICAGO**, ATTENTION EXPORT SERVICES MONEY TRANSFER A/C #7521-7657, QUOTING OUR REFERENCE NUMBER.

	Acknowledge receipt by ☐ airmail ☐ cable		Protest non-payment/non-acceptance
	Deliver documents against ☐ payment ☐ acceptance		Do not protest
	All collection charges and expenses for account of Drawee		Advise acceptance and maturity date by ☐ airmail ☐ cable
	Waive charges and expenses if refused: ☐ yours ☐ ours		Advise non-acceptance/non-payment by ☐ airmail ☐ cable
	Do not waive charges or expenses: ☐ yours ☐ ours		Return accepted draft to us by registered airmail
	At Drawee's request you may hold for arrival of goods		Hold accepted draft and collect at maturity
	If U.S. dollar exchange is not immediately available on presentation, or at maturity if draft is not drawn at sight, you may accept provisional payment in local currency pending availability of U.S. dollar exchange if it is explicitly understood that the Drawee shall remain liable for all exchange differences. At the time of deposit of local currency, deliver documents against Drawee's written undertaking to take all necessary actions to obtain U.S. dollar exchange and to remain responsible for any exchange differences. Do not release the draft until you remit payment to us in U.S. dollars.		
	Allow a discount of if paid within / before		
	Collect interest at the rate of % p.a. from until ☐ Do not waive interest		

In case of need refer to

Case of need ☐ is ☐ is not authorized to alter these instructions

PAYMENT INSTRUCTIONS:
Remit proceeds by cable quoting our reference number and Money Transfer A.C #7521 7657
Cable expense for ☐ Drawee's ☐ Principal's account

This collection is subject to the Uniform Rules for Collections published by the International Chamber of Commerce in effect on the date hereof.

DETACH DRAFT HERE

ACCEPTED

DATE
REF. NO.
TO MATURE ON
AUTHORIZED SIGNATURE

SOLE BILL OF EXCHANGE

US$ ______ DATE ______ NO. ______

TENOR ______

PAY TO THE ORDER OF **THE FIRST NATIONAL BANK OF CHICAGO, CHICAGO, ILLINOIS**

______ U.S. DOLLARS

DRAWN ON ______

______ ______

______ ______
AUTHORIZED SIGNATURE

Figure 4–29. Sight draft.

SOLE BILL OF EXCHANGE

US $ 250,000 DATE March 1, 1990 NO. 1

TENOR At sight

PAY TO THE ORDER OF ABC Export Company — Payee must endorse draft on reverse side prior to payment

Two hundred fifty thousand and no/100 U.S. Dollars

DRAWN UNDER LETTER OF CREDIT NO. 2738 DATED January 31, 1990

ISSUED BY The Mitsui Bank, Ltd.

DRAWN ON XYZ Import Company

2-3, Toranomon 1-chome — ABC Export Company

Tokyo, Japan — AUTHORIZED SIGNATURE

Courtesy of The First National Bank of Chicago.

Figure 4–30. Time draft.

SOLE BILL OF EXCHANGE

US $ $250,000 DATE March 1, 1990 NO. 2

TENOR 90 days after sight

PAY TO THE ORDER OF ABC Export Company — Payee must endorse draft on reverse side prior to payment

Two hundred fifty thousand and no/100 U.S. Dollars

DRAWN UNDER LETTER OF CREDIT NO. 2021 DATED January 31, 1990

ISSUED BY The Mitsui Bank, Ltd.

DRAWN ON XYZ Import Company

2-3, Toranomon 1-chome — ABC Export Company

Tokyo, Japan — AUTHORIZED SIGNATURE

Courtesy of The First National Bank of Chicago.

bank. The advice will specify the exact documents that the exporter must provide to the bank in order to receive payment. Since the foreign and U.S. banks are acting as agent and subagent, respectively, for the buyer, the U.S. bank will refuse to pay unless the exact documents specified in the letter of credit are provided. The banks never see the actual shipment or inspect the goods; therefore, they are extremely meticulous about not releasing payment unless the documents required have been provided. The issuing bank and advising bank each have up to seven banking days to review the documents presented before making payment. When the exporter receives the advice of the opening of a letter of credit, the exporter should review in detail the exact documents required in order to be paid under the letter of credit. A list of common "discrepancies" which may prevent payment is shown in Figure 4–32. A checklist that the exporter (beneficiary of the letter of credit) should follow in reviewing the letter of credit and other documents is shown in Figure 4–33. Sometimes, if an ex-

Figure 4–31. Letter of credit instructions.

Date:

LETTER OF CREDIT INSTRUCTIONS

TO

FROM

NAME		
COMPANY		
ADDRESS		
CITY	STATE	ZIP CODE
TELEPHONE	TELEX	

GENTLEMEN:

Following are the particular details we wish to have included in your documentary Letter of Credit, issued in reply to our Pro Forma invoice number ________ dated ________________.

Please instruct your bank to open and issue this credit, by telecommunication or by mail, in accordance with the following terms and subject to the Uniform Customs and Practices for Documentary Credits, International Chamber of Commerce Publication 400 (revision currently in force).

We have made every effort in these instructions to provide you with terms which can be easily accommodated. If you or your bank are unable to comply with these terms and conditions, please consult with our offices prior to the issuance of the credit to avoid delay or non-shipment. Thank you for your cooperation.

____

1. The Letter of Credit shall be irrevocable.
2. The credit shall be ☐ advised by ________________ ☐ confirmed by ________________
3. The credit shall be payable at the counters of ________________
4. The credit shall show as the beneficiary ________________
5. The credit shall be payable in ________ (currency), in the amount ☐ not to exceed ________ ☐ exactly ________ ☐ about ________
6. The credit shall be payable ☐ at sight ☐ ________ days sight ☐ ________ days from ________________ Date, upon presentation at the counters of the bank stated in item #3 above
7. The Letter of Credit ☐ shall ☐ shall not be transferrable.
8. The credit shall show that all banking charges incurred ☐ inside ☐ outside the beneficiary's country are for the account of the applicant
9. The credit shall show that all charges for amendments to the credit, including related communications expenses, are for the account of ☐ applicant ☐ beneficiary
10. Partial shipments ☐ shall be allowed ☐ shall not be allowed
11. Transshipments ☐ shall be allowed ☐ shall not be allowed
12. The credit shall allow for required transport documents dated
    - ☐ No later than ________________
    - ☐ No later than ________ days from the advising bank's issuance of written notice to the beneficiary
13. The credit shall allow for a minimum of ______ days after the required transport document date for presentation of documents at the counters of the bank stated in item #3
14. The required documents should include
    - ☐ Commercial Invoice Totaled ☐ F O B ☐ C & F ☐ F A S ☐ C I F ________ (named point)
    - ☐ Commercial invoice shall cover ☐ Pro Forma invoice # ________ or ☐ the following
    - ☐ Packing list for above
    - ☐ Insurance certificate showing insurance policy provided by seller in the amount of ________
    - ☐ Ocean Bill of Lading
      - ☐ The credit ☐ shall ☐ shall not allow for NVOCC bills of lading
      - ☐ The Bill of Lading shall be consigned ☐ to ________________ ☐ to the order of ________________
      - ☐ The Bill of Lading ☐ shall ☐ need not be marked on board
    - ☐ Air Waybill consigned to ________________
      - ☐ The credit ☐ shall ☐ shall not allow for air consolidators Airway Bills
    - ☐ The transport document shall be marked freight ☐ prepaid ☐ collect
    - ☐ Inland straight bill of lading consigned to ________________
    - ☐ Any shipping documents required shall show as the origin ________________ and as the destination ________________
    - ☐ Other required documents: ________________
15. If designated, the forwarder shall be shown as ________________
16. If designated, the carrier shall be shown as ________________
17. Special instructions:

Form 18-400 Printed and Sold by UNZCO 190 Baldwin Ave., Jersey City, NJ 07306 • (800) 631-3098 • (201) 795-5400

UNITRAK™

(continues)

Figure 4–31. *(continued)*

[*reverse*]

DOCUMENTATION CHECKLIST
FOR LETTER OF CREDIT (L/C) SHIPMENTS

On any L/C transaction, the commercial and shipping documents must meet the conditions of the L/C exactly. In order to help you avoid costly discrepancy charges by banks, we are pleased to provide you with this checklist for use in preparing and reviewing your documents prior to shipment.

Do your documents show:

- Correct name and address of exporter?
- Correct name and address of buyer?
- Third parties or "notify" information (banks, etc.)?
- Description of goods identical to L/C?
- Unit prices and extensions identical to L/C?
- Number of packages, and consistent weight and measurements?
- Marks and numbers as stipulated in the L/C?
- Terms of Sale (FOB, C&F, etc.) as stipulated in the L/C?
- Any Import License number or other statements required by the L/C?
- Ports of loading or discharge, or ultimate destination, where required?
- "Freight Prepaid [Collect]", where required by the L/C?
- The L/C number and date of issue, or other statements as required?
- An original signature or endorsement?

Finally, have you prepared the correct number of copies, as stipulated by the L/C?

Form 18-400 Printed and Sold by UNZCO 190 Baldwin Ave Jersey City NJ 07306 • (800) 631-3098 • (201) 795-5400

porter is a good customer of the advising bank, the bank may be willing to make payment even when there are discrepancies if the exporter signs a letter of indemnity (see Figure 4–34). The buyer can also instruct the bank to waive discrepancies. If, for any reason, the exporter anticipates that it cannot provide a document exactly as required, it should contact the buyer immediately and have the buyer instruct its bank and the U.S. correspondent bank to amend the letter of credit. If this is not done, even though the exporter has shipped the goods, payment will not be made by the bank. It is also important to note the date for presentation of documents and the expiration date of the letter of credit, and if for any reason shipment cannot be made within the time period, the seller should contact the buyer and the buyer must instruct the banks to amend the letter of credit to extend the presentation and/or expiration date. (Sample advices of an irrevocable, confirmed letter of credit and an irrevocable, unconfirmed letter of credit are shown in Figures 4–35 and 4–36, respectively. A sample letter of credit is shown in Figure 4–37.) Sometimes letters of credit are issued in "SWIFT" telex format. In such cases, standardized field codes are used (see Figure 4–38).

Figure 4–32. Common discrepancies in letters of credit.

- Documents presented after the expiration date of the letter of credit.
- Documents presented more than twenty-one days after shipment (or other date specified in the letter of credit).
- Missing documents, such as a full set of bills of lading, insurance certificates, inspection certificates.
- Description of merchandise on the invoice differs from the description in the letter of credit (such as being written in a different language or different wording in the same language).
- Shipment terms and charges (ex-works, CFR, CIF) on invoice differ from the terms specified in the letter of credit.
- Transshipment when it is not allowed.
- Shipment made after the date specified in the letter of credit.
- On board stamp on bills of lading not dated and signed or initialed by the carrier or his agent.
- Bills of lading improperly consigned, not endorsed, or show damage to goods.
- Documents inconsistent with one another (e.g., weights or packing information not the same on all documents presented).
- Insurance document not as per the credit terms, not in a sufficient amount, not endorsed, or after the shipment date.
- Drafts drawn on wrong person or for wrong amount or not signed or endorsed.
- Invoice not made out in the name of the applicant shown on the letter of credit.

S. Shipper's Export Declarations

The Shipper's Export Declaration (SED) is important because it is the only one of all of the export documents that is filed with and U.S. governmental agency. (Two samples are shown in Figures 4–39 and 4–40.) The SED is given to the exporting steamship carrier or air carrier and is filed by them with the U.S. Customs Service prior to clearing the port. This document may be prepared by the exporter, or it may be prepared by the exporter's agent, the freight forwarder, and the exporter may not see it. Nevertheless, the SED form specifically states that any false statements in the form (which is interpreted to include accidentally false statements as well as intentionally false statements) will subject the exporter to various civil and criminal penalties, including a $10,000 fine and up to five years' imprisonment. Consequently, the exporter has a real interest in making sure that any agent, such as the freight forwarder, prepares the SED correctly and that the information being submitted to the U.S. Cus-

(*Text continues on page 186.*)

Figure 4–33. Checklist for a letter of credit beneficiary.

CHECKLIST FOR A COMMERCIAL LETTER OF CREDIT—BENEFICIARY

The following checklist identifies points that a beneficiary of a commercial letter of credit should consider when receiving the letter of credit and when preparing required documents.

Letters of Credit

1. Are the names and addresses of the buyer and seller spelled correctly?
2. Is the credit irrevocable and issued in accordance with the latest International Chamber of Commerce (ICC) publication of the Uniform Customs and Practice for Documentary Credits (UCP)?
3. Which bank issued the credit? Is this bank satisfactory, or should a U.S. bank add its confirmation?
4. Do the terms of the letter of credit agree with the terms of the contract? Can you meet these terms?
5. Is the shipping schedule, as stipulated in the letter of credit, realistic? If necessary, is partial shipment or transshipment allowed?
6. Is the merchandise described correctly, including unit price, weight, and quantities?
7. Can presentation of documents be made on time? Will documents arrive before the expiration date and any other time limits indicated in the letter of credit?
8. Are the points of shipment and destination as agreed?
9. Are the terms of sale regarding freight charges and insurance as agreed?
10. If necessary, is the credit transferable?
11. Are the payment terms as agreed? If time payment terms are stated, which party is responsible for discount and acceptance charges?
12. Which party is responsible for banking charges?

Drafts

1. Are the drafts drawn by the beneficiary for the amount shown on the commercial invoice and in accordance with the tenor indicated?
2. Are drafts properly identified with the letter of credit?
3. Are the drafts drawn on (addressed to) the proper drawee and signed by authorized parties, with their titles indicated?

Courtesy of Continental Bank N.A. (Bank of America Illinois).

Figure 4–33. *(continued)*

4. Are the drafts endorsed in blank if made out "to order" of the beneficiary (drawer)?

Commercial Invoices

1. Is the commercial invoice in the name of the beneficiary?
2. Is the commercial invoice addressed to the applicant named in the letter of credit?
3. Did you sign the commercial invoice if required?
4. Was the commercial invoice countersigned by any other party if required in the letter of credit?
5. Does the commercial invoice conform to the letter of credit's terms relative to the following items:
   - Total amount?
   - Unit prices and computations?
   - Description of merchandise and terms (FOB, CFR, CIF, and so on)?
   - Foreign language used for the merchandise description, if used in the letter of credit?
   - Description of packing, if required?
   - Declarations or clauses properly worded?
6. Do the shipping marks on the commercial invoice agree with those appearing on the bill of lading?
7. Do the shipping charges on the commercial invoice agree with those on the bill of lading?
8. If partial shipments are prohibited, is all merchandise shipped? Or, if partial shipments are permitted, is the value of the merchandise invoiced in proportion to the quantity of the shipment when the letter of credit does not specify unit prices?

Consular Invoices (If Required)

1. Does the consular invoice match the commercial invoice and bill of lading?
2. Is the description of merchandise in a foreign language, if it is shown that way in the letter of credit?
3. Is the official form completed in all the indicated places?
4. Are there no alterations, except by a Letter of Correction issued by the consulate?
5. If legalized commercial invoices are required, have the required number of copies been properly legalized?

(continues)

Figure 4–33. *(continued)*

Marine Bills of Lading (Ocean Shipments)

1. Are bills of lading in negotiable form if required in the letter of credit?
2. Are all originals being presented to the bank or accounted for?
3. Are all originals properly endorsed when consigned "to the order" of the shipper?
4. Are bills of lading clean (no notation showing defective goods or packaging)?
5. Do bills of lading indicate that merchandise was loaded on board and loaded within the time specified in the letter of credit? If this provision is not part of the text but in the form of a notation, is the notation dated and signed (initialed) by the carrier or its agent?
6. Are the bills of lading made out as prescribed in the letter of credit (in other words, with names and addresses of beneficiary, applicant, notify parties, and flag, if any)?
7. If freight was prepaid, is this payment clearly indicated by either "FREIGHT PREPAID" or "FREIGHT PAID"?
8. If charter party, sailing vessel, on deck, forwarder's, or consolidator's bills of lading are presented, does the credit specifically allow for them?
9. Do marks and numbers, quantities, and the general description of goods agree with the commercial invoice and letter of credit, with no excess merchandise shipped?
10. Does the bill of lading show transshipment if prohibited in the letter of credit?
11. Is the document signed by the carrier or its agent? Are corrections, if any, signed or initialed by the carrier or agent?

Insurance Documents

1. Are you presenting an insurance policy or a certificate? (Acknowledgements or a broker's cover are acceptable only if expressly allowed in the letter of credit.)
2. Is the insured amount sufficient?
3. Is the insurance coverage complete and in conformity with the letter of credit as it relates to:
   - Special risks where required?
   - Coverage of destination and time (in other words, carried through to proper point and covering the entire period of shipment)?
   - Proper warehouse clauses?
4. Has the insurance document been countersigned where required?

Figure 4–33. *(continued)*

5. Was the insurance document endorsed in blank if payable to the shipper?
6. Are shipping marks identical to those on the commercial invoice and bill of lading?
7. Are all corrections signed or initialed, and are riders or binders attached or cross-referenced?

Other Shipping Documents—Air Waybills, Inland Bills of Lading, Parcel Post Receipts

1. Do marks and numbers, quantities, and the general description of goods agree with the invoice and letter of credit, with no excess merchandise shipped?
2. Are the documents made out as prescribed by the letter of credit (including names and addresses of beneficiary, applicant, notify parties, flag, flight number, and visa, if any)?
3. If freight or dispatch expenses were to be prepaid, is this clearly indicated?
4. Are the documents dated within the terms specified by the letter of credit?
5. Are the bills of lading signed by the carrier or its agent? Are corrections, if any, initialed by the carrier or agent?

Certificates of Origin, Weight, Inspection, and Analysis

1. Are names and addresses as per the commercial invoice and letter of credit?
2. Is the country of origin, if required, as per the commercial invoice and letter of credit?
3. Have they been issued by the proper party and signed?
4. Do they show a description relative to the commercial invoice and letter of credit?
5. Are they in exact compliance with the letter of credit and dated with a reasonably current date?

Packing and Weight List

1. Does the packing type shown agree with the commercial invoice?
2. Does the quantity, or do the units, match the commercial invoice?
3. Is the exact breakdown of merchandise per individual packages shown, if required?

Have you made a final comparative check of all documents to make sure they are consistent with one another?

Figure 4–34. Letter of indemnity.

(Company Letterhead)

The First National Bank of Chicago
Export Services Unit
Suite 0812
Chicago, Illinois 60670-0812

BLANKET INDEMNITY

Gentlemen:

In consideration of your honoring/negotiating our drawings presented to you under any and all letters of credit issued in our favor notwithstanding any discrepancies which might exist therein, we hereby agree to indemnify and hold you harmless, on demand, for the amount of each such drawing, together with any losses, costs, and expenses incurred in connection therewith, in the event that the documents included in the drawing are refused by the issuing bank.

Name: ______________________________

Title: ______________________________

toms Service is accurate. In that connection, the person preparing the SED is required to certify that he or she has read the instructions set forth in a booklet issued by the U.S. Department of Commerce entitled *Correct Way to Complete the Shipper's Export Declaration.* A copy is included in Appendix C. If the exporter discovers that the Shipper's Export Declaration which it or its freight forwarder has prepared is inaccurate, it should file an amended Declaration at the same port as the original export.

There is an exemption from filing an SED where the value of the shipment is $2,500 or less per Schedule B number and for most shipments to Canada. Any shipment that requires an export license (see discussion in Chapter 5) is not exempt even if the value is less than $2,500. Exporters or freight forwarders engaging in many shipments are encouraged (and may soon be required by law or by the transportation carriers) to file electronic SEDs rather than hard copies.

The form was substantially revised and became effective April 1, 2001. Certain

(*Text continues on page 194.*)

Figure 4–35. Advice of irrevocable letter of credit (confirmed).

FIRST CHICAGO
The First National Bank of Chicago

EXPORT SERVICES
ONE NORTH DEARBORN—
9TH FLOOR, MAIL SUITE 0812
CHICAGO, ILLINOIS 60670-0812 U.S.A.

SWIFT Address: FNBCUS44
Telex: TRT 190201 FNBC UT
ITT 4330253 FNBCUI
FAX: (312) 407-1065

CONFIRMED IRREVOCABLE STRAIGHT CREDIT

BENEFICIARY:

DATE:

ALL DRAFTS DRAWN MUST BE
MARKED:
FNBC REFERENCE NO.
OPENER'S REFERENCE NO.

GENTLEMEN:

WE ENCLOSE THE ABOVE-REFERENCED IRREVOCABLE CREDIT ISSUED BY:

THE ATTACHED INSTRUMENT AND THIS LETTER ARE TO ACCOMPANY ALL DRAFTS AND DOCUMENTS. WHEN PRESENTING YOUR DRAFT(S) AND DOCUMENTS OR WHEN COMMUNICATING WITH US, PLEASE INDICATE OUR REFERENCE NUMBER SHOWN ABOVE.

WE CONFIRM THE CREDIT AND HEREBY UNDERTAKE TO HONOR EACH OF YOUR DRAFTS DRAWN AS SPECIFIED IN THE ABOVE-REFERENCED CREDIT WHEN PRESENTED TO US.

PLEASE TAKE SPECIAL NOTE OF THE FOLLOWING TERMS AND CONDITIONS OF THE CREDIT AND OUR INTERPRETATIONS THEREOF:

PLEASE BE AWARE THAT THE FOLLOWING CHARGES UNDER THE CREDIT ARE FOR YOUR ACCOUNT:

THE CREDIT IS SUBJECT TO THE UNIFORM CUSTOMS AND PRACTICE FOR DOCUMENTARY CREDITS (1983 REVISION), INTERNATIONAL CHAMBER OF COMMERCE PUBLICATION 400.

PLEASE ADDRESS ALL CORRESPONDENCE REGARDING THIS LETTER OF CREDIT TO OUR EXPORT SERVICES UNIT, TRADE FINANCE DIVISION, ATTENTION: , MENTIONING OUR REFERENCE NUMBER AS IT APPEARS ABOVE.

NOTICE: INQUIRIES REGARDING THIS LETTER OF CREDIT MAY BE PLACED DIRECTLY TO TELEPHONE NUMBER WHO IS HANDLING THIS TRANSACTION.

VERY TRULY YOURS,

PREPARER/AUTHORIZED SIGNER

AUTHORIZED SIGNER

Figure 4–36. Advice of irrevocable letter of credit (unconfirmed).

FIRST CHICAGO
The First National Bank of Chicago

EXPORT SERVICES
ONE NORTH DEARBORN—
9TH FLOOR, MAIL SUITE 0812
CHICAGO, ILLINOIS 60670-0812 U.S.A.

SWIFT Address: FNBCUS44
Telex: TRT 190201 FNBC UT
ITT 4330253 FNBCUI
FAX: (312) 407-1065

CORRESPONDENT'S IRREVOCABLE NEGOTIABLE CREDIT

BENEFICIARY:

DATE:

ALL DRAFTS DRAWN MUST BE MARKED:
FNBC REFERENCE NO.
OPENER'S REFERENCE NO.

GENTLEMEN:

WE ENCLOSE THE ABOVE-REFERENCED IRREVOCABLE CREDIT ISSUED BY:

THE ATTACHED INSTRUMENT AND THIS LETTER ARE TO ACCOMPANY ALL DRAFTS AND DOCUMENTS. WHEN PRESENTING YOUR DRAFT(S) AND DOCUMENTS OR WHEN COMMUNICATING WITH US, PLEASE INDICATE OUR REFERENCE NUMBER SHOWN ABOVE.

OUR ABOVE-NAMED CORRESPONDENT ENGAGES WITH THE DRAWERS, ENDORSERS, AND BONAFIDE HOLDERS THAT EACH DRAFT DRAWN UNDER, AND IN COMPLIANCE WITH, THE TERMS OF THE SAID CREDIT AND ACCOMPANIED BY THE SPECIFIED DOCUMENTS WILL BE DULY HONORED IF NEGOTIATED BEFORE THE EXPIRATION DATE. THIS CREDIT IS SOLELY AN ADVICE OF THE OPENING OF THE AFORESAID CREDIT AND CONVEYS NO ENGAGEMENT BY US.

PLEASE TAKE SPECIAL NOTE OF THE FOLLOWING TERMS AND CONDITIONS OF THE CREDIT AND OUR INTERPRETATIONS THEREOF:

PLEASE BE AWARE THAT THE FOLLOWING CHARGES UNDER THE CREDIT ARE FOR YOUR ACCOUNT:

THE CREDIT IS SUBJECT TO THE UNIFORM CUSTOMS AND PRACTICE FOR DOCUMENTARY CREDITS (1983 REVISION), INTERNATIONAL CHAMBER OF COMMERCE PUBLICATION 400.

PLEASE ADDRESS ALL CORRESPONDENCE REGARDING THIS LETTER OF CREDIT TO OUR EXPORT SERVICES UNIT, TRADE FINANCE DIVISION, ATTENTION: , MENTIONING OUR REFERENCE NUMBER AS IT APPEARS ABOVE.

NOTICE: INQUIRIES REGARDING THIS LETTER OF CREDIT MAY BE PLACED DIRECTLY TO , TELEPHONE NUMBER , WHO IS HANDLING THIS TRANSACTION.

VERY TRULY YOURS,

PREPARER/AUTHORIZED SIGNER

AUTHORIZED SIGNER

Figure 4–37. Letter of credit.

The Hongkong and Shanghai Banking Corporation Limited **Original for Beneficiary**

Incorporated in Hong Kong with limited liability

TELEX: 30381 HSBCKL MA30381
Cable Address: HongBank

KUALA LUMPUR MAIN OFFICE
2 LEBOH AMPANG P O BOX 10244
KUALA LUMPUR MALAYSIA

DATE OF ISSUE:
11 December 1993

IRREVOCABLE DC NO.: KLH932199

BENEFICIARY:	APPLICANT:
Troy Ohio 45374 U S A	Segambut Industrial Estate 51200 Kuala Lumpur Malaysia
ADVISING BANK: The First National Bank of Chicago Trade Finance Dept 9/F One North Dearbon Suite 0236 Chicago Illinois 60602-0236 U S A	AMOUNT: USD13,341.75 U S Dollars THIRTEEN THOUSAND THREE HUNDRED AND FORTY ONE 75/100 ONLY
PARTIAL SHIPMENTS: not allowed TRANSHIPMENT: not allowed	EXPIRY DATE AND PLACE: 27 January 1994 U S A
SHIPMENT FROM: any port in U S A TO: Port Klang, Malaysia LATEST: 6 January 1994	CREDIT AVAILABLE WITH: Any Bank in U S A by negotiation

Dear Sirs,
We hereby issue this irrevocable documentary credit in your favour which is available by negotiation of your draft(s) at sight drawn on The Hongkong and Shanghai Banking Corporation Limited, Kuala Lumpur, Main Office bearing the clause: 'Drawn under documentary credit No. KLH932199', for full invoice value of goods accompanied by the following documents:

+ Invoices in triplicate.
+ Shipping agent's certificate certifying that vessel falls within the category of Institute Classification clauses.
+ Full set of original clean on board marine bills of lading made out to shipper's order, endorsed in blank, marked freight collect and notify the applicant and The Hongkong and Shanghai Banking Corporation Limited Kuala Lumpur Main Office.
+ Beneficiary's certificate evidencing that a set of non-negotiable documents has been airmailed directly to the applicant immediately after shipment.

GOODS:
KITCHEN EQUIPMENT
AS PER PROFORMA INVOICE NO. 664083 AND 668872

.... TO BE CONTINUED ON PAGE 2 ....

For The Hongkong and Shanghai Banking Corporation Limited	Advising Bank's notification
ZAFINAS ZAINU ABIDIN LAI SIEW LIAN Authorized Signatures 3074	Place, date, name and signature of the Advising Bank.

Telex: Telegrams: Hongbank Malaysia
Please address all letters to The Manager

Except so far as otherwise expressly stated, this documentary credit is subject to Uniform Customs and Practice for Documentary Credits (1983 Revision), International Chamber of Commerce Publication No. 400.

(*continues*)

Figure 4–37. *(continued)*

The Hongkong and Shanghai Banking Corporation Limited **Original for Beneficiary**

Incorporated in Hong Kong with limited liability

TELEX: 30381 HSBCKL MA30381
Cable Address: HongBank

KUALA LUMPUR MAIN OFFICE
This page is attached to and forms part of Credit No. KLH932199 Page 2

BENEFICIARY:	DATE OF ISSUE:
Troy Ohio 45374 U S A	11 December 1993

FOB
Documents to be presented within 21 days after the issuance of the shipping documents but within the validity of the credit.
ADDITIONAL CONDITIONS:
+ A USD30-00 (or equivalent) fee should be deducted from the reimbursement claim for each presentation of discrepant documents under this Documentary Credit. Notwithstanding any instructions to the contrary, this charge shall be for the account of the beneficiary.
All banking charges other than DC opening charges are for the account of the beneficiary.
DIRECTIONS TO ADVISING BANK:
Please add your confirmation to this credit and all confirmation charges are for the account of beneficiary.
INFO TO PRESENTING BK:
+ Documents to be despatched to us by courier service in one lot
+ On receipt of documents conforming to the terms of this documentary credit, we undertake to reimburse you in the currency of this letter of credit in accordance with your instructions. Negotiating bank's discount and/or interest, if any, prior to reimbursement by us are for the account of the beneficiary.

THIS CREDIT CONSISTS OF 2 SIGNED PAGES

****

For The Hongkong and Shanghai Banking Corporation Limited

Advising Bank's notification

ZAFINAS ZAINU ABIDIN LAI SIEW LIAN
Authorised Signatures 3074

Place, date, name and signature of the Advising Bank.

Except so far as otherwise expressly stated, this documentary credit is subject to Uniform Customs and Practice for Documentary Credits (1983 Revision), International Chamber of Commerce Publication No. 400.

Telex: Telegrams: Hongbank Malaysia
Please address all letters to The Manager

Figure 4–38. SWIFT letter of credit codes.

Line Number	*Description of Field*	*Tag Number*
1	Sequence of total (pages)	27
2	Form of documentary credit (revocable, irrevocable)	40A
3	Documentary credit number	20
4	Reference to preadvice	23
5	Date of issue	31C
6	Date and place of expiry	31D
7	Applicant bank	51a
8	Applicant	50
9	Beneficiary	59
10	Currency code, amount	32B
11	Percentage credit amount tolerance	39A
12	Maximum credit amount	39B
13	Additional amounts covered	39C
14	Available with . . . by . . .	41a
15	Drafts at (tenor)	42C
16	Drawee	42a
17	Mixed payment details	42M
18	Deferred payment details	42P
19	Partial shipments	43P
20	Transhipment	43T
21	Loading on board/dispatch/taking in charge at/from . . .	44A
22	For transportation to	44B
23	Latest date of shipment	44C
24	Shipment period	44D
25	Description of goods and/or services	45A
26	Documents required	46A
27	Additional conditions	47A
28	Charges	71B
29	Period for presentation	48
30	Confirmation instructions	49
31	Reimbursing bank	53a
32	Instructions to the paying/accepting/ negotiating bank	78
33	Advise through bank	57a
34	Sender to receiver information	72

Figure 4–39. Shipper's export declaration.

U.S. DEPARTMENT OF COMMERCE — U.S. CENSUS BUREAU – Economics and Statistics Administration — BUREAU OF EXPORT ADMINISTRATION

FORM **7525-V** (7-25-2000) **SHIPPER'S EXPORT DECLARATION** OMB No. 0607-0152

1a. U.S. PRINCIPAL PARTY IN INTEREST (USPPI) *(Complete name and address)*

ZIP CODE

2. DATE OF EXPORTATION

3. TRANSPORTATION REFERENCE NO.

b. USPPI EIN (IRS) OR ID NO.

c. PARTIES TO TRANSACTION

__ Related __ Non-related

4a. ULTIMATE CONSIGNEE *(Complete name and address)*

b. INTERMEDIATE CONSIGNEE *(Complete name and address)*

5. FORWARDING AGENT *(Complete name and address)*

6. POINT (STATE) OF ORIGIN OR FTZ NO.

7. COUNTRY OF ULTIMATE DESTINATION

8. LOADING PIER *(Vessel only)*

9. METHOD OF TRANSPORTATION *(Specify)*

14. CARRIER IDENTIFICATION CODE

15. SHIPMENT REFERENCE NO.

10. EXPORTING CARRIER

11. PORT OF EXPORT

16. ENTRY NUMBER

17. HAZARDOUS MATERIALS

Yes __ No

12. PORT OF UNLOADING *(Vessel and air only)*

13. CONTAINERIZED *(Vessel only)*

Yes No

18. IN BOND CODE

19. ROUTED EXPORT TRANSACTION

__ Yes __ No

20. SCHEDULE B DESCRIPTION OF COMMODITIES *(Use columns 22–24)*

D/F or M (21)	SCHEDULE B NUMBER (22)	QUANTITY – SCHEDULE B UNIT(S) (23)	SHIPPING WEIGHT *(Kilograms)* (24)	VIN/PRODUCT NUMBER/ VEHICLE TITLE NUMBER (25)	VALUE (U.S. dollars, omit cents) *(Selling price or cost if not sold)* (26)

27. LICENSE NO./LICENSE EXCEPTION SYMBOL/AUTHORIZATION

28. ECCN *(When required)*

29. Duly authorized officer or employee

The USPPI authorizes the forwarder named above to act as forwarding agent for export control and customs purposes.

30. I certify that all statements made and all information contained herein are true and correct and that I have read and understand the instructions for preparation of this document, set forth in the **"Correct Way to Fill Out the Shipper's Export Declaration."** I understand that civil and criminal penalties, including forfeiture and sale, may be imposed for making false or fraudulent statements herein, failing to provide the requested information or for violation of U.S. laws on exportation (13 U.S.C. Sec. 305; 22 U.S.C. Sec. 401; 18 U.S.C. Sec. 1001; 50 U.S.C. App. 2410).

Signature

Confidential – For use solely for official purposes authorized by the Secretary of Commerce (13 U.S.C. 301 (g)).

Title

Export shipments are subject to inspection by U.S. Customs Service and/or Office of Export Enforcement.

Date

31. AUTHENTICATION *(When required)*

Telephone No. *(Include Area Code)*

E-mail address

This form may be printed by private parties provided it conforms to the official form. For sale by the Superintendent of Documents, Government Printing Office, Washington, DC 20402, and local Customs District Directors. The **"Correct Way to Fill Out the Shipper's Export Declaration"** is available from the U.S. Census Bureau, Washington, DC 20233.

Figure 4–40. Shipper's export declaration (in-transit).

ENG FORM **7513**
(1-1-88)

UNITED STATES DEPARTMENT OF THE ARMY
U.S. ARMY CORPS OF ENGINEERS

OMB No. 0710-0013

See Export Administration Regulations, Foreign Trade Statistics Regulations and USACE Navigation Regulations.

This space for number, date of Entry, bond, etc.

No. ____________

(Class of entry)

SHIPPER'S EXPORT DECLARATION FOR IN-TRANSIT GOODS

NOTE – This form is to be used for merchandise: (a) Shipped in transit *through* the United States by marine vessel, (b) transshipped in ports of the United States for foreign countries by marine vessel, (c) exported from General Order Warehouse by marine vessel, and (d) rejected and exported by marine vessel. For these transactions the Shipper's Export Declarations, Commerce Form 7525-V, should not be used.

Custom File No.	
District	Port of Exportation
Country from -	Country to -
Pier No.	

1. Exporting carrier	**2.** From *(U.S. Customs port of exportation)*	**3.** Date filed
4. Exporter *(Actual shipper or agent)*	*Address: (Number, street, place, state)*	
5. For account of *(Principal or seller)*	*Address: (Number, street, place, state)*	
6. Consignee *(Ultimate consignee)*	*Address: (Place, country)*	
7. Foreign port of unloading	**8.** Final foreign destination *(Country)*	
9. U.S. port of arrival	**10.** From *(Country from which last shipped)*	
11. Date of arrival into the United States		

Marks and numbers and origin of merchandise (12)	Gross weight[1] *(Kilos)* (13)	Numbers and kinds of packages, description of merchandise and export license number[2] *(Describe in sufficient detail to permit Classification according to Schedule B. Do not use general terms)* (14)	Schedule B number *(Report only the first 6 digits)* (15)	Net quantity in Schedule B unit(s) *(Nearest whole unit)* (16)	Value at time and place of export *(Selling price, or cost if not sold, including inland freight, insurance, and other charges to place of export) (Nearest whole dollar)* (17)

18. I certify that the above statement is correct and true to the best of my knowledge and belief in all particulars.

, Exporter.

[1] If gross weight is not available for each Schedule B item listed in column (14) included in one or more packages, insert the approximate gross weight for each Schedule B item. The total of these estimated weights should equal the actual weight of the entire package or packages.
[2] Insert the appropriate export license number on the line below the description of each item.

aspects of the form deserve further comment. Formerly, Field 2 called for the name of the "exporter." This often caused confusion, particularly where the seller passed title or made delivery in the United States, such as in "Ex-Works" or FOB factory sales. Under the revised form, the seller's name will be inserted in Field 1 (except in very unusual circumstances) no matter what the terms of sale or delivery are. Where the sales terms are such that the foreign buyer is arranging for export from the United States through a U.S. freight forwarder this "routed export transaction" must be declared in Field 19 of the form. In such cases, the law requires the seller to provide certain information to the buyer's U.S. freight forwarder to complete the form, including the seller's tax identification number, Schedule B number, Schedule B description of the goods, whether the goods are "domestic" or "foreign," the quantity, and the value. The buyer's freight forwarder must supply the information for the remaining fields. In return, the seller should obtain a copy of the completed Declaration from the buyer's freight forwarder and check its accuracy.

The form calls for the Employer Identification Number (EIN). If the seller is a corporation, it will use its Federal Employer Identification Number issued by the Internal Revenue Service, and if the seller is an individual, he or she will use his or her Social Security Number as the EIN. The SED also requires that the seller specify whether the transaction is a related party transaction. This means that the seller has a 10 percent or more stockholding or similar interest in the foreign consignee, or vice versa.

The seller must specify the Schedule B Commodity Number for the product being exported. Since the adoption of the Harmonized Tariff System (HTS) on January 1, 1989, in the United States, the Schedule B classification number is the same as the import classification number. One problem that has arisen since the adoption of the HTS is that due to different duty rates that may be imposed on the same commodity when imported in different countries of the world, the seller may find that the buyers in various countries are arguing, perhaps in good faith, that the description of the product falls under a certain tariff classification that would reduce its customs duties. The result can be that various buyers will enter the same product under different HTS classifications in different countries, and each buyer will want the exporter to issue an SED using the Schedule B classification corresponding to its HTS classification. This may place the seller in a difficult position, because it will have to file SEDs, sworn to under oath, with different Schedule B numbers for the same product. This is highly risky. The seller should generally make its own good faith classification based upon consultations with attorneys, freight forwarders, and customs brokers, and select a single Schedule B number for the same product for export to all destinations. Thereafter, it would be the responsibility of the importer to determine whether or not it can persuade its local customs authorities that a different tariff classification should be applied.

The seller must designate whether the product being shipped is "D" (domestic) or "F" (foreign). Domestic products are those grown, produced, or manufactured in the United States or imported and enhanced in value. Foreign products are those that have been imported into the United States and exported in the same condition as when imported.

For the SED form, the seller must declare the value of the goods. This is defined to mean the selling price, or if not sold, the cost including the inland freight, insurance, and other charges, to the U.S. port of export. It does not include unconditional discounts and commissions. This value declaration is extremely important, because if it varies from the selling price stated in the commercial invoice, consular invoice, special customs invoice, insurance certificate, or, especially, any forms filed by the buyer with the foreign customs or exchange control authorities, a charge of false statement may arise, subjecting the exporter and/or the foreign buyer to civil or criminal penalties.

Finally, the SED calls for an export license number or exception symbol, and the Export Control Classification Number (ECCN). This information relates to the export licensing system applicable in the United States. A detailed discussion of that system follows in Chapter 5. The important thing to note at this point is that prior to clearance for shipment from the United States, the "exporter" or its agent must declare, under penalty of perjury, that no export license is required, or that the export can be made under a license exception, and the correct license exception symbol must be inserted in the SED, or that a license is required and has been obtained, and the license number issued by the U.S. Department of Commerce is stated in the SED. When an individual license is required, there will be an ECCN that also must be inserted in the SED. If this information is not put in the form, the shipment will be detained and will not be permitted to clear. Under the revised regulations, the seller will be responsible for making the license determination unless the buyer has expressly agreed in writing to accept such responsibility and has appointed a U.S. agent (such as a freight forwarder) to share such responsibility.

Many exporters are already filing their Shipper's Export Declarations electronically under the Automated Export System (AES). Many carriers are already requiring their customers to file electronically, and filing electronically is mandatory for all items listed on the Commerce Control List and the U.S. Munitions List beginning March 2002. A description of AES, the four options for filing, and Internet filing through "AES Direct" is contained in Appendix D.

T. Freight Forwarder's Invoices

The freight forwarder will issue a bill to the exporter for its services. Sometimes the forwarder will include certain services in its standard quotation while other services will be add-ons. It is important to make clear at the outset of the transaction which services will be performed by the exporter, the freight forwarder, and others, such as the bank. (A sample of a freight forwarder's invoice is shown in Figure 4–41.)

Figure 4–41. Freight forwarder's invoice.

INVOICE NO.

DATE

YOUR REF. NO.

CONSIGNEE:

FROM: TO:	☐ AIR ☐ OCEAN	CARRIER: B/L OR AWB NO

INLAND FREIGHT/LOCAL CARTAGE
EXPORT PACKING
AIR FREIGHT CHARGES
OCEAN FREIGHT/TERMINAL CHARGES
CONSULAR FEES
INSURANCE/CERTIFICATE OF INSURANCE
CHAMBER OF COMMERCE
BROKERAGE FEES
FORWARDING
HANDLING AND EXPEDITING
DOCUMENT PREPARATION
MESSENGER FEES
POSTAGE
TELEPHONE
CABLES
CERTIFICATE OF ORIGIN
BANKING: (LETTER OF CREDIT/SIGHT DRAFT)
MISCELLANEOUS

As amended by the United States Shipping Act of 1984.

TOTAL $

______________________ has a policy against payment, solicitation, or receipt of any rebate, directly or indirectly, which would be unlawful under the United States Shipping Act, 1916, as amended

FORM NO. 16-524 Printed and Sold by UNZ&CO 190 Baldwin Ave., Jersey City, NJ 07306 • (800) 631-3098 • (201) 795-5400

Reprinted with permission of Unz & Co., 190 Baldwin Ave., Jersey City, NJ 07306, USA.

Chapter 5
Export Controls and Licenses

A. Introduction

There are a number of laws that control exports from the United States, including the Arms Export Control Act, the Atomic Energy Act of 1954, the International Emergency Economic Powers Act, the Trading with the Enemy Act, the Munitions Act, the Food, Drug and Cosmetic Act, and the Comprehensive Anti-Apartheid Act. The Department of State, Office of Defense Trade Controls; the Drug Enforcement Administration; the Food and Drug Administration; the Department of Interior; the Department of Treasury, Office of Foreign Assets Control; the Department of Energy; the Nuclear Regulatory Commission; the Department of Commerce, Patent and Trademark Office; the Department of Transportation; and the U.S. Maritime Administration all have responsibilities regarding the regulation and control of exports. The law which is of most general application to the broadest range of commodities is known as the Export Administration Act and is administered by the Department of Commerce. In March 1996, the Department of Commerce issued completely rewritten regulations interpreting the responsibilities under the Export Administration Act. Although one of the important changes under the new regulations is that products are controlled only if they are listed on the Commerce Control List, in fact for every export shipment from the United States, the exporter must determine that the product does not require a license or that a license exception applies and indicate that on the Shipper's Export Declaration. If the exporter neglects this task, the shipment could be seized and the exporter subjected to serious penalties.

Not only must an exporter do this once, but it must be constantly alert to product modifications which may make a product previously eligible for export without a license subject to an export license requirement. For example, in recent years, process control computers have been added to numerous machine tools, which has rendered those products ineligible for export to some destinations without a license.

How, then, does one determine whether the product requires an export license, it may be shipped "No License Required" or is eligible for a license exception? Under the new Export Administration Regulations (EAR), an exporter may be shocked to learn, the regulations require the exporter to proceed through a twenty-nine-step analysis for each of its products to determine eligibility. This process can be grouped into four major steps: First, analyzing the scope of the EAR; second, determining the applicability of the ten general prohibitions; third, determining the applicability of the various license exceptions; and fourth, complying with the export documentation requirements. The following discussion is divided between the export of products, on the one hand, and the export of technology, software, and technical assistance on the other. It also distinguishes between the initial export from the United States and re-exports of U.S.-origin products from one foreign country to another. The following discussion is a summary of over 350 pages under the new EAR, and exporters should seek legal advice for specific export transactions.

B. Scope of the EAR

The first step in determining whether or not an export license is required is to determine whether the contemplated activity is "subject to," that is, within the scope of, the EAR. In general, the coverage of the EAR is very broad. Items subject to the EAR include all items in the United States, including any U.S. foreign trade zone or moving in transit through the United States, all U.S.-origin items wherever located, U.S.-origin parts, components, materials, or other commodities incorporated abroad in foreign-made products (in quantities exceeding de minimis levels), and certain foreign-made direct products of U.S.-origin technology. Items not subject to the EAR include prerecorded phonograph records reproducing the content of printed books, pamphlets, newspapers and periodicals, children's picture and painting books, music books, sheet music, calendars and calendar blocks, paper, maps, charts, atlases, gazetteers, globes and covers, exposed and developed microfilm reproducing the contents of any of the foregoing and exposed and developed motion picture film and soundtrack, and advertising printed matter exclusively related thereto. Step 1 is to determine whether or not the item being exported is subject to the exclusive export control jurisdiction of another governmental agency. If it is, the item is outside the scope of the EAR and administrative control of the Department of Commerce but will be subject to the regulations and administration of that other governmental agency. Steps 4 and 5 relate to determining whether or not a product manufactured in a foreign country contains more than the permitted (de minimis) level of U.S.-origin parts, components, or materials. For embargoed countries, the U.S.-origin parts, components, or materials cannot exceed 10 percent of the total value of the foreign-made product; for all other countries, the limit is 25 percent. If an exporter is unsure whether or not its proposed transaction is within the scope of the EAR, it may request an advisory opinion which would normally be answered within thirty calendar days after receipt. (Steps 2 and 6, pertaining to technology and software exports, and Step 3, pertaining to re-export of US.-origin items, are discussed below.)

C. Commerce Control List

The first of the Ten General Prohibitions is concerned with exporting (or re-exporting) controlled items to countries listed on the Country Chart without a license.

All products manufactured or sold in the United States are classified somewhere in the Commerce Control List. Specific products which are of concern for various reasons are specifically listed by name in great detail using scientific and engineering specifications. At the end of each category of commodity group classifications, there is a catch-all, or basket, category, "EAR 99," which applies to all other commodities not specifically named but which fall within that general commodity category.

The general commodity categories are:

0—Nuclear materials, facilities, and equipment and miscellaneous products
1—Materials, chemicals, microorganisms, and toxins
2—Materials processing
3—Electronics
4—Computers
5—Telecommunications and information security
6—Lasers and sensors
7—Navigation and avionics
8—Marine
9—Propulsion systems, space vehicles, and related equipment

Within each of the foregoing categories, controlled items are arranged by group. Each category contains the same five groups. The groups are as follows:

A—Equipment, assemblies, and components
B—Test, inspection, and production equipment
C—Materials
D—Software
E—Technology

It should be noted, that with the rewrite of the EAR, the numbering system has changed and products previously classified under one number in the Commerce Control List may now be classified under a new number or deleted, or additional items may be included.

Additionally, the Commerce Department has issued "Interpretations" relating to various products, including anti-friction bearings and parts; parts of machinery, equipment, or other items; wire or cable cut to length; telecommunications equipment and systems; numerical control systems; parts, accessories, and equipment exported as scrap; scrap arms, ammunition, and implements of war; military automotive vehicles and parts for such vehicles; aircraft parts, accessories, and components; civil aircraft inertial navigation equipment; "precursor" chemicals; technology and software; and chemical mixtures. An alphabetical index to the Commerce Control List is included in the EAR but, in fact, it is not very helpful in actually finding a product. It is much more useful to conduct a computerized search of the EAR. A further complication is that technology changes constantly, and new products do not fit well into the old classifications.

The descriptions in the Commerce Control List are extremely detailed, containing engineering and scientific language, and it is unlikely that a person in the export sales or traffic department will be able to determine whether his company's products are covered by a particular description without the assistance of company engineers. If it is unclear whether a product falls under one of the classifications, the exporter can request a classification by submitting a completed application for an export license, Form BXA-748P. Such requests will ordinarily be answered within fourteen calendar days after receipt.

Step 7 is the process of reviewing the Commerce Control List and determining whether or not the item being exported falls under a specific classification number and reviewing the "Reasons for Control" specified within the Commerce Control List for that item. Items are controlled for one of the following nine reasons:

AT—Anti-Terrorism
CB—Chemical and Biological Weapons
CC—Crime Control
MT—Missile Technology
NS—National Security
NP—Nuclear Nonproliferation
RS—Regional Stability
SS—Short Supply
XP—Computers

For each product listed in the Commerce Control List, the reason for control is specified. Some products are subject to multiple reasons for control, and some reasons apply to only some of the products listed within the Export Control Classification Number (ECCN). In order to proceed with the analysis, it is necessary to obtain the Reason for Control and "column" shown for the controlled product within the ECCN for that product.

Certain products are controlled because they are in short supply within the United States and are listed on the Commerce Control List. But for these, unlike other products, the Commerce Control List does not specify the "Column" or possible license exceptions. These products include crude oil, petroleum products (which is rather an extensive list), unprocessed western red cedar, and horses exported by sea for slaughter. For such products, the applicable licensing requirements and exceptions are specified under part 754 of the EAR.

Sample pages from the Commerce Control List for ECCN 2B001, "Machine tools . . . which . . . can be equipped with electronic devices for numerical control," are shown in Figure 5–1. In reviewing this, an exporter will learn that certain, specified numerical controlled machine tools are a controlled commodity, that the reasons for control include "NS" (National Security), "AT" (Anti-Terrorism), and, for certain items within the classification, "NP" (Nuclear Nonproliferation). It also indicates that certain common license exceptions, "LVS," "GBS," and "CIV" are not available.

If the item being exported is not specifically described on the Commerce Control

(*Text continues on page 203.*)

Figure 5–1. Sample pages from the Commerce Control List (ECCN 2B001).

2B001 Machine tools and any combination thereof, for removing (or cutting) metals, ceramics or "composites", which, according to the manufacturer's technical specification, can be equipped with electronic devices for "numerical control".

License Requirements

Reason for Control: NS, NP, AT

Control(s)	*Country Chart*
NS applies to entire entry	NS Column
NP applies to 2B001.a,b,c, and d, EXCEPT:(1) turning machines under 2B001.a with a capacity equal to or less than 35 mm diameter; (2) bar machines (Swissturn), limited to machining only bar feed through, if maximum bar diameter is equal to or less than 42 mm and there is no capability of mounting chucks. (Machines may have drilling and/or milling capabilities for machining parts with diameters less than 42 mm); or (3) milling machines under 2B001.b. with x-axis travel greater than two meters and overall "positioning accuracy" on the x-axis more (worse) than 0.030 mm	NP Column 1
AT applies to entire entry	AT Column 1

License Requirement Notes: See §743.1 of the EAR for reporting requirements for exports under License Exceptions.

License Exceptions

LVS: N/A
GBS: N/A
CIV: N/A

List of Items Controlled

Unit: Equipment in number; parts and accessories in $ value
Related Controls :1.) See also 2B290 and 2B991; 2.) See also 1B101.d for cutting equipment designed or modified for removing prepregs and preforms controlled by 9A110.
Related Definitions: N/A
Items:

a. Machine tools for turning, having all of the following characteristics:

a.1. Positioning accuracy with "all compensations available" of less (better) than 6 µm along any linear axis; *and*

a.2. Two or more axes which can be coordinated simultaneously for "contouring control";

Note: 2B001.a does not control turning machines specially designed for the production of contact lenses.

b. Machine tools for milling, having any of the following characteristics:

b.1.a. Positioning accuracy with "all compensations available" of less (better) than 6 µm along any linear axis; *and*

b.1.b. Three linear axes plus one rotary axis which can be coordinated simultaneously for "contouring control";

Export Administration Regulations **January 2001**

Figure 5–1. *(continued)*

b.2. Five or more axes which can be coordinated simultaneously for "contouring control"; *or*

b.3. A positioning accuracy for jig boring machines, with "all compensations available", of less (better) than 4 µm along any linear axis;

c. Machine tools for grinding, having any of the following characteristics:

c.1.a. Positioning accuracy with "all compensations available" of less (better) than 4 µm along any linear axis; *and*

c.1.b. Three or more axes which can be coordinated simultaneously for "contouring control"; *or*

c.2. Five or more axes which can be coordinated simultaneously for "contouring control";

Notes: 2B001.c does not control grinding machines, as follows:

1. Cylindrical external, internal, and external-internal grinding machines having all the following characteristics:

a. Limited to cylindrical grinding; *and*

b. Limited to a maximum workpiece capacity of 150 mm outside diameter or length.

2. Machines designed specifically as jig grinders having any of following characteristics:

a. The c-axis is used to maintain the grinding wheel normal to the work surface; *or*

b. The a-axis is configured to grind barrel cams.

3. Tool or cutter grinding machines limited to the production of tools or cutters.

4. Crank shaft or cam shaft grinding machines.

5. Surface grinders.

d. Electrical discharge machines (EDM) of the non-wire type which have two or more rotary axes which can be coordinated simultaneously for "contouring control";

e. Machine tools for removing metals, ceramics or "composites":

e.1. By means of:

e.1.a. Water or other liquid jets, including those employing abrasive additives;

e.1.b. Electron beam; *or*

e.1.c. "Laser" beam; *and*

e.2. Having two or more rotary axes which:

e.2.a. Can be coordinated simultaneously for "contouring control"; *and*

e.2.b. Have a positioning accuracy of less (better) than 0.003°;

f. Deep-hole-drilling machines and turning machines modified for deep-hole-drilling, having a maximum depth-of-bore capability exceeding 5,000 mm and specially designed components therefor.

List, it thereby falls within EAR 99 and no license will be required for export, but records analyzing and demonstrating that the item falls outside of any of the classifications must be maintained and proper export documentation must be completed (see Section J below).

D. Export Destinations

If an item is listed in the Commerce Control List it is prima facie subject to an export license requirement. However, to determine whether or not an export license will actually be required, it is necessary to proceed to determine the country of ultimate destination (Step 8). Products being exported may pass through one or more countries (except certain prohibited countries), but licenses are issued based on the country of ultimate destination—the country which, according to the representation of the purchaser is the last country of delivery and use.

The Commerce Country Chart is divided into four main groups: Group A (four subgroups), B, D (four subgroups), and E (two subgroups). These country listings overlap and are different depending upon the Reason for Control (see Figures 5–2 through 5–6).

Using the "Reason for Control" listed in the Commerce Control List for the product being exported and the "Column" listed there, the exporter can review the Commerce Country Chart by country of destination. Wherever the exporter observes that an "X" is shown for that country in the same "Reason for Control" and "Columns" specified in the ECCN for that product, an export license will be required (Step 9).

Where the item being exported is not a finished good but is a part or component being exported for incorporation in a product being manufactured abroad, if the part or component which is being exported is described in an entry on the Commerce Control List and the Country Chart requires a license to the intended export destination, then a license will be required unless the parts or components meet the de minimis 10 percent or 25 percent standards (Step 10).

Where the export is to certain embargoed destinations, it is unlikely that a license will be granted. Presently, the EAR prohibit exports to Cuba, Iran, Iraq, and Libya. All exports to North Korea also require a license. The Department of Treasury, Office of Foreign Assets Control, also maintains controls on the foregoing destinations plus Afghanistan, Angola (sales to UNITA), Syria (government-owned entities), and Sudan. The analysis of whether or not the intended export is subject to control under those regulations is Step 14.

Related to the country of destination, there are certain countries through which the goods cannot transit on the way to their ultimate destination. These countries include the following: Albania, Armenia, Azerbaijan, Belarus, Bulgaria, Cambodia, Cuba, Estonia, Georgia, Kazakhstan, Kyrgyzstan, Laos, Latvia, Lithuania, Mongolia, North Korea, Russia, Tajikistan, Turkmenistan, Ukraine, Uzbekistan, and Vietnam (Step 8).

(*Text continues on page 210.*)

Figure 5–2. Country group A.

Country Group A

Country	[A:1]	[A:2] Missile Technology Control Regime	[A:3] Australia Group	[A:4] Nuclear Suppliers Group
Argentina		X	X	X
Australia	X	X	X	X
Austria[1]		X	X	X
Belgium	X	X	X	X
Brazil		X		
Bulgaria				X
Canada	X	X	X	X
Czech Republic			X	X
Denmark	X	X	X	X
Finland[1]		X	X	X
France	X	X	X	X
Germany	X	X	X	X
Greece	X	X	X	X
Hong Kong[1]				
Hungary		X	X	X
Iceland		X	X	
Ireland[1]		X	X	X
Italy	X	X	X	X
Japan	X	X	X	X
Korea, South[1]			X	X
Luxembourg	X	X	X	X
Netherlands	X	X	X	X
New Zealand[1]		X	X	X
Norway	X	X	X	X
Poland			X	X
Portugal	X	X	X	X
Romania			X	X
Russia		X		X
Slovakia			X	X
South Africa		X		X
Spain	X	X	X	X
Sweden[1]		X	X	X
Switzerland[1]		X	X	X
Turkey	X			
United Kingdom	X	X	X	X
United States	X	X	X	X

[1] Cooperating Countries

Figure 5–3. Country group B.

Country Group B

Countries

Afghanistan
Algeria
Andorra
Angola
Antigua
Argentina
Australia
Austria
Bahamas
Bahrain
Bangladesh
Barbados
Barbuda
Belgium
Belize
Benin
Bhutan
Bolivia
Bosnia & Herzegovina
Botswana
Brazil
Brunei
Burkina Faso
Burma
Burundi
Cameroon
Canada
Cape Verde
Central African Republic
Chad
Chile
Colombia
Comoros
Congo
Costa Rica
Cote d'Ivoire
Croatia
Cyprus
Czech Republic
Denmark
Djibouti
Dominica
Dominican Republic
Ecuador
Egypt
El Salvador
Equatorial Guinea
Eritrea
Ethiopia
Fiji
Finland
France
Gabon
Gambia, The
Germany
Ghana
Greece
Grenada
Guatemala
Guinea
Guinea-Bissau
Guyana
Haiti
Honduras
Hong Kong
Hungary
Iceland
India
Indonesia
Ireland
Israel
Italy
Jamaica
Japan
Jordan
Kenya
Kiribati
Korea, South
Kuwait
Lebanon
Lesotho
Liberia
Liechtenstein
Luxembourg
Macedonia, the Former Yugoslav Republic of
Madagascar
Malawi
Malaysia
Maldives
Mali
Malta
Marshall Islands
Mauritania
Mauritius
Mexico
Micronesia, Federated States of
Monaco
Morocco
Mozambique
Namibia
Nauru
Nepal
Netherlands
New Zealand
Nicaragua
Niger
Nigeria
Norway
Oman
Pakistan
Palau
Panama
Papua New Guinea
Paraguay
Peru
Philippines
Poland
Portugal
Qatar
Rwanda
Saint Kitts & Nevis
Saint Lucia
Saint Vincent
San Marino
Sao Tome & Principe
Saudi Arabia
Senegal
Seychelles
Sierra Leone
Singapore
Slovakia
Slovenia
Solomon Islands
Somalia
South Africa
Spain
Sri Lanka
Surinam
Swaziland
Sweden
Switzerland
Taiwan
Tanzania
Thailand
Togo
Tonga
Trinidad & Tobago
Tunisia
Turkey
Tuvalu
Uganda
United Arab Emirates
United Kingdom
United States
Uruguay
Vanuatu
Vatican City
Venezuela
Western Sahara
Western Samoa
Yemen
•Yugoslavia (Serbia and Montenegro), Federal Republic of
Zaire
Zambia
Zimbabwe

Figure 5–4. Country group D.

Country Group D

Country	[D: 1] National Security	[D: 2] Nuclear	[D: 3] Chemical & Biological	[D: 4] Missile Technology
Afghanistan			X	
Albania	X			
Armenia	X		X	
Azerbaijan	X		X	
Bahrain			X	X
Belarus	X		X	
Bulgaria	X		X	
Burma			X	
Cambodia	X			
China (PRC)	X		X	X[1]
Cuba		X	X	
Egypt			X	X
Estonia	X			
Georgia	X		X	
India		X	X	X[1]
Iran		X	X	X[1]
Iraq		X	X	X
Israel		X	X	X
Jordan			X	X
Kazakhstan	X		X	
•Korea, North	X	X	X	X[1]
Kuwait			X	X
Kyrgyzstan	X		X	
Laos	X			
Latvia	X			
Lebanon			X	X
Libya		X	X	X
Lithuania	X			
Macau	X		X	X
Moldova	X		X	
Mongolia	X		X	
Oman			X	X
Pakistan		X	X	X[1]
Qatar			X	X

Figure 5–4. *(continued)*

Country	[D: 1] National Security	[D: 2] Nuclear	[D: 3] Chemical & Biological	[D: 4] Missile Technology
Romania	X			
Russia	X		X	
Saudi Arabia			X	X
Syria			X	X
Taiwan			X	
Tajikstan	X		X	
Turkmenistan	X		X	
Ukraine	X		X	
United Arab Emirates			X	X
Uzbekistan	X		X	
Vietnam	X		X	
Yemen			X	X

[1] Certain Missile Technology projects have been identified in the following countries:

China	M Series Missiles CSS-2
India	Agni, Prithvi, SLV-3 Satellite Launch Vehicle, Augmented Satellite Launch Vehicle (ASLV), Polar Satellite Launch Vehicle (PSLV), Geostationary Satellite Launch Vehicle (GSLV).
Iran	Surface-to-Surface Missile Project, Scud Development Project
Korea, North	No Dong I, Scud Development Project
Pakistan	Haft Series Missiles

Figure 5–5. Country group E.

License Exceptions **Supplement No. 1 to Part 740–page 6**

Country Group E

Country	[E:1] UN Embargo	[E:2] Unilateral Embargo
Angola	X	
Cuba		X
Iraq	X	
Libya	X	X
Rwanda	X	
Serbia & Montenegro	X	

Export Administration Regulations **January 2001**

Figure 5–6. Excerpts from Commerce Country Chart.

Commerce Country Chart

Reason for Control

Countries	Chemical & Biological Weapons			Nuclear Nonproliferation		National Security		Missile Tech	Regional Stability		Firearms Convention	Crime Control			Anti-Terrorism	
	CB 1	CB 2	CB 3	NP 1	NP 2	NS 1	NS 2	MT 1	RS 1	RS 2	FC 1	CC 1	CC 2	CC 3	AT 1	AT 2
Barbados	X	X		X		X	X	X	X	X	X	X		X		
Belarus	X	X	X	X		X	X	X	X	X		X	X			
Belgium	X					X		X	X							
Belize	X	X		X		X	X	X	X	X	X	X		X		
Benin	X	X		X		X	X	X	X	X		X		X		
Bhutan	X	X		X		X	X	X	X	X		X		X		
Bolivia	X	X		X		X	X	X	X	X	X	X		X		
Bosnia & Herzegovina	X	X		X		X	X	X	X	X		X		X		
Botswana	X	X		X		X	X	X	X	X		X		X		
Brazil	X	X				X	X	X	X	X	X	X		X		
Brunei	X	X		X		X	X	X	X	X		X		X		
Bulgaria	X	X	X			X	X	X	X	X		X	X			
Burkina Faso	X	X		X		X	X	X	X	X		X		X		
Burma	X	X	X	X		X	X	X	X	X		X		X		

E. Customers, End Users, and End Uses

The Commerce Department issues and updates on an ongoing basis the "Denied Persons List." This list identifies persons who have previously violated U.S. export control laws and who are under prohibition of engaging in export activities. The Department of Treasury maintains a similar list of "Specially Designated Nationalists and Terrorists." It is a violation of the export control laws for a person on such lists to be involved in any export either as a purchaser, consignee, freight forwarder, or in any other role. Whenever an exporter is engaged in a transaction, it is incumbent upon the exporter to check the Denied Persons List and the List of Specially Designated Nationalists and Terrorists to avoid potential serious export violations (Step 12).

Even where an export may be ordinarily made, if the product being exported will be used in certain end-use activities, a license may be required or the license may be unavailable. These include nuclear explosive activities; unsafeguarded nuclear activities; exports of items for nuclear end uses that are permitted for countries in Supplement Number 3 to part 744; design, development, production or use of missiles in a country listed in Country Group D:4; and design, development, production, stockpiling, or use of chemical or biological weapons.

Finally, "U.S. persons" are prohibited from engaging in or supporting proliferation activities. This includes the design, development, production, or use of nuclear explosive devices in or by a country listed in Country Group D:2; the design, development, production, or use of missiles in or by a country listed in Country Group D:4; and the design, development, production, stockpiling, or use of chemical and biological weapons in any country listed in Country Group D:3. This includes any action such as financing, employment, transportation and/or freight forwarding. The definition of "U.S. person" includes any individual who is a citizen of the United States, a permanent resident alien of the United States or a protected individual; any juridical person organized under the laws of the United States, including foreign branches; and any person in the United States. This prohibition relates to any activities including products produced entirely abroad without any U.S.-origin parts, components, or technology, and services provided entirely abroad—it need not involve a U.S. export or import. Confirming that the intended transaction does not violate the prohibition on proliferation activities is Step 15.

The Commerce Department expects exporters to know their customer. Step 18 involved deciding whether there are any "red flags" in the transaction. If there are red flags, the exporter is under a duty to inquire further, employees must be instructed how to handle red flags, and the exporter must refrain from the transaction or advise the Department of Commerce, Bureau of Export Administration, and wait for its guidance. The "red flags" are listed in Figure 5–7.

F. Ten General Prohibitions

Step 19 involves a review of the "Ten General Prohibitions" to confirm whether or not the intended export violates any of the prohibitions. Proceeding with the trans-

Figure 5–7. Red flags.

Possible indicators that an unlawful diversion might be planned by your customer include the following:

1. The customer or purchasing agent is reluctant to offer information about the end use of a product.
2. The product's capabilities do not fit the buyer's line of business: for example, a small bakery places an order for several sophisticated lasers.
3. The product ordered is incompatible with the technical level of the country in which the product is being shipped. For example, semiconductor manufacturing equipment would be of little use in a country without an electronics industry.
4. The customer has little or no business background.
5. The customer is willing to pay cash for a very expensive item when the terms of the sale call for financing.
6. The customer is unfamiliar with the product's performance characteristics but still wants the product.
7. Routine installation, training, or maintenance services are declined by the customer.
8. Delivery dates are vague, or deliveries are planned for out-of-the-way destinations.
9. A freight forwarding firm is listed as the product's final destination.
10. The shipping route is abnormal for the product and destination.
11. Packaging is inconsistent with the stated method of shipment or destination.
12. When questioned, the buyer is evasive or unclear about whether the purchased product is for domestic use, export, or re-export.

action with knowledge that a violation has occurred or is about to occur is itself prohibited. This prohibition includes selling, transferring, exporting, re-exporting, financing, ordering, buying, removing, concealing, storing, using, loaning, disposing of, transferring, transporting, forwarding, or otherwise servicing any item subject to the EAR.

The Ten General Prohibitions are as follows:

1. Exporting or re-exporting controlled items to listed countries without a license
2. Re-exporting and exporting from abroad foreign-made items incorporating more than a de minimis amount of controlled U.S. content
3. Re-exporting and exporting from abroad the foreign-produced direct product of U.S. technology and software to Cuba, North Korea, Libya, or a destination in Country Group D:1

4. Engaging in actions prohibited by Denial Orders
5. Exporting or re-exporting to prohibited end uses or end users
6. Exporting or re-exporting to embargoed destinations
7. Support of proliferation activities
8. Shipping goods through, transiting, or unloading in prohibited countries
9. Violating any order, terms, and conditions of the EAR or any license or exception
10. Proceeding with transactions with knowledge that a violation has occurred or is about to occur

If none of the Ten General Prohibitions will be violated by the intended export transaction, then no license is required (Step 20).

G. License Exemptions and Exceptions

If an item is outside of the scope of the EAR, that is, it is not subject to the EAR, then, assuming it is not subject to licensing by and the requirements of any other agency, it can be exported "No License Required" (NLR). In addition, an item which is subject to the EAR because it is a U.S. export or certain type of re-export but is not specifically identified on the Commerce Control List (therefore falling in the basket category "EAR 99"), can also be exported "NLR" provided it is not subject to any of the Ten General Prohibitions. Finally, if the item is listed on the Commerce Control List but there is no "X" in the country box of ultimate destination, it may be exported "NLR" provided, again, that it does not violate any of the Ten General Prohibitions.

Assuming, however, the foregoing analysis indicates that a license will be required for export, before applying for a license, the exporter can review the license exceptions designated in the EAR. Although there are numerous license exceptions specified, Step 21 involves reviewing a list of restrictions that apply to all license exceptions contained in section 740.2 of the EAR. Again, assuming that none of those restrictions apply, the exporter may review each of the available license exceptions and assess whether or not the intended export transaction qualifies for one of the specific exceptions.

One large group of exceptions is based upon the Commerce Control List. As discussed above in regard to the Commerce Control List, identifying a product intended for export on the List will also show under the ECCN various types of license exceptions that may be available. For example, "LVS" (Low Value Shipments) may be available for small shipments, "GBS" may be available for shipments to Country Group B, "CIV" may be available for shipments to civil (nonmilitary) end users, and "CTP" may apply to certain types of computers. All the foregoing license exceptions are based on the Commerce Control List. Another exception, "TMP," encompasses both temporary exports (TEMP) and temporary imports (TUS). Likewise, "RPL" includes both replacement parts (PTS) and service and repair exports (SNR). Exports to governmental end users may qualify for "GOV." "GFT" covers gifts and humanitarian donations. "BAG" covers the export of commodities and software which are personal effects, household effects, vehicles, and tools of trade. (They must be owned by the individual and intended for and necessary and appropriate for the use of the individual. Such items must accompany the traveler or in certain cases may be shipped within three months before or after the individual's departure.) "AVS" is an exception for the export of aircraft and vessels and "APR" (Additional Permissive Re-exports) is a license exception for re-exports from Country Group A:1 destined for: (1) a country in Country Group B that is not also included in Country Group D:2, D:3, D:4, Cambodia, or Laos, and the commodity being re-exported is both controlled for national security reasons and not controlled for export to Country Group A:1, or (2) a country in Country Group D:1 other than Cambodia, Laos, or North Korea and the commodity being re-exported is controlled for national security reasons. (This exception does not include computers with a CTP greater than 45,000 MTOPS to Hong Kong and South Korea and commodities controlled for nuclear nonproliferation or missile technology reasons.) Analyzing whether an export qualifies for an exception comprises Steps 22 and 23. If the exporter believes an exception applies, it must export in accordance with the terms and conditions of the exception (Steps 17 and 24).

In completing the export documentation, including specifically the Shipper's Export Declaration, designation of "NLR" license exception is made under penalty of perjury and subjects any false or inaccurate designation to the penalties described in Section M, below.

H. License Applications and Procedures

If the transaction is subject to the EAR, the product is on the Commerce Control List and there is an "X" in the Country Chart for the intended destination, and no exception applies, the exporter will have to apply for a license (see Figure 5–8).

The first step in applying for a license is determining what documentation is required from the buyer.

1. Documentation From Buyer

If the item being exported is controlled for national security reasons and destined for one of the following countries, an Import or End-User Certificate from the buyer's government is required: Argentina, Australia, Austria, Belgium, Bulgaria, China (PRC), Czech Republic, Denmark, Finland, France, Germany, Greece, Hong Kong, Hungary, India, Republic of Ireland, Italy, Japan, Korea, Principality of Liechtenstein, Luxembourg, Netherlands, New Zealand, Norway, Pakistan, Poland, Portugal, Romania, Singapore, Slovakia, Spain, Sweden, Switzerland, Taiwan, Turkey, United Kingdom. A list of government agencies issuing Import Certificates is contained in the EAR. Import Certificates are required where the total value of the shipment exceeds $5,000 (a sam-

Figure 5–8. Decision tree for exporters.

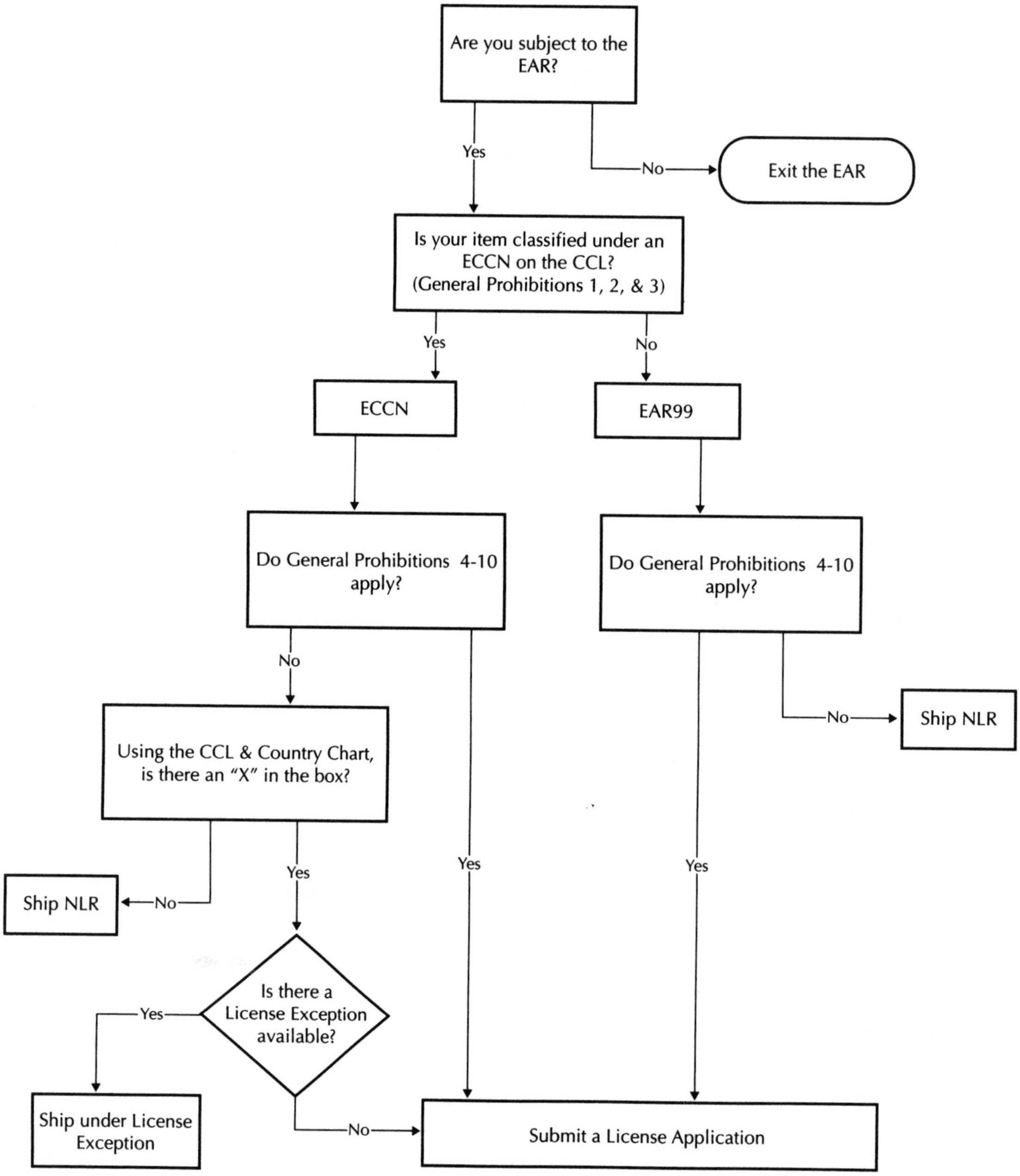

ple of the form used for U.S. imports is shown in Figure 5–9). In a number of situations, no support documentation is required from the buyer to apply for an export license. These include exports and re-exports involving ultimate consignees located in any of the following countries: Bahamas, Barbados, Belize, Bermuda, Bolivia, Brazil, Canada, Chile, Colombia, Costa Rica, Dominican Republic, Ecuador, El Salvador, French Guiana, French West Indies, Greenland, Guatemala, Guiana, Haiti, Honduras, Jamaica, Leeward and Windward Islands, Mexico, Miquelon and Saint Pierre Islands, Netherlands Antilles, Nicaragua, Panama, Paraguay, Peru, Surinam, Trinidad and Tobago, Uruguay, and Venezuela. No support documentation is required for license applications where the ultimate consignee or purchaser is a foreign government or foreign government agency except for the People's Republic of China, India, Bulgaria, Czech Republic, Hungary, Poland, Romania, and Slovakia. Likewise, no support documentation is required for items exported for temporary exhibit, demonstration, or testing purposes.

All other export transactions require a "Statement by Ultimate Consignee and Purchaser." This is a revised form, BXA-711. A sample is shown in Figure 5–10. No Statement by Ultimate Consignee and Purchaser is required where the transaction is valued at $5,000 or less. If the country of ultimate destination is listed in either Country Group D:2, D:3, or D:4, a copy of the Statement must be submitted with the license application. Otherwise, the Statement must be maintained in the records of the applicant for the license.

2. *License Application Form*

Figure 5–11 shows the new license application form, BXA-748P. The form contains instructions for its completion. Additional items may be listed in an "Item Appendix," and additional end users may be listed in an "End User Appendix" (see Figures 5–12 and 5–13, respectively). In addition to the general instructions, specific information must be provided for certain items or types of transactions ("unique license application requirements"). These include the export of chemicals, medicinals, and pharmaceuticals; communications intercepting devices; digital computers; telecommunications and related equipment; gift parcels; goods transiting in the United States; goods transiting other countries; nuclear nonproliferation items and end uses; numerical control devices; motion control boards; numerically controlled machine tools; dimensional inspection machines; direct numerical control systems; specially designed assemblies and specially designed software; parts, components, and materials incorporated abroad in foreign-made products; ship stores and plane stores, supplies, and equipment; regional stability controlled items; re-exports; robots; short-supply controlled items; technology; temporary exports or re-exports; and exports of chemicals controlled for "CW" reasons by ECCN 1C350 to countries not listed on Supplement No. 2 to Part 745 of the EAR.

The specific instructions for such items and transactions are contained in the EAR. Completion of the license application form comprises Steps 25 and 26.

(*Text continues on page 223.*)

Figure 5–9. Import certificate (U.S.).

Forms Supplement page - 1

FORM BXA-645P/ATF-4522/DPS-53 (REV 3/98)

Form Approved: OMB No. 0694-0017 - Modele approuvé: OMB No. 0694-0017

U.S. DEPARTMENT OF COMMERCE
Bureau of Export Administration
U.S. DEPARTMENT OF THE TREASURY
Bureau of Alcohol, Tobacco and Firearms
U.S. DEPARTMENT OF STATE
Office of Munitions Control

INTERNATIONAL IMPORT CERTIFICATE
(CERTIFICAT INTERNATIONAL D'IMPORTATION)

NOTE: **Read instructions on the reverse side before completing and submitting this form.** (Lire les instructions au verso avant de remplir et de presenter la présente formule.)

Certificate Number

1. U.S. Importer/Importateur (Name and address—Nom et adresse)

FOR U.S. GOVERNMENT USE (Réservé pour le Gouvernment des Etats-Unis)

2. Exporter/Exportateur (Name and address—Nom et adresse)

If this form has been approved by the Department of Commerce or the Department of State, it is not valid unless the official seal of the Department of Commerce, or the Department of State, appears in this space. If this form is approved by the Treasury Department, a seal is not required. (Si ce formulaire a été approuvé par le Ministère du Commerce, ou le Ministère des Affaires Etrangères, il n'est pas valide à moins qu'un sceau officiel du Ministère du Commerce ou du Ministère des Affaires Etrangères soit apposé sur le document. Si ce formulaire est approuvé par le Ministère des Finances, un sceau officiel n'est pas nècessaire.

3. Description of goods (Désignation de la Marchandise)	TSUS Anno. No. (Numéro de la liste)	Quantity (Quantité)	Value (Valeur) (FOB, CIF, etc.)

4. Representation and undertaking of U.S. importer or principal

The undersigned hereby represents that he has undertaken to import into the United States of America under a U.S. Consumption Entry or U.S. Warehouse Entry the commodities in quantities described above, or, if the commodities are not so imported into the United States of America, that he will not divert, transship, or reexport them to another destination except with explicit approval of the Department of Commerce, the Department of State, or the Department of the Treasury, as appropriate. The undersigned also undertakes to notify the appropriate Department immediately of any changes of fact or intention set forth herein. If a delivery verification is required, the undersigned also undertakes to obtain such verification and make disposition of it in accordance with such requirement. **Any false statement willfully made in this declaration is punishable by fine and imprisonment.** (See experts from U.S. Code on reverse side.)

Déclaration et engagement de l'importateur ou du commettant des Etats-Unis

Le soussigné déclare par la présente qu'il a pris l'engagement d'importer aux Etats-Unis d'Amérique, en vertu d'une Déclaration américaine de Mise en Consommation, ou d'une Declaration américaine d'Entrée en entrepôt, la quantité de produits ci-dessus et que, dans le cas ou ces produits ne seraient pas ainsi importés aux Etats-Unis d'Amérique, il ne le détournera, ne les transbordera, ni les réexportera a destination d'un autre lieu, si ce n'est avec l'approbation explicite du Ministère du Commerce, du Ministère des Affaires Etrangères ou du Ministère des Finances, comme il est requis. Le soussigné prend également l'èngagement d'aviser le Ministère intéressé des Etats-Unis de tous changements survenus dans les actes ou les intentions énoncés dans la présente déclaration. Si demande est faite d'une confirmation de la livraison le soussignè prend également l'engagement d'obtenir cette confirmation et d'en disposer de la manière prescrite par cette demande. **Toute fausee déclaration faite intentionnellement espose l'auteur aux pénalités prévues par la loi.** (Voir Extrait du Code des Etats-Unis au verso.)

Type or Print (Prière d'écrire a la machine ou en caractères d imprimerie)

Name of Firm or Corporation (Nom de la Firme ou de la Société)

Type or Print (Prière d'écrire a la machine ou en caractères d imprimerie)

Name and Title of Authorized Official (Nom et titre de l'agent ou employé autorisé)

Signature of Authorized Official (Signature de l'agent ou employé autorisé)

Date of Signature (Date de la signature)

This document ceases to be valid unless presented to the competent foreign authorities within six months from its date of issue. (Le présent document perd sa validité s'il n'est pas remis aux autorités étrangères compétentes dans un délai de six mois à compter de sa délivrance.)

No import certification may be obtained unless this International Import Certificate has been completed and filed with the appropriate U.S. Government agency (Department of Commerce: 50 U.S.C. app. §2411, E.O. 12214 15 C.F.R. §368; Department of the Treasury; 22 U.S.C. §2778, E.O. 11959, 27 C.F.R. §47; Department of State: 22 U.S.C. 2778, 2779, E.O. 11958, 22 C.F.R. §123). Information furnished herewith is subject to the provisions of Section 12(c) of the Export Administration Act of 1979, 50 U.S.C. app. 2411(c), and its unauthorized disclosure is prohibited by law.

FOR U.S. GOVERNMENT USE (Réservé au Gouvernement des Etats-Unis)

Certification: This is to certify that the above declaration was made to the U.S. Department of Commerce, State, or Treasury through the undersigned designated official thereof and a copy of this certification is placed in the official files.

Certification : Il est certifié par la présente que la déclaration ci-dessus a été faite au Ministère du Commerce, des Affaires Etrangères, ou des Finances des Etats-Unis par l'intermédiaire du fonctionnaire autorisé soussigné de ce Ministère et qu'une copie de ce certificat a été conservée dans les archives officielles.

Designated Commerce, State, or Treasury Official (Fonctionnaire competent du Ministère du Commerce, d'Etat, ou du Trésor) Date

USCOMM DC 89-24414

ORIGINAL COPY

Export Administration Regulations January 2001

Figure 5–10. Statement by ultimate consignee and purchaser.

FORM BXA-711
FORM APPROVED: OMB NO. 0694-0088

U.S. DEPARTMENT OF COMMERCE
Bureau of Export Administration

Information furnished herewith is subject to the provisions of Section 12(c) of the Export Administration Act of 1979, as amended, 50 U.S.C. app. 2411(c), and its unauthorized disclosure is prohibited by law.

DATE RECEIVED
(Leave Blank)

STATEMENT BY ULTIMATE CONSIGNEE AND PURCHASER

1. ULTIMATE CONSIGNEE	CITY	
ADDRESS LINE 1	COUNTRY	
ADDRESS LINE 2	POSTAL CODE	TELEPHONE OR FAX

2. DISPOSITION OR USE OF ITEMS BY ULTIMATE CONSIGNEE NAMED IN BLOCK 1
We certify that the items:

A. ☐ Will be used by us (as capital equipment) in the form in which received in a manufacturing process in the country named in Block 1 and will not be reexported or incorporated into an end product.

B. ☐ Will be processed or incorporated by us into the following product(s) ______
to be manufactured in the country named in Block 1 for distribution in ______

C. ☐ Will be resold by us in the form in which received in the country named in Block 1 for use or consumption therein.
The specific end-use by my customer will be ______

D. ☐ Will be reexported by us in the form in which received to ______

E. ☐ Other (describe fully) ______

NOTE: If BOX (D) is checked, acceptance of this form by the Bureau of Export Administration as a supporting document for license applications shall not be construed as an authorization to reexport the items to which the form applies unless specific approval has been obtained from the Bureau of Export Administration for such reexport.

3. NATURE OF BUSINESS OF ULTIMATE CONSIGNEE NAMED IN BLOCK 1
A. The nature of our usual business is ______
B. Our business relationship with the U.S. exporter is ______
and we have had this business relationship for ______ year(s).

4. ADDITIONAL INFORMATION

5. ASSISTANCE IN PREPARING STATEMENT

STATEMENT OF ULTIMATE CONSIGNEE AND PURCHASER
We certify that all of the facts contained in this statement are true and correct to the best of our knowledge and we do not know of any additional facts which are inconsistent with the above statement. We shall promptly send a supplemental statement to the U.S. Exporter, disclosing any change of facts or intentions set forth in this statement which occurs after the statement has been prepared and forwarded. Except as specifically authorized by the U.S. Export Administration Regulations (15 CFR Parts 730-774), or by prior written approval of the Bureau of Export Administration, we will not reexport, resell, or otherwise dispose of any items approved on a license supported by this statement: (1) to any country not approved for export as brought to our attention by means of a bill of lading, commercial invoice, or any other means; or (2) to any person if we know that it will result directly or indirectly, in disposition of the items contrary to the representations made in this statement or contrary to Export Administration Regulations.

6. SIGNATURE OF OFFICIAL OF ULTIMATE CONSIGNEE	7. NAME OF PURCHASER
NAME OF OFFICIAL	SIGNATURE OF OFFICIAL OF PURCHASER
TITLE OF OFFICIAL	NAME OF OFFICIAL
DATE	TITLE OF OFFICIAL
CERTIFICATION FOR USE OF U.S. EXPORTER We certify that no corrections, additions, or alterations were made on this form by us after the form was signed by the (ultimate consignee)(purchaser).	DATE

8. NAME OF EXPORTER	SIGNATURE OF PERSON AUTHORIZED TO CERTIFY FOR EXPORTER	
NAME OF PERSON SIGNING THIS DOCUMENT	TITLE OF PERSON SIGNING THIS DOCUMENT	DATE

We acknowledge that the making of any false statements or concealment of any material fact in connection with this statement may result in imprisonment or fine, or both and denial, in whole or in part, of participation in U.S. exports and reexports.

Public reporting burden for this collection of information is estimated to average 15 minutes per response plus one minute for recordkeeping, including the time for reviewing instruments, searching existing data sources, gathering and maintaining the data needed, and completing and reviewing the collection of information. Send comments regarding this burden estimate or any other aspect of this collection of information, including suggestions for reducing this burden, to The Director of Administration, Room 3889, Bureau of Export Administration, U.S. Department of Commerce, Washington, D.C. 20230; and to the Office of Management and Budget Paperwork Reduction Project (0694-0021), Washington, D.C. 20503.

Notwithstanding any other provision of law, no person is required to respond to nor shall a person be subject to a penalty for failure to comply with a collection of information subject to the requirements of the Paperwork Reduction Act unless that collection of information displays a currently valid OMB Control Number.

USCOMM-DC 96-24082

Figure 5–11. Multipurpose application.

FORM **BXA-748P**
FORM APPROVED: OMB NO. 0694-0088,0694-0089

U.S. DEPARTMENT OF COMMERCE
Bureau of Export Administration

MULTIPURPOSE APPLICATION FORM

GENERAL INSTRUCTIONS

A. USE OF THIS FORM. Use this form to submit either a classification request or an application for a license to export or reexport items subject to the export licensing authority of the U.S. Department of Commerce.

B. WHO MAY APPLY. Anyone may submit a classification request or a license application for the reexport of commodities, software, or technology. License applications for the export of items from the United States may be made only by a person subject to the jurisdiction of the United States. An application may be made on behalf of a person not subject to the jurisdiction of the United States by an authorized agent in the United States. Refer to §748.5 of the Export Administration Regulations (EAR) for additional information.

C. WHAT TO SUBMIT. Consult Part 748 of the EAR for instructions on documentation that you may need to submit with your application. Remove this cover page along with the last page of this application and firmly attach any required support documentation. (Do not separate the remaining pages in this packet and note the Application Control Number on all attached support documents.) This last page contains your Application Control Number, necessary to track your application during processing at the Bureau of Export Administration (BXA). Refer to §750.5 of the EAR for additional information on these services.

D. DUPLICATE APPLICATIONS. You may not submit a second application for a license covering the same proposed transaction while your first application is pending with BXA.

E. ASSISTANCE AND ADDITIONAL COPIES. To order small quantities of this form, or to request assistance on this or other export control matters, contact the Exporter Counseling Division on (202) 482-4811 or BXA's Western Regional Office in Newport Beach, California on (714) 660-0144 or Santa Clara, California on (408) 748-7450. Copies may also be obtained from any U.S. Department of Commerce, International Trade Administration District Office. To order large quantities of this form, write BXA's Operations Support Division, P.O. Box 273, Washington, D.C. 20044, or telephone (202) 482-3332.

F. COMPLIANCE WITH THE EAR. Additional information necessary to properly complete and file this application is contained in the EAR, codified at 15 CFR 730 et seq with changes published in the Federal RegistBXA also publishes a looseleaf version of the EAR, with changes issued in the form of supplements titled Export Administration Bulletins. BXA also offers the EAR on-line. If you wish to subscribe to the print or electronic version of the EAR, contact the Department of Commerce's National Technical Information Service at 5285 Port Royal Road, Springfield, VA 22161; or by telephone during the hours of 8:30 a.m.-5:00 p.m., Eastern Standard Time, Monday - Friday on (703) 487-4630; or by facsimile 24 hours a day/7 days a week on (703) 321-8547.

SPECIFIC INSTRUCTIONS

This application will be processed using an Optical Character Recognition (OCR) System. Type using 10 or 12 pitch. Do not use script type faces. Information must be placed within the space provided. Do not go through or outside Failure to complete the form as requested will significantly delay processing of the form.

All information must be legibly typed within the lines for each Block or Box except where a signature is required. Where there is a choice of entering telephone numbers or facsimile numbers, and you wish to provide a facsimile number instead of a telephone number, identify the facsimile number with the letter "F" immediately after the number (e.g., 011-358-0-123456F).

Block 1: CONTACT PERSON. Enter the name of the person who can answer questions concerning the application.

Block 2: TELEPHONE. Enter the telephone number of the person who can answer questions concerning the application.

Block 3: FACSIMILE. Enter the facsimile number, if available, of the person who can answer questions concerning the application.

Block 4: DATE OF APPLICATION. Enter the current date.

Block 5: TYPE OF APPLICATION. **Export**. If the items are located within the United States, and you wish to export those items, mark the Box labeled "Export" with an (X). **Reexport**. If the items are located outside the United States, mark the Box labeled "Reexport" with an (X). **Classification Request**. If you are requesting BXA to classify your item against the Commerce Control List (CCL), mark the Box labeled "Classification Request" with an (X). **Special Comprehensive License.** If you are submitting a Special Comprehensive License application in accordance with procedures described in Part 752 of the EAR, mark the Box labeled "Special Comprehensive License" with an (X).

Block 6: DOCUMENTS SUBMITTED WITH APPLICATION. Review the documentation you are required to submit with your application in accordance with the provisions of Part 748 of the EAR, and mark all applicable Boxes with an (X).

Mark the Box "Foreign Availability" with an (X) if you are submitting an assertion of foreign availability with your license application. See Part 768 of the EAR for instructions on foreign availability submissions.

Mark the "Tech. Specs." box with an (X) if you are submitting descriptive literature, brochures, technical specifications, etc. with your application.

Block 7: DOCUMENTS ON FILE WITH APPLICANT. Certify that you have retained on file all applicable documents as required by the provisions of Part 748 of the EAR by placing an (X) in the appropriate Box(es).

Block 8: SPECIAL COMPREHENSIVE LICENSE. Complete this Block only if you are submitting an application for a Special Comprehensive License in accordance with Part 752 of the EAR.

Block 9: SPECIAL PURPOSE. Complete this Block for certain items or types of transactions only if specifically required in Supplement No. 2 to Part 748 of the EAR.

Block 10: RESUBMISSION APPLICATION CONTROL NUMBER. If your original application was returned without action, provide the Application Control Number for that application.

Block 11: REPLACEMENT LICENSE NUMBER. If you have received a license for identical items to the same ultimate consignee, but would like to make a change to the license as originally approved that is not excepted in §750.7(c) of the EAR, enter the license number here, and a statement in Block 24 regarding what changes you wish to make to the original license.

Block 12: ITEMS PREVIOUSLY EXPORTED. This Block should be completed only if you have marked the "Reexport" box in Block 5. Enter the license number, License Exception symbol (for exports under General Licenses, enter the appropriate General License symbol), or other authorization under which the items were originally exported, if known.

Block 13: IMPORT/END-USER CERTIFICATE. Enter the name of the country and number of the Import or End User Certificate obtained in accordance with provisions of Part 748 of the EAR.

Block 14: APPLICANT. Enter the applicant's name, street address, city, state/country, and postal code. Refer to §748.5(a) of EAR for a definition of "applicant". If you have marked "Export" in Block 5, you must include your company's Employer Identification Number unless you are filing as an individual or as an agent on behalf of the exporter. The Employer Identification Number is assigned by the Internal Revenue Service for tax identification purposes. Accordingly, you should consult your company's financial officer or accounting division to obtain this number.

Block 15: OTHER PARTY AUTHORIZED TO RECEIVE LICENSE. If you would like BXA to transmit the approved license to another party designated by you, complete all information in this Block, including name, street address, city, country, postal code and telephone number. Leave this space blank if the license is to be sent to the applicant. Designation of another party to receive the license does not alter the responsibilities of the applicant.

Block 16: PURCHASER. Enter the purchaser's complete name, street address, city, country, postal code and telephone or facsimile number. Refer to §748.5(c) of the EAR for a definition of "purchaser". If the purchaser is also the ultimate consignee, enter the words "same as Block 18".

SEE CONTINUATION OF SPECIFIC INSTRUCTIONS ON REVERSE SIDE.

Figure 5–11. *(continued)*

Block 17: INTERMEDIATE CONSIGNEE. Enter the intermediate consignee's complete name, street address, city, country, postal code and telephone or facsimile number. Provide a complete street address. P.O. Boxes are not acceptable. Refer to §748.5(d) of the EAR for a definition of "intermediate consignee". If this party is identical to that listed in Block 16, you may simply type the words "Same as Block 16". If your proposed transaction does not involve use of an intermediate consignee, enter "None". If your proposed transaction involves use of more than one intermediate consignee, provide the information in Block 24 for each additional Intermediate Consignee.

Block 18: ULTIMATE CONSIGNEE. Enter the ultimate consignee's complete name, street address, city, country, postal code and telephone or facsimile number. Provide a complete street address. P.O. Boxes are not acceptable. The ultimate consignee is the party who will actually receive the material for the end-use designated in Block 21. Refer to §748.5(e) of the EAR for the definition of "ultimate consignee" A bank, freight forwarder, forwarding agent, or other intermediary may not be identified as the ultimate consignee. Government purchasing organizations are the sole exception to this requirement. This type of entity may be identified as the government entity that is the actual ultimate consignee in those instances when the items are to be transferred to the government entity that is the actual end-user, provided the actual end-use and end-user is clearly identified in Block 21 or in additional documentation attached to the application.

If your application is for the reexport of items previously exported, enter the new ultimate consignee's complete name, street address, city, country postal code and telephone or facsimile number. If your application involves a temporary export or reexport, the applicant should be shown as the ultimate consignee in care of a person or entity who will have control over the items abroad.

Block 19: END-USER. Complete this Block only if the ultimate consignee identified in Block 18 is not the actual end-user. If there will be more than one end-user enter the word "various" in this Block, and use Form BXA-748P-B to identify each of the end-users. Enter each end-user's complete name, street address, city, country, postal code and telephone or facsimile number. Provide a complete street address. P.O. Boxes are not acceptable.

Block 20: ORIGINAL ULTIMATE CONSIGNEE. If your application involves the reexport of items previously exported, enter the original ultimate consignee's complete name, street address, city, country, postal code and telephone or facsimile number. The original ultimate consignee is the entity identified in the original application for export as the ultimate consignee or the party currently in possession of the items. Provide a complete street address. P.O. Boxes are not acceptable.

Block 21: SPECIFIC END-USE. Provide a complete and detailed description of the end-use intended by the ultimate consignee and/or end-user(s). If you are requesting approval of a reexport, provide a complete and detailed description of the end-use intended by the new ultimate consignee or end-user(s) and indicate any other countries for which resale or reexport is requested. If additional space is necessary, use Block 21 on Form BXA-748P-A or B. Be specific. Such vague descriptions as "research," "manufacturing," or "scientific uses" are not acceptable.

Block 22: FOR A LICENSE APPLICATION YOU MUST COMPLETE EACH OF THE SUB-BLOCKS CONTAINED IN THIS BLOCK. If you are submitting a classification request, you need not complete Blocks (e), (f), (g), and (h). Enter "N/A" in these Blocks. If you wish to export, reexport or have BXA classify more than one item, use Form BXA-748P-A for additional items:

(a) ECCN. Enter the Export Control Classification Number (ECCN) that corresponds to the item you wish to export or reexport. If you are asking BXA to classify your item, provide a recommended classification for the item in this Block.

(b) CTP. You must complete this Block if your application involves a digital computer or equipment containing a digital computer as described in Supplement No. 2 to Part 748 of the EAR. Instructions on calculating the CTP are contained in a Technical Note at the end of Category 4 in the CCL. If your application does not involve these items, insert "N/A" in this Block.

(c) Model Number. Enter the correct model number for each item.

(d) CCATS Number. If you have received a classification for this item from BXA, provide the CCATS number shown on the classification issued by BXA. Otherwise, enter "N/A" in this Block.

(e) Quantity. Identify the quantity to be exported or reexported, in terms of the "Units" identified for the ECCN entered in Block 21 (a). If the "Unit" for an item is "$ value", enter the quantity in units commonly used in the trade.

(f) Units. The "Unit" paragraph within each ECCN will list a specific "Unit" for those items controlled by the entry. The "Unit" must be entered on all license applications submitted to BXA. If an item is licensed in items of "$ value", the unit of quantity commonly used in trade must also be shown on the license application. If the unit for your particular item is shown as "N/A" in the appropriate entry on the CCL, enter "N/A" in this Block.

(g) Unit Price. Provide the fair market value of the items you wish to export or reexport. Round all prices to the nearest whole dollar amount. Give the exact unit price only if the value is less than $0.50. If normal trade practices make it impractical to establish a firm contract price, state in Block 24 the precise items upon which the price is to be ascertained and from which the contract price may be objectively determined.

(h) Total Price. Provide the total price of the item(s) described in Block 22(j).

(i) Manufacturer. Provide the name only of the manufacturer, if known, for each of the items you wish to export, reexport, or have BXA classify, if different from the applicant.

(j) Technical Description. Provide a description of the item(s) you wish to export, reexport, or have BXA classify. Provide details when necessary to identify the specific item(s), and include all characteristics or parameters shown in the applicable ECCN using measurements identified in the ECCN (e.g., basic ingredients, composition, electrical parameters, size, gauge, grade, horsepower, etc.). These characteristics must be identified for the items in the proposed transaction when they are different from the characteristics described in promotional brochure(s).

Block 23: TOTAL APPLICATION DOLLAR VALUE. Enter the total value of all items contained on the application in U.S. Dollars. The use of other currencies is not acceptable.

Block 24: ADDITIONAL INFORMATION. Enter additional data pertinent to the application as required in the EAR. Include special certifications, names of parties in interest not disclosed elsewhere, explanation of documents attached, etc. Do not include information concerning Block 22 in this space.

If your application represents a previously denied application, you must provide the Application Control Number for the original application.

If you are asking BXA to classify your product, use this space to explain why you believe the ECCN entered in Block 22(a) is appropriate. This explanation must contain an analysis of the item in terms of the technical control parameters specified in the appropriate ECCN. If you do not identify a recommended classification in Block 22(a), you must state the reason you cannot determine the appropriate classification, identifying any ambiguities or deficiencies in the regulations that precluded you from determining the correct classification.

If additional space is necessary, use Block 24 on Form BXA-748P-A or B.

Block 25: YOU, AS THE APPLICANT OR DULY AUTHORIZED AGENT OF THE APPLICANT, MUST MANUALLY SIGN THE APPLICATION. If you are an agent of the applicant, in addition to providing your name and title in this Block you must enter your company's name in Block 24. Note: rubber-stamped or electronic signatures are not acceptable. Type both your name and title in the spaces provided.

MAIL APPLICATION TO:	COURIER DELIVERIES TO:
OFFICE OF EXPORTER SERVICES P.O. BOX 273 WASHINGTON, D.C. 20044	OFFICE OF EXPORTER SERVICES ROOM 2705 14TH & PENNSYLVANIA AVE., N.W. WASHINGTON, D.C. 20230

Public reporting burden for this collection of information is estimated to average 45 minutes per response, including the time for reviewing instructions, searching existing data sources, gathering and maintaining the data needed, and completing and reviewing the collection of information. Send comments regarding this burden estimate or any other aspect of this collection of information, including suggestions for reducing this burden, to Robert F. Kugleman, Director of Administration, U.S. Department of Commerce, Bureau of Export Administration, Room 3889, Washington, D.C. 20230

INCOMPLETE APPLICATIONS WILL BE RETURNED FOR THE NECESSARY INFORMATION AND/OR DOCUMENTATION. DETACH THIS SHEET AT PERFORATION.

(continues)

Figure 5–11. *(continued)*

B
FORM **BXA-748P**
FORM APPROVED: OMB NO. 0694-0088, 0694-0089

U.S. DEPARTMENT OF COMMERCE
Bureau of Export Administration
MULTIPURPOSE APPLICATION

DATE RECEIVED (Leave Blank) **X**

1. CONTACT PERSON

Information furnished herewith is subject to the provisions of Section 12(c) of the Export Administration Act of 1979, as amended, 50 U.S.C. app. 2411(c), and its unauthorized disclosure is prohibited by law.

2. TELEPHONE

APPLICATION CONTROL NUMBER
This is NOT an export license number.
Z 029074

3. FACSIMILE

4. DATE OF APPLICATION

5. TYPE OF APPLICATION
- ☐ EXPORT
- ☐ REEXPORT
- ☐ CLASSIFICATION REQUEST
- ☐ SPECIAL COMPREHENSIVE LICENSE
- ☐ OTHER

6. DOCUMENTS SUBMITTED WITH APPLICATION
- ☐ BXA-748P-A
- ☐ BXA-748P-B
- ☐ BXA-711
- ☐ IMPORT/END-USER CERTIFICATE
- ☐ TECH. SPECS.
- ☐ NUCLEAR CERTIFICATION
- ☐ LETTER OF EXPLANATION
- ☐ FOREIGN AVAILABILITY
- ☐ OTHER

7. DOCUMENTS ON FILE WITH APPLICANT
- ☐ BXA-711
- ☐ LETTER OF ASSURANCE
- ☐ IMPORT/END-USER CERTIFICATE
- ☐ OTHER

8. SPECIAL COMPREHENSIVE LICENSE
- ☐ BXA-752 OR BXA-752-A
- ☐ INTERNAL CONTROL PROGRAM
- ☐ COMPREHENSIVE NARRATIVE
- ☐ CERTIFICATIONS
- ☐ OTHER

9. SPECIAL PURPOSE

10. RESUBMISSION APPLICATION CONTROL NUMBER

11. REPLACEMENT LICENSE NUMBER

12. FOR ITEM(S) PREVIOUSLY EXPORTED, PROVIDE LICENSE EXCEPTION SYMBOL OR LICENSE NUMBER

13. IMPORT/END-USER CERTIFICATE COUNTRY: NUMBER:

14. APPLICANT		15. OTHER PARTY AUTHORIZED TO RECEIVE LICENSE	
ADDRESS LINE 1		ADDRESS LINE 1	
ADDRESS LINE 2		ADDRESS LINE 2	
CITY	POSTAL CODE	CITY	POSTAL CODE
STATE/COUNTRY	EMPLOYER IDENTIFICATION NUMBER	STATE/COUNTRY	TELEPHONE OR FAX
16. PURCHASER		17. INTERMEDIATE CONSIGNEE	
ADDRESS LINE 1		ADDRESS LINE 1	
ADDRESS LINE 2		ADDRESS LINE 2	
CITY	POSTAL CODE	CITY	POSTAL CODE
COUNTRY	TELEPHONE OR FAX	COUNTRY	TELEPHONE OR FAX
18. ULTIMATE CONSIGNEE		19. END-USER	
ADDRESS LINE 1		ADDRESS LINE 1	
ADDRESS LINE 2		ADDRESS LINE 2	
CITY	POSTAL CODE	CITY	POSTAL CODE
COUNTRY	TELEPHONE OR FAX	COUNTRY	TELEPHONE OR FAX
20. ORIGINAL ULTIMATE CONSIGNEE		21. SPECIFIC END-USE	
ADDRESS LINE 1			
ADDRESS LINE 2			
CITY	POSTAL CODE		
COUNTRY	TELEPHONE OR FAX		

22. (a) ECCN	(b) CTP	(c) MODEL NUMBER		(d) CCATS NUMBER	23. TOTAL APPLICATION DOLLAR VALUE
(e) QUANTITY	(f) UNITS	(g) UNIT PRICE	(h) TOTAL PRICE	(i) MANUFACTURER	$

(j) TECHNICAL DESCRIPTION

24. ADDITIONAL INFORMATION

LICENSE APPLICATION CERTIFICATION: I hereby make application for a license to export or reexport, and I certify that (a) to the best of my knowledge, information and belief all statements in this application, including the description of the commodities, software or technology and their end-uses, and any documents submitted in support of this application are correct and complete and that they fully and accurately disclose all the terms of the order and other facts of the transaction; (b) this application conforms to the instructions accompanying this application and the Export Administration Regulations; (c) I obtained the order from the order party or I negotiated with and secured the order directly from the purchaser or ultimate consignee, or through his or their agent(s); (d) I will retain records pertaining to this transaction and make them available as required by the Export Administration Regulations; (e) I will report promptly to the Bureau of Export Administration any material changes in the terms of the order or other facts or intentions of the transaction as reflected in this application and supporting documents, whether the application is still under consideration or a license has been granted; and (f) if the license is granted, I will be strictly accountable for its use in accordance with the Export Administration Regulations and all the terms and conditions of the license.

25. SIGNATURE (of person authorized to execute this application)	NAME OF SIGNER	TITLE OF SIGNER

This license application and any license issued pursuant thereto are expressly subject to all rules and regulations of the Bureau of Export Administration. Making any false statement or concealing any material fact in connection with this application or altering in any way the license issued is punishable by imprisonment or fine, or both, and by denial of export privileges under the Export Administration Act of 1979, as amended, and any other applicable Federal statutes. No license will be issued unless this form is completed and submitted in accordance with Export Administration Regulation.

X	X	ORIGINAL B

USCOMM-DC 96-24024

Figure 5–12. Item appendix.

C FORM BXA-748P-A FORM APPROVED: OMB NO. 0694-0088,0694-0089	U.S. DEPARTMENT OF COMMERCE Bureau of Export Administration **ITEM APPENDIX**	DATE RECEIVED (Leave Blank) X
1. APPLICATION CONTROL NUMBER (Insert from BXA-748P)	Information furnished herewith is subject to the provisions of Section 12(c) of the Export Administration Act of 1979, as amended, 50 U.S.C. app. 2411(c), and its unauthorized disclosure is prohibited by law.	2. SUBTOTAL

22. (a) ECCN	(b) CTP	(c) MODEL NUMBER		(d) CCATS NUMBER
(e) QUANTITY	(f) UNITS	(g) UNIT PRICE	(h) TOTAL PRICE	(i) MANUFACTURER
(j) TECHNICAL DESCRIPTION				
22. (a) ECCN	(b) CTP	(c) MODEL NUMBER		(d) CCATS NUMBER
(e) QUANTITY	(f) UNITS	(g) UNIT PRICE	(h) TOTAL PRICE	(i) MANUFACTURER
(j) TECHNICAL DESCRIPTION				
22. (a) ECCN	(b) CTP	(c) MODEL NUMBER		(d) CCATS NUMBER
(e) QUANTITY	(f) UNITS	(g) UNIT PRICE	(h) TOTAL PRICE	(i) MANUFACTURER
(j) TECHNICAL DESCRIPTION				
22. (a) ECCN	(b) CTP	(c) MODEL NUMBER		(d) CCATS NUMBER
(e) QUANTITY	(f) UNITS	(g) UNIT PRICE	(h) TOTAL PRICE	(i) MANUFACTURER
(j) TECHNICAL DESCRIPTION				
22. (a) ECCN	(b) CTP	(c) MODEL NUMBER		(d) CCATS NUMBER
(e) QUANTITY	(f) UNITS	(g) UNIT PRICE	(h) TOTAL PRICE	(i) MANUFACTURER
(j) TECHNICAL DESCRIPTION				
21. CONTINUATION OF SPECIFIC END-USE INFORMATION				
24. CONTINUATION OF ADDITIONAL INFORMATION				

X	X	ORIGINAL C

USCOMM-DC96-24021

Figure 5–13. End user appendix.

D FORM BXA-748P-B FORM APPROVED; OMB NO. 0694-0088,0694-0089	U.S. DEPARTMENT OF COMMERCE Bureau of Export Administration **END-USER APPENDIX**	DATE RECEIVED X (Leave Blank)
1. APPLICATION CONTROL NUMBER (Insert from BXA-478P)	Information furnished herewith is subject to the provisions of Section 12(c) of the Export Administration Act of 1979, as amended, 50 U.S.C. app. 2411(c) and its unauthorized disclosure is prohibited by law.	

19. END-USER		19. END-USER	
ADDRESS LINE 1		ADDRESS LINE 1	
ADDRESS LINE 2		ADDRESS LINE 2	
CITY	POSTAL CODE	CITY	POSTAL CODE
COUNTRY	TELEPHONE OR FAX	COUNTRY	TELEPHONE OR FAX
19. END-USER		19. END-USER	
ADDRESS LINE 1		ADDRESS LINE 1	
ADDRESS LINE 2		ADDRESS LINE 2	
CITY	POSTAL CODE	CITY	POSTAL CODE
COUNTRY	TELEPHONE OR FAX	COUNTRY	TELEPHONE OR FAX
19. END-USER		19. END-USER	
ADDRESS LINE 1		ADDRESS LINE 1	
ADDRESS LINE 2		ADDRESS LINE 2	
CITY	POSTAL CODE	CITY	POSTAL CODE
COUNTRY	TELEPHONE OR FAX	COUNTRY	TELEPHONE OR FAX
19. END-USER		19. END-USER	
ADDRESS LINE 1		ADDRESS LINE 1	
ADDRESS LINE 2		ADDRESS LINE 2	
CITY	POSTAL CODE	CITY	POSTAL CODE
COUNTRY	TELEPHONE OR FAX	COUNTRY	TELEPHONE OR FAX
19. END-USER		19. END-USER	
ADDRESS LINE 1		ADDRESS LINE 1	
ADDRESS LINE 2		ADDRESS LINE 2	
CITY	POSTAL CODE	CITY	POSTAL CODE
COUNTRY	TELEPHONE OR FAX	COUNTRY	TELEPHONE OR FAX

21. CONTINUATION OF SPECIFIC END-USE INFORMATION

24. CONTINUATION OF ADDITIONAL INFORMATION

X X	D **ORIGINAL**

USCOMM-DC 96-24020

3. Procedures

The license application form must be filed with the Bureau of Export Administration, U.S. Department of Commerce, 14th Street and Pennsylvania Avenue, N.W., Room 2705, Washington, D.C. 20044. In addition, when the exporter establishes proper electronic communication, applications may be filed electronically. Under the new EAR, all license applications will be resolved or referred to the President of the United States no later than ninety calendar days from the date of "registration" of the license application. If the license application is not complete, it will be returned without action ("RWA"). If the Department of Commerce intends to deny the license ("ITD"), it will inform the applicant, specifying the reasons, and permit the applicant to respond before finally denying the license application. In some cases, the Commerce Department can hold the application without action ("HWA"). If the exporter desires to know the status of a license application, it can telephone the BXA's system for tracking export license applications ("STELA").

Licenses which are issued are computer generated and carry a license number and validation date (a sample is shown in Figure 5–14). Usually the license will be issued for a period of two years. The license number must be entered on the Shipper's Export Declaration for export clearance. When a license has been issued, the export must be carried out in accordance with the terms and conditions of the license (Step 17).

I. Re-Exports

Items that originated in the United States and were originally exported with or without a license continue to potentially be subject to the EAR. Step 3 requires a person engaging in a re-export transaction to determine whether the re-export can be made without a license, whether a license exception applies, or whether a license must be obtained.

As explained above, if a transaction is subject to the EAR, it is necessary to assess whether or not the transaction is also prohibited by one of the Ten General Prohibitions. General Prohibition 1 includes re-export of controlled items to listed countries; 2 includes re-export from abroad of foreign-made items incorporating more than the de minimis amount of controlled U.S. content (parts and components of re-exports); 3 includes re-exports from abroad of the foreign-produced direct product of U.S. technology and software; 4 includes re-export to prohibit end uses or end users; and 5 includes re-exports to embargoed destinations without a license.

J. Export Documentation and Record-Keeping

In order to complete the exportation, whether a license is required or not, it is necessary for the exporter to complete certain export documentation and maintain certain records. The EAR requires an exporter to complete a Shipper's Export Declaration declaring the eligibility of the export. Specifically, fields 21 and 22 of the Declaration require certain information. In field 21 the exporter will be required to enter

Figure 5–14. Sample export license.

Forms Supplement **page - 10**

EXPORT LICENSE

EXPORT LICENSE NO.: A030043

VALIDATED: 7/19/88

EXPIRATION DATE: 7/31/90

UNITED STATES DEPARTMENT OF COMMERCE
BUREAU OF EXPORT ADMINISTRATION
P.O. BOX 273
BEN FRANKLIN STATION
WASHINGTON, D.C. 20044

CONSIGNEE IN COUNTRY OF ULTIMATE DESTINATION:
ABU DHABI TRADING ESTABLISHMENT
2345 LIAM DUK WAY
ABU DHABI, UNITED ARAB EMIRATES

APPLICANT'S REFERENCE NO.: A030043

PURCHASER:
AEG TELEFUNKEN
STEINHOEFT 9
HAMBURG, WEST GERMANY

LICENSEE:
A P CIRCUIT CORPORATION
513 EAST 86 STREET
NEW YORK, NY 10028

INTERMEDIATE CONSIGNEE:
ZINCOR INFOSYSTEMS, INC.
4456 PASQUATCH LET
BOMBAY, INDIA

PROCESSING CODE: CS

COMMODITIES:

QUANTITY	DESCRIPTION	ECCN	UNIT PRICE	TOTAL PRICE
50 EACH	MODEL 2345 6.50 MATH COPROCESSORS	1565	14000.00	700000.00
2 EACH	MCS68 3.40 HUMPHREY ANALYZERS	1565	30000.00	60000.00

VOID

TOTAL: 760000

THE EXPORT ADMINISTRATION REGULATIONS REQUIRE YOU TO TAKE THE FOLLOWING ACTIONS WHEN EXPORTING UNDER THE AUTHORITY OF THIS LICENSE.

A. RECORD THE EXPORT CONTROL COMMODITY NUMBER IN PARENTHESES DIRECTLY BELOW THE CORRESPONDING SCHEDULE B NUMBER ON EACH SHIPPERS EXPORT DECLARATION (SED).

B. RECORD YOUR LICENSE NUMBER IN THE COMMODITY DESCRIPTION COLUMN ON EACH SED.

C. PLACE A DESTINATION CONTROL STATEMENT ON ALL BILLS OF LADING. AIRWAY BILLS, AND COMMERCIAL INVOICES.

THIS LICENSE AUTHORIZES THE LICENSEE TO CARRY OUT THE EXPORT TRANSACTION DESCRIBED ON THE LICENSE (INCLUDING ALL ATTACHMENTS). IT MAY NOT BE TRANSFERRED WITHOUT PRIOR WRITTEN APPROVAL OF THE BUREAU OF EXPORT ADMINISTRATION. THIS LICENSE HAS BEEN GRANTED IN RELIANCE ON REPRESENTATIONS MADE BY THE LICENSEE AND OTHERS IN CONNECTION WITH THE APPLICATION FOR EXPORT AND IS EXPRESSLY SUBJECT TO ANY CONDITIONS STATED ON THE LICENSE, AS WELL AS ALL APPLICABLE EXPORT CONTROL LAWS, REGULATIONS, RULES, AND ORDERS. THIS LICENSE IS SUBJECT TO REVISION, SUSPENSION, OR REVOCATION WITHOUT PRIOR NOTICE.

Export Administration Regulations **January 2001**

"NLR" when no license is required; the license exception symbol where the export qualifies for a license exception, for example, GBS; or the license number where a license has been obtained. In general, the ECCN number must also be shown in field 22.

In addition to the Shipper's Export Declaration, a destination control statement must be entered on all copies of the bill of lading, the air waybill, and the commercial invoice for an export. If the export requires a license, the export is made under the license exceptions GBS, CIV, LVS, RPL (PTS, SNR), or TEMP (TMP, TUS), or the export is made under "NLR" (if the Reason for Control of the item as stated on the entry in the Commerce Control List is "NS" or "NP"), at a minimum, the destination control statement "These commodities, technology or software were exported from the United States in accordance with the Export Administration Regulations. Diversion contrary to law is prohibited" must be entered on such documents.

An additional document that may be required is a "Delivery Verification" (see Figure 5–15). When an export is being made to a country where an Import Certificate issued by the government of a foreign country is required for application for the export license, the Department of Commerce will on a selective basis require the exporter to obtain a Delivery Verification. If verification of delivery is required, the requirement will appear as a condition on the face of the license when issued. The list of countries issuing Import Certificates and Delivery Verification is contained in Supplement Number 4 to part 748 of the EAR.

Frequent exporters may apply for and obtain permission to file Shipper's Export Declarations on a monthly basis. Where a Shipper's Export Declaration was incorrect or the transaction is altered, a corrected Shipper's Export Declaration must be filed with the Customs Director at the port of exportation.

Exporters are required to maintain the originals of all documents pertaining to export transaction, including license applications, memoranda, notes, correspondence, contracts, invitations to bid, books of account, and financial records. If the exporter complies with certain specific requirements, the exporter may maintain the records in microfilm or electronic digital storage. The system must be able to record and reproduce all marks, information, and other characteristics of the original record, including both sides of the paper; the system must preserve the initial image and record all changes, who made them, and when they were made; and this information must be stored in such manner that none of it may be altered once it is initially recorded. The records must be maintained for a period of five years from the time of the export from the United States, any known re-export, or any other termination of the transaction. The record-keeping requirement extends to records maintained outside the United States if they pertain to any U.S. export transaction or any re-export. Any person subject to the jurisdiction of the United States may be required to produce the records in response to an inquiry from the Department of Commerce. (In some cases, a request for records located abroad may conflict with the laws and regulations of a foreign country.)

K. Special Comprehensive Licenses

Formerly, under the previous EAR, an exporter could apply for a Distribution License, a Service Supply License, or a Project License. Under the new EAR, all such

Figure 5–15. Delivery verification certificate.

Forms Supplement page - 2

Form Approved: OMB No. 0694-0016

FORM BXA 647P
(REV. 4-98)

U.S. DEPARTMENT OF COMMERCE
BUREAU OF EXPORT ADMINISTRATION

DELIVERY VERIFICATION CERTIFICATE

Public reporting burden for this collection of information is estimated to average 30 minutes per response, including the time for reviewing instruments, searching existing data sources, gathering and maintaining the data needed, and completing and reviewing the collection of information. Send comments regarding this burden estimate or any other aspect of this collection of information, including suggestions for reducing this burden, to The Director of Administration, room 3889, Bureau of Export Administration, U.S. Department of Commerce, Washington, D.C., 20230; and to the Office of Management and Budget Paperwork Reduction Project (0694-0016) Washington, D.C. 20503

Notwithstanding any other provision of law, no person is required to respond to nor shall a person be subject to a penalty for failure to comply with a collection of information subject to the requirements of the Paperwork Reduction Act unless that collection of information displays a currently valid OMB Control Number.

Instructions - When required to obtain a delivery verification, the U.S. Importer shall submit this form in duplicate, to the Customs Office. U.S. importer is required to complete all items on this form except the portion to be completed by the U.S. Customs Service. The Customs Office will certify a Delivery Verification Certificate only after the import has been delivered to the U.S. importer. The duly certified form shall then be dispatched by the U.S. importer to the foreign exporter or otherwise disposed of in accordance with instructions of the exporting country.

No delivery verificaton may be obtained unless a completed application form has been received. (50 U.S.C. App § 2401 et seq., 15 C.F.R.§ 748)

EXPORTER *(Name and address)*

This certification applies to the goods described below, shown on U.S. Department of Commerce International Import Certificate No.__________

ARRIVED *(Name of port)*

DATE OF ARRIVAL

IMPORTER *(Name and address)*

NAME OF SHIP, AIRCRAFT, OR CARRIER *(Include numbers on bills of lading, airway bills, etc.)*

DESCRIPTION OF GOODS	QUANTITY	VALUE *(FOB, CIF, etc)*

TO BE COMPLETED BY U.S. CUSTOMS SERVICE

REGION NO:

(Customs's Seal)

CERTIFICATION - It is hereby certified that the importer has produced evidence that the goods specified above have been delivered and brought under the Export Administration Regulations of the United States.

____________________ Signature

__________ Date

ENTRY ☐ WAREHOUSE ☐ CONSUMPTION | NUMBER | DATE

licenses are combined as a Special Comprehensive License. Ordinary licenses granted by the Bureau of Export Administration cover only single export transactions. With an SCL, multiple exports and re-exports can be authorized. All items subject to EAR are eligible for export under an SCL except the following:

1. Items controlled for missile technology reasons that are identified by the letters "MT" in the applicable Reason for Control paragraph of the Commerce Control List
2. Items controlled by ECCN 1C351, 1C352, 1C353, 1C354, 1C991, 1E001, 1E350, 1E351, 2B352, 2E001, 2E002, and 2E301 on the Commerce Control List that can be used in the production of chemical and biological weapons
3. Items controlled by ECCN 1C350, 1C355, 1D390, 2B350, and 2B351 on the Commerce Control List that can be used in the production of chemical weapons, precursors, and chemical warfare agents to destinations listed in Country Group D:3
4. Items controlled for short supply reasons that are identified by the letters "SS" in the applicable Reason for Control paragraph on the Commerce Control List
5. Items controlled for "EI" reasons on the Commerce Control List
6. Maritime (civil) nuclear propulsion systems or associated design or production
7. Communications intercepting devices controlled by ECCN 5A980 on the Commerce Control List
8. Hot section technology for the development, production, or overhaul of commercial aircraft engines controlled under ECCN 9E003.a.1 through a.12.f and related controls
9. Items specifically identified as ineligible by the Bureau of Export Administration on the SCL
10. Additional items consistent with international commitments

Shipments under an SCL may be made to all countries specified in the SCL except Cuba, Iran, Iraq, Libya, North Korea, Sudan, and Syria and other countries that the Bureau of Export Administration may designate on a case-by-case basis. Servicing items owned or controlled by or under the lease of entities in the foregoing countries is also prohibited.

In order to apply for an SCL, an exporter prepares the regular license application, Form BXA 748P, the Item Appendix, and the End User Appendix. In addition, the applicant must submit a comprehensive narrative statement containing the information specified in the EAR; a Form BXA-752, "Statement by Consignee in Support of Special Comprehensive License" (see Figure 5–16); Form BXA-752-A, "Reexport Territories" (see Figure 5–17); certain certifications by the consignee on their company letterhead; and the description of the "Internal Control Program." The Internal Control Program must state the procedures and safeguards that have been put in place by the

(*Text continues on page 230.*)

Figure 5–16. Statement by consignee in support of special comprehensive license.

F

FORM **BXA-752**
FORM APPROVED: OMB NO. 0694-0089

U.S. DEPARTMENT OF COMMERCE
Bureau of Export Administration

DATE RECEIVED
(Leave Blank) **X**

STATEMENT BY CONSIGNEE IN SUPPORT OF SPECIAL COMPREHENSIVE LICENSE

1. APPLICATION CONTROL NUMBER (Insert from BXA-748P)	2. CONSIGNEE ID NUMBER (Leave Blank)	Information furnished herewith is subject to the provisions of Section 12(c) of the Export Administration Act of 1979, as amended, 50 U.S.C. app. 2411(c), and its unauthorized disclosure is prohibited by law.

3. TYPE OF REQUEST

A. ☐ ADD A NEW CONSIGNEE B. ☐ CHANGE AN EXISTING CONSIGNEE C. ☐ DELETE A CONSIGNEE

4. ULTIMATE CONSIGNEE		5. SCL HOLDER	
ADDRESS LINE 1		ADDRESS LINE 1	
ADDRESS LINE 2		ADDRESS LINE 2	
CITY	POSTAL CODE	CITY	ZIP CODE
COUNTRY	CONSIGNEE NUMBER	STATE	SCL CASE NUMBER

6. DESCRIPTION OF ITEMS
We expect to use, sell, install, or reexport the following items:

7. CONSIGNEE'S BUSINESS AND RELATIONSHIP WITH SCL HOLDER NAMED IN BLOCK 5

A. Nature of Business	B. Our relationship with the exporter is:	C. We have had this business relationship for years.	D. Past Sales Volume $	E. Projected Sales Volume $

8. DISPOSITION OR USE OF ITEMS BY ULTIMATE CONSIGNEE NAMED IN BLOCK 4
We certify that the items:

A. ☐ Used by us (as captial equipment) in the form in which received in the country named in Block 4 and will not be reexported or incorporated into an end product.

B. Will be processed or incorporated by us into the following product(s) for distribution in the countries authorized on the attached BXA-752-A.

C. Will be used to service the following commodities in the countries authorized on the attached BXA-752-A.

D. Will be resold by us in the form in which received in the country named in Block 4 for use or consumption therein. The specific end-use by my customer(s) will be:

E. ☐ Will be reexported by us in the form in which received to countries authorized on the attached BXA-752-A.

F. Other

9. ADDITIONAL INFORMATION

CERTIFICATION OF CONSIGNEE

We certify that all of the facts contained in this statement are true and correct to the best of our knowledge and belief and we do not know of any additional facts which are inconsistent with the above statement. We shall promptly send a supplemental statement to the SCL Holder named in Block 5, disclosing any change of facts or intentions set forth in this statement which occurs after the statement has been prepared and forwarded, except as specifically authorized by the U.S. Export Administration Regulations (15 CFR Parts 730-774). We (a) will not use, reexport, sell, distribute, install or otherwise dispose of any items covered by this statement contrary to U.S. Export Administration Regulations; and (b) will not sell or otherwise dispose of any of these items to any person or firm listed on the Bureau of Export Administration Denied Persons List or where there is reason to believe that the items will be reexported to destinations or activities not authorized by the Bureau of Export Administration.

10. SIGNATURE OF OFFICIAL OF ULTIMATE CONSIGNEE	DATE SIGNED
NAME OF OFFICIAL OF ULTIMATE CONSIGNEE	TITLE OF PERSON SIGNING THIS DOCUMENT

REQUEST AND CERTIFICATION OF SCL HOLDER

We request that the firm named in Block 4 be approved as an ultimate consignee to whom we may export items, under the Special Comprehensive License Case Number specified in Block 5. We understand that all undertakings, commitments, obligations, and responsibilities under the special comprehensive licensing procedure, and the Export Administration Regulations related thereto, are fully applicable to any export to the above mentioned ultimate consignee if this form is validated by the Bureau of Export Administration. No corrections, additions, or alterations were made on this form by us after the form was signed by the official named in Block 10 above. We certify that we will not export or otherwise dispose of any items covered by the Special Comprehensive License to the ultimate consignee named in Block 4, until this form has been validated or after it has expired or been revoked.

SIGNATURE OF PERSON AUTHORIZED TO CERTIFY FOR SCL HOLDER	NAME OF PERSON SIGNING THIS DOCUMENT	
NAME OF SCL HOLDER FIRM	TITLE OF PERSON SIGNING THIS DOCUMENT	DATE SIGNED

We acknowledge that the making of any false statements or concealment of any material fact in connection with this statement may result in imprisonment or fine, or both and denial, in whole or in part, of participation in U.S. exports and reexports.

X	**X**	**ORIGINAL F**

USCOMM-DC 96-24022

Figure 5–17. Reexport territories.

G

FORM BXA-752-A
FORM APPROVED: OMB NO. 0694-0089

U.S. DEPARTMENT OF COMMERCE
Bureau of Export Administration

DATE RECEIVED (Leave Blank) X

REEXPORT TERRITORIES

1. APPLICATION CONTROL NUMBER (insert from BXA-748P)	2. SCL LICENSE NUMBER	3. CONSIGNEE NUMBER	4. CONTINUATION OF BXA-752 QUESTION NUMBER: ☐ 8B ☐ 8C ☐ 8E ☐ 8F

☐ AFGHANISTAN	☐ CANADA	☐ GERMANY	☐ LIBERIA	☐ PAKISTAN	☐ SWAZILAND
☐ ALBANIA	☐ CAPE VERDE	☐ GHANA	☐ LIECHTENSTEIN	☐ PALAU	☐ SWEDEN
☐ ALGERIA	☐ CENTRAL AFRICAN REPUBLIC	☐ GREECE	☐ LITHUANIA	☐ PANAMA	☐ SWITZERLAND
☐ ANDORRA	☐ CHAD	☐ GRENADA	☐ LUXEMBOURG	☐ PAPUA NEW GUINEA	☐ TAIWAN
☐ ANGOLA	☐ CHILE	☐ GUATEMALA	☐ FYROM (MACEDONIA)	☐ PARAGUAY	☐ TAJIKISTAN
☐ ANTIGUA & BARBUDA	☐ CHINA (PRC)	☐ GUINEA	☐ MADAGASCAR	☐ PERU	☐ TANZANIA
☐ ARGENTINA	☐ COLOMBIA	☐ GUINEA-BISSAU	☐ MALAWI	☐ PHILIPPINES	☐ THAILAND
☐ ARMENIA	☐ COMOROS	☐ GUYANA	☐ MALAYSIA	☐ POLAND	☐ TOGO
☐ AUSTRALIA	☐ CONGO	☐ HAITI	☐ MALDIVES	☐ PORTUGAL	☐ TONGA
☐ AUSTRIA	☐ COSTA RICA	☐ HONDURAS	☐ MALI	☐ QATAR	☐ TRINIDAD & TOBAGO
☐ AZERBAIJAN	☐ COTE d'IVOIRE	☐ HONG KONG	☐ MALTA	☐ ROMANIA	☐ TUNISIA
☐ BAHAMAS, THE	☐ CROATIA	☐ HUNGARY	☐ MARSHALL ISLANDS	☐ RUSSIA	☐ TURKEY
☐ BAHRAIN	☐ CYPRUS	☐ ICELAND	☐ MAURITANIA	☐ RWANDA	☐ TURKMENISTAN
☐ BANGLADESH	☐ CZECH REPUBLIC	☐ INDIA	☐ MAURITIUS	☐ ST KITTS & NEVIS	☐ TUVALU
☐ BARBADOS	☐ DENMARK	☐ INDONESIA	☐ MEXICO	☐ ST. LUCIA	☐ UGANDA
☐ BELARUS	☐ DJIBOUTI	☐ IRELAND	☐ MICRONESIA	☐ ST. VINCENT & GRENADINES	☐ UKRAINE
☐ BELGIUM	☐ DOMINICA	☐ ISRAEL	☐ MOLDOVA	☐ SAN MARINO	☐ UNITED ARAB EMIRATES
☐ BELIZE	☐ DOMINICAN REPUBLIC	☐ ITALY	☐ MONACO	☐ SAO TOME & PRINCIPE	☐ UNITED KINGDOM
☐ BENIN	☐ ECUADOR	☐ JAMAICA	☐ MONGOLIA	☐ SAUDI ARABIA	☐ URUGUAY
☐ BHUTAN	☐ EGYPT	☐ JAPAN	☐ MOROCCO	☐ SENEGAL	☐ UZBEKISTAN
☐ BOLIVIA	☐ EL SALVADOR	☐ JORDAN	☐ MOZAMBIQUE	☐ SEYCHELLES	☐ VANUATU
☐ BOSNIA & HERZEGOVINA	☐ EQUATORIAL GUINEA	☐ KAZAKHSTAN	☐ NAMIBIA	☐ SIERRA LEONE	☐ VATICAN CITY
☐ BOTSWANA	☐ ERITREA	☐ KENYA	☐ NAURU	☐ SINGAPORE	☐ VENEZUELA
☐ BRAZIL	☐ ESTONIA	☐ KIRIBATI	☐ NEPAL	☐ SLOVAKIA	☐ VIETNAM
☐ BRUNEI	☐ ETHIOPIA	☐ KOREA, SOUTH	☐ NETHERLANDS	☐ SLOVENIA	☐ WESTERN SAHARA
☐ BULGARIA	☐ FIJI	☐ KUWAIT	☐ NEW ZEALAND	☐ SOLOMON ISLANDS	☐ WESTERN SAMOA
☐ BURKINA FASO	☐ FINLAND	☐ KYRGYZSTAN	☐ NICARAGUA	☐ SOMALIA	☐ YEMEN
☐ BURMA	☐ FRANCE	☐ LAOS	☐ NIGER	☐ SOUTH AFRICA	☐ ZAIRE
☐ BURUNDI	☐ GABON	☐ LATVIA	☐ NIGERIA	☐ SPAIN	☐ ZAMBIA
☐ CAMBODIA	☐ GAMBIA, THE	☐ LEBANON	☐ NORWAY	☐ SRI LANKA	☐ ZIMBABWE
☐ CAMEROON	☐ GEORGIA	☐ LESOTHO	☐ OMAN	☐ SURINAM	

☐ OTHER SPECIFY: ☐ OTHER SPECIFY: ☐ OTHER SPECIFY:

X X ORIGINAL G

USCOMM-DC 96-24023

exporter and the consignee to ensure compliance with the U.S. export and re-export control laws. It must address thirteen specific items specified in the EAR. The consignee must agree to maintain records and make them available for inspection by the U.S. Department of Commerce. The EAR contains additional instructions for completing all these forms.

An SCL, when issued, is valid for four years and may be extended for an additional four years. Certain changes in the export relationship or procedures require prior written approval from the Bureau of Export Administration, whereas other changes must be notified to the Bureau of Export Administration within thirty days after their occurrence.

L. Technology, Software, and Technical Assistance Exports

A significant portion of the EAR is concerned with the export of technology, software, and technical assistance. Within each category of the Commerce Control List, there is a "group" which includes software ("D") and technology ("E") pertaining to that category. Such exports would normally take place pursuant to a license agreement between the U.S. licensor and the foreign licensee. However, in fulfillment of a license agreement, tangible documents as well as oral information may be communicated. The definition of "export" includes an actual shipment or transmission of items subject to the EAR out of the United States and, with regard to the export of technology or software, includes any "release" of technology or software subject to the EAR in a foreign country or any release of technology or source code subject to the EAR to a foreign national, in the United States or in another country. "Release" of technology or software includes visual inspection by foreign nationals of U.S.-origin equipment and facilities, the oral exchange of information in the United States or abroad, or the application to situations abroad of personal knowledge or technical experience acquired in the United States. "Technology" is defined as information necessary for the development, production, or use of a product. Information may take the form of "technical data" or "technical assistance." Controlled "technology" is defined in the General Technology Note (Supplement Number 1 to part 774). "Technical data" may include blueprints, plans, diagrams, models, formulas, tables, engineering designs, specifications, manuals, and instructions written or recorded on other media or devices such as disk, tape, or read-only memories. "Technical assistance" may take the form of instruction, skills training, working knowledge, or consulting services.

Two steps in analyzing the scope of the EAR, Step 2 and Step 6, pertain to technology. Step 2 exempts from control of the EAR publicly available technology and software. This is both for exports and re-exports. Publicly available technology and software includes that which has already been published or will be published, which includes software generally accessible to the interested public in any form either free or at a price that does not exceed the cost of reproduction and distribution; patents and open, published patent applications; information readily available at libraries open to the public; and/or information released at an "open" conference meeting, seminar, or trade show. The EAR contains questions and answers further developing and clarifying what type of technology and software is publicly available. It also includes information arising from "fundamental" (as opposed to "proprietary") and educational research. Step 6 of the EAR pertains to foreign-made items produced with certain U.S. technology. If the foreign-produced item is described in an entry on the Commerce Control List, and the Country Chart requires a license for a direct export from the United States for national security reasons or, if the destination is Cuba, North Korea, Libya, or a country in Group D:1 and the technology or software that was used to create the foreign-produced direct product required a written assurance from the licensee as a supporting document for the license or as a condition to utilizing license exception "TSR," a license is required. This restriction also applies to direct products of a complete plant. If the technology or software is outside the scope of the EAR, the exporter should use "TPSA" in field 21 of the Shipper's Export Declaration. (This analysis is also required by Step 11 of the EAR.)

In addition to the exemption for publicly available technology and software, several exceptions from license requirements are also available. License exception "TSR" (Technology and Software under Restriction) permits exports and re-exports of technology and software when so specified on the specific entry in the Commerce Control List and the export is to destinations in Country Group B. The exporter must receive written assurances from the consignee prior to export that the technology or software will not e released to a national in Country Groups D:1 or E:2 and will not export to those same countries the direct product of the technology if the produce is subject to national security controls.

Another license exception, "TSU" (Technology and Software Unrestricted), permits the export of "Operating Technology and Software" (OTS) and "Sales Technology" (STS). Operating technology is the minimum technology necessary for the installation, operation, maintenance (checking), and repair of products lawfully exported. It must be in object code and exported to the destination to which the equipment for which it is required has been legally exported. Sales Technology is data supporting a prospective or actual quotation, bid, or offer to sell, lease, or otherwise supply any item. It does not include information that discloses the design, production, or manufacture of the item being offered for sale. Software updates that are intended for and are limited to correction of errors is also authorized. Finally, "mass market" software may be exported under this exception. Generally, this is software sold from stock at retail selling points or by mail order and designed for installation by the user without further substantial support by the supplier.

License exception, "TMP," authorizes temporary exports. Within that exception is included exports of "beta test" software ("BETA"). This pertains only to software which the producer intends to market to the general public, is provided free of charge or at a price that does not exceed the cost of reproduction and distribution, does not require further substantial support from the supplier, and for which the importer provides a certification that it will not be transferred. The software must be returned or destroyed within thirty days after completion of the test.

An "Interpretation" has been issued by the Bureau of Export Administration for the purposes of clarifying what technology and software may be exported to Country Group D:1. Under the controls relating to end users and end use, technology pertaining to maritime nuclear propulsion plants may not be exported without a license.

M. Violations and Penalties

For violation of the Export Administration Act, penalties can be assessed of up to $1 million or five times the value of the exports involved, whichever is greater, and/or violators can be imprisoned for up to ten years. In addition, export privileges can be denied up to ten years. Since these are extremely serious penalties, it is important to make every effort not to violate the law, even accidentally. Exports in violation of the law may be seized by the U.S. Customs Service. A Customs Export Enforcement Subpoena is shown in Figure 5-18. If the exporter, its freight forwarder, or any other of the exporter's agents receive such a subpoena or even an informal inquiry from Customs or the Office of Export Enforcement, Bureau of Export Administration, the exporter should take it very seriously and make sure that it is in compliance with the law before responding.

N. Munitions and Arms Exports

Under the Arms Export Control Act, exports and imports of defense articles and services are prohibited without a license. Export licenses are issued by the Department of State, Office of Defense Trade Controls (ODTC), under the International Traffic in Arms Regulations. Import licenses are issued by the Department of the Treasury, Bureau of Alcohol, Tobacco and Firearms. Items that are inherently military in character or that have substantial military applicability and have been specifically designed or modified for military purposes are included in the U.S. Munitions List. Prior to exporting any such item, the exporter must register with the ODTC on Form DSP-2032, and an application to export the item must be filed on Form DSP-5. For some items, specified as "significant military equipment," the applicant must obtain a signed Non-Transfer and Use Certificate (DSP-83) from the consignee and end user prior to making application. In come cases, as a condition of granting the license, the ODTC may require that the applicant obtain an Import Certificate signed by the government of the foreign country and/or provide verification of delivery of the item to the foreign country. Different procedures and license forms apply to classified articles and technical data. Different procedures and forms also apply to direct, commercial sales and to sales to the United States Department of Defense for resale to foreign countries under the Foreign Military Assistance program. Before appointing any foreign distributors who are authorized to resell the products, the exporter must submit the distributorship agreement to the ODTC for approval. Agreements to grant manufacturing licenses or provide technical assistance must also be approved in advance. Applications for li-

Figure 5–18. Customs export enforcement subpoena.

CUSTOMS EXPORT ENFORCEMENT SUBPOENA

1 TO (Name, Address, City, State, ZIP)	DEPARTMENT OF THE TREASURY UNITED STATES CUSTOMS SERVICE **SUBPOENA** TO APPEAR AND/OR PRODUCE RECORDS

By the service of this subpoena upon you, YOU ARE HEREBY SUMMONED AND REQUIRED TO:

(A) ☐ APPEAR before the Customs officer named in Block 2 below at the place, date, and time indicated, to testify and give information.

(B) ☐ PRODUCE the records (including statements, declarations, and other documents) indicated in Block 3 below, before the Customs officer named in Block 2 at the place, date, and time indicated.

Your testimony and/or the production of the indicated records is required in connection with an investigation or inquiry to insure compliance with: 1) the Export Administration Act of 1979, as amended; 2) the Arms Export Control Act; and/or 3)____________________; and to determine liability for any penalty, forfeiture, or other sanction arising thereunder.

Failure to comply with this subpoena will render you liable to proceedings in a U.S. District Court to enforce compliance with this subpoena as well as other sanctions.

2 (A) NAME, TITLE, ADDRESS, AND TELEPHONE NUMBER OF CUSTOMS OFFICER BEFORE WHOM YOU ARE TO APPEAR	(B) DATE (C) TIME

3 RECORDS REQUIRED TO BE PRODUCED FOR INSPECTION

Issued under authority of: section 12(a) of the Export Administration of 1979, as amended, 50 USC, App. 2411(a)(1); the Arms Export Control Act, 22 USC 2778(e); or ____________________.

4 NAME OF PERSON AUTHORIZED TO SERVE SUBPOENA: or any other Customs officer.	5 DATE OF ISSUE COMMISSIONER OF CUSTOMS BY (Signature):
If you have any questions regarding this subpoena, contact the Customs officer identified in Block 2.	6 NAME, TITLE, ADDRESS, AND TELEPHONE NUMBER OF PERSON ISSUING THIS SUBPOENA

Customs Form 337 (041886)

(*continues*)

Figure 5–18. *(continued)*

[*reverse*]

CERTIFICATE OF SERVICE AND ACKNOWLEDGMENT OF RECEIPT

A. CERTIFICATE OF SERVICE OF SUBPOENA

I certify that I served the subpoena on the front of this form as follows:

☐	I delivered a copy of the subpoena to the person to whom it was directed, as follows:	ADDRESS OR LOCATION	DATE TIME
☐	*(For corporations, partnerships, and unincorporated associations which may be sued under a common name)* I delivered a copy of the subpoena to an officer, managing or general agent, or agent authorized to accept service of process as follows:	PERSON TO WHOM SUBPOENA WAS DELIVERED: NAME ADDRESS OR LOCATION	Title DATE TIME
☐	I left a copy of the subpoena at the last and usual dwelling or place of abode of the person to whom it was directed as follows:	ADDRESS OR LOCATION NAME OF PERSON WITH WHOM SUBPOENA LEFT (If Any)	DATE TIME

SIGNATURE	TITLE	DATE

B. ACKNOWLEDGMENT OF RECEIPT

I acknowledge receipt of a copy of the subpoena on the front of this form.

SIGNATURE	TITLE	
X	DATE	TIME

Customs Form 337 (041886) (Back)

☆U.S. GOVERNMENT PRINTING OFFICE: 1988 - 542-156/61130

censes will be denied for exports to Afghanistan, Armenia, Azerbaijan, Belarus, Burma, China (PRC), Cuba, Haiti, Iran, Iraq, Liberia, Libya, Mongolia, North Korea, Rwanda, Somalia, Sudan, Syria, Tajikistan, Vietnam, the Federal Republic of Yugoslavia (Serbia and Montenegro), and Zaire. Those who broker sales of defense articles are required to register with the ODTC.

An area of particular sensitivity is the requirement that if the amount of the export sales is $500,000 or more, the license applicant must disclose to the ODTC the names and detailed payment information of any fees of commissions of $1,000 or more paid to any person to promote or secure the sale of a defense article or service to the armed forces of a foreign country. The applicant must also report any political contributions of $1,000 or more to any government employee, political party, or candidate. The applicant must also survey its suppliers, subcontractors, and agents to ascertain whether they have paid or agreed to make any such payments. In addition to the disclosure to the ODTC, such payments may violate foreign law.

Persons who violate the Arms Export Control Act are subject to the civil and criminal penalties under the Export Administration Regulations (see Section M, above) and can be debarred from exporting for a period of up to three years. The ODTC's policy is that persons engaged in the export of defense articles and services should maintain an export procedures manual containing ODTC-specified policies and procedures to reduce the risk of violations.

Part III

Importing: Procedures and Documentation

Chapter 6

Importing: Preliminary Considerations

Before beginning to import, and on each importation, the importer/buyer should consider a number of preliminary matters that will make a great deal of difference in smooth and efficient importing.

A. Products

Before actually importing, or whenever the importer is considering importing a new item, the characteristics of that item should be reviewed. That is, is the product being imported as a raw material or component to be used in the manufacturing process? Is it a finished product that is going to be resold in the form imported or with some slight or significant modification? Is it a replacement or spare part? Is the item sold singly or as a part of a set or system? Does the product need to be modified, such as to size, weight, or color, to be suitable in the U.S. market? Often the appropriate method of manufacturing, marketing, the appropriate purchase and import documentation, the appropriate procedures for importation, and the treatment under U.S. law, including U.S. customs law, will depend upon these considerations (for example, whether or not the product may be imported duty-free or what the correct classification and duty will be).

In addition to the general procedures and documents, some products are subject to special import restrictions, permits, licenses, standards, and/or procedures. These include foods, drugs, cosmetics, alcoholic beverages, tea, medical devices, certain energy-using commercial and industrial equipment, civil aircraft and parts, educational and scientific apparatus, ethyl alcohol, master records and matrices, vegetable oils, seed potatoes and corn, works of art, antiques, engines for vehicles and off-road, bolting cloths, purebred animals for breeding, products subject to quotas, certain radiation-producing electronic products, wildlife, pets, certain mammals, fish, snails, clams, crustaceans, mollusks and amphibians, migratory birds, meat and meat products, watches and watch movements, sugar, textiles, wool, cheese, milk and dairy products, fruits, vegetables, nuts, insects, livestock and animals, plant and plant products, poultry and poultry products, seafood, seeds, arms, ammunition and explosives, cigarette lighters, radioactive materials and devices, household appliances, flammable fabrics, animal drugs, narcotic drugs, drug paraphernalia, certain fireworks, monetary instruments in excess of $10,000, bicycles and bicycle helmets, lead paint, precursor chemicals, automobiles, boats, pesticides, toxic and hazardous substances, postage stamps, petroleum and petroleum products, archaeological and ethnological material, pre-Columbian sculpture and murals, and "foreign excess property." Importation of white or yellow phosphorous matches; certain fireworks; "cultural property"; switchblades; lottery tickets; most endangered species; African elephant ivory and articles; counterfeit articles; treasonable or obscene material; and products of convict, child, and forced labor are prohibited.

B. Volume

What is the expected volume of imports of the product? Will this be an isolated purchase of a small quantity or an ongoing series of transactions amounting to substantial quantities? Small quantities may be imported under purchase orders and purchase order acceptance documentation. Large quantities may require more formal international purchase agreements; more formal methods of payment; special shipping, packing, and handling procedures; an appointment as the U.S. sales agent and/or distributor from the foreign exporter; or commitments to perform after-sales service. (See the discussion in Chapter 7, Section B.)

C. Country Sourcing

One of the principal preliminary considerations will be to identify those countries that have products the importer is seeking for purchase. If the importer seeks to import a raw material or natural resource, the importer may be limited to purchasing from those countries where such products are grown or mined. If the importer is looking for a manufactured product, it is more likely that the number of countries where such products are available for sale will be much greater; however, identifying the low-cost countries based upon proximity to raw materials, labor costs of manufacturing, current exchange rates with the United States, or transportation costs may require considerable study and analysis. This information is not always easy to obtain. Since the U.S. government is more interested in promoting exports, it does not regularly collect and make available such information to U.S. companies wishing to import. Importers will probably have to contact foreign governments directly (or through their U.S. embassies and consulates), foreign chambers of commerce, and foreign trade associations. Sometimes, foreign banks operating in the United States, U.S. accounting firms or law firms that have offices in the foreign country, or U.S. banks with offices in the foreign country can be helpful in supplying information. The United Nations publishes its *International Trade Statistics Yearbook* showing what countries are selling and exporting all types of products. In identifying the potential country, the importer should ascertain whether the products of that country are eligible for duty-free or reduced duty treatment under the Generalized System of Preferences, the Caribbean Basin Economic Recovery Act, the North American Free Trade Agreement, the African Growth and

Opportunity Act or other programs. Under the U.S. Foreign Assets Control Regulations, importation from Cuba, Libya, Iran (except for certain carpets and food), Iraq, North Korea, and Sudan is prohibited without a license or approval from the Department of the Treasury, and imports from such countries will be immediately seized by the U.S. Customs Service. Under the Antiterrorism Act, importations from the governments (or any government-owned entity) of Syria and Angola (UNITA) are prohibited (in addition to Cuba, Iran, Iraq, Libya, and North Korea). Diamonds cannot be imported from Angola (UNITA), Liberia, or Sierra Leone.

D. Identification of Suppliers

Once the countries with the products available for supply have been identified, of course, the importer still needs to identify a specific supplier. This will be just as important as identifying which countries can provide the products at the lowest cost. An unreliable supplier or one that has poor product quality control will certainly result in disaster for the importer. The importer should spend a significant amount of time in evaluating the potential supplier if there are going to be ongoing purchase transactions. The importer should ascertain the business reputation and performance of the potential supplier. If possible, the importer should inspect the plant and manufacturing facilities of the supplier. The importer should determine whether there are other customers within its own country who might be able to confirm quality and supply reliability of the potential supplier. Related thereto, if the importer will be acting as the distributor or sales agent for the foreign manufacturer, the importer needs to ascertain whether the supplier has already appointed (on either an exclusive or nonexclusive basis) other U.S. distributors or sales agents. The importer should also determine if a supplier is acting as an agent for the manufacturer or if the supplier will be acting as the buying agent for the buyer. If the latter, the buyer should enter into a separate agency agreement and pay all commissions separately, since the importer need not pay customs duties on buying commissions but must do so on commissions paid to the seller's agent.

Once potential suppliers have been identified, if an ongoing relationship is contemplated, a personal visit to evaluate the supplier is essential. One efficient way that the author has used is to arrange a schedule of interviews at its foreign law office where the U.S. importer could meet with numerous potential suppliers in that country in the course of a two- or three-day period. Based on such meetings, one or more suppliers can be selected and the capabilities of the suppliers can be clearly understood.

In evaluating potential suppliers, it is important to obtain a credit report. International credit reports are available from Dun & Bradstreet, Parsippany, New Jersey, telephone number (973) 605-6000; Graydon America, New York, New York, telephone number (212) 385-9580; Justitia International, Bristol, Connecticut, telephone number (860) 283-5714; Teikoku Data Bank America, Inc. [Japan], New York, New York, telephone number (212) 421-9805; Owens Online, Tampa, Florida, telephone number (813) 877-2008; and local offices of the U.S. Department of Commerce (International Company Profiles).

E. Compliance With Foreign Law

Prior to importing from a foreign country or even agreeing to purchase from a supplier in a foreign country, a U.S. importer should be aware of any foreign laws that might affect the purchase. Information about foreign law can often be obtained from the supplier from whom the importer intends to purchase. However, if the supplier is incorrect in the information that it gives to the importer, the importer may have to pay dearly for having relied solely upon the advice of the supplier. Incorrect information about foreign law may result in the prohibition of importation of the supplier's product; or it may mean that the importer cannot resell the product as profitably as expected. Unfortunately, suppliers often overlook those things that may be of the greatest concern to the importer. As a result, it may be necessary for the U.S. importer to confirm its supplier's advice with third parties, including attorneys, banks, or government agencies, to feel confident that it properly understands the foreign law.

1. *Foreign Export Controls*

A number of countries, particularly those politically allied with the United States, enforce a system of export controls. The previous COCOM controls have been superseded by the "Wassenaar Arrangement." Currently, thirty-three countries are members of the agreement. In order to export certain products from those countries, even to the United States, certain procedures of the foreign country must be followed. The first step is for the importer to ascertain whether or not the product is a controlled commodity under the foreign country's laws. If it is, the U.S. importer will be required to furnish a document to the foreign supplier to enable the foreign supplier to obtain a license from its own government to export the product to the United States. The importer will have to identify the documents required either through the potential supplier or directly from the foreign government agency, but in most cases an Import Certificate (see Chapter 5, Figure 5–9) will be required. The U.S. importer must have this document signed by the United States Department of Commerce and it must be forwarded to the foreign supplier to enable it to apply for and obtain the necessary foreign government license for exporting the product.

In addition, there may be other documents that the supplier must provide to its own government in order to obtain an export license. When an export license will be required, the importer should clearly ascertain the time period required in order to adequately plan its import schedule. The importer should also take certain steps in its purchase and sale documentation with the supplier to adequately obligate the supplier to obtain the necessary export licenses. (See discussion in Chapter 7, Section B.2.k.)

2. *Exchange Control Licenses*

Many countries of the world control their foreign exchange. Consequently, before an exporter can export valuable products produced or manufactured in its own country to a U.S. importer, the exporter's government will insist that the exporter have adequate assurance of payment by the U.S. importer. The foreign exporter will need a license in order to convert U.S. dollars received from the U.S. importer into its local currency to obtain payment. This is important for the importer to confirm in order to make sure that the products are not detained prior to export because the necessary exchange control license has not been obtained. Of significant importance to the importer is the requirement by the exporter's country that payment must be made by certain means, such as confirmed irrevocable letter of credit. In order to protect their companies against nonpayment, some governments impose strict payment requirements on foreign trade contracts. If the importer is unable or unwilling to pay by letter of credit, importation from that country may be practically impossible.

3. Export Quotas

Generally, the importing country establishes quotas for imported products. These are discussed in Section F.6 below. However, the U.S. government, through its negotiating representatives such as the United States Trade Representative's office, often requires the foreign government to agree to impose export quotas on products destined for the United States. These are sometimes designated Voluntary Restraint Agreements (VRA); for example, in the area of textiles, steel, and machine tools, foreign government "visas" are required. (This "visa" should not be confused with the visa required by the immigration laws of foreign countries in order to travel there.) Ordinarily, the foreign supplier should be aware of any export quotas or export visa requirements, but if the foreign supplier has only been selling domestically in the past, the supplier may not be familiar with those requirements. The U.S. importer should double-check on the existence of any foreign government quotas or visas prior to entering into purchase transactions that cannot be fulfilled. Sometimes these export visas or export rights are auctioned in the foreign country, and a potential exporter must participate in the government auction at the correct time in order to get an allocation for the coming year. Where export quotas or VRAs have been established, competition for such export visas is usually intense, and an importer will be unable to enter into spot transactions on short notice for the purchase of the products from suppliers who have not obtained the necessary governmental visas.

F. U.S. Customs Considerations

Various aspects of the U.S. Customs laws as they affect potential importers will be discussed in greater detail throughout subsequent chapters; however, there are a number of items that should be part of the importer's preliminary planning.

1. Utilization of Customs Brokers

Whether or not an importer should utilize a customs broker primarily depends upon the amount of imports the importer will have, and the number and expertise of its own personnel. If the importer has sufficient personnel with sufficient expertise, these people can be trained to handle the importing procedures and documentation themselves. Even large importers, however, often use the services of a customs broker. The most difficult problem may be the selection of a customs broker. There are many customs brokers with varying levels of expertise and various levels of financial stability. More importantly, some customs brokers are more familiar with certain types of products. Today, it is becoming increasingly important that the customs broker have automated electronic interface with the U.S. Customs Service and the ability to process documentation electronically. Interviews with a number of potential brokers and a frank discussion of the products and quantities that the importer intends to import, the source countries, and the brokers' capabilities are worthwhile. A visit to the brokers' premises may be even more helpful.

This concern and effort is more than merely academic. The broker acts as the agent for the importer, and, therefore, even though the importer may pay a fee to the broker expecting to obtain the broker's expertise, if the broker makes a mistake or error, the U.S. Customs Service ill attribute the responsibility therefor to the importer, the principal. For example, if the broker fails to pay customs duties to the Customs Service that were paid to the broker by the importer, the importer may be required to pay twice. In performing its services, the broker will require a power of attorney from the importer. (A sample power of attorney acceptable to the U.S. Customs Service is shown in Figure 6–1.) However, the importer should be aware that many customs brokers expand upon the standard power of attorney and include a number of other provisions (which are designed to protect the broker and not the importer) in the form that they furnish to the importer. The importer should review the power of attorney and make appropriate modifications. The broker should at least agree to indemnify and hold the importer harmless from any penalties, costs, or damages due to the broker's negligence or errors. Another form useful in instructing the broker what services the importer desires on each importation is an importer's letter of instruction (see Figure 6–2).

In the event that a broker is intransigent and refuses to perform its services as required by law, an importer can request that license revocation proceedings be initiated by the U.S. Treasury Department Customs Service.

2. *Importation Bonds*

In order to import merchandise into the United States, it is necessary for the importer to obtain a bond from a surety company. This is to guarantee that all customs duties, customs penalties, and other charges assessed by Customs will be properly paid, even if the importer goes bankrupt. There are essentially two types of bonds: the single transaction bond and the continuous bond. Single transaction bonds cover single importations, may be for as much as three times the value of the goods depending upon the goods, and are only practical for the importer engaged in very few importations. Continuous bonds are issued to cover all of the importations of an importer for a particular time period, usually one year. The amount is usually equal to 10 percent of the total customs duties paid for the previous year or reasonably estimated for the current year, but not less than $50,000. Obviously, before a surety company will provide the importation bond, it will be necessary for the importer to make application, undergo a credit investigation, and show financial stability. Customs brokers have their own customs bonds, and will sometimes handle imports for importers under the coverage of their bond. An application to file a continuous bond and the bond must be filed with the District Director of Customs where the goods are entered. (A sample application and customs bond are shown in Figures 6–3 and 6–4, respectively.)

(*Text continues on page 250.*)

Figure 6–1. Power of attorney for customs broker.

Department of the Treasury
U.S. Customs Service
19 CFR 141.32

POWER OF ATTORNEY

Check appropriate box:
☐ Individual
☐ Partnership
☐ Corporation
☐ Sole Proprietorship

KNOW ALL MEN BY THESE PRESENTS: That, ______________________________
(Full Name of person, partnership, or corporation, or sole proprietorship; Identify)

a corporation doing business under the laws of the State of ______________________ or a ______________________

doing business as ______________________ residing at ______________________

having an office and place of business at ______________________, hereby constitutes and appoints each of the following persons

____
(Give full name of each agent designated)

as a true and lawful agent and attorney of the grantor named above for and in the name, place, and stead of said grantor from this date and in Customs Port __________, and in no other name, to make, endorse, sign, declare, or swear to any entry, withdrawal, declaration, certificate, bill of lading, or other document required by law or regulation in connection with the importation, transportation, or exportation of any merchandise shipped or consigned by or to said grantor; to perform any act or condition which may be required by law or regulation in connection with such merchandise; to receive any merchandise deliverable to said grantor;

To make endorsements on bills of lading conferring authority to make entry and collect drawback, and to make, sign, declare, or swear to any statement, supplemental statement, schedule, supplemental schedule, certificate of delivery, certificate of manufacture, certificate of manufacture and delivery, abstract of manufacturing records, declaration of proprietor on drawback entry, declaration of exporter on drawback entry, or any other affidavit or document which may be required by law or regulation for drawback purposes, regardless of whether such bill of lading, sworn statement, schedule, certificate, abstract, declaration, or other affidavit or document is intended for filing in said port or in any other customs port;

To sign, seal, and deliver for and as the act of said grantor any bond required by law or regulation in connection with the entry or withdrawal of imported merchandise or merchandise exported with or without benefit of drawback, or in connection with the entry, clearance, lading, unlading or navigation of any vessel or other means of conveyance owned or operated by said grantor, and any and all bonds which may be voluntarily given and accepted under applicable laws and regulations, consignee's and owner's declarations provided for in section 485, Tariff Act of 1930, as amended, or affidavits in connection with the entry of merchandise;

To sign and swear to any document and to perform any act that may be necessary or required by law or regulation in connection with the entering, clearing, lading, unlading, or operation of any vessel or other means of conveyance owned or operated by said grantor;

And generally to transact at the customhouses in said port any and all customs business, including making, signing, and filing of protests under section 514 of the Tariff Act of 1930, in which said grantor is or may be concerned or interested and which may properly be transacted or performed by an agent and attorney, giving to said agent and attorney full power and authority to do anything whatever requisite and necessary to be done in the premises as fully as said grantor could do if present and acting, hereby ratifying and confirming all that the said agent and attorney shall lawfully do by virtue of these presents; the foregoing power of attorney to remain in full force and effect until the _____ day of ______________, 19 _____, or until notice of revocation in writing is duly given to and received by the Port Director of Customs of the port aforesaid. If the donor of this power of attorney is a partnership, the said power shall in no case have any force or effect after the expiration of 2 years from the date of its receipt in the office of the Port Director of Customs of the said port.

IN WITNESS WHEREOF, the said ______________________________

has caused these presents to be sealed and signed: (Signature) ______________________________

(Capacity) ______________________ (Date) ______________

WITNESS: ______________________ ______________________

(Corporate seal)*(Optional)

Customs Form 5291 (120195) **(SEE OVER)**

INDIVIDUAL OR PARTNERSHIP CERTIFICATION *(Optional)

CITY ______________________
COUNTY ______________________ } SS:
STATE ______________________

On this ______ day of ______________, 19 _____, personally appeared before me ______________________

residing at ______________________, personally known or sufficiently identified to me, who certifies that

______________________ (is)(are) the individual(s) who executed the foregoing instrument and acknowledge it to be ______________ free act and deed.

(Notary Public)

CORPORATE CERTIFICATION *(Optional)

(To be made by an officer other than the one who executes the power of attorney)

I, ______________________, certify that I am the ______________________

of ______________________, organized under the laws of the State of ______________________

that ______________________, who signed this power of attorney on behalf of the donor, is the ______________________ of said corporation; and that said power of attorney was duly signed, sealed, and attested for and on behalf of said corporation by authority of its governing body as the same appears in a resolution of the Board of Directors passed at a regular meeting held on the ______ day of ______________, now in my possession or custody. I further certify that the resolution is in accordance with the articles of incorporation and bylaws of said corporation.

IN WITNESS WHEREOF, I have hereunto set my hand and affixed the seal of said corporation, at the City of ______________ this ______ day of ______________, 19 _____

______________________ (Signature) ______________________ (Date)

If the corporation has no corporate seal, the fact shall be stated, in which case a scroll or adhesive shall appear in the appropriate, designated place.

Customs powers of attorney of residents (including resident corporations) shall be without power of substitution except for the purpose of executing shipper's export declarations. However, a power of attorney executed in favor of a licensed customhouse broker may specify that the power of attorney is granted to the customhouse broker to act through any of its licensed officers or any employee specifically authorized to act for such customhouse broker by power of attorney.

NOTE: The corporate seal may be omitted. Customs does not require completion of a certification. The grantor has the option of executing the certification or omitting it.

☆GOVERNMENT PRINTING OFFICE: 1998 – 606-491

Customs Form 5291 (120195)(Back)

Figure 6–2. Importer's letter of instruction.

TO: BROKER		REFERENCE NUMBER	DATE
		FOREIGN SELLER	
FROM: IMPORTER/CONSIGNEE		NOTIFY INTERMEDIATE CONSIGNEE	
IMPORTER'S TELEPHONE	CONTACT		
IMPORTING CARRIER	FLIGHT VESSEL	ROUTE	B L AWB

IMPORTER'S LETTER OF INSTRUCTION

Enclosed you will find the documents listed below to clear referenced shipment for our account.

- ☐ ORIGINAL B/L NO. ____________
- ☐ NON-NEGOTIABLE B/L AND ________ COPIES
- ☐ ORIGINAL COMMERCIAL INVOICE AND ________ COPIES
- ☐ PACKING LIST AND ________ COPIES
- ☐ GSP FORM A
- ☐ ____________
- ☐ ____________
- ☐ ____________

Please prepare the necessary documents for the following entry type:

- ☐ CONSUMPTION ENTRY
- ☐ WAREHOUSE ENTRY
- ☐ TEMPORARY IMPORT BOND ENTRY
- ☐ FREE TRADE ZONE ENTRY
- ☐ IMMEDIATE TRANSPORTATION ENTRY

  To: ____________

- ☐ ARRANGE FOR INSURANCE ON CARGO

ROUTING INSTRUCTIONS

- ☐ STANDARD INSTRUCTIONS
- ☐ VIA ____________
- ☐ TO ____________
- ☐ Please call prior to delivery.

  (TELEPHONE) ____________

  (CONTACT) ____________

- ☐ PREPAID ☐ COLLECT
- ☐ BILL TO ____________
- ☐ REQUEST CUSTOMS OVERTIME
- ☐ In the event that this merchandise is subject to examination by Customs, please deliver to CES: ____________

SPECIAL INSTRUCTIONS

Form 16-305 Printed and Sold by UNZ&CO 190 Baldwin Ave., Jersey City, NJ 07306 • (800) 631-3098 • (201) 795-5400

BROKER

Reprinted with permission of Unz & Co., 190 Baldwin Ave., Jersey City, N.J. 07306, USA.

Figure 6–3. Application for customs bond.

APPLICATION TO PORT DIRECTOR U.S. CUSTOMS SERVICE
TO FILE C.F. 301 — CONTINUOUS

Bond Serial No: ____________ CHB Name: ____________

Importer Name: ____________ Importer Number: ____________

Street: ____________ City: ____________ State: ______ Zip: ______

Describe Merchandise (Attach additional sheet if necessary)	Country of Origin
1.	
2.	
3.	
4.	
5.	
6.	

	Last Calendar Year			Estimate Next Calendar Year		
Type Merchandise	Value	Est. Duties	No. Entries	Value	Est. Duties	No. Entries
Dutiable						
Conditionally Free						
Unconditional Free						
Total						

Total amount of Penalties & Liquidation Damages assessed: ____________ Total number of cases: ______

Importer requests that customs approve the filing of C.F. 301
Continuous in an amount determined by Customs to be effective on: ____________

Activity Code	Activity Name and Customs Regulation in which conditions codified	Bond Amount Requested	Bond Amount Approved	Activity Code	Activity Name and Customs Regulation in which conditions codified	Bond Amount Requested	Bond Amount Approved
☐ 1	Importer or Broker................113.62			☐ 3	International Carrier............113.64		
☐ 1a	Drawback Payment Refunds.. 113.65			☐ 3a	Instrument of International Traffic..............................113.66		
☐ 2	Custodian of Bonded Merchandise ....113.63 (Includes bonded carriers, freight forwarders, cartmen and lightermen, all classes of warehouses, container station operators)			☐ 4	Foreign Trade Zone Operator...........................113.73		
				☐ 5	Public Gauger....................113.67		

U.S. Customs district where bond is to be filed: ____________

Other districts through which I will import: ____________

LIST CURRENT ANNUAL BONDS (Attach additional sheet if necessary)				
BOND TYPE	BOND AMOUNT	EFFECTIVE DATE	SURETY	WHERE FILED
1.				
2.				
3.				
4.				
5.				

State of Incorporation: ____________ ______ Years in Business

Local district additional information: ____________

☐ Proprietorship
☐ Partnership
☐ Corporation
☐ Individual

CERTIFICATION

I certify that the factual information contained in this application is true and accurate and any information provided which is based upon estimates is based upon the best information available on the date of this application.

BY: ____________ TITLE: ____________ DATE: ____________

____
(Signature)

Template provided by: Roanoke Trade Services, Inc. 3/00

Figure 6–4. Customs bond.

Approved through 00/00/00;OMB No 1515-0144
See back of form for Paperwork Reduction Act Notice.

DEPARTMENT OF THE TREASURY
UNITED STATES CUSTOMS SERVICE

CUSTOMS BOND

19 CFR Part 113

CUSTOMS USE ONLY	BOND NUMBER[1] (Assigned by Customs)
	FILE REFERENCE

In order to secure payment of any duty, tax or charge and compliance with law or regulation as a result of activity covered by any condition referenced below, we, the below named principal(s) and surety(ies), bind ourselves to the United States in the amount or amounts, as set forth below. | Execution Date

SECTION I—Select Single Transaction OR Continuous Bond (not both) and fill in the applicable blank spaces.

☐ SINGLE TRANSACTION BOND	Identification of transaction secured by this bond (e.g., entry no., seizure no., etc.)	Date of transaction	Transaction district & port code
☐ CONTINUOUS BOND	Effective date	This bond remains in force for one year beginning with the effective date and for each succeeding annual period, or until terminated. This bond constitutes a separate bond for each period in the amounts listed below for liabilities that accrue in each period. The intention to terminate this bond must be conveyed within the time period and manner prescribed in the Customs Regulations.	

SECTION II— This bond includes the following agreements.[2] (Check one box only, except that, 1a may be checked independently or with 1, and 3a may be checked independently or with 3. Line out all other parts of this section that are not used.

Activity Code	Activity Name and Customs Regulations in which conditions codified	Limit of Liability
☐ 1	Importer or broker 113.62	
☐ 1a	Drawback Payment Refunds 113.65	
☐ 2	Custodian of bonded merchandise .... 113.63 (Includes bonded carriers, freight forwarders, cartmen and lightermen, all classes of warehouses, container station operators) ☐ a.- Bonded carriers ☐ b.- Bonded Warehouses ☐ c.- CFS, freight forwarder, cartman, lighterman ☐ d.- Centralized Examination Station	
☐ 3	International Carrier 113.64	
☐ 3a	Instruments of International Traffic 113.66	
☐ 4	Foreign Trade Zone Operator 113.73	

Activity Code	Activity Name and Customs Regulations in which conditions codified	Limit of Liability
☐ 5	Public Gauger 113.67	
☐ 6	Wool & Fur Products Labeling Acts Importation (Single Entry Only) 113.68	
☐ 7	Bill of Lading (Single Entry Only) 113.69	
☐ 8	Detention of Copyrighted Material (Single Entry Only) 113.70	
☐ 9	Neutrality (Single Entry Only) 113.71	
☐ 10	Court Costs for Condemned Goods (Single Entry Only) 113.72	

REMARKS

SECTION III— List below all tradenames or unincorporated divisions that will be permitted to obligate this bond in the principal's name including their Customs Identification Number(s).[3] (If more space is needed, use Section III (Continuation) on back of form.)

Importer Number	Importer Name	Importer Number	Importer Name

Total number of importer names listed in Section III:

Principal and surety agree that any charge against the bond under any of the listed names is as though it was made by the principal(s).

Principal and surety agree that they are bound to the same extent as if they executed a separate bond covering each set of conditions incorporated by reference to the Customs Regulations into this bond.

If the surety fails to appoint an agent under Title 6, United States Code, Section 7, surety consents to service on the Clerk of any United States District Court or the U.S. Court of International Trade, where suit is brought on this bond. That clerk is to send notice of the service to the surety at:

Mailing Address Requested by the Surety

PRINCIPAL[4]	Name and Address	Importer No.[3] SIGNATURE[5]	SEAL
PRINCIPAL[4]	Name and Address	Importer No.[3] SIGNATURE[5]	SEAL
SURETY[4,6]	Name and Address[6]	Surety No.[7] SIGNATURE[5]	SEAL
SURETY[4,6]	Name and Address[6]	Surety No.[7] SIGNATURE[5]	SEAL

SURETY AGENTS	Name[8]	Identification No.[9]	Name[8]	Identification No.[9]

Customs Form 301 (073197)

PART 1 - U.S. CUSTOMS

Figure 6–4. *(continued)*

SECTION III (Continuation)

Importer Number	Importer Name	Importer Number	Importer Name

WITNESSES

Two witnesses are required to authenticate the signature of any person who signs as an individual or partner; however a witness may authenticate the signatures of both such non-corporate principals and sureties. No witness is needed to authenticate the signature of a corporate official or agent who signs for the corporation.

SIGNED, SEALED, and DELIVERED in the PRESENCE OF:

Name and Address of Witness for the Principal	Name and Address of Witness for the Surety
SIGNATURE:	SIGNATURE:
Name and Address of Witness for the Principal	Name and Address of Witness for the Surety
SIGNATURE:	SIGNATURE:

EXPLANATIONS AND FOOTNOTES

1 .The Customs Bond Number is a control number assigned by Customs to the bond contract when the bond is approved by an authorized Customs official.

2 .For all bond coverage available and the language of the bond conditions refer to Part 113, subpart G, Customs Regulations.

3 .The Importer Number is the Customs identification number filed pursuant to section 24.5, Customs Regulations. When the Internal Revenue Service employer identification number is used the two-digit suffix code must be shown.

4 .If the principal or surety is a corporation, the name of the State in which incorporated must be shown.

5 .See witness requirement above.

6 .Surety Name, if a corporation, shall be the company's name as it is spelled in the Surety Companies Annual List published in the Federal Register by the Department of the Treasury (Treasury Department Circular 570).

7 .Surety Number is the three digit identification code assigned by Customs to a surety company at the time the surety company initially gives notice to Customs that the company will be writing Customs bonds.

8 .Surety Agent is the individual granted a Corporate Surety Power of Attorney, CF 5297, by the surety company executing the bond.

9 .Agent Identification No. shall be the individual's Social Security number as shown on the Corporate Surety Power of Attorney, CF 5297, filed by the surety granting such power of attorney.

Paperwork Reduction Act Notice. The Paperwork Reduction Act of 1980 says we must tell you why we are collecting this information, how we will use it and whether you have to give it to us. We ask for this information to carry out the U.S. Customs Service laws of the United States. We need it to ensure that persons transacting business with Customs have the proper bond coverage to secure their transactions as required by law and regulation. Your response is required to enter into any transaction in which a bond is a prerequisite under the Tariff Act of 1930, as amended.

Privacy Act Statement: The following notice is given pursuant to Section 7(b) of the Privacy Act of 1974 (5 U.S.C. 552a). Furnishing the information on this form, including the Social Security Number, is mandatory. The primary use of the Social Security Number is to verify, in the Customs Automated System, at the time an agent submits a Customs bond for approval that the individual was granted a Corporate Surety Power of Attorney by the surety company. Section 7 of Act of July 30, 1947, chapter 390, 61 Stat. 646, authorizes the collection of this information.

Statement Required by 5 CFR 1320.21: The estimated average burden associated with this collection of information is 15 minutes per respondent or recordkeeper depending on individual circumstances. Comments concerning the accuracy of this burden estimate and suggestions for reducing this burden should be directed to U.S. Customs Service, Paperwork Management Branch, Washington DC 20229. ***DO NOT send completed form(s) to this office.***

Customs Form 301 (050798)(Back)

3. *Importer's Liability and Reasonable Care*

The company that intends to import should fully comprehend that liability for all U.S. customs duties, penalties, and charges is the responsibility of the importer. The U.S. Customs Service generally will not have jurisdiction (or it will be too much trouble for it to obtain jurisdiction) over the foreign supplier to collect or assess any customs penalties. Ordinarily, the importer may feel that there is a reasonable risk in importing and paying the normal (for example, 5 percent) customs duties. However, if certain events occur, such as the imposition of antidumping duties, or if false documents, even documents furnished by the foreign supplier (such as commercial invoices), are filed with the U.S. Customs Service in connection with the importation, whether intentionally or accidentally, the importer's liability can dramatically escalate, including the imposition of substantial criminal fines and civil penalties amounting to the full domestic value of—not just the customs duties on—the merchandise. This liability can extend backward up to five years from the date of violation or, in the case of fraud, five years from the date of discovery of the violation by the U.S. Customs Service. Under the Customs Modernization Act, the importer is now required to use "reasonable care" in determining the value, classification, and admissibility of imported merchandise. A checklist released by U.S. Customs is shown in Appendix E.

In order to avoid some of these risks, the buyer may decide to insist that the exporter act as the importer of record. This can be done if the exporter establishes a branch office or subsidiary company in the United States, or if the exporter obtains a bond from a surety company incorporated in the United States and the exporter appoints a person in the United States in the state of the port of entry who is authorized to accept service of process in the event of any court action commenced against the exporter. The broker can also act as the importer of record but, because of the potential liability, it will normally seek to relieve itself from this responsibility by asking the importer to sign an Owner's Declaration (see Figure 6–5).

4. *Application for Importer's Number*

Companies that have not previously engaged in importing must file an application for an importer's number with the U.S. Customs Service (either the Data Center in Washington, D.C., or the nearest Customs District Office). (When the importer's name or address changes, it should file an amendment to this application.) A sample application is shown in Figure 6–6. Thereafter, Customs will notify the applicant of its assigned importer's number. This number must be used on many documents that the importer or its broker will file with the U.S. Customs Service on future importations. Usually, it will be the importer's Federal Employer Identification Number or, in the case of an individual importer, the Social Security number.

5. *Ports of Entry*

The importer should determine what the appropriate ports of entry in the United States should be. If goods are traveling by air or by ship, it will be easy enough to

(*Text continues on page 254.*)

Figure 6–5. Owner's declaration.

DEPARTMENT OF THE TREASURY
UNITED STATES CUSTOMS SERVICE

OMB No. 1515-0050
See back of form for Paperwork Reduction Act Notice and Privacy Act Notice.

DECLARATION OF OWNER

FOR MERCHANDISE OBTAINED *(Otherwise than)* IN PURSUANCE OF A PURCHASE OR AGREEMENT TO PURCHASE

19 CFR 24.11(a)(1), 141.20

This declaration must be presented at the port of entry within 90 days after the date of entry in order to comply with sec. 485(d), of the Tariff Act of 1930. LINE OUT EACH PHRASE SHOWN IN ITALICS NOT APPLICABLE TO THIS DECLARATION.

1. NAME OF OWNER
2. ADDRESS OF OWNER (Street, city, state, ZIP code)
3. SUPERSEDING BOND SURETY CODE
4. PORT OF ENTRY
5. PORT CODE
6. IMPORTER NUMBER OF AUTHORIZED AGENT (Show hyphens)
7. VESSEL/CARRIER ARRIVED FROM
8. IMPORTER NUMBER OF OWNER (Show hyphens)
9. ENTRY NUMBER
10. DATE OF ENTRY
11. DATE OF ARRIVAL

I, the undersigned, representing the above named owner in the capacity indicated herein, declare that they are the actual owners for Customs purposes of the merchandise covered by the entry identified in Blocks 9 and 10 above, and that they will pay all additional and increased duties thereon pursuant to section 485(d), of the Tariff Act of 1930, and that such entry exhibits a full and complete account of all the merchandise imported by them in the vessel identified in the entry and obtained by them *(otherwise than)* in pursuance of a purchase, or an agreement to purchase, except as listed in columns 20-26 below.

I also declare to the best of my knowledge and belief that all statements appearing in the entry and in the invoice or invoices and other documents presented therewith and in accordance with which the entry was made, are true and correct in every respect; that the entry and invoices set forth the true prices, values, quantities, and all information as required by the law and the regulations made in pursuance thereof; that the invoices and other documents are in the same state as when received; that I have not received and do not know of any other invoice, paper, letter, document, or information showing a different currency, price, value, quantity, or description of the said merchandise; and that if at any time hereafter I discover any information showing a different state of facts, I will immediately make the same known to the port director of Customs at the port of entry.

I further declare, if the merchandise was entered by means of a seller's or shipper's invoice, that no Customs invoice for any of the merchandise covered by the said seller's or shipper's invoice can be produced due to causes beyond my control, and that if entered by means of a statement of the value or the price paid in the form of an invoice it is because neither seller's, shipper's, nor Customs invoice can be produced at this time.

12. EXCEPTIONS (If any)
13. NOMINAL CONSIGNEE OR AUTHORIZED AGENT

FILED BY:

14. I request that:
☐ Bills, Refunds, and Notices of Liquidation
☐ Checks for Refunds only
☐ Bills only
☐ Notices of Liquidation only

be addressed to me in care of the authorized agent whose importer number is shown above.

15. SIGNATURE OF PRINCIPAL MEMBER OF FIRM
16. DATE
17. ADDRESS OF PRINCIPAL MEMBER OF FIRM (Street, city, state, ZIP code)
18. TITLE

19. EXECUTE THIS PORTION ONLY IF OWNER DOES NOT HAVE AN IMPORTER NUMBER (i.e., has not filed Customs Form 5106)

IRS Employer Number of Firm Owner

Suffix

NAME

ADDRESS (Street, city, state, ZIP code)

OR IF NO EMPLOYER NUMBER: Social Security Number of Individual Owner

OR IF NEITHER OF THE ABOVE NUMBERS: Customs Serial Number

NOTE: If owner has no IRS or Social Security Number or a Customs Serial Number has not been previously assigned, file an additional copy of this form. The copy will be returned to owner with Customs Serial Number assigned. Such number shall be used by owner in all future Customs transactions requiring the Importer Number.

20. Number of Packages	21. Seller or Shipper	22. Place and Date of Invoice	23. Amount Paid or to be Paid in Foreign Currency	24. Rate of Exchange	25. Entered Value (Foreign Currency)	26. Entered Value (U.S. Dollars)

Customs Form 3347 (052296)

Figure 6–6. Application for importer's number and instructions.

Approved through 12/31/95. OMB NO. 1515-0191
See back of form for Paperwork Reduction Act Notice.

DEPARTMENT OF THE TREASURY
UNITED STATES CUSTOMS SERVICE

IMPORTER ID INPUT RECORD

19 CFR 24.5

1. TYPE OF ACTION *(Mark all applicable)*

☐ Notification of importer's number
☐ Change of address*
☐ Change of name*
☐ Check here if you also want your address updated in the Fines, Penalties, and Forfeitures Office

*NOTE–If a continuous bond is on file, a bond rider must accompany this change document.

2. IMPORTER NUMBER *(Fill in one format):*--

2A. I.R.S. Number

2B. Social Security Number

2C. ☐ Check here if requesting a Customs-assigned number and indicate reason(s). *(Check all that apply.)* ☐ I have no IRS No. ☐ I have no Social Security No. ☐ I have not applied for either number. ☐ I am not a U.S. resident.

2D. Customs-Assigned Number

3. Importer Name

4. DIV/AKA/DBA ☐ DIV ☐ AKA ☐ DBA

5. DIV/AKA/DBA Name

6. Type
☐ Corporation ☐ Partnership ☐ Sole Proprietorship ☐ Individual ☐ U.S. Government ☐ Other

7. Importer Mailing Address *(2 32-character lines maximum)*

8. City

9. State Code

10. ZIP

11. Country ISO Code *(Non-U.S. Only)*

12. Importer Physical Location Address *(2 32-character lines maximum; see instructions)*

13. City

14. State Code

15. ZIP

16. Country ISO Code *(Non-U.S. Only)*

17a. Has importer ever been assigned a Customs Importer Number using the <u>same</u> name as in Block 3?
☐ No ☐ Yes *(List number(s) and/or name(s) in Block 17c.)*

17b. Has importer ever been assigned a Customs Importer Number using a name <u>different</u> from that in Block 3?
☐ No ☐ Yes *(List number(s) and/or name(s) in Block 17c.)*

17c. If "Yes" to 17a and/or 17b, list number(s) and/or name(s)

I CERTIFY: That the information presented herein is correct; that if my Social Security Number is used it is because I have no IRS Employer Number; that if my Customs-assigned number is used it is because I have neither a Social Security Number nor an IRS Employer Number; that if none of these numbers is used, it is because I have none, and my signature constitutes a request for assignment of a number by Customs.

18. Printed or Typed Name and Title

19. Telephone No. Including Area Code

20. Signature
X

21. Date

22. Broker Use Only

See Back of Form for Privacy Act Statement.

Customs Form 5106 (031595)

Figure 6–6. *(continued)*

Paperwork Reduction Act Notice: We need this information to establish the importer's name, address, and importer number. We will use this information as basis for establishing bond coverage, release and entry of merchandise, liquidation, issuance of bills and refunds, and processing of drawback and FP&F actions. Your response is mandatory.

Statement Required by 5 CFR 1320.21: The estimated average burden associated with this collection of information is 6 minutes per respondent or recordkeeper depending on individual circumstances. Comments concerning the accuracy of this burden estimate and suggestions for reducing this burden should be directed to U.S. Customs Service, Paperwork Management Branch, Washington DC 20229. ***DO NOT** send completed form(s) to this office.*

PRIVACY ACT STATEMENT: Pursuant to the requirements of Public Law 93-579 (Privacy Act of 1974, notice is hereby given that 19 CFR 24.5 authorizes the disclosure of Social Security numbers (SSN) on the Customs Form 5106. The principal purpose for disclosure of the Social Security number is to assure maintenance of records that have a high degree of usefulness in regulatory investigations or proceedings. The information collected may be provided to those officers and employees of the Customs Service and any constituent unit of the Department of the Treasury who have a need for the records in the performance of their duties. The records may be referred to any department or agency of the federal government upon the request of the head of such department or agency. The authority to collect the SSN is 31 CFR 103.25. The SSN will be used to identify the individuals conducting business with the Customs Service.

BLOCK 1 - TYPE OF ACTION

Notification of Importer's Number - Check this box if you are a first time importer, using an importer number for the first time, or if you have not engaged in Customs business within the last year.

Change of Name - Check this box if this importer number is on file but there is a change in the name on file.

Change of Address - Check this box if this importer number is on file but there is a change in the address on file.

BLOCK 2 - IMPORTER NUMBER

2A -IRS Number - Complete this block if you are assigned an Internal Revenue Service employer identification number.

2B -Social Security Number - Complete this block if no Internal Revenue Service employer identification number has been assigned. The Social Security number should belong to the principal or owner of the company or the individual who represents the importer of record.

2C -Requesting a Customs-Assigned Number - Complete this block if no Internal Revenue Service employer identification number has been assigned, or no Social Security number has been assigned. If this box is checked, all corresponding boxes in 2C must also be marked.

PLEASE NOTE: A Customs-Assigned Number is for Customs use **only** and does not replace a Social Security number or Internal Revenue Service employer identification number. In general, a Customs Assigned Number will only be issued to foreign businesses or individuals, provided no IRS or Social Security number exists for the applicant. If Block 2C is completed, this form must be submitted in duplicate. Customs will issue an Assigned Number and return a copy of the completed form with the Assigned Number to the requester. This identification number will be used for all future Customs transactions when an importer number is required. If an Internal Revenue Service employer identification number and/or a Social Security number are obtained after an importer number has been assigned by Customs, the importer will continue to use the assigned number unless otherwise instructed.

2D -Customs-Assigned Number - Complete this block if you are assigned a Customs-Assigned Number but there is an Action change (Block 1).

BLOCK 3 - IMPORTER NAME

If the name is an individual, input the last name first, first name, and middle initial. Business names should be input first name first.

BLOCK 4 - DIV/AKA/DBA

Complete this block if an importer is a division of another company (DIV), is also known under another name (AKA), or conducts business under another name (DBA).

BLOCK 5 - DIV/AKA/DBA NAME

Complete this block only if Block 4 is used.

BLOCK 6 - TYPE OF COMPANY

Check applicable box. *Please Note:* Place an "X" after U.S. Gov't **only** for a U.S. federal government department, agency, bureau or office. All federal agencies are assigned I.R.S. numbers which should be used for any Customs transactions by that agency.

BLOCK 7 - IMPORTER MAILING ADDRESS

This block must always be completed. It may or may not be the importer's business address. Insert a post office box number, or a street number representing the first line of the importer's mailing address (up to 32 characters). For a U.S. or Canadian mailing address, additional mailing address information may be inserted (up to 32 characters). If a P.O. box number is given for the mailing address, a second address (physical location) must be provided in Block 12.

BLOCK 8 - CITY

Insert the city name of the importer's mailing address.

BLOCK 9 - STATE

For a U.S. mailing address, insert a valid 2-position alphabetic U.S. state postal code (see list below). For a Canadian mailing address, insert a 2-character alphabetic code representing the province of the importer's mailing address (see list below).

BLOCK 10 - ZIP CODE

For a U.S. mailing address, insert a 5 or 9 digit numeric ZIP code as established by the U.S. Postal Service. For a Canadian mailing address, insert a Canadian postal routing code. For a Mexican mailing address, leave blank. For all other foreign mailing addresses, a postal routing code may be inserted.

BLOCK 11 - COUNTRY ISO CODE

For a U.S. mailing address, leave blank. For any foreign mailing address, including Canada and Mexico, insert a 2 character alphabetic International Standards Organization (ISO) code representing the country. *Please Note:* Valid ISO codes may be found in Annex A of the Harmonized Tariff Schedule of the United States; Customs Directive 099 5610-002, "Standard Guidelines for the Input of Names and Addresses into ACS Files"; or Customs Directive 099-3550-061 "Instructions for Preparation of CF 7501".

BLOCK 12 - SECOND IMPORTER ADDRESS

If the importer's place of business is the same as the mailing address, leave blank. If different from the mailing address, insert the importer's business address in this space. A second address representing the importer's place of business is to be provided if the mailing address is a post office box or drawer.

BLOCK 13 - CITY

Insert the city name for the importer's business address.

BLOCK 14 - STATE

For a U.S. address, insert a 2 character alphabetic U.S. state postal code (see list below). For a Canadian address, insert a 2 character alphabetic code representing the province of the importer's business address (see list below).

BLOCK 15 - ZIP CODE

For a U.S. business address, insert a 5 or 9 digit numeric ZIP code as established by the U.S. Postal Service. For a Canadian address, insert a Canadian postal routing code. For a Mexican address, leave blank. For all other foreign addresses, postal routing code may be inserted.

BLOCK 16 - COUNTRY ISO CODE

For a U.S. address, leave blank. For any foreign address, including Canada and Mexico, insert a 2 character alphabetic ISO code representing the country.

BLOCK 17 - PREVIOUSLY ASSIGNED CUSTOMS IMPORTER NUMBER

Indicate whether or not importer has previously been assigned a Customs Importer Number under the same name or a different name. If "Yes" to either question, list name(s) and/or number(s) in Block 17c.

OFFICIAL UNITED STATES POSTAL SERVICE
TWO-LETTER STATE AND POSSESSION ABBREVIATIONS

AL	Alabama	MT	Montana
AK	Alaska	NE	Nebraska
AZ	Arizona	NV	Nevada
AR	Arkansas	NH	New Hampshire
AS	American Samoa	NJ	New Jersey
CA	California	NM	New Mexico
CO	Colorado	NY	New York
CT	Connecticut	NC	North Carolina
DE	Delaware	ND	North Dakota
DC	District of Columbia	MP	Northern Mariana Islands
FM	Federated States of Micronesia	OH	Ohio
FL	Florida	OK	Oklahoma
GA	Georgia	OR	Oregon
GU	Guam	PW	Palau
HI	Hawaii	PA	Pennsylvania
ID	Idaho	PR	Puerto Rico
IL	Illinois	RI	Rhode Island
IN	Indiana	SC	South Carolina
IA	Iowa	SD	South Dakota
KS	Kansas	TN	Tennessee
KY	Kentucky	TX	Texas
LA	Louisiana	UT	Utah
ME	Maine	VT	Vermont
MH	Marshall Islands	VA	Virginia
MD	Maryland	VI	Virgin Islands
MA	Massachusetts	WA	Washington
MI	Michigan	WV	West Virginia
MN	Minnesota	WI	Wisconsin
MS	Mississippi	WY	Wyoming
MO	Missouri		

OFFICIAL TWO-LETTER CANADIAN PROVINCE CODES

AB	Alberta	NS	Nova Scotia
BC	British Columbia	ON	Ontario
MB	Manitoba	PE	Prince Edward Island
NB	New Brunswick	PQ	Quebec
NF	Newfoundland (Incl. Labrador)	SK	Saskatchewan
NT	Northwest Territories	YT	Yukon Territory

Customs Form 5106 (031595)(Back)

determine their place of arrival. However, where the goods are unloaded is not necessarily the place where customs entry will be made. Goods can be unloaded on the East or West Coast and transported in-bond to an inland port of entry for the filing of entry documents and release from Customs custody. Because of the congestion that may occur at certain ports, sometimes efficient importing may mandate the use of ports that would not normally be considered. In addition, there are situations where different U.S. Customs offices will treat importations differently. This port shopping is not illegal; however, if an importer has sought a determination of a classification and proper duty for a prospective import at one port, under new Customs regulations, the importer must disclose its inquiry and answer to any other port where it may enter merchandise. Finally, in some cases, such as the importation of livestock and animals, entry is permitted only at certain designated ports of entry.

6. Import Quotas

Through legislation, enacted as often as yearly, the U.S. Congress imposes quotas on different imported merchandise. Quotas may be worldwide or related to specific countries. Some quotas are absolute; that is, once a specific quantity has been entered into the United States, no further imports are permitted. Currently, wheat gluten is the only commodity subject to an absolute quota.

Most quotas are tariff-rate quotas, meaning that a certain quantity of the merchandise is entered at one duty rate, and once that quantity has been exceeded—for the United State as a whole, not for the specific importer—the tariff duty rate increases. Thus, the importer can continue to import, but it will have to pay a higher tariff duty. Examples of tariff-rate quotas are certain milks and creams, anchovies, brooms, ethyl alcohol, olives, mandarin oranges, tuna, upland cotton, and tobacco.

Additionally, there are specific tariff-rate quotas for products under the jurisdiction of the U.S. Department of Agriculture, which require the importer to have an import license. With a license, the importer may import at a lesser duty rate; without a license, the importer may still import the product, but it must pay a higher duty rate. Examples of the Department of Agriculture quotas are certain butters, sour creams, dried milks or creams, butter substitutes, blue-molded cheese, cheddar cheese (except Canadian cheddar), American-type cheese, Edam and Gouda cheeses, Italian-type cheeses, Swiss or Emmentaler cheese, and cheese substitutes.

Under the NAFTA agreement, there are also specific tariff-rate quotas for products imported from Mexico including certain dried milks and creams, condensed and evaporated milks and cream, cheese, tomatoes, onions and shallots, eggplants, chili peppers, watermelons, peanuts, sugars derived from sugarcane or sugar beets, orange juice, cotton, and brooms. Imports of some products from both Canada and Mexico are subject to tariff-rate quotas such as certain cotton, man-made fiber, or wool apparel, and cotton or man-made fiber fabrics and yarns.

Following the Uruguay Round negotiations of the General Agreement on Tariffs and Trade (GATT), specific tariff-rate quotas on certain products were also implemented. These quotas include beef, milk and cream, dried milk and cream, dairy products, condensed or evaporated milk and cream, dried whey, Canadian cheddar cheese, peanuts, sugar (including sugarcane), certain articles containing sugar, blended syrups, cocoa powder, chocolate, chocolate crumb, infant formula, mixes and doughs, peanut butter and paste, mixed condiments and seasonings, ice cream, animal feed, cotton, card strips made from cotton, and fibers of cotton.

The importation of textiles and textile products may, pursuant to Section 204 of the Agricultural Act of 1956, be subject to quota, visa, or export-license requirements and additional entry requirements including declarations identifying the fabricated components from some countries. Mere possession of the export visa will not guarantee entry into the United States, since only a finite quantity is allowed admission throughout the year. If the quota closes between the time the visa is issued by the foreign government and the shipment arrives in the United States, it will not be released until the quota re-opens for the next period. There are currently sixty countries subject to textile controls.

Finally, so as not to harm U.S. farm production, there are tariff-rate preferences for certain vegetables and fresh produce when entered during the peak growing season in the United States. Importers of produce during peak season will be assessed a lower duty rate. However, in the off season, the tariff classification and associated duty rate are higher.

Before agreeing to purchase products for importation and in planning the cost of the product, the importer must ascertain in advance whether any absolute or tariff-rate quotas exist on the merchandise.

7. Antidumping, Countervailing, and Other Special Duties

Before entering into an agreement to purchase products for importation, the importer should specifically confirm whether that product is subject to an antidumping or countervailing duty order of the U.S. Department of Commerce (administered by the U.S. Customs Service) or to a special duty imposed under Sections 201 or 406 of the Trade Act of 1974. When goods are subject to one of these orders, the amount of customs duties (which are payable by the importer) can be much greater than on ordinary importations. While in recent years manufactured items have been subject to a relatively low rate of normal duty (in the range of 3–5 percent), cases under these laws exist where duties of as much as 300 percent of the value of the goods have been assessed. Furthermore, U.S. Customs regulations prohibit the reimbursement by the foreign supplier to the U.S. importer if the U.S. importer pays antidumping or countervailing duties. Where goods are subject to an antidumping or countervailing duty order, the importer will be required to sign a certificate for the U.S. Customs Service under penalty of perjury that it has not entered into any agreement for reimbursement of such duties. When an importer is negotiating the price for purchase from the foreign supplier, it is important for the importer to ascertain the price at which the foreign supplier is selling in its own country and for export to third countries. This will help the importer determine whether there is a risk that an antidumping investigation can be initiated in the future on the imports of the product being purchased. Furthermore, if the importer determines that the goods are already subject to an antidumping order, it can take certain steps, such as insisting that the exporter act as the importer of record, becoming a related party to the seller or substantially transforming the merchandise in a third country, to reduce or eliminate the dumping risks.

8. Classification

Before importing and during the time that the importer is trying to calculate the potential duties payable on the imported product, it will be necessary for the importer to ascertain the correct customs classification for the product. Under the Customs Modernization Act, an importer must use "reasonable care" in classifying the product. As of January 1, 1989, the United States became a party to the Harmonized Tariff System (HTS), a new commodity classification system that has been adopted in sixty-five countries. The attempt has been to standardize among those countries a common classification system for all merchandise. The HTS classification system is extensive. A copy of the table of contents of the HTS, the General Rules of Interpretation used to classify merchandise, the symbols for special tariff reduction programs, and a sample page relating to men's suits are included in Appendix F. All merchandise is classified in some provision of this tariff system, including a catch-all provision for items not elsewhere specified. Only by identifying the appropriate classification in the HTS can the importer ascertain the duty that will be payable on the imported product. Sometimes, in order to attempt to classify the merchandise, the importer will have to obtain information from the exporter—for example, which material constitutes the chief value when the goods are classified by component material.

Unfortunately, identification of the correct classification is not always easy. Not only can an item be classified under two or more classifications (such as individual items or as a set or system), but in some cases, such as the development of new commercial products, no classification may be immediately apparent. In that event, it may be necessary to request a classification ruling from the U.S. Customs Service. Some rulings are informal and can provide useful guidance for planning purposes. However, if the importer wants to have assurance of a certain duty rate (and not a surprise duty increase at some later date), it is necessary to seek a binding, formal ruling from the U.S. Customs Service. (See subsection 18, below.) It goes without saying that tariff classification opinions offered by customs brokers are not binding on the U.S. Customs Service and can only be regarded as knowledgeable guesses. The classification should be checked each year since products are sometimes reclassified by the Customs Service.

9. Valuation

When the importer imports merchandise, it is generally required to state a value for the merchandise on the documents filed with the U.S. Customs Service, and the seller will be required to furnish the buyer with a commercial invoice evidencing the sales price. Under the Customs Modernization Act, an importer must use "reasonable care" in determining the value of the merchandise. Even when the item is duty-free, for U.S. import balance of payment statistical purposes, the Department of Commerce through the U.S. Customs Service wants to know the value of the merchandise. Where the goods are dutiable at an ad valorem duty, that is, a percentage of the value, obviously it makes a great deal of difference whether the value is $100 or $100,000. In general, the value will be the price of the merchandise paid or payable by the importer/buyer to the exporter/seller. This is known as the transaction value. This must include any indirect payments, such as when the merchandise is being provided free or at a reduced price to satisfy a previous debt. There are a number of deductions permitted from the invoice price, such as foreign inland freight from the seller's factory to the port of export if such charges are separately identified on the invoice and shipment is made on a through bill of lading, and ocean or air international transportation charges and insurance. Similarly, the law permits certain additions to the price paid or payable in order to arrive at the transaction value, such as packing costs incurred by the buyer, selling commissions incurred by the buyer, assists, royalties or license fees that the buyer is required to pay as a condition of the sale, and any proceeds accruing to the seller upon subsequent resale, disposal, or use of the merchandise, provided that such amounts were not included in the original price. This means that the value for customs purposes may be different from the price that the buyer and the seller have negotiated.

One area of concern occurs when the buyer and the seller are related parties. That is, if the buyer or the seller owns 5 percent or more of the stock or a similar interest in the other, or if the buyer and the seller are commonly owned by a third party, the U.S. Customs Service suspects that the price paid between the buyer and the seller may not be a true arm's-length value. Customs assumes that the price may have been manipulated, for example, to reduce income taxes in the seller's country or to avoid antidumping duties in the buyer's country. Consequently, when the importation is between a related seller and buyer, Customs will ordinarily request, and the importer will be required to furnish, information designed to establish to Customs' satisfaction that the price paid or payable is equivalent to a true arm's-length price.

In certain circumstances, for example, where Customs has determined that the transaction value is not equivalent to a true arm's-length price, or any element of the price cannot be determined, Customs will use other valuation methods to calculate the customs value. Customs may use the transaction value of identical or similar merchandise, the deductive value, or the computed value. When Customs determines that one of these alternative valuation methods is required, the importer can often be surprised by a retroactive increase in customs duties that can substantially and adversely affect the importer.

Where the purchase is in a foreign currency, Customs requires the price to be converted to U.S. dollars for valuation of the merchandise on the date of export, even though the date of payment will probably be different.

10. Duty-Free and Reduced Duty Programs

Before importing, the importer should ascertain whether or not the product is eligible for one of the special duty-free or reduced duty programs which Congress has allowed.

The largest program is known as the Generalized System of Preferences (GSP). This program was designed to encourage the economic development of less-developed countries by permitting the importation of those countries' products duty-free. The HTS contains a list of the approximately 101 countries eligible for this program. (See Appendix F.) (Under the North American Free Trade Agreement, Mexico was eliminated as a beneficiary country as of January 1, 1994.) The fact that a product will be imported from one of the GSP beneficiary countries, however, does not guarantee duty-free treatment. Some specific products even from eligible countries have been excluded, and it is necessary for the importer to identify whether the particular product is on the exclusion list. In addition, at least 35 percent of the final appraised value must be added in that country. The importer must claim the duty-free status by putting an "A" in the Entry Summary and, if requested by Customs, obtain a GSP Declaration from the exporter (see Figure 8–11).

For imports from the twenty-four countries located in the Caribbean Basin, a similar duty-free program is available, along with imports from Israel under the Israel Free Trade Agreement; imports from Bolivia, Colombia, Peru, and Ecuador under the Andean Trade Preference Act; and imports from thirty-five countries under the African Growth and Opportunity Act.

The final program is a duty-free and reduced duty program, the North American Free Trade Agreement, which was implemented on January 1, 1994. Under the North American Free Trade Agreement, products of Canadian and Mexican origin eventually can be imported duty-free to the United States if various requirements are met. Usually, this means that the product must be of Canadian or Mexican origin under one of six eligibility rules and the exporter must provide the importer with a Certificate of Origin (see Figure 4–17). Many items were granted duty-free status immediately, but other items will be eligible for duty-free status over a phase-out period of five to fifteen years. Nevertheless, if the importer can comply with the requirements, the duty will be less than on ordinary imports from Canada or Mexico.

11. Column 2 Imports

The HTS presently classifies imports according to their source. Products coming from nations that are members of the General Agreement on Tariffs and Trade (GATT) are entitled to be imported at the lowest duty rates ("Normal Tariff Rate [NTR]"—generally 0–10 percent). Products from certain countries, including Laos, Cuba, and North Korea, are assessed duties at much higher rates, in the range of 20 to 110 percent. (Importations from certain countries—Cuba, Libya, Iran, North Korea, and Iraq—are prohibited without a license from the Department of Treasury.)

In addition, under Section 406 of the Trade Act of 1974, if there is a substantial increase in products from a Communist country which causes market disruption and injury to the U.S. industry, the International Trade Commission, with the approval of the President, can impose quotas or assess additional duties. An importer contemplating importation from a Communist country should confirm whether such quotas or duties have been imposed.

12. Deferred Duty Programs (Bonded Warehousing and Foreign Trade Zones)

An importer may wish to plan its importations in a manner to defer the payment of duties. Two possible programs exist for this purpose. The first is bonded warehouse importations. Importers can apply for and obtain authorization from the U.S. Customs Service to establish a bonded warehouse on their own premises, or they can utilize the services of a public warehouse that has received similar Customs authorization. When such authorization has been received, goods can be imported and placed in such warehouses to be withdrawn for use or consumption at a later date (up to five years) with a warehouse entry. In the meantime, no customs duties are payable. When the goods are withdrawn for consumption, the goods will be dutiable at the value at the time of withdrawal rather than the time of entry into the warehouse. A bond must be secured to prevent loss of duties in case the merchandise is accidentally or intentionally released into U.S. commerce. The importer can manipulate, mark, re-label, re-package, and perform a number of other operations (except manufacturing) on the merchandise. A Warehouse Entry is made on the regular Entry Summary form by designating the correct type code. (See Chapter 8, Section K.)

The second program for the deferral of duties is the use of a foreign trade zone. Foreign trade zones are operations authorized by the U.S. Foreign Trade Zones Board and are operated on a charge basis for importers using them. In authorized locations, importers may place imported merchandise for manipulation, and more importantly, actual manufacturing operations can occur there. (Further manufacturing is not permitted in bonded warehouse operations.) The merchandise can then be entered for consumption in the United States or exported. While the merchandise is in the foreign trade zone (there is no time limit), no duty is payable, and, if the merchandise is exported, no U.S. duties will be paid at all. A number of importers, such as automobile manufacturers, have established very large foreign trade zone operations on their own premises, called subzones, and customs duties are reduced by importing components and raw materials and finishing them into final products in the subzone. The final product is then entered into the United States at the classification and duty rate applicable to the final product, which is often lower than that for the raw materials and components. The establishment of bonded warehousing and foreign trade zone operations requires significant lead time and the importer should take this into account in its pre-importation planning. (Samples of applications to admit merchandise to a foreign trade zone and to perform activities there are shown in Figures 8–9 and 8–10.)

Under the North American Free Trade Agreement, beginning January 1, 1996, on exports to Canada and January 1, 2001, on exports to Mexico, U.S. duty will be payable on U.S. bonded warehouse and foreign trade zone importations, reduced by the amount of duty payable upon importation to Canada or Mexico.

13. Temporary Importations

In some situations, an importer may intend to import merchandise only temporarily. For example, an importer may be importing samples for testing, inspection, or for making purchasing decisions; an importer may wish to display a sample at a trade fair or other sales show; or an importer may wish to import merchandise and to further manufacture it and then export the finished product. In such cases, the importer can enter the goods under a Temporary Importation Bond (TIB). (Under the North American Free Trade Agreement, products meeting the rules of origin imported from Canada or Mexico may be admitted temporarily without posting a bond. However, beginning January 1, 1996, on imports from Canada and January 1, 2001, on imports from Mexico, U.S. duty will be payable if the goods are subsequently exported to Canada or Mexico.) Under a TIB entry, the importer establishes a bond covering the imported merchandise and guaranteeing that it will be exported within one year, unless extended (up to two more years). If the goods are not exported, the bond is forfeited, usually in the amount of twice the value of the customs duties that would have been payable on the products. TIBs are not available for merchandise that is subject to an absolute quota. The importer should be aware of its obligation to account for the exportation of products prior to the deadline, and should file an Application for Exportation of Articles under Special Bond—Form 3495 (see Figure 6–7) with Customs prior to the export so that Customs can inspect and confirm that the exportation indeed occurs. Without this, the importer will be unable to cancel the bond and avoid payment of double duties.

14. Country of Origin

Determination of the proper country of origin can affect the duty rate payable on imported goods or whether they are subject to quotas. In addition, Section 304 of the Tariff Act of 1930 requires that imported merchandise be clearly and conspicuously marked in a permanent manner with the English name of the foreign country of origin. Some types of merchandise are exempt from the marking requirement but, in such cases, usually the outermost container that will go to the end user must be marked. This is an important preliminary planning consideration because the Customs regulations specify that certain types of products must be marked in certain ways, such as die-stamping, cast-in-the-mold lettering, or etching, during the manufacturing process. The importer should check the country of origin regulations prior to purchasing products to ascertain whether or not it must advise the supplier or seller of any special marking methods prior to the manufacture of the products. Sometimes off-the-shelf inventory manufactured in a foreign country cannot be modified after manufacture to comply with the U.S. country of origin marking requirements. Merchandise which is not properly marked may be seized by the U.S. Customs Service. In some cases, the products can be marked after such seizure, but only upon payment of a marking penalty, which increases the cost of importing the products. More seriously, sometimes Customs will release the merchandise to the importer, and the importer may resell it. Then, the U.S. Customs Service may issue a notice of redelivery of the products (see Figure 8–18). If the importer is unable to redeliver the products, a substantial customs penalty may be payable. The marking must remain on the product (including after any repacking) until it reaches the ultimate purchaser, which is usually the retail customer. Recently, penalties for any intentional removal of markings were raised to a $100,000 fine and/or imprisonment for one year.

15. Assists

One of the situations in which the U.S. Customs Service can increase the value of imported merchandise and assess additional customs duties is where the importer has provided an "assist" to the manufacturer/exporter. This may occur when the importer furnishes tooling, dies or molds, raw materials or components, or other items used in the manufacture of the product to the seller at a reduced price or free of charge. Any technical data such as engineering drawings or know-how furnished by the importer to the supplier that was not produced in the United States is also an assist. If the

Figure 6–7. Exportation of articles under special bond.

DEPARTMENT OF THE TREASURY
UNITED STATES CUSTOMS SERVICE

Form Approved
O.M.B. No. 1515-0009

APPLICATION FOR EXPORTATION OF ARTICLES UNDER SPECIAL BOND

19 CFR 10.38

TO DISTRICT DIRECTOR OF CUSTOMS

1. TO: District Director of Customs *(Address)*	2. FROM: *(Name and Address of Importer or Agent)*

ATTACH COPY OF EXPORT INVOICE DESCRIBING ARTICLES TO BE EXPORTED

3. Name of Exporting Carrier	4. Date of Departure	5. Country of Origin	6. No. of Export Packages
7. Port of Entry	8. Entry Number and Date		9. Date Bonded Period Expires
10. Date Articles Available for Customs Examination	11. Signature of Importer or Agent		12. Date

(FOR CUSTOMS USE ONLY)

NOTICE TO IMPORTER TO DELIVER ARTICLES TO BE EXAMINED AND IDENTIFIED FOR EXPORTATION

13. Place and Date of Customs Examination

14. DATE	15. DISTRICT DIRECTOR OF CUSTOMS BY:

REPORT OF EXAMINATION

☐ 16. The articles covered by this application have been examined and agree with the invoice in content and No. of export pkgs. and are approved for export.

17. No. of Export Packages	18. Date of Delivery for Exportation	19. Marks and Numbers on Export Packages

☐ 20. The articles covered by this application do not agree with the invoice in content or in number of packages as follows

21. SIGNATURE OF EXAMINING CUSTOMS OFFICER	22. DATE

REPORT OF EXPORTATION

23. Home of Exporting Conveyance *(Vessel, Railroad, Airline and Flight Number)*

24. Date of Departure	25. Manifest No.	Paperwork Reduction Act Notice: The Paperwork Reduction Act of 1980 says we must tell you why we are collecting this information, and whether you have to give it to us. We need this information to ensure that importers and exporters are complying with the customs laws of the United States and allow us to figure and collect the right amount of revenue. Your response is mandatory.
26. SIGNATURE OF CUSTOMS OFFICER		Statement Required by 5 CFR 1320.21: The estimated average burden associated with this collection of information is 8 minutes per respondent or recordkeeper depending on individual circumstances. Comments concerning the accuracy of this burden estimate and suggestions for reducing this burden should be directed to U.S. Customs Service, Paperwork Management Branch, Washington DC 20229. ***DO NOT send completed form(s) to this office.***

(Customs officer must return one copy of this form to port of origin upon exportation.)

(EDITIONS PRIOR TO 11/67 ARE OBSOLETE)

Customs Form 3495 (080195)

*U.S. Government Printing Office: 1995 — 387-594/25991

importer will be providing any assists, this should be considered at the time the seller makes up the commercial invoices and sales documentation, and the importer should determine the appropriate way to pay customs duties on the value thereof.

16. Specialized Products

Certain products imported into the United States must comply with the regulations of various U.S. governmental agencies. For example, foods, drugs, cosmetics, and medical devices must comply with the Food, Drugs and Cosmetics Act; electronic products must comply with the Federal Communications regulations; hazardous materials and dangerous goods must comply with the regulations of the Environmental Protection Agency and the Department of Transportation. Foods must also comply with the Department of Agriculture regulations. Specialized forms must be filed upon importation of such products, and the importer may need to get the information from the exporter to complete such forms prior to arrival of the goods. (Sample forms are shown in Figures 8–11, 8–12, 8–13, and 8–14.)

17. Record-Keeping Requirements

Under the U.S. Customs regulations, importers are required to keep copies of all documents relating to their importations for a period of five years. In the event of any question, Customs has the right to expect such records (on reasonable advance notice) to ascertain that the importer has complied with U.S. customs laws. Prior to engaging in importing, the importer should establish record retention policies and procedures which will ensure that the relevant records are kept for the appropriate period of time. (See the fuller discussion of this issue in Chapter 1, Section E.)

18. Customs Rulings

Where the importer has questions about the proper application of the customs laws, it may be necessary for the importer to seek a ruling from the U.S. Customs Service. Without such rulings, the importer may take the risk that it is violating customs laws. For example, rulings may be requested relating to the proper classification of merchandise, the proper valuation of merchandise, whether merchandise qualifies for a duty-free or deferred duty treatment, or the proper country of origin marking. Sometimes the waiting period for such rulings is substantial—several months to one year. In the event of a substantial volume of planned importations and significant ambiguity regarding the appropriate method of compliance, a ruling may be advisable, and enough lead time to obtain the ruling must be allowed.

G. Import Packing and Labeling

Prior to the exportation of the purchased products, the importer should ascertain the type of packaging and labeling the exporter will use. Different packaging is often required to withstand the rigors of international transportation and to ensure that the importer is going to receive the products in an undamaged condition. Generally, container transportation will protect best against damage and pilferage. Certain types of containers may be needed, such as ventilated, refrigerated, flat, open top or high-cube. If the merchandise is a hazardous material, it cannot be transported unless it complies with the United Nations' Performance Oriented Packaging Standards which went into effect on January 1, 1991, and unless the packaging has been certified by a government-approved independent testing agency. (A list of common hazardous materials is in Chapter 2, Section L.) The M.S. packing, labeling, and invoicing requirements for such hazardous materials must be communicated to the seller before shipment. Where the supplier sells FOB factory or any term or condition of sale other than delivered to the buyer, the buyer/importer will be taking the risk of loss during the transportation. Under the Carriage of Goods by Sea Act, steamship lines are not responsible for damage to cargo which is insufficiently packed. Even with insurance, the importer should make an effort to prevent losses due to improper packing. Identification marks on the packages should be put in the packing list. Containerized shipments may be eligible for lower insurance rates compared to breakbulk cargo. The buyer should keep in mind that upon arrival, the goods will have to be examined by the U.S. Customs Service. Packing that facilitates such examination will minimize delays in release from Customs custody. Furthermore, if goods subject to different duty rates are not segregated, all of the merchandise will be dutiable at the highest value. The buyer should ascertain the classification and duty rates of different goods and instruct the buyer to segregate the merchandise prior to shipment. As of January 1, 1996, wood pallets or other solid wood packing materials used with imported cargo are subject to inspection and must be certified free of bark and live plant pests.

Similarly, in order to sell or transport some merchandise after its arrival in the United States, it must be labeled in a certain way. Through its own investigation or through consultation with third parties, the importer should determine if any special labeling is required and should notify the exporter of this prior to exportation of the merchandise. For example, the Consumer Product Safety Act; the regulations of the Bureau of Alcohol, Tobacco and Firearms; the Energy Policy Conservation Act; the Food, Drugs, and Cosmetics Act; the Wool Products Labeling Act; the Textile Fiber Products Identification Act; the Hazardous Substances Act; and the Fur Product Labeling Act are some U.S. laws that impose requirements relating to the proper labeling of imported products. Shipments not properly labeled may be refused entry.

H. U.S. Commercial Considerations

There are several commercial considerations that the importer must take into account.

1. Prevailing Market Price

In planning its import purchases, the importer must pay attention to the prevailing market price. Obviously, if raw materials or components can be purchased in the United States at a lower price than they can be purchased abroad, depending upon the source country, importation will not be economically feasible. In purchasing for resale, if the purchase price is not sufficiently low to permit an adequate markup when resold at the prevailing U.S. market price, the importation will not be economic. If the product is resold in the U.S. market below the prevailing market price, competitors may charge that the sales are predatory pricing (sales below fully allocated costs) or dumping (sales below the price at which the same products are sold to customers in the country of origin).

2. *Buy American Policies*

In planning import transactions, the importer should determine if there are any Buy American policies applicable to the resale of the products. In particular, in sales to the U.S. federal or state governments or their agencies, there may be certain preferences given to U.S. manufactured products. Sometimes there is a maximum foreign content limitation or there are price preferences. If the importer expects to make such sales, it may be necessary to determine if the cost savings of the foreign product is sufficient to overcome the potential sales differential under Buy American policies.

3. *U.S. Industry Standards*

Merchandise manufactured abroad may not comply with standards adopted by U.S. trade associations or enacted into law, such as local building codes. Prior to agreeing to purchase foreign products, the importer should check any applicable U.S. industry standards to make sure that the products will comply. The importer may need to advise the manufacturer of the appropriate specifications so that the products can be manufactured to meet U.S. industry standards.

I. Terms of Purchase

Although there are ordinarily many terms and conditions that the buyer will include in its import purchase agreements, one of the terms of purchase upon which seller and buyer must agree is that relating to passage of title, risk of loss, price, and payment. Although a buyer can purchase on different terms of sale from different sellers in accordance with whatever terms are expressed in each seller's quotation or purchase order acceptance, it is ordinarily much better for the buyer to think about and formulate policies relating to its terms of purchase in advance of placing its order. There are a number of considerations, the first of which relates to the use of abbreviations.

In order to standardize the understanding of the seller and buyer relating to their obligations in international purchase agreements, various nomenclatures have been developed which use abbreviations such as *ex-factory, FOB plant, CIF,* and *landed.* While these shorthand abbreviations can be useful, they can also be sources of confusion. The International Chamber of Commerce developed the "Incoterms," which were revised in 2000 (see Chapter 2, Figures 2–4 and 2–5). There are also the Revised American Foreign Trade Definitions, the Warsaw Terms, and the abbreviations in the

U.S. Uniform Commercial Code. Although these abbreviated terms of sale are similar, they also differ from nomenclature to nomenclature, and it is important to specify in the purchase agreement which nomenclature is being used when an abbreviation is utilized. For example, on a CIF purchase under the Uniform Commercial Code, the seller is required to furnish war risk along with the other coverage. Under the Incoterms, however, the seller need provide war risk coverage only if requested by the buyer. Furthermore, even though it is assumed that sellers and buyers know the responsibilities and obligations which flow from utilizing specific terms such as *FOB plant,* the parties in fact may not always understand all of their rights and responsibilities in the same way, and disputes and problems may arise. For example, even though on an FOB seller's plant sale the buyer is responsible for obtaining and paying for ocean insurance, often the buyer will want the seller to obtain such insurance, which the buyer will reimburse the seller for paying. It is also possible that the seller will arrange for such insurance at the same time that the buyer does so, resulting in expensive duplication. Or, even though the buyer may be responsible for paying freight, the buyer may expect the seller to arrange for shipment "freight collect." Finally, under the new Incoterms certain traditional terms such as "C & F," "FOR," "FOT," and "FOB airport" have been abolished and certain new terms such as "CFR," "DES," "DEQ," and "DDU" have been created. In the author's experience, even if the parties choose to use an abbreviation to specify the way in which title will pass, the author strongly recommends that the "who does what" be stated in detail in the purchase agreement to avoid the possibility of a misunderstanding.

It is also important for the buyer to realize that the price term may differ from the place of passage of title and risk of loss or time of payment. For example, under an INCO CFR or CIF term, the seller will be quoting a price to the buyer which includes the seller's cost of shipping the merchandise to the destination, but, in actuality, title and risk of loss will pass to the buyer when the merchandise is loaded on the ship at the time of export. Similarly, in a sales quotation CIF means only that the price quoted by the seller will include all expenses to the point of destination—it does not mean payment will be made upon arrival. Payment may be made earlier or later depending upon the agreement of the parties. Buyers should be sure that their import purchase documentation distinguishes between price terms, title and risk of loss terms, and payment terms.

Under the new Convention on the International Sale of Goods (discussed in Chapter 7, Section B.2.l), if the parties do not agree upon a place for transfer of title and delivery in their sale agreement, title and delivery will transfer when the merchandise is delivered to the first transportation carrier, and payment by the buyer will be due at that time.

In most international transactions, the buyer will be responsible for importing the products to its own country, clearing customs, and paying any applicable customs duties. This is because the importer is liable for all customs duties, even antidumping duties. However, if the seller agrees to sell landed, duty paid, or delivered to the buyer's place of business (so-called "free domicile" or "free house" delivery), the seller will be responsible for such customs duties. Ordinarily, the seller cannot act as the importer of record in the United States unless it obtains a bond from a U.S. surety company and appoints an agent in the United States for all claims for customs duties.

Generally, a seller would not want to sell delivered, duty paid, but sometimes the buyer's bargaining leverage is such or competition is such that the seller cannot get the business unless it is willing to do so. Similarly, if the buyer is wary of paying dumping duties, she may insist that the seller act as the importer of record. Another situation is when the buyer is buying from a related seller, such as a parent company. In such a case, the parent company may want to sell landed, duty paid and assume such expenses.

In general, if the seller sells ex-factory, it will have the least responsibilities and risks. The buyer will then be responsible for arranging and paying for inland transportation to the port of export, ocean transportation, and U.S. importation. In some cases an ex-factory purchase can result in the buyer being able to avoid U.S. customs duties on the inland freight from the seller's factory to the port of export. In such cases, the buyer will have the responsibility for complying with all foreign export laws, such as obtaining export control licenses, export visas, and exchange control licenses, arranging insurance, and complying with foreign laws. In order to ensure that the seller has the responsibility to complete all of these requirements of foreign law, ordinarily the buyer should not buy ex-factory, but FOB port of export, CIF, or landed. If the buyer buys landed, it should discuss with the seller and make sure that the seller understands its responsibilities during the formation of the purchase agreement. If the seller is unable to effect import, the fact that the buyer is not legally responsible will be of little consolation and will lead to lawsuits, nondelivery, and loss of future supply.

Even though purchasing on a landed, delivered duty-paid basis may be attractive to the buyer, there are many reasons why the buyer may need or want to purchase on other terms. For example, the seller may be inexperienced in arranging international shipments, the buyer's competitors may be willing to purchase ex-factory, the buyer may be buying from an affiliated company, and the buyer may have warehouse-to-warehouse marine insurance under a blanket policy, and, therefore, by agreeing to pay the insurance costs can save the seller some money. Sometimes the buyer is in a better position to obtain lower ocean transportation or insurance rates. For all of these reasons, a thorough discussion of the terms and conditions of purchase between the seller and buyer, rather than simply following a set policy, may be advantageous.

J. Consignments

In addition to purchase transactions, where title to the merchandise transfers to the U.S. buyer in the foreign country or sometime up to delivery in the United States in accordance with the terms of purchase between the parties, in consignment transactions the exporter/seller maintains ownership of the goods and the consignee in the United States takes possession of the goods. The consignee then offers the goods for sale, and when a customer purchases the goods, title transfers from the exporter/seller to the importer/buyer and to the customer simultaneously. Such transactions have various procedural and documentary considerations. As the owner, the exporter/seller will be responsible for all transportation costs, insurance, filing of export declaration, and obtaining foreign export control license. While U.S. Customs regulations may permit the consignee to effect customs clearance, legally the goods are owned by the exporter/seller, and the exporter/seller will be liable for the U.S. Customs duties. Additional taxes may be assessed, such as personal property taxes assessed on the goods while they are awaiting sale and income taxes, because title will pass to the importer/buyer at the buyer's place of business in the United States. In addition, to avoid the inability to take possession of the goods in case of bankruptcy of the importer/buyer or other claims by the importer's creditors, special arrangements under the buyer's law, such as public notices or security interests, may be required. Because the export/import transaction is not a sale at the time of entry, transaction value cannot be used—the U.S. Customs Service will assess customs duties based upon an alternative valuation method.

K. Leases

In import transactions that are leases, no purchase documentation should be used. The ability of the exporter/lessor to retain title and ownership, repossess the goods at the end of the lease, and obtain income tax benefits depends upon using lease documentation rather than sales agreements. Similar to the consignment, the exporter/seller is legally responsible for all exporting and importing obligations, although those obligations can be delegated to the importer in the lease agreement. For U.S. customs valuation purposes, a lease is not a sale; therefore, transaction value will not be used, and the customs duties payable will depend upon an alternative valuation method.

L. Marine and Air Casualty Insurance

If the supplier sells FOB factory or port of export, the importer will be responsible for the ocean (marine) or air insurance covering the shipment. The importer should make arrangements for or make sure that the insurance is properly obtained prior to exportation. Without such insurance, even when the carrier can be proven liable, responsibility is limited to $500 per "package" on ocean shipments and $20 per kilogram on air shipments unless a higher value is disclosed in advance and a higher transportation charge paid. The importer's letter of credit or payment instructions should require insurance unless the importer already has its own or, under the terms of purchase, the importer has agreed to be responsible for the insurance. Even when the importer believes that the terms of sale are clear, the importer should coordinate with the exporter to avoid a situation where both the importer and exporter obtain such insurance, and the importer is billed twice, or neither party obtains the insurance. Importers can obtain single shipment insurance or use open cargo policies covering all of their imports during a specific time period. "Warehouse to warehouse" and "all risk" rather than "named peril" coverage is best. Even "all risk" coverage does not include war risk or "strike, riot, and civil commotion" coverage and the buyer must specifically request the seller to obtain such coverage if the buyer desires it. (A sample marine insurance policy and certificate are shown in Figures 4–11 and 4–12, respectively.) For additional information see Chapter 2, Section P, and Chapter 4, Section G.

M. Method of Transportation; Booking Transportation

When the importer is responsible for the transportation of the merchandise from the foreign country to the United States, the importer will have to make a decision relating to the mode of transportation and arrange for shipment. Transportation may be made by air or by ship. Transportation can be arranged directly with air carriers or steamship companies or through freight forwarders. Air transportation is obviously much quicker, but is more expensive. Large shipments cannot be shipped by air. In obtaining quotations from various carriers, it is important to record and confirm any such quotations to avoid future increases and discrepancies. When checking with transportation carriers, the name of the person making the quotation, the date, the rate, and the appropriate tariff classification number used by the carrier should be recorded. (A sample steamship tariff, Figure 2–7, and a booking confirmation, Figure 2–8, are shown and additional information is contained in Chapter 2, Section Q.)

N. Import Financing

Some foreign governments offer financing assistance to U.S. importers who are purchasing merchandise from exporters in their countries. Some state government agencies even offer financing to purchase imported components if the finished products will be exported. If the importer intends to utilize any import financing program, the program should be investigated sufficiently in advance of commencing imports. The necessary applications and documentation must be filed and approvals obtained prior to importation of the merchandise.

O. Patent, Trademark, and Copyright Registrations and Infringements

In purchasing foreign products for importation to the United States, the importer should satisfy itself that the products will not infringe the patent, trademark, and/or copyright registration (sometimes called intellectual or industrial property rights) of another person. If the trademark or copyright has been registered with the U.S. Customs Service, entry of the merchandise may be prohibited and the merchandise seized. Under the Anti-Counterfeiting Consumer Protection Act of 1996, importing or trading in counterfeit goods is punishable by a fine of up to $1 million. Even though the foreign manufacturer may have a patent, trademark, or copyright in its own country, unless such patent, trademark, or copyright has been registered in the United States, importation of the product may infringe a valid right of another person. That person may be a U.S. manufacturer or a foreign company which has registered its rights in the United States. Under the new Convention on the International Sale of Goods (discussed in Chapter 7, Section B.2.l) and contrary to U.S. law, there is no implied warranty that a foreign-manufactured product will not infringe on U.S. intellectual property rights as long as the foreign seller was not aware of an infringement. The importer should initiate a patent, trademark, or copyright search to make sure that the patent, trademark, or copyright has not been registered in the United States, and in its purchase documentation the importer should receive warranties and representations from its supplier that it will indemnify and hold the importer harmless from any such infringement actions. Obviously, if the supplier is a small company without much financial strength or has no offices in, and is not subject to the jurisdiction of the U.S. courts, the complaining party may proceed only against the importer in an infringement action. The importer will be unable to obtain indemnification from the supplier unless the supplier has consented to jurisdiction in the United States in the purchase agreement or the importer files another lawsuit against the supplier in the foreign country.

If the foreign supplier has not registered its patents, trademarks, or copyrights in the United States, the importer may wish to do so. To avoid disputes, generally the importer should do so only with the authorization of the foreign supplier. If the supplier is manufacturing the product with the importer's brand or trademark in a private branding arrangement, the importer should register such trademark and the supplier should disclaim all rights therein.

A related area concerns gray market imports. Even though the importer may have obtained an exclusive purchase right, distributorship, or sales agency in the United States, products manufactured by the supplier may be diverted from other customers in the manufacturer's home country or third countries for sale in the United States. Such situations will only occur where the price at which the manufacturer sells in its home market or to third countries is below the prevailing market price in the United States, and, therefore, third persons can make a profit by buying at the lower price and reselling in the United States. However, this may arise as a result of exchange rate fluctuations rather than intentional disregard of the importer's exclusive rights. Under current U.S. Customs regulations, trademarks and copyrights can be registered with the U.S. Customs Service and products which are counterfeit will be seized. Genuine products manufactured by the original manufacturer or its authorized licensee (gray market goods) will also be seized unless they were manufactured by a foreign affiliated company of the U.S. trademark or copyright owner.

P. Confidentiality and Non-Disclosure Agreements

If the importer will be furnishing any samples to the exporter, for example, when the foreign manufacturer is manufacturing products in accordance with specifications of the importer in a contract manufacturing arrangement, or when the importer will be providing other confidential or proprietary information regarding its business or products, the importer should require the manufacturer/exporter to sign a confidentiality and non-disclosure agreement in advance of disclosure of any proprietary information. In some countries where laws against counterfeiting are weak, this contractual agreement may be the importer's only protection against unauthorized copying or unfair competition by the manufacturer/exporter or dishonest third parties.

Q. Payment

An importer may be required to pay for merchandise it purchases by cash in advance or a letter of credit, unless the exchange control regulations of the government of the buyer do not require it or the buyer has sufficient bargaining leverage to purchase on more liberal terms. The buyer's methods of payment are discussed in Chapter 7, Section B.2.e. If a letter of credit is required, the seller will often provide instructions to the importer (see Chapter 4, Figure 4–28), and the importer will have to make an application in the nature of a credit application to a bank that offers letter of credit services. A sample application is shown in Figure 6–8. An applicant's checklist for a commercial letter of credit is shown in Figure 6–9. Two samples of advices of letter of credit as they will be issued to the seller are shown in Chapter 4, Figures 4–35 and 4–36. A sample credit notification sent by the importer's bank to a correspondent bank in the seller's country (who will advise the seller that the letter of credit has been opened) is shown in Figure 6–10. For payment by documentary collection, a sample of the seller's instructions to the bank is shown in Chapter 4, Figure 4–28. Sample sight or time drafts which the seller will present to the correspondent bank under a letter of credit to obtain payment when the goods are shipped are shown in Figures 4–29 and 4–30, respectively.

A buyer should realize in using a letter of credit that the bank does not verify the quantity, quality, or even the existence of the goods. The bank will make payment as long as the seller presents documents that appear on their face to be in compliance with the terms of the letter of credit. For this reason, a buyer may wish to arrange for a preshipment inspection by an inspection service.

R. Translation

The importer must also give consideration to the necessity of translating into English any foreign language documents, such as advertising materials, instruction manuals, warranties, and labeling. The importer may be able to get the seller to agree to perform such translations and bear the cost. These translations may be necessary to achieve sales and adequately protect the importer's rights. For example, if a patent application is incorrectly translated, the patent owner may lose its rights. The location of a competent translator and completion of the translation may require significant lead time and, depending on the volume of material, may involve significant expense.

S. Foreign Branch Operations, Subsidiaries, Joint Ventures, and Licensing

Sometimes the importer will be importing from its or its parent company's existing branch or subsidiary company in a foreign country. Or, rather than purchasing from an independent manufacturer or distributor, the importer may decide to establish such a branch operation or subsidiary company. If personnel are available to staff the foreign branch or company, this may increase the importer's sourcing capability and may smooth export and import operations. Similarly, the importer may form a joint venture with a foreign company to manufacture or export the importer's desired product to the United States and perhaps other countries. Where the laws prohibit the

(*Text continues on page 276.*)

Figure 6–8. Application for letter of credit.

FIRST CHICAGO
The First National Bank of Chicago

APPLICATION FOR IRREVOCABLE COMMERCIAL LETTER OF CREDIT

Import Services Unit
Mail Suite 0236
Chicago, Illinois 60670-0236

F.N.B.C. No. ____________ (For Bank Use Only)

Date ____________

Please issue an irrevocable Letter of Credit substantially as set forth below and forward same by:

☐ Airmail ☐ Full Cable, directly to the beneficiary, telex number: ________ ☐ Full Cable, for delivery to the beneficiary by the advising bank ☐ Return original Credit to us ☐ Other: ________

In issuing the credit you are expressly authorized to make such changes from the terms of this application as you, in your sole discretion, may deem advisable provide no such changes shall vary the principal terms hereof.

	FOR ACCOUNT OF (APPLICANT)
IN FAVOR OF (BENEFICIARY)	AMOUNT
	Drafts must be presented for Negotiation or to Drawee on or before (Expiry Date) [896]

Shipment from: Latest Shipping Date ____________ ☐ Partial Shipments Prohibited

To: ☐ Transshipments Prohibited

☐ Documents must be presented to negotiating or paying bank within ________ days after the date of issuance of documents evidencing shipment or dispatch or taken in charge (shipping documents) but within validity of letter of credit.

Available by drafts ____________ drawn, at your option, on you or your correspondent for ____________ % of the Invoice value.

Discount charges are for ☐ Applicant ☐ Beneficiary. Banking charges other than FNBC are for ☐ Applicant ☐ Beneficiary.

When accompanied by the following documents, as checked:

CHECK DOCUMENTS REQUIRED

[111] ☐ Commercial Invoice [110] ☐ Packing List

[112] ☐ Customs Invoice

[890] ☐ Marine and War Risk Insurance Policy and/or Certificate ____________ (Indicate Special Instructions for Insurance, if any)

☐ Certificate of Origin

[912] ☐ GSP Certificate of Origin Form A ☐ Other Documents ____________

☐ Full Set of Clean On Board Original Ocean Bills of Lading (If more than one original has been issued all are required)

Issued to order of: ____________

Marked Freight: Collect/Paid and Notify: ____________

☐ Air Waybill Consigned to: ____________

Marked Freight: Collect/Paid and Notify: ____________

COVERING: Merchandise described in the invoice as: (Mention commodity only in generic terms omitting details as to grade, quality, etc.)

Check one: Terms ☐ EX FACTORY ☐ FAS ☐ FOB ☐ C&F ☐ CIF ☐ C&I ____________

[113] ☐ Insurance effected by applicant. Applicant agrees to keep insurance coverage in force until this transaction is completed

[886] ☐ Please instruct the negotiating or Drawee Bank to forward one set of negotiable documents to ☐ Customs House Broker ☐ Applicant

Other Instructions: ☐ L/C is transferable ☐ Combined shipment permitted
Unless otherwise instructed, documents shall be forwarded to you in one airmail.

Without limiting and in addition to the provisions, terms and conditions set forth on the reverse hereof, you are hereby expressly authorized and directed to honor any request for payment which is made under and in compliance with the terms of the Credit requested by this application without regard to, and without any duty on your part to inquire into, the existence of any disputes or controversies between any of the undersigned, the beneficiary of the Credit or any other person, firm or corporation; or the respective rights, duties or liabilities of any of them; or whether any facts or occurrences represented in any of the documents presented under the Credit are true or correct. Furthermore, we fully understand and agree that your sole obligation to us shall be limited to honoring requests for payment made under and in compliance with the terms of the Credit and this application and your obligation remains so limited even if you may have assisted us in the preparation of the wording of the Credit or any documents required to be presented thereunder and even if you may otherwise be aware of the underlying transaction giving rise to the Credit and this application.

PLEASE DATE AND OFFICIALLY SIGN THE AGREEMENT ON THE REVERSE SIDE OF THIS APPLICATION

XEL 2012 (R-11-86) Any and all attachments and / or alterations must be individually signed

Courtesy of The First National Bank of Chicago.

(continues)

Figure 6–8. *(continued)*

[*reverse*]

SECURITY AND REIMBURSEMENT AGREEMENT FOR IRREVOCABLE COMMERCIAL LETTER OF CREDIT

In consideration of your issuing a commercial letter of credit (the "Credit"), substantially according to the Application appearing on the reverse side hereof or as attached hereto and individually signed by us, we, the undersigned, hereby jointly and severally contract as follows:

1. We agree: (a) in the case of each sight draft under or purporting to be under the Credit in United States currency, to reimburse you at your head office in Chicago on demand, in United States currency, the amount paid on such draft, or, if so demanded by you, to pay you at your office in advance in United States currency the amount required to pay such draft; and (b) in the case of each acceptance under or purporting to be under the Credit in United States currency, to pay to you at your head office in Chicago in United States currency the amount thereof on demand but in any event not later than the date of maturity.

2. We agree: (a) in the case of each sight draft under or purporting to be under the Credit in currency other than United States currency, to reimburse you on demand at your head office in Chicago the equivalent of the amount paid in United States currency at the rate of exchange then current in Chicago for cable transfer to the place of payment in the currency in which such draft is drawn, together with interest thereon from the date of payment to the date of reimbursement; or if so required by you, to pay you at your head office in Chicago in advance in United States currency the equivalent of the amount required to pay the same; and (b) in the case of each acceptance under or purporting to be under the Credit in currency other than United States currency, to pay you on demand at your head office in Chicago the equivalent of the acceptance in United States currency (i) if payment is made by us in time to reach your head office in Chicago not later than the date of maturity, at the rate of exchange current in Chicago at the time of transmission for cable or wire transfer to the place of payment in the currency in which the acceptance is payable or (ii) if payment is made at your head office in Chicago on the maturity date, at the rate of exchange then current in Chicago for cable or wire transfer to the place of payment in the currency in which the acceptance is payable.

If, for any cause whatsoever, there exists at the time in question no rate of exchange generally current in Chicago for effective cable or wire transfers of the sort above provided for, we agree to pay you on demand an amount in United States currency equivalent to the actual cost of settlement of your obligation to the payor of the draft or acceptance or any holder thereof, as the case may be, and however and whenever such settlement may be made by you, including interest on the amount of United States currency payable by us from the date of payment of such draft or drawing to the date of our payment to you.

3. In the event that any drafts are drawn by us on you in order to refinance any obligation set forth in the preceding two sections, and such drafts, at your option, are accepted by you, we agree to pay you at your head office in Chicago on demand, but in any event not later than the maturity date, the amount of each such acceptance.

4. We agree to pay you on demand a commission on the Credit at such rate as you may determine to be proper in the market for such credits and to reimburse you on demand for any and all charges and expenses which may be paid or incurred by you in connection with the Credit (whether incurred before or after the stated expiration date of the Credit), together with interest at the rate customarily charged by you at the time in like circumstances on any and all such amounts from the date of demand until paid in full, including without limitation (a) any and all out-of-pocket expenses and charges in connection with the administration, collection and enforcement of this Agreement and the Credit, including attorney's fees related thereto, and (b) any and all applicable reserve or similar requirements and any and all premiums, assessments, or levies imposed upon you by any agency or instrumentality of any government, including, without limitation, FDIC assessments or charges.

5. If any change in law or any governmental rule, regulation, policy, guideline or directive (whether or not having the force of law) or the interpretation thereof affects the amount of capital required or expected to be maintained by you or any corporation controlling you and you determine the amount of capital required is increased by or based upon the existence of this Agreement, the Credit or the Application or upon agreements or letters of credit of similar type, then you may notify us of such fact. We and you shall thereafter attempt to negotiate an adjustment to the commission payable hereunder which will adequately compensate you in light of these circumstances. If we and you are unable to agree to such adjustment within 30 days of the date on which we receive such notice, then, commencing on the date of such notice (but not earlier than the effective date of any such change), the commission payable shall increase by an amount which will, in your sole determination, provide adequate compensation.

6. Any and all amounts which may become due and payable to you under this Agreement shall be paid in immediately available funds without setoff or deduction and may, in your discretion, and if not otherwise paid, be charged by you to any available funds then held by you for our account.

7. As security for all of our obligations and liabilities to you, we hereby recognize and admit your security interest in all property shipped under or pursuant to or in connection with the Credit or in any way related thereto or to the drafts drawn thereunder, whether or not released to us or to our agents under security agreements, and in and to all shipping documents, warehouse receipts, policies or certificates of insurance and other documents accompanying or related to drafts drawn under or in connection with the Credit, and in and to the proceeds of the foregoing, until such time as all of our obligations and liabilities to you at any time existing under or with reference to the Credit or this Agreement, or any other obligation or liability to you have been fully paid and discharged. All or any of such property and documents, and the proceeds thereof, coming into your possession or that of any of your correspondents, may be held and disposed of as provided herein. We hereby grant to you all of the rights of a secured party under the Uniform Commercial Code in the aforesaid property, in addition to all of the rights specified herein. We agree to execute such financing statements and other writings as shall be necessary to perfect and maintain your security interest in all of said property and to pay all costs of filing financing, continuation and termination statements with respect to your security interest hereunder. The receipt by you or any of your correspondents at any time of other security of whatsoever nature, including cash, shall not be deemed a waiver of any of your rights or powers herein recognized.

8. In the absence of written instructions expressly to the contrary, we agree that you or any of your correspondents may receive and accept as a "transport document", a "bill of lading" or a "cargo receipt" under the Credit any document issued or purporting to be issued by or on behalf of any carrier which acknowledges receipt of property for transportation (whatever the other specific provisions of such document) and that the date of each such document shall be regarded as the date of shipment of the property mentioned therein, provided, that, with respect to an ocean bill of lading, the date of an onboard notation is to be considered the shipment date. Any transport document issued by or on behalf of an ocean carrier may be accepted by you as an "ocean bill of lading" whether or not the entire transportation is by water. Unless otherwise specifically agreed in writing, partial shipments may be made and you may honor the related drafts, provided, that, our liability to reimburse you for payments made or obligations incurred on such drafts is limited to the amount of the Credit. If the Credit specifies shipments in installments within given periods and any installment is not shipped within the period allowed for such installment, the Credit ceases to be available for that or any subsequent installment, unless otherwise expressly provided in the Credit. You and any of your correspondents may receive and accept as documents of insurance under the Credit either insurance policies or insurance certificates which need not be for an amount of insurance greater than the amount paid by you under or relative to the Credit. You and any of your correspondents may receive, accept, or pay as complying with the terms of Credit, any drafts or other documents, otherwise in order, which may be signed by, or issued to, the administrator or executor of, or the trustee in bankruptcy or the receiver for any of the property of, the party in whose name it is provided in the Credit that any drafts or other documents should be drawn or issued.

Figure 6–8. *(continued)*

9. If, at our special request, the Credit is issued in transferable form, it is understood and agreed that you are under no duty to determine the proper identity of anyone appearing in the draft or documents as transferee, nor shall you be charged with responsibility of any nature or character for the validity or correctness of any transfer or successive transfers, and payment by you to any purported transferee or transferees as determined by you is hereby authorized and approved. We further agree to hold you harmless and indemnified against any liability or claim in connection with or arising out of the foregoing.

If it is a condition of the Credit that payment may be made upon receipt by you of a cable advising negotiation, we hereby agree to reimburse you on demand for the amount indicated in such cable advice, and further agree to hold you harmless if the documents fail to arrive, or if, upon the arrival of the documents, you should determine that the documents are not in order.

10. We agree that you and your branches, affiliates and correspondents shall not be liable or responsible in any respect for: (a) the use which may be made of the Credit or any acts or omissions of the users of the Credit; (b) the existence of the property purporting to be represented by documents; (c) any difference in character, quality, quantity, condition or value between any property description in documents presented under the Credit and the property purporting to be represented by such documents: (d) the validity, sufficiency or genuineness of documents which you have determined in good faith to comply on their face with the terms of the Credit, even if such documents should in fact prove to be in any or all respects invalid, fraudulent, or forged; (e) particular conditions stipulated in the documents or superimposed thereon; (f) the time, place, manner or order in which shipment is made; (g) partial or incomplete shipment, or failure or omission to ship any and all of the property referred to in the Credit; (h) the character, adequacy, validity, or genuineness of any insurance, the solvency or responsibility of any insurer, or any other risk connected with insurance; (i) any deviation from instructions, delay, default, or fraud by the shipper or anyone else in connection with the property or the shipment thereof; (j) the solvency, responsibility, or relationship to the property of any party issuing any documents in connection with such property; (k) any delay in arrival or failure to arrive of the property or any of the documents relating thereto; (l) any delay in giving or failure to give notice of arrival or any other notice; (m) any breach of contract between the shippers or vendors and ourselves or any of us; (n) the failure of any instrument to bear any reference or adequate reference to the Credit, or the failure of any draft to be accompanied by documents at negotiation, or the failure of any person to note the amount of any draft on the reverse of the Credit or to surrender or take up the Credit or to send forward documents apart from drafts as required by the terms of the Credit (each of which provisions, if contained in the Credit itself, it is agreed may be waived by you; (o) any error, omission, interruption or delay in transmission or delivery of any message or advice in connection with the Credit whether transmitted by courier, mail, cable, telex, telegraph, wireless, any other telecommunication or otherwise and despite any cipher or code which may be employed.

The happening of any one or more of the contingencies referred to in the preceding paragraph shall not affect, impair, or prevent the vesting of any of your rights or powers hereunder or our obligation to make reimbursement. In furtherance and extension and not in limitation of the specific provisons hereinabove set forth, we agree that any action, inaction or omission by you or any of your branches, affiliates or correspondents under or in connection with the Credit or the related drafts, documents or property, if taken in good faith, shall be binding on us and shall not put you or any of your branches, affiliates or correspondents under any resulting liability to us. You shall not be responsibile for any act, error, neglect, default, omission, insolvency or failure in the business of any of your affiliates or correspondents or for any refusal by you or any of your branches, affiliates or correspondents to pay or honor drafts drawn under the Credit because of any United States or foreign laws or regulations now or hereafter in force or for any other matter beyond your control.

11. If it is a condition of this Credit that the beneficiary is authorized to draw clean drafts, you are authorized and instructed to accept and pay drafts without requiring, and without responsibility for, the delivery of shipping documents, either at the time of acceptance or of payment or thereafter.

12. We hereby certify and agree that no shipments or other transactions in connection with the Credit will be undertaken in violation of any United States or foreign laws or regulations. We agree to procure promptly any necessary import, export or other licenses for the import, export or shipping of the property and to comply with all United States and foreign governmental regulations in regard to the shipment of the property or the financing thereof, and to furnish such certificates in that respect as you may at any time require. We also agree to keep the property adequately covered by insurance acceptable to you, to assign the policies or certificates of insurance to you or, at your option, to make any loss or adjustment payable to you, and upon your request, to furnish you with evidence of acceptance of any such assignment by the insurers.

13. In the event that you deliver to us or to a Customs House Broker at our request any of the documents of title pledged hereunder prior to having received payment in full of all of our liabilities to you, we agree to obtain possession of any goods represented by such documents within twenty-one days after the date of delivery of such documents, and, if we should fail to do so, we agree to return such documents or to have them returned by the Customs House Broker to you prior to the expiration of the twenty-one day period. We further agree to execute and deliver to you receipts for such documents and the goods represented thereby identifying and describing such documents and goods, which receipts shall constitute a part of this Agreement.

14. We hereby authorize you, in the event that you become aware that we have claimed from the carrier any goods identified in the shipping documents required under the Credit and that such goods have been released to us or to a customs broker or agent acting on our behalf, to immediately, and without further inquiry and consideration, charge the amount of the Credit represented by such goods to any available funds then held by you.

15. We agree to deliver, convey, transfer or assign to you, at any time and from time to time on demand, as security for any and all of our obligations and liabilities, contingent or absolute, due or to become due, which are now or may at any time hereafter be owning by us to you, additional security of a character and value satisfactory to you, or to make such payment as you may require. We agree that all property belonging to any of us in which any of us may have an interest, of every name and nature whatsoever, now or at any time hereafter delivered, conveyed, transferred, assigned or paid to you or coming into your possession in any manner whatsoever, whether expressly as security for any of our obligations or liabilities to you or for safekeeping or otherwise, including any items received for collection or transmission and the proceeds thereof, whether or not such property is in whole or in part released to us under a security agreement, is hereby made security for the above-described obligations and liabilities. We further agree to execute and deliver such instruments, security agreements, financing statements and other documents as you may request to evidence the security interest granted hereby and to perform such other acts as may be necessary to perfect such interest.

16. In the event of (a) any default hereunder, (b) the death, failure in business, dissolution or termination of existence of any of us, (c) the filing of any petition in bankruptcy by or against any of us, (d) the commencement of any proceedings in bankruptcy or relating to the relief of debtors for the relief or readjustment of any indebtedness of any of us, either through reorganization, composition, extension or otherwise, (e) an assignment by any of us for the benefit of creditors or the utilization by any of us of any insolvency law, (f) the appointment of a receiver of any property of any of us at any time or (g) any attachment or distrainment of property of any of us which may be in, or come into, your possession and control or that of any third party acting for you or the subjection of such property at any time to any mandatory order of court or other legal process; then, or at any time after the happening of any such event, the amount of the Credit, both drawn and undrawn, as well as any and all other amounts payable hereunder to you (to the extent not theretofore paid to you hereunder), shall become immediately due and payable without demand or notice, and full power and authority are hereby given to you to sell, assign and deliver the whole of the property upon which you have heretofore been given a lien, or any part thereof, or any substitution therefor, or any additions thereto, at any broker's board or at public or private sale at your option, either for cash or on credit or for future delivery, without demand, advertisement or notice of any kind, all of which are hereby expressly waived.

(continues)

Figure 6–8. *(continued)*

[reverse]

At any sale hereunder, you may purchase the whole or any part of the property sold, free from any rights of redemption on our part, all of which rights are hereby waived and released. In the event of any sale or other disposition of any of the aforesaid property, after deducting all costs or expenses of every kind for care, safekeeping, collection, sale, delivery or otherwise, you may apply the remainder of the proceeds of the sale or other disposition thereof to the payment or reduction, either in whole or in part, of all or any of the obligations hereunder, whether then due or not due, and may return any overplus to us, all without prejudice to your rights as against us with respect to any and all obligations which may be or remain unpaid hereunder at any time.

17. The rights and liens which you possess hereunder shall continue unimpaired, and we shall remain obligated in accordance with the terms and provisions hereof, notwithstanding the release or substitution of any property which may be held as security hereunder at any time, or of any right or interest therein. If this Agreement should be terminated or revoked as to us by operation of law, we will indemnify and save you harmless from any loss which may be incurred by you in acting hereunder prior to the receipt by you or your successors, transferees, or assigns of notice in writing of such termination or revocation. No delay, extension of time, renewal, compromise or other indulgence which may occur shall impair your rights or powers hereunder. You shall not be deemed to have waived any of your rights hereunder unless you or your authorized agent shall have signed such waiver in writing. No such waiver, unless expressly stated therein, shall be effective as to any transaction which occurs subsequent to the date of such waiver or as to any continuance of a breach after such waiver.

18. Except as otherwise expressly provided in the Application and this Agreement or as you and we may otherwise expressly agree with regard to and prior to your issuance of the Credit, the "Uniform Customs and Practice for Documentary Credits (1983 Revision), International Chamber of Commerce, Publication 400", or such subsequent Uniform Customs and Practice as established by the International Chamber of Commerce and in effect at the time of reference thereto (hereinafter referred to as the "UCP"), shall be deemed a part hereof as fully as if incorporated herein, shall be binding on the Credit and shall serve, in the absence of proof expressly to the contrary, as evidence of general banking usage.

19. The word "property" as used herein includes goods and merchandise (as well as any and all documents related thereto), securities, funds, monies (whether United States currency or otherwise), choses in action, and any and all other forms of property, whether real, personal or mixed and any right or interest of us, or any one or more of us, therein.

20. If this Agreement is signed by one party, the terms "we," "our," "us," shall be read throughout as "I," "my," "me," as the case may be. If this Agreement is signed by two or more parties, it shall constitute the joint and several agreement of such parties. If we are a corporation, we hereby represent and warrant to you that: (a) we are duly organized and validly existing and duly authorized to enter into this Agreement and to perform obligations hereunder; and (b) the execution and delivery of this Agreement do not, and the performance of the obligations under this Agreement will not, violate any provisions of law, of our certificate of incorporation or by-laws or of any agreement, indenture, note or other instrument which is binding on us.

21. This Agreement shall become effective upon your receipt thereof and shall be governed by the laws of the State of Illinois, United States of America, and shall be binding upon us and our heirs, successors, assigns and legal representatives. We hereby irrevocably submit to the non-exclusive jurisdiction of any United States Federal or state court sitting in Chicago in any action or proceeding related to the Credit or this Agreement.

Very Truly Yours

____
Company or Individual Name (Applicant / Obligor)

____
Official Signature and Title

____
Address Street

____
City State Zip

____
Contact Party Telephone

Commissions will be debited to the Demand Deposit Account of the Applicant / Obligor unless otherwise agreed.

FOR BANK USE ONLY: Liabilities outstanding:	Approved by:
Import Contingent __________	__________ Signature of Relationship Manager with authority to initial notes for this Applicant / Obligor.
Standby Contingent __________	
Acceptances __________	Credit Responsibility: MAS No. __________
Total __________	Group Name __________
IF THE LETTER OF CREDIT IS SECURED BY A SEGREGATED CASH DEPOSIT TO BE DEBITED TO THE CUSTOMER'S ACCOUNT AT ISSUANCE, PLEASE CHECK ☐	

Figure 6–9. Applicant's checklist for letter of credit.

CHECKLIST FOR A COMMERCIAL LETTER OF CREDIT—APPLICANT

The following checklist identifies points that an applicant for a commercial letter of credit should consider when making an agreement with the seller (beneficiary) and completing an application for a letter of credit.

1. Does the beneficiary agree that the letter of credit should be irrevocable?
2. Do you have the complete name and address of the beneficiary, including street address and postal code, if applicable? If the beneficiary is a large company, what is the name of the person to whom correspondence should be addressed?
3. Is the letter of credit to be delivered to the beneficiary by the issuing bank through its correspondent bank, by the issuing bank directly, or by you directly?
4. How is the letter of credit to be delivered to the beneficiary—by air mail or by telex?
5. Do you or the beneficiary wish to designate an advising bank to deliver the letter of credit to the beneficiary, or do you want the issuing bank to choose the advising bank? If you wish to designate the advising bank, do you have its complete name and address?
6. Is the advising bank or another bank going to confirm the letter of credit? Or does the beneficiary wish another bank to act as the confirming bank? Do you have the complete name and address of the confirming bank, if any?
7. What is the total amount of credit, and in what currency is it to be denominated? If you want to approximate the total value of the transaction, is the credit amount preceded by a qualification such as "not exceeding" or "approximately" (meaning 10 percent more or less)?
8. What is the expiration date of the letter of credit?
9. What is the location for presentation of documents?
10. To what bank (nominated bank) is the beneficiary going to present documents?
11. How many days does the beneficiary have after shipment of goods to present documents to the nominated bank?
12. What is the method of payment under the letter of credit—sight draft, time draft, deferred payment?
13. What is the tenor of the draft(s), and what percentage of the invoice value is each draft to cover?
14. Is the draft(s) to be drawn on you or another drawee?
15. How many copies of the commercial invoice should the beneficiary present to the nominated bank?
16. What is the agreed-upon description of the merchandise and/or services to be itemized in the commercial invoice? (Include quantity and unit price, if applicable.)

(*continues*)

Courtesy of Continental Bank N.A. (Bank of America Illinois)

Figure 6–9. *(continued)*

17. What are the origin and destination of the shipment?
18. What are the terms of shipment (FOB, CFR, CIF, other)?
19. Are the freight charges to be collect or prepaid?
20. What is the last date on which the beneficiary can ship in order to comply with the shipping terms?
21. Are partial shipments allowed?
22. Are transshipments allowed?
23. What transportation document(s) do you require the beneficiary to present to the nominated bank? How many copies of each do you require?
24. Do you require that an extra set of transportation documents accompany an air shipment?
25. What is the name, address, and phone number of the person to be notified when the shipment arrives?
26. Is the beneficiary responsible for insuring the shipment, or are you? What percentage of the invoice value is the insurance to cover? Where are the risks to be covered?
27. What other documents do you require the beneficiary to present? How many copies of each do you require? When appropriate, who is to issue each document, and what should its wording be?
28. Who is responsible for the bank charges other than those of the issuing bank?
29. Who is responsible for discount charges, if any?
30. What is the complete name and address of the person to whom the nominated bank should send the documents submitted by the beneficiary?
31. Is the credit transferable?

establishment of branches, subsidiaries, or satisfactory joint ventures, the importer may need to license or contract with a foreign company to manufacture the product for sale to the importer. All of these methods of doing business will require some modifications to the purchase and other export and import documentation and procedures. For example, purchases from affiliated entities often raise income tax issues of transfer pricing and the related issue of proper customs valuation. License royalties may in certain circumstances be dutiable, and licensed technology may require export control approvals.

T. Electronic Commerce

The development of the Internet and e-mail and the proliferation of Web sites have created a revolution in electronic commerce. Because of the essentially worldwide availability of the Internet and access to Web sites, new issues for cross-border importing and exporting have arisen. This has opened a new channel of direct marketing using electronic catalogs and has created conflict with the seller's traditional foreign distribution channels, such as distributors and sales agents. Sellers are more interested

Figure 6–10. Instructions by importer's bank to correspondent bank in seller's country regarding opening of letter of credit.

FIRST CHICAGO
The First National Bank of Chicago

IMPORT SERVICES GROUP
MAIL SUITE 0236
CHICAGO, ILLINOIS 60670-0236
U.S.A.
Swift Address: FNBCUS44
Telex number: ITT 4330253 FNBCUI
TRT 190201 FNBC UT
Fax: (312) 407-1065

IRREVOCABLE NEGOTIABLE CREDIT

ADVISING BANK:

DATE:

ALL DRAFTS DRAWN MUST BE MARKED:
FNBC REFERENCE NO.
ADVISING BANK REF. NO.

GENTLEMEN:

BY THE ORDER OF
FAVOR OF:

WE HEREBY ISSUE THROUGH YOU IN

OUR IRREVOCABLE CREDIT FOR THE ACCOUNT OF FOR AN AMOUNT NOT TO EXCEED, IN THE AGGREGATE, US DOLLARS AVAILABLE BY YOUR DRAFTS AT ON THE FIRST NATIONAL BANK OF CHICAGO, CHICAGO, ILLINOIS, U.S.A., WHEN ACCOMPANIED BY THE DOCUMENTS INDICATED BELOW, EFFECTIVE AND EXPIRING ON

THIS CREDIT IS SUBJECT TO THE FOLLOWING:

SHIP FROM: SHIP TO:

DOCUMENTS REQUIRED:

COVERING SHIPMENT OF:
SHIPPING TERMS:

NEGOTIATING BANK MUST AIRMAIL ONE ORIGINAL COMMERCIAL INVOICE, CUSTOMS INVOICE, AND BILL OF LADING TO FOR OUR ACCOUNT AND A CERTIFICATE TO THIS EFFECT MUST BE SUBMITTED WITH THE REMAINING DOCUMENTS.

WE HEREBY ENGAGE WITH THE DRAWERS AND WITH NEGOTIATING BANKS AND BANKERS THAT EACH DRAFT DRAWN UNDER AND IN COMPLIANCE WITH THE TERMS OF THIS CREDIT WILL BE DULY HONORED IF PRESENTED FOR NEGOTIATION ON OR BEFORE THE EXPIRY DATE.

THE AMOUNT OF EACH DRAFT MUST BE ENDORSED ON THE REVERSE OF THIS CREDIT BY THE NEGOTIATING BANK.

THIS CREDIT IS SUBJECT TO THE UNIFORM CUSTOMS AND PRACTICE FOR DOCUMENTARY CREDITS (1983 REVISION), INTERNATIONAL CHAMBER OF COMMERCE PUBLICATION 400.

VERY TRULY YOURS,
THE FIRST NATIONAL BANK OF CHICAGO

ADVISING BANK'S NOTIFICATION

AUTHORIZED SIGNATURE

PLACE, DATE, NAME AND SIGNATURE

AUTHORIZED SIGNATURE

Courtesy of The First National Bank of Chicago.

in marketing internationally and are forced to cope with the logistical issues that arise from purchase orders from abroad. Some of the more important issues that must be considered and managed include the following:

- *Validity and enforceability of electronic sales contracts.* This concern has required the consideration and development of legal terms of sale on the Web site that are modified and appropriate for foreign as well as domestic customers. It has also forced the use of "click-wrap" agreements to record the purchaser's agreement to the sales terms and authentication procedures to confirm that the person purporting to place the order is actually that person. For low-price items, sellers may be willing to accept the risk of lack of enforceability of the sales contract but, for expensive items or ongoing business this is not feasible. Many sellers have required their distributors and customers who are making ongoing purchases to sign hard-copy "umbrella" agreements at the outset of the relationship before undertaking electronic sales. This is a less satisfactory solution for onetime purchasers.
- *Delivery and logistics.* At least with direct sales to consumers, and for consumer goods, the customer wants and expects the convenience of direct delivery to his or her door. These "delivered duty paid" terms of sale are almost a necessity for this type of business. Customers also want prompt delivery, which is difficult to achieve if there is no stock of inventory in the buyer's country. For smaller products, delivery by international courier services such as UPS, Federal Express, and DHL has become more practical. In such cases, the transportation carrier is also able to act as the customs broker in the United States, paying customs duties and value-added taxes and billing them back to the seller. For large, capital goods, however, such as in B2B transactions, the issues of containerized or other packing, transportation booking, export licenses or permits, U.S. customs clearance, and lack of skilled in-house personnel, thereby requiring the use of a freight forwarder, have limited the expansion of Internet sales. Challenges continue to exist relating to establishing in-country inventory for immediate delivery without the expenses of establishing branch offices or subsidiary companies.
- *Price.* Since many customers want to have delivery to their door, when they see a price quotation on a Web site, they expect to see an "all-in" (delivered duty paid) price. The difficulty of maintaining up-to-date quotations online, including freight charges, insurance, duties, quotas, and value-added taxes for multiple countries, has forced many sellers to hire software companies that offer such services.
- *Payment.* For low-price consumer goods, payment by credit card has enabled sellers to increase Internet sales. However, since credit card purchases do not guarantee payment to the seller (the buyer can instruct the credit card company not to pay the seller in certain circumstances, such as a dispute over quality), the seller is always at risk when payment is by credit card. That fact, together with the virtual impossibility of pursuing a collection lawsuit against the buyer overseas due to prohibitive costs, has limited the expansion of internet sales. For expensive purchases or ongoing accounts, the seller may need the security of a letter of credit or documents against payment. On the other side, buyers dislike having to pay for purchases in advance

without inspection of the goods. Where the seller has done business in the past on open account, or is willing to do so in the future, Internet sales can be practical.

- *Taxation.* Although one of the great spurs to the growth of electronic commerce in the past has been the ability to avoid certain taxes in certain countries, such as sales, value-added, corporate franchise or personal property taxes, there is an increasing demand by governments to recover those tax revenues that are being lost. It is likely that some forms of taxation will increase and sellers and buyers may have to comply with U.S. and foreign tax claims.
- *Information security.* Although there has been significant progress in maintaining the confidentiality of information transmitted over the Internet, the sophistication of "hackers" has also increased. For information from credit card numbers to purchase order numbers and customer lists, confidentiality, particularly from competitors and fraud artists, is crucial. The most secure current technologies using "key" systems are cumbersome, especially for small orders and onetime sales. Furthermore, exporting such software may require an export license.

Despite the foregoing difficulties, the outlook is good that more creative ways of dealing with these problems will evolve and that Internet sales will continue to expand.

Chapter 7

Importing: Purchase Documentation

The single most important document in importing is the purchase agreement. Just as in exporting, most of the problems that occur in importing can be eliminated or greatly reduced by using a suitable purchase agreement. Generally, different types of documentation are used for isolated purchase transactions as opposed to ongoing purchase transactions. The various types of documentation, including the important provisions in international purchase agreements, import distribution agreements, and import sales agent agreements will be discussed. (In order to understand how the seller views the transaction, you may wish to read Chapter 3.)

A. Isolated Purchase Transactions

For the purposes of discussion in this chapter, isolated purchase transactions are defined as situations where, for example, the importer purchases infrequently or purchases are made on a trial basis in anticipation of establishing an ongoing purchase relationship, or when the exporter is unwilling to grant any credit to the importer until a satisfactory history of payment has been established. Purchase agreements for such transactions should be in writing and the seller and buyer may use a variety of common, preprinted forms. The importer/buyer should check carefully to try to eliminate as much as possible any conflicting provisions between the seller/exporter's forms and the forms used by the buyer.

1. Importance of Written Agreements

In some industries (for example, the commodities industry), it is common to conduct purchases and sales orally through telephone orders and acceptances. Sometimes oral agreements occur in international purchasing when the buyer gives an order at a trade show, by long-distance telephone, or in a meeting. Under the new Convention on the International Sale of Goods (discussed in Section B.2.l), a sales agreement may be formed or modified orally. It is highly advisable to formalize the purchase and sale agreement in a written document, even for domestic purchases, and there are many additional reasons why import purchases should be memorialized in a written agreement. Under the Uniform Commercial Code applicable in the United States, an agreement to purchase, and therefore to require delivery, is enforceable by the buyer only if the agreement is in writing if the purchase exceeds $500 in value. While there are some exceptions to this law and sometimes even informal notes will be sufficient to create an enforceable purchase agreement, by far the safest practice is to formalize the purchase agreement in a written document.

In addition to legal issues, an old Chinese proverb states: "The lightest ink is better than the brightest memory." This is one way of saying that often disputes arise in international purchase transactions because the parties did not record their agreement, or failed to discuss an issue and reach agreement. A written purchase agreement acts both as a checklist to remind the buyer and seller what they should discuss and agree upon and as a written record of their agreement. All modifications of the agreement should also be in writing.

2. *Telex or Facsimile Orders*

While a telex or facsimile order and acceptance can satisfy the legal requirements as written evidence of an agreement, such communications commonly contain only the specification of the quantity, sometimes an offering price, and possibly a shipment date. There are many other terms and conditions of purchase which should be inserted in a good purchase agreement, and a simple order by the buyer in response to such telex or facsimile offers to sell will fall far short of adequately protecting the buyer in case of problems in the transaction. Consequently, acceptances of offers to sell by telex or facsimile should specifically and expressly state that the purchase incorporates the buyer's other standard terms and conditions of purchase. Those additional terms and conditions of purchase should be included in the buyer's earliest telex or facsimile response to the seller, so that there can be no argument that the seller was not aware of such terms and conditions of purchase before proceeding with the transaction.

3. *The Formation of Purchase Agreements*

The purchase agreement is a formal contract governed by law. In general, a purchase agreement is formed by agreement between the seller and the buyer and is the passing of title and ownership to goods for a price. An agreement is a mutual manifestation of assent to the same terms. Agreements are ordinarily reached by a process of offer and acceptance. This process of offer and acceptance can proceed by the seller and the buyer preparing a purchase agreement contained in a single document that is signed by both parties, by the exchange of documents such as purchase orders and purchase order acceptances, or by conduct, such as when the buyer offers to purchase and the seller ships the goods.

From the view of clarity and reducing risks, preparation of a purchase agreement contained in a single document is best. Both parties negotiate the agreement by exchanges of letters, faxes, or in person. Before proceeding with performance of any part of the transaction, both parties reach agreement and sign the same purchase agreement. This gives both the seller and the buyer the best opportunity to understand the terms and conditions under which the other intends to transact business, and to negotiate and resolve any differences or conflicts. This type of purchase agreement is often used if the size of the transaction is large, if the seller is concerned about payment or the buyer is concerned about manufacture and shipment, or if there are particular risks involved, such as government regulations or exchange controls, or differences in culture, language, or business customs that might create misunderstandings.

Quite often, however, the process of formation of the purchase agreement is an exchange of documents that the seller and buyer have independently prepared, and that, in the aggregate, constitute the purchase agreement. These documents may contain differences and conflicts. Figure 3–1 in Chapter 3 shows the chronology of exchange and common documents used in many purchase transactions. Although all documents will not be used in all purchase transactions, these documents are in common use.

Several questions arise when a purchase transaction is formed by such an exchange of documents. The first relates to the time of formation of the purchase agreement. For example, a seller or buyer may send certain preliminary inquiries or information such as a price list, not intending to actually offer to sell or place an order, but may find that the other party's understanding (or the applicable law) has created a binding purchase agreement prior to that party's intention. This can arise because under some countries' laws, an offer to sell or buy is accepted when the acceptance is dispatched, rather than when it is received. It can also arise because silence can be considered as acceptance if the parties are merchants.

The second issue that arises relates to the governing law. Contracts are often governed by the law of the country where the contract is negotiated and performed or where the offer to sell or buy was accepted. Since an international agreement may be partly negotiated and partly performed in both countries, and since there may be a question as to whether the buyer accepted the offer to sell or the seller accepted the offer to purchase, situations can arise where the purchase agreement is governed by the law of the seller's country. Since foreign law may be quite different from U.S. law, the buyer's rights and responsibilities may differ greatly from what he or she anticipated. Customary local ways of doing business, called trade usages, may unknowingly become a part of the purchase agreement under the sales laws of some countries. Sellers and buyers sometimes try to resolve this problem by including a governing law term in their documents, but again, these may conflict.

A final method of formation of a purchase agreement involves conduct. A simple example is where a buyer sends a purchase order, and the seller, without communicating, simply ships the goods, or if the seller offers to sell the goods and the buyer simply sends payment. In such cases, the conduct in accepting the offer will include all of the terms and conditions of the offer. If the buyer is not satisfied with the seller's terms and conditions of sale, he should send some communication to negotiate those terms before simply sending an order or making payment.

4. Common Forms for the Formation of Purchase Agreements

There are a number of forms customarily used in the formation of purchase agreements. In order to save time (and discourage changes by the other party), both buyers and sellers often purchase preprinted forms from commercial stationers or develop and preprint their own forms. Not all of the same documents are used by the seller or the buyer in all purchase transactions. For example, a seller may submit a quotation to a potential buyer without receiving any request for quotation, or the first communication the seller receives may be a purchase order from the buyer. However, it is important to be familiar with the various forms.

a. Price Lists

Sometimes a seller will send a price list to a prospective buyer as its first communication. Ordinarily, a buyer should not consider such lists as offers to sell entitling the buyer to accept. The buyer should ordinarily communicate with the seller (specifying that he is not making an order), asking for a quotation and confirming that the terms of the price list are still current.

b. Requests for Quotations and Offers to Purchase

Sometimes the first document involved in the formation of a purchase agreement is a request from the buyer to the seller for a quotation (RFQ) (see Figure 3–2). Ordinarily, such a request—whether it be informal, in a telex, facsimile, or letter, or formal, in a printed form—will ask for a price quotation from the seller for a specific quantity and often a shipping date. When requesting a quotation, the buyer should be particularly careful to specify that its request is not an offer to purchase and that such offer will be made only by the buyer's subsequent purchase order. Another method is to expressly state that the buyer's request is subject to or incorporates all of the buyer's standard terms and conditions of purchase. The most cautious approach is for the buyer to print all of its terms and conditions of purchase in its request for quotation. In that way, there is absolutely no argument that the seller was not aware of all the terms and conditions on which the buyer is willing to purchase, and if the seller has any objection thereto, it should so state in its quotation to the buyer. The buyer should request that the seller's quotation be in writing.

c. Quotations

In response to a request for a quotation, the seller ordinarily prepares and forwards a quotation or a pro forma invoice. In making quotations, the seller may use a printed form which may contain all of its terms and conditions of sale on the front or back thereof (see samples in Figures 3–4, 3–5, 3–6, and 3–10). If this is the first communication from the seller to the buyer, the buyer should be careful to ascertain whether the quotation contains other terms and conditions of sale in addition to the price, quantity, and shipment date. This may be expressly stated as in fine print boiler plate provisions on the front or back or by reference to the seller's terms and conditions of sale by incorporation by reference. If the seller refers to terms and conditions not expressly stated in the quotation, the best course is for the buyer to ask the seller to provide a copy of such terms and conditions of sale prior to sending any order. If such terms and conditions are stated, the buyer should carefully review them to determine if there are any discrepancies between the buyer's standard terms and conditions of purchase or if there are any terms and conditions that are objectionable to the buyer. If there are objectionable terms, it is far better to negotiate and resolve these items before placing any order. The quotation may expressly state that the offer is firm or irrevocable for a certain period of time or it may also state that it is not an offer to sell and that the seller is not agreeing to sell until it has received a purchase order from the buyer and has issued an acceptance of the order. If the quotation does not state that it is firm for a certain period of time, the buyer may wish to immediately inquire if it is so; otherwise, the seller is generally free to withdraw its quotation anytime before acceptance, which could mean even after the buyer has sent a purchase order, especially if the seller has reserved the right not to sell until it accepts the buyer's purchase order.

d. Purchase Orders

The next document that may occur in a purchase transaction is a purchase order (PO) issued by the buyer. Again, the purchase order may be informal, such as in a telex, facsimile, or letter, or it may be on a printed form. This is the most important document for the buyer because it should contain all of the additional terms and conditions that the buyer wants to be a part of the purchase agreement when the purchase order is accepted by the seller. (See samples in Figures 3–7 and 3–8.) Before issuing a purchase order in response to a quotation, the buyer should carefully calculate its costs. The buyer should determine whether the quotation is ex-factory, FOB port, CIF, or delivered, since all expenses of transportation from the point quoted will be the expenses of the buyer, including U.S. Customs duties. If the buyer intends to resell the product in its imported form, it should determine if the quoted price plus additional expenses of importation will still permit the buyer to sell at the prevailing U.S. market price with a reasonable profit or, if the product will be used as a raw material or component, that its delivered cost will be lower than that from U.S. suppliers (compare Figure 3–3). If the price is unacceptable, the buyer should make a counteroffer at a lower price before sending a purchase order. Even though the buyer may expect that no purchase agreement is formed until he has sent its purchase order, if the seller has previously sent a quotation to the buyer, the terms and conditions stated in the seller's quotation may govern the purchase agreement. Of course, the terms and conditions contained in the seller's quotation or purchase order acceptance are always written to be most favorable to the seller. An important way in which the buyer can try to guard against such a result is for the buyer to specify in its purchase order that its purchase order is an offer to purchase only on the terms and conditions stated therein and that any acceptance with different terms and conditions will be void unless expressly accepted by the buyer in writing. The purchase order should also limit acceptance to a certain time period so that the offer to purchase is not open indefinitely. Finally, the purchase order should specify that any acceptance and purchase agreement will be governed by the law of the buyer's state and the United States, excluding the Convention on the International Sale of Goods, to avoid a purchase order acceptance being issued in the foreign country and the formation of a purchase agreement governed by foreign law.

e. Purchase Order Acknowledgments, Acceptances, and Sales Confirmations

When a purchase order is received, some sellers prepare a purchase order acknowledgment, purchase order acceptance, or sales confirmation form (see sample in Figure 3–9). A purchase order acknowledgment may state that the seller has received the purchase order from the buyer and is in the process of evaluating it, such as checking on the credit of the buyer or determining the availability of raw materials for manufacture, but that the seller has not yet accepted the purchase order and will issue a purchase order acceptance at a later date. In other cases, the language of the purchase order acknowledgment is also clearly an acceptance of the order and no further communication is issued. Sales confirmations usually perform the same role as purchase order acceptances. The seller will normally include its detailed terms and conditions of sale in its purchase order acknowledgment or purchase order acceptance. If this is the first time that the buyer has seen such terms and conditions of sale (they were not included in the seller's earlier quotation), even if the buyer has stated in its purchase order that it is offering to purchase only on its own terms and conditions, the buyer should confirm that there is no conflict and that the seller has not purported to accept the purchase order only on its own terms and conditions. If a conflict exists, the buyer should immediately negotiate and resolve such conflicts; otherwise, the seller may proceed with manufacture and shipment and the buyer may be bound by the seller's terms and conditions. If the seller's quotation and purchase order acceptance do not contain detailed terms and conditions of sale, the buyer can feel reasonably comfortable that its terms or conditions will control.

f. Commercial Invoices

Later, when manufacture is complete and the product is ready for shipment, ordinarily the seller will prepare a commercial invoice, which is the formal statement for payment to be sent directly to the buyer or submitted through banking channels for payment by the buyer. Such invoices may also contain the detailed terms or conditions of sale on the front or back of the form (see sample in Figure 3–11). However, if this is the first time that the seller has brought such terms to the attention of the buyer, and the buyer has previously advised the seller of its detailed terms and conditions of purchase in its request for quotation or purchase order, the buyer should immediately object if the seller's terms and conditions are in conflict.

g. Conflicting Provisions in Seller and Buyer Sales Documentation

It is common in international trade for sellers and buyers to use preprinted forms that are designed to reduce the amount of negotiation and discussion required for each sales agreement. Undoubtedly, such forms have been drafted by attorneys for each side and contain terms and conditions of purchase or terms and conditions of sale which are favorable to the buyer and seller, respectively. Consequently, it is not unusual for sellers and buyers intent on entering into a sales transaction to routinely issue such documentation with little or no thought regarding the consistency of those provisions. Afterward, if the sales transaction breaks down and either the buyer or seller consults its attorney regarding its legal rights and obligations, the rights of the parties may be very unclear. In the worst case, the buyer may find that a purchase agreement has been validly formed on all of the terms and conditions of the seller's quotation or purchase order acceptance and is governed by the law of the seller's country. In order to reduce or eliminate this problem, often the buyer's attorney drafts requests for quotations and purchase orders with language which states that, notwithstanding any terms or conditions that might be contained in the seller's quotation or purchase order acceptance, the buyer agrees to make the purchase only on its own terms or conditions.

While this can be of some help, sometimes the seller's quotation and purchase order acceptance also contain such language, and consequently, the buyer's terms and conditions may not win out. In fact, the only way to be comfortable regarding the terms or conditions of sale that will govern a purchase agreement is to actually review the terms or conditions contained in the seller's forms and compare them with the terms and conditions that the buyer desires to utilize. Where specific conflicts exist or where the seller's terms or conditions of purchase differ from the buyer's terms or conditions of purchase, the buyer should expressly bring that to the attention of the seller, the differences should be negotiated to the satisfaction of the buyer, and appropriate changes should be made in the form of a rider to the purchase agreement or a letter to clarify the agreement reached between the parties (which should be signed by both parties).

In some isolated sales transactions where the quantities are small, the buyer may simply choose to forego this effort and accept the risk that the transaction will be controlled by the seller's terms and conditions of sale. However, the buyer should establish some dollar limit over which a review is to be made and should not continue a practice that might be appropriate for small purchases but would be very dangerous for large purchases.

h. Side Agreements

Occasionally, the seller may suggest that the seller and buyer enter into a side or letter agreement. In some cases, the suggestion may be innocent enough, for example, where the parties wish to clarify how they will interpret or carry out a particular provision of the purchase agreement. Even then, however, it is better practice to incorporate all of the agreements of the parties in a single document. Unfortunately, more often the seller's proposal of a side agreement is designed to evade the seller's foreign exchange control, tax, or antitrust laws. Buyers should be wary of entering into such agreements unless they fully understand the consequences. Such agreements may be unenforceable, the buyer may not be able to get delivery of the goods for which it paid, and/or the buyer may be prosecuted as a co-conspirator for violating such laws.

B. Ongoing Purchase Transactions

When an importer begins to purchase on a regular basis, or when the importer desires to make regular purchases from a particular supplier, the buyer and the seller should enter into a more comprehensive agreement to govern their relationship. Often these types of agreements are a result of the buyer being willing to commit to regular purchases, and, therefore, to purchase a larger quantity of the goods, in return for obtaining a lower price. Or, they may result from the buyer's desire to tie-up, that is, to obtain more assurance from the seller to commit to supply the buyer's requirements, or from the seller's desire to plan its production. The three major types of agreements used in ongoing sales transactions are: (1) international purchase agreements, that is, supply agreements where the seller sells directly to the buyer who either incorporates the seller's product as a component into a product the buyer manufactures, or who consumes the product itself and does not resell the product; (2) distributor agreements, where the buyer buys the product from a foreign seller and resells the product in the

United States or for export, usually in the same form but sometimes with modifications; and (3) sales agent or sales representative agreements, where a U.S. person is appointed to solicit orders from potential customers in the United States for a foreign seller. In the last case, the sale is not made to the sales agent, but is made directly to the U.S. customer, with payment of a commission or other compensation to the sales agent.

In any of the three foregoing agreements, there is a correlation between the documentation used in isolated purchase transactions and the documentation used in ongoing purchase transactions. Furthermore, there are a number of important provisions in international purchase, distributor, and sales agent agreements not relevant to domestic purchases that should be included in such agreements.

1. Correlation With Documentation for Isolated Purchase Transactions

As discussed in Section A.4, it is common for sellers and buyers to use forms such as requests for quotation, purchase orders, purchase order acknowledgments, purchase order acceptances, sales confirmations, and invoices during the course of buying and selling products. When an ongoing purchase relationship is being established with a particular seller, it is usual to enter into an umbrella or blanket agreement, which is intended to govern the relationship between the parties over a longer period of time, for example, one year, five years, or longer. Sometimes the parties will enter into a trial purchase agreement that will last for a short period of time, such as one year, before deciding to enter into a longer-term agreement. In any event, the international purchase (supply) agreement, the distributor agreement, and the sales agent (representative) agreement define the rights and obligations of the parties over a fairly long period of time and commit the buyer and the seller to doing business with each other so that both sides can make production, marketing, and advertising plans and expenditures. Special price discounts in return for commitments to purchase specific quantities are common in such agreements. Such agreements may contain a commitment to purchase a specific quantity over the life of the agreement and may designate a specific price or a formula by which the price will be adjusted over the life of the agreement. To this extent, these agreements serve as an umbrella over the parties' relationship with certain specific acts to be accomplished as agreed by the parties. For example, it is usually necessary during the term of such agreements for the buyer to advise the seller as to the specific quantity it wishes to order at that time to be applied against the buyer's overall purchase commitment.

If the price of the product is likely to fluctuate, no price may be specified in the umbrella agreement. Instead, the price may be changed from time to time by the seller depending upon the seller's price at the time the buyer submits an order, perhaps with a special discount from such price because the buyer has committed to buy a substantial quantity over the life of the agreement. In such cases, depending upon whether or not a specific price has been set in the umbrella agreement, the buyer will send a request for quotation and the seller will provide a quotation, or a purchase order will be sent describing the specific quantity the buyer wishes to order at that time, a suggested shipment date, and the price. The seller will still use a purchase order acknowledgment and/or a purchase order acceptance form to agree to ship the specific quantity on the specific shipment date at the specific price. The seller will continue to provide a commercial invoice against which the buyer must make payment.

In summary, where the seller and buyer wish to enter into a longer-term agreement, they will define their overall relationship in an umbrella agreement, but the usual documentation utilized in isolated purchase transactions will also be utilized to order specific quantities and to confirm prices and shipment dates. Sometimes conflicts can arise between the terms and conditions in the umbrella agreement and the specific documentation. Usually the parties provide that, in such cases, the umbrella agreement will control, but this can also lead to problems in situations where the parties wish to vary the terms of their umbrella agreement for a specific transaction.

2. *Important Provisions in International Purchase Agreements*

There are numerous terms and conditions in an international purchase agreement that require special consideration different from the usual terms and conditions in a domestic purchase agreement. A sample international purchase agreement is included as Appendix G.

a. *Purchasing and Selling Entities*

One consideration that may arise in an international purchase agreement is the identity of the purchasing and selling entity. In some cases, the buyer may want to organize a separate company to handle all importations. One reason for this is to insulate the U.S. company's assets against claims related to the imported article such as product liability claims. If the U.S. company will be reselling the products, it may wish to conduct such business in a separate, subsidiary company that conducts the importing and resale operations. (Ordinarily, unless the parent corporation is in the chain of ownership and takes title to the products, it would not be liable for product liability claims.) Generally, however, a U.S. company will not be able to protect its assets against unforeseen U.S. Customs liability by organizing a subsidiary to act as the importer. That usually will make no difference, as the importer will be required to post a bond to guarantee payment of all customs duties and penalties. If the importing company has limited assets, the bonding company will not issue the bond unless the parent company guarantees the debts of the subsidiary/importer.

If the seller and the buyers are related entities, such as a subsidiary and parent corporation, the U.S. Customs treatment may be different, for example, in the valuation of the merchandise or assessment of dumping duties. Some transactions may be structured to involve the use of a trading company, on either the exporting side, the importing side, or both. Depending upon whether the trading company takes title or is appointed as the agent (of either the buyer or the seller), or whether the trading company is related to the seller or the buyer, the customs value may be different. For example, commissions paid to the seller's agent are ordinarily subject to customs duties in the United States, but commissions paid to the buyer's agent are not.

b. *Quantity*

The quantity term is even more important than the price. Under U.S. law, if the parties have agreed on the quantity, the purchase agreement is enforceable even if the parties have not agreed on price—a current, or market, price will be implied. When no quantity has been agreed upon, however, the purchase agreement will not be enforceable.

One reason for forming a formal purchase agreement is for the buyer to obtain a lower price by committing to purchase a large quantity, usually over a year or more. The seller may be willing to grant a lower price in return for the ability to plan ahead, schedule production and inventory, develop economies of scale, and reduce shipping and administrative costs. The buyer should be aware that price discounts due to quantity may violate U.S. price discrimination laws, unless the amount of the discount can be directly related to the cost savings of the seller for that particular quantity.

Quantity agreements can be for a specific quantity or a target quantity. Generally, if the commitment is a target only, failure to actually purchase such amount will not justify the seller in claiming damages or terminating the agreement (although sometimes the buyer may agree to a retroactive price increase). Failure to purchase a minimum purchase quantity, however, will justify termination and a claim for breach.

Sometimes the buyer may wish to buy the seller's entire output or the seller may seek a commitment that the buyer will purchase all of its requirements for the merchandise from the seller. Usually, such agreements are lawful, but in certain circumstances they can violate the U.S. antitrust laws, such as when the seller is the only supplier or represents a large amount of the supply, or the buyer is the only buyer or represents a large segment of the market.

c. Pricing

There are a number of considerations in formulating the buyer's pricing policy for international purchase agreements. A delivered price calculation sheet will identify all additional costs of importing to make sure that the price of resale results in a net profit acceptable to the buyer. The buyer also has to be aware of several constraints in formulating its pricing policy.

The first constraint relates to dumping. The United States has laws prohibiting dumping. This generally means that the price at which products are sold for export to the United States cannot be lower than the price at which such products are sold for domestic consumption in the country from which they are exported. The mere fact that sales are made at lower prices to the United States does not automatically mean that a dumping investigation will be initiated or that a dumping finding will occur. Under the laws of the United States, no dumping will occur if the price to the United States is above the current U.S. market price, even if the seller's price to the United States is lower than its sale price in its own country.

Additionally, there are U.S. legal constraints on the extent to which a price quoted for import can vary from buyer to buyer. The antitrust laws in the United States (in particular the price discrimination provisions of the Robinson-Patman Act) apply when two or more sales to two or more buyers are being made in the United States. If the seller is selling to two or more buyers in the United States at different prices, such sales may violate the price discrimination provisions of U.S. law. The buyer who is paying the higher price may sue the foreign seller. Moreover, if the buyer purchasing at the lower price induced the price discrimination, the buyer would also violate U.S. law. In order to gain some assurance that it is getting the best price, sometimes a buyer will obtain a covenant from the seller in the purchase agreement that the seller agrees to grant the buyer the best price that it grants to any other purchaser during the term of the agreement. Such covenants may be helpful, but the buyer must have the right to inspect the sales records of the seller to confirm that it is getting the best price.

If the price is below the seller's total cost of production, there is a risk that such purchases will be attacked as predatory pricing in violation of U.S. antitrust laws. The accounting calculation of cost is always a subject of dispute, particularly where the seller may feel that the costs of foreign advertising or other costs should not be allocated to export sales. However, in general, any sales below total, fully allocated costs are at risk. Obviously, it will be the importer's competitors who will object to, and sue to stop, such sales.

Another very important pricing area relates to rebates, discounts, allowances, and price escalation clauses. Sometimes the buyer will ask for and the seller will be willing to grant some form of rebate, discount, or allowance under certain circumstances, such as the purchase of large quantities of merchandise. Such price concessions generally do not, in and of themselves, violate U.S. or foreign law, but if such payments are not disclosed to the proper governmental authorities, both the U.S. importer and the foreign seller can violate various U.S. and foreign laws and may be charged with conspiracy to violate or aiding and abetting the other's violation of those laws. For example, the U.S. importer must file customs entry documents on each shipment and must declare the price at which the goods are being purchased. If, in fact, this price is false (because the exporter has agreed to grant some rebate, discount, or allowance, or, in fact, does so), the U.S. importer will violate U.S. law and be subject to civil and criminal penalties. Similarly, when the seller exports the goods to the United States, the seller will be required to state a value for export purposes in its country. If the seller sends the buyer two invoices for different amounts, or if the seller asks the buyer to pay any part of the purchase price outside of the seller's country (for example, by deposit in a bank account in the United States, Switzerland, or some other country), there is considerable risk that the intended action of the seller will violate the seller's foreign exchange control, tax, and/or customs laws. If the buyer cooperates by making any such payment, or is aware of the scheme, the buyer can also be charged with conspiracy to violate those foreign laws and can risk fines, arrest, and imprisonment in that country. Similarly, retroactive price increases (for example, due to currency fluctuations), or price increases under escalation clauses, may cause a change in the final price, which may have to be reported to foreign exchange authorities or to U.S. Customs. Before agreeing to accept any price rebate, discount, or allowance, or to use a price escalation clause, or to implement a retroactive price increase, or to make any payment to the seller in any place except the seller's own country by check or wire transfer (not cash), the buyer should satisfy itself that its actions will not result in the violation of any U.S. or foreign law.

If the purchase is from an affiliated company, such as a foreign parent or subsidiary, additional pricing considerations arise. Because the buyer and seller are related, pricing can be artificially manipulated. For example, a U.S. importer that is taxable on its U.S. sales profits at a rate of 35 percent when purchasing from an affiliated seller in a country that has a higher tax rate may attempt to minimize taxes in the foreign country by purchasing at a low price from its foreign affiliate. Thus, when the foreign affiliate sells the product, its profit will be small and its taxes reduced. When the purchase is from a country where the tax rate is lower than in the United States, the considerations are reversed and the transfer price is set at a high rate, in which case the U.S. profits will be low. These strategies are well known to the tax authorities in foreign countries and to the Internal Revenue Service in the United States. Consequently, purchases from affiliated companies are always susceptible to attack by the tax authorities. In general, the tax authorities in both countries require that the buyer purchase from its affiliated seller at an arm's length price, as if it were purchasing from an unaffiliated seller. Often, preserving evidence that the seller was selling to its unaffiliated customers at the same price as its affiliated customers will be very important in defending a tax audit. When the U.S. buyer is purchasing from a country with a higher tax rate, the U.S. Customs authorities will also be suspicious that the transfer price is undervalued, and, therefore, customs duties may be underpaid. Under U.S. tax regulations, the U.S. importer cannot claim any income tax deduction for cost of goods greater than the value declared for U.S. Customs purposes.

Another consideration in the pricing of goods for import concerns parallel imports or gray market goods. If buyers in one country are able to purchase at a lower price than in the United States, an economic incentive will exist for customers in the lower-price country to divert such goods to the United States in hopes of making a profit. Obviously, the seller's distributor in the United States will complain about such unauthorized imports and loss of sales. Recently, the U.S. Supreme Court has held that genuine goods, that is, those which are made by the same manufacturer and are not mere copies or imitations, can be imported into the United States under the U.S. Customs laws. An importer who experiences such gray market goods may have other legal remedies available to stop or prevent such import, but the best remedy is to make sure that the seller is not selling at lower prices in other markets. Unfortunately, maintaining pricing parity is not always easy because of floating exchange rates, not only between the United States and other countries, but among those other countries.

Finally, the import price as shown in the seller's invoice and as declared to the U.S. Customs for duty purposes affects the "cost of goods" for U.S. income tax purposes as is specified in section 1059A of the Internal Revenue Code.

d. Currency Fluctuations

Related to the issue of pricing are the currency fluctuations which occur between the countries of the seller and the buyer. If the U.S. importer purchases only in U.S. dollars, the fluctuation of the foreign currency will not affect the final U.S. dollar amount that the importer makes as payment. However, if the seller is a much larger company than the buyer and has more negotiating and bargaining leverage, or if the buyer is anxious to make the purchase, it may be necessary to agree to a purchase agreement denominated in foreign currency, such as Japanese yen or German marks. In such cases, if the foreign currency strengthens between the time of the price agreement and the time of payment, the U.S. importer will have to pay more U.S. dollars than it had anticipated when it agreed to the price and calculated the expected cost. In such cases, the importer is assuming the foreign exchange fluctuation risk. Sometimes, when the term of the agreement is long, or when major currency fluctuations are anticipated, neither the seller nor the buyer is comfortable in entirely assuming such risk. Consequently, they may agree to some sharing of the risk such as a 50/50 price adjustment due to any exchange fluctuations that occur during the life of the agreement, or to some other formula that attempts to protect both sides against such fluctuations.

e. *Payment Methods*

In a domestic sales transaction, the buyer may be used to purchasing an open account, receiving credit, or paying cash on delivery. In international purchases, it is more customary to utilize certain methods of payment that are designed to give the overseas seller a greater level of protection. The idea is that if the buyer fails to pay, it is much more difficult for a seller to come to the United States, institute a lawsuit, attempt to attach the buyer's assets, or otherwise obtain payment. When a seller is dealing with a buyer who is essentially unknown to it, with whom it has no prior payment experience, or who is small, the seller often requires that the buyer pay by cash in advance or obtain a documentary letter of credit from a bank in the buyer's country. The seller may also require that the letter of credit be confirmed by a bank in the seller's country to guarantee payment by the buyer's bank. The seller may still sell on terms with payment to be made at the time of arrival or the seller may give the buyer some longer period of time (for example, from 30 days to 180 days) to make payment, but the letter of credit acts as an umbrella obligation of the bank guaranteeing such payment, and the buyer does not pay the seller directly but through the bank that issues the letter of credit. In some cases, however, the buyer will be unable to obtain a letter of credit, for example, because the buyer's bank does not feel comfortable with the buyer's financial solvency. Furthermore, the issuance of letters of credit involves the payment of bank fees which are normally paid for by the buyer, and the buyer usually does not wish to incur such expenses in addition to the cost of purchasing the goods. Another disadvantage to the buyer is that it will be unable to inspect the goods before its bank is obliged to make payment. In such cases, particularly if the seller is anxious to make the sale, or if other sellers are willing to offer more liberal payment terms, the buyer may be able to force the seller to give up a letter of credit and agree to make the sale on some other, more liberal, method of payment.

The best method of purchase for the buyer is on open account, where the seller makes the sale and the shipment by forwarding the bill of lading and a commercial invoice directly to the buyer for payment. Because the bill of lading is sent directly to the buyer, once it leaves the possession of the seller, the seller will be unable to control what happens to the goods and the buyer will be able to obtain the goods whether or not payment is made. This also gives the buyer an opportunity to inspect the goods prior to making payment. When a seller agrees to sell on open account, the seller may request that the buyer open a standby letter of credit or grant a security interest under U.S. law to protect the seller's right to payment in case the buyer goes bankrupt or otherwise fails to pay at the agreed time (see Subsection g, below).

The next best method of payment for the buyer is to utilize a time draft, commonly known as a document against acceptance or D/A transaction. The bill of lading and time draft (that is, a document like a check in the amount of the sale drawn by the seller on the buyer—rather than a bank—and payable to the seller) are forwarded through banking channels, but the buyer agrees to make payment within a certain number of days (for example, 30 to 180) after it receives and accepts the draft. Normally, this permits the buyer to obtain possession of the goods and may give the buyer enough time to resell them before its obligation to pay comes due. However, documents against acceptance transactions are a significantly greater risk for the seller because, if the buyer does not pay at the promised time, the seller's only recourse is to file a lawsuit—the goods have already been released to the buyer. Where the buyer is financially strong, sometimes such acceptances can be discounted by the seller, however, permitting the seller to get immediate payment but giving the buyer additional time to pay. This discounting may be done with recourse or without recourse, depending upon the size of the discount the seller is willing to accept. The seller may decide to waive the interest charge for the delay in payment in order to make the sale.

The next best method of payment for the buyer is by sight draft documentary collection, commonly known as documents against payment or D/P transactions. In this case, the seller uses the services of a bank to effect collection but neither the buyer's bank nor the seller's bank guarantees payment by the buyer. The seller will ship the goods, and the bill of lading and a draft will be forwarded to the seller's bank. The seller's bank will forward such documents to a correspondent bank in the United States (sometimes the seller or its freight forwarder sends the documents directly to the buyer's bank—this is known as direct collection), and the U.S. bank will collect payment from the buyer prior to the time that the goods arrive. If payment is not made by the buyer, the U.S. bank does not release the bill of lading to the buyer, and the buyer will be unable to take possession of the goods or clear U.S. Customs. Although it can still be a significant problem for the seller if the buyer does not make payment and the shipment has already arrived in the United States, the seller should still be able to control the goods upon arrival, for example, by asking the bank to place them in a warehouse or by requesting that they be shipped to a third country or back to the seller at the seller's expense. Direct collections are often used for air shipments to avoid delays through the seller's bank and, also, because air waybills are non-negotiable.

Sometimes a buyer will begin purchasing from a particular seller under letters of credit, and as the seller becomes more familiar with the buyer (the buyer honors its obligations, increases its purchases, or enters into an ongoing purchase relationship agreement), the seller will be willing to liberalize its payment terms.

In addition, in international transactions the buyer may be required to use alternative payment methods, such as wire transfers via banking channels, since payment by check will often involve an inordinate length of time if the check is first sent to the seller in the foreign country and then sent back to the United States to be collected from the buyer's bank. Direct telegraphic transfer from bank account to bank account is a highly efficient and useful way to deal with international payments. However, the buyer should resist making a wire transfer until after the goods have arrived and have been inspected, or at least until after the goods are shipped under a non-negotiable (straight) bill of lading. Other methods of payment, such as cash payments made by employees traveling from the buyer to the seller or vice versa, or payment made in third countries, all carry the risk of violating the seller's foreign exchange control and/or tax laws and should only be agreed to after detailed investigation of the possible risks. A chart comparing these various methods of payment is shown in Figure 3–12.

Finally, an additional method of payment that sellers sometimes use is the factoring of export accounts receivable. This may represent an opportunity for a foreign seller to obtain its money immediately on open account sales in return for accepting a lesser amount, at some discount from the sales price. Such factoring arrangements usually involve a disadvantage for the buyer, however, because the buyer may be obligated to pay the factor when the obligation is due even though the buyer may have a dispute, such as a claim for defective goods, with the seller. To guard against that problem, the buyer should try to make sure that the purchase agreement provides that the seller cannot assign its accounts receivable without the buyer's consent.

f. Import Financing

The substantive aspects of import financing were discussed in Chapter 6, Section N. If import financing is going to be utilized, it should be discussed in the international purchase agreement. The seller will thus be clearly aware that the buyer intends to use such financing. The documentation that the seller is required to provide in order for the buyer to obtain such financing should be specified in the agreement, and the buyer's obligation to purchase should be excused if such import financing is not granted.

g. Security Interest

As discussed in subsection e, above, on payment methods, if the buyer intends to purchase on open account or on documents against acceptance, the seller may request a security interest to protect its rights to payment. Under U.S. law, unless the seller has registered its lien or security interest with a government agency, if the buyer goes into bankruptcy or falls into financial difficulties, the seller will be unable to repossess the merchandise it sold, even if the merchandise is still in the possession of the buyer. Also, the seller may be unable to obtain priority over other creditors, and after such creditors are paid, nothing may remain for the seller. Although granting a security interest does reduce the buyer's flexibility in negotiating with creditors in the event that the buyer falls into financial difficulties, in practice, the buyer will have a difficult time objecting to granting such a security interest. However, the buyer should not accept responsibility for preparing or filing such security interest or notifying other creditors since, if it does so improperly, the seller may sue the buyer for negligence. If a security interest is granted by the buyer and the buyer does experience financial difficulties, it should make sure it makes payments in accordance with the priority of the security interests or the directors of the company may become personally liable. Sometimes, the buyer's bank or other creditor will have been granted a security interest in the assets of the buyer. In order for a seller to take priority over the previous creditors, it may try to impose upon the buyer an obligation to obtain subordination agreements from the buyer's other creditors. Generally, the buyer should resist this and insist that the seller obtain such agreements itself.

h. Passage of Title, Delivery, and Risk of Loss

Ownership is transferred from the seller to the buyer by the passage of title. Under the Convention on the International Sale of Goods (discussed in subsection l), unless otherwise agreed, title and risk of loss will pass to the buyer when the seller delivers the merchandise to the first transportation carrier. The buyer's payment will be due at that time. Under U.S. law, title passes at the time and place agreed to by the parties to the international purchase agreement. It can pass at the seller's plant, at the port of export, upon arrival in the United States after clearance of Customs, upon arrival at the buyer's place of business, or at any other place, time, or manner agreed to by the parties. Usually the risk of loss for any subsequent casualty or damage to the products will pass to the buyer at the same time the title passes. However, it is possible in the purchase agreement to specify that it will pass at a different time.

i. Warranties and Product Defects

From the buyer's point of view, one of the most important provisions in the international purchase agreement is the one that specifies the warranty terms. Under the law of the United States and the Convention on the International Sale of Goods (discussed in subsection l), unless the seller limits its warranty expressly in writing in the international purchase agreement, the seller will be responsible and liable for all foreseeable consequential damages which result to the buyer from defective products. Consequently, it is common for the seller to try to eliminate all or most warranties. The purchase agreement should specify exactly what warranty the seller is giving for the products, whether the products are being sold "as is" with no warranty, whether there is a limited warranty such as repair or replacement, whether there is a dollar limit on the warranty, whether there is a time period within which the warranty claim must be made, and/or whether there is any limitation on consequential damages. In the United States, as a matter of public policy, the law prohibits certain types of warranty disclaimers or exclusions. For example, imported products have to comply with the Magnuson-Moss Warranty Act. Consequently, in reviewing the warranty limitation, the buyer may need to consult with an attorney to make sure that the warranty will be effective. If the sales agreement is formed by a mere exchange of preprinted forms, the buyer may find that the seller's terms or conditions control the sale and that no warranty exists. Therefore, the buyer should carefully read the seller's communications, and, if the warranty is too limited, the buyer must negotiate a warranty acceptable to both sides before going ahead with the purchase.

j. Preshipment Inspections

Even if the buyer has not paid in advance, if the products arrive in the United States and are defective, the buyer may be faced with substantial losses or the necessity of re-exporting the merchandise to the seller. Consequently, the buyer should generally insist upon preshipment inspection in the international purchase agreement. In an international purchase agreement, if the buyer can get the seller to agree that the buyer is entitled to purchase at the lowest price at which it sells to any of its other customers, the inspection company may be able to review more than the quality of the goods. For example, the inspection company may require the seller to produce documentation relating to sales of the same product to other customers to ascertain the prices at which such sales were made. If the buyer getting the preshipment inspection determines that the price it is paying is higher than the prices the seller had charged other customers, the buyer can refuse to go forward in the transaction or renegotiate the price.

The buyer should realize, however, that asking for a preshipment inspection will usually delay the shipment anywhere from twenty to forty days and that it will have to pay for such inspection unless it can get the seller to agree to share the costs.

k. Export Licenses

The importance of an export license has been touched upon in Chapter 6, Section E.1. In an international purchase agreement, the buyer should require the seller to warrant that no export license is required, or the exporter should state that an export license is required and should promise to obtain the license in a timely manner. If the seller fails to obtain the license, the buyer could claim damages. The buyer should be aware that, if the seller is required to obtain an export license, the buyer will usually be required to provide an International Import Certificate issued by the U.S. Department of Commerce. The seller will be unable to apply for its export license until it obtains the Certificate and the buyer should obtain it and send it to the seller as soon as possible to avoid delays in obtaining the export license. (Under the Incoterms, the buyer is responsible for obtaining the export license on "ex-works" sales.)

l. Governing Law

In any international purchase agreement, whether the agreement is formed by a written agreement between the parties or whether it is an oral agreement, the rights and obligations of the parties will be governed either by the law of the country of the seller or the law of the country of the buyer. The laws of most countries permit the seller and buyer to specifically agree on which law will apply, and that choice will be binding upon both parties whether or not a lawsuit is brought in either the buyer's or the seller's country. Of course, whenever the subject is raised, the seller will prefer the agreement to be governed by the laws of the seller's country, and the buyer will prefer it to be governed by the laws of the buyer's country. If the bargaining leverage of the parties is approximately equal, it is fair to say that it is more customary for the buyer to agree that the seller's law will govern the agreement. However, if the buyer has more bargaining leverage, the buyer may be able to prevail. Before agreeing to have the foreign seller's law govern the agreement, however, the buyer should check on what differences exist between the foreign law and U.S. law, so that the buyer can fully appreciate the risks it is assuming by agreeing to the application of foreign law. The buyer can also determine whether or not the risk is serious enough to negotiate a specific solution to that particular problem with the seller. Frequently, however, the parties do not raise, negotiate, or expressly agree upon the governing law. This may occur as a result of an exchange of preprinted forms wherein the buyer and seller each have specified that their own law governs, which results in a clear conflict between these two provisions. It may also occur when the parties have not discussed the governing law, as in a situation where an oral agreement or sale has occurred, or when the facsimile, telex, or other purchase or sale documentation does not contain any express specification of the governing law. In such cases, if a dispute arises between the parties, it will be extremely difficult to determine with any confidence which law governs the purchase agreement. Often the buyer believes that the law of the country where the offer is accepted will govern. However, the laws of the two countries may be in conflict on this point, and it may be unclear whether this means an offer to sell or an offer to buy, and whether or not the acceptance must be received by the offeror before the formation of the purchase agreement.

An additional development relating to this issue is the relatively new Convention on the Contracts for the International Sale of Goods (the Convention). On January 1, 1988, this multinational treaty went into effect among the countries that have signed it, including the United States. The following list includes the parties to the Convention as of November 1996.

Parties to the Convention on the Contracts for the International Sale of Goods

Argentina	Georgia	Poland
Australia	Germany	Romania
Austria	Greece	Russian Federation
Belarus	Guinea	Singapore
Belgium	Hungary	Slovak Republic
Bosnia-Herzegovina	Iraq	Slovenia
Bulgaria	Italy	Spain
Burundi	Kgrgyzstan	Sweden
Canada	Latvia	Syria
Chile	Lesotho	Uganda
China	Lithuania	Ukraine
Croatia	Luxembourg	United States
Czech Republic	Mexico	Uruguay
Denmark	Moldova	Uzbekistan
Ecuador	Mongolia	Venezuela
Egypt	Netherlands	Yugoslavia
Estonia	New Zealand	Zambia
Finland	Norway	
France	Peru	

Because the Convention is relatively new and because the United States has signed it, it is expected that many more countries will sign it hereafter and it will become a major force in international trade. The Convention is a detailed listing of over one hundred articles dealing with the rights and responsibilities of the buyer and the seller in international purchase agreements. It is similar in some respects to Article 2 of the U.S. Uniform Commercial Code. Nevertheless, there are many concepts, such as fundamental breach, avoidance, impediment, and nonconformity, that are not identical to U.S. law.

The Convention permits buyers and sellers located in countries which are parties to the Convention to exclude the application of the Convention (by expressly referring to it) and to choose the law of either the seller or the buyer to apply to the international purchase agreement. However, for companies located in any of the countries which are parties to the Convention (including U.S. companies), if the seller and buyer cannot or do not agree on which law will apply, the provisions of the Convention will automatically apply.

In summary, the buyer should include provisions on governing law in its international purchase agreement, and if the seller disagrees, the buyer should negotiate this provision. The buyer should also determine what differences exist between the Convention and U.S. law in case the parties cannot agree and the Convention thereby becomes applicable.

m. Dispute Resolution

One method of resolving disputes which may arise between the parties is litigation in the courts. For a U.S. importer, the most likely dispute to arise relates to defective goods. In such cases, the importer may be limited to going to the courts of the seller's country in order to institute litigation and seek a judgment to obtain assets of the seller. Even if the parties have agreed that U.S. law will govern the purchase agreement, there is a risk that a foreign court may misapply U.S. law, disregard U.S. law, or otherwise favor and protect the seller located in its own country. Furthermore, there can be significant delays in legal proceedings (from two to five years), court and legal expenses can be high, and the outcome may be questionable. In order to reduce such risks, the importer can specify in the international purchase agreement that all disputes must be resolved in the courts of the importer's country, that the seller consents to jurisdiction there, and to the commencement of any such lawsuit by the simple forwarding of any form of written notice by the importer to the seller. Of course, sellers may resist such provisions and whether the buyer will be able to finally obtain this agreement will depend upon the negotiating and bargaining strength of the parties.

Another form of dispute resolution which is common in international purchase agreements is arbitration. In many foreign countries, sellers take a less adversarial approach to the resolution of contractual disputes and they feel more comfortable with a less formal proceeding, such as arbitration. While arbitration can be included in an international purchase agreement, an importer should thoroughly understand the advantages and disadvantages of agreeing to resolve disputes by arbitration. First, arbitration is unlikely to save much in expenses and quite often may not involve a significantly shorter time period to resolve the dispute. In fact, from the point of view of expense, in some cases, if the seller refuses to go forward with the arbitration, the buyer will have to advance the seller's portion of the arbitration fees to the arbitration tribunal, or the arbitrators will not proceed with the dispute. Furthermore, in litigation, of course, the judges or juries involved are paid at the public expense, whereas in arbitration, the parties must pay the expenses of the arbitrators, which can be very substantial, especially if there are three arbitrators.

Second, the administering authority must be selected. The International Chamber of Commerce is commonly designated as the administering authority in arbitration clauses, but the fees which they charge are very high. The American Arbitration Association also handles international disputes, but the foreign seller may be unwilling to agree to arbitration by a U.S. administering authority. Other administering authorities, such as the Inter-American Commercial Arbitration Commission, the London Court of International Arbitration, the Stockholm Chamber of Commerce Arbitration Institute, the British Columbia International Arbitration Centre, or an arbitration authority in the seller's country, may be acceptable.

Third, the number of arbitrators should be specified. Since the parties will be paying for them, the author recommends that one arbitrator be utilized to resolve disputes of a smaller amount (a specified dollar figure) and that three arbitrators be utilized for larger disputes.

Fourth, the place of arbitration must be specified. Again, the seller and buyer will have a natural conflict on this point, so some third country or intermediate location is probably most likely to be mutually agreeable. Another variation that has developed, although its legal validity has been questioned, is an agreement that if the seller commences the arbitration, arbitration will be conducted in the buyer's country, and if the buyer commences the arbitration, the arbitration will be conducted in the seller's country. This has the effect of discouraging either party from commencing arbitration and forcing the parties to reach amicable solutions to their disputes.

Finally, the buyer should ascertain beforehand whether an arbitral award would be enforced in the courts of the seller's country. Some fifty-five countries have become parties to a multinational treaty known as the New York Convention, which commits them to enforcing the arbitral awards of member countries. Without this assurance, the entire dispute may have to be relitigated in the seller's country.

n. Termination

Protection against termination of an international purchase agreement or distributor or sales agent agreement may prove to be difficult for the U.S. buyer. No federal law specifically protects U.S. buyers, distributors, or sales agents against unfair terminations, although some states such as Wisconsin have enacted protective legislation. Although the U.S. buyer may have invested a great deal of time in purchasing products or building up a market for resale of such products, the seller may terminate the agreement on short notice or without payment of compensation. In general, the buyer may be able to claim damages if the termination is the result of conspiracy such as the agreement of two or more suppliers not to sell to the buyer (concerted refusal to deal), if the termination is by a seller with monopoly power (such as a 60 percent or greater market share), or the termination is for an anti-competitive, rather than a business, reason (such as a refusal of the buyer to adhere to the seller's suggested resale prices). The buyer should try to get some protection by entering into an ongoing purchase agreement (rather than simply dealing on a purchase order by purchase order basis) and inserting a provision that there be a long lead time prior to termination or that the seller will pay the buyer some termination compensation for goodwill created by the buyer's market development. (If the purchaser is selling the goods under its own trademark, the seller will not be able to appoint another distributor to sell under the same brand name unless the seller is willing to buy the trademark from the buyer.) Of course, the buyer should always specify in the purchase agreement that it will have no obligation to continue to purchase from the seller if there is a change in control, bankruptcy, insolvency, or breach of the agreement by the seller.

C. Import Distributor and Sales Agent Agreements

In addition to the foregoing provisions, which arise in all international purchase agreements, there are other, specific provisions that arise in import distributor agreements and sales agent agreements.

1. *Distinction Between Distributor and Sales Agent*

A distributor is a company that buys products from a seller, takes title thereto, and assumes the risk of resale. A distributor will purchase at a specific price and will be compensated by reselling the product at a higher price. Under the antitrust laws of the United States, the seller cannot restrict or require a distributor to resell the product at any specific price, although it may be able to restrict the customers to whom or the territories in which the buyer resells.

A sales agent does not purchase from the seller. The sales agent or representative locates customers and solicits offers to purchase the product from the potential buyers. In order to avoid tax liability for the seller in the United States, the sales agent normally will not have any authority to accept offers to purchase from potential customers. Instead, the offers from the customer are forwarded to the seller for final acceptance, and shipment and billing is direct between the seller and the customer. Furthermore, since the sales agent normally does not take title, it will ordinarily not act as importer of record and will not assume liabilities for customs duties or penalties. For such services, the sales agent is paid a commission or some other type of compensation. Because no sale occurs between the seller and the sales agent, the seller can specify the price at which it will sell to customers and the sales agent can be restricted to quoting only that price to a potential customer. Likewise, the sales agent can be restricted as to its territory or the types of customers from which it has been given the right to solicit orders. Sometimes the sales agent will guarantee payment by the customers or perform other services, such as after-sales service or invoicing of the customers.

A chart summarizing these differences is shown in Figure 3–13. Another chart analyzing the financial comparison of acting as a distributor or sales agent is shown in Figure 3–14.

2. *Import Distributor Agreements*

As previously indicated, when a distributor agreement is utilized, such agreement will act as an umbrella agreement, and specific orders for specific quantities, shipment dates, and, possibly, prices will be stated in purchase orders, purchase order acceptances, and similar documentation discussed in relation to isolated purchase transactions. A checklist for negotiation issues for a distributor agreement is shown in Figure 3–15.

The important provisions in an import distributor agreement include the following:

a. Territory and Exclusivity

The distributor will normally want to be the exclusive distributor in a territory, whereas the seller would generally prefer to make a nonexclusive appointment so that if the distributor fails to perform, it can appoint other distributors. Also, the seller may simply wish from the outset to appoint a number of distributors in the United States to adequately serve the market. A possible compromise is that the appointment will be exclusive unless certain minimum purchase obligations are not met, in which case the seller has the right to convert the agreement to a nonexclusive agreement.

Usually the entire United States or the part of the United States that is granted to the distributor is specified. The distributor may be required to agree not to solicit sales from outside the territory. The distributor may be prohibited from establishing any warehouse or sales outlet outside of the territory.

b. Pricing

As indicated, normally it is illegal for the seller to specify the price at which the U.S. distributor can resell the merchandise. Of course, ordinarily the distributor would not mark the product up too much, gouging end users and resulting in less sales and market penetration for the products. In addition, because of the gray market problem, the price at which the buyer resells should not be set too high, thereby attracting diversions from other countries. Gray markets can occur as a result of exchange rate fluctuations; where one of the seller's other distributors in another country is able to obtain a product at a lower price in its own currency than is available in the United States.

Currency fluctuations must be monitored, and the right to price reductions is normally necessary to make sure that the buyer is fairly participating in the profits which are being created along the chain of distribution. For example, if a French seller sells a product for $1 at a time when the French exchange rate is 5 francs to $1, the seller will be receiving $1 (or 5 francs) when its cost of production may be 4 francs, or a 1 franc profit. However, if the franc weakens to 10 francs to $1, and the seller still sells the product for $1, now it will receive 10 francs and its profit will increase. Sometimes the seller will continue to ask for price increases from the buyer even though the seller has had a very favorable exchange rate movement. Normally the buyer's interest is that the seller reduce the price whenever the foreign currency weakens (or the dollar strengthens). When the seller does decrease its price to the U.S. distributor, however, normally the seller will also want the U.S. distributor to reduce its price on resale to the end users so that more sales will be made, volume will increase, and the seller can increase its market share.

c. Minimum Purchase Quantities

In most long-term purchase agreements or distributor agreements, the seller will ask for a commitment for purchase of a significant quantity. The buyer should request some price discount for such commitment. Ordinarily, it is in the buyer's interest to commit only to a target amount or to use its best efforts to make sales. In such cases, if the buyer fails to make the target, there is no breach of the agreement and the seller cannot sue the buyer for damages. If the buyer commits to purchase fixed quantities or dollar amounts, however, and fails to perform, the seller may be able to sue for damages and terminate the distributor agreement.

d. Handling Competing Products

Normally a seller will want a provision wherein the distributor agrees not to handle competing products. If the distributor is already handling any competing products (either manufacturing them or purchasing them from alternative sources), the distributor may not want to agree to this provision, and there is no legal requirement that it do so. In fact, in certain situations, such as where other competing sellers do not have adequate outlets for their products, a violation of the U.S. antitrust laws can result if the buyer is required not to handle competing products. However, the seller will normally be unwilling to give the distributor an exclusive appointment in the territory unless the distributor agrees not to handle competing products.

e. Appointment of Subdistributors

Whether or not the distributor has the right to appoint subdistributors should be expressly stated in the distributor agreement. If this right is not discussed, the distributor may not have the right under U.S. law to appoint subdistributors. This can cause various problems for the distributor. Not only will the distributor be unable to meet its purchase commitments to the seller, which could result in termination of the distributor agreement, but the distributor may lose chances to multiply its sales. In appointing subdistributors, the distributor needs to control the resale territories (but not the prices) to maximize distribution and sales potential. If the right to appoint subdistributors is granted, the distributor should try to avoid responsibility for their activities in the distribution agreement, such as sales outside their territories; otherwise, the distributor may find its master distribution agreement with the seller is being terminated due to breaches by the independent subdistributors.

f. Use of Trade Names, Trademarks, and Copyrights

As discussed in Chapter 6, Section O, control of intellectual property rights is quite important. Sometimes U.S. distributors can protect their market position by registering their intellectual property rights, such as trademarks, in the United States. This is a particular disadvantage for the foreign seller, because if the seller wishes to terminate the distributor and to appoint a new distributor, the past distributor may own the intellectual property rights to distribute the products in the United States. Until the distributor consents to the assignment of the intellectual property rights to the seller or the new distributor, any sales by the seller into the United States or by the new distributor will be an infringement of the intellectual property rights owned by the former distributor. This puts the former distributor in a very strong bargaining position to negotiate a substantial termination compensation payment. The distributor may do this in a private branding arrangement where the seller, if it is a manufacturer, puts the distributor's own trademark or brand on the product. In the international purchase agreement, the distributor could specify that it has the exclusive rights to that name or brand and the distributor should register the name with the U.S. Patent and Trademark Office. Upon termination of the distributorship agreement, the seller could not sell the products under that name or appoint another distributor to do so (but the seller could sell identical products under another brand name).

g. Warranties and Product Liability

In addition to the considerations discussed in Section B.2.i, the importer should require the seller to maintain product liability insurance in its own name and to name the importer as an additional insured in amounts deemed satisfactory by the importer. Product liability claims are not as common overseas as they are in the United States and foreign sellers may not have product liability insurance. Furthermore, the customer will find it easier to sue the importer in the United States. The overseas seller may have no office in the United states and the importer may be unable to sue the seller in the United States for warranty claims by the importer's customers. The seller should use a U.S. insurance company or a foreign insurance company that is doing business in the United States and is subject to jurisdiction in the United States. Before modifying or adding to any of the seller's warranties, the buyer should obtain the seller's consent. If the distributor agrees to perform warranty or after-sale service for the seller, it should make sure that it clearly understands its responsibilities and the terms for reimbursement for warranty labor it performs.

3. *Import Sales Agent Agreements*

Like distributor agreements, sales agent agreements often contain many of the same provisions that are included in an international purchase agreement, but there are certain provisions peculiar to the sales agent agreement that must be considered. A checklist for negotiation issues for a sales agent agreement is shown in Figure 3–16.

a. Commissions

The sales agent is compensated for its efforts by payment of a commission by the seller. The sales agent is appointed to solicit orders, and when such orders are accepted by the seller, the agent is paid a commission. The U.S. sales agent should try to have its commission due upon solicitation or acceptance of the order instead of when the customer actually makes payment to the seller. The sales agent is not normally guaranteeing payment by the customers or making credit decisions, so it should not have to wait for its commission—its work is done when it brings a customer to the seller. Generally, the seller should not bill the agent for the price of the product (less commission) because such practice could result in characterizing the relationship as a distributorship rather than a sales agency.

b. Pricing

Because there is no sale between the seller and the sales agent, the seller can lawfully require the sales agent to quote only prices that the seller has authorized. For sellers who wish to establish uniform pricing on a worldwide basis, eliminate gray market, and control markups, use of the sales agent appointment can be highly beneficial. However, the trade-off is that the seller will ordinarily assume the credit risk and will have to satisfy itself in regard to the ability of the customer to pay. This sometimes presents difficulties in obtaining sufficient information, although the sales agent can be given the responsibility of forwarding and gathering such information for the seller prior to acceptance of any orders. In addition, some sales agents are willing to be appointed as *del credere* agents, wherein the sales agent guarantees the payment by any customer from whom it solicits an order. Obviously, a sales agent should require higher commissions for guaranteeing payment.

c. Shipment

Shipment is not made to the sales agent; it is made directly to the customer from whom the sales agent solicited the order. Generally there will be problems associated with trying to maintain an inventory at the agent's place of business in the United States. If the seller maintains an inventory in its own name or through an agent, the seller can become taxable on its own sales profits to customers in the United States. If the customer cannot wait for shipment from the foreign country, or if it is important to maintain an inventory in the United States, the appropriate way to do so while using sales agents must be investigated with a knowledgeable attorney.

Chapter 8

Import Process and Documentation

In addition to the purchase agreement, there are numerous other documents that the importer will commonly encounter in the process of importing merchandise. Since some of these documents may be prepared by the customs broker or others, the importer may not see or realize that such documents have been prepared. Nevertheless, because the importer is responsible for the actions of its agent, the customs broker, it is imperative that the importer understand what documents are being prepared and filed on each importation. Furthermore, since the documents filed by the customs broker may be based on information provided by the importer, if the importer does not understand the documents or provides incorrect information, the customs broker will disclaim any responsibility therefor.

An overview of the U.S. Customs import process, which will be described in more detail in this chapter, is shown in Figure 8–1.

A. Bills of Lading

The bill of lading or loading is issued by the transportation carrier, either the airline or steamship company. It evidences receipt of the merchandise for transportation to the destination specified in the bill. In the case of ocean shipments, the original bill of lading will have been obtained by the exporter and will be forwarded by air courier service through banking channels (or directly to the buyer on open account purchases) for arrival in advance of the shipment. Customs requires that the person making entry of the goods into the United States (the importer of record) present a properly endorsed bill of lading with the other customs entry documents in order to establish that that person has the right to make entry of the goods. Where the transportation is under a negotiable bill of lading, the importer will also have to present the bill of lading to the transportation carrier in order to obtain release of the goods. On import transactions the Uniform Commercial Code requires that the bill of lading be negotiable unless the parties agree to a non-negotiable bill of lading in their purchase agreement. Where a negotiable bill of lading has been lost or the importer cannot pre-

Figure 8–1. Import process.

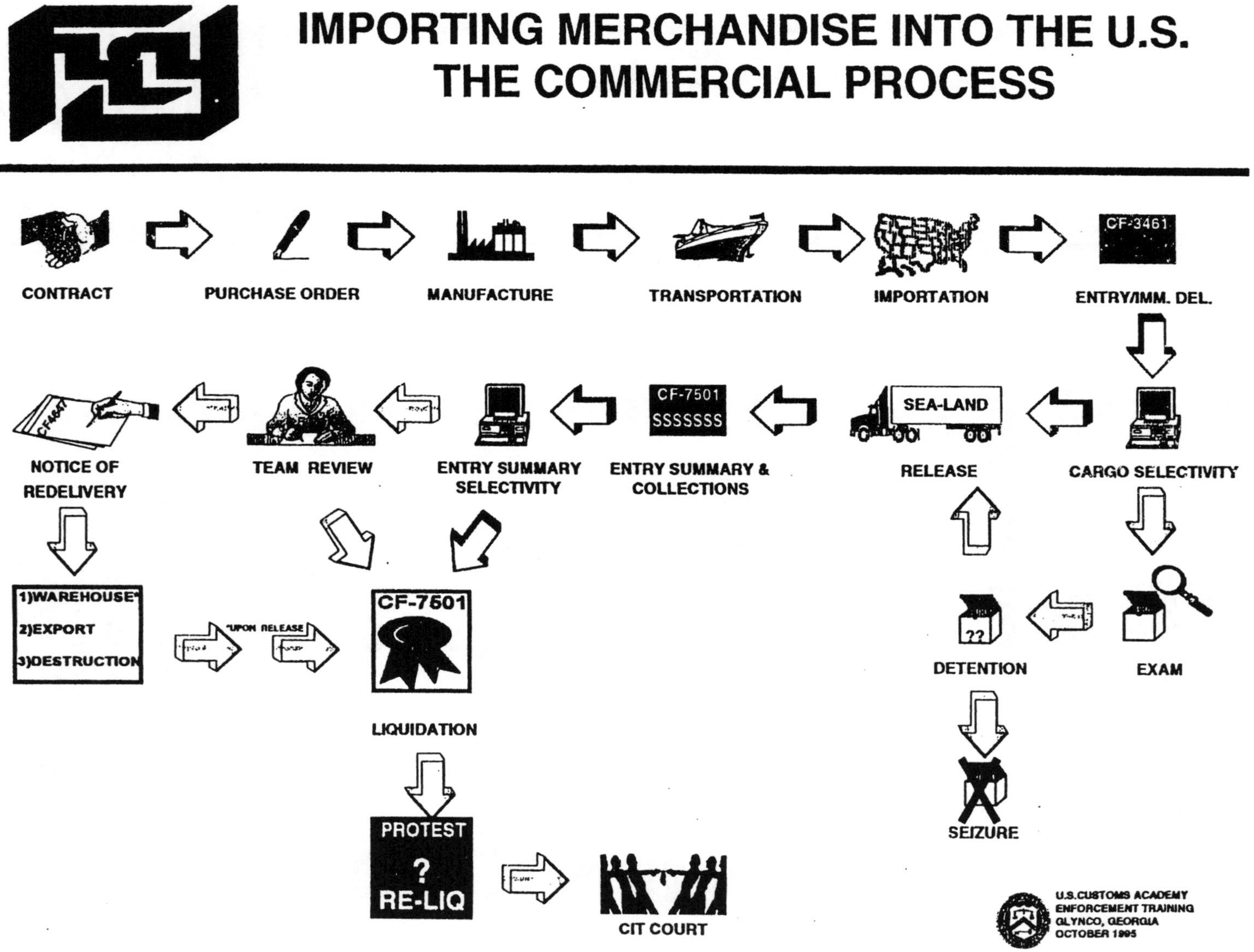

sent it, the steamship line may permit the importer to obtain the merchandise if it signs a "letter of indemnity" and the importer is determined to be a good credit risk. Sample ocean and air bills of lading are shown in Figures 4–5, 4–6, and 4–7. Additional information on bills of lading is contained in Chapter 4, Section D.

B. Commercial Invoices

At the same time that the exporter forwards the bill of lading, it will include a commercial invoice (which must be in the English language) itemizing the merchandise sold and the amount due for payment. There must be one invoice for each separate shipment. Under U.S. Customs regulations, those commercial invoices must contain very specific items of information, such as quantities, description, purchase price, country of origin, assists, transportation charges, commissions, installation service, and financing charges. For forty-five classes of products, the commercial invoice must contain certain additional information. Prior to exportation, the importer should identify what specialized information is required by the U.S. Customs regulations and communicate that to the exporter. A summary of the required contents is shown in Figure 4–3. Recently, the U.S. Customs Service has indicated that it will detain and refuse to release shipments where the invoice does not contain all of the necessary information. (A sample invoice is shown in Figure 3–11.) Showing the package numbers and quantities on the commercial invoice facilitates Customs' examination of the merchandise. Putting the commercial invoice number on all of the shipping documents helps to tie the documents together. The importer should understand that the invoice amount and the declared value have consequences for the "cost of goods" calculation for U.S. income tax purposes under section 1059A of the Internal Revenue Code.

C. Pro Forma Invoices

When the importer receives a shipment and no commercial invoice is available, it can prepare its own invoice, known as a pro forma invoice, and submit it to Customs for entry of the merchandise, provided it supplies a bond for its production. (A sample pro forma invoice is shown in Figure 8–2. This should not be confused with the pro forma invoice the seller provides to the buyer, shown in Figure 3–10.) This is merely the representation by the buyer as to the price which it paid or is payable for purchase of the goods. The commercial invoice signed by the exporter must be furnished to Customs within fifty days or the bond will be forfeited.

D. Packing Lists

The buyer may request or the seller may include a packing list with the merchandise. Although this is not strictly required by U.S. Customs laws, if one is sent, it must also be filed with the U.S. Customs Service. It is important where different types of

Figure 8–2. Pro forma invoice.

PRO FORMA INVOICE

Importers Statement of Value or the Price Paid in the Form of an Invoice

Not being in possession of a special or commercial seller's or shipper's invoice I request that you accept the statement of value or the price paid in the form of an invoice submitted below:

Name of shipper ______________________ address ______________________

Name of seller ______________________ address ______________________

Name of purchaser ______________________ address ______________________

Name of consignee ______________________ address ______________________

The merchandise (has) (has not) been purchased or agreed to be purchased by importer named.

The prices, or in the case of consigned goods the values, given below are true and correct to the best of my knowledge and belief, and are based upon: (Check basis with an "X")

(a) The price paid or agreed to be paid ( ) as per order dated ______________________
(b) Advices from exporter by letter ( ) by cable ( ) dated ______________________
(c) Comparative values of shipments previously received ( ) dated ______________________
(d) Knowledge of the market in the country of exportation ( ) ______________________
(e) Knowledge of the market in the United States (if U.S. Value) ( ) ______________________
(f) Advices of the District Director of Customs ( ) ______________________
(g) Other ( ) ______________________

Check below charges, included/not included, in price, columns "D" and "E"

	AMT. INC.	AMT. NOT INCL.		AMT. INC.	AMT. NOT INCL.
Package	$	$	Lighterage	$	$
Cartage	$	$	Ocean Freight	$	$
Inland Freight	$	$	U.S. duties	$	$
Wharfage & loading abroad	$	$	Total	$	$

A	B	C	D	E	F	G
MARKS AND NUMBERS	MANUFACTURERS ITEM NO. SYMBOL OR BRAND	QUANTITIES AND FULL DESCRIPTION OF MERCHANDISE	UNIT PURCHASE PRICE IN CURRENCY	TOTAL PURCHASE PRICE IN CURRENCY	UNIT FOREIGN VALUE	TOTAL FOREIGN VALUE

Country of Origin:

If any other invoice is received, I will immediately file it with the Collector of Customs.

Signature of person making invoice

Date: ______________________ ______________________

Firm: ______________________

Title: ______________________

merchandise subject to different rates of duty are shipped in one shipment. In the event that there is any shortage, damage, or defects, the packing list is also important for making insurance claims. When the buyer is responsible for obtaining such insurance, the buyer/importer should require the seller to send a packing list (see Figure 4–8).

E. Inspection Certificates

If the buyer requires a preshipment inspection in its purchase agreement, the inspection certificate should be furnished by the third party company that performed the inspection prior to exportation. This need not be filed with the U.S. Customs Service, but in the event of any discrepancy between the merchandise upon arrival and the inspection certificate, the importer should notify the inspection service (and the courier and insurance company) immediately. (A sample is shown in Figure 4–10.)

F. Drafts for Payment

Where the seller/exporter has made shipment under a letter of credit opened by the buyer/importer, or under an agreement with a bank for documentary collection, the buyer's bank will pay the amount owed on sight drafts to the seller's bank immediately and will present any time drafts to the buyer/importer for acceptance. (Samples are shown in Figures 4–29 and 4–30, respectively.)

G. Arrival Notices

The transportation carrier (steamship company or airline) will send an arrival notice to the customs broker or to the importer (the consignee or notify party in the bill of lading) upon arrival of the merchandise in the port. The party who is notified will be in accordance with the instructions that the transportation carrier received from the seller/exporter or the seller's freight forwarder in the foreign country, which is usually based on the instructions of the buyer to the seller. After receiving an arrival notice, the importer or its customs broker will ordinarily have five days within which to supply the necessary documents to the U.S. Customs Service to make entry and obtain release and delivery of the merchandise. (See sample steamship company Arrival Notice in Figure 8–3.)

H. Pick-Up and Delivery Orders

If the foreign exporter has agreed to deliver the merchandise to the buyer/importer's premises, the foreign exporter or, more usually, its freight forwarder will issue a delivery order to the freight forwarder in the United States upon arrival of the goods in the United States to effect the inland transportation between the U.S. port of arrival

Figure 8–3. Arrival notice.

SeaLand

Asia/Hawaii/Alaska: 1-800-759-9000
Europe/Mid-East: 1-800-759-7100
Carib/Cen & So Americas: 1-800-759-9100

NOTIFICATION OF CARGO ARRIVAL **DATE MAILED:**

MAIL TO:

Shipper:
Consignee:
Notify:
Also Notify:
Bill To:
Pickup Location:

Bill of Lading No:
Est. Arrival Date At Destination:

See original Bill of Lading for additional container numbers and full description

ARRIVING VESSEL:	Quan	Pkg	Lead Marks & Numbers	Abbreviated Desc. of Goods
I.T. No:				
I.T. Date:				
I.T. Destination:				
Service Type:				
Sailing Date:				
Origin:				
Port of Loading:				
Port of Discharge:				
Destination:				

Container Numbers	Size Type	Charges (Subject to Correction)	Rated As	Per Code	Rate	Amount
Total Container Count:		Total Weight	Total Measure			
THIS IS NOT AN INVOICE		PLEASE NOTE, ARRIVAL DATE IS ESTIMATED TO CONFIRM, CALL ABOVE REFERENCED PHONE NUMBERS			TOTAL COLLECT	
		ALL GOVERNING BILL OF LADING, FREETIME PROVISIONS, TARIFF AND CUSTOMS REGULATIONS APPLY				

and the buyer's premises. (A sample is shown in Figure 8–4.) Or, if the title has passed to the buyer prior to or upon arrival, the importer will instruct the customs broker to make entry with the U.S. Customs Service. Once entry has been made, the customs broker will instruct the trucking company to pick up the merchandise from the international transportation carrier and deliver it to the importer.

I. Entry/Immediate Delivery

Usually, when an importer imports merchandise, it must prepare the necessary customs entry documents and present them to the U.S. Customs Service along with payment of estimated duties before release of the goods can be authorized by the U.S. Customs Service to the importer. However, where the importer has provided a customs bond (and is not in default on the payment of its customs bills), the importer can apply for immediate release of the goods by filing an Entry/Immediate Delivery form (Customs Form 3461). (See sample in Figure 8–5.) Customs brokers who have been accepted under the Automated Broker Interface may file this form electronically. If entry is made using this form, the importer is required to file an Entry Summary form (with the additional information required by that form and payment of estimated duties) within ten days thereafter or Customs will make a liquidated damages assessment, a form of customs penalty. In certain situations, such as the importation of fresh fruit and vegetables from Canada or Mexico, this form can be filed prior to arrival of the merchandise. Upon filing of the Entry/Immediate Delivery form, Customs will examine the merchandise or waive examination.

J. Entry Summary

The Entry Summary is the main document used to enter goods into the United States. Either the Entry/Immediate Delivery form or the Entry Summary must be filed with the U.S. Customs Service within five working days after arrival of the shipment at the port of entry (or the port of destination for in-bond shipments). Where no Entry/Immediate Delivery form was filed before the filing of the Entry Summary, the Entry Summary is referred to as a "live entry." Customs brokers who have qualified with Customs may file this information electronically and, under the Customs Modernization Act, importers may submit "import activity summary" statements covering entries made during a calendar month. The entry may specify that the merchandise is for consumption or is for storage in a warehouse, to be withdrawn for consumption at a later date. If no entry is made, the merchandise will be transferred to a "general order" warehouse. If no entry is made within six months (immediately for perishable goods), the merchandise will be sold. (An Order for Public Sales is shown in Figure 8–6. An Entry Summary and Continuation Sheet is shown in Figure 8–7.) The instructions for completing the Entry Summary are shown in Appendix H. Several items on the Entry Summary are worthy of note:

In box 4, if an export visa is required, the number must be listed.

(*Text continues on page 317.*)

Figure 8–4. Pick-up order.

PICK UP ORDER/D.O.

DATE

IMPORTING CARRIER	FROM PORT OF/ORIGIN AIRPORT	OUR REF. NUMBER	ARRIVAL DATE	FREE TIME EXP.

LOCATION OF MERCHANDISE

DELIVER TO →

THE CARRIER OR CARTMAN TO WHOM THIS ORDER IS ASSIGNED WILL BE RESPONSIBLE FOR ANY STORAGE AND DEMURRAGE CHARGES RESULTING FROM NEGLIGENCE.

IMPORTANT: NOTIFY US AT ONCE IF DELIVERY CANNOT BE EFFECTED AS INSTRUCTED.

BROKER/IMPORTER NAME	AUTHORIZED SIGNATURE	FREIGHT CHARGES
		☐ COD ☐ PREPAID ☐ COLLECT ☐ BANK RELEASE

TRUCKING COMPANY NAME → IS AUTHORIZED TO PICK UP THE MERCHANDISE INDICATED BELOW.

DATE & SIGNATURE OF RECEIVER	NO. PKGS. REC'D.

MARKS & NUMBERS	ENTRY NUMBER	PKGS. BY ENTRY	IMPORTING CARRIER & B/L OR AWB NO.	DESCRIPTION OF GOODS & WT

ORIGINAL

THE RECEIPT OF THIS DELIVERY ORDER WILL SERVE AS A PRELIMINARY NOTICE OF INTENT TO FILE CLAIM AGAINST THE IMPORTING CARRIER FOR ANY DAMAGE TO, AND/OR LOSS OF THE SHIPMENT WITH THE UNDERSTANDING THAT THE FINAL CLAIM WILL BE MADE BY THE IMPORTER OR THEIR INSURANCE COMPANY.

PACKAGE COUNT VALIDATION

DATE ____________ **NO. OF PKGS.**

AGENT OF DELIVERING CARRIER ____________ (NAME) ____________ (TITLE)

DELIVERED QUANTITIES VERIFIED ____________ (SIGNATURE OF CUSTOMS OFFICER) ____________ (BADGE NO.)

CUSTOMS PERMIT	PKG. NOS. HELD BY U.S. CUSTOMS TO FOLLOW	GO NO.
☐ ATTACHED ☐ LODGED WITH U.S. CUSTOMS		

DOCUMENTS ATTACHED	DELIVERY CHARGES	
☐ DELIVERY ORDER ☐ DOCK RECEIPT ☐ B/L ☐		PER

DELIVERY CLERK: ALL DEMURRAGE FOR ACCOUNT OF DRAWEE OF THIS ORDER

Courtesy of Apperson Business Forms, Inc.

Figure 8–5. Entry/Immediate Delivery form.

TABS:

DEPARTMENT OF THE TREASURY
UNITED STATES CUSTOMS SERVICE

Form Approved
OMB No. 1515-0069

ENTRY/IMMEDIATE DELIVERY

19 CFR 142.3, 142.16, 142.22, 142.24

1. ARRIVAL DATE	2. ELECTED ENTRY DATE	3. ENTRY TYPE CODE/NAME	4. ENTRY NUMBER
5. PORT	6. SINGLE TRANS. BOND	7. BROKER/IMPORTER FILE NUMBER	
	8. CONSIGNEE NUMBER		9. IMPORTER NUMBER
10. ULTIMATE CONSIGNEE NAME		11. IMPORTER OF RECORD NAME	
12. CARRIER CODE	13. VOYAGE/FLIGHT/TRIP	14. LOCATION OF GOODS-CODE(S)/NAME(S)	
15. VESSEL CODE/NAME			
16. U.S. PORT OF UNLADING	17. MANIFEST NUMBER	18. G.O. NUMBER	19. TOTAL VALUE
20. DESCRIPTION OF MERCHANDISE			

21. IT/BL/AWB CODE	22. IT/BL/AWB NO.	23. MANIFEST QUANTITY	24. H.S. NUMBER	25. COUNTRY OF ORIGIN	26. MANUFACTURER NO.

27. CERTIFICATION

I hereby make application for entry/immediate delivery. I certify that the above information is accurate, the bond is sufficient, valid, and current, and that all requirements of 19 CFR Part 142 have been met.

SIGNATURE OF APPLICANT

X

PHONE NO. | DATE

29. BROKER OR OTHER GOVT. AGENCY USE

28. CUSTOMS USE ONLY

☐ OTHER AGENCY ACTION REQUIRED, NAMELY:

☐ CUSTOMS EXAMINATION REQUIRED.

☐ ENTRY REJECTED, BECAUSE:

DELIVERY AUTHORIZED: | SIGNATURE | DATE

Paperwork Reduction Act Notice: This information is needed to determine the admissibility of imports into the United States and to provide the necessary information for the examination of the cargo and to establish the liability for payment of duties and taxes. Your response is necessary.

Statement Required by 5 CFR 1320.21: The estimated average burden associated with this collection of information is 15 minutes per respondent or recordkeeper depending on individual circumstances. Comments concerning the accuracy of this burden estimate and suggestions for reducing this burden should be directed to U.S. Customs Service, Paperwork Management Branch, Washington, DC 20229, or the Paperwork Reduction Project (1515-0069), Office of Management and Budget, Washington, DC 20503.

Customs Form 3461 (010189)

Figure 8–6. Order for public sale.

DEPARTMENT OF THE TREASURY
U.S. CUSTOMS SERVICE
19 CFR 127.24

ORDER TO TRANSFER
MERCHANDISE FOR PUBLIC AUCTION (SALE)

LOT NO. | ENTRY NO.

G.O. NO.

DATE SENT TO G.O.

VESSEL

DATE OF ARRIVAL

DISTRICT

PORT

DATE OF MAILING

TO CONSIGNEE

[redacted]

LOCATION

DATE OF SALE

PUBLIC SALE LOCATION *(City — State)*

FOR FULL INFORMATION CALL OR WRITE

MARKS AND NOS.	DESCRIPTION	APPRAISED VALUE	RATE OF DUTY	DOMESTIC VALUE

SIGNATURE OF CUSTOMS OFFICER *(Print & Sign)*

THE ABOVE - DESCRIBED GOODS EXCEPT AS NOTED WERE RECEIVED AT THE PLACE OF SALE.

EXCEPTIONS:

SIGNATURE OF CUSTOMS OFFICER *(Print & Sign)*

DATE

LIQUIDATED DUTIES

LIQUIDATED I. R. TAX

INITIALS

TO LIENHOLDER

ORIGINAL-FILE COPY

Customs Form 5251 (020384)

Figure 8–7. Entry summary and continuation sheet.

DEPARTMENT OF THE TREASURY
UNITED STATES CUSTOMS SERVICE

ENTRY SUMMARY

Form Approved OMB No. 1515-0065

(1) Entry No.	(2) Entry Type Code	3. Entry Summary Date
4. Entry Date	(5) Port Code	
6. Bond No.	7. Bond Type Code	8. Broker/Importer File No.

9. Ultimate Consignee Name and Address	10. Consignee No.	(11) Importer of Record Name and Address	(12) Importer No.
		(13) Exporting Country	14. Export Date
		(15) Country of Origin	16. Missing Documents
	State	(17) I.T. No.	(18) I.T. Date
(19) B/L or AWB No.	20. Mode of Transportation	21. Manufacturer I.D.	22. Reference No.
(23) Importing Carrier	24. Foreign Port of Lading	25. Location of Goods/G.O. No.	
26. U.S. Port of Unlading	(27) Import Date		

(28) Line No.	(29) Description of Merchandise: 30. (A) T.S.U.S.A. No. B. ADA/CVD Case No.	31. (A) Gross Weight B. Manifest Qty.	(32) Net Quantity in T.S.U.S.A. Units	33. (A) Entered Value B. CHGS C. Relationship	34. (A) T.S.U.S.A. Rate B. ADA/CVD Rate (C) I.R.C. Rate D. Visa No.	(35) Duty and I.R. Tax: Dollars	Cents

(36) Declaration of Importer of Record (Owner or Purchaser) or Authorized Agent

I declare that I am the

☐ Importer of record and that the actual owner, purchaser, or consignee for customs purposes is as shown above. OR ☐ owner or purchaser or agent thereof.

I further declare that the merchandise

☐ was obtained pursuant to a purchase or agreement to purchase and that the prices set forth in the invoices are true. OR ☐ was not obtained pursuant to a purchase or agreement to purchase and the statements in the invoices as to value or price are true to the best of my knowledge and belief.

I also declare that the statements in the documents herein filed fully disclose to the best of my knowledge and belief the true prices, values, quantities, rebates, drawbacks, fees, commissions, and royalties and are true and correct, and that all goods or services provided to the seller of the merchandise either free or at reduced cost are fully disclosed. I will immediately furnish to the appropriate customs officer any information showing a different state of facts.

Notice required by Paperwork Reduction Act of 1980: This information is needed to ensure that importers/exporters are complying with U.S. customs laws, to allow us to compute and collect the right amount of money, to enforce other agency requirements, and to collect accurate statistical information on imports. Your response is mandatory. (Continued on back of form.)

▼ U.S. CUSTOMS USE ▼		TOTALS
A. Liq. Code	B. Ascertained Duty	(37) Duty
	C. Ascertained Tax	(38) Tax
	D. Ascertained Other	(39) Other
	E. Ascertained Total	(40) Total

(41) Signature of Declarant, Title, and Date

PART 1 -- RECORD COPY

Customs Form 7501 (112295)

(continues)

Figure 8–7. *(continued)*

DEPARTMENT OF THE TREASURY
UNITED STATES CUSTOMS SERVICE

ENTRY SUMMARY CONTINUATION SHEET

Form Approved, OMB No. 1515-0065. See Customs Form 7501 for Paperwork Reduction Act Notice.

(1) Entry No.

(28) Line No.	(29) Description of Merchandise			33. (A) Entered Value B. CHGS C. Relationship	34. (A) HTSUS Rate B. ADA/CVD Rate (C) I.R.C. Rate D. Visa No.	(35) Duty and I.R. Tax	
	30. (A) HTSUS No. B. ADA/CVD Case No.	31. (A) Gross Weight B. Manifest Qty.	(32) Net Quantity in HTSUS Units			Dollars	Cents

PART 1 – RECORD COPY

Customs Form 7501A (032796)

Box 21 of the Entry Summary requires the importer to show the manufacturer's/shipper's identification. This is a special code which must be constructed from the name and address of the manufacturer. Customs' instructions for the construction of such code is shown in Appendix I.

Column 33 of the Entry Summary requires the importer to state the entered value. CHGS stands for charges, and means those items such as foreign inland freight, ocean transportation, and ocean insurance, which are not dutiable. The "relationship" line is asking whether or not the seller and buyer are affiliated companies.

In addition to the customs duties, the importer is required to calculate the Merchandise Processing Fee (currently .21 percent) and the Harbor Maintenance Fee (currently .125 percent) and make payment at the times of entry (see Chapter 4, section S).

At the bottom of the form, the signer is required to declare that the statements in the Entry Summary fully disclose the true prices, values, quantities, rebates, drawbacks, fees, commissions, and royalties on the purchase, and that all goods or services provided to the seller of the merchandise either free or at reduced costs have been fully disclosed. The signer represents that it will immediately furnish to the appropriate U.S. Customs officer any information showing facts different than those stated in the Entry Summary. This is extremely important, because incorrect and therefore false statements on the Entry Summary can be the basis for both criminal and civil penalties assessed by the U.S. Customs Service against the importer. Such errors need not be intentional, and even accidental errors can be the basis for penalties.

K. Other Entries

In place of the Entry Summary used for consumption entries, transportation and exportation entries and immediate transportation entries, and entries for admission to a foreign trade zone are listed on their own forms. (Samples are shown in Figures 8–8 and 8–9. An Application for a Foreign Trade Zone Activity Permit is shown in Figure 8–10.) Transportation and exportation entries are used when the importer knows at the time of import that the product will be exported and the merchandise is merely being transported temporarily through the United States. No manipulation or modification of the merchandise is permitted during the time that it is in the United States, and the merchandise technically remains in Customs' custody. No customs duties are payable, but the importer must have a customs bond to guarantee payment of the customs duties in case the shipment is accidentally diverted into the United States. Immediate transit entries are used to move merchandise from the port of arrival to an inland port of entry nearer to the buyer where the customs entries and formalities are completed and the merchandise is released to the importer. The foreign trade zone entry is used when the goods are to be entered into a foreign trade zone for manipulation or further manufacturing. Finally, when merchandise is to be stored in a public or private customs-bonded warehouse for future consumption, entry is made on the regular Entry/Immediate Delivery or Entry Summary, marked with the type code for warehouse entries, in which case no estimated duties need be paid until the merchandise is later withdrawn for consumption.

(*Text continues on page 322.*)

Figure 8–8. Transportation entry.

O.M.B. No. 1515-0005

19 CFR 10.60, 10.61, 123.41, 123.42

Entry No. ....
Port ....
Date ....

TRANSPORTATION ENTRY AND MANIFEST OF GOODS SUBJECT TO CUSTOMS INSPECTION AND PERMIT

U.S. CUSTOMS SERVICE

Entry No. ....
Class of Entry ....
(I.T.) (T.E.) (WD.1E) (Drawback, etc.)

PORT CODE NO. .... FIRST U.S. PORT OF UNLADING ....

PORT OF .... DATE ....

Entered or imported by .... Importer/IRS # .... to be shipped in bond via .... (C.H.L. number) (Vessel or carrier) (Car number and initial) (Pier or station) consigned to Customs Port Director .... Final foreign destination .... (For exportations only)

Consignee .... (At customs port of exit or destination)

Foreign port of lading .... B/L No. .... Date of sailing ..../..../....
(Above information to be furnished only when merchandise is imported by vessel)

Imported on the .... (Name of vessel or carrier and motive power) Flag .... on .... (Date imported) via .... (Last foreign port)

Exported from .... (Country) on .... (Date) Goods now at .... (Name of warehouse, station, pier, etc.)

Marks and Numbers of Packages	Description and Quantity of Merchandise Number and Kind of Packages (Describe fully as per shipping papers)	Gross Weight in Pounds	Value (Dollars only)	Rate	Duty

G.O. No. .... ☐ Check if withdrawn for Vessel supplies (19 U.S.C. 1309)

CERTIFICATE OF LADING FOR TRANSPORTATION IN BOND AND/OR LADING FOR EXPORTATION FOR

.... (Port)

WITH THE EXCEPTIONS NOTED ABOVE, THE WITHIN-DESCRIBED GOODS WERE:

Delivered to the Carrier named above, for delivery to the Customs Port Director at destination sealed with Customs seals Nos. .... or the packages (were) (were not) labeled, or corded and sealed.

.... (Inspector)

.... (Date)

Laden on the—

.... (Vessel, vehicle, or aircraft)

which cleared for—

....

on .... (Date)

as verified by export records.

.... (Inspector)

.... (Date)

I truly declare that the statements contained herein are true and correct to the best of my knowledge and belief.

Entered or withdrawn by ....

To the Inspector: The above-described goods shall be disposed of as specified herein.

.... For the Port Director

Received from the Port Director of the above Customs location the merchandise described in this manifest for transportation and delivery into the custody of the customs officers at the port named above, all packages in apparent good order except as noted hereon.

.... Attorney or Agent of Carrier.

Customs Form 7512 (0598)

Figure 8–8. *(continued)*

INSTRUCTIONS

Consult customs officer or Part 18, Customs Regulations, for the appropriate number of copies required for entry, withdrawal, or manifest purposes.

For the purpose of transfer under the cartage or lighterage provisions of a proper bond to the place of shipment from the port of entry, extra copies bearing a stamp or notation as to their intended use may be required for local administration.

As the form is the same whether used as an entry or withdrawal or manifest, all copies may be prepared at the same time by carbon process, unless more than one vessel or vehicle is used, in which case a separate manifest must be prepared for each such vessel or vehicle.

Whenever this form is used as an entry or withdrawal, care should be taken that the kind of entry is plainly shown in the block in the upper right-hand corner of the face of the entry.

This form may be printed by private parties provided that the supply printed conforms to the official form in size, wording, arrangement, and quality and color of paper and ink. For sale by Customs Port Directors.

RECORD OF CARTAGE OR LIGHTERAGE
Delivered to Cartman or Lighterman in apparent good condition except as noted on this form

Conveyance	Quantity	Date	Delivered	Received	Received	
			(Inspector)	(Cartman or Lighterman)	(Date)	(Inspector)
			(Inspector)	(Cartman or Lighterman)	(Date)	(Inspector)
			(Inspector)	(Cartman or Lighterman)	(Date)	(Inspector)
Total						

(Warehouse proprietor)

CERTIFICATES OF TRANSFER. (If required)

I certify that within-described goods were transferred by reason of .... to .... on ...., at .... and sealed with .... or seals Nos. ...., and that goods were in same apparent condition as noted on original lading except ....

Inspector, Conductor, or Master

I certify that within-described goods were transferred by reason of .... to .... on ...., at .... and sealed with .... or seals Nos. ...., and that goods were in same apparent condition as noted on original lading except ....

Inspector, Conductor, or Master

INSPECTED

at ....

on .... (Date)

and seals found ....

Inspector.

If transfer occurs within city limits of a customs port or station, customs officers must be notified to supervise transfer.

INSPECTOR'S REPORT OF DISCHARGE AT DESTINATION

Port ...., *Station* ...., ... (Date)

TO THE PORT DIRECTOR: Delivering line .... Car No. .... Initial ....

Arrived .... (Date) Condition of car ...., of seals ...., of packages ....

Date of Delivery to Importer, or Gen. Order	Packages	No. and Kind of Entry or General Order	Bonded Truck or Lighter No.	Conditions, Etc.

I certify above report is correct.

.................., *Inspector.*

Paperwork Reduction Act Notice: The Paperwork Reduction Act of 1980 says we must tell you why we are collecting this information, how we will use it, and whether you have to give it to us. We ask for the information in order to carry out the laws and regulations administered by the U.S. Customs Service. These regulations and forms apply to carriers and brokers who are transporting merchandise in-bond from a port of importation to another Customs port prior to final release of the merchandise from Customs custody. This is governed by regulation and to your benefit.

Customs Form 7512 (0598)(Back)

Figure 8–9. Application for foreign trade zone admission.

OMB No. 1515-0086.

CENSUS USE ONLY

DEPARTMENT OF THE TREASURY
UNITED STATES CUSTOMS SERVICE

APPLICATION FOR FOREIGN-TRADE ZONE ADMISSION AND/OR STATUS DESIGNATION

19 CFR 146.22, 146.32, 146.35-146.37, 146.39-146.41, 146.44, 146.53, 146.66

1. ZONE NO. AND LOCATION *(Address)*

2. PORT CODE

3. IMPORTING VESSEL (& FLAG)/OTHER CARRIER	4. EXPORT DATE	5. IMPORT DATE	6. ZONE ADMISSION NO.

7. U.S. PORT OF UNLADING	8. FOREIGN PORT OF LADING	9. BILL OF LADING/AWB NO.	10 INWARD M'FEST NO.

11. INBOND CARRIER	12. I.T. NO. AND DATE	13. I.T. FROM *(Port)*

14. STATISTICAL INFORMATION FURNISHED DIRECTLY TO BUREAU OF CENSUS BY APPLICANT? ☐ YES ☐ NO

15. NO. OF PACKAGES AND COUNTRY OF ORIGIN CODE	16. DESCRIPTION OF MERCHANDISE	17. HTSUS NO.	18. QUANTITY (HTSUS)	19. GROSS WEIGHT	20. SEPARATE VALUE & AGGR CHGS.
		21. HARBOR MAINTENANCE FEE (19 CFR 24.24)			

2 2 .I hereby apply for admission of the above merchandise into the Foreign-Trade Zone. I declare to the best of my knowledge and belief that the above merchandise is not prohibited entry into the Foreign-Trade Zone within the meaning of section 3 of the Foreign-Trade Zones Act of 1934, as amended, and section 146.31, Customs Regulations.

23. I hereby apply for the status designation indicated:

☐ NONPRIVILEGED FOREIGN (19 CFR 146.42) ☐ PRIVILEGED FOREIGN (19 CFR 146.41) ☐ ZONE RESTRICTED (19 CFR 146.44) ☐ DOMESTIC (19 CFR 146.43)

24. APPLICANT FIRM NAME	25. BY *(Signature)*	26. TITLE	27. DATE
F.T.Z. AGREES TO RECEIVE MERCHANDISE INTO THE ZONE	28. FOR THE F.T.Z. OPERATOR *(Signature)*	29. TITLE	30. DATE
PERMIT — Permission is hereby granted to transfer the above merchandise into the Zone.	31. PORT DIRECTOR OF CUSTOMS: BY *(Signature)*	32. TITLE	33. DATE
PERMIT — The above merchandise has been granted the requested status.	34. PORT DIRECTOR OF CUSTOMS: BY *(Signature)*	35. TITLE	36. DATE

PERMIT TO TRANSFER

37. The goods described herein are authorized to be transferred: ☐ without exception ☐ except as noted below

38. CUSTOMS OFFICER AT STATION *(Signature)*	39. TITLE	40. STATION	41. DATE
42. RECEIVED FOR TRANSFER TO ZONE *(Driver's Signature)*	43. CARTMAN	44. CHL NO.	45. DATE

FTZ OPERATOR'S REPORT OF MERCHANDISE RECEIVED AT ZONE

46. To the Port Director of Customs: The above merchandise was received at the Zone on the date shown except as noted below:

47. FOR THE FTZ OPERATOR *(Signature)*	48. TITLE	49. DATE

(See back of form for Paperwork Reduction Act Notice.)

Customs Form 214 (08/00)

Figure 8–10. Application for foreign trade zone activity permit.

DEPARTMENT OF THE TREASURY
UNITED STATES CUSTOMS SERVICE

APPLICATION FOR FOREIGN-TRADE ZONE ACTIVITY PERMIT

19 CFR 146.52, 146.66

Approved through OMB No. 1515-0086.

1. ZONE NO. AND LOCATION *(Address)*

2. ZONE ADMISSION NO.

3. APPLICATION DATE

4. TYPE OF ACTIVITY FOR WHICH PERMIT REQUESTED

☐ Manipulate ☐ Manufacture ☐ Exhibit ☐ Destroy ☐ Temporary Removal

5. FULL DESCRIPTION OF THE ACTIVITY *(Include designation of the exact place in the zone where the operation is to be performed and, in the case of a proposed manipulation or manufacture, a statement as to whether merchandise with one zone status is to be packed, commingled, or combined with merchandise having a different zone status. If additional space required, attach separate sheet. If first application for manufacturing of this kind, state whether Foreign-Trade Zones Board has concurred in proposed operation.)*

6. ZONE LOT NO. OR UNIQUE IDENTIFIER	7. MARKS AND NUMBERS	8. DESCRIPTION OF MERCHANDISE	9. QUANTITY	10. WEIGHTS, MEASURES	11. ZONE STATUS

If any merchandise is to be manipulated in any way or manufactured, I agree to maintain the records provided for in sections 146.21(a), 146. 23, and 146.52(d) of the Customs Regulations and to make them available to customs officers for inspection.

12. APPLICANT FIRM NAME

13. BY *(Signature)*

14. TITLE

APPROVED BY FOREIGN-TRADE ZONE OPERATOR ➧

15. BY *(Signature)*

16. TITLE

PERMIT

The application made above is hereby approved and permission is granted to manipulate, manufacture, exhibit, destroy, or temporarily remove, as requested, on condition that the applicable regulations are complied with and the records required to be maintained will be available for inspection.

17. PORT DIRECTOR OF CUSTOMS: By *(Signature)*

18. TITLE

19. DATE

FTZ OPERATOR'S RETURN

20. TO THE PORT DIRECTOR OF CUSTOMS:

I certify that the goods described herein have been disposed of as directed except as noted below.

21. FOR THE FTZ OPERATOR: *(Signature)*

22. TITLE

23. DATE

Customs Form 216 (01/01)

L. Reconciliation

Sometimes, the importer may not have the final information necessary to complete and file an Entry Summary at the time of importation. In some cases, such situations may be routine, for example, when the importer is using the constructed value method of calculation or importing under Harmonized Tariff classification 9802 and the costs of manufacture or processing are based on standard costs subject to revision at the end of the accounting period. It can also arise when regional value content calculations are necessary for NAFTA eligibility. Customs has developed a program, first offered in 1998 as a prototype, but now extended indefinitely for filing the usual Entry Summary at the time of entry with the "best information available," but "flagging" individual entries or all entries during a specified period. The result is that the importer is allowed fifteen months (twelve months for NAFTA claims) to file a "reconciliation" containing the final information. This process is available for missing information relating to the correct value of the imported merchandise (including value under 9802), classification, and NAFTA eligibility. In order to participate in the program, it is necessary to file an application with the U.S. Customs Service and to provide a rider to the importer's customs bond to cover the open import entries. Once accepted, reconciliation may be filed either with entry-by-entry adjustments or with an aggregate calculation for all the entries covered by the reconciliation (aggregate adjustment is not allowed when the reconciler claims a refund and refunds may not be netted against duties owed).

M. GSP, CBI, ATPA, AGOA—Special Programs

Where the importer is claiming duty-free importation of the merchandise under the terms of the Generalized System of Preferences (GSP) program, it is necessary for the exporter to indicate that on the Entry Summary. If requested, the exporter must provide a "GSP Declaration" to U.S. Customs. (A sample is shown in Figure 8–11.) An importer wishing to claim the benefits of the Caribbean Basin Economic Recovery Act, the Andean Trade Preference Act, or the African Growth and Opportunity Act may also be required to obtain a similar declaration from the exporter. It is strongly recommended that an importer obtain such declarations from its exporter on a contemporaneous basis and keep them with its records against a future request by Customs.

N. NAFTA Certificate of Origin

Under the North American Free Trade Agreement, articles from Canada and Mexico may be imported duty-free or at a reduced rate of duty. In order to qualify for the tariff concession, however, the articles must be a product of Canada or Mexico under one of six eligibility rules. The exact method of determining eligibility is specific to each type of merchandise involved and must be checked in the Headnotes of the Harmonized Tariff Schedules. The importer must obtain a certificate from the Canadian or

Figure 8–11. GSP declaration.

GSP DECLARATION

I, ________________ (name), hereby declare that the articles described below were produced or manufactured in ______________________ (country) by means of processing operations performed in that country as set forth below and were also subjected to processing operations in the other country or countries which are members of the same association of countries as set forth below and incorporate materials produced in the country named above or in any other country or countries which are members of the same association of countries as set forth below.

		Processing operations performed on articles		Materials produced in a beneficiary developing country or member of the same association	
Number and date of invoices	Description of articles and quantity	Description of processing operation and country of processing	Direct costs of processing operations	Description of material, production process, and country of production	Cost of value of material

Signature ____________________ Date ____________________

Title ____________________ Address ____________________

Mexican exporter certifying the country of origin. (A sample of the certificate is shown in Figure 4–18.)

O. Specialized Products Customs Entry Forms

Food, drug, cosmetic, and medical device imports are monitored by the Food and Drug Administration (FDA) through the U.S. Customs Service. Consequently, importers of such items must file Customs Form 3461 (Entry/Immediate Delivery) with the FDA at the time of entry. The FDA inspector will then determine whether the product is being imported in compliance with U.S. law. Importers of certain radiation-producing electronic products such as televisions, monitors, microwave ovens, X-ray equipment, laser products, ultrasound equipment, sunlamps, CD Rom players, and cellular and cordless telephones are required to file FDA Form 2877 and importers of certain radio-frequency devices such as radios, tape recorders, stereos, televisions, and citizen's band radios are required to file FCC Form 740 (see Figures 8–12 and 8–13, respectively). Importers of plants are required to file U.S. Department of Agriculture Form 368, Notice of Arrival (see Figure 8–14). When importing (or exporting) fish or wildlife, U.S. Fish and Wildlife Service Form 3-177 must be filed (see Figure 8–15). Importers of textiles composed of cotton, wool, or man-made fibers are required to file certain declarations, a Single Country Declaration if a product of a single country (Figure 8–16), or a Multiple Country Declaration if processed in more than one country (Figure 8–17).

Importers of "precursor" and "essential" chemicals that can be used to manufacture illegal drugs are required to file DEA Form 486 (sometimes fifteen days in advance) (see Chapter 4, Section O and Figure 4–25).

P. Examination and Detention

After a customs entry is filed (Entry/Immediate Delivery or Entry Summary along with any other specialized forms), Customs will decide whether to examine the merchandise. If Customs elects not to examine the merchandise and is otherwise satisfied from the entry documents that the goods are entitled to entry, it will release the goods by stamping the Entry/Immediate Delivery or Entry Summary form, perforate the form, or issue an electronic release. This releases the merchandise and authorizes the transportation carrier to surrender possession of the goods to the importer and is effective when the importer presents the release to the transportation carrier.

If Customs elects to examine the merchandise it has a period of five days following presentation for examination to determine whether to detain the merchandise. If it determines to detain the merchandise it must give a notice to the importer within an additional five days specifying the reason for the detention, the anticipated length of the detention, and additional information being requested (see Figure 8–18). If Customs determines that the merchandise is not eligible for entry it may pursue the procedures for seizure and forfeiture of the merchandise. If Customs takes no action within thirty days after presentation of the merchandise for examination, the importer may

(Text continues on page 334.)

Figure 8–12. FDA Form 2877.

DEPARTMENT OF HEALTH AND HUMAN SERVICES PUBLIC HEALTH SERVICE FOOD AND DRUG ADMINISTRATION **DECLARATION FOR IMPORTED ELECTRONIC PRODUCTS SUBJECT TO RADIATION CONTROL STANDARDS**		*Form Approved OMB No. 0910-0025* *Expiration Date: 11/30/2003* **INSTRUCTIONS** 1. If submitting entries electronically through ACS/ABI, hold FDA-2877 in entry file. Do not submit to FDA unless requested. 2. If submitting paper entry documents, submit the following to FDA: a. 2 copies of Customs Entry Form (e.g. CF 3461, CF 3461 Alt, CF 7501, etc.) b. 1 copy of FDA 2877 c. Commercial Invoice(s) in English.	
U.S. CUSTOMS PORT OF ENTRY		ENTRY NUMBER	DATE OF ENTRY
NAME & ADDRESS OF MANUFACTURING SITE; COUNTRY OF ORIGIN		NAME & ADDRESS OF IMPORTER & ULTIMATE CONSIGNEE *(if not importer)*	
PRODUCT DESCRIPTION	QUANTITY *(Items/Containers)*	MODEL NUMBER(S) & BRAND NAME(S)	

DECLARATION: I / WE DECLARE THAT THE PRODUCTS IDENTIFIED ABOVE: ***(Mark X applicable statements, fill in blanks, & sign)***

☐ **A. ARE NOT SUBJECT TO RADIATION PERFORMANCE STANDARDS BECAUSE THEY:**

☐ 1. Were manufactured prior to the effective date of any applicable standard; Date of Manufacture ____________

☐ 2. Are excluded by the applicability clause or definition in the standard or by FDA written guidance.
Specify reason for exclusion ____________.

☐ 3. Are personal household goods of an individual entering the U.S. or being returned to a U.S. resident. (Limit: 3 of each product type).

☐ 4. Are property of a party residing outside the U.S. and will be returned to the owner after repair or servicing.

☐ 5. Are components or subassemblies to be used in manufacturing or as replacement parts (NOT APPLICABLE to diagnostic x-ray parts).

☐ 6. Are prototypes intended for on going product development by the importing firm, are labeled "FOR TEST/EVALUATION ONLY," and will be exported, destroyed, or held for future testing (i.e., not distributed). (Quantities Limited - see reverse.)

☐ 7. Are being reprocessed in accordance with P.L. 104-134 or other FDA guidance, are labeled "FOR EXPORT ONLY," and will not be sold, distributed, or transferred without FDA approval.

☐ **B. COMPLY WITH THE PERFORMANCE STANDARDS** WHICH ARE APPLICABLE AT DATE OF MANUFACTURE AND THAT A CERTIFICATION LABEL OR TAG TO THIS EFFECT IS AFFIXED TO EACH PRODUCT. COMPLIANCE DOCUMENTED IN:

☐ 1. Last annual report or Product/Initial report

____________ ____________ ____________

ACCESSION NUMBER of Report   Name of MANUFACTURER OF RECORD *(Filed report with FDA/CDRH)*

☐ 2. Unknown manufacturer or report number; State reason: ____________

☐ **C. DO NOT COMPLY WITH PERFORMANCE STANDARDS;** ARE BEING HELD UNDER A TEMPORARY IMPORT BOND; WILL NOT BE INTRODUCED INTO COMMERCE; WILL BE USED UNDER A RADIATION PROTECTION PLAN; AND WILL BE DESTROYED OR EXPORTED UNDER U.S. CUSTOMS SUPERVISION WHEN THE FOLLOWING MISSION IS COMPLETE:

☐ 1. Research, Investigations/Studies, or Training (attach Form FDA 766)

☐ 2. Trade Show/Demonstration; List dates & use restrictions ____________

☐ **D. DO NOT COMPLY WITH PERFORMANCE STANDARDS;** ARE HELD AND WILL REMAIN UNDER BOND; AND WILL NOT BE INTRODUCED INTO COMMERCE UNTIL NOTIFICATION IS RECEIVED FROM FDA THAT PRODUCTS HAVE BEEN BROUGHT INTO COMPLIANCE IN ACCORDANCE WITH AN FDA APPROVED PETITION. *(See Form FDA 766.)*

☐ 1. Approved Petition is attached.   ☐ 2. Petition Request is attached.   ☐ 3. Request will be submitted within 60 days.

WARNING: Any person who knowingly makes a false declaration may be fined not more than $10,000 or imprisoned not more than 5 years or both, pursuant to Title 18 U.S.C. 1001. Any person importing a non- compliant electronic product may also be subject to civil penalties of $1000 per violation, up to a maximum $300,000 for related violations pursuant to Title 21 U.S.C. 360pp.	SIGNATURE OF IMPORTER OF RECORD NAME AND TITLE OF RESPONSIBLE PERSON

Public reporting burden for this collection of information is estimated to average 0.2 hour per response, including the time for reviewing instructions, searching existing data sources, gathering and maintaining the data needed, and completing reviewing the collection of informat ion. Send comments regarding this burden estimate or any other aspect of this collection of information, including suggestions for reducing this burden to:

Food and Drug Administration
CDRH (HFZ-342)
2094 Gaither Road
Rockville, MD 20850

An agency may not conduct or sponsor, and a person is not required to respond to, a collection of information unless it display s a currently valid OMB control number.

FORM FDA 2877 (12/00)   PREVIOUS EDITION IS OBSOLETE.   Created by: PSC Media Arts (301) 443-2454   PAGE 1 OF 2 PAGES   EF

Figure 8–12. *(continued)*

INSTRUCTIONS TO IMPORTERS/BROKERS OF ELECTRONIC PRODUCTS

PURPOSE: The Form FDA 2877 must be completed for electronic products subject to Radiation Control Standards (21 CFR 1010 and 1020-1050) prior to entry into the United States. The local Food and Drug Administration (FDA) district office will review the declaration and notify the importer/agent if the products may be released into U.S. commerce or if they must be held under bond until exported, destroyed, or reconditioned. Until the shipment is released, it may be subject to redelivery for FDA examination.

PAPER OR ELECTRONIC SUBMISSION: Paper entries may be made by submitting the signed original FDA 2877 along with U.S. Customs forms to the local FDA district office; if electronic products are given a MAY PROCEED, a signed copy of CF 3461 will be returned, or if not given a MAY PROCEED, a FDA Notice of Action will be issued. For electronic entries, follow U.S. Customs Service ACS/ABI format and procedures, supported by a signed copy of this form or similar letter. Multiple entries of the same product and model families that are filed electronically may be supported by one form dated not more than 12 months previously.

DECLARATION: Select A, B, C, or D and then select the appropriate number; fill in requested information and sign. For electronic entries, AofC (affirmation of compliance) = RA#, RB#, RC#, or RD# (e.g., Radiation Declaration A5 = RA5). **Transmit model number using AofC code MDL and transmit brand name using FDA line level brand name field. If RA3 or RA6 is selected, you must transmit quantity (number of units) using the Quantity and Unit of Measure Pairs at the FDA line level.**

DECLARATION A: Importers should be prepared to demonstrate compliance to or non-applicability of FDA standards, regulations, or guidance. Components or sub-assemblies must be non-functioning. Products being reprocessed must be exported by the importer, without intermediate transfer of ownership. For RA3 the quantity limit is 3 and for RA6 the limit = 50 units TV products, microwave ovens, and Class 1 laser products limit = 200 units CD-ROM and DVD (digital versatile disc) laser products; see May 14, 1997, notice to industry issued by the Center for Devices and Radiological Health (CDRH).

DECLARATION B: If declaration RB1 is selected, provide the FDA Establishment Identifier (FEI) of the manufacturer who filed the radiation product/abbreviated report to FDA, CDRH, Rockville, Maryland. To transmit the accession number of that report use AofC code ACC. If the manufacturer cannot be determined or located, the importer must be able to provide evidence showing a certification (certifi.) label on each product and state reason: returned to orig exporter or certifi. label evidence. The new AofC codes (RB1, RB2) for this declaration will not be activated until a process is made available to determine the FEI of the responsible firm. Continue to use RAB in electronic transmission until the FEI query is available and industry is notified of its availability.

DECLARATION C: Noncompliant products may be imported only for research, investigations/studies, demonstration or training. They should be used only by trained personnel and under controlled conditions to avoid unnecessary radiation exposure. Product(s) will be detained by the local FDA district office. Since product(s) for which "C" Declarations are made will be under Temporary Import Bond (TIB) or equivalent, ultimate disposition is limited to export or destruction under U.S. Customs supervision when the purpose has been achieved or the length of time stated has expired. For purposes other than demonstration, the Form FDA 766, outlining protections, must be approved by FDA prior to use. The importer/broker must include with the FDA 766:

1. A full description of the subject electronic product(s).
2. The purpose for which the product(s) is being imported.
3. How the product(s) will be used.
4. Where the product(s) will be located.
5. The approximate length of time and dates the product(s) will be in this country.

For product(s) being used for trade shows/demonstrations, list the dates and use restrictions (Form FDA 766 is not required). A sign stating that the product does not comply with FDA performance standards must be displayed and viewable at all times during the use of product(s). All medical products, cabinet x-ray, or Class IIIb and IV lasers may NOT operate (turn on product(s)) at trade shows.

DECLARATION D: Noncompliant products must be brought into compliance with standards under FDA supervision and following a plan approved by FDA. The plan, documented on the Form FDA 766, must address technical requirements, labeling, and reporting. Some plans may need approval by both the CDRH and the local FDA district office. Use of this declaration is limited to occasional shipments; ongoing reconditioning is considered manufacturing that is handled through other means. Product(s) will be detained by the local FDA district office. An FDA 766 must be filed indicating the procedure intended to bring the product into compliance. This procedure will include a satisfactory corrective action plan and/or a product report. The FDA 766 must include all of the information requested under Declaration C. The approximate length of time will be for the amount of time needed to bring product(s) into compliance. Declaration D is also made for failure to provide reports, failure to certify, etc.

If an importer/broker intends to import equipment into the United States for purposes of research, investigation, studies, demonstrations, or training but also wishes to retain the option of bringing the product into compliance with the performance standard, check Declarations C and D on the FDA 2877 and insert the word "or " between the Affirmations. Note: The U.S. Customs Service will treat this entry as a "D" Declaration for purposes of duty. Such requests must be made on the FDA 766; include Items 1, 2, and 3 under Declaration C, a statement of the need to use the option "C" or "D" Declaration, a statement of how the product(s) will be brought into compliance and the approximate length of time necessary to evaluate or demonstrate the product(s) and the time necessary to bring the product(s) into compliance (both actions must be accomplished within the period of time granted by FDA). For electronic entries select Declaration RD3.

Ultimately, product(s) must be brought into compliance with the applicable standard in accordance with a corrective action plan which has been approved by the FDA. If the product(s) are not brought into compliance within the allotted time frame of the approved application and an extension is not requested of, or granted by, the FDA, the local FDA district office shall refuse entry on the shipment and require the product(s) to be either exported or destroyed under U.S. Customs supervision.

If additional guidance is needed, please contact your local FDA district office or consult the following FDA web pages: www.fda.gov/cdrh, www.fda.gov/ora/hier/ora_field_names.txt, and www.fda.gov/ora/compliance_ref/rpm_new2/contens.html.

[Ref: 21 U.S.C. 360mm, 21 CFR 1005, 19 CFR 12.90-12.91.] FDA: CP 7382.007/.007A

FORM FDA 2877 (12/00) PREVIOUS EDITION IS OBSOLETE. PAGE 2 OF 2 PAGES

Figure 8–13. FCC Form 740.

FEDERAL COMMUNCATIONS COMMISSION
Washington, D.C. 20554

Approved by OMB
3060-0059
Expires 08-31-2003

STATEMENT REGARDING THE IMPORTATION OF RADIO FREQUENCY DEVICES CAPABLE OF CAUSING HARMFUL INTERFERENCE

(Read instructions before completing form. Please type or print clearly in ink.)

Part I - All Blocks **MUST** Be Completed

Date of Entry	Entry Number	Port of Entry¹	Harmonized Tariff Number ²	Quantity of Item (not number of containers) ³

Device Model/Type Name or #	Trade Name	FCC ID	Description of Equipment

Manufacturer's Name and Address	Consignee's Name and Address	Importer's Name and Address

Printed or Typed Name of Importer or Consignee	Signature of Importer or Consignee	Date (Month/Day/Year)

Warning: Any person who knowingly makes a false declaration may be fined not more than $250,000 or imprisoned not more than 5 years, or both, pursuant to 18 U.S.C. § 1001.

Part II - With Regard to the Importation of the Described Radio Frequency Device(s), **I DECLARE THAT:**
(Place an "X" in only one box)

	1. The FCC has issued a grant of equipment authorization for the FCC ID listed above.
	2. An FCC grant of equipment authorization and an FCC ID are not required, but the equipment complies with FCC technical requirements.
	3. The described equipment is being imported in limited quantities for testing and evaluation for compliance with technical requirements or marketing suitability. The equipment will not be offered for sale or otherwise marketed. (See Instructions)
	4. The described equipment is being imported in limited quantities for demonstration at industry trade shows and will not be offered for sale or otherwise marketed. (See Instructions)
	5. The described equipment is being imported solely for export. It will not be offered for sale or otherwise marketed in the U.S.
	5(a). The described equipment is a non-U.S. standard cellular phone that can only function outside of the U.S. (See Instructions)
	6. The described equipment is being imported for use exclusively by the U.S. Government.
	7. Three or fewer radio receivers, computers, or other unintentional radiators as defined in Part 15 of the FCC Rules, are being imported for an individual's personal use and are not intended for sale.
	8. The described equipment is being imported for repair and will not be offered for sale or otherwise marketed.

1. Port of Entry Use Schedule D – Classification of U.S. Customs Districts and Ports for U.S. Foreign Trade Statistics – a four digit code i.e., New York City, NY 1001.
2. Harmonized Tariff Number – Harmonized Tariff Schedule of the United States.
3. This quantity must be total number of items, not number of containers.

FCC Form 740 August 2000

Figure 8–13. *(continued)*

INSTRUCTIONS FOR COMPLETION OF FCC FORM 740

This form must be completed for each radio frequency device, as defined in 47 U.S.C. 302 and 47 C.F.R. 2.801, which is imported into the Customs territory of the United States. The original shall be filed with the U.S Customs Service on or before the date the shipment is delivered to a U.S. port of entry.

The completed form must accompany each such entry.

The following are typical examples of devices that require the use of FCC Form 740: radio and TV receivers, converters, transmitters, transmitting devices, radio frequency amplifiers, microwave ovens, industrial heaters, ultrasonic equipment, transceivers, and computers.

Marketing, as used in this form (and 47 C.F.R. 2.1201 et seq.), means sale or lease (including advertising for sale or lease, or display at a trade show) or import, ship or distribute for the purpose of selling or leasing or offering for sale or lease.

Limited quantities, as used in this form, are the number specified in 47 C.F.R. 2.1204(a)(3). Waivers of this limit are infrequently granted but may be requested from the FCC office listed in 47 C.F.R. 2.1204(a)(3)(iii). Written waiver requests must contain specific information required by that office.

Equipment imported for test, evaluation or display (see import conditions 3 or 4 of Part II of this form) may not be marketed (sold or leased, offered for sale or lease, advertised, etc.). Display of this equipment must include markings clearly indicating that the device(s) are not eligible for sale. See 47 C.F.R. 2.803 for details regarding this labeling.

Wireless telephony devices that do not have a FCC grant of equipment authorization must either comply with 47 C.F.R. 2.1204(a)(5) or 47 C.F.R. 2.803(a)(2) (e.g., Verification or Declaration of Conformity is required).

The identification (company name and model number/FCC ID) of the radio frequency device specified on the front of this form must be identical to the company name and model number/FCC ID inscribed on the device. If the device being imported requires an equipment authorization to be issued by the FCC (e.g., Certification), it is important that the name of the company, description of the device and FCC ID specified on the grant of equipment authorization agree exactly with the same information shown on the front of this form. Any discrepancy between the information on this form and the FCC grant of equipment authorization may result in unnecessary delays, additional expense, or enforcement action.

FCC Form 740 may be reproduced provided the following conditions are met (see 47 C.F.R. 0.409, Commission Policy on Private Printing of FCC Forms.) Some of the conditions are listed below:

1. That private companies reproducing the form use a printing process resulting in a product that is comparable to the original document;

2. That private companies reproducing the form refrain from including therein or attaching thereto any advertising matter or deleting any material from the form;

3. That private companies reproducing the form exercise care that the form being reproduced or distributed is the current edition presently used by the FCC for the type of application involved: such private company to be advised that, though the Commission will endeavor to keep the public advised of revisions of the form, it cannot assume responsibility to the extent of eliminating any element or risk against overstocking, etc.

PAPERWORK REDUCTION ACT STATEMENT AND PRIVACY ACT STATEMENT

The solicitation of information requested on this form is authorized by the Communications Act of 1934, as amended. The information collected will be used to ascertain whether equipment authorization is required, and if so, whether or not it has been granted. If all the information is not provided the importation of this or other shipments may be delayed or prevented. Accordingly, every effort should be made to provide all necessary information. Your response is required to obtain a benefit.

Public reporting for this collection of information is estimated to average .04 seconds per response, including the time for reviewing instructions searching existing data sources, gathering and maintaining the data needed, and completing and reviewing the collection of information. Comments regarding this burden estimate or any other aspect of this collection of information, including suggestions for reducing the burden, should be sent to the Federal Communications Commission, Performance and Evaluations and Records Management, Washington, DC 20554, Paperwork Reduction Project (3060-0059) DO NOT SEND COMPLETED FORMS TO THIS ADDRESS. Individuals are not required to respond to a collection of information unless it displays a currently valid OMB control number.

THE FOREGOING NOTICE IS REQUIRED BY THE PRIVACY ACT OF 1974, P.L. 93-579, DECEMBER 31, 1974, 5 U.S.C. 552A(E)(3), AND THE PAPERWORK REDUCTION ACT OF 1995, P.L. 104-13, OCTOBER 1, 1995, 44 U.S.C. 3507.

FCC Form 740 instructions – Page 2 August 2000

Figure 8–14. U.S. Department of Agriculture Form 368 Notice of Arrival.

This notice informs the PPQ Office of the arrival of a restricted article at a port of entry.
The information is used to schedule required inspections. (7 CFR 319.321, .322, .352)

U.S. DEPARTMENT OF AGRICULTURE
ANIMAL PLANT HEALTH INSPECITON SERVICE
PLANT PROTECTION AND QUARANTINE

NOTICE OF ARRIVAL

INSTRUCTIONS: Immediately upon arrival, the permittee or his agent should prepare original and one copy of this form. Submit copies to the Plant Protection and Quarantine office having jurisdiction over the port of arrival.	1. NAME OF CARRIER
3. NAME OF PERMITTEE/CONSIGNEE	2. DATE OF ARRIVAL 4. PORT OF ARRIVAL 5. PERMIT NO.
6. PORT OF DEPARTURE	7. CUSTOMS ENTRY NO.
8. CONSIGNOR/SHIPPER (Name and Address)	9. PRESENT LOCATION 10. COUNTRY AND LOCALITY WHERE GROWN 11. NAME OF PREVIOUS U.S. PORT (In Transit Only) 12. I.T. NO. (In Transit Shipments Only)

13. DESCRIPTION OF PRODUCT

MARKS, BILL OF LADING AND/OR CONTAINER NO.	QUANTITY AND NET WEIGHT	COMMODITY

14. SIGNATURE OF IMPORTER OR BROKER	15. FULL BUSINESS ADDRESS OF IMPORTER OR BROKER
16. DATE SIGNED	TELEPHONE NUMBER (INCLUDE AREA CODE)

TO BE COMPLETED BY PPQ OFFICIAL

17. DISPOSITION OF PRODUCT	
18. SIGNATURE OF PPQ OFFICIAL	20. DATE SIGNED

PPQ FORM 368 (LOCALLY PRODUCED)Ekz.N.J. 6/00

Figure 8–15. U.S. Fish and Wildlife Service Form 3-177.

USFWS Form 3-177
(Revised 10/17/2000)
O.M.B. No. 1018-0012
Expiration Date: 10/31/2003

U.S. FISH AND WILDLIFE SERVICE

Page ___ of ___

DECLARATION FOR IMPORTATION OR EXPORTATION OF FISH OR WILDLIFE

Please Type or Print Legibly

1. Date of Import/Export: (mm/dd/yyyy) __ __ / __ __ / __ __ __ __
2. I/E License Number:
3. Indicate One: ☐ Import ☐ Export
4. Port of Clearance: ___ ___
5. Purpose Code: ___
6. Customs Entry Number:
7. Name of Carrier:
8. Air Way Bill or Bill of Lading Number:
   Master:
   House:
9. Transportation Code: ___
   ________ License ___ State
10. Bonded Location for Inspection:
11. Number of Cartons Containing Wildlife:
12. Package Markings Containing Wildlife:

13. (indicate one) (complete name / address / phone number)
☐ U.S. Importer of Record
☐ U.S. Exporter

14a. Foreign Supplier / Receiver:
(complete name / address / phone number)

14b. __ __

15. Customs Broker, Shipping Agent or Freight Forwarder:

Phone Number / Fax Number: Contact Name:

Species Code (Official Use)	16a. Scientific Name / 16b. Common Name	17a. Foreign CITES Permit Number / 17b. U.S. CITES Permit Number	18a. Description Code / 18b. Source	19a. Quantity / Unit / 19b. Total Monetary Value	20. Country of Origin of Animal

Knowingly making a false statement in a Declaration for Importation or Exportation of Fish or Wildlife may subject the declarant to the penalty provided by 18 U.S.C 1001 and 16 U.S.C. 3372 (d)

21. I certify under penalty of perjury that the information furnished is true and correct:

________ Signature ________ Date

________ Type or Print Name

FOR OFFICIAL USE ONLY

Action/Comments:

Wildlife Inspected:
None / Partial / Full

SEE REVERSE OF THIS FORM FOR PRIVACY ACT NOTICE

Figure 8–16. Textile declaration form—single country.

TEXTILE DECLARATION (Single Country Declaration)

I ________________ (name), declare that the articles listed below and covered by the invoice or entry to which this declaration relates are wholly the growth, product, or manufacture of a single foreign territory or country or insular possession of the United States, or were assembled in the single foreign territory or country or insular possession of the United States of fabricated components which are in the whole the product of the United States and/or the single foreign territory or country, or insular possession of the United States as identified below. I declare that the information set forth in this declaration is correct and true to the best of my information, knowledge, and belief.

A________________ (Country*)   C________________ (Country*)

B________________ (Country*)   D________________ (Country*)

Marks of identification, numbers	Description of article and quantity	Country* of origin	Date of exportation

Signature: ________________   Company: ________________

Name: ________________   Address: ________________

Title: ________________   Date: ________________

A 12 Rev. 01/31/97

Figure 8–17. Textile declaration form—multiple countries.

Multiple Country Textile Declaration

I,____________________, hereby declare that the articles described below and covered by the invoice or entry to which this declaration relates were exported from the country identified below on the dates listed and were subjected to assembling, manufacturing or processing operations in, and/or incorporate materials originating in, the foreign territory or country* or countries*, or the U.S. or an insular possession of the U.S., identified below. I declare that the information set forth in this declaration is correct and true to the best of my information, knowledge and belief.

A ____________________(country) C ____________________(country)

B ____________________(country) D ____________________(country) Page #____ of ____

Marks of Identification, numbers	Description of Articles and quantity Include stitch count if knit article	Description of Manufacturing and/or processing operations	*Color	Date and country of manufacture and/or processing		Materials		Country of Production		
				Country	Date of Export-ation	Description of Materials	Woven or Knit	Fabric	Yarn	Fiber

Date: ________________

Name: ________________

Signature: ________________

*Color:
B = Blue Denim
O = Other

Title: ________________

Company: ________________

Address: ________________

____

(*Country or Countries when used in this declaration includes territories and U.S. insular possessions. The country will be identified in the above declaration by the alphabetical designation appearing next to the named country.)

Figure 8–18. Notice of detention.

FORM A
cc importer

Detention Number ______________ **Date of Detention** ______________

NOTICE OF DETENTION/INADMISSIBILITY
CHICAGO DISTRICT

Entry Number ______________________
Importer ______________________
Broker ______________________
Broker Contact ______________________
Location of Merchandise ______________________

TREASURY
U S CUSTOMS SERVICE

Reason for Detention/Inadmissibility ______________________

____
____
____
____
____
____
____
____
____
____
____
____
____
____
____
____
____
____
____
____

Customs Inspector ______________________ **Phone** ______________ file a protest and seek expedited review in the appropriate court (usually the Court of International Trade).

Q. Liquidation Notices

After entry has been made, the U.S. Customs Service will process the entry documentation and liquidate the entry. When the importer makes the original entry, it is required to declare (state its opinion of) the correct classification, value, and duties payable and to tender those duties. After Customs has reviewed the classification, value, and duties payable and if it agrees with the importer's entry, liquidation will occur with no change. Currently, entries are scheduled by Customs for liquidation 314 days after entry. Sometimes, when information is needed by Customs to verify the classification or value (or when the importer requests for good cause), liquidation may be suspended up to a maximum of four years from the date of entry. The official notice of liquidation, known as the Bulletin Notice, is published in the port where entry was made at the Customs office. The official notice is the only one binding upon the Customs Service. (A sample form is shown as Figure 8–19, but these are generally now produced as a computer printout.) However, it is the practice of the U.S. Customs Service to mail to the importer (or its customs broker) a non-binding Courtesy Notice of Liquidation (Form 4333A), advising the importer that the entry has been liquidated. (A sample is shown in Figure 8–20.)

R. Notices of Redelivery

Where merchandise has been released to the importer and Customs comes to believe that the merchandise has been entered in violation of the laws of the United States, for example, the goods have not been properly marked with the foreign country of origin, Customs may issue a Notice of Redelivery (see Figure 8–21) to the importer. The form will specify the law that has been violated and will order the redelivery of the merchandise to Customs' custody within a thirty-day period. If no redelivery is made, the customs bond covering the entry of the merchandise will be declared forfeited and the importer will become liable for liquidated damages.

S. Requests for Reliquidation

When the entry is liquidated with an increase in duties, or, if the importer later discovers that its original entry was incorrect, another avenue available to the importer is to file a Request for Reliquidation. No particular form is required, but a request must be filed with the District Director of Customs at the port of entry within one year from the date of liquidation. Under the Customs regulations, reliquidation is permitted when the reason for the importer's original mistake is a clerical error or a mistake of fact—mistakes of law are not grounds for reliquidation. In this way, if the importer has overpaid the customs duties, it may seek a refund.

(Text continues on page 339.)

Figure 8–19. Bulletin notice of liquidation.

DEPARTMENT OF THE TREASURY
UNITED STATES CUSTOMS SERVICE

BULLETIN OF ENTRIES LIQUIDATED

DISTRICT

PORT

DATE

ENTRIES LIQUIDATED AND SO STAMPED (Increase, Decrease, No Change) 19 CFR 159.9 - 159.11

KIND OF ENTRY AND NUMBER	DATE OF ENTRY	IMPORTER OR CLAIMANT	REMARKS

Editions prior to 7-12-74 are obsolete.

If you are dissatisfied with the liquidated amount, a protest may be filed within 90 days of the date of notice of liquidation according to the procedures set forth in Part 174 of the Customs Regulations (19 CFR Part 174).

Customs Form 4333 (041092)

Figure 8–20. Courtesy notice of liquidation.

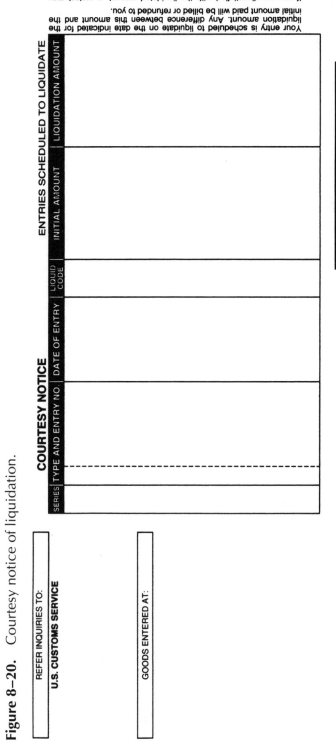

REFER INQUIRIES TO:
U.S. CUSTOMS SERVICE

GOODS ENTERED AT:

COURTESY NOTICE

ENTRIES SCHEDULED TO LIQUIDATE

SERIES	TYPE AND ENTRY NO.	DATE OF ENTRY	LIQUID CODE	INITIAL AMOUNT	LIQUIDATION AMOUNT

Your entry is scheduled to liquidate on the date indicated for the liquidation amount. Any difference between this amount and the initial amount paid will be billed or refunded to you.

If you are dissatisfied with the liquidated amount, a protest may be filed within 90 days of the date of liquidation according to the procedures set forth in Part 174 of the Customs Regulations (19 CFR Part 174).

IMPORTER NUMBER	DATE OF LIQUIDATION

+ INDICATES REFUND TO DIFFERENT ADDRESS
• INDICATES OFFSET OF REFUNDS

DEPARTMENT OF THE TREASURY
U.S. CUSTOMS SERVICE
Customs Form 4333A (041593)

Figure 8–21. Notice of redelivery.

DEPARTMENT OF THE TREASURY
UNITED STATES CUSTOMS SERVICE

NOTICE TO MARK
AND/OR
NOTICE TO REDELIVER

19 CFR 134.51, 134.52, 141.113

SECTION I (To Be Completed By Customs)

1. FROM

2. NAME OF CONTACT PERSON

3. TELEPHONE NO.

4. TO *(Importer of Record Name and Address)*:

ENTRY DATA

5. PORT OF ENTRY

6. ENTRY NO.

7. DATE OF ENTRY

8. BROKER OR IMPORTER FILE NO.

The merchandise described below is in violation of statutes(s)/regulation(s) as indicated, and cannot be entered into the commerce of the U.S. until brought into conformity as noted below in Section II. If it is not brought into conformity, redelivered, exported, or destroyed under Customs supervision within 30 days from the date of this Notice or the time specified by another Government agency having jurisdiction over the importation, **liquidated damages and/or criminal/civil penalties shall apply.**

9. STATUTE(S)/REGULATION(S) VIOLATED

☐ 19 U.S.C. 1304 (Section 304, Tariff Act of 1930) (Country of Origin Marking Violation) ☐ Other, Namely:

10. DESCRIPTION OF MERCHANDISE	11. QUANTITY	12. IDENTIFYING MARKS AND NUMBERS	13. SHIPPER/MANUFACTURER

SECTION II (To Be Completed By Customs)

14. ACTION REQUIRED OF IMPORTER

☐ Merchandise must be brought into compliance as specified below or returned to Customs custody within 30 days of this Notice or other time specified.

☐ Marking or other corrective action must be done under Customs supervision.

☐ Customs supervision of marking or other corrective action not required. After all merchandise has been brought into conformity with cited statute(s)/regulation(s), complete the certification below and return copy to Customs ☐ with ☐ without a sample.
WARNING: All merchandise must be retained until you are notified by Customs that corrective action is acceptable.

☐ Merchandise must be redelivered to Customs within 30 days from date of this notice or other time specified.

15. REMARKS/INSTRUCTIONS/OTHER ACTION REQUIRED OF IMPORTER

16. SIGNATURE OF CUSTOMS OFFICER

17. DATE

SECTION III – IMPORTER CERTIFICATION ***(To Be Completed By Importer/Authorized Agent)***
IMPORTER:— APPROPRIATE ITEMS MUST BE COMPLETED, SIGNED, AND DATED BEFORE ACCEPTANCE BY CUSTOMS.

☐ Merchandise to be ☐ exported. ☐ destroyed under Customs supervision in lieu of marking or other required corrective measures.

☐ I certify that all merchandise has been marked to indicate the country of origin as required by 19 U.S.C. 1304, or otherwise brought into compliance with cited statute(s) or regulation(s). Sample ☐ is ☐ is not submitted herein. Merchandise and original containers being held intact and available for Customs inspection at: *(Indicate Place and Phone No.)*

PLACE | DATE | TIME

I (We) guarantee the payment of all expenses incident to the above action.

SIGNATURE OF IMPORTER OR AUTHORIZED AGENT
X
TITLE | TELEPHONE | DATE

SECTION IV (To Be Completed By Customs)

☐ Merchandise excepted from marking under

☐ Merchandise has been legally marked or otherwise brought into conformity with cited statute(s)/regulation(s): ☐ under Customs supervision ☐ certification accepted.

☐ Merchandise was ☐ exported ☐ destroyed under Customs supervision. ☐ Other, namely:

SIGNATURE OF CUSTOMS OFFICER | DATE

PART 1 - IMPORTER - RETURN TO CUSTOMS

Customs Form 4647 (121592)

(*continues*)

Figure 8–21. *(continued)*

CUSTOMS FORM 4647 INFORMATION AND INSTRUCTIONS

This form is notification that the imported merchandise is not in conformity with statutory or regulatory requirements and must be marked, labeled, or otherwise brought into conformity with the applicable requirements within 30 days of this notice. The form also serves as a redelivery notice and requires redelivery to Customs custody within the specified time.

The following instructions are provided to assist importers in fulfilling the statutory and regulatory obligations.

SECTIONS I AND II: COMPLETED BY THE CUSTOMS SERVICE.

SECTION III: COMPLETED BY THE IMPORTER OF RECORD OR AUTHORIZED AGENT.

1. Retain control of all merchandise described on the Customs Form 4647. The merchandise must be held intact; it cannot be moved or distributed until authorized by the Customs Service.

2. Marking and/or additional instructions are provided in SECTION II.

3. Upon completion of marking, complete the appropriate item(s). **SIGNATURE MUST BE THAT OF THE IMPORTER OR AUTHORIZED AGENT.**

4. Identify the location where the merchandise will be available for Customs verification and provide a contact telephone number.

5. Upon completion of SECTION III, submit the "Return to Customs" copy of the form with a sample, if requested, to the office specified in SECTION I of this form. NOTE: Appropriate items must be completed, signed, and dated before acceptance by Customs.

SECTION IV: COMPLETED BY THE CUSTOMS SERVICE.

Upon return of the Customs Form 4647, Customs will review the form to ensure that SECTION III has been completed, signed, and dated by the IMPORTER OF RECORD OR AUTHORIZED AGENT, and take one of the following actions:

1. A Customs officer will visit your premises to verify your certification of marking and to notify you whether or not it is acceptable.

2. Notify you (in writing) that (a) the marking or corrective action is acceptable and the merchandise is officially released by Customs; or (b) the marking or corrective action is not acceptable and that the merchandise must be redelivered to Customs custody within the prescribed time.

If you have any questions or find that the marking procedure or other corrective action requires more than 30 days, contact the office indicated in SECTION I.

Customs Form 4647 (121592)(Back)

T. Requests for Information

Sometimes after the importer has made entry of merchandise, Customs will decide that it needs additional information in order to decide whether or not it agrees with the classification, value, and duties payable declared by the importer at the time of entry. Ordinarily, in such cases, Customs will send the importer a Request for Information (see Figure 8–22). A common request by Customs is for more information relating to the relationship between the seller and the buyer (Field 12.A.). Other standard items of request include brochures or catalogs describing the merchandise, or information about the dutiable and non-dutiable charges. Customs may request any information, however, which it believes is necessary in order to confirm that the merchandise is being entered in accordance with the customs laws of the United States.

U. Notices of Action

When Customs determines that it disagrees with the way in which the importer originally entered the merchandise, either prior to sending a Request for Information or after receiving a response to a Request for Information, it will send a Notice of Action to the importer (see Figure 8–23). A Notice of Action may indicate that the Customs Service proposes to take certain action and may invite the importer to give its reasons as to why that action should not be taken within twenty days, or the notice may specify that Customs has already taken that action. Often, the action taken is an advance in value, where Customs has determined that the value declared by the importer at the time of entry was too low, and therefore, additional customs duties are being assessed. Other actions, such as re-classification of the merchandise, can also be taken. If Customs receives no response from the importer, the entry will be liquidated in accordance with Customs' Notice. This means that additional customs duties will be payable and a bill for such duties will be sent to the importer.

V. Protests, Supplemental Information Letters, and Post-Entry Amendments

Where the entry is liquidated with an increase in duty or merchandise is excluded from entry, the importer may request a written explanation from Customs for the duty increase. The importer also may protest such action by filing Customs Form 19. (A sample Protest and Instructions form is shown in Figure 8–24.) This form must be filed within ninety days of the bulletin notice of liquidation or date of exclusion. Consequently, if the importer does not receive the courtesy notice of liquidation and the entry is liquidated by posting the bulletin at the customs house, the importer may miss the protest deadline. For this reason, it is important for the importer to establish a procedure whereby the status of entries is checked from time to time at the customs

(*Text continues on page 345.*)

Figure 8–22. Request for information.

DEPARTMENT OF THE TREASURY
UNITED STATES CUSTOMS SERVICE

REQUEST FOR INFORMATION

Approved through 01/31/96. OMB No. 1515-0068.
See back of form for Paperwork Reduction Act Notice.

1. DATE OF REQUEST

2. DATE OF ENTRY AND IMPORTATION

(General Information/Instructions on reverse) 19 CFR 151.11

3. MANUFACTURER/SELLER/SHIPPER | 4. CARRIER | 5. ENTRY NO.

6A. INVOICE DESCRIPTION OF MERCHANDISE | 6B. INVOICE NO. | 7. HTSUS ITEM NO.

8. COUNTRY OF ORIGIN/EXPORTATION | 9. CUSTOMS BROKER AND REFERENCE OR FILE NO.

10. TO: | 11. FROM:

PRODUCTION OF DOCUMENTS AND/OR INFORMATION REQUIRED BY LAW: If you have provided the information requested on this form to U.S. Customs at other ports, please indicate the port of entry to which it was supplied, and furnish a copy of your reply to this office, if possible. | A. PORT | B. DATE INFORMATION FURNISHED

12. PLEASE ANSWER INDICATED QUESTION(S)

☐ A. Are you related (see reverse) in any way to the seller of this merchandise? If you are related, please describe the relationship, and explain how this relationship affects the price paid or payable for the merchandise.

☐ B. Identify and give details of any additional costs/expenses incurred in this transaction, such as.

- ☐ (1) packing
- ☐ (2) commissions
- ☐ (3) proceeds that accrue to the seller (see reverse)
- ☐ (4) assists (see reverse)
- ☐ (5) royalties and/or license fees (see reverse)

13. PLEASE FURNISH INDICATED ITEM(S)

☐ A. Copy of contract (or purchase order and seller's confirmation thereof) covering this transaction, and any revisions thereto.

☐ B. Descriptive or illustrative literature or information explaining what the merchandise is, where and how it is used, and exactly how it operates.

☐ C. Breakdown of components, materials, or ingredients by weight and the actual cost of the components at the time of assembly into the finished article.

☐ D. Submit samples:
Article no. and description ____
from container no. ____
mark(s) and no. ____
Samples consumed in analysis, and other samples whose return is not specifically requested, will not normally be returned.

☐ E. See Item 14 below.

14. CUSTOMS OFFICER MESSAGE

15. REPLY MESSAGE *(Please print or type. Use additional sheets if more space is needed.)*

16. CERTIFICATION | It is required that an appropriate corporate/company official execute this certificate and/or endorse all correspondence in response to the information requested. (NOTE: NOT REQUIRED IF FOREIGN FIRM COMPLETES THIS FORM.)

I hereby certify that the information furnished herewith or upon this form in response to this inquiry is true and correct, and that any samples provided were taken from the shipment covered by this entry.

A. NAME AND TITLE/POSITION OF SIGNER *(Owner, Importer, or Corporate/Company Official--Print or Type)* | B. SIGNATURE | C. TELEPHONE NO. | D. DATE

17. CUSTOMS OFFICER *(Print or Type)* | 18. TEAM DESIGNATION | 19. TELEPHONE NO.

Customs Form 28 (030195)

ORIGINAL

(continues)

Figure 8–22. *(continued)*

GENERAL INFORMATION AND INSTRUCTIONS

1. The requested information is necessary for proper classification and/or appraisement of your merchandise and/or for insuring import compliance of such merchandise. Your reply is required in accordance with section 509(a), Tariff Act of 1930, as amended (19 U.S.C. 1509).
2. All information, documents, and samples requested must relate to the shipment of merchandise described on the front of this form.
3. Please answer all indicated questions to the best of your knowledge.
4. All information submitted will be treated confidentially.
5. If a reply cannot be made within 30 days from the date of this request or if you wish to discuss any of the questions designated for your reply, please contact the Customs officer whose name appears on the front of this form.
6. Return a copy of this form with your reply.

DEFINITIONS OF KEY WORDS IN BLOCK 12.

Question A: RELATED--The persons specified below shall be treated as persons who are related:

(A) Members of the same family, including brothers and sisters (whether by whole or half blood), spouse, ancestors, and lineal descendants.

(B) Any officer or director of an organization and such organization.

(C) An officer or director of an organization and an officer or director of another organization, if each such individual is also an officer or director in the other organization.

(D) Partners.

(E) Employer and employee.

(F) Any person directly or indirectly owning, controlling, or holding with power to vote, 5 percent or more of the outstanding voting stock or shares of any organization and such organization.

(G) Two or more persons directly or indirectly controlling, controlled by or under common control with, any person.

PRICE PAID OR PAYABLE--This term is defined as the total payment (whether direct or indirect and exclusive of any costs, charges, or expenses incurred for transportation, insurance, and other C.I.F. charges) made, or to be made, for imported merchandise by the buyer to, or for the benefit of, the seller.

Question B: ASSISTS--The term "assist" means any of the following if supplied directly or indirectly, and free of charge or at reduced cost, by the buyer of the imported merchandise for use in connection with the production or the sale for export to the United States of the merchandise:

(1) Materials, components, parts, and similar items incorporated in the imported merchandise.

(2) Tools, dies, molds,and similar items used in the production of the imported merchandise.

(3) Merchandise consumed in the production of the imported merchandise.

(4) Engineering, development, artwork, design work, and plans and sketches that are undertaken elsewhere than in the United States and are necessary for the production of the imported merchandise.

PROCEEDS THAT ACCRUE TO THE SELLER--This term is defined as the amount of any subsequent resale, disposal, or use of the imported merchandise that accrues, directly or indirectly, to the seller.

ROYALTIES AND/OR LICENSE FEES--This term relates to those amounts that the buyer is required to pay, directly or indirectly, as a condition of the sale of the imported merchandise for exportation to the United States.

PAPERWORK REDUCTION ACT NOTICE: The Paperwork Reduction Act of 1980 says we must tell you why we are collecting this information, how we will use it, and whether you have to give it to us. We ask for the information to carry out the laws of the United States. We need it to ensure importers/brokers are complying with these laws and to allow us to properly appraise and classify imported merchandise or correct duties and determine import admissibility, where appropriate. Your response is mandatory.

Statement Required by 5 CFR 1320.21: The estimated average burden associated with this collection of information is 33 minutes per respondent or recordkeeper depending on individual circumstances. Comments concerning the accuracy of this burden estimate and suggestions for reducing this burden should be directed to U.S. Customs Service, Paperwork Management Branch, Washington DC 20229. ***DO NOT** send completed form(s) to this office.*

Customs Form 28 (030195)(Back)

Figure 8–23. Notice of action.

DEPARTMENT OF THE TREASURY
UNITED STATES CUSTOMS SERVICE
19 CFR 152.2

NOTICE OF ACTION
This is NOT a Notice of Liquidation

1. DATE OF THIS NOTICE			
2. CARRIER	3. DATE OF IMPORTATION	4. DATE OF ENTRY	5. ENTRY NO.
6. MFR/SELLER/SHIPPER	7. COUNTRY	8. CUSTOMS BROKER AND FILE NO.	
9. DESCRIPTION OF MERCHANDISE			
10. TO ▶		11. FROM	

12. THE FOLLOWING ACTION, WHICH WILL RESULT IN AN INCREASE IN DUTIES,—

☐ IS **PROPOSED** — IF YOU DISAGREE WITH THIS PROPOSED ACTION, PLEASE FURNISH YOUR REASONS IN WRITING TO THIS OFFICE WITHIN 20 DAYS FROM THE DATE OF THIS NOTICE. AFTER 20 DAYS THE ENTRY WILL BE LIQUIDATED AS PROPOSED.

☐ HAS BEEN **TAKEN** — THE ENTRY IS IN THE LIQUIDATION PROCESS AND IS NOT AVAILABLE FOR REVIEW IN THIS OFFICE.

TYPE OF ACTION

A. ☐ RATE ADVANCE

B. ☐ VALUE ADVANCE

C. ☐ EXCESS ☐ WEIGHT ☐ QUANTITY

D. ☐ OTHER *(See below)*

13. EXPLANATION *(Refer to Action letter designations above)*

14. CUSTOMS OFFICER *(Print or Type)*	15. TEAM DESIGNATION	16. TELEPHONE

Customs Form 29 (031795)

ORIGINAL (WHITE) - IMPORTER

Figure 8–24. Protest and instructions.

DEPARTMENT OF THE TREASURY
UNITED STATES CUSTOMS SERVICE

PROTEST

Pursuant to Sections 514 & 514(a), Tariff Act of 1930 as amended, 19 CFR Part 174 et. seq.

Form Approved, OMB No. 1515-0056. See back of form for Paperwork Reduction Act Notice.

1. PROTEST NO. *(Supplied by Customs)*

NOTE: If your protest is denied, in whole or in part, and you wish to CONTEST the denial, you may do so by bringing a civil action in the U.S. Court of International Trade within 180 days after the date of mailing of Notice of Denial. You may obtain further information concerning the institution of an action by writing the Clerk of U.S. Court of International Trade, One Federal Plaza, New York NY 10007 (212-264-2800).

2. DATE RECEIVED *(Customs Use Only)*

SECTION I – IMPORTER AND ENTRY IDENTIFICATION

3. PORT

4. IMPORTER NO.

6. NAME AND ADDRESS OF IMPORTER OR OTHER PROTESTING PARTY

5. ENTRY DETAILS

PORT CODE	FILER CODE	ENTRY NO.	CHECK DIGIT	DATE OF ENTRY	DATE OF LIQUIDATION

SECTION II – DETAILED REASONS FOR PROTEST

7. With respect to each category of merchandise, set forth, separately, (1) each decision protested, (2) the claim of the protesting party, and (3) the factual material and legal arguments which are believed to support the protest. All such material and arguments should be specific. General statements of conclusions are not sufficient.

(Attach Additional Sheets if necessary.)

SECTION III – REQUEST FOR DISPOSITION IN ACCORDANCE WITH ACTION ON PREVIOUSLY FILED PROTEST

Protesting party may request disposition in accordance with the action taken on a previously filed protest that is the subject of a pending application for further review and is alleged to involve the same merchandise and the same issues. (See 19 CFR 174.13(a)(7).) To request such disposition, enter in Blocks 8 and 9 the protest number and date of receipt of such previously filed protest. ▶

8. PROTEST NO. OF PREVIOUSLY FILED PROTEST

9. DATE OF RECEIPT

SECTION IV – SIGNATURE AND MAILING INSTRUCTIONS

10. NAME AND ADDRESS OF PERSON TO WHOM ANY NOTICE OF APPROVAL OR DENIAL SHOULD BE SENT

11. NAME, ADDRESS, AND CUSTOMS IDENTIFICATION NUMBER TO WHICH REFUND SHOULD BE SENT

12. IF FILING AS ATTORNEY OR AGENT, TYPE OR PRINT YOUR NAME, ADDRESS AND IMPORTER NUMBER, IF ANY

13. SIGNATURE AND DATE

X

(Optional) **SECTION V – APPLICATION FOR FURTHER REVIEW** *(Fill in Item 1 above if this is a separate Application for Further Review.)*

14. MARK BOX CORRESPONDING TO YOUR ANSWER TO EACH OF THE FOLLOWING QUESTIONS

YES	NO	
☐	☐	(A) Have you made prior request of a port director for a further review of the same claim with respect to the same or substantially similar merchandise?
☐	☐	(B) Have you received a final adverse decision from the U.S. Court of International Trade on the same claim with respect to the same category of merchandise or do you have action involving such a claim pending before the U.S. Court of International Trade?
☐	☐	(C) Have you previously received an adverse administrative decision from the Commissioner of Customs or his designee or have you presently pending an application for an administrative decision on the same claim with respect to the same category of merchandise?

15. JUSTIFICATION FOR FURTHER REVIEW UNDER THE CRITERIA IN 19 CFR 174.24 AND 174.25

(Attach Additional Sheets If Necessary.)

SECTION VI – DECISION *(CUSTOMS USE ONLY)*

16. APPLICATION FOR FURTHER REVIEW ☐ Approved* ☐ Denied for the reason checked: ☐ Untimely filed ☐ Does not meet criteria ☐ Other, namely
EXPLANATION:

*When further review only is approved the decision on the protest is suspended, pending issuance of a protest review decision.

17. PROTEST ☐ Approved ☐ Rejected as non-protestable ☐ Denied in full for the reason checked: ☐ Denied in part for the reason checked: ☐ Untimely filed ☐ See attached protest review decision ☐ Other, namely
EXPLANATION:

18. TITLE OF CUSTOMS OFFICER

19. SIGNATURE AND DATE

Editions Prior to 090883 Are Obsolete.

Customs Form 19 (120495)

(*continues*)

Figure 8–24. *(continued)*

Paperwork Reduction Act Notice: The U.S. Customs Service requires the information in this form to ensure compliance with Customs laws, to identify documents and statements in order to allow or deny the protest, and to advise protestant. Your response is required to obtain a benefit.

The estimated average burden associated with this collection of information is 1 hour and 3 minutes per respondent or recordkeeper depending on individual circumstances. Comments concerning the accuracy of this burden estimate and suggestions for reducing this burden should be directed to U.S Customs Service, Paperwork Management Branch, Washington DC 20229. *DO NOT send completed form(s) to this office.*

INSTRUCTIONS

PLEASE REFER TO: Part 174, Customs Regulations

Definitions:

"Liquidation" means the final computation or ascertainment of the duties or drawback accruing on an entry.

"Protest" means the seeking of review of a decision of an appropriate Customs officer. Such a review may be conducted by Customs officers who participated directly in the underlying decision.

"Further Review" means a request for review of the protest to be performed by a Customs officer who did not participate directly in the protested decision, or by the Commissioner, or his designee as provided in the Customs Regulations. This request will only be acted upon in the event that the protest would have been denied at the initial level of review. If you are filing for further review, you must answer each question in Item 14 on Customs Form 19 and provide justification for further review in Item 15.

What matters may be protested?

1. The appraised value of merchandise;
2. The classification and rate and amount of duties chargeable;
3. All charges within the jurisdiction of the Secretary of the Treasury;
4. Exclusion of merchandise from entry or delivery, or demand for redelivery;
5. The liquidation or reliquidation of an entry;
6. The refusal to pay a claim for drawback; and
7. The refusal to reliquidate an entry under Sec. 520(c), Tariff Act of 1930, as amended.

Who may file a protest or application for further review?

1. The importer or consignee shown on the entry papers, or their sureties;
2. Any person paying any charge or exaction;
3. Any person seeking entry or delivery, or upon whom a demand for redelivery has been made;
4. Any person filing a claim for drawback; or
5. Any authorized agent of any of the persons described above.

Where to file protests:

With the port director whose decision is protested (at the port where entry was made).

When to file a protest:

Within 90 days after either: 1) the date of notice of liquidation or reliquidation; or 2) the date of the decision, involving neither a liquidation nor reliquidation, as to which the protest is made (e.g., the date of an exaction, the date of written notice excluding merchandise from entry or delivery or demand for redelivery); or 3) a surety may file within 90 days after the date of mailing of notice of demand for payment against its bond.

Contents of protest:

1. Name and address of the protestant;
2. The importer number of the protestant;
3. The number and date(s) of the entry(s);
4. The date of liquidation of the entry (or the date of a decision);
5. A specific description of the merchandise;
6. The nature of and justification for the objection set forth distinctly and specifically with respect to each category, claim, decision, or refusal;
7. The date of receipt and protest number of any protest previously filed that is the subject of a pending application for further review; and
8. If another party has not filed a timely protest, the surety's protest shall certify that the protest is not being filed collusively to extend another authorized person's time to protest.

NOTE: Under Item 5, Entry Details, "Check Digit" information is optional; however, Customs would appreciate receiving the information if you can provide it. All attachments to a protest (other than samples or similar exhibits) must be filed in quadruplicate.

Customs Form 19 (120495)(Back)

office. Similarly, sometimes liquidation will be suspended. In general, entries will be liquidated 314 days from the date of entry. If an entry is not liquidated, the importer should investigate why it is being suspended to avoid a future liquidation with a duty increase long after the time of importation. A protest gives the importer an additional opportunity to present its reasons why the entry should be liquidated as originally entered with no increase in duties. Customs must grant or deny a protest within two years of filing (thirty days for excluded merchandise). In order to obtain a decision more quickly, ninety days after a protest has been filed, a request for accelerated disposition may be filed, which Customs must act upon within an additional thirty days. In certain circumstances an importer may request that its protest be reviewed by Customs Headquarters as an Application for Further Review.

If the importer (or its customs broker) makes an error and overpays the customs duties owed, Customs has instituted two procedures that allow the importer to seek a refund without waiting for the 314 days to expire to file a protest. The first is to file a Supplemental Information Letter (SIL) at the port where entry was made. SILs can also be used to "amend" an entry where the importer has underpaid the duties owed. The second procedure is the Post-Entry Amendment Program. Under this program, in some cases corrections can be made on a quarterly basis.

W. Administrative Summons

If Customs suspects that a violation of the customs laws has occurred, it may issue a summons to an importer or to third-party record-keepers, such as customs brokers, accountants, and attorneys, requesting them to produce documents or to give testimony relating to the importations. (A sample summons is shown in Figure 8–25.) When a summons is being issued to a third-party record-keeper, Customs sends a copy of the notice to the importer of record (see Figure 8–26). If the recipient does not comply with the summons, the U.S. Customs Service can seek an order from the U.S. District Court compelling the importer to produce the documents or provide the testimony requested. Upon receipt of a summons and before providing any documents or answering any questions from a Customs agent, the importer should consult with its attorney.

X. Search Warrants

When Customs believes a criminal or intentional violation of the customs laws has occurred, it may apply to the appropriate U.S. district court for a search warrant to inspect the premises or seize records of an importer. A sample affidavit, which must be filed with the court, and a search warrant are shown in Figures 8–27 and 8–28, respectively. When Customs agents approach an importer with a search warrant, the importer should realize that the case is a criminal case and that individuals as well as the company may be subject to fines or imprisonment. The importer should not discuss the case with the Customs agent without consulting its attorney.

(*Text continues on page 350.*)

Figure 8–25. Administrative summons.

1 TO (Name, Address, City, State, ZIP)

DEPARTMENT OF THE TREASURY
UNITED STATES CUSTOMS SERVICE

SUMMONS

TO APPEAR AND/OR PRODUCE RECORDS

By the service of of this summons upon you, YOU ARE HEREBY SUMMONED AND REQUIRED TO:

(A) ☐ APPEAR before the Customs officer named in Block 2 below at the place, date, and time indicated, to testify and give information.
(B) ☐ PRODUCE the records (including statements, declarations, and other documents) indicated in Block 3 below, before the Customs officer named in Block 2 at the place, date, and time indicated.

Your testimony and/or the production of the indicated records is required in connection with an investigation or inquiry to ascertain the correctness of entries, to determine the liability for duties, taxes, fines, penalties or forfeitures, and/or to insure compliance with the laws or regulations administered by the U.S. Customs Service.

Failure to comply with this summons will render you liable to proceedings in a U.S. District Court to enforce compliance with this summons as well as other sanctions

2 (A) NAME, TITLE, ADDRESS, AND TELEPHONE NUMBER OF CUSTOMS OFFICER BEFORE WHOM YOU ARE TO APPEAR

(B) DATE

(C) TIME

3 RECORDS REQUIRED TO BE PRODUCED FOR INSPECTION

Issued under authority of section 509, Tariff Act of 1930, as amended by Public Law 95-410 (19 U.S.C. 1509); Customs Delegation Order No. 55 (44 F.R. 2217).

4 NAME OF PERSON AUTHORIZED TO SERVE SUMMONS:

or any other Customs officer.

5 DATE OF ISSUE

COMMISSIONER OF CUSTOMS

BY
(Signature):

6 NAME, TITLE, ADDRESS, AND TELEPHONE NUMBER OF PERSON ISSUING THIS SUMMONS

If you have any questions regarding this summons, contact the Customs officer identified in Block 2.

Customs Form 3115 (101091)

*U.S. GPO: 1991-312-754/50236

Figure 8–26. Summons notice to importer of record.

TO

DEPARTMENT OF THE TREASURY
UNITED STATES CUSTOMS SERVICE

SUMMONS NOTICE

section 509(c)(2), Tariff Act of 1930, as amended

REFERENCE

Enclosed is a copy of a Summons served by the United States Customs Service to examine records or to request testimony relating to records of your business transactions or affairs which have been made or kept by the person named in Block 1 of the Summons. If you object to the examination of these records, you may stay (prevent) examination of the records until a summons enforcement proceeding is commenced in court. Compliance with the Summons will be stayed if, not later than the day before the date indicated in Block 2 of the Summons, you advise the person summoned (the person named in Block 1), in writing, not to comply with the Summons, and you send a copy of that notice by registered or certified mail to the officer who issued the Summons at the address shown in Block 6 of the Summons.

The United States Customs Service may begin an action to enforce the Summons in the appropriate United States District Court. In such cases, you will be notified and you will have the right to intervene and present your objections before the court. The court will decide whether the person summoned should be required to comply with the Summons.

If the court issues an order to comply with the Summons and the person summoned fails to comply, the court may punish such failure as a contempt of court. Other sanctions may be provided by law.

If you have any questions regarding this matter, please contact the Customs officer before whom the summoned person is required to appear. The officer's name and telephone number are given in Block 2 of the Summons.

Customs Form 3115-B (1-19-79)

Figure 8–27. Affidavit.

Affidavit for
Search Warrant

Form A. O. 106

United States District Court

FOR THE

Commissioner's Docket No.

Case No.

UNITED STATES OF AMERICA

vs.

AFFIDAVIT FOR
SEARCH WARRANT

BEFORE — Name of Commissioner — Address of Commissioner

The undersigned being duly sworn deposes and says:

That he (has reason to believe) (is positive)[1] that (on the person of) (on the premises known as)

in the District of

there is now being concealed certain property, namely — here describe property

which are — here give alleged grounds for search and seizure

And that the facts tending to establish the foregoing grounds for issuance of a Search Warrant are as follows:

Signature of Affiant.

Official Title, if any.

Sworn to before me, and subscribed in my presence, , 19

United States Commissioner.

[1] The Federal Rules of Criminal Procedure provide: "The warrant shall direct that it be served in the daytime, but if the affidavits are positive that the property is on the person or in the place to be searched, the warrant may direct that it be served at any time." (Rule 41C)

Figure 8–28. Search warrant.

Form A. O. 93 (Revised June 1964) **Search Warrant**

United States District Court

FOR THE

____

UNITED STATES OF AMERICA vs.	Commissioner's Docket No. Case No. **SEARCH WARRANT**

To

Affidavit having been made before me by

that he { has reason to believe / is positive[1] } that { on the person of / on the premises known as }

in the District of

there is now being concealed certain property, namely

here describe property

which are

here give alleged grounds for search and seizure

and as I am satisfied that there is probable cause to believe that the property so described is being concealed on the { person / premises } above described and that the foregoing grounds for application for issuance of the search warrant exist.

You are hereby commanded to search forthwith the { person / place } named for the property specified, serving this warrant and making the search { in the daytime / at any time in the day or night[1] } and if the property be found there to seize it, leaving a copy of this warrant and a receipt for the property taken, and prepare a written inventory of the property seized and return this warrant and bring the property before me within ten days of this date, as required by law.

Dated this day of , 19

______________________________,
U. S. Commissioner.

[1] The Federal Rules of Criminal Procedure provide: "The warrant shall direct that it be served in the daytime, but if the affidavits are positive that the property is on the person or in the place to be searched, the warrant may direct that it be served at any time." (Rule 41C)

(*continues*)

Figure 8–28. *(continued)*

[*reverse*]

RETURN

I received the attached search warrant , 19 , and have executed it as follows:

On , 19 at o'clock M, I searched { the person / the premises } described in the warrant and

I left a copy of the warrant with ....
name of person searched or owner or "at the place of search"
together with a receipt for the items seized.

The following is an inventory of property taken pursuant to the warrant:

This inventory was made in the presence of

and

I swear that this Inventory is a true and detailed account of all the property taken by me on the warrant.

....

Subscribed and sworn to and returned before me this day of , 19

....,
U. S. Commissioner.

Y. Grand Jury Subpoenas

When Customs investigates a criminal violation of the customs laws, the U.S. Attorney may convene a grand jury. The grand jury may subpoena persons employed by the importer or other persons to testify before the grand jury. Obviously, these are extremely serious proceedings, and before any person testifies before a grand jury, he should be advised by legal counsel. (A sample subpoena is shown in Figure 8–29.)

Z. Seizure Notices

When Customs believes that goods have been imported into the United States in violation of the customs laws, it may issue a seizure notice and information for claim-

Figure 8–29. Grand jury subpoena.

United States District Court

______________ DISTRICT OF ______________

TO: SAMPLE ONLY

SUBPOENA TO TESTIFY BEFORE GRAND JURY

SUBPOENA FOR:
☐ PERSON ☐ DOCUMENTS OR OBJECT(S)

YOU ARE HEREBY COMMANDED to appear and testify before the Grand Jury of the United States District Court at the place, date, and time specified below.

PLACE	ROOM
	DATE AND TIME

YOU ARE ALSO COMMANDED to bring with you the following document(s) or object(s):*

VOID SAMPLE ONLY

☐ *Please see additional information on reverse*

This subpoena shall remain in effect until you are granted leave to depart by the court or by an officer acting on behalf of the court.

CLERK	DATE
VOID SAMPLE ONLY	
(BY) DEPUTY CLERK	SAMPLE
VOID SAMPLE ONLY	

This subpoena is issued upon application of the United States of America	NAME, ADDRESS AND PHONE NUMBER OF ASSISTANT U.S. ATTORNEY

*If not applicable, enter "none." To be used in lieu of AO110 FORM OBD-227 JAN. 86

(*continues*)

Figure 8–29. *(continued)*

[*reverse*]

RETURN OF SERVICE[1]		
RECEIVED BY SERVER	DATE	PLACE
SERVED	DATE	PLACE
SERVED ON (NAME)		
SERVED BY		TITLE

STATEMENT OF SERVICE FEES		
TRAVEL	SERVICES	TOTAL

DECLARATION OF SERVER[2]

I declare under penalty of perjury under the laws of the United States of America that the foregoing information contained in the Return of Service and Statement of Service Fees is true and correct.

Executed on ______________________ ______________________________________
Date *Signature of Server*

____
Address of Server

ADDITIONAL INFORMATION

(1) As to who may serve a subpoena and the manner of its service see Rule 17(d), Federal Rules of Criminal Procedure, or Rule 45(c), Federal Rules of Civil Procedure.

(2) "Fees and mileage need not be tendered to the witness upon service of a subpoena issued on behalf of the United States or an officer or agency thereof (Rule 45(c), Federal Rules of Civil Procedure; Rule 17(d), Federal Rules of Criminal Procedure) or on behalf of certain indigent parties and criminal defendants who are unable to pay such costs (28 USC 1825, Rule 17(b) Federal Rules of Criminal Procedure)".

ants (see Figure 8–30). Once a seizure notice has been issued, the importer must proceed by means of the procedures specified in the Customs regulations to try to repossess the merchandise. Sometimes, in order to avoid additional assessments of customs penalties or the expenses of further proceedings, the importer may agree or consent to abandon the merchandise which has been seized. (A form of consent is shown in Figure 8–31.) However, the importer should not be pressured into abandoning the merchandise by threats that Customs will pursue further penalties against the importer unless it abandons the merchandise. Although no particular form is required, a sample form of a petition for remission or mitigation is shown in Figure 8–32, which is filed to try to obtain release of the seized merchandise.

AA. Prepenalty Notices

When Customs determines that a civil violation of the customs laws has occurred, it issues a prepenalty notice (see Figure 8–33). The prepenalty notice states the customs law or regulation that has been violated. This notice is also used where Customs claims liquidated damages, for example, because merchandise was released to the importer under an Entry/Immediate Delivery and the importer failed to file the Entry Summary and other necessary customs entry documents within the allotted time period. The importer will normally be given thirty days to present reasons explaining why the penalty should be reduced or forgiven.

BB. Penalty Notices

After the Customs Service receives the importer's explanation or, if the importer files no explanation, Customs will issue a penalty notice. This is the formal assessment of penalty (see Figure 8–34). A petition for remission or mitigation may be filed within the time period specified on the penalty notice (see Figure 8–32). Thereafter, if the importer fails to pay, collection will be referred to the U.S. Department of Justice Civil Division, for the filing of a civil collection action in the Court of International Trade.

CC. Customs Audits

The U.S. Customs Service has always had the authority to conduct audits in which it reviews an importer's records to determine compliance with the customs laws, but such audits have assumed a new significance following enactment of the Customs Modernization Act. The Act enables importers to file customs entries electronically. Since additional documents traditionally attached to the customs entries, such as hard copies of the exporter's commercial invoice and bills of lading, are not available to the Customs officers at the time of electronic filing, post-importation audits become much more critical in Customs' ability to ensure compliance and detect fraud.

(*Text continues on page 362.*)

Figure 8–30. Notice of seizure.

U.S. Customs Service
610 S. Canal Street
Chicago, IL 60607-4523

FILE: ENF-4-02 PD:P
CASE NO:

Dear :

The records of this office indicate that you might have an interest in certain property seized by U. S. Customs in (location)______________ on (date)_______________. The property was seized under the provisions of Title 19, United States Code, Section 1595a(c). Specifically, it violates (citation of law)._______________. The property consists of the following items:

(DESCRIPTION OF SEIZED MERCHANDISE)

The value of the merchandise is _______________ .

Under the provisions of Title 19, United States Code, Section 1618, you may petition for relief from the above liability(ies). The enclosed Notice of Seizure and Information for Claimants explains your options with regard to the remission of the forfeiture and possible return to you of the seized property. If you decide to petition for relief, you must check the first box on the enclosed Election of Proceeding/Waiver form indicating that you wish this office to consider your petition administratively. By checking this box you are providing an express agreement to defer judicial or administrative forfeiture proceedings until completion of the administrative process. Checking the second or third box indicates that you desire Customs to begin appropriate forfeiture proceedings. No matter which box you check, you must also sign and return the form.

All petitions should be filed, in triplicate, at the following address: Port Director, U. S. Customs Service, (address), _____________, Attn: FP&F Section. If a petition is not received within 30 days from the date of this letter, appropriate forfeiture action will be initiated.

Sincerely,

Fines, Penalties & Forfeitures Officer

Enclosure

TRADITION
★
SERVICE
★
HONOR

Figure 8–30. *(continued)*

NOTICE OF SEIZURE AND INFORMATION FOR CLAIMANTS
FORM AF

PORT DIRECTOR OF CUSTOMS
610 SOUTH CANAL ST, FP&F
CHICAGO, IL 60607

PLEASE TAKE PARTICULAR
NOTE OF INFORMATION
FOLLOWING CHECKED BOXES

(312) 983-1324

To The Party Named in The Attached Letter:

You are hereby notified that the merchandise, conveyances, monetary instruments, or other property shown on the attached document(s), or other property shown on the attached document(s) were seized for violation of the Customs laws or the other laws enforced or administered by the U. S. Customs Service, as indicated on the attachment.

The facts available to the U. S. Customs Service indicate that you have an interest in the seized property. The purpose of this letter is to advise you of the options available to you concerning this seizure:

1. You may choose to take no action. If you take no action, the Customs Service will seek to forfeit the property by administrative action in accordance with section 607, Tariff Act of 1930, as amended (19 U.S.C. 1607) and section 162.45, Title 19, Code of Federal Regulations. In order to obtain forfeiture, the Customs Service must publish a notice of seizure and intent to forfeit in a newspaper for three successive weeks. After that time, the Government acquires full title to the seized property. The first notice will be published on or about 30 days in the Chicago Sun Times.

2. You may request the Port (or Area) Director of Customs to publish the first notice sooner than the scheduled date which appears above.

In either case (#1 or #2 above), once the first notice is published, and within 20 days of the publication, you may appear before the Port (or Area) Director of Customs and file a claim and a bond in the amount of $5,000.00 or 10 percent of the value of the claimed property, whichever is lower, but not less than $250. If you file the claim and bond, the matter will immediately be referred to the appropriate United States Attorney for the institution of judicial proceedings in Federal court to forfeit the seized property, in accordance with section 608, Tariff Act of 1930, as amended (19 U.S.C. 1608) and section 162.47, Title 19, Code of Federal Regulations. If you wish the Government to seek judicial forfeiture proceedings but cannot afford to post the bond, you should contact the Port (or Area) Director of Customs. Upon satisfactory proof of financial inability to pay the bond, it will be waived; or

Figure 8–30. *(continued)*

FORM AF
-2-

3. If you wish to seek administrative relief, you must, within 30 days from the date of the attached letter (unless some other period is stated in the letter), file a completed copy of the attached form waiving your right to prompt commencement of administrative forfeiture proceedings in accordance with section 609, Tariff Act of 1930, as amended (19 U.S.C. 1609) and request administrative action, and:

(a) File a petition for administrative relief with the Port (Area) Director of Customs in accordance with section 618, Tariff Act of 1930, as amended (19 U.S.C. 1618) and section 171.11, Title 19, Code of Federal Regulations; or

(b) Submit an offer in compromise to the Port (or Area) Director of Customs in accordance with section 617, Tariff Act of 1930, as amended (19 U.S.C. 1617) and section 161.5, Title 19, Code of Federal Regulations; or

(c) Unless the seized property is prohibited entry into the United States, submit an offer to pay the appraised domestic value of the seized property accompanied by payment or an irrevocable letter of credit with the Port (or Area) Director of Customs in accordance with section 614, Tariff Act of 1930, as amended (19 U.S.C. 1614) and section 162.44, Title 19, Code of Federal Regulations. If Customs accepts your offer, the property will be immediately released, the security will be substituted for the seized property, and you may still petition for relief [see 3(a) above] or submit an offer in compromise [see 3(b) above].

If you complete and submit the attached waiver requesting administrative proceedings, together with any of the options in 3(a), (b), or (c) above, you will be requesting the Customs Service NOT to begin administrative forfeiture proceedings by publication of the notice of seizure and intent to forfeit while your petition or offer is pending administratively, or to halt proceedings if they have already commenced. However, if the matter has been referred to the United States attorney for the institution of judicial forfeiture proceedings because a claim and bond were filed with Customs, your petition or offer will be forwarded to the United States Attorney for consideration under Department of Justice Regulations.

If your petition or offer is NOT accompanied by the attached waiver, or you request immediate commencement of administrative forfeiture proceedings on that form, publication of the notice of seizure and intent to forfeit will begin promptly, unless the matter has been referred to the United States Attorney because a claim and cost bond were filed by another party. If a claim and cost bond have been filed, your petition or offer will be forwarded to the United States Attorney for consideration.

Figure 8–30. *(continued)*

FORM AF
- 3 -

If you decide to file a petition for relief, an offer in compromise, or an offer to pay the value to obtain release, with the Customs Service, you should address it to the Commissioner of Customs and submit it in triplicate (3 copies) to the Port (or Area) Director of Customs at the address shown in the attached letter.

If you follow any of the options in #3 above and you do not believe that the Customs Service is acting expeditiously on your request, you may notify the Port (or Area) Director of Customs in writing that you are withdrawing your request and the Customs Service will, within 14 days from receipt of your notice, begin to publish the notice of seizure and intent to forfeit in a newspaper (see #1 and #2 above).

If you have any questions concerning the reasons for, or the circumstances surrounding the seizure, or the procedures to be followed in connection with this matter, or if you require additional information, you may request an informal conference with the Port (or Area) Director of Customs or one of his designated employees.

[ ] SPECIAL NOTICE TO MULTIPLE CLAIMANTS AND HOLDERS OF LIENS OR SECURITY INTERESTS

The information available to Customs indicates that another party has an ownership interest in the seized property identified on the attachment. Although you may avail yourself of the options listed above, no relief will be granted to you until AFTER forfeiture unless your petition, offer, or request is accompanied by an agreement to hold the United States, its officers and employees harmless, and a release from the registered owner, and/or the person from whom the property was seized [contact the Port (or Area) Director of Customs for details]. If you do not submit the hold harmless agreement and release(s), the administrative forfeiture proceedings will proceed, unless you file a claim and a bond in the amount of $5,000 or 10 percent of the value of the claimed property, whichever is lower, but not less than $250, in which case the matter will be referred to the United States Attorney for the institution of judicial forfeiture proceedings.

[ ] PENALTY INFORMATION

In addition to the seizure(s) and forfeiture liability, a civil penalty has been or will be assessed in this matter. Details on the civil penalty are:

[ ] in the attached letter; or

[ ] being prepared and will be mailed shortly.

Figure 8–30. *(continued)*

ELECTION OF PROCEEDINGS
FORM AF- PUBLISH

NOTE: READ THE ATTACHED "NOTICE OF SEIZURE AND INFORMATION FOR CLAIMANTS" BEFORE YOU FILL OUT THIS FORM. THIS FORM MUST BE COMPLETED AND RETURNED WITH YOUR PETITION OR OFFER. IF YOU DO NOT COMPLETE AND RETURN THIS FORM, WE SHALL PROCEED TO FORFEIT THE PROPERTY ADMINISTRATIVELY, REGARDLESS OF WHETHER YOU FILE A PETITION OR OFFER.

TO: CUSTOMS FINES, PENALTIES AND FORFEITURE OFFICER:

I understand that property in which I have an interest has been seized by the U.S. Customs Service, under Case Number: ______________________.

Check ONLY ONE (1) of the following choices:

[ ] I REQUEST THAT THE CUSTOMS SERVICE CONSIDER MY PETITION OR OFFER ADMINISTRATIVELY. That document is attached. By making this request, I understand that I am giving up my right to (1) begin administrative forfeiture proceedings immediately, as provided under title19, United States Code (U.S.C.), section 1607 and title 19, Code of Federal Regulations (CFR), section 162.45, or (2) immediate referral to the U.S. Attorney for court action, as provided by 19 U.S.C. 1608 and 19 CFR 162.47. If administrative forfeiture has begun, it will be stopped until my petition or offer is considered. However, I understand that *at any time* I can request, in writing, that you begin adminstrative proceedings, and you will continue to consider my petition or offer. I also understand that *at any time* I can file a claim and cost bond with you, and Customs consideration of my petition or offer will stop and the case will be sent to the U.S. Attorney for court action.

[ ] I REQUEST THAT THE CUSTOMS SERVICE BEGIN ADMINISTRATIVE PROCEEDINGS TO FORFEIT THE PROPERTY. Please immediately begin publication of the notice of seizure and intent to forfeit, and consider my petition or offer, if any. I understand that within 20 days of the first publication of the notice, I can request that you send the case to the U.S. Attorney for court action.

( ) I REQUEST THAT THE CUSTOMS SERVICE SEND MY CASE FOR COURT ACTION. Please immediately send the case to the U.S. Attorney for a court decision. I am filing /will file a claim and cost bond with you.

______________________ ______________________

Signature Date

Figure 8–31. Consent to forfeiture.

DEPARTMENT OF THE TREASURY
UNITED STATES CUSTOMS SERVICE

NOTICE OF ABANDONMENT AND ASSENT TO FORFEITURE OF PROHIBITED OR SEIZED MERCHANDISE AND CERTIFICATE OF DESTRUCTION

19 CFR Part 162

1. PORT	2. DATE	3. SEIZURE NO.

4. DESCRIPTION OF MERCHANDISE

PLEASE PRINT:

5. NAME	6. ADDRESS

I hereby abandon all claim to the above-described articles, and waive any further rights or proceedings relative to these articles, other than my right to file a petition for administrative relief.

7. SIGNATURE OF IMPORTER	8.DATE	9. WITNESS (CUSTOMS OFFICER)	10.DATE

CUSTOMS USE ONLY — CERTIFICATE OF DESTRUCTION

11. LOCATION	12. DATE	13. METHOD OF DESTRUCTION

14. SIGNATURE OF CUSTOMS OFFICER	15. WITNESS

Customs Form 4607 (09/00)

Figure 8–32. Petition for remission or mitigation.

DEPARTMENT OF THE TREASURY
UNITED STATES CUSTOMS SERVICE

Approved Through 06/30/96
OMB No. 1515-0052

PETITION FOR REMISSION OR MITIGATION OF FORFEITURES AND PENALTIES INCURRED

19 U.S.C. 1618; 19 CFR 171.11

1. PORT	2. SEIZURE CASE NO.

3. DESCRIPTION OF MERCHANDISE

4. NAME	5. ADDRESS

I petition for the release of the seized above-described merchandise and for relief from the liability incurred because of the following mitigating circumstances.

6. SIGNATURE	7. ADDRESS	8. DATE

Paperwork Reduction Act Notice: The Paperwork Reduction Act of 1980 says we must tell you why we are collecting this information, how we will use it, and whether you have to give it to us. We ask for this information to carry out the Customs Service laws of the United States. This form is used by those persons who are requesting mitigation of a penalty or remission of a forfeiture which has been incurred under the Customs laws or a law administered by Customs. Completion of the form will permit the authorized Customs officer to grant mitigation or remission. It is required that the form be completed to obtain this benefit.

The estimated average burden associated with this collection of information is 15 minutes per respondent or recordkeeper depending on individual circumstances. Comments concerning the accuracy of this burden estimate and suggestions for reducing this burden should be directed to U.S. Customs Service, Paperwork Management Branch, Washington DC 20229. *DO NOT send completed form(s) to this office.*

*U.S. Government Printing Office: 1996 - 405-483/36053

Customs Form 4609 (120495)

Figure 8–33. Prepenalty notice.

U.S. Customs Service
610 S. Canal Street
Chicago, IL 60607-4523

ENF 4-02 PD:P
Port Case

Gentlemen:

This is to inform you that pursuant to Title 19, Code of Federal Regulations, Section 162, notice is hereby given that the United States Customs Service is contemplating assessing a penalty against you in the amount of $_________. This amount represents the maximum penalty for (culpability) for your introduction of merchandise into the United States in violation of Title 19, United States Code, Section 1592.

Prior to the issuance of a notice of penalty, you have the right to make an oral and written presentation as to why the claim for monetary penalty should not be issued in the amount proposed. The written presentation must be made within thirty (30) business days from the date of the mailing of the pre-penalty notice as provided for in sections 162.77/78 of the Customs Regulations. Should you wish to make an oral presentation, please contact ___________ of my staff at the above telephone number to arrange a mutually convenient time and date for the presentation. Please be advised that we prefer the oral presentation be arranged after submission of the written response. The penalty notice will be issued automatically should you fail to respond to the pre-penalty notice within the effective period.

Exhibit A contains relevant information concerning the penalty action, i.e. specific details of the violation. Exhibit B represents the consumption entries involved in the penalty action.

If we do not hear from you within the time frame stipulated above the matter will be referred to the Court of International Trade for the institution of judicial proceedings.

Sincerely,

Fines, Penalties & Forfeitures Officer

TRADITION
★
SERVICE
★
HONOR

Figure 8–33. *(continued)*

EXHIBIT A

1. **Description of Merchandise:**
2. **Shipper/Manufacturer:**
3. **Broker:**
4. **Consignee:**
5. **Details of Entry Introduction:**
6. **Loss of Revenue:**
7. **Law(s) Violated:**
8. **Facts Establishing Violation:**
9. **Culpability**
10. **Penalty Amount:**

Under the Customs Modernization Act, Customs is required to follow certain procedures in conducting audits. It must give the importer an estimate of the duration of the audit, explain the purpose of the audit at the entry conference, explain the preliminary results of the audit at the closing conference, and, subject to certain exceptions, provide a copy of the final audit report to the importer within 120 days of the closing conference.

Customs has issued certain documents to the trade community to inform them of the compliance issues which Customs will review, called "Focused Assessments." Appendix J contains sample Internal Control and Electronic Data Processing Questionnaires. Reviewing these documents will assist an importer in establishing proper importing procedures and compliance.

If, as a result of an audit, Customs assesses additional duties and penalties, the importer may file a protest and/or a petition for remission or mitigation.

DD. Prior Disclosure

An importer who has become aware that it has accidentally violated the customs laws or who determines that one of its employees intentionally violated the customs laws, can utilize a procedure called "prior disclosure," which permits an

Figure 8–34. Notice of penalty.

U.S. Customs Service
610 S. Canal Street
Chicago, IL 60607-4523

FILE: ENF-4-02 PD:P
CASE NO:

Dear :

Consideration has been given to the prepenalty response submitted in the above referenced case number. The letter was submitted in response to a prepenalty notice issued to on , informing them that U. S. Customs was contemplating issuing a penalty for (level of culpability). The claim arose due to (facts of violation).

Based upon information in your prepenalty response, it has been determined that the facts indicate a finding that the violation occurred as a result of (culpability) on the part of __________. Exhibit A contains relevant information concerning the penalty action, i.e., specific details of the violation. Exhibit B represents the entries involved in this penalty action.

Pursuant to Section 171.12 of the Customs Regulations, your client has the right to submit a petition. The petition must be submitted within 30 days from the date of this letter. If payment or a petition is not submitted within the effective period, the matter will be referred to the Court of International Trade for the institution of judicial proceedings. If you have any questions in this matter, please contact ____________ of my staff at the above listed telephone number.

Sincerely,

Fines, Penalties & Forfeitures Officer

TRADITION

Enclosures

★

SERVICE

★

HONOR

Figure 8–34. *(continued)*

DEPARTMENT OF THE TREASURY
UNITED STATES CUSTOMS SERVICE

NOTICE OF PENALTY OR LIQUIDATED DAMAGES INCURRED
AND DEMAND FOR PAYMENT

19 USC 1618, 19 USC 1623

Case Number

Port Name and Code

Investigation File No.

TO:

DEMAND IS HEREBY MADE FOR PAYMENT OF $ ____________, representing ☐ Penalties or ☐ Liquidated Damages
assessed against you for violation or law or regulation, or breach of bond, as set forth below:

LAW OR REGULATION VIOLATED	BOND BREACHED

DESCRIPTION OF BOND (if any)	Form Number	Amount $	Date

Name and Address of Principal on Bond

Name and Address of Surety on Bond | Surety Identification No.

If you feel there are extenuating circumstances, you have the right to object to the above action. Your petition should explain why you should not be penalized for the cited violation. Write the petition as a letter or in legal form; submit in (duplicate) (triplicate), addressed to the Commissioner of Customs, and forward to the FP&F Officer at

Unless the amount herein demanded is paid or a petition for relief is filed with the FP&F Officer within the indicated time limit, further action will be taken in connection with your bond or the matter will be referred to the United States Attorney.

TIME LIMIT FOR PAYMENT OR FILING PETITION FOR RELIEF (Days from the date of this Notice)

Signature	Title	Date
By		

Customs Form 5955A (08/00)

importer to voluntarily tender the customs duties that were avoided and reduce the penalties it would otherwise have to pay if the Customs authorities discover the violation themselves. If the violation was accidental, the only penalty is payment of interest in addition to the duties; if fraudulent, a penalty equal to the amount of the duties is payable. Nevertheless, these penalties are far lower than the ordinary penalties which can be assessed, including the full domestic value of the goods for fraud.

In order to make a prior disclosure, information detailing the nature of the error, the entries affected by the error, the ports of entry, and the merchandise affected must be furnished to Customs before Customs commences any investigation. The duties must be paid in order to qualify for the reduced penalty.

EE. Court of International Trade

If the importer's protest is denied, the importer may appeal the decision of the U.S. Customs Service to the Court of International Trade. It must file its "summons" and Information Statement with the Court of International Trade within 180 days following the denial of the protest (see Figures 8–35 and 8–36). All additional duties must also be paid. Within thirty days thereafter, the importer must file its complaint with the Court. In the meantime, the U.S. Customs Service will transmit all of the documents relating to the case to the Court of International Trade (see Figure 8–37).

FF. Appeals

Following the decision of the Court of International Trade, the importer may appeal to the U.S. Court of Appeals for the Federal Circuit in Washington, D.C. No special form is used to docket an appeal on a customs matter. The Notice of Appeal form must be filed within thirty days following the decision of the Court of International Trade. If the decision of the Court of Appeals is adverse to the importer, the importer may seek review by the U.S. Supreme Court via a petition for certiorari, but such petitions are not granted frequently.

GG. Offers of Compromise

If Customs has assessed a penalty, the importer may make an offer of compromise addressed to the Secretary of Treasury in Washington, D.C. While there is no guarantee that such offer will be accepted, this is one avenue to resolve a customs penalty without the necessity of court proceedings or admission of guilt. Normally, such an offer would not be made until some later stage in the administrative process, for example, after denial of a protest, request for reliquidation, or the initiation of court proceedings.

(*Text continues on page 372.*)

Figure 8–35. Court of International Trade summons.

Form 1-1

UNITED STATES COURT OF INTERNATIONAL TRADE **FORM 1**

Plaintiff,
v.
UNITED STATES, **Defendant.**

SUMMONS
In Actions Under
28 U.S.C. § 1581 (a)

TO: The Attorney General and the Secretary of the Treasury:

PLEASE TAKE NOTICE that a civil action has been commenced pursuant to 28 U.S.C. § 1581(a) to contest denial of the protest specified below (and the protests listed in the attached schedule).

L. S.

Clerk of the Court

PROTEST

Port of Entry:	Date Protest Filed:
Protest Number:	Date Protest Denied:
Importer:	
Category of Merchandise:	

ENTRIES INVOLVED IN ABOVE PROTEST

Entry Number	Date of Entry	Date of Liquidation	Entry Number	Date of Entry	Date of Liquidation

District Director,

Address of Customs District in Which Protest was Denied

Name, Address and Telephone Number of Plaintiff's Attorney

Figure 8–35. *(continued)*

Form 1-2

CONTESTED ADMINISTRATIVE DECISION

Appraised Value of Merchandise

	Statutory Basis	Statement of Value
Appraised:		
Protest Claim:		

Classification, Rate or Amount

	Assessed		Protest Claim	
Merchandise	Paragraph or Item Number	Rate	Paragraph or Item Number	Rate

Other

State Specifically the Decision [as Described in 19 U.S.C. § 1514(a)] and the Protest Claim:

The issue which was common to all such denied protests:

Every denied protest included in this civil action was filed by the same above-named importer, or by an authorized person in the importer's behalf. The category of merchandise specified above was involved in each entry of merchandise included in every such denied protest. The issue or issues stated above were common to all such denied protests. All such protests were filed and denied as prescribed by law. All liquidated duties, charges or exactions have been paid, and were paid at the port of entry unless otherwise shown.

____
Signature of Plaintiff's Attorney

____
Date

Figure 8–35. *(continued)*

Form 1-3

SCHEDULE OF PROTESTS

____
Port of Entry

Protest Number	Date Protest Filed	Date Protest Denied	Entry Number	Date of Entry	Date of Liquidation

District Director of Customs,

If the port of entry shown above is different from the port of entry shown on the first page of the summons, the address of the District Director for such different port of entry must be given in the space provided.

Figure 8–36. Information statement.

Form 5-1

FORM 5

UNITED STATES COURT OF INTERNATIONAL TRADE

INFORMATION STATEMENT

(Place an "X" in applicable [ ])

PLAINTIFF: **ATTORNEY** *(Name, Address, Telephone No.)*:	**PRECEDENCE** If the action is to be given precedence under Rule 3(g), indicate the applicable paragraph of that section: [ ] (1) [ ] (3) [ ] (5) [ ] (2) [ ] (4)

J U R I S D I C T I O N

28 U.S.C. § 1581(a) - Tariff Act of 1930, Section 515 - 19 U.S.C. § 1515

[ ] Appraisal [ ] Classification [ ] Charges or Exactions

[ ] Exclusion [ ] Liquidation [ ] Drawback

[ ] Refusal to Reliquidate [ ] Rate of Duty [ ] Redelivery

28 U.S.C. § 1581(b) - Tariff Act of 1930, Section 516 - 19 U.S.C. § 1516

[ ] Appraisal [ ] Classification [ ] Rate of Duty

28 U.S.C. § 1581(c) - Tariff Act of 1930, Section 516A(a)(1), (a)(2) or (a)(3) - 19 U.S.C. § 1516a *(Provide a brief description of the administrative determination you are contesting, including the relevant* ***Federal Register*** *citation(s) and the product(s) involved in the determination. For Section 516A(a)(1) or (a)(2), cite the specific subparagraph and clause of the section.)*

Subparagraph and Clause ________________ Agency________________

Federal Register Cite(s)________________________________

Product(s) ________________________________

28 U.S.C. § 1581(d) - Trade Act of 1974 - 19 U.S.C. §§ 2273, 2341, 2371

[ ] U.S. Secretary of Labor [ ] U.S. Secretary of Commerce

28 U.S.C. § 1581(e) - Trade Agreements Act of 1979, Section 305(b)(1) - 19 U.S.C. § 2515
(Provide a brief statement of the final determination to be reviewed.)

28 U.S.C. § 1581(f) - Tariff Act of 1930, Section 777(c)(2) - 19 U.S.C. § 1677f(c)(2)

Agency: [ ] U.S. International Trade Commission [ ] Administering Authority

28 U.S.C. § 1581(g) - Tariff Act of 1930, Section 641 - 19 U.S.C. § 1641 - or Section 499 - 19 U.S.C. § 1499

[ ] Sec. 641(b)(2) [ ] Sec. 641(b)(3) [ ] Sec. 641(c)(1) [ ] Sec. 641(b)(5)

[ ] Sec. 641(c)(2) [ ] Sec. 641(d)(2)(B) [ ] Sec. 499(b)

(Continued on reverse side)

Figure 8–36. *(continued)*

Form 5-2

JURISDICTION
(Continued)

28 U.S.C. § 1581(h) - Ruling relating to:

[ ] Classification	[ ] Valuation	[ ] Restricted Merchandise
[ ] Rate of Duty	[ ] Marking	[ ] Entry Requirements
[ ] Drawbacks	[ ] Vessel Repairs	[ ] Other: ______________

28 U.S.C. § 1581(i) - *(Cite any applicable statute and provide a brief statement describing jurisdictional basis.)*

28 U.S.C. § 1582 - Actions Commenced by the United States

[ ] (1) Recover civil penalty under Tariff Act of 1930:

[ ] Sec. 592	[ ] Sec. 593A	[ ] Sec. 641(b)(6)
[ ] Sec. 641(d)(2)(A)	[ ] Sec. 704(i)(2)	[ ] Sec. 734(i)(2)

[ ] (2) Recover upon a bond

[ ] (3) Recover customs duties

RELATED CASE(S)

To your knowledge, does this action involve a common question of law or fact with any other action(s) previously decided or now pending?

	PLAINTIFF	COURT NUMBER	JUDGE
[ ] Decided:			
[ ] Pending:			

(Attach additional sheets, if necessary.)

(As amended, eff. Jan. 1, 1985; Jan. 25, 2000, eff. May 1, 2000.)

Figure 8–37. Transmittal to the Court of International Trade.

DEPARTMENT OF THE TREASURY
UNITED STATES CUSTOMS SERVICE

DISTRICT
DATE

Clerk of the Court
U.S. Court of International Trade
1 Federal Plaza
New York, NY 10007

Re: U.S. Court of International Trade (Summons)
No.

In compliance with Section 2635 of Title 28, United States Code, there are transmitted herewith a copy of the Protest(s) and Denial of Protest(s) required in connection with the above summons. There are also transmitted all the additional items required by that section, which have been found to exist for the above civil action, subject to the exceptions noted below. Any of the required items which are not herewith submitted or noted below do not exist for this civil action.

EXCEPTION(S)

PROTEST NUMBER	ENTRY NUMBER	EXPLANATION

DISTRICT DIRECTOR

cc: Assistant Chief Counsel

SUMMONS DOCUMENTATION TRANSMITTAL — Customs Form 322 (031684)

HH. ITC and Commerce Questionnaires

Another type of document that importers may see in the course of importation is a questionnaire sent to the importer by the International Trade Commission (ITC). The ITC has an investigatory or adjudicatory role under a number of different trade laws relating to the importation of merchandise. Sections 201 and 406 of the Trade Act of 1974 permit the ITC, with Presidential approval, to assess additional customs duties or impose quotas when importation of merchandise has increased substantially and is injuring U.S. producers. Under Section 301 of the Trade Act of 1974, the ITC can impose similar sanctions when a foreign government is unjustifiably or unreasonably burdening U.S. export commerce. Under the antidumping and countervailing duty laws, the ITC seeks to determine the quantity of imports, prices, and whether U.S. manufacturers have been injured by imported products. Under Section 337 of the Tariff Act, the ITC may impose restrictions on the import of merchandise if it determines that there have been unfair practices in the import trade, such as patent infringement. Under Section 332, the ITC may conduct general investigations simply to determine the quantity of imports, changes in import trends, and to advise Congress on appropriate legislation to regulate international trade. In all of these investigations, the ITC normally issues lengthy (sometimes fifty- or sixty-page) questionnaires to importers. Under these laws, the importers are required to respond to the questionnaires; however, the ITC will normally grant an extension of time if the importer needs it.

The Department of Commerce conducts national security investigations under Section 232 of the Trade Act of 1974 to determine whether U.S. national security is being endangered by overdependence on foreign products.

Part IV

Specialized Exporting and Importing

Chapter 9

Specialized Exporting and Importing

The transactions described in this Part are distinguished by the fact that they involve a combination of both exporting and importing. Several such transactions are described in this chapter.

A. Drawback

Drawback is a program administered by the United States Customs Service which permits a refund of 99 percent of the U.S. Customs duties paid on merchandise that has been imported into the United States and is thereafter exported (certain duties, such as antidumping duties, Harbor Maintenance fees, and merchandise-processing fees are not eligible for drawback). In order to claim the refund, Customs must be able to trace that the merchandise was actually imported and then exported. Several types of drawback programs exist.

The first is called manufacturing drawback. Under this program, merchandise may be imported by a manufacturer and used as a raw material or component in manufacturing a finished product, which is then exported. This is known as direct identification manufacturing drawback. In order to encourage U.S. manufacturers to use U.S.-origin raw materials and components, however, Congress has provided for substitution drawback. In this type of drawback, the U.S. manufacturer that imports a foreign-origin raw material or component and then decides instead to substitute a U.S.-origin raw material or component in the manufacturing process can also claim a refund of duties on the imported raw materials or components that were not used. Under the North American Free Trade Agreement, beginning January 1, 1996, on exports to Canada and January 1, 2001, on exports to Mexico, the amount of direct identification drawback will be limited to the lower of the amount of duties paid at the time of importation to the United States or the amount of duties paid on the exported goods when imported into Canada or Mexico. Substitution drawback was eliminated on such exports as of January 1, 1994. In both types of manufacturing drawback, the manufacturer must maintain records showing the amount of waste in the manufacturing process. The manufacturer must also maintain records from which the utilization of raw materials or components in the manufacture of the finished product can be verified for a period of three years from the date of payment of the drawback claim or five years from the date of importation, whichever is longer. The manufacturer must have applied for and obtained an importer's identification number and must apply for a drawback contract. In order to meet the needs of most manufacturers, Customs has issued general drawback offers, specifying the terms and conditions under which the manufacturing must take place. The manufacturer must file an acceptance of the offer that contains certain information and undertakings. Where the manufacturer's case is unusual or does not fit the general drawback offer, it must apply for and enter into a specific drawback contract with U.S. Customs.

Anytime within three years after exportation, the exporter can file its Drawback Entry (see Figure 9–1), along with evidence of exportation, which is a claim for the refund. The merchandise for which a refund is being sought must have been imported within five years prior to the filing of the claim (for substitution manufacturing drawback, the exported merchandise also must have been produced within three years from the time the manufacturer received the imported merchandise). Where the manufacturer is the exporter of the imported articles, the manufacturer files the Drawback Entry. However, where the exporter is not the manufacturer, the exporter must obtain a Delivery Certificate (see Figure 9–2) from the importer and each intermediate transferee and file it with the Drawback Entry. It should be noted that the exporter is the one entitled to the refund of the duties, not the importer (unless the exporter has expressly assigned its right to the importer). Congress assumes that the exporter paid the customs duties as part of the price when it purchased the merchandise from the importer.

The second type of drawback is the Unused Merchandise drawback. This arises where an article has been imported into the United States but is exported without being "used"; that is, the imported article has not been processed into a new and different article having a distinctive name, character, or use and has not been processed in a manner that has made it fit for a particular use (direct unused merchandise drawback). Alternatively, the importer can substitute commercially interchangeable merchandise and export that merchandise (substitution unused merchandise drawback). If the exporter is not the importer, the exporter must file Delivery Certificates with its Drawback Entry. At least two days prior to export (seven days if the exporter intends to destroy the merchandise under Customs' supervision), the exporter must file the Notice of Intent to Export with Customs (see Figure 9–3). Customs will either examine the merchandise prior to export or waive examination. Exportation must occur within three years after importation.

The third kind of drawback is rejected merchandise. This arises where the buyer/importer receives merchandise from a foreign supplier that does not conform to sample or specifications, is defective at the time of import, or was shipped without the consent of the consignee. Rejected merchandise must be returned to Customs' custody within three years of import. If the exporter was not the importer, the exporter must submit a statement signed by the importer and every other intermediate owner that no other claim for drawback was made on the goods. The Notice of Intent to Export must be submitted to U.S. Customs at least five working days prior to the intended return to

(*Text continues on page 382.*)

Figure 9–1. Drawback entry.

DEPARTMENT OF THE TREASURY
UNITED STATES CUSTOMS SERVICE

DRAWBACK ENTRY

19 CFR 191

Paperwork Reduction Act Notice: This information is requested in order to carry out U.S. Department of Treasury laws and regulations, to determine the eligibility for refund of taxes on domestic alcohol (if applicable), and to determine the proper amount of drawback. Your response is required to obtain or retain a benefit.

The estimated average burden associated with this collection of information is 10 minutes per respondent or recordkeeper depending on individual circumstances. Comments concerning the accuracy of this burden statement and suggestion for reducing this burden should be directed to U.S. Customs Service, Information Services Group, Washington DC 20229. DO NOT send completed form(s) to this office.

Section I - Claim Header **OMB 1515-0213**

1. DRAWBACK ENTRY NUMBER	2. ENTRY TYPE CODE	3. PORT CODE	4. SURETY CODE	5. BOND TYPE
6. CLAIMANT ID NUMBER	7. BROKER ID NUMBER (CF 4811)		8. DBK RULING NO.	
9. TOTAL DRAWBACK CLAIMED	10. PUERTO RICO DRAWBACK CLAIMED		11. TOTAL I.R. TAX CLAIMED	
12. METHOD OF FILING ☐ MANUAL ☐ DISK ☐ ABI	13. NAFTA DBK ☐ YES ☐ NO	14. PRIVILEGES AUTHORIZED ☐ Accelerated Payment ☐ W PN	15. DRAWBACK PROVISION	
16. NAME AND ADDRESS OF CLAIMANT	17. CONTACT NAME, ADDRESS, PHONE & FAX NUMBER OF PREPARER			

Section II - Imported Duty Paid, Designated Merchandise or Drawback Product

18. IMPORT ENTRY OR CM&D NO.	19. PORT CODE	20. IMPORT DATE	21. CD	22. IF USING 1313(b) A. DATE(S) RECEIVED	B. DATE(S) USED	23. HTSUS NO.	24. DESCRIPTION OF MERCHANDISE INCLUDE PART NUMBER(S)	25. QUANTITY & UNIT OF MEASURE	26. ENTERED VALUE PER UNIT	27. DUTY RATE	28. 99% DUTY
										29. TOTAL	

30. STATUS -- THE IMPORT ENTRIES LISTED ON THIS FORM ARE SUBJECT TO (Must be identified on claim or coding sheet):

☐ Reconciliation ☐ Protest

☐ 520 (c) (1) ☐ 520 (d)

DATE RECEIVED

U.S. CUSTOMS SERVICE USE ONLY

Class Code	Accelerated	Liquidated	Net
364 Drawback			
365 Tax			
369 Puerto Rico			

☐ Bill ☐ Refund ☐ No Change

Reason Code

Specialist Code

Customs Form 7551 (042498)

Figure 9–1. *(continued)*

Section III -- MANUFACTURED ARTICLES

31. QUANTITY & DESCRIPTION OF MERCHANDISE USED	32. DATE(S) OF MANUFACTURE OR PRODUCTION	33. DESCRIPTION OF ARTICLES MANUFACTURED OR PRODUCED	34. QUANTITY & UNIT OF MEASURE	35. FACTORY LOCATION

36. EXHIBITS TO BE ATTACHED FOR THE FOLLOWING:

☐ RELATIVE VALUE ☐ PETROLEUM ☐ DOMESTIC TAX PAID ALCOHOL ☐ PIECE GOODS ☐ WASTE CALCULATION ☐ SUGAR

Section IV -- INFORMATION ON EXPORTED OR DESTROYED MERCHANDISE

37. DATE (MMDDYYYY)	38. ACTION CODE	39. UNIQUE IDENTIFIER NO.	40. NAME OF EXPORTER/DESTROYER	41. DESCRIPTION OF ARTICLES (INCLUDE PART NUMBER(S))	42. QUANTITY AND UNIT OF MEASURE	43. EXPORT DESTINATION	44. HTSUS NO.

Section V -- DECLARATIONS

☐ NAFTA - The undersigned hereby certifies that the merchandise herein described is in the same condition as when it was imported under above import entry(s) and further certifies that this merchandise was not subjected to any process of manufacture or other operation except the following allowable operations: ____________

☐ The undersigned hereby certifies that the merchandise herein described is unused in the U.S. and further certifies that this merchandise was not subjected to any process of manufacture or other operation except the following allowable operations: ____________

☐ The undersigned hereby certifies that the merchandise herein described is commercially interchangeable with the designated imported merchandise and further certifies that the substituted merchandise is unused in the U.S. and that the substituted merchandise was in our possession prior to exportation or destruction.

☐ Merchandise does not conform to sample or specifications. ☐ Merchandise was defective at time of importation. ☐ Merchandise was shipped without consent of the consignee.

☐ The undersigned hereby certifies that the merchandise herein described is same kind and quality as defined in 19 USC 1313(p)(3)(B), with the designated imported merchandise or the article manufactured or produced under 1313(a) or (b), as appropriate.

☐ The article(s) described above were manufactured or produced and disposed of as stated herein in accordance with the drawback ruling on file with Customs and in compliance with applicable laws and regulations.

The undersigned acknowledges statutory requirements that all records supporting the information on this document are to be retained by the issuing party for a period of 3 years from the date of payment of the drawback claim. The undersigned is fully aware of the sanctions provided in 18 U.S.C. 1001 and 18 U.S.C. 550 and 19 U.S.C. 1593a.

I declare that according to the best of my knowledge and belief, all of the statements in this document are correct and that the exported article is not to be relanded in the United States or any of its possessions without paying duty.

☐ Member of Firm with Power of Attorney ☐ Officer of Corporation ☐ Broker with Power of Attorney

Printed Name and Title	Signature and Date

Customs Form 7551 (Back) (042498)

Figure 9–2. Delivery certificate.

DEPARTMENT OF THE TREASURY
UNITED STATES CUSTOMS SERVICE
DELIVERY CERTIFICATE
FOR PURPOSES OF DRAWBACK
19 CFR Part 191

☐ **CERTIFICATE OF DELIVERY**

☐ **CERTIFICATE OF MANUFACTURE AND DELIVERY**

OMB 1515-0213

1. C M & D NO.	2. PORT CODE	3. DRAWBACK RULING NO.
4. TYPE CODE	5. ID NO.	

6. FROM TRANSFEROR:	7. TO TRANSFEREE:	RECEIVED DATE
COMPANY NAME AND COMPLETE ADDRESS	COMPANY NAME AND COMPLETE ADDRESS	

IMPORTED DUTY PAID, DESIGNATED MERCHANDISE OR DRAWBACK PRODUCT

8. USE	9. IMPORT ENTRY OR CM&D NO.	10. PORT CODE	11. IMPORT DATE (MMDDYYYY)	12. CD	13. IF USING 1313b A. DATE(S) REC'D	B. DATE(S) USED	14. DATE DELIVERED	15. HTSUS NO.	16. DESCRIPTION OF MERCHANDISE (INCLUDE PART NUMBER(S))	17. QUANTITY & UNIT OF MEASURE	18. ENTERED VALUE PER UNIT	19. 100% DUTY
											TOTAL	

20. CONTACT NAME, ADDRESS, PHONE & FAX NUMBER OF PREPARER

Paperwork Reduction Act Notice: The Paperwork Reduction Act Notice of 1980 says we must tell you why we are collecting this information, how we will use it, and whether you have to give it to us. We ask for the information on this form to enforce the laws of the United States, to fulfill the Customs Regulations, to ensure that the claimant is entitled to drawback, and to have the necessary information which permits Customs to calculate and refund (or increase) the correct amount of duty and/or tax. Your response is required to obtain a benefit. Statement Required by 5 CFR 1320.21: The estimated average burden associated with this collection of information is 10 minutes per respondent or recordkeeper depending on individual circumstanced. Comments concerning the accuracy of this burden estimate and suggestions for reducing this burden should be directed to U.S. Customs Service, Information Services Group, Washington DC 20229, and to the Office of Management and Budget, Paperwork Reduction Project (1515-0213), DO NOT send completed form(s) to either of these offices.

Customs Form 7552 (042498)

Figure 9–2. *(continued)*

21. QUANTITY & DESCRIPTION OF MERCHANDISE USED	22. DATE(S) OF MANUFACTURE (MMDDYYYY)	23. DESCRIPTION OF ARTICLES MANUFACTURED OR PRODUCED (INCLUDE PART NO.'S)	24. QUANTITY & UNIT OF MEASURE	25. DATE DELIVERED

26. DUTY AVAILABLE ON MANUFACTURE ARTICLES (TOTAL OF DUTIES IN BLK 19)	27. DBK AVAILABLE PER UNIT OF MEASURE ON MANUFACTURED ARTICLE

29. FACTORY LOCATION

30. STATUS - IMPORT ENTRIES LISTED ON THIS FORM ARE SUBJECT TO: (IF CD IDENTIFY ON THIS FORM. IF CM & D, IDENTIFY ON CODING SHEET.)

☐ Reconciliation ☐ 520 (c) (1)

☐ Protest, 514 ☐ 520 (d)

By signing this document the party acknowledges statutory requirements that all records supporting the information on this document are to be retained by the issuing party for 3 years from the date of payment of the related drawback entry.

Assignment of Rights is transferred when this form is prepared as a CD or CM & D.

TITLE: ☐ MEMBER OF FIRM WITH POWER OF ATTORNEY ☐ BROKER WITH POWER OF ATTORNEY ☐ OFFICER OF CORP.

28. EXHIBITS TO BE ATTACHED FOR THE FOLLOWING

☐ RELATIVE VALUE ☐ WASTE CALCULATION

☐ PETROLEUM ☐ SUGAR

☐ DOMESTIC TAX PAID ALCOHOL ☐ PIECE GOODS

DECLARATIONS

☐ THE MERCHANDISE TRANSFERRED ON THIS C.D. IS THE IMPORTED MERCHANDISE

☐ THE MERCHANDISE TRANSFERRED ON THIS CD IS PURSUANT TO 19 USC 1313(j)(2) AND WILL NOT BE DESIGNATED FOR ANY OTHER DRAWBACK PURPOSES.

☐ THE ARTICLE(s) DESCRIBED ABOVE WERE MANUFACTURED OR PRODUCED AND DELIVERED AS STATED HEREIN IN ACCORDANCE WITH THE DRAWBACK RULING ON FILE WITH CUSTOMS & IN COMPLIANCE WITH APPLICABLE LAWS & REGULATIONS.

☐ THIS CERTIFICATE OF DELIVERY IS A SUBSEQUENT TRANSFER & THE MERCHANDISE IS THE SAME AS RECEIVED.

I DECLARE THAT ACCORDING TO THE BEST OF MY KNOWLEDGE & BELIEF ALL THE STATEMENTS IN THIS DOCUMENT ARE CORRECT & AM FULLY AWARE OF THE SANCTIONS PROVIDED IN 18 USC 1001, 18 USC 550 & 19 USC 1593a

PRINTED NAME AND TITLE

SIGNATURE AND DATE SIGNED

Customs Form 7552 (Back) (042498)

Figure 9–3. Notice of intent to export.

OMB 1515-0213

DEPARTMENT OF THE TREASURY
UNITED STATES CUSTOMS SERVICE

NOTICE OF INTENT TO EXPORT, DESTROY OR RETURN MERCHANDISE FOR PURPOSES OF DRAWBACK

19 CFR Part 191

Paperwork Reduction Act Notice: The Paperwork Reduction Act Notice of 1980 says we must tell you why we are collecting this information, how we will use it, and whether you have to give it to us. We ask for the information on this form to enforce the laws of the United States, to fulfill the Customs Regulations, to ensure that the claimant is entitled to drawback, and to have the necessary information which permits Customs to calculate and refund (or increase) the correct amount of duty and/or tax. Your response is required to obtain a benefit. Statement Required by 5 CFR 1320.21: The estimated average burden associated with this collection of information is 10 minutes per respondent or recordkeeper depending on individual circumstanced. Comments concerning the accuracy of this burden estimate and suggestions for reducing this burden should be directed to U.S. Customs Service, Information Services Group, Washington DC 20229, and to the Office of Management and Budget, Paperwork Reduction Project (1515-0213), **DO NOT** send completed form(s) to either of these offices.

1. EXPORTER'S OR DESTROYER'S NAME AND ADDRESS AND ID NUMBER	2. DRAWBACK ENTRY NO.	3. INTENDED ACTION ☐ EXPORT ☐ DESTROY	4. INTENDED DATE OF ACTION (MMDDYYYY)	**DATE RECEIVED**
	5. DRAWBACK CENTER	6. CONTACT NAME, ADDRESS, PHONE & FAX NO.		

7. LOCATION OF MERCHANDISE	8. METHOD OF DESTRUCTION AND LOCATION	9. EXPORTING CARRIER NAME (IF KNOWN)	10. INTENDED PORT OF EXPORT	11. UNIQUE IDENTIFIER NO.
			12. T & E NO.	13. COUNTRY OF ULTIMATE DESTINATION

14. DESCRIPTION AND VALUE MERCHANDISE (INCLUDE PART NO.)	15. Export Value	16. QTY & UNIT OF MEASURE	17. H.T.S.U.S. NO.

18. Drawback To Be Filed As:

- ☐ UNUSED MERCHANDISE DRAWBACK
  - ☐ J1 ☐ J2
- ☐ MANUFACTURING DRAWBACK
- ☐ REJECTED MERCHANDISE
  - ☐ SHIPPED WITHOUT CONSENT
  - ☐ DEFECTIVE AT TIME OF IMPORTATION
  - ☐ NOT CONFORMING TO SAMPLE OR SPECIFICATIONS
- ☐ SAME CONDITION DRAWBACK UNDER NAFTA
- ☐ DISTILLED SPIRITS, WINE OR BEER UNDER SECTION 5062(C), INTERNAL REVENUE CODE

19. Preparer's Signature, Title and Date

THIS FORM MUST BE SUBMITTED WITH THE DRAWBACK CLAIM

CUSTOMS USE ONLY

20. EXAMINATION ☐ WAIVED ☐ REQUIRED **(ADDITIONAL INFORMATION MAY BE REQUIRED IF EXAM REQUESTED, T & E MAY BE REQUIRED.)**	23. PRINTED NAME & PHONE NUMBER	
21. PRESENT MERCHANDISE TO CUSTOMS AT:	24. SIGNATURE AND BADGE NO.	
22. **DESTRUCTION** TO BE WITNESSED BY CUSTOMS ☐ YES ☐ NO	25. DATE	26. PORT

CUSTOMS USE ONLY

27. COMMENTS/RESULTS OF EXAMINATION OR WITNESSING OF DESTRUCTION. (MERCHANDISE MATCHES INVOICE DESCRIPTION)	
28. DATE DESTROYED OR EXAM CONDUCTED	29. BADGE NO.
30. PRINTED NAME AND PHONE NO. OF EXAMINING OFFICER	31. SIGNATURE AND DATE

CUSTOMS FORM 7553 (042498)

Customs' custody (seven days if the exporter intends to destroy the merchandise). Customs will examine the merchandise or waive examination. In some situations, rejected merchandise may also qualify for an unused merchandise drawback claim.

When an importer has established some history of drawback claims, for example, five claims substantiated properly, the importer may apply for the accelerated drawback payment program. The importer must file the application with the information required by the regulations, including a description of the claimant's drawback compliance program, procedures, and controls. The exporter must post a customs bond to guarantee a refund of any overpayments made by Customs to the exporter in an amount equal to the estimated amount of the drawback to be claimed during the term of the bond (usually twelve months). When the exporter has qualified for the accelerated program, it may obtain payment of drawback claims as soon as three weeks after filing the claim electronically or three months if filed manually.

B. Foreign Processing and Assembly Operations

In some circumstances, U.S. companies may wish to export U.S.-origin products to foreign countries, such as Mexico, for further manufacture, processing, or assembly, and then re-import the resulting products into the United States. Ordinarily, the products when imported to the United States would be subject to U.S. Customs duties on the full value of the product, notwithstanding the fact that part of the value of the product was originally U.S.-origin products exported to that country. There are three exceptions from the general rule.

First, when goods originally the product of the United States (not imported) are exported, and then imported without having been advanced in value or improved in condition by any process of manufacture or other means while abroad, and the U.S. importer certifies that no drawback was claimed when the goods were exported, then the goods can be imported into the United States without payment of duty (under classification 9801.00.10 of the HTS). (A sample form Declaration by Foreign Shipper and Importer's Endorsement is shown in Figure 9–4.)

Second, where the exporter exported merchandise for alteration, repair, use abroad, replacement, or processing, thereafter, when the goods are imported (under 9802.00.40 or 9802.00.50 of the HTS), they will not be subject to U.S. Customs duties except that duties will be assessed on the cost or value of the alterations, repairs, or processing. (A sample declaration is shown in Figure 9–5.)

Finally, an exporter intending to export U.S.-origin commodities, assemble them abroad, and import the finished product may qualify for reduced duty under classification 9802.00.80 of the HTS. This provision, previously known as classification 807 of the Tariff Schedules of the United States, permits only assembly operations; manufacturing operations are prohibited. Since this is a point of importance, 807 operations should be discussed with and approved by Customs in advance. Sometimes Customs rulings are necessary. If the operation qualifies as an assembly operation, the imported finished article is dutiable on the full value of the article reduced by the value of the U.S.-origin parts or components. The person or entity performing the assembly

Figure 9–4. Declaration by foreign shipper and importer's endorsement.

FOREIGN SHIPPER'S DECLARATION AND IMPORTER'S ENDORSEMENT
(U.S. Goods Returned - HS 9801.00.10)

I, _______________, declare that to the best of my knowledge and belief the articles herein specified were exported from the United States, from the port of ____________ on or about __________, 19__, and that they are returned without having been advanced in value or improved in condition by any process of manufacture or other means.

Marks	Number	Quantity	Description	Value, in U.S. coin
	________	________	________	________
	________	________	________	________
	________	________	________	________
	________	________	________	________

____________________ (Date)

____________________ (Address)

____________________ (Signature)

____________________ (Capacity)

I, _____________, declare that the above declaration by the foreign shipper is true and correct to the best of my knowledge and belief, that the articles were manufactured by ______ ________ (name of manufacturer) located in ______________ (city and state), that the articles were not manufactured or produced in the United States under subheading 9813.00.05, HTSUS, and that the articles were exported from the United States without benefit of drawback.

____________________ (Date)

____________________ (Address)

____________________ (Signature)

____________________ (Capacity)

Figure 9–5. Foreign repairer's declaration and importer's endorsement.

FOREIGN REPAIRER'S DECLARATION AND IMPORTER'S ENDORSEMENT
(Repairs and Alterations - HS 9802.00.40 and 9802.00.50)

I, ________________, declare that the articles herein specified are the articles which, in the condition in which they were exported from the United States, were received by me (us) on _________, 19____, from ____________ (name and address of owner or exporter in the United States); that they were received by me (us) for the sole purpose of being repaired or altered; that only the repairs or alterations described below were performed by me (us); that the full cost or (when no charge is made) value of such repairs or alterations are correctly stated below; and that no substitution whatever has been made to replace any of the articles originally received by me (us) from the owner or exporter thereof mentioned above.

Marks and numbers	Description of articles and of repairs or alterations	Full cost or (when no charge is made) value of repairs or alterations (see subchapter II, chapter 98, HTSUS)	Total value of articles after repairs or alterations

_______________ (Date)

_______________ (Signature)

_______________ (Address)

_______________ (Capacity)

I, ____________, declare that the (above) (attached) declaration by the person who performed the repairs or alterations abroad is true and correct to the best of my knowledge and belief; that the articles were not manufactured or produced in the United States under subheading 9813.00.05 HTSUS; that such articles were exported from the United States for repairs or alterations and without benefit of drawback from ___________________ (port) on _______, 19__; and that the articles entered in their repaired or altered condition are the same articles that were exported on the above date and that are identified in the (above) (attached) declaration.

_______________ (Date)

_______________ (Signature)

_______________ (Address)

_______________ (Capacity)

operations must file an Assembler's Declaration, and any unreported change in the operation or a false declaration can lead to serious customs penalties. A sample Foreign Assembler's Declaration is shown in Figure 9–6. Customs must be notified of any variation in the assembly operation of more than 5 percent of the total cost or value. Where cost data is estimated or standard costs are being used at the time of entry that must be stated on the entry, liquidation of the entry must be suspended and actual cost data must be submitted as soon as accounting procedures permit. This is submitted via the "reconciliation" procedure (see Chapter 8, Section L). 807 treatment is not available on foreign-origin components imported into the United States and then exported for assembly, unless the foreign components were subjected to additional processing in the United States resulting in a substantial transformation into a new and different article of commerce and the imported components were not imported under a temporary importation bond. Foreign-origin components can be used in the assembly process; however, no reduction of U.S. duties is allowed for their value. Articles assembled abroad are considered to be a product of the country of assembly for country of origin marking requirements.

When U.S.-origin commodities are exported to foreign countries and further processed, if the country of processing is a beneficiary country under the Generalized System of Preferences (or Caribbean Basin Initiative) and at least 35 percent of the value is added in the foreign country, the foreign country becomes the new country of origin, and importation of the articles to the United States may be made duty-free.

Recently, under law enacted in Mexico, *maquiladora* operations have become popular. Due to the low labor rates and the close proximity to the U.S. market, many U.S. and foreign companies have established assembly or processing operations under Mexican law. Mexican law provides for the equivalent of temporary importations under bond which permit the U.S.-origin raw materials or components to be brought into Mexico, assembled or further processed, and then exported to the United States without payment of Mexican customs duties. In order to establish a successful *maquiladora* operation, it is necessary to comply with both Mexican and U.S. Customs requirements. Otherwise, the full value of the articles can be dutiable both in Mexico and in the United States. Under the North American Free Trade Agreement, beginning January 1, 2001, the duty-free treatment of raw materials or components was eliminated and they became dutiable at the regular duty rate or the lower duty rate applicable to products meeting the eligibility rules of NAFTA.

C. Plant Construction Contracts

Sometimes an exporter will be a person who has contracted with a foreign purchaser to build an entire plant, sometimes pursuant to a turn-key contract. In such cases, thousands of items may be exported and all of the many considerations discussed in Part II on exporting will be applicable. However, one significant provision in the export control laws is the availability of a special project license from the U.S. Department of Commerce, Office of Export Licensing, where some of the items being exported require individual validated licenses for export. By applying for a project license, the exporter can obtain a blanket license covering all of the items, thereby

Figure 9–6. Foreign assembler's declaration.

FOREIGN ASSEMBLER'S DECLARATION

I, ______________________________, declare that to the best of my knowledge and belief the ____________________________ were assembled in whole or in part from fabricated components listed and described below, which are products in the United States:

Marks of identification, numbers	Description of component	Quality	Unit value at time and place of export from United States	Port and date of export from United States	Name and address of manufacturer

Date Signature

Address Capacity

U.S. IMPORTER'S ENDORSEMENT

I declare that to the best of my knowledge and belief the (above), (attached) declaration, and any other information submitted herewith, or otherwise supplied or referred to, is correct in every respect and there has been compliance with all pertinent legal notes to the Harmonized Tariff Schedule of the United States (19 U.S.C. 1202).

Date Signature

Address Capacity

substantially reducing the effort required to obtain individual validated licenses for each product exported.

D. Barter and Countertrade Transactions

Presently in international trade, an exporter may be asked to accept payment in merchandise rather than cash (barter). Moreover, in other situations, such as compensation arrangements or switch transactions, both export and import transactions may be involved. Such transactions give rise to unique documentation and procedural problems. First, the U.S. company having a role in such a transaction should not try to use its standard-form sales or purchase documents. These transactions require special terms and conditions to protect the participant and should be specifically tailored to the transaction. Second, even though no money will change hands, the parties should value the merchandise or services that will be exchanged. This will be necessary for tax, customs, and foreign exchange control purposes. The U.S. Customs Service recommends that the parties seek an advance ruling. In most countries, attempts to engage in barter transactions for the purpose of avoiding these laws will subject the participants to prosecution for evasion. Correlatively, the participant should satisfy itself that all necessary government notifications and forms are filed, just as if it were a cash transaction, and that all values stated are accurate, consistent, and supportable.

Appendices

Appendix A

Government Agencies and Export Assistance

TIC 1-800-USA-TRADE Trade Information Center

INTERNATIONAL TRADE ADMINISTRATION | U.S. DEPARTMENT OF COMMERCE

Export Programs Guide

About Us | Search | Home | E-Mail Counseling | Site Map

How May We Help You?
Export Questions?
Country Information
Tariff & Tax Information
Export Resources
Trade Offices Nationwide
Trade Promotion
Country Commercial Guide
Business Holidays
Industry Information

Table of Contents

2001 Edition produced by the
Trade Information Center
U.S. Department of Commerce
Washington, DC 20230

Chapter 1: General Export Counseling and Assistance

Chapter 2: Industry-Specific Counseling and Assistance

Chapter 3: Country-Specific Counseling and Assistance

Chapter 4: Trade Contact and Market Research Programs

- Customized Programs
- Electronic Matchmaking and Trade Contact Programs
- Computerized and Published Market Information

Chapter 5: Making Contacts Through Trade Promotion Events

- Domestic Trade Promotion Events
- Foreign Trade Promotion Events

Chapter 6: Special Market Access and Technical Assistance

Chapter 7: Export Finance, Insurance, and Grants (Non-Agricultural)

- Export Finance
- Investment Finance
- Grants for Feasibility Studies and Other Export-Related Needs

Chapter 8: Agriculture Export and Finance Programs

- Agriculture Export Programs
- Agriculture Technical Assistance
- Agriculture Finance and Grant Programs

Chapter 9: Food, Health, and Safety Inspection/Certification Programs

Chapter 10: Export Licenses and Controls

To download the entire EPG 2001 document, please click on the icon:

EPG2001.pdf (2.8 Mb)

Get Acrobat® Reader

For assistance with exporting U.S. products please contact:

Trade Information Center, International Trade Administration
U.S. Department of Commerce, Washington, DC 20230
Phone: 1-800-USA-TRADE,
Fax: (202) 482-4473; Email: TIC@ita.doc.gov

Contact the Webmaster at **TICwebmaster@ita.doc.gov**

54959

TIC INTERNATIONAL TRADE ADMINISTRATION | U.S. DEPARTMENT OF COMMERCE
1-800-USA-TRADE
Trade Information Center
Export Programs Guide

About Us | Search | Home | E-Mail Counseling | Site Map

How May We Help You?
Export Questions?
Country Information
Tariff & Tax Information
Export Resources
Trade Offices Nationwide
Trade Promotion
Country Commercial Guide
Business Holidays
Industry Information

1. General Export Counseling and Assistance

2001 Edition produced by the
Trade Information Center
U.S. Department of Commerce
Washington, DC 20230

International Trade Administration (ITA)/U.S. Department of Commerce - The International Trade Administration is dedicated to opening markets for U.S. products and providing assistance and information to exporters. ITA units include: 1) 104 domestic Export Assistance Centers and 158 overseas commercial export-focused offices in the **U.S. & Foreign Commercial Service** network; 2) industry experts and market and economic analysts in its **Trade Development** unit; and 3) trade compliance and market access experts in its **Market Access and Compliance** offices. The units perform analyses, promote products, and offer services and programs for the U.S. exporting community, including export promotion, counseling, and information programs listed elsewhere in this booklet.

Contact: 1-800-USA-TRAD(E) (1-800-872-8723); Internet home page: **http://www.trade.gov**

Trade Information Center (TIC)/ITA/U.S. Department of Commerce - The Trade Information Center is the first stop for companies seeking export assistance from the federal government. TIC trade specialists: 1) advise exporters on how to find and use government programs; 2) guide businesses through the export process; 3) provide country and regional business counseling on standards and trade regulations, distribution channels, opportunities and best prospects for U.S. companies, import tariffs/taxes and customs procedures, and common commercial difficulties; 4) direct businesses to market research and trade leads; 5) provide information on overseas and domestic trade events and activities; and 6) supply sources of public and private export financing. The TIC trade specialists also direct businesses to state and local trade organizations that provide additional assistance. Country information is available on Western Europe, Asia, Western Hemisphere, Africa, and the Near East.

The Trade Information Center website provides a variety of information, including the most frequently asked questions and answers on exporting, the National Export Directory of international trade contacts for each state, a directory of foreign trade offices in the United States, an alternative finance guide, an Internet guide to export trade leads, and the most up-to-date *Export Programs Guide*. Extensive regional and country market and regulatory information is also available, including assistance with NAFTA Certificate of Origin forms and tariff and border tax rates.

Contact: TIC staff, 1-800-USA-TRAD(E) (1-800-872-8723); fax (202) 482-4473; e-mail: **tic@ita.doc.gov**; Internet home page: **http://tradeinfo.doc.gov**

http://www.export.gov - This new interagency trade portal brings together U.S. Government export-related information under one easy-to-use web site, organized according to the intended needs of the exporter. Whether a company is exploring the possibility of doing international business, searching for trade partners, seeking information on new markets, or dealing with trade problems, this web site can help. Additionally, the site has easy links to information on advocacy, trade events, trade statistics, tariffs and taxes, market research, NAFTA Rules of Origin, export documentation, financing export transactions, and much more.

Contact: Internet home page: **http://www.export.gov**

U.S. and Foreign Commercial Service (US&FCS)/ITA/U.S. Department of Commerce - The mission of the US&FCS is to promote the export of goods and services from the United States, particularly by small- and medium-sized businesses, and protect United States business interests abroad. The 1,800 trade experts in the US&FCS work in more than 100 Export Assistance Centers conveniently located throughout the country and in more than 80 overseas posts.

Contact: For information on the US&FCS and its programs, call 1-800-USA-TRAD(E) (1-800-872-8723) or consult the US&FCS home page at: **http://www.usatrade.gov**

The Export Assistance Center Network (USEACs/EACs)/ITA/U.S. Department of Commerce - The U.S. Department of Commerce, the U.S. Small Business Administration (SBA), the Export-Import Bank (Ex-Im), the U.S. Agency for International Development (USAID), and the U.S. Department of Agriculture (USDA) have formed a unique partnership to establish a nationwide network of Export Assistance Centers (EACs). EACs are located in over 100 cities throughout the United States and serve as one-stop shops that provide small- and medium-sized American businesses with hands-on export marketing and trade finance support. EACs work closely with federal, state, local, public and private organizations to provide unparalleled export assistance to American businesses seeking to compete in the global marketplace. EACs are responsible for providing in-depth, value-added counseling to U.S. firms seeking to expand their international activities, as well as to companies that are just beginning to venture overseas. EAC Trade Specialists provide global business solutions by: 1) identifying the best markets for their clients' products; 2) developing an effective market entry strategy based on information generated from overseas commercial offices; 3) facilitating the implementation of these strategies by advising clients on distribution channels, key factors to consider in pricing, and relevant trade shows and missions; and 4) providing assistance in obtaining trade finance available through federal government programs, as well as access to state, local, public and private sector entities.

Several initiatives have been designed by the EAC network to meet the international trade goals of traditionally under-served communities. The *Rural Export Initiative* provides companies in rural areas with better access to export assistance and global market research by facilitating their access to international trade services and increasing the number of companies in rural areas engaged in exporting. The *Global Diversity Initiative* provides minority businesses with the international trade information and industry connections that can make their product or service successful in the global marketplace. The *Women in International Trade Initiative* offers the expertise, network, and experience of the Commercial Service to meet the needs of women in international trade. The Commercial Service piloted several E-Commerce products through these initiatives that are now available to all Commercial Service clients. These E-Commerce products and services include Video Market Briefs, Video Conferences, Video Gold Keys, and E-Expo USA, a virtual trade show.

Contact: For the address and phone number of the Export Assistance Center nearest you, see the Apendix, call 1-800-USA-TRAD(E) (1-800-872-8723), or consult the web site at **http://www.usatrade.gov**

USA Trade Center/U.S. Department of Commerce - Emphasizing customer service and seamless assistance, the USA Trade Center brings together key components of the Department of Commerce to serve as a single source in Washington, D.C., for a complete range of export-related products and information. The USA Trade Center, located in the Ronald Reagan Building and International Trade Center in our nation's capital, offers general export counseling, country-specific information and counseling covering the globe, access to extensive market research and on-line trade leads, innovative e-commerce programs, and a trade reference assistance center.

Contact: 1-800-USA-TRAD(E) (1-800-872-8723); e-mail: tic@ita.doc.gov; Internet home page: **http://usatc.doc.gov**

District Export Councils (DECs)/ITA/U.S. Department of Commerce - DECs are organizations of leaders from local business communities whose knowledge of international business provides a source of professional advice for local firms. Closely affiliated with the Export Assistance Centers, the 55 nationwide DECs combine the energies of over 1,500 volunteers to supply specialized expertise to small- and medium-sized businesses in their local community who are interested in exporting. For example, DECs organize seminars that make trade finance understandable and accessible to small exporters, host international buyer delegations, design export resource guides, help design Internet home pages, and create export assistance partnerships to strengthen the support given to local businesses.

Contact: For more information on DECs, consult the DEC website at **http://www.usatrade.gov/dec** or contact your local Department of Commerce Export Assistance Center (EAC). For the address and phone number of the EAC nearest you, see the Appendix, call 1-800-

USA-TRAD(E) (1-800-872-8723), or visit the Internet website: **http://www.usatrade.gov**

Office of International Trade (OIT)/Small Business Administration (SBA) -The Office of International Trade works in coordination with other federal agencies and public and private sector organizations to encourage small businesses to expand their export activities and to assist small businesses seeking to export. OIT directs and coordinates SBA's export finance and export development assistance. OIT's outreach efforts include regional initiatives with Russia, Ireland, Argentina, Mexico, and Egypt. In addition, OIT develops how-to and market-specific publications for exporters. OIT oversees the SBA's loan guarantee programs to small business exporters, including the Export Working Capital Program, which is available to exporters through the U.S. Export Assistance Centers (USEACs) and SBA field offices across the country. The office also spearheads a program, through the USEAC network, called E-TAP (Export Trade Assistance Partnership), which focuses on small groups of export-ready companies, teaches assistance needed to develop export markets, acquire orders or contracts, and provides access to export financing in preparation for a trade mission or show overseas.

Contact: Office of International Trade, (202) 205-6720; fax (202) 205-7272; Internet home page: **http://www.sba.gov/oit**

Small Business Development Centers (SBDCs)/Small Business Administration (SBA) - The Small Business Development Centers, located throughout the United States, provide a range of export assistance, particularly to new-to-export companies. They offer assistance services to small businesses, including counseling, training, and managerial assistance. They provide counseling services at no cost to the small business exporter, but they generally charge fees for export training seminars and other SBDC-sponsored export events. Many SBDCs are involved in the E-TAP program.

Contact: Jorge F. Cardona, Office of Small Business Development Centers, (202) 205-7303; fax (202) 205-7727; Internet home page: **http://www.sba.gov/SBDC** For the location of the SBDC nearest you, please contact the Trade Information Center at 1-800-USA-TRAD(E) (1-800-872-8723)

Export Legal Assistance Network (ELAN)/Small Business Administration (SBA) - The Export Legal Assistance Network is a nationwide group of private law firm attorneys experienced in international trade that provides free initial consultations to new-to-export businesses on export-related matters.

Contact: The ELAN service is available through SBA district offices, Service Corps of Retired Executives (SCORE) offices, and Small Business Development Centers (SBDCs). For the address and phone number of the SBA office nearest you, call 1-800-U-ASK-SBA; or contact Judd Kessler, ELAN National Coordinator, (202) 778-3080, fax (202) 778-3063, e-mail: jkessler@porterwright.com; Internet home page: **http://www.fita.org/elan**

Service Corps of Retired Executives (SCORE) - Members of the SCORE program, many of whom have years of practical experience in international trade, provide one-on-one counseling and training seminars. Specialists assist small firms in evaluating export potential and in strengthening domestic operations by identifying financial, managerial, or technical problems.

Contact: National SCORE office, 1-800-634-0245; fax (202) 205-7636; Internet home page: **http://www.score.org**

Minority Business Development Agency (MBDA)/U.S. Department of Commerce - The Minority Business Development Agency (MBDA) provides management and technical assistance, as well as access to domestic and international markets. MBDA's mission is to promote the establishment and growth of minority-owned business enterprises in the United States. Consequently, it is constantly seeking to create new and innovative ways to engage U.S. minority firms in the international business arena. MBDA assists minority firms in gaining international access in many ways, including: trade missions, matchmaker programs, one-on-one client counseling, seminars, and special international program events.

Contact: MBDA International Trade Office, (202) 482-5061; fax (202) 501-4698; Internet home page: **http://www.mbda.gov**

For assistance with exporting U.S. products please contact:

Trade Information Center, International Trade Administration
U.S. Department of Commerce, Washington, DC 20230
Phone: 1-800-USA-TRADE,
Fax: (202) 482-4473; Email: TIC@ita.doc.gov

Contact the Webmaster at **TICwebmaster@ita.doc.gov**

13071

INTERNATIONAL TRADE ADMINISTRATION | U.S. DEPARTMENT OF COMMERCE
TIC 1-800-USA-TRADE
Trade Information Center
Export Programs Guide

About Us | Search | Home | E-Mail Counseling | Site Map

How May We Help You?
Export Questions?
Country Information
Tariff & Tax Information
Export Resources
Trade Offices Nationwide
Trade Promotion
Country Commercial Guide
Business Holidays
Industry Information

4. Trade Contact and Market Research Programs

2001 Edition produced by the
Trade Information Center
U.S. Department of Commerce
Washington, DC 20230

CUSTOMIZED PROGRAMS

International Partner Search (IPS)/ITA/U.S. Department of Commerce - IPS provides a customized search that helps identify well-matched agents, distributors, licensees and strategic alliance partners. A fee of $600 per country is charged.

Contact: For more information on the IPS, contact your local Department of Commerce Export Assistance Center (EAC). For the address and phone number of the EAC nearest you, call 1-800-USA-TRAD(E) (1-800-872-8723) or visit the Internet web site: **http://www.usatrade.gov**

Gold Key Service/ITA/U.S. Department of Commerce - Offered by many Commercial Service overseas offices, the Gold Key Service is a custom-tailored service for U.S. firms planning to visit a country. This service provides assistance in developing a sound market strategy, orientation briefings, introductions to pre-screened potential partners, interpreters for meetings, and effective follow-up planning. The fees range from $150 to $700 (for the first day) per country.

Contact: For more information on the Gold Key Service, contact your local Department of Commerce Export Assistance Center (EAC). For the address and phone number of the EAC nearest you, call 1-800-USA-TRAD(E) (1-800-872-8723) or visit the Internet web site: **http://www.usatrade.gov**

Platinum Key Service/ITA/U.S. Department of Commerce - Offers customized, long-term assistance to U.S. companies seeking to enter a new market, win a contract, lower a trade barrier, or resolve complex issues. Fees depend on the scope of work.

Contact: For more information on the Platinum Key Service, contact your local Department of Commerce Export Assistance Center (EAC). For the address and phone number of the EAC nearest you, call 1-800-

USA-TRAD(E) (1-800-872-8723) or visit the Internet web site: **http://www.usatrade.gov**

Flexible Market Research (FMR)/ITA/U.S. Department of Commerce - Provides customized responses to questions and issues related to a client's product or service. Available on a quick turnaround basis, the research addresses overall marketability of the product, key competitors, price of comparable products, customary distribution and promotion practices, trade barriers, potential business partners, and more. Fees vary according to scope of work.

Contact: For more information on FMR, contact your local Department of Commerce Export Assistance Center (EAC). For the address and phone number of the EAC nearest you, call 1-800-USA-TRAD(E) (1-800-872-8723) or visit the Internet web site: **http://www.usatrade.gov**

International Company Profile (ICP)/ITA/U.S. Department of Commerce - A service for checking the reputation, reliability, and financial status of a prospective trading partner. A U.S. exporter can obtain this information, as well as detailed answers to specific questions about the prospective partner, in a confidential report. In addition, commercial officers at the U.S. Embassy will provide a recommendation on the suitability of the profiled company as a business partner. A fee of $500 per company is charged.

Contact: For more information on the ICP, contact your local Department of Commerce Export Assistance Center (EAC). For the address and phone number of the EAC nearest you, call 1-800-USA-TRAD(E) (1-800-872-8723) or visit the Internet web site: **http://www.usatrade.gov**

Video Conferencing Programs/ITA/U.S. Department of Commerce - The "Virtual Matchmaker," "Video Gold Key," and "Video Market Briefing" programs provide an effective tool to help U.S. companies assess an overseas market or overseas business contacts before venturing abroad to close a deal. Companies can use these cost-effective video services to interview international contacts, get a briefing from overseas industry specialists on prospects and opportunities, or develop a customized solution to international business needs.

- ***Virtual Matchmaker*** - Meet and talk face-to-face with a pre-screened foreign partner via videoconferencing without the cost of traveling overseas.

- ***Video Gold Key*** - The Video Gold Key helps a firm identify and meet with qualified international partners. This service offers 3-5 scheduled meetings with pre-screened business partners and an industry briefing with trade professionals. All meetings take place via videoconference, saving time and travel expenses. Prices vary according to location.

- ***Video Market Briefing*** - The Video Market Briefing provides time-sensitive, custom market research for specific products and services. Benefits include a market entry evaluation and written report and then a follow-up videoconference with an industry professional so a firm can get immediate answers to market questions. Prices vary according to location.

Contact: For more information on these video conferencing services and a schedule of upcoming Virtual Matchmakers, contact your local Department of Commerce Export Assistance Center (EAC). For the address and phone number of the EAC nearest you, call 1-800-USA-TRAD(E) (1-800-872-8723) or visit the Internet web site: **http://www.usatrade.gov**

***Commercial News USA*/ITA/U.S. Department of Commerce -** *Commercial News USA*, a catalog-magazine containing advertisements of U.S. products, is published twelve times per year by the Commercial Service through its private sector partner, ABP International, to promote U.S. products and services to more than 400,000 potential buyers and partners in 145 countries.

Contact: For information and costs on advertising in *Commercial News USA*, call 1-800-USA-TRAD(E) (1-800-872-8723) or call ABP International at (212) 490-3999, fax (212) 822-2028; Internet home page: **http://www.cnewsusa.com**

ELECTRONIC MATCHMAKING AND TRADE CONTACT PROGRAMS

E-Expo USA/ITA/U.S. Department of Commerce - E-Expo USA is a virtual trade show/on-line catalog of U.S. products and services across a broad array of industries. Companies exhibiting on E-Expo USA receive worldwide exposure 24 hours a day, 7 days a week, 365 days per year. Potential foreign buyers can view photos and videos of U.S. products, post leads, link to exhibltors' web sites, and send e-mail inquiries. E-Expo USA is regularly promoted at key trade shows throughout the world, and trade leads collected at the shows are sent directly to U.S. participants. The worldwide network of the Commercial Service provides technical assistance to U.S. exhibitors and to foreign buyers. Assistance includes how to promote products online, financing, packaging, business protocol, customs, logistics, and more. For more information or to register online, visit the E-Expo USA home page at: **http://e-expousa.doc.gov**

***MyExports.com*™/ITA/U.S. Department of Commerce** - U.S. firms can register their business profile free at **http://www.myexports.com** to promote their products before a worldwide audience. Foreign buyers use *MyExports.com*™ to source U.S. goods and services. *MyExports.com*™ also helps U.S. producers find export partners and locate export companies, freight forwarders and other service firms that can facilitate export business. Registrants receive both a free online listing and a free listing in the annual publication *MyExports.com*™ "Buyers' Guide to U.S. Products and Services" distributed nationwide through the Department of Commerce's Export Assistance Centers (EACs) and through U.S. Embassies and Consulates. Hyperlink, display advertising and other export facilitation services are available for a small fee.

Contacts: *MyExports.com™* is coordinated by ITA's Office of Export Trading Company Affairs **http://www.trade.gov/oetca** and produced by its private sector partner, Global Publishers LLC. For more information on *MyExports.com™*, call toll-free at 1-877-390-2629. To receive a free copy of the *MyExports.com™* "Buyers' Guide" and information on other export programs, contact your local EAC. For the EAC closest to you, call 1-800-USA-TRADE, or visit the home page at: **http://www.usatrade.gov**

Global Technology Network (GTN)/U.S. Agency for International Development (USAID) - Operated by USAID's Business Development office, the Global Technology Network receives technology requests from Asia, Latin America, Sub-Saharan Africa, Central and Eastern Europe, the Newly Independent States, and the Near East in areas of agriculture, communications and information, environment, and health technologies. GTN distributes these trade leads, via fax and e-mail, to appropriate U.S. businesses, service firms, and trade associations that are registered with GTN. GTN representatives are located in ten Latin American countries, five Sub-Saharan countries, and ten Asian nations. GTN transmits these leads to U.S. firms within 48 hours of receipt from GTN offices.

Contact: U.S. Agency for International Development/ Global Technology Network (GTN), 1-800-872-4348; fax (202) 466-4597; Internet home page: **http://www.usgtn.org**

Trade Mission OnLine/Small Business Administration (SBA) - Trade Mission OnLine is a searchable database of U.S. small businesses that wish to export their products to be used by foreign firms and U.S. businesses seeking U.S. business partners or suppliers for trade-related activity. It is designed to facilitate small business international sales, franchising, joint ventures, and licensing. Trade Mission OnLine will also be used by the SBA to recruit for foreign trade missions and to provide time-sensitive trade leads to registered companies. To visit and/or register, the Trade Mission OnLine website can be found at: **http://www.sba.gov/tmonline**

Contact: U.S. Small Business Administration, Office of International Trade, (202) 205-6720; fax (202) 205-7272; Internet website: **http://www.sba.gov/oit**

COMPUTERIZED AND PUBLISHED MARKET INFORMATION

http://www.export.gov - This new interagency trade portal brings together U.S. Government export-related information under one easy-to-use web site, organized according to the intended needs of the exporter. Whether a company is exploring the possibility of doing international business, searching for trade partners, seeking information on new markets, or dealing with trade problems, this web site can help. Additionally, the site has easy links to information on advocacy, trade events, trade statistics, tariffs and taxes, market research, NAFTA Rules of Origin, export documentation, financing export transactions, and much more.

Contact: Internet home page: **http://www.export.gov**

Trade Opportunity Program (TOP)/ITA/U.S. Department of Commerce – TOP provides companies with current sales leads from international firms seeking to buy or represent their products and services. TOP leads are accessible free of charge on the Department of Commerce's Commercial Service web site and as a component of the subscription service through STAT-USA. TOP leads are also printed weekly in leading commercial newspapers.

Contact: For more information on TOP, visit the U.S. Department of Commerce's Commercial Service home page at **http://www.usatrade.gov** or for STAT-USA/Internet subscription information, call 1-800-STAT-USA (1-800-782-8872) or (202) 482-1986; fax (202) 482-2164; Internet web site: **http://www.stat-usa.gov**

Trade and Economic Analysis/ITA/U.S. Department of Commerce - The Office of Trade and Economic Analysis provides a broad range of U.S. foreign trade data useful in evaluating trends in U.S. export performance by major export categories and foreign markets. Its major publication is *U.S. Industry and Trade Outlook.* The Office of Trade and Economic Analysis web site includes state and metropolitan area trade data, national trade and industry statistics, and links to key foreign country data sources.

Contact: Jeffrey Lins at (202) 482-5145; fax (202) 482-4614; e-mail jeffrey_lins@ita.doc.gov; Internet home page: **http://www.trade.gov/tradestats**

STAT-USA Electronic Information Products/U.S. Department of Commerce - STAT-USA, the federal government's premier office for the publication of market information, trade leads, and other trade-related data, offers information through the following electronic products:

1. National Trade Data Bank (NTDB) **-** The NTDB is a one-stop source for export promotion and international trade data collected by more than 40 U.S. Government agencies. The NTDB is accessible on the Internet or on CD-ROM (see ordering information below) and enables the user to view more than 200,000 trade-related documents. The NTDB contains: 1) the complete set of Country Commercial Guides; 2) current market research reports compiled by the Commercial Service; 3) State Department country reports on economic policy and trade practices; 4) trade publications; and 5) the Export Promotion Calendar and many other data series.

The NTDB is available as part of STAT-USA/Internet. The cost is $75 for three months and $175 for one year. The Internet address is **http://www.stat-usa.gov**

Contact: The NTDB can be purchased in the form of a CD-ROM for $59 per monthly issue or $575 for a 12-month subscription. Non-U.S. shipments will be charged $75 monthly or $775 for an annual subscription. Additional charges apply for network or redistribution use. For ordering and other specific information, call (202) 482-1986 or 1-800-STAT-USA (1-800-782-8872), fax (202) 482-2164. The NTDB is also available at over 1,100 federal depository libraries nationwide. Call 1-800-USA-TRAD(E) (1-800-872-8723) for a list of these libraries.

2. STAT-USA/Internet - Trade, economic, and business information is available on the Internet at one worldwide web address: http://www.stat-usa.gov. Here, you will find the contents of the National Trade Data Bank (NTDB) plus all of the contents of the former Economic Bulletin Board, on-line, fully searchable and accessible 24 hours a day, seven days a week. *GLOBUS & NTDB* has all of the market research reports, agricultural and business trade leads, and export guides of the NTDB CD-ROM, as well as U.S. Government procurement opportunities. *State of the Nation* provides businesses with the economic news, statistics, and indicators necessary to gauge the direction of the American economy.

Contact: Subscriptions to STAT-USA/Internet are $75 for three months or $175 for a year of unlimited access. Call 1-800-STAT-USA (1-800-782-8872) or (202) 482-1986, fax (202) 482-2164, or subscribe on-line at **http://www.stat-usa.gov**

3. USA Trade CD-ROM and USA Trade Online - How many parachutes does the U.S. export to France? How many printed circuit boards does the U.S. import and what percentage comes from Asia? USA Trade CD-ROM and USA Trade Online can tell you. These two products provide U.S. import and export statistics for over 18,000 commodities trade worldwide. Both versions of USA Trade offer the most current merchandise trade statistics available in a dynamic spreadsheet format. The CD-ROM version offers the convenience of portability and the power for real number crunching. The Online version, **http://www.usatradeonline.gov**, offers immediate delivery of the current numbers 24 hours a day and the ability to store queries. Both use the statistics generated by the Foreign Trade Division of the U.S. Census Bureau and are available through STAT-USA.

Contact: USA Trade CD-ROM can be purchased for $65 per monthly issue or $650 for a 12-month subscription. Non-U.S. shipments will be charged $80 monthly or $800 for an annual subscription. The Internet-based version, USA Trade Online, is available at $50 per month or $300 for an annual subscription. Call 1-800-STAT-USA (1-800-782-8872) or (202) 482-1986; fax (202) 482-2164

Top Targets for Trade Promotion/ITA/U.S. Department of Commerce - "Top Targets for Trade Promotion" and "Top Market Opportunites for Small Business" highlight outstanding markets for American industries--ranked by potential gain in export sales over the next two years. Among 40 key countries with strong sales potential for U.S. goods and services, there are some 400 individual market sectors judged as "Top Targets" for increasing U.S. exports through the coming year. Top targets were initially identified by Foreign Commercial Service staff overseas--and then analyzed by Trade Development's Export Promotion Office according to a common set of market factors, which gauge both potential demand for the individual product and expected overall economic growth of the countries. Market factors include measures of the size and projected growth of the total market, imports, and U.S. exports--as well as judgments on local and third-country competition.

Contact: Alan O. Maurer, Ph.D. (202) 482-3486 or the Trade Information Center at 1-800-USA-TRAD(E) (1-800-872-8723); Internet web site: **http://tradeinfo.doc.gov**

***Export America*/ITA/U.S. Department of Commerce** - The official magazine of the International Trade Administration (ITA) in the U.S. Department of Commerce offers practical export advice and serves as a valuable resource for small and medium-sized exporters (SMEs). Each month, *Export America* draws on the resources of the ITA and other government agencies to feature regional developments, country- and industry-specific opportunities, trade events listings, technical advice, online marketing tips and export statistics. Each article specifically focuses on SMEs' needs and includes information on technical topics, such as export documentation and market research. This combination of feature stories and hands-on exporting advice makes *Export America* an essential resource for any exporter looking to enter or expand in the global marketplace.

Contact: For subscription information, please contact the Government Printing Office at 202-512-1800 or visit the *Export America* home page at: **http://exportamerica.doc.gov**. For all other comments or questions about the magazine, or to receive a sample copy, please contact *Export America's* editorial offices at Tel: 202-482-3809, fax: 202-482-5819, or e-mail: Export_America@ita.doc.gov

Webcast Library/ITA/U.S. Department of Commerce - Webcasts are on-line series of video streamed seminars and briefings on current international business topics from tips on exporting health care products to Argentina to selling globally via the Internet. To view "Featured Webcasts," visit the Internet web site: **http://www.usatrade.gov/webcasts**

National Technical Information Service (NTIS)/U.S. Department of Commerce - NTIS is the official source for government-sponsored U.S. and world-wide scientific, technical, engineering, and business-related information for the benefit of U.S. industry. NTIS offers a wide variety of export promotion and international trade resources, including Country Commercial Guides.

Contact: NTIS Sales Desk, 1-800-553-NTIS (1-800-553-6847) or (703) 605-6000; Internet home page: **http://www.ntis.gov**

International Data Base/U.S. Census Bureau/U.S. Department of Commerce -The International Programs Center compiles and maintains up-to-date global demographic and social information for all countries in its International Data Base (IDB), which is available to U.S. companies seeking to identify potential markets overseas.

Contact: Peter Johnson or Pat Dickerson, Information Resources Branch, (301) 457-1403; fax (301) 457-1539; e-mail: peterj@census.gov. Information about the IDB, including online access and free download, is available on the Internet at:

http://www.census.gov/ipc/www/idbnew.html

Export and Import Trade Data Base/U.S. Census Bureau//U.S. Department of Commerce - This database contains U.S. export and import statistics tracked by mode of transportation and district of entry or exit. Various levels of classification, including the Harmonized System of Commodity Classification, Standard International Trade Classification (SITC), North American Industry Classification System (NAICS) based codes, and End-Use Classification are available. Customized tabulations and reports can be prepared to user specifications. Prices begin at $25 and vary depending upon user requirements and job size. Export and import databases can also be purchased on CD-ROM at a price of $1,200 a year, $500 a quarter, or $150 a month.

Contact: Data Dissemination Branch, (301) 457-2311; fax (301) 457-4615 for reports, (301) 457-4100 for CD-ROM; Internet home page: **http://www.census.gov/foreign-trade/www**

SBA Online BBS/Small Business Administration (SBA) - SBA Online is an electronic bulletin board developed to expedite dissemination of information to the small business community on starting, expanding, and financing a business. The system operates 23 hours a day and 365 days a year. All that is needed is a computer, modem, phone line, and communications software. Data parameters are 14.4, N, 8, 1. Access different SBA Online services by calling the following numbers on a modem:

Contact: 1-800-697-4636 (This line provides SBA and other government agency information and some downloadable text files.) 1-900-463-4636 (This number allows access, for $0.14 a minute to SBA and other government information, a wide range of downloadable files, including application and software files, the gateway, mail, Internet mail, news groups, and on-line searchable data banks.) While information can also be obtained by calling (202) 401-9600, technical support for SBA Online BBS is available by calling (202) 205-6400.

SBA Internet Home Page/Small Business Administration (SBA) - The SBA Home Page provides SBA services, downloadable files, plus services from agency resource partners, links to other federal and state governments, and direct connections to additional outside resources. Special areas of interest focus on assisting U.S. companies that are setting up an operation, seeking financing, looking to expand, and beginning to engage in exporting. There are special features that include Year 2000 (Y2K) help for small businesses and current SBA outreach initiatives. SBA's home page also contains information on SBA programs that assist minority- and women-owned businesses. In addition, large libraries of business-focused shareware, downloadable SBA loan forms, and agency publications are available. A wide variety of services listed by state are provided, including calendars of local training courses sponsored by SBA. On-line workshops are offered for individuals to work through self-paced activities that help them start and expand their business. In addition, the home page links directly to the White House home page and the U.S. Business Advisor, which houses a large volume of regulatory information for small businesses. SBA provides full text search capabilities as well as an area for user comments and suggestions.

Contact: SBA Help Desk (202) 205-6400; Internet home page: **http://www.sba.gov**

Overseas Security Advisory Council (OSAC)/U.S. Department of State -OSAC is the point of contact between the Department of State and the U.S. private sector on all overseas security-related matters such as political unrest, crime, terrorism, and the protection of information. OSAC manages an Internet-based electronic database available to U.S. businesses with overseas interests. The electronic database provides comprehensive and timely security-related and country-specific information. OSAC also works closely with U.S. Embassies and Consulates worldwide to expedite contacts between U.S. business representatives and State Department security officers.

Contact: Nickolas W. Proctor, Executive Director, OSAC, (202) 663-0533; fax (202) 663-0868

***Foreign Labor Trends*/U.S. Department of Labor -** *Foreign Labor Trends* is a series of annual reports that describe and analyze labor trends in some 75 foreign countries. The reports cover labor-management relations, labor and government, international labor activities, and other significant developments. A list of key labor indicators is also included. The U.S. Department of Labor's Office of Foreign Relations publishes additional reports on four foreign countries each year.

Contact: Sudha Haley, Office of Foreign Relations, (202) 219-6234 ext. 168; fax (202) 219-5613

For assistance with exporting U.S. products please contact:

Trade Information Center, International Trade Administration
U.S. Department of Commerce, Washington, DC 20230
Phone: 1-800-USA-TRADE,
Fax: (202) 482-4473; Email: TIC@ita.doc.gov

Contact the Webmaster at **TICwebmaster@ita.doc.gov**

7888

Appendix B

International Sales Agreement (Export)

FORM

AGREEMENT made January 4, 1982, between Panoramic Export Company, Inc., a New York corporation having its principal place of business at 71 West 42d Street, New York, New York (the "Seller"), and Miguel Vellos, of 31 Avenida de Cortez, Lima, Peru (the "Purchaser").

1. *Sale.* The Seller shall cause to be manufactured, and shall sell and deliver to the Purchaser certain machinery and equipment (the "goods"), to be manufactured specially for the Purchaser by Rollo Manufacturing Company (the "Manufacturer"), at the Manufacturer's plant in Detroit, Michigan, according to the specifications appearing in Exhibit A annexed.

2. *Price.* The purchase price shall be $1,857.60 F.O.B. mill, freight prepaid to New Orleans, Louisiana, payable in currency of the United States of America. The term "F.O.B. mill" means delivery free on board cars at the Manufacturer's works.

3. *Payment.* The terms are net cash on presentation of invoice and inland bill of lading to bankers approved by the Seller, with whom credit in favor of the Seller for the full amount of the purchase price is to be established forthwith. This credit shall be confirmed to the Seller by the bankers, and shall remain in full force until this contract shall have been completely performed. Delay by the Purchaser in establishing this credit shall extend the time for the performance of this contract by the Seller to such extent as may be necessary to enable it to make delivery in the exercise of reasonable diligence after such credit has been established; or, at the Seller's option, such delay may be treated by the Seller as a wrongful termination of this contract on the part of the Purchaser.

4. *Delivery.* The Seller shall notify the Purchaser when the goods are ready for shipment. Thereupon the Purchaser shall furnish shipping instructions to the Seller, stating the date of shipment, the carrier, and the routing. The

Purchaser shall be entitled to select any routing officially authorized and published by the transportation companies, provided that the Seller may change the routing if inability to secure cars promptly, or other reasons, would involve delay in forwarding the goods over the route selected by the Purchaser. The Seller shall not be required to ship the goods until it has received shipping instructions from the Purchaser. If the Purchaser fails to furnish shipping instructions promptly, so as to enable the Seller to perform this contract in accordance with its terms, the Seller may, at its option, and in addition to all other rights it may possess, cancel such portion of this contract as may remain unexecuted, or make shipment in accordance with any routing of its own selection.

5. *Freight charges.* Any prepayment by the Seller of freight charges shall be for the account of the Purchaser, and shall be included in the amount of the invoice and repaid by the Purchaser on presentation thereof, and shall not affect the obligations of the Seller with respect to delivery. Insofar as the purchase price includes freight charges, such price is based upon the lowest official freight rate in effect at the date of this contract. Any difference between such rate and the rate actually paid, when the goods are shipped from the Manufacturer's plant, shall be for the Purchaser's account, and shall be reflected in the invoice, whether such difference results from a change in rate or a change in route.

6. *Insurance.* In no case does the purchase price, even though inclusive of freight, cover the cost of any insurance; but if the route selected involves movement of the goods by water, or by rail and water, for which the freight rate does not include insurance, the Seller shall effect marine insurance for the account of the Purchaser, and the Purchaser shall repay to the Seller the cost of such insurance.

7. *Partial delivery.* The Seller may ship any portion of the goods as soon as completed at the Manufacturer's plant, upon compliance with the terms of paragraph 4; and payment for any portion of the goods as shipped shall become

due in accordance with the terms of payment stated in paragraph 3.

8. *Contingencies.* The Seller shall not be liable for any delay in manufacture or delivery due to fires, strikes, labor disputes, war, civil commotion, delays in transportation, shortages of labor or material, or other causes beyond the control of the Seller. The existence of such causes of delay shall justify the suspension of manufacture, and shall extend the time of performance on the part of the Seller to the extent necessary to enable it to make delivery in the exercise of reasonable diligence after the causes of delay have been removed. However, that in the event of the existence of any such causes of delay, the Purchaser may cancel the purchase of such portion of the goods as may have been subjected to such delay, provided such portion of the goods has not been manufactured nor is in process of manufacture at the time the Purchaser's notice of cancellation arrives at the Manufacturer's plant.

9. *Warranty.* The Seller guarantees that the goods will generate or utilize electrical energy to their rated capacities without undue heating, and will do their work in a successful manner, provided that they are kept in proper condition and operated under normal conditions, and that their operation is properly supervised. THE WARRANTIES SPECIFIED IN THIS CONTRACT ARE IN LIEU OF ANY AND ALL OTHER WARRANTIES, EXPRESS OR IMPLIED, INCLUDING ANY WARRANTY OF MERCHANTABILITY OR FITNESS FOR A PARTICULAR PURPOSE.

10. *Inspection.* The Purchaser may inspect the goods at the Manufacturer's plant, and such inspection and acceptance shall be final. Reasonable facilities shall be afforded to inspectors representing the Purchaser to make the inspection, and to apply, before shipment from the Manufacturer's plant, tests in accordance with the specifications contained in paragraph 1. If the Purchaser fails to inspect

the goods, the failure shall be deemed an acceptance of the goods, and any acceptance shall be deemed a waiver of any right to revoke acceptance at some future date with respect to any defect that a proper inspection would have revealed.

11. *Claims.* The Seller shall not be liable for any claims unless they are made promptly after receipt of the goods and due opportunity has been given for investigation by the Seller's representatives. Goods shall not be returned except with the Seller's permission.

12. *Country of importation.* The Purchaser represents that the goods are purchased for the purpose of exportation to Peru, and the Purchaser covenants that the goods will be shipped to that destination, and shall furnish, if required by the Seller, a landing certificate duly executed by the customs authorities at the port of importation, certifying that the goods have been landed and entered at that port.

13. *Duties.* All drawbacks of duties paid on materials entering into the manufacture of the goods shall accrue to the Seller, and the Purchaser shall furnish the Seller with all documents necessary to obtain payment of such drawbacks, and to cooperate with the Seller in obtaining such payment.

14. *Cancellation by purchaser.* The Purchaser may cancel this contract, as to any goods not manufactured or in process of manufacture at the time the Purchaser's notice of cancellation arrives at the Manufacturer's plant, in any of the following events:

(a) if the country of importation becomes involved in civil or foreign war, insurrection, or riot, or is invaded by armed forces; or if, as a result of war, treaty, or otherwise, it is added to or becomes a part of the domain of any other sovereignty; or

(b) if a countervailing duty is declared or imposed on the goods by the country of importation; or

(c) if by reason of an embargo the goods cannot be exported from the United States; or

(d) if the Purchaser is unable to obtain an export shipping license for the purpose of exporting the goods to Peru.

15. *Benefit.* This agreement shall be binding upon and shall inure to the benefit of the parties, their legal representatives, successors, and assigns, provided that the Purchaser shall not assign this contract without the prior written consent of the Seller.

16. *Construction.* This contract shall be construed under the laws of New York.

In witness whereof the parties have executed this contract.

Corporate Seal Attest:	Panoramic Export Company, Inc. by . . . . President
. . . . Secretary	. . . . (L.S.) Miguel Vellos

Appendix C

Correct Way to Complete the Shipper's Export Declaration

CORRECT WAY TO COMPLETE THE SHIPPER'S EXPORT DECLARATION FORM 7525-V

Title 15 Code of Federal Regulations, Part 30

(www.census.gov/foreign-trade)

U.S. Department of Commerce
Donald L. Evans, Secretary

Bureau of the Census
(Vacant), Director

Foreign Trade Division
Bureau of the Census
C. Harvey Monk, Jr., Chief

Issued: February 14, 2001

THE CORRECT WAY TO COMPLETE THE SHIPPER'S EXPORT DECLARATION (SED)

This booklet explains how to properly complete the SED and contains references to the major rules, regulations, and guidelines to assist you in preparing the SED. If, at any time, you have a question regarding the completion of the SED please contact the Regulations, Outreach, & Education Branch on 301-457-2238 or visit our website at <www.census.gov/foreign-trade>

Correct Way to Complete the Shipper's Export Declaration

TABLE OF CONTENTS

TOPIC	PAGE NO.
1. When is a SED REQUIRED OR NOT REQUIRED	1
2. Purpose of the SED	2
3. Form or Method of Data Collection	2
4. Preparation and Signature of the SED	2
5. Requirement for Separate SEDs	3
6. Presentation of the SED	3
7. Correction to a SED	4
8. A SED is not Required In the Following Instances (SED Exemptions)	4
9. Retention of Shipping Documents	6
10. Administrative Provisions	6
11. Regulations	7
12. Office of Management & Budget Response Burden Paragraph	8
13. References	8
14. Information to be Reported on the SED (data element descriptions)	9
APPENDIX (Export Assistance Telephone Contacts)	15

Appendix C

THE CORRECT WAY TO COMPLETE THE SED

(Follow these instructions carefully to avoid delay at shipping point. Refer to the Foreign Trade Statistics Regulations (FTSR) for specific details on these provisions, 15 CFR Part 30)

1a. Shipper's Export Declarations (SEDs) are Required in the Following Instances:

From	To	No. of Copies
United States	Canada	1 (only if a license is required)
United States (Postal & Non-Postal)	Foreign Countries	Postal (1), Non-Postal (2)
United States	Puerto Rico	1
United States	U.S. Virgin Islands	1
Puerto Rico	United States	1
Puerto Rico	Foreign Countries	1
Puerto Rico	U.S. Virgin Islands	1
U.S. Virgin Islands	Foreign Countries	1

1b. Shipper's Export Declarations ARE NOT REQUIRED in the Following Instances:

From	To
United States	Canada (unless an export license is required)
U.S. Virgin Islands	United States
U.S. Virgin Islands	Puerto Rico
United States/Puerto Rico	Other U.S. Possessions**
Other U.S. Possessions	United States

** American Samoa, Baker Island, Commonwealth of the Northern Mariana Islands, Guam, Howland Island, Jarvis Island, Johnston Atoll, Kingmen Reef, Midway Islands, Navassa Island, Palmyra Atoll, Wake Island.

2. Purpose of the SED

The Shipper's Export Declaration (SED), Commerce Form 7525-V, is used for compiling the official U.S. export statistics for the United States and for export control purposes. The regulatory provisions for preparing, signing and filing the SED are contained in the Foreign Trade Statistics Regulations (FTSR), Title 15 Code of Federal Regulations (CFR) Part 30.

3. Form or Method of Data Collection

(a) Paper

The Commerce Form 7525-V and its continuation sheet may be purchased from the Government Printing Office, (202) 512-1800, local Customs District Directors, or can be privately printed. **Privately printed SEDs must conform in every respect to the official form.** The SED Form 7525-V can also be downloaded from the Foreign Trade Division website at <**www.census.gov/foreign-trade**> on buff (yellow) or goldenrod colored paper. Customs will not accept SEDs on white paper.

(b) Electronic: Automated Export System (AES)

The U.S. Census Bureau and the U.S. Customs Service jointly offer an electronic method for filing shipper's export declaration information known as the Automated Export System (AES). Participants in the AES include exporters (U.S. principal party in interest), forwarding or other agents, carriers, non-vessel operating common carriers (NVOCCs), consolidators, port authorities, software vendors, or service centers. Once certified by the Census Bureau, participants may file shipper's export data electronically using the AES in lieu of filing an individual paper SED for each shipment. The Census Bureau also offers a free Internet service for filing SED information through the AES called AES*Direct*. For additional information on AES and AES*Direct* go to the Foreign Trade Division web sites at **<www.census.gov/foreign-trade > or <*www.aesdirect.gov*>.**

For regulatory requirements on filing shipper's export information electronically through the AES refer to the FTSR, Sections 30.60 through 30.66.

4. Preparation and Signature of the SED

The SED must be prepared in English, be typewritten or in other non-erasable medium. The original should be signed (signature stamp acceptable) by the exporter (U.S. principal party in interest) or its authorized forwarding or other agent. In all cases where a forwarding or other agent is preparing a SED or AES record on behalf of a principal party in interest (i.e. U.S. or foreign), the principal party in interest must authorize the forwarding or other agent to prepare and sign and file the SED or transmit the AES record on its behalf through a formal power of attorney, written authorization, or, for USPPIs only, by signing block 29 on the paper SED.

5. **Requirement for Separate SEDs**

A separate SED is required for each shipment per USPPI, including each rail car, truck, ocean vessel, airplane, or other vehicle.

A shipment is defined as - All merchandise sent from one exporter (U.S. principal party in interest) to one foreign consignee, to a single foreign country of ultimate destination, on a single carrier, on the same day.

The exporter (U.S. principal party in interest) may list more than one Commerce Department (BXA) license or license exception or a combination of licenses and license exceptions on the same SED or AES shipment. In addition, the exporter may combine "No License Required" (NLR) items with licensed items and license exceptions on the same SED or AES shipment. To avoid confusion when preparing the paper SED, goods licensed by other U.S. agencies, such as the State Department, should be reported on a separate SED from goods licensed by the Commerce Department. For AES transactions, multiple licenses can be reported on one shipment.

Where two or more items are classified under the same Schedule B number, the Schedule B number should appear only once on the SED with a single quantity, shipping weight, and value, unless a validated license requires otherwise or, the shipment consists of a combination of foreign and domestic merchandise classified under the same Schedule B number.

Shipments involving multiple invoices or packages should be reported on the same SED.

6. **Presentation of the SED**

(a) Postal (mail) Shipments - the SED must be delivered to a Post Office official with the package at the time of mailing. (See the U.S. Postal Service's International Mail Manual). All mail shipments valued at $2,500 or over, or that require an export license, require a SED.

(b) All other shipments - the SEDs shall be delivered to the exporting carrier with the merchandise.

(c) Exporting carriers are required to file the SED and manifest with Customs at the port of export.

The SED may accompany the merchandise or it may be delivered directly to the exporting carrier at the port of exportation.

In cases where a shipment does not require a SED based on the FTSR, a reference to the applicable section of the FTSR that exempts the merchandise from the requirement to file a SED, must be noted on the bill of lading, air waybill, or other loading document. Detailed exemption provisions for when a SED is not required are contained in the FTSR, Subpart D, sections 30.50 through 30.58. For acceptable SED exemption statements refer to Foreign Trade Statistics Letter 168 (amendment 1). Also, see Section 8 below.

7. Correction to a SED

Corrections or amendments of data to a previously filed SED should be made on a copy of the originally filed SED. Mark "**CORRECTED COPY**" on the top of the SED, line through the appropriate field(s) requiring correction and insert the correction. File the corrected SED with the Customs Director at the port of export.

For mail exports, corrections must be sent directly to the U.S. Census Bureau, National Processing Center. Attention: Foreign Trade Section, 1201 East 10th Street, Jeffersonville, Indiana 47132 as soon as the need to make such correction or cancellation is determined.

8. A SED is not Required In the Following Instances (SED Exemptions):
(Reference Sections 30.50 thru 30.58 of the FTSR)

A. Shipments where the value of commodities classified under each individual Schedule B number is $2,500 or less and for which an export license is not required, except that a SED is required for exports destined to Cuba, Iran, Iraq, Libya, North Korea, Serbia, (excluding Kosovo), Sudan, and Syria. (See §30.55(h))

If a shipment contains a mixture of individual Schedule B numbers valued at $2,500 or less and individual Schedule B numbers valued at over $2,500, only those valued at $2,500 or more should be reported on the SED. (See §30.55(h)(1))

When either all or part of the shipment does not require a SED, one of the following statements must appear on the bill of lading, air waybill, or other loading documents for carrier use:

1. "No SED required, FTSR Section 30.55 (h)".

2. "No SED required - no individual Schedule B number valued over $2,500".

3. "Remainder of shipment valued $2,500 or less per individual Schedule B number".

[Note: Refer to FTSR Letter 168 (amendment 1) for more detailed information on acceptable SED exemption statements.]

B. Shipments from the **United States to Canada, except those:** (See §30.58)

(1) Requiring a Department of Commerce export license.

(2) Subject to the Department of State, International Traffic in Arms Regulations regardless of license requirements.

(3) Subject to Department of Justice, Drug Enforcement Administration, export declaration requirements.

[Note: For merchandise transhipped from the United States through Canada for ultimate destination to a foreign country, other than Canada, a SED or AES record is required.]

C. Shipments through the U.S. Postal Service that do not require an export license and the shipment is valued at $2500 or under.

D. Shipments from one point in the United States to another point in the United States by routes passing through Mexico, and shipments from one point in Mexico to another point in Mexico by routes passing through the United States.

E. Shipments to the U.S. Armed Services

(1) All commodities consigned to the U.S. Armed Service, including exchange systems. (See §30.52)

(2) Department of Defense Military Assistance Program Grant-Aid shipments being transported as Department of Defense cargo. (See §30.52)

F. Shipments to U.S. Government agencies and employees for their exclusive use. (See §30.53)

G. Other miscellaneous shipments. (See §30.55)

(1) Diplomatic pouches and their contents.

(2) Human remains and accompanying receptacles and flowers.

(3) Shipments of gift parcels moving under General License GFT.

(4) Shipments of interplant correspondence and other business records from a U.S. firm to its subsidiary or affiliate.

(5) Shipments of pets as baggage, accompanying or not accompanying persons leaving the United States.

H. Merchandise not moving as cargo under a bill of lading or air waybill and not requiring a validated export license.

(1) Baggage and household effects of persons leaving the United States when such are owned by the person, in his possession at the time of departure and not intended for sale.

(2) Carriers' stores, supplies, equipment, bunker fuel, and so forth, when not intended for unlading in a foreign country.

(3) Usual and reasonable kinds and quantities of dunnage necessary to secure and stow cargo. (For sole use on board the carrier)

If the above shipments are moving under a bill of lading or air waybill, a SED is required, but Schedule B numbers should **not** be shown, and the SED should include a statement that the shipment consists of baggage, personal effects, and so forth.

If these shipments require a validated export license, the SED must identify the shipment as baggage, personal effects, and so forth, and must contain all of the information required on the SED.

I. SED for Personal Effects and Household Goods

(1) A SED is required for personal effects and household goods only when the value of such items is $2,500 or over. A schedule B number is not required for such items.

(2) Personal effects and household goods destined for Canada do not require a SED regardless of value.

9. Retention of Shipping Documents

Exporters or their agents must maintain copies of shipping documents for a period of 5 years for statistical purposes. Additional record retention requirements for licensed shipments appear in the Export Administration Regulations. Exporters or their agents must also be aware of the record retention policies of other Government agencies.

10. Administration Provisions

The SED and its content is strictly confidential and used solely for official purposes authorized by the Secretary of Commerce in accordance with 13 U.S.C. Section 301(g). Neither the SED nor its contents may be disclosed to anyone except the exporter or its agent by those having possession of or access to any official copy. (See §30.91)

Information from the SED (except common information) may not be copied to manifests or other shipping documents. The exporter (U.S. principal party in interest) or the forwarding or other agent may not furnish the SED or its content to anyone for unofficial purposes.

Copies of the SED may be supplied to the exporter (U.S. principal party in interest) or its agent only when such copies are needed to comply with official U.S. Government requirements.

A SED presented for export constitutes a representation by the exporter (U.S. principal party in interest) that all statements and information are in accordance with the export control regulations. The commodity described on the declaration is authorized under the particular license as identified on the declaration, all statements conform to the applicable licenses, and all conditions of the export control regulations have been met.

It is unlawful to knowingly make false or misleading representation for exportation. This constitutes a violation of the Export Administration Act, 50, U.S.C. App. 2410. It is also a violation of export control laws and regulations to be connected in any way with an altered SED to effect export.

Commodities that have been, are being, or for which there is probable cause to believe they are intended to be exported in violation of laws or regulations are subject to seizure, detention, condemnation, or sale under 22 U.S.C. Section 401.

To knowingly make false or misleading statements relating to information on the SED is a criminal offense subject to penalties as provided for in 18 U.S.C. Section 1001.

Violations of the Foreign Trade Statistics Regulations are subject to civil penalties as authorized by 13 U.S.C. Section 305. (See §30.95)

11. Regulations

Detailed legal and regulatory requirements regarding the SED and its preparation are contained in the Foreign Trade Statistics Regulations (FTSR) (15 CFR, Part 30). Questions concerning the FTSR may be directed to the Regulations, Outreach, & Education Branch Foreign Trade Division, U.S. Census Bureau on (301) 457-2238. Up to date copies of regulations, FTSR Letters, *Federal Register* Notices, and other current information can also be accessed on the Foreign Trade Division's web site at <www.census.gov/foreign-trade>

Information concerning export control laws and regulations including additional SED requirements is contained in the Export Administration Regulations (EAR) (15 CFR Parts 730 - 774) which may be purchased from the Superintendent of Documents, U.S. Government Printing Office, Washington, DC 20402. The EAR can also be accessed on the Bureau of Export Administration (BXA) web site at <www.bxa.doc.gov>

12. Office of Management and Budget Response Burden Paragraph

Public reporting burden for this collection of information is estimated to average slightly more than 11 minutes (.186 hour) per response for the paper SED, Commerce Form 7525-V, and approximately 3 minutes (.05 hour) per response for the Automated Export System, including the time for reviewing instructions, searching existing data sources, gathering and maintaining the data needed, and completing and reviewing the collection of information. Send comments regarding this burden or any other aspect of this collection of information, including suggestions for reducing this burden to the Associate Director for Administration, Room 3104, Federal Office Building 3, Bureau of the Census, Washington, DC 20233-0001; and to the Office of Management and Budget, Washington, DC 20503.

13. References

Schedule B - Statistical Classification of Domestic and Foreign Commodities Exported from the United States. For sale by the Superintendent of Documents, U.S. Government, U.S. Government Printing Office, Washington, DC 20402 and local U.S. Customs District Directors. A Schedule B search engine is also available on the FTD web site. (www.census.gov/foreign-trade)

Schedule C - Classification of Country and Territory Designations for U.S. Foreign Trade Statistics. Free from the Bureau of the Census, Washington, DC 20233-0001. Also included as part of Schedule B. Schedule C codes are also available on the FTD web site. (www.census.gov/foreign-trade)

Schedule D - Classification of Customs Districts and Ports for U.S. Foreign Trade Statistics. Free from the Bureau of the Census, Washington, DC 20233-0001. Also included as part of Schedule B. The Schedule D codes are also available on the FTD web site. (www.census.gov/foreign-trade)

Foreign Trade Statistics Regulations (FTSR).
Free from the Bureau of the Census, Washington, DC 20233-0001. The FTSR is also available for downloading on the FTD web site. (www.census.gov/foreign-trade)

Export Administration Regulations (EAR). For sale by the Superintendent of Documents, U.S. Government Printing Office, Washington, DC 20402 and U.S. Department of Commerce District Offices. The EAR is also available on the BXA web site (www.bxa.doc.gov)

Note: This is an instructional pamphlet summarizing the preparation of the SED. It is in no way intended as a substitute for either the Foreign Trade Statistics Regulations, the Export Administration Regulations, or the regulations of any other agency.

See the Appendix for a List of Telephone Contacts Providing Additional Information

INFORMATION TO BE REPORTED ON THE SHIPPER'S EXPORT DECLARATION FORM 7525-V

Block Number and Data Required

1(a) **U.S. Principal Party In Interest (USPPI)** - Provide the name and address of the U.S. exporter (U.S. principal party in interest). The USPPI is the person in the United States that receives the primary benefit, monetary or otherwise, of the export transaction. Generally that person is the U.S. seller, manufacturer, order party, or foreign entity. The foreign entity must be listed as the USPPI if in the United States when the items are purchased or obtained for export. Report only the first five digits of the ZIP code. (See §30.4, 30.7)

1(b) **USPPI Employer Identification Number (EIN) or ID Number**- Enter the USPPI's Internal Revenue Service Employer Identification Number (EIN) or Social Security Number (SSN) if no EIN has been assigned. Report the 9-digit numerical code as reported on your latest Employer's Quarterly Federal Tax Return, Treasury Form 941. The EIN is usually available from your accounting or payroll department. If an EIN or SSN is not available a border crossing number, passport number, or a Customs identification number must be reported. (See §30.7(d)(2))

1(c) **Parties To Transaction** - Indicate if this is a related or non-related party transaction. A related party transaction is a transaction between a USPPI and a foreign consignee, (e.g., parent company or sister company), where there is at least 10 percent ownership of each by the same U.S. or foreign person or business enterprise.

2 **Date of Exportation** - Enter the date the merchandise is scheduled to leave the United States for all methods of transportation . If the actual date is not known, report the best estimate of departure. The date format should be indicated by MM/DD/YYYY.

3 **Transportation Reference Number** - Report the booking number for ocean shipments. The booking number is the reservation number assigned by the carrier to hold space on the vessel for the cargo being shipped. For air shipments the airway bill number must be reported. For other methods of transportation leave blank.

4(a) **Ultimate Consignee** - Enter the name and address of the foreign party actually receiving the merchandise for the designated end-use or the party so designated on the export license. For overland shipments to Mexico, also include the Mexican state in the address.

4(b) **Intermediate Consignee** - Enter the name and address of the party in a foreign country who makes delivery of the merchandise to the ultimate consignee or the party so named on the export license.

5 **Forwarding Agent** - Enter the name and address of the forwarding or other agent authorized by a principal party in interest.

6 **Point (State) of Origin or Foreign Trade Zone (FTZ) Number**

(a) If from a FTZ enter the FTZ number for exports leaving the FTZ, otherwise enter the:

(b) two-digit U.S. Postal Service abbreviation of the state in which the merchandise actually starts its journey to the port of export, or

(c) State of the commodity of the greatest value, or

(d) State of consolidation.

7 **Country of Ultimate Destination** - Enter the country in which the merchandise is to be consumed, further processed, or manufactured; the final country of destination as known to the exporter at the time of shipment; or the country of ultimate destination as shown on the export license. Two-digit (alpha character) International Standards Organization (ISO) codes may also be used.

8 **Loading Pier** - (For vessel shipments only) Enter the number or name of the pier at which the merchandise is laden aboard the exporting vessel.

9 **Method of Transportation** - Enter the method of transportation by which the merchandise is exported (or exits the border of the United States). Specify the method of transportation by name, such as, vessel, air, rail, truck, etc. Specify "own power" if applicable.

10 **Exporting Carrier** - Enter the name of the carrier transporting the merchandise out of the United States. For vessel shipments, give the name of the vessel.

11 **Port of Export**

(a) For Overland Shipments - Enter the name of the U.S. Customs port at which the surface carrier (truck or railcar) crosses the border.

(b) For Vessel and Air Shipments - Enter the name of the U.S. Customs port where the merchandise is loaded on the carrier (airplane or ocean vessel) that is taking the merchandise out of the United States.

(c) For Postal (mail) Shipments - Enter the U.S. Post Office from which the merchandise is mailed.

12 **Foreign Port of Unloading** - For vessel shipments between the United States and foreign countries, enter the foreign port and country at which the merchandise will be unloaded from the exporting carrier. For vessel and air shipments between the United States and Puerto Rico, enter the Schedule C code, "U.S. Customs District and Port Code".

13 **Containerized** - (For vessel shipments only) Check the **YES** box for cargo originally booked as containerized cargo and for cargo that has been placed in containers at the vessel operator's option.

14 **Carrier Identification Code** - Enter the 4-character Standard Carrier Alpha Code (SCAC) of the carrier for vessel, rail and truck shipments, or the 2- or 3-character International Air Transport Association (IATA) Code of the carrier for air shipments. In a consolidated shipment, if the ultimate carrier is unknown, the consolidators carrier ID code may be reported. The National Motor Freight Traffic Association (703) 838-1831 or www.nmfta.org issues the SCAC's for ocean carriers, trucking companies and consolidators. The American Association of Railroads, Railinc (919) 651-5006 issues the SCAC codes for rail carriers. The International Air Transportation Association (IATA) issues the air carrier codes. The IATA codes are available on the Foreign Trade Division web site under "Air Carrier Codes" at <www.census.gov/foreign-trade>.

15 **Shipment Reference Number** - Enter the unique reference number assigned by the filer of the SED for identification purposes. This shipment reference number must be unique for five years. For example, report an invoice number, bill of lading or airway bill number, internal file number or so forth.

16 **Entry Number** - Enter the Import Entry Number when the export transaction is used as proof of export for import transactions, such as In-Bond, Temporary Import Bond or Drawback's and so forth. Also, an Entry Number is required for merchandise that is entered as an import (CF 7501 or Automated Broker Interface (ABI) entries) and is then being exported out of the United States.

17 **Hazardous Materials** - Check the appropriate "Yes" or "No" indicator that identifies the shipment as hazardous as defined by the Department of Transportation.

18 **In Bond Code** - Report one of the 2 - character In-Bond codes listed in Part IV of Appendix C of the FTSR (15 CFR Part 30) to include the type of In-Bond or not In-Bond shipment.

19 **Routed Export Transaction** - Check the appropriate "Yes" or "No" indicator that identifies the transaction as a routed export transaction. A routed export transaction is where the foreign principal party in interest authorizes a U.S. forwarding or other agent to export the merchandise out of the United States.

20 **Schedule B Description of Commodities** - Use columns 22 - 24 to enter the commercial description of the commodity being exported, its schedule B number, the quantity in

schedule B units, and the shipping weight in kilograms. Enter a sufficient description of the commodity as to permit verification of the Schedule B Commodity Number or the commodity description as shown on the validated export license. Include marks, numbers, or other identification shown on the packages and the numbers and kinds of packages (boxes, barrels, baskets, etc.)

21 **"D" (Domestic) , "F" (Foreign) or M (Foreign Military Sales)**

(a) Domestic exports (D) - merchandise that is grown, produced, or manufactured in the United States (including imported merchandise which has been enhanced in value or changed from the form in which imported by further manufacture or processing in the United States).

(b) Foreign exports (F) - merchandise that has entered the United States and is being re-exported in the same condition as when imported.

(c) Foreign Military Sales (M) - exports of merchandise that are sold under the foreign military sales program.

22 **Schedule B Number -** Enter the commercial description of the commodity being exported and the ten-digit commodity number as provided in Schedule B - Statistical Classification of Domestic and Foreign Commodities Exported from the United States. See item 5 (page 2) for a discussion of not repeating the same Schedule B numbers on the SED. If necessary, the Harmonized Tariff Schedule (HTS) number can be reported on the SED. See the Appendix showing a list of telephone numbers for assistance with Schedule B numbers.

23 **Quantity** (Schedule B Units) - Report whole unit(s) as specified in the Schedule B commodity classification code. Report also the unit specified on the export license if the units differ. See the Appendix showing a list of telephone numbers for assistance with units of quantity.

24 **Shipping Weight** (kilograms) - (For vessel and air shipment only) Enter the gross shipping weight in kilograms for each Schedule B number, including the weight of containers but excluding carrier equipment. To determine kilograms use pounds (lbs) Multiplied by 0.4536 = kilograms (report whole units.)

25 **VIN/Product Number/Vehicle Title Number -** (For used self-propelled vehicles only). Report the following items of information for used self-propelled vehicles as defined in Customs regulations 19 CFR 192.1: (1) Report the unique Vehicle Identification Number (VIN) in the proper format; (2) Report the Product Identification Number (PIN) for those used self propelled vehicles for which there are no VINs; and (3) the Vehicle Title Number.

26 **Value** (U.S. dollars) - Enter the selling price or cost if not sold, including freight, insurance, and other charges to U.S. port of export, but excluding unconditional discounts and commissions (nearest whole dollar, omit cents). The value to be reported on the SED is the exporter's (U.S. principal party in interest) price or cost if not sold, to the foreign principal party in interest. Report one value for each Schedule B number.

27 **License No./License Exception Symbol/Authorization - Whenever a SED or AES record is required:**

(a) Enter the license number on the SED or AES record when you are exporting under the authority of a Department of Commerce, Bureau of Export Administration (BXA) license, a Department of State, Office of Defense Trade Controls (ODTC) license, a Department of the Treasury, Office of Foreign Assets Control (OFAC) license (enter either the general or specific OFAC license number), a Department of Justice, Drug Enforcement Agency (DEA) permit, or any other export license number issued by a Federal government agency. For the BXA license the expiration date of the license must be entered on the paper version of the SED only.

(b) Enter the correct License Exception symbol (e.g. LVS, GBS, CIV) on the SED or AES record when you are exporting under the authority of a License Exception. See § 740.1, § 740.2, and § 758.1 of the Export Administration Regulations (EAR).

(c) Enter the "No License Required" (NLR) designator when you are exporting items under the NLR provisions of the EAR:

(1) When the items being exported are subject to the EAR but not listed on the Commerce Control List (CCL) (i.e. items that are classified as EAR99); and

(2) When the items being exported are listed on the CCL but do not require a license.

28 **Export Control Classification Number (ECCN)** - Whenever a SED or AES record is required, you must enter the correct Export Control Classification Number (ECCN) on the SED or AES record for all exports authorized under a license or License Exception, and items being exported under the "No License Required" (NLR) provisions of the EAR that are listed on the CCL and have a reason for control other than anti-terrorism (AT).

29 **Duly authorized officer or employee** - Provide the signature of the exporter (U.S. principal party in interest) authorizing the named forwarding or agent to effect the export when such agent does not have a formal power of attorney or written authorization.

30 **Signature/Certification** - Provide the signature of the exporter (U.S. principal party in interest) or authorized forwarding or other agent certifying the truth and accuracy of the information on the SED, the title of exporter (U.S. principal party in interest) or authorized agent, the date of signature, the telephone number of the exporter (U.S. principal party in interest) or authorized agent preparing the SED and who can best answer questions for resolving problems on the SED, and the email address of the exporter (U.S. principal party in interest) or authorized agent.

31 **Authentication** - For Customs use only.

APPENDIX

List of telephone Numbers Providing Additional Assistance in Filling Out the Shipper's Export Declaration (SED)

(Census Bureau) Foreign Trade Division Contacts

Commodity Classification (Schedule B Number) Assistance		***Schedule B***
Food, Animal and Wood Products (Including paper and printed matter)	301-457-3484	Chapters 1-24; 41; 43-49
Minerals	301-457-3484	Chapters 25-27; 68-71
Metals	301-457-3259	Chapters 72-83
Textiles and Apparel	301-457-3484	Chapters 41-43; 50-67
Machinery and Vehicles (including computers, other electronic equipment and transportation)	301-457-3259	Chapters 84-85; 86-89
Chemical and Sundries	301-457-3259	Chapters 28-40; 90-98

Foreign Trade Statistics Regulations 301-457-2238

Automated Export System (AES) 1-800-549-0595

Other Agency Export Control Telephone Contacts

Bureau of Export Administration, Department of Commerce <www.bxa.doc.gov>

Washington, DC	Newport Beach, CA	San Jose, CA
202-482- 4811 or 202-482-2642	949-660-0144	408-998-7402

International Trade Administration, Export Assistance Center 1-800-872-8723
<www.ita.doc.gov>

Department of State, Office of Defense Trade Controls (ODTC)
(International Traffic In Arms Regulations (ITAR)) 202-663-2714 <www.pmdtc.org>

Department of the Treasury, Office of Foreign Assets Control (OFAC)
(Sanctioned countries and trade restrictions) 202-622-2490 <www.treas.gov/ofac>

U.S. Customs Import (Inbound) Questions (Summary Management Office) 202-927-0625
<www.customs.treas.gov>

U.S. Customs Export (Outbound) Questions (Outbound Programs) 202-927-6060
<www.customs.treas.gov>

NAFTA (hotline) 972-574-4061 <www.mac.doc.gov/nafta/nafta2.htm>

To Order Paper SEDs Contact the: **Government Printing Office (GPO)**
Publication Order & Information Office
202-512-1800

Appendix D

Automated Export System (AES) and AES Direct

Automated Systems | Automated Export System | About AES-Automated Export System

Easy Steps

Getting Started

The Automated Export System (AES) is the paperless way to file the Shipper's Export Declaration (SED) and the ocean manifest information directly to U.S. Customs. On these web pages you will find information on the history and future of AES, technical documentation, software vendors, and many other items of interest related to AES.

These instructions provide you with a short description on how to file your letter of intent with the government and a example of estimated costs associated.

Participation Procedures

Participation in the AES program may be phased in.

Process for AES:

Step 1	**File Letter of Intent**	The Letter of Intent provides basic company profile information.
Step 2	**Choose Implementation Method**	You will be contacted by a Customs Client Representative to discuss your implementation method. Are you self-programing, using a vendor or using a service center? A list of AES certified vendors and service centers can be found at the Vendors web page. Record formats are available on the AESTIR web page. Information on AES*Direct*, the free internet application supported by the Census Bureau is available on the AES*Direct* website.
Step 3	**Certification**	This tests your ability to send and receive messages, including responding to error messages. If you utilize an AES certified vendor or service center, the test is minimal. If you utilize AES*Direct*, the test is part of the registration process. Once certified, you are ready to go. ***No more paper SEDs!!!***

Process for AES-Option 4:

Option 4 post-departure filing privileges are only granted to exporters (U.S. Principal Party in Interest). Forwarders cannot have Option 4 privileges, but may transmit to AES for their Option 4 approved clients.

Step 1	**File Letter of Intent**	File a written *Letter of Intent*(LOI) on company letterhead, signed by an officer of the company. The letter is reviewed by participating agencies who have 30 days to deny AES-Option 4 privileges. Exporter (USPPI) will receive a letter indicating AES-Option 4 approval, denial (with the denying agency identified), or indicating that more time is required for the approval process.
Step 2	**Choose Implementation Method**	Exporters (USPPIs) can implement AES-Option 4 on their own or have their forwarder transmit the information (see above).
Step 3	**Certification Testing**	Works the same as above. Once approved for AES-Option 4, you must begin transmitting within six months.

Cost Estimates

The following are estimated start-up costs for accessing AES, as gathered from current organizations participating in AES. These figures are estimated averages and should be taken as such.

	Mini/Mainframe	LAN or Client Server	PC with Modem
Software	$3,000 - $25,000	$3,000 - $20,000	$1,500 - $5,000
Communications Package		Up to $1,200	Up to $1,200
Maintenance Costs	5% - 10% of program cost	Up to $600 per year	Up to $600 per year
Installation & Training *		Included or up to $2,000	Included or up to $2,000

* Some firms include Installation & Training in the price: others charge seperately.

Service Center - Basic SED filing Service ONLY (Some have other add-on services for an additional cost)	Up to $200 per month
Charge per SED filed	$0.50 up to $5.00 per SED

Once you are connected to the Internet, using AES*Direct* is **FREE!**

▲ Top

Automated Systems Automated Export System Letter of Intent

How to Register for AES and/or AES Option-4

The first requirement for participation in the Automated Export System (AES) is a Letter of Intent. The Letter of Intent (LOI) is a written statement of a company's commitment to develop, maintain, and adhere to Customs and Census performance requirements and operations standards as participants in AES.

Letters of Intent should be on company letterhead and must include:

- Company Name, Address (***NO*** *P.O. Boxes*), City, State, Postal Code
- Company Contact Person, Phone Number, Fax Number
- Technical Contact Person, Phone Number, Fax Number
- Corporate Office Address, City, State, Postal Code
- Computer Site Location Address, City, State, Postal Code
- Type of Business - Exporter (U.S. Principal Party in Interest), Freight Forwarder/Broker, Carrier, NVOCC, Port Authority, Software Vendor, Service Center, etc. (Indicate all that apply)

    Freight Forwarder/Brokers, indicate the number of exporters (U.S. Principal Party in Interest) for whom you file export information (SEDs).

- U.S. Ports of Export Currently Utilized
- Average Monthly Paper SEDs submitted
- Average Monthly Value of Export Shipments
- Filer Code - EIN, DUNS, SSN or SCAC (Indicate all that apply)
- Software Vendor Name, Contact and Phone Number (if using vendor provided software)
- Look-a-Like Remote to Copy (as provided by vendor)
- Modes of Transportation used for export shipments (Air, Vessel, Truck, Rail, etc.)
- Types of Merchandise exported
- Types of Licenses or Permits
- Anticipated Implementation Date

The following self-certification statement, signed by an officer of the company must be included in your letter of intent:

> We (COMPANY NAME) certify that all statements made and all information provided herein are true and correct. I understand that civil and criminal penalties, including forfeiture and sale, may be imposed for making false or fraudulent statements herein, failing to provide the requested information or for violation of U.S. laws on exportation (13 U.S.C. Sec. 305; 22 U.S.C. Sec 401; 18 U.S.C. Sec. 1001; 50 U.S.C. App. 2410)

Send AES or Option 4 Letter of Intent to:

Chief, Foreign Trade Division
Bureau of the Census
Suitland and Silver Hills Road

Washington, DC 20233
Or, the copy can be faxed to: 301-457-1159

The LOI requirement can be satisfied by submitting the completed LOI Form provided on-line for your convenience. However, if the USPPI is applying for Option 4 filing privileges, the LOI must be written on company letterhead and signed by an official of the company. Option 4 filing privileges can not be accomplished electronically. If you register to file exports to AES using the free internet application,AES*Direct*, your on-line registration satisfies the requirement for the LOI. A written letter is still required for AES*Direct* Option 4 filing privileges as described above.

Upon receipt of your LOI, a Customs Client Representative and a Census Client Representative will be assigned to serve as your technical advisors during development, testing and implementation.

Top

Automated Systems   Automated Export System   About AES-Automated Export System

AES Frequently Asked Questions

AES Frequently Asked Questions

Listed below are the most frequently asked questions about AES. If your question isn't answered below, please feel free to contact us on the AES Hotline 1-800-549-0595

Q: Using the Census Bureau's Automated Export Reporting Program (AERP), I am approved to report my export shipments on a monthly basis directly to Census. Can I stay with AERP instead of using AES?

A: The Census Bureau's AERP ended on December 31, 1999. AERP was not Y2K compliant and was turned off as advertised. You will need to file export shipments electronically in AES or revert to filing paper SEDs.

Q: What filing options are available to me for filing SED information?

A: Option 1 provides for the filing of paper SEDs, pre-departure. The AES electronic filing options include Option 2 which requires full pre-departure transmission and is the basic way of reporting export shipments in AES. Option 3, implemented in September 1999, requires partial information reported pre-departure followed by complete information filed within five days of export. Option 3 does not require prior approval. Option 4 was implemented in March 1999 and is available to approved exporters only. It allows the approved exporter to send his shipment without pre-departure notification to AES. Full post-departure information must be reported within ten working days from the date of exportation. In addition to these filing options, AES-PASS is available to approved filers until March 2000.

Q: How much will AES cost me for hardware, software and transmissions?

A: The cost will vary depending on the size and business needs of your organization. There are several options available to you, including cost free filing over the internet using AES*Direct* or other relatively inexpensive filing options using the internet. As an AES participant, you may develop your own software from the specifications we provide. You may contract with a vendor that has developed and tested software with AES. You may file using a Value Added Network (VAN) electronic mailbox or using the facilities of a service center, port authority or a freight forwarder acting as your agent. The cost will be proportionate to the sophistication of the system you choose.

Q: How can I find a software vendor that has successfully tested their software with AES?

A: While we do not endorse one vendor over another, we do make available a list of software vendor and service providers that have completed or are in the process of developing software for AES. That listing is available by a link to Census from this site.

Q: I want to develop AES software in-house. What data formats are acceptable to AES and how can I find the technical specifications?

A: AES accepts data programmed using the Customs Proprietary Record Formats, UNEDIFACT or ANSIX.12 formats. The specifications for each of these formats is provided in the AESTIR (Automated Export System Trade Interface Requirements) at http://www.customs.gov

Q: I don't always know all the information required to file a complete SED prior to departure. Does AES allow for this business reality?

A: Yes, AES allows you to correct estimated information with the accurate information once it is known. In addition, AES does offer various filing options that accommodates full post-departure filing or limited pre-departure filing.

Q: Why does AES require pre-departure filing of the Shipper's Export Declaration (SED)? Don't I have four days after departure to file my SED? Why is AES changing this after all these years?

A: No, as the exporter, you do not have four days after departure to file the SED. By regulation (15CFR, Sec. 30.12) the SED must be submitted by the shipper to the carrier PRIOR to departure. The carrier under bond has four days to submit the manifest, with the SEDs attached, to Customs. AES is not changing this regulation. Customs and Census efforts to raise the compliance level with these regulations have highlighted this misinterpretation. While AES requires pre-departure filing of SED commodity information as per these regulations, there is a post-departure filing option available to exporters in AES.

Q: Does AES require a lot more data elements then the paper SED?

A: No. Most conventional export shipments require about 20 data elements. There are a number of data elements that may be conditionally required from time to time, for various licensed shipments. If you are trying to export a used vehicle powered by a nuclear reactor and containing a Cray super-computer which will transit two countries before it is delivered to the buyer in Libya, then you would come close to needing to report all 72 possible elements.

Q: Will AES hold up my export cargo? I have heard AES referred to as an enforcement system, is it?

A: No, AES is simply an electronic tool that supports the enforcement system that currently exists. AES's verifications, up-front edits, and selectivity allows us to focus our attention on high risk shipments and expedite other shipments. With the pre-departure filing of export shipments, inspectors are able to make informed decisions regarding examinations similar to the way imports are handled. Chances of low risk shipments being delayed are actually decreased.

Q: I have heard that AES requires a DUNS number. What do I do if I don't have one?

A: AES will accept an Employer Identification Number (EIN), Social Security Number (SSN) or a Data Universal Numbering System (DUNS) number. "DUNS" is a registered trademark of The Dun and Bradstreet Corporation. You may contact them directly if you wish to register with them, but AES does not require it.

Q: Is the Schedule B export commodity classification system being eliminated?

A: No, both Schedule B and the Harmonized Tariff Schedule (HTS) are acceptable for reporting export shipments in AES. Please note that there are a few exceptions, spelled out in front of the HTS, when reporting HTS numbers as export classifications are not allowed. Schedule B numbers can not be reported in lieu of the import HTS number for import shipments.

Q: What if I have questions, either technical or subject matter related? Is there a help desk?

A: Once you have informed us of your intention to participate in AES, you will be assigned a Customs Client Representative and a Census Client Representative to help you get established in AES. In addition, there is a toll-free AES Answerline at 1-800-549-0595 to take your questions.

E-mail comments to askAES@census.gov

▲ Top

AESDirect
Reduce Exporting Stress with AES

Getting Started
- Tour
- How To Register
- Registration Form
- Terms & Conditions
- Privacy Policy

Log In
- Tutorial & Quiz
- AES*Direct*

Using AES*Direct*
- User Guide
- Support Center
- Browser Support
- Developers Center
- News

Related Sites
- AES
- Census Bureau
- U.S. Customs
- USATrade.gov
- Partner Sites

AES*Direct* Newsflash Check the News section for the latest AES*Direct* Updates

Welcome to **AES***Direct*

AES*Direct* is the U.S. Census Bureau's free, internet based system for filing Shipper's Export Declaration (SED) information to the Automated Export System (AES). It is the electronic alternative to filing a paper SED, and can be used by U.S. Principal Parties in Interest (USPPIs), forwarders, or anyone else responsible for export reporting.

Why **AES***Direct*?

AES*Direct* significantly streamlines the export reporting process by reducing the paperwork burden on the trade community, reducing costly document handling and storage, and ensuring that export information is filed in a timely manner. AES*Direct* improves the quality of the export trade statistics, helping the Census Bureau provide the Government and the public more accurate information.

AES*Direct* System Requirements
AES*Direct* does not require any software or hardware investment, however there are some minimum system requirements. Check the Browser Support page for details.

AES*WebLink* and EDI Upload
If you are a software or internet application vendor you can connect your application to AES*Direct* using AES*WebLink* or EDI Upload. More information on AES*WebLink* and EDI Upload is contained in the Developers Center.

FOREIGN TRADE STATISTICS YOUR KEY TO TRADE
U. S. CENSUS BUREAU

[top of page]

AESDirect

Reduce Exporting Stress with AES

Home

Getting Started
- Tour
- How To Register
- Registration Form
- Terms & Conditions
- Privacy Policy

Log-In
- Tutorial & Quiz
- AES*Direct*

Using AES*Direct*
- User Guide
- Support Center
- Browser Support
- Developers Center
- News

Related Sites
- AES
- Census Bureau
- U.S. Customs
- USATrade.gov
- Partner Sites

How to Register for **AES***Direct*

It's easy for your company to become a registered user of AES*Direct*

How To Register | EDI Upload | Post Departure Filing | Data Entry Centers (DECs)

How To Register

Online Registration covers on-line interactive Option 2 (pre departure) AES*Direct* filing for all companies, and Option 4 (post departure) filing only for companies that have already been certified for Option 4. Any USPPI can apply for Option 4. Additional information about EDI Upload submission to AES*Direct* is located in the Support Center.

AES*Direct* Online Registration Process

- Complete and submit the Online AES*Direct* Registration Form.
- Complete the AES*Direct* Online Tutorial

After you submit the registration form the following will happen:

- An AES*Direct* filing account will be created for your company
- As soon as your AES*Direct* account has been set up you will receive an e-mail that will provide your AES*Direct* User ID and Password. Please note it is your responsibility to keep these secure.

When it is first set up, your AES*Direct* account will only be validated to provide access to the AES*Direct* Tutorial. In order to become a fully authorized user of AES*Direct* (and begin to file your SEDs into AES) you must first complete this tutorial.

Use your User ID and Password to Log on to AES*Direct* (click on the "Tutorial" Option) and complete the tutorial. AES*Direct* support staff will be notified when you have completed the tutorial.

After you have completed the tutorial and Bureau of the Census has set up your AES Account, your AES*Direct* account will be opened up to allow you to begin filing SEDs electronically with AES.

You will be notified by e-mail when your AES*Direct* account has been fully activated for filing.

Your activation notice will also specify which AES filing status your AES*Direct* account has been authorized for. The options are:

- AES Option 2 predeparture filing approved - You have been certified to report export information predeparture. If you are applying for postdeparture, we are still awaiting confirmation from the approving federal agencies. For questions, please call Census at 1-800-549-0595.

- AES Option 4 postdeparture filing approved.

EDI Upload

Appendix D

When you register for AES*Direct* you should fill out the EDI Upload section of the registration form if you intend to use AES*Direct* for EDI upload filing of SEDs.

Important: If you have already registered for AES*Direct* and now wish to start using EDI Upload, please contact us at 1-877-715-4433 or boc-support@tradegate2000.com

If you are using an AES*Direct* Certified Software Vendor:

Please contact your vendor when you register for AES*Direct*. They will need to check that the software that you are using is the version that has been certified, and will need to confirm that to us.

If you are using another software vendor or custom developed software:

Once you have finished the tutorial, we will create a test account for you to start testing your EDI Upload. Once you have passed the AES*Direct* EDI upload certification script we will update your production account to include EDI Upload filing and inform you when you can begin filing.

Additional information about EDI upload is available in the Support Center.

Post Departure

Post Departure filing is available to approved USPPIs, or forwarders filing on behalf of approved USPPIs.

If you have applied for or are already approved for option 4 indicate that in the appropriate question on the registration form. If you are approved then your AES*Direct* account will be set up as option 4. If you are not yet approved for option 4 your account will be set up as option 2 and switched to option 4 status when it becomes approved for option 4.

If you have not applied for option 4 but would like to do so, see the Option 4 Information page. You will need to mail or fax a letter of intent to the Census Bureau to apply for option 4.

Data Entry Centers (DECs)

If you are a Carrier or NVOCC and need to file with AES, you can use AES*Direct*. In addition to submiting an online registration, you will need to sign the DEC Agreement. Additional information on signing up as a DEC and submitting the DEC agreement.

FOREIGN TRADE STATISTICS YOUR KEY TO TRADE
U. S. CENSUS BUREAU

[top of page]

Required Pre-Departure Data Elements for filing Option 3

(1) Identifier of Exporter - EIN, etc.

(2) Forwarding Agent I.D. - EIN, etc.

(3) Carrier I.D. (SCAC or IATA).

(4) Country of Ultimate Destination - ISO code.

(5) Name of Ultimate Consignee.

(6) (a) Commodity description or

(b) Optional - Schedule B No. or HTS code

(7) Shipment reference number (17 characters or less). The filer of the export shipment provides a unique shipment reference number that allows for the identification of the shipment in their system. This shipment reference number must be unique for five years.

(8) Intended U.S. Port of Export

(9) Estimated Date of Export

(10) Transportation Reference Number, e.g., vessel booking number

(11) Method of Transportation (MOT) code

(12) HAZMAT - Y/N

(13) License code

(14) Export License Number

Electronic (AES) Filing Codes

PART I – METHOD OF TRANSPORTATION CODES

10	Sea
11	Sea Containerized
12	Sea (Barge)
20	Rail
21	Rail Containerized
30	Truck
31	Truck Containerized
32	Auto
33	Pedestrian
34	Road, Other
40	Air
41	Air Containerized
50	Mail
60	Passenger, Hand Carried
70	Fixed Transport (Pipeline and Powerhouse)

PART II – EXPORT INFORMATION CODES

LC	Shipments valued $2,500 or less per classification number that are required to be reported
TP	Temporary exports of domestic merchandise
IP	Shipments of merchandise imported under a Temporary Import Bond for further manufacturing or processing
IR	Shipments of merchandise imported under a Temporary Import Bond for repair
DB	Drawback
CH	Shipments of goods donated for charity
FS	Foreign Military Sales
OS	All other exports
HV	Shipments of personally owned vehicles
HH	Household and personal effects
SR	Ship's stores
TE	Temporary exports to be returned to the United States
TL	Merchandise leased for less than a year
IS	Shipments of merchandise imported under a Temporary Import Bond for return in the same condition
CR	Shipments moving under a carnet
GP	U.S. government shipments
LV	Shipments valued $2,500 or less that are not required to be reported
SS	Carriers' stores for use on the carrier
MS	Shipments consigned to the U.S. Armed Forces
GS	Shipments to U.S. government agencies for their use
DP	Diplomatic pouches
HR	Human remains
UG	Gift parcels under Bureau of Export Administration License Exception GFT
IC	Interplant correspondence
SC	Instruments of international trade
DD	Other exemptions: Currency Airline tickets Bank notes Internal revenue stamps State liquor stamps Advertising literature Shipments of temporary imports by foreign entities for their use
RJ	Inadmissible merchandise
	(For Manifest Use Only by AES Carriers)
RP	Shipment information filed through Census Bureau's AERP
AE	Shipment information filed through AES

(See §§30.50 through 30.58 for information on filing exemptions.)

PART III — LICENSE CODES

Department of Commerce, Bureau of Export Administration (BXA) Licenses

C30	BXA Licenses	**C41**	RPL
C31	SCL	**C42**	GOV
C32	NLR (CCL/NS Column 2)	**C43**	GFT
C33	NLR (All Others)	**C44**	TSU
C34	Future Use	**C45**	BAG
C35	LVS	**C46**	AVS
C36	GBS	**C47**	APR
C37	CIV	**C48**	KMI
C38	TSR	**C49**	TAPS
C39	CTP	**C50**	ENC
C40	TMP		

Nuclear Regulatory Commission (NRC) Codes

N01 NRC Form 250/250A
N02 NRC General License

Department of State, Office of Defense Trade Controls (ODTC) Codes

SAG Agreements
S00 License Exemption Citation
S05 DSP-5
S61 DSP-61
S73 DSP-73
S85 DSP-85

Department of Treasury, Office of Foreign Assets Control (OFAC) Codes

T10 OFAC Specific License
T11 OFAC General License

Other License Types

OPA Other Partnership Agency Licenses not listed above

PART IV — IN-BOND CODES

70	Not-In-Bond
36	Warehouse Withdrawal for Immediate Exportation
37	Warehouse Withdrawal for Transportation and Exportation
62	Transportation and Exportation
63	Immediate Exportation
67	Immediate Exportation from a Foreign Trade Zone
68	Transportation and Exportation from a Foreign Trade Zone

Appendix E

U.S. Customs Reasonable Care Checklists

U.S. CUSTOMS REASONABLE CARE CHECKLISTS:
(Federal Register December 4, 1997)

GENERAL QUESTIONS FOR ALL TRANSACTIONS:

1. If you have not retained an expert to assist you in complying with Customs requirements, do you have access to the Customs Regulations (Title 19 of the Code of Federal Regulations), the Harmonized Tariff Schedule of the United States, and the GPO publication "Customs Bulletin and Decisions?" Do you have access to the Customs Internet Website, Customs Electronic Bulletin Board or other research service to permit you to establish reliable procedures and facilitate compliance with Customs laws and regulations?

2. Has a responsible and knowledgeable individual within your organization reviewed the Customs documentation prepared by you or your expert to insure that it is full, complete and accurate? If that documentation was prepared outside your own organization, do you have a reliable system in place to insure that you receive copies of the information as submitted to Customs; that it is reviewed for accuracy; and that Customs is timely apprised of any needed corrections?

3. If you use an expert to assist you in complying with Customs requirements, have you discussed your importations in advance with that person and have you provided that person with full, complete and accurate information about the import transactions?

4. Are identical transactions or merchandise handled differently at different ports or Customs offices within the same port? If so, have you brought this to the attention of the appropriate Customs officials?

QUESTIONS ARRANGED BY TOPIC:

Merchandise Description & Tariff Classification

Basic Question: Do you know or have you established a reliable procedure or program to ensure that you know what you ordered, where it was made and what it is made of?

1. Have you provided or established reliable procedures to ensure you provide a complete and accurate description of your merchandise to Customs in accordance with 19 U.S.C. 1481? (Also, see 19 CFR 141.87 and 141.89 for special merchandise description requirements.)

2. Have you provided or established reliable procedures to ensure you provide a correct tariff classification of your merchandise to Customs in accordance with 19 U.S.C. 1484?

3. Have you obtained a Customs "ruling" regarding the description of the merchandise or its tariff classification (See 19 CFR Part 177), and if so, have you established reliable procedures to ensure that you have followed the ruling and brought it to Customs attention?

4. Where merchandise description or tariff classification information is not immediately available, have you established a reliable procedure for providing that information, and is the procedure being followed?

5. Have you participated in a Customs "pre-importation review or pre-classification" of your merchandise relating to proper merchandise description and classification?

6. Have you consulted the tariff schedules, customs informed compliance publications, court cases and/or Customs rulings to assist you in describing and classifying the merchandise?

7. Have you consulted with a Customs "expert" (e.g., lawyer, broker, accountant, or Customs consultant) to assist in the description and/or classification of the merchandise?

8. If you are claiming a conditionally free or special tariff classification/provision for your merchandise (e.g., GSP, HTS Item 9802, NAFTA, etc.), how have you verified that the merchandise qualifies for such status? Have you obtained or developed reliable procedures to obtain any required or necessary documentation to support the claim? If making a NAFTA preference claim, do you already have a NAFTA certificate of origin in your possession?

9. Is the nature of your merchandise such that a laboratory analysis or other specialized procedure is suggested to assist in proper description and classification?

10. Have you developed a reliable program or procedure to maintain and produce any required Custom entry documentation and supporting information?

Valuation

Basic Questions: Do you know or have you established reliable procedures to know the "price actually paid or payable" for your merchandise? Do you know the terms of sale; whether there will be rebates, tie-ins, indirect costs, and additional payments, whether "assists" were provided, commissions or royalties paid? Are amounts actual or estimated? Are you and the supplier "related parties"?

1. Have you provided or established reliable procedures to provide Customs with a proper declared value for your merchandise in accordance with 19 U.S.C. 1484 and 19 U.S.C. 1401a?

2. Have you obtained a Customs "ruling" regarding the valuation of the merchandise (See 19 CFR Part 177), and if so, have you established reliable procedures to ensure that you have followed the ruling and brought it to Customs attention?

3. Have you consulted the Customs valuation laws and regulations, Customs Valuation Encyclopedia, Customs informed compliance publications, court cases and Customs rulings to assist you in valuing merchandise?

4. Have you consulted with a Customs "expert" (e.g., lawyer, broker, accountant, or Customs consultant) to assist in the valuation of the merchandise?

5. If you purchased the merchandise from a "related" seller, have you established procedures to ensure that you have reported that fact upon entry and taken measures or established reliable procedures to ensure that value reported to Customs meets one of the "related party" tests?

6. Have you taken measures or established reliable procedures to ensure that all of the legally required costs or payments associated with the imported merchandise have been reported to Customs (e.g., assists, all commissions, indirect payments or rebates, royalties, etc.)?

7. If you are declaring a value based on a transaction in which you were/are not the buyer, have you substantiated that the transaction is a bona fide sale at arms length and that the merchandise was clearly destined to the United States at the time of sale?

8. If you are claiming a conditionally free or special tariff classification/provision for your merchandise (e.g., GSP, HTS Item 9802, NAFTA, etc.), have you established a reliable system or program to ensure that you reported the required value information and obtained any required or necessary documentation to support the claim?

9. Have you established a reliable program or procedure to produce any required entry documentation and supporting information?

Country of Origin/Marking/Quota

Basic Question: Have you taken reliable measures to ascertain the correct country of origin for the imported merchandise?

1. Have you taken established reliable procedures to ensure that you report the correct country of origin on Customs entry documents?

2. Have you established reliable procedures to verify or ensure that the merchandise is properly marked upon entry with the correct country of origin (if required) in accordance with 19 U.S.C. 1304 and any other applicable special marking requirement (watches, gold, textile labeling, etc.)?

3. Have you obtained a Customs "ruling" regarding the proper marking and country of origin of the merchandise (See 19 CFR Part 177), and if so, have you established reliable procedures to ensure that you followed the ruling and brought it to Customs attention?

4. Have you consulted with a Customs "expert" (e.g., lawyer, broker, accountant, or Customs consultant) regarding the correct country or origin/proper marking of your merchandise?

5. Have you taken reliable and adequate measures to communicate Customs country of origin marking requirements to your foreign supplier prior to importation of your merchandise?

6. If you are claiming a change in the origin of the merchandise or claiming that the goods are of U.S. origin, have you taken required measures to substantiate your claim (e.g. Do you have U.S. milling certificates or manufacturer's affidavits attesting to the production in the U.S.)?

7. If you are importing textiles or apparel, have you developed reliable procedures to ensure that you have ascertained the correct country of origin in accordance with 19 U.S.C. 3592 (Section 334, Pub Law 103-465) and assured yourself that no illegal transshipment or false or fraudulent practices were involved?

8. Do you know how your goods from raw materials to finished goods? If so, by whom and where?

9. Have you checked with Customs and developed a reliable procedure or system to ensure that the quota category is correct?

10. Have you checked or developed reliable procedures to check the Status Report on Current Import Quotas (Restraint Levels) issued by Customs to determine if your goods are subject to a quota category which has "part" categories?

11. Have you taken reliable measures to ensure that you have obtained the correct visas for your goods if they are subject to visa categories?

12. In the case of textile articles, have you prepared or developed a reliable program to prepare the proper country declaration for each entry, i.e., a single country declaration (if wholly obtained/produced) or a multi-country declaration (if raw materials from one country were produced into goods in a second)?

13. Have you established a reliable maintenance program or procedure to ensure you can produce any required entry documentation and supporting information, including any required certificates of origin?

Intellectual Property Rights

Basic Question: Have you determined or established a reliable procedure to permit you to determine whether your merchandise or its packaging bear or use any trademarks or copyrighted matter or are patented and, if so, that you have a legal right to import and/or use those items into, and/or those items in, the U.S.?

1. If you are importing goods or packaging bearing a trademark registered in the U.S., have you checked or established a reliable procedure to ensure that it is genuine and not restricted from importation under the "gray-market" or parallel import requirements of U.S. law (see 19 CFTR 133.21), or that you have permission from the trademark holder to import such merchandise?

2. If you are importing goods or packaging, which consist of, or contain registered copyrighted material, have you checked or established a reliable procedure to ensure that it is authorized and genuine? If you are importing sound recordings of live performances, were the recordings authorized?

3. Have you checked or developed a reliable procedure to see if your merchandise is subject to an International Trade Commission or court ordered exclusion order?

4. Have you established a reliable procedure to ensure that you maintained and can you produce any required entry documentation and supporting information?

Some Miscellaneous Questions

1. Have you taken measures or developed a reliable procedure to ensure that your merchandise complies with other agency requirements (e.g., FDA, EPA/DOT, CPSC, FTC, Agriculture, etc.) prior to or upon entry, including the procurement of any necessary licenses or permits?

2. Have you taken measures or developed a reliable procedure to check to see if your goods are subject to a Commerce Department dumping or countervailing duty investigation or determination, and if so, have you complied or developed reliable procedures to ensure compliance with Customs reporting requirements upon entry (e.g., 19 CFR 141.61)?

3. Is your merchandise subject to quota/visa requirements, and if so, have you provided or developed a reliable procedure to provide a correct visa for the goods upon entry?

4. Have you taken reliable measures to ensure and verify that you are filing the correct type of Customs entry (e.g., TIB, T&E, consumption entry, mail entry, etc.), as well as ensure that you have the right to make entry under the Customs Regulations?

Additional Questions for Textile and Apparel Importers

Note: Section 333 of the Uruguay Round Implementation Act (19 U.S.C. §1592a) authorizes the Secretary of the Treasury to publish a list of foreign producers, manufacturers, suppliers, sellers, exporters, or other foreign persons who have been found to have violated 19 U.S.C. §1592 by using certain false, fraudulent or counterfeit documentation, labeling, or prohibited transshipment practices in connection with textiles and apparel products. Section 1592a also requires any importer of record entering, introducing, or attempting to introduce into the commerce of the United States textile or apparel products that were either directly or indirectly produced, manufactured, supplied, sold, exported, or transported by such named person to show, to the satisfaction of the Secretary, that such importer has exercised reasonable care to ensure that the textile or apparel products are accompanied by documentation, packaging, and labeling that are accurate as to its origin. Under §1592a, reliance solely upon information regarding the imported product from a person named on the list does not constitute the exercise of reasonable care. Textile apparel importers who have some commercial relationship with one or more of the listed parties must exercise a degree of reasonable care in ensuring that the documentation covering the imported merchandise, as well as its packaging and labeling, is accurate as to the country of origin of the merchandise. This degree of reasonable care must rely on more than information supplied by the named party.

In meeting the reasonable care standard when importing textile or apparel products and when dealing with a party named on the list published pursuant to section §1592a an importer should consider the following questions in attempting to ensure that the documentation, packaging, and labeling is accurate as to the country or origin of the imported merchandise. The list of questions is not exhaustive but is illustrative.

1. Has the importer had a prior relationship with the named party?

2. Has the importer had any detentions and/or seizures of textile or apparel products that were directly or indirectly produced, supplied, or transported by the named party?

3. Has the importer visited the company's premises and ascertained that the company has the capacity to produce the merchandise?

4. Where a claim of an origin conferring process is made in accordance with 19 C.F.R. §102.21, has the importer ascertained that the named party actually performed the required process?

5. Is the named party operating from the same country as is represented by that party on the documentation, packaging or labeling?

6. Have quotas for the imported merchandise closed or are they nearing closing from the main producer countries for this commodity?

7. What is the history of this country regarding this commodity?

8. Have you asked questions of your supplier regarding the origin of the product?

9. Where the importation is accompanied by a visa, permit, or license, has the importer verified with the supplier or manufacturer that the visa, permit, and/or license is both valid and accurate as to its origin? Has the importer scrutinized the visa, permit, or license as to any irregularities that would call its authenticity into question?

Appendix F

Harmonized Tariff Schedules (Excerpts)

United States International Trade Commission

Harmonized Tariff Schedule
of the United States
2001

For Use in Classification of Imported Merchandise
for Rate of Duty and Statistical Purposes

USITC PUBLICATION 3378

U.S. GOVERNMENT PRINTING OFFICE
WASHINGTON, D.C.

Appendix F

TABLE OF CONTENTS

GENERAL NOTES; GENERAL RULES OF INTERPRETATION;
GENERAL STATISTICAL NOTES

SECTION I

LIVE ANIMALS; ANIMAL PRODUCTS

Section Notes

Chapter 1 Live animals

2 Meat and edible meat offal

3 Fish and crustaceans, molluscs and other aquatic invertebrates

4 Dairy produce; birds eggs; natural honey; edible products of animal origin, not elsewhere specified or included

5 Products of animal origin, not elsewhere specified or included

SECTION II

VEGETABLE PRODUCTS

Section Notes

Chapter 6 Live trees and other plants; bulbs, roots and the like; cut flowers and ornamental foliage

7 Edible vegetables and certain roots and tubers

8 Edible fruit and nuts; peel of citrus fruit or melons

9 Coffee, tea, maté and spices

10 Cereals

11 Products of the milling industry; malt; starches; inulin; wheat gluten

12 Oil seeds and oleaginous fruits; miscellaneous grains, seeds and fruits; industrial or medicinal plants; straw and fodder

13 Lac; gums, resins and other vegetable saps and extracts

14 Vegetable plaiting materials; vegetable products not elsewhere specified or included

SECTION III

ANIMAL OR VEGETABLE FATS AND OILS AND THEIR CLEAVAGE PRODUCTS; PREPARED EDIBLE FATS; ANIMAL OR VEGETABLE WAXES

Chapter 15 Animal or vegetable fats and oils and their cleavage products prepared edible fats; animal or vegetable waxes

SECTION IV

PREPARED FOODSTUFFS; BEVERAGES, SPIRITS, AND VINEGAR; TOBACCO AND MANUFACTURED TOBACCO SUBSTITUTES

Section Notes

Chapter 16 Preparations of meat, of fish or of crustaceans, molluscs or other aquatic invertebrates

17 Sugars and sugar confectionery

18 Cocoa and cocoa preparations

19 Preparations of cereals, flour, starch or milk; bakers' wares

20 Preparations of vegetables, fruit, nuts or other parts of plants

21 Miscellaneous edible preparations

22 Beverages, spirits and vinegar

23 Residues and waste from the food industries; prepared animal feed

24 Tobacco and manufactured tobacco substitutes

SECTION V

MINERAL PRODUCTS

Chapter 25 Salt; sulfur; earths and stone; plastering materials, lime and cement

26 Ores, slag and ash

27 Mineral fuels, mineral oils and products of their distillation; bituminous substances; mineral waxes

SECTION VI

PRODUCTS OF THE CHEMICAL OR ALLIED INDUSTRIES

Section Notes

Chapter 28 Inorganic chemicals; organic or inorganic compounds of precious metals, of rare earth metals, of radioactive elements or of isotopes

29 Organic chemicals

30 Pharmaceutical products

31 Fertilizers

32 Tanning or dyeing extracts; tannins and their derivatives; dyes, pigments and other coloring matter; paints and varnishes; putty and other mastics; inks

33 Essential oils and resinoids; perfumery, cosmetic or toilet preparations

34 Soap, organic surface-active agents, washing preparations, lubricating preparations, artificial waxes, prepared waxes, polishing or scouring preparations, candles and similar articles, modeling pastes, "dental waxes" and dental preparations with a basis of plaster

35 Albuminoidal substances; modified starches; glues; enzymes

36 Explosives; pyrotechnic products; matches; pyrophoric alloys; certain combustible preparations

37 Photographic or cinematographic goods

38 Miscellaneous chemical products

SECTION VII

PLASTICS AND ARTICLES THEREOF RUBBER AND ARTICLES THEREOF

Section Notes

Chapter 39 Plastics and articles thereof

40 Rubber and articles thereof

SECTION VIII

RAW HIDES AND SKINS, LEATHER, FURSKINS AND ARTICLES THEREOF; SADDLERY AND HARNESS; TRAVEL GOODS, HANDBAGS AND SIMILAR CONTAINERS; ARTICLES OF ANIMAL GUT (OTHER THAN SILKWORM GUT)

Chapter 41 Raw hides and skins (other than furskins) and leather

42 Articles of leather; saddlery and harness; travel goods, handbags and similar containers; articles of animal gut (other than silkworm gut)

43 Furskins and artificial fur; manufactures thereof

SECTION IX

WOOD AND ARTICLES OF WOOD; WOOD CHARCOAL; CORK AND ARTICLES OF CORK; MANUFACTURERS OF STRAW, OF ESPARTO OR OF OTHER PLAITING MATERIALS; BASKETWARE AND WICKERWORK

Chapter 44 Wood and articles of wood; wood charcoal

45 Cork and articles of cork

46 Manufactures of straw, of esparto or of other plaiting materials; basketware and wickerwork

SECTION X

PULP OF WOOD OR OF OTHER FIBROUS CELLULOSIC MATERIAL; WASTE AND SCRAP OF PAPER OR PAPERBOARD; PAPER AND PAPERBOARD AND ARTICLES THEREOF

Section Notes

Chapter 47 Pulp of wood or of other fibrous cellulosic material; waste and scrap of paper or paperboard

48 Paper and paperboard; articles of paper pulp, of paper or of paperboard

49 Printed books, newspapers, pictures and other products of the printing industry; manuscripts, typescripts and plans

SECTION XI

TEXTILE AND TEXTILE ARTICLES

Section Notes

Chapter 50 Silk

51 Wool, fine or coarse animal hair; horsehair yarn and woven fabric

52 Cotton

53 Other vegetable textile fibers; paper yarn and woven fabric of paper yarn

54 Man-made filaments

55 Man-made staple fibers

56 Wadding, felt and nonwovens; special yarns, twine, cordage, ropes and cables and articles thereof

57 Carpets and other textile floor coverings

58 Special woven fabrics; tufted textile fabrics; lace, tapestries; trimmings; embroidery

59 Impregnated, coated, covered or laminated textile fabrics; textile articles of a kind suitable for industrial use

60 Knitted or crocheted fabrics

61 Articles of apparel and clothing accessories, knitted or crocheted

62 Articles of apparel and clothing accessories, not knitted or crocheted

63 Other made up textile articles; sets; worn clothing and worn textile articles; rags

SECTION XII

FOOTWEAR, HEADGEAR, UMBRELLAS, SUN UMBRELLAS, WALKING STICKS, SEATSTICKS, WHIPS, RIDING-CROPS AND PARTS THEREOF; PREPARED FEATHERS AND ARTICLES MADE THEREWITH; ARTIFICIAL FLOWERS; ARTICLES OF HUMAN HAIR

Chapter 64 Footwear, gaiters and the like; parts of such articles

65 Headgear and parts thereof

66 Umbrellas, sun umbrellas, walking sticks, seatsticks, whips, riding-crops and parts thereof

67 Prepared feathers and down and articles made of feathers or of down; artificial flowers; articles of human hair

SECTION XIII

ARTICLES OF STONE, PLASTER, CEMENT, ASBESTOS, MICA OR SIMILAR MATERIALS; CERAMIC PRODUCTS; GLASS AND GLASSWARE

Chapter 68 Articles of stone, plaster, cement, asbestos, mica or similar materials

69 Ceramic products

70 Glass and glassware

SECTION XIV

NATURAL OR CULTURED PEARLS, PRECIOUS OR SEMI-PRECIOUS STONES, PRECIOUS METALS, METALS CLAD WITH PRECIOUS METAL AND ARTICLES THEREOF; IMITATION JEWELRY; COIN

Chapter 71 Natural or cultured pearls, precious or semi-precious stones, precious metals, metals clad with precious metal and articles thereof; imitation jewelry; coin

SECTION XV

BASE METALS AND ARTICLES OF BASE METAL

Section Notes

Chapter 72 Iron and steel

73 Articles of iron or steel

74 Copper and articles thereof

75 Nickel and articles thereof

76 Aluminum and articles thereof

77 (Reserved for possible future use)

78 Lead and articles thereof

79 Zinc and articles thereof

80 Tin and articles thereof

81 Other base metals; cermets; articles thereof

82 Tools, implements, cutlery, spoons and forks, of base metal; parts thereof of base metal

83 Miscellaneous articles of base metal

SECTION XVI

MACHINERY AND MECHANICAL APPLIANCES; ELECTRICAL EQUIPMENT; PARTS THEREOF; SOUND RECORDERS AND REPRODUCERS, TELEVISION IMAGE AND SOUND RECORDERS AND REPRODUCERS, AND PARTS AND ACCESSORIES OF SUCH ARTICLES

Section Notes

Chapter 84 Nuclear reactors, boilers, machinery and mechanical appliances; parts thereof

85 Electrical machinery and equipment and parts thereof; sound recorders and reproducers, television image and sound recorders and reproducers, and parts and accessories of such articles

SECTION XVII

VEHICLES, AIRCRAFT, VESSELS AND ASSOCIATED TRANSPORT EQUIPMENT

Section Notes

Chapter	86	Railway or tramway locomotives, rolling-stock and parts thereof; railway or tramway track fixtures and fittings and parts thereof; mechanical (including electro-mechanical) traffic signalling equipment of all kinds
	87	Vehicles other than railway or tramway rolling stock, and parts and accessories thereof
	88	Aircraft, spacecraft, and parts thereof
	89	Ships, boats and floating structures

SECTION XVIII

OPTICAL, PHOTOGRAPHIC, CINEMATOGRAPHIC, MEASURING, CHECKING, PRECISION, MEDICAL OR SURGICAL INSTRUMENTS AND APPARATUS; CLOCKS AND WATCHES; MUSICAL INSTRUMENTS; PARTS AND ACCESSORIES THEREOF

Chapter	90	Optical, photographic, cinematographic, measuring, checking, precision, medical or surgical instruments and apparatus; parts and accessories thereof
	91	Clocks and watches and parts thereof
	92	Musical instruments; parts and accessories of such articles

SECTION XIX

ARMS AND AMMUNITION; PARTS AND ACCESSORIES THEREOF

Chapter	93	Arms and ammunition; parts and accessories thereof

SECTION XX

MISCELLANEOUS MANUFACTURED ARTICLES

Chapter 94 Furniture; bedding, mattresses, mattress supports, cushions and similar stuffed furnishings; lamps and lighting fittings, not elsewhere specified or included; illuminated sign illuminated nameplates and the like; prefabricated buildings

95 Toys, games and sports requisites; parts and accessories thereof

96 Miscellaneous manufactured articles

SECTION XXI

WORKS OF ART, COLLECTORS' PIECES AND ANTIQUES

Chapter 97 Works of art, collectors' pieces and antiques

SECTION XXII

SPECIAL CLASSIFICATION PROVISIONS;
TEMPORARY LEGISLATION; TEMPORARY MODIFICATIONS PROCLAIMED
PURSUANT TO TRADE AGREEMENTS LEGISLATION; ADDITIONAL IMPORT
RESTRICTIONS PROCLAIMED PURSUANT TO SECTION 22 OF THE AGRICULTURAL
ADJUSTMENT ACT, AS AMENDED

Chapter 98 Special classification provisions

99 Temporary legislation; temporary modifications proclaimed pursuant to trade agreements legislation; additional import restrictions proclaimed pursuant to section 22 of the Agricultural Adjustment Act, as amended

Chemical Appendix to the Tariff Schedule

Pharmaceutical Appendix to the Tariff Schedule

Intermediate Chemicals for Dyes Appendix to the Tariff Schedule

Statistical Annexes
- Annex A - Schedule C, Classification of Country and Territory Designations for U.S. Import Statistics
- Annex B - International Standard Country Codes
- Annex C - Schedule D, Customs District and Port Codes

Alphabetical Index

Change Record

Harmonized Tariff Schedule of the United States (2001)

Annotated for Statistical Reporting Purposes

Gen.Rs.Int.

GENERAL RULES OF INTERPRETATION

Classification of goods in the tariff schedule shall be governed by the following principles:

1. The table of contents, alphabetical index, and titles of sections, chapters and sub-chapters are provided for ease of reference only; for legal purposes, classification shall be determined according to the terms of the headings and any relative section or chapter notes and, provided such headings or notes do not otherwise require, according to the following provisions:

2. (a) Any reference in a heading to an article shall be taken to include a reference to that article incomplete or unfinished, provided that, as entered, the incomplete or unfinished article has the essential character of the complete or finished article. It shall also include a reference to that article complete or finished (or falling to be classified as complete or finished by virtue of this rule), entered unassembled or disassembled.

   (b) Any reference in a heading to a material or substance shall be taken to include a reference to mixtures or combinations of that material or substance with other materials or substances. Any reference to goods of a given material or substance shall be taken to include a reference to goods consisting wholly or partly of such material or substance. The classification of goods consisting of more than one material or substance shall be according to the principles of rule 3.

3. When, by application of rule 2(b) or for any other reason, goods are, *prima facie*, classifiable under two or more headings, classification shall be effected as follows:

   (a) The heading which provides the most specific description shall be preferred to headings providing a more general description. However, when two or more headings each refer to part only of the materials or substances contained in mixed or composite goods or to part only of the items in a set put up for retail sale, those headings are to be regarded as equally specific in relation to those goods, even if one of them gives a more complete or precise description of the goods.

   (b) Mixtures, composite goods consisting of different materials or made up of different components, and goods put up in sets for retail sale, which cannot be classified by reference to 3(a), shall be classified as if they consisted of the material or component which gives them their essential character, insofar as this criterion is applicable.

   (c) When goods cannot be classified by reference to 3(a) or 3(b), they shall be classified under the heading which occurs last in numerical order among those which equally merit consideration.

4. Goods which cannot be classified in accordance with the above rules shall be classified under the heading appropriate to the goods to which they are most akin.

5. In addition to the foregoing provisions, the following rules shall apply in respect of the goods referred to therein:

   (a) Camera cases, musical instrument cases, gun cases, drawing instrument cases, necklace cases and similar containers, specially shaped or fitted to contain a specific article or set of articles, suitable for long-term use and entered with the articles for which they are intended, shall be classified with such articles when of a kind normally sold therewith. This rule does not, however, apply to containers which give the whole its essential character;

   (b) Subject to the provisions of rule 5(a) above, packing materials and packing containers entered with the goods therein shall be classified with the goods if they are of a kind normally used for packing such goods. However, this provision is not binding when such packing materials or packing containers are clearly suitable for repetitive use.

6. For legal purposes, the classification of goods in the subheadings of a heading shall be determined according to the terms of those subheadings and any related subheading notes and, *mutatis mutandis*, to the above rules, on the understanding that only subheadings at the same level are comparable. For the purposes of this rule, the relative section, chapter and subchapter notes also apply, unless the context otherwise requires.

Harmonized Tariff Schedule of the United States (2001)

Annotated for Statistical Reporting Purposes

Add.U.S.Rs.Int.

ADDITIONAL U.S. RULES OF INTERPRETATION

1. In the absence of special language or context which otherwise requires--

   (a) a tariff classification controlled by use (other than actual use) is to be determined in accordance with the use in the United States at, or immediately prior to, the date of importation, of goods of that class or kind to which the imported goods belong, and the controlling use is the principal use;

   (b) a tariff classification controlled by the actual use to which the imported goods are put in the United States is satisfied only if such use is intended at the time of importation, the goods are so used and proof thereof is furnished within 3 years after the date the goods are entered;

   (c) a provision for parts of an article covers products solely or principally used as a part of such articles but a provision for "parts" or "parts and accessories" shall not prevail over a specific provision for such part or accessory; and

   (d) the principles of section XI regarding mixtures of two or more textile materials shall apply to the classification of goods in any provision in which a textile material is named.

Harmonized Tariff Schedule of the United States (2001)–Supplement 1

Annotated for Statistical Reporting Purposes

(c) Products Eligible for Special Tariff Treatment.

(i) Programs under which special tariff treatment may be provided, and the corresponding symbols for such programs as they are indicated in the "Special" subcolumn, are as follows:

Generalized System of Preferences	A, A* or A+
Automotive Products Trade Act	B
Agreement on Trade in Civil Aircraft	C
North American Free Trade Agreement:	
Goods of Canada, under the terms of general note 12 to this schedule	CA
Goods of Mexico, under the terms of general note 12 to this schedule	MX
African Growth and Opportunity Act	D
Caribbean Basin Economic Recovery Act	E or E*
United States-Israel Free Trade Area	IL
Andean Trade Preference Act	J or J*
Agreement on Trade in Pharmaceutical Products	K
Uruguay Round Concessions on Intermediate Chemicals for Dyes	L
United States-Caribbean Basin Trade Partnership Act	R

(ii) Articles which are eligible for the special tariff treatment provided for in general notes 4 through 14 and which are subject to temporary modification under any provision of subchapters I, II and VII of chapter 99 shall be subject, for the period indicated in the "Effective Period" column in chapter 99, to rates of duty as follows:

(A) if a rate of duty for which the article may be eligible is set forth in the "Special" subcolumn in chapter 99 followed by one or more symbols described above, such rate shall apply in lieu of the rate followed by the corresponding symbol(s) set forth for such article in the "Special" subcolumn in chapters 1 to 98; or

(B) if "No change" appears in the "Special" subcolumn in chapter 99 and subdivision (c)(ii)(A) above does not apply, the rate of duty in the "General" subcolumn in chapter 99 or the applicable rate(s) of duty set forth in the "Special" subcolumn in chapters 1 to 98, whichever is lower, shall apply.

(iii) Unless the context requires otherwise, articles which are eligible for the special tariff treatment provided for in general notes 4 through 14 and which are subject to temporary modification under any provision of subchapters III or IV of chapter 99 shall be subject, for the period indicated in chapter 99, to the rates of duty in the "General" subcolumn in such chapter.

(iv) Whenever any rate of duty set forth in the "Special" subcolumn in chapters 1 to 98 is equal to or higher than, the corresponding rate of duty provided in the "General" subcolumn in such chapters, such rate of duty in the "Special" subcolumn shall be deleted; except that, if the rate of duty in the "Special" subcolumn is an intermediate stage in a series of staged rate reductions for that provision, such rate shall be treated as a suspended rate and shall be set forth in the "Special" subcolumn, followed by one or more symbols described above, and followed by an "s" in parentheses. If no rate of duty for which the article may be eligible is provided in the "Special" subcolumn for a particular provision in chapters 1 to 98, the rate of duty provided in the "General" subcolumn shall apply.

Harmonized Tariff Schedule of the United States (2001)--Supplement 1

Annotated for Statistical Reporting Purposes

GN 4(a)

4. Products of Countries Designated Beneficiary Developing Countries for Purposes of the Generalized System of Preferences (GSP).

(a) The following countries, territories and associations of countries eligible for treatment as one country (pursuant to section 507(2) of the Trade Act of 1974 (19 U.S.C. 2467(2)) are designated beneficiary developing countries for the purposes of the Generalized System of Preferences, provided for in Title V of the Trade Act of 1974, as amended (19 U.S.C. 2461 *et seq.*):

Independent Countries

Albania
Angola
Antigua and Barbuda
Argentina
Armenia
Bahrain
Bangladesh
Barbados
Belize
Benin
Bhutan
Bolivia
Bosnia and Hercegovina
Botswana
Brazil
Bulgaria
Burkina Faso
Burundi
Cambodia
Cameroon
Cape Verde
Central African Republic
Chad
Chile
Colombia
Comoros
Congo (Brazzaville)
Congo (Kinshasa)
Costa Rica
Cote d'Ivoire
Croatia
Czech Republic
Djibouti
Dominica
Dominican Republic
Ecuador
Egypt
El Salvador
Equatorial Guinea
Eritrea
Estonia
Ethiopia
Fiji
Gabon
Gambia, The
Georgia
Ghana
Grenada
Guatemala
Guinea
Guinea-Bissau
Guyana
Haiti
Honduras
Hungary
India
Indonesia
Jamaica
Jordan
Kazakhstan
Kenya
Kiribati
Kyrgyzstan
Latvia
Lebanon
Lesotho
Lithuania
Macedonia, Former Yugoslav Republic of
Madagascar
Malawi
Mali
Malta
Mauritania
Mauritius
Moldova
Mongolia
Morocco
Mozambique
Namibia
Nepal
Niger
Nigeria
Oman
Pakistan
Panama
Papua New Guinea
Paraguay
Peru
Philippines
Poland
Romania
Russia
Rwanda
St. Kitts and Nevis
Saint Lucia
Saint Vincent and the Grenadines
Samoa
Sao Tome and Principe
Senegal
Seychelles
Sierra Leone
Slovakia
Slovenia
Solomon Islands
Somalia
South Africa
Sri Lanka
Suriname
Swaziland
Tanzania
Thailand
Togo
Tonga
Trinidad and Tobago
Tunisia
Turkey
Tuvalu
Uganda
Ukraine
Uruguay
Uzbekistan
Vanuatu
Venezuela
Republic of Yemen
Zambia
Zimbabwe

Harmonized Tariff Schedule of the United States (2001)--Supplement 1

Annotated for Statistical Reporting Purposes

GN 4(a) (con.)

Non-Independent Countries and Territories

Anguilla
British Indian Ocean Territory
Christmas Island (Australia)
Cocos (Keeling) Islands
Cook Islands
Falkland Islands (Islas Malvinas)
French Polynesia
Gibraltar
Heard Island and McDonald Islands
Montserrat
New Caledonia
Niue
Norfolk Island
Pitcairn Islands
Saint Helena
Tokelau
Turks and Caicos Islands
Virgin Islands, British
Wallis and Futuna
West Bank and Gaza Strip
Western Sahara

Associations of Countries (treated as one country)

Member Countries of the Cartagena Agreement (Andean Group)

Consisting of:

Bolivia
Colombia
Ecuador
Peru
Venezuela

Member Countries of the West African Economic and Monetary Union (WAEMU)

Consisting of:

Benin
Burkina Faso
Cote d'Ivoire
Guinea-Bissau
Mali
Niger
Senegal
Togo

Member Countries of the Association of South East Asian Nations (ASEAN)

Currently qualifying:

Cambodia
Indonesia
Philippines
Thailand

Member Countries of the Southern Africa Development Community (SADC)

Currently qualifying:

Botswana
Mauritius
Tanzania

Member Countries of the Caribbean Common Market (CARICOM), except The Bahamas

Consisting of:

Antigua and Barbuda
Barbados
Belize
Dominica
Grenada
Guyana
Jamaica
Montserrat
St. Kitts and Nevis
Saint Lucia
Saint Vincent and the Grenadines
Trinidad and Tobago

Harmonized Tariff Schedule of the United States (2001)

Annotated for Statistical Reporting Purposes

XI
61-6

Heading/ Subheading	Stat. Suf- fix	Article Description	Unit of Quantity	Rates of Duty 1 General	Rates of Duty 1 Special	Rates of Duty 2
6103		Men's or boys' suits, ensembles, suit-type jackets, blazers, trousers, bib and brace overalls, breeches and shorts (other than swimwear), knitted or crocheted:				
		Suits:				
6103.11.00	00	Of wool or fine animal hair (443)	No. kg	50.3¢kg + 13%	Free (CA,IL,MX)	77.2¢/kg + 54.5%
6103.12		Of synthetic fibers:				
6103.12.10	00	Containing 23 percent or more by weight of wool or fine animal hair (443)	No. kg	65.4¢/kg + 16.9%	Free (CA,IL,MX)	77.2¢/kg + 54.5%
6103.12.20	00	Other (643)	No. kg	28.7%	Free (CA,IL,MX)	72%
6103.19		Of other textile materials:				
		Of artificial fibers:				
6103.19.10	00	Containing 23 percent or more by weight of wool or fine animal hair (443)	No. kg	23.2¢/kg + 6%	Free (CA,IL,MX)	77.2¢/kg + 54.5%
6103.19.15	00	Other (643)	No. kg	9%	Free (CA,IL,MX)	72%
6103.19.20		Of cotton		12.2%	Free (CA,IL,MX)	90%
	10	Jackets imported as parts of suits (333)	doz. kg			
	15	Trousers, breeches and shorts imported as parts of suits (347)	doz. kg			
	30	Waistcoats imported as parts of suits (359)	doz. kg			
6103.19.60	00	Containing 70 percent or more by weight of silk or silk waste (743)	No. kg	2.4%	Free (CA,E,IL,J, MX)	45%
6103.19.90		Other		5.7%	Free (CA,E*,IL, MX)	45%
		Subject to cotton restraints:				
	10	Jackets imported as parts of suits (333)	doz. kg			
	20	Trousers, breeches, and shorts imported as parts of suits (347)	doz. kg			
	30	Waistcoats imported as parts of suits (359)	doz. kg			
	40	Subject to wool restraints (443)	No. kg			
	50	Subject to man-made fiber restraints (643)	No. kg			
	80	Other (843)	No. kg			

Appendix G

International Purchase Agreement (Import)

FORM

AGREEMENT made December 6, 1981, between Renoir Industrielles et Cie., of Paris, France, a corporation organized under the laws of France (the "Seller"), and H. A. Pannay, Inc., of 142 Trimble Avenue, St. Louis, Missouri, U.S.A., a Missouri corporation (the "Buyer").

1. *Sale.* The Seller shall sell to the Buyer 100,000 long tons of No. 1 heavy steel melting scrap up to a length of 1.50 meters, not over 40 centimeters in width, and not less than five millimeters in thickness.

2. *Price.* The purchase price is $27.18 per long ton, F.A.S. Vessel Cherbourg. The price is free alongside the vessel designated by the Buyer (the "Buyer's vessel"), at Cherbourg, the port of shipment. Payment for all merchandise shall be made in currency of the United States of America.

3. *Delivery.* The Seller shall deliver the scrap, in the kind and quantity specified in paragraph 1, alongside the Buyer's vessel, within reach of its loading tackle, at the port of shipment. The scrap shall be delivered by the Seller at a minimum rate of 14,000 long tons every 30 days. If this minimum rate of delivery is not maintained by the Seller during any 30-day period, the total quantity stated in paragraph 1 shall be reduced by an amount equal to the difference between the amount actually delivered and the minimum rate of delivery for such 30-day period.

4. *Notice.* The Seller shall give notice to the Buyer by cable of the quantity of scrap available for loading, the price

(Text continued on page 4–1097)

thereof, and the date on which the Seller is ready to commence loading for transportation to the port of shipment. Thereafter, the Buyer shall give adequate notice to the Seller by cable of the date on which it is ready to commence loading upon the Buyer's vessel. The notice shall contain the name, sailing date, loading berth, and date of delivery alongside the Buyer's vessel. Upon the receipt of such notice from the Buyer, the Seller shall prepare and commence loading the scrap for transportation to the port of shipment in sufficient quantities for the Buyer to load at the rate of 700 tons per working day; provided that the Seller shall not be required to have the scrap prepared or loaded for transportation to the port of shipment until after receipt of the letter of credit provided for in paragraph 12, and receipt of notice in writing from the bank, referred to in paragraph 12, that the Buyer has made the deposit of earnest money provided for in paragraph 11.

5. *Insurance.* The Buyer shall obtain and pay for all marine insurance for its own account, provided that all marine insurance obtained by the Buyer shall include, for the protection of the Seller, standard warehouse to warehouse coverage.

6. *Demurrage.* The Seller shall be liable for demurrage charges in excess of one day incurred by the Buyer by reason of the Seller's default. The Buyer shall be liable for demurrage or storage charges in excess of one day incurred by the Seller by reason of the Buyer's failure to load or to have his vessel ready for loading on any stipulated date.

7. *Invoices.* The Seller shall issue provisional invoices and final invoices for every shipment of scrap. The weights as established at the time and place of loading upon the Buyer's vessel shall be used in determining the amounts of the provisional invoices. The Buyer shall forward to the Seller certified weight certificates issued at the time and place of loading upon rail or barge, at the point of importation, for shipment to the Buyer's destination, and the weights as established at such time and place shall be final

in determining the total amounts of the final invoices; provided, that if a shipment is lost after loading upon the Buyer's vessel, the weights as established at the time and place of loading upon the Buyer's vessel shall be final in determining the total amounts of the final invoices.

8. *Inspection.* The Buyer shall have the right to inspect the scrap at the yards of the Seller, or at the place of loading upon the Buyer's vessel. All rejected scrap shall be replaced by scrap meeting the description and specifications stated in paragraph 1. The Buyer, or its agent, shall execute a certificate of inspection and acceptance, at its own cost. Failure of the Buyer to inspect shall constitute a waiver of the right of inspection, and shall be deemed acceptance of the scrap as delivered for loading.

9. *Title.* Title to the scrap shall pass to the Buyer upon delivery alongside the Buyer's vessel, provided the Buyer has established the letter of credit and made the deposit of the earnest money provided for in paragraphs 11 and 12.

10. *Covenant against reexportation.* The Buyer covenants that the scrap will be shipped to and delivered in the United States of America, and that the Buyer will not ship the scrap to, or deliver it in, any other country, and will not reexport the scrap after it is delivered in the United States of America.

11. *Earnest money.* Within ten days after the execution of this agreement, the Buyer shall deposit, at the bank at which the Buyer establishes the letter of credit provided for in paragraph 12, the sum of $40,000, in the form of bank cashier's or certified checks payable to the order of the Seller, for disposition in accordance with the terms of this paragraph. Upon full performance of the conditions of this agreement by the Buyer, the earnest money shall be refunded either by direct payment to the Buyer or by application toward the payment for the last shipment. If the Buyer fails to perform all the conditions of this agreement, the earnest money shall be delivered to the Seller as liqui-

dated damages, and not as a penalty, and this agreement shall thereafter become null and void.

12. *Letter of credit.* Within ten days after receipt of the notice from the Seller provided for in paragraph 4, stating the quantity of scrap available for loading and the price thereof, the Buyer shall establish with a bank in New York, New York, a confirmed, revolving, irrevocable letter of credit in favor of the Seller in the amount stated in the notice, for the term of six months, to cover the first shipment. The amount of the letter of credit shall be replenished, and the term thereof extended, to cover any additional shipments, upon receipt of notice from the Seller stating the quantity of additional scrap available for loading and the price thereof. The letter of credit shall provide that partial shipments against the letter of credit shall be permitted, and shall also provide that payment therefrom shall be made in the amount of 90% of the provisional invoice upon presentation of the following documents: (a) provisional commercial invoice; (b) consular invoice, if required; (c) clean dock or ship's receipt, or received-for-shipment ocean bill of lading, or other transportation receipt; (d) certified weight certificate; (e) Buyer's certificate of inspection and acceptance, but if the Buyer has waived his right of inspection under paragraph 8 the Seller shall so state in the invoices.

13. *Adjustment of payment.* Any difference between the amount of the final invoices, determined as provided in paragraph 7, and the amount paid on the provisional invoices shall be paid against the letter of credit upon presentation of the final invoices.

14. *Cancellation.* In the event that delivery in whole or in part, for a period not exceeding 30 days, shall be prevented by causes beyond the control of the Seller, including but not limited to acts of God, labor troubles, failure of essential means of transportation, or changes in policy with respect to exports or otherwise by the French government, this agreement shall be extended for an additional period equal

to the period of delay. In the event, however, that such nondelivery continues after such extended period, the Buyer or the Seller shall have the right to cancel this agreement to the extent of such nondelivery by written notice, and in such case there shall be no obligation or liability on the part of either party with respect to such undelivered scrap; provided that any such notice from the Buyer shall not apply with respect to any scrap which the Seller has prepared or loaded for transportation to the port of shipment prior to the receipt by the Seller of such notice.

15. *Assignment.* The Buyer shall not assign its rights nor delegate the performance of its duties under this contract without the prior written consent of the Seller.

16. *Export license.* This agreement shall be subject to the issue of an export license to the Buyer by the appropriate agency of the French government.

17. *Modifications.* All modifications of this agreement shall be in writing signed by both parties.

18. *Benefit.* This agreement shall be binding upon and shall inure to the benefit of the parties, their successors, and assigns, subject, however, to the limitation of paragraph 15.

In witness whereof the parties have executed this agreement.

Corporate Seal
Attest:
....
Secretary

Renoir Industrielles et Cie.
by ....
President

Corporate Seal
Attest:
....
Secretary

H. A. Pannay, Inc.
by ....
President

Appendix H

Rules for Completing an Entry Summary

CD 099 3550-061, Sept. 18, 1992

INSTRUCTIONS FOR PREPARATION OF CF 7501

ALL PORTS WILL ACCEPT CF 7501'S COMPLETED IN ACCORDANCE WITH THE INSTRUCTIONS CONTAINED HEREIN. NO ADDITIONAL INFORMATION OR AGENDA MAY BE REQUIRED ON THE CF 7501 BY ANY REGION, DISTRICT, AREA, OR PORT, WITHOUT THE EXPRESS WRITTEN APPROVAL OF CUSTOMS HEADQUARTERS. IT IS ESSENTIAL THAT UNIFORMITY IN THE PREPARATION AND ACCEPTANCE OF THE CF 7501 BE MAINTAINED. **THE INSTRUCTIONS CONTAINED HEREIN ARE APPLICABLE TO BOTH CONSUMPTION AND WAREHOUSE ENTRY SUMMARIES AND ENTRY/ENTRY SUMMARIES.**

1. ENTRY NUMBER

Record the 11 digit alphanumeric code. Always begin with the three digit code assigned to the filer, followed by the seven digit number, and finally, the one digit check digit. Due to a space limitation in this block, the three character entry filer code is to be printed outside and immediately to the left of this block. The assigned entry number, with hyphen and check digit, is to be shown inside the block. See example below.

Entry Filer Code XXX   Entry No. NNNNNNN-N

XXX represents the three character alphanumeric filer code assigned to the broker or importer by Customs.

NNNNNNN represents the seven digit number assigned by the filer. The number may be assigned in any manner convenient, provided that the same number is not assigned to more than one CF 7501. Leading zeros must be shown.

N represents the check digit which is computed on the previous 10 characters.

Detailed instructions concerning the entry number are contained in Customs Directive 3500-08, dated June 19, 1986, (Customs), and **Customs Directive 3500-058, dated September 10, 1991.** The formula for computing the check digit is included in this issuance as Appendix A.

An entry number, in this format, is required on all broker/importer prepared informal (which require a CF 7501) and warehouse entries.

Where the entry summary covers more than one release (consolidated entry summary), refer to the instructions on page 28 of this directive.

Where the entry summary consists of more than one page, record the entry number on the first page of the CF 7501, as well as on each additional page.

2. ENTRY TYPE CODE

Record the appropriate entry type code by selecting the two digit code for the type of entry summary being filed. The first digit of the code identifies the general category of the entry (i.e., consumption =0, informal =1, warehouse =2, etc.). The second digit further defines the specific processing type within the entry category. Therefore, a consumption quota entry should be recorded under code 02, an informal free or dutiable entry under code 11, etc.

Automated Broker Interface (ABI) processing requires an ABI status indicator. This indicator must be recorded in block 2 following the two digit entry type code. It is to be shown for those entry summaries with ABI status only, and must be shown in one of the following formats:

(1) ABI/S = ABI statement entry summaries **paid by check or cash**
(2) ABI/A = ABI statement entry summaries paid through the Automated Clearinghouse (ACH)
(3) ABI/N = ABI non-statement entry summaries
(4) ABI/P = ABI periodic payment statement entry summaries (this capability not yet operational)

Note: Either a slash (/) or hyphen (-) may be used to separate ABI from the indicator (i.E., ABI/S or ABI-S).

If an entry/entry summary (live entry) is presented, an additional indicator is required to be shown in the following formats:

(1) ABI/A/L = ABI statement live entry summaries **paid through ACH**
(2) ABI/N/L = ABI non-statement live entry summaries
(3) ABI/P/L = ABI periodic payment statement live entry summaries
(4) "LIVE" or "L" for non-ABI entry summaries

An entry/entry summary is considered "LIVE" when duties are deposited and which results in release of the merchandise.

Note: The word "ACH" is no longer required to be written in the upper right hand corner of the CF 7501.

ENTRY TYPE CODES

ENTRY TYPE	ENTRY TYPE CODE
Consumption Entries	
Free and Dutiable	01
Quota/Visa	02
Countervailing/Antidumping Duty	03
Appraisement	04
Vessel Repair	05
Foreign Trade Zone (Consumption)	06
Quota/Visa and AD/CVD combinations	07
Informal Entries	
Free and Dutiable	11
Quota (Other than textiles)	12
Warehouse Entries	
Warehouse	21
Re-Warehouse	22
Temporary Importation Bond	23
Trade Fair	24
Permanent Exhibition	25
Foreign Trade Zone (Admission)	26
Warehouse Withdrawal	
For Consumption	31
Quota/Visa	32
Aircraft and Vessel Supply (Immediate Export)	33
Countervailing and Antidumping Duty	34
For Transportation	35
For Immediate Exportation	36
For Transportation and Exportation	37
Quota/Visa and ADA/CVD combinations	38
Drawback Entries	
Manufacturer	41
Same condition	42
Rejected Importation	43
Government Entries	
Defense Contract Management Command - International (DCMC-I) (formerly DCASR) is the importer of record <u>and</u> filer of the entry.	**51**
Any U.S. Federal Government agency (other than DCMAO) is the importer of record.	**52**

Note: When the importer of record of emergency war materials under HTS #9808.00.3000 <u>is not</u> a government agency, entry type codes 01, 02, 03, etc., as appropriate, are to be used. ALSO, ENTRY TYPE CODE 53 HAS BEEN DELETED.

*Transportation Entries
Immediate Transportation. 61
Transportation and Exportation. 62
Immediate Exportation 63
Barge Movement. 64
Permit to Proceed 65
Baggage 66
****

3. ENTRY SUMMARY DATE

This block is to record the date the entry summary is filed with Customs (six digit numeric code showing month, day, and year - MMDDYY). The record copy of the entry summary will be time stamped by the filer at the time of presentation of the entry summary. In the case of entry summaries submitted on an ABI Statement, only the statement is required to be time stamped.

This block should not be printed or typed prior to presentation of the entry/entry summary. Use of this field is optional for ABI statement entries. The time stamp mandated by Customs Directive #3550-24 date September 8, 1987, entitled "Entry Summary and Entry/Entry Summary Flow" will serve as the entry summary date. This mandate was also published as Treasury Decision 88-27.

The filer will record the **proper** import specialist team number designation in the upper right portion of this block (three character team number code). **For ABI entry summaries, the team number is supplied by ACS in the summary processing output message.**

All dates required to be shown on the CF 7501 may use slashes, dashes, and spaces.

4. ENTRY DATE

Record the six digit numeric code: month, day, and year (MMDDYY). Normally, it is the date the goods are released except for immediate delivery, quota goods, or where importer/broker requests another date prior to release (see 19 CFR 141.68).

It is the responsibility of the filer to ensure that the entry date shown for entry/entry summaries is the date of presentation (i.e., the time stamp date).

5. PORT CODE

Record the four digit numeric code of the U.S. port where the merchandise was entered under an entry or released under an immediate delivery permit. U.S. port codes can be found in Annex C of the Harmonized Tariff Schedule. The port code should be shown as follows:

NNN (no spaces or hyphens)

Do not show the name of the port instead of the numeric code.

6. BOND NUMBER

Record the three digit numeric code that identifies the surety company on the bond. This code number can be found in block #7 of the Customs Form 301/Customs Bond. This code number is also available through ACS to ABI filers, via the importer bond query transaction. For U.S. Government importations and entry types not requiring surety, the code 999 should appear in this block. When cash or Government securities are used in lieu of surety, use code 998.

7. BOND TYPE CODE

Record the single digit numeric code as follows:

0 - U.S. Government or entry types not requiring a bond
8 - Continuous
9 - Single Transaction

Bond type "0" should be used in conjunction with surety code "999" for government entries secured by stipulation cited in C.R. 10.101(d).

Bond type "8" or "9", as appropriate, should be used in conjunction with surety code "998" when cash or government securities are deposited in lieu of surety.

Bond type "9" should be used in conjunction with surety code "999" when surety has been waived in accordance with C.R. 142.4 (c).

8. BROKER/IMPORTER FILE NO.

This block is reserved for a broker's or importer's internal file or reference number.

9. ULTIMATE CONSIGNEE NAME AND ADDRESS

For a period of 90 days from the date of issuance of this directive, record the name and address of the individual or firm for whose account the merchandise is shipped. If this information is the same as the importer of record, leave blank. Effective on the 91st day from the date of issuance of this directive, record the name and address of the individual or firm purchasing the merchandise or, if a consigned shipment to whom the merchandise is consigned, or if those parties are not known, to whose premises the merchandise is being shipped. If this information is the same as the importer of record, leave blank.

In the space provided for indicating the state, report the ultimate state of destination of the imported merchandise, as known at the time of entry summary filing. If the contents of the shipment are destined to more than one state or if the entry summary represents a consolidated shipment, report the state of destination with the greatest aggregate value. If, in either case, this information is unknown, the state of the ultimate consignee, or the state where the entry is filed, in that order, should be reported. However, before either of these alternatives are used, a good faith effort should be made by the entry filer to ascertain the state where the imported merchandise will be delivered. In all cases, the state code reported should be derived from the standard postal two-letter state or territory abbreviation. The reporting of the ultimate state of destination was made mandatory for all entry summaries and entry/entry summaries filed on or after July 1, 1991.

NOTE: A list of two-letter U.S. Postal Service state and territory codes are listed as Appendix F to this issuance.

To facilitate mailing of requests and/or notices on Customs Form 28 or 29 to a party other than the importer of record, the following alternate procedure shall be used. Where this block is modified by the legend "c/o" followed by the name and address of a different party, Customs Form 28 or 29 will be sent to the name and address that follows the "c/o" legend. The broker's copy will continue to be sent to the broker when **they are** involved (Manual Supplement 2112-04, 9/22/78).

10. CONSIGNEE NUMBER

Record the IRS, Social Security, or Customs assigned number of the consignee. **This number must reflect a valid identification number filed with Customs via the CF 5106 or its electronic (ACS) equivalent.** When the consignee number is the same as the importer of record number, the word "SAME" may be used in lieu of repeating the importer of record number.

Only the following formats shall be used:

IRS Number	NN-NNNNNNN
IRS Number with suffix	NN-NNNNNNNXX
Social Security Number	NNN-NN-NNNN
Customs Assigned Number.	**YYDDPP-NNNNN**

For **permitted and proper** consolidated shipments, enter zeros in this block in the "IRS Number" format shown **above** (e.g. 00-0000000). **The reporting of zeros on the entry summary document is limited to consolidated shipments only.**

11. IMPORTER OF RECORD NAME AND ADDRESS

Record the name and address, including the standard two letter postal state or territory abbreviation, of the importer of record. The importer of record is the individual or firm liable for payment of all duties and meeting all statutory and regulatory requirements incurred as a result of importation.

12. IMPORTER NUMBER

Record the IRS, Social Security, or Customs assigned number of the importer of record. For format, see instructions under "Consignee Number."

13. **EXPORTING COUNTRY**

Record the exporting country utilizing the two character alpha ISO country codes specified in the International Standard ISO 3166 (a list of the ISO two character alpha codes is provided as Appendix C in this issuance).

The country of exportation is that country from which the merchandise was shipped to the United States having last been a part of the commerce of the country and without contingency of diversion.

For merchandise entering the U.S. Customs territory from a U.S. Foreign Trade Zone, leave blank.

For multiple countries of export, record the word "MULTI" in this block, and associate the country of export with each line number (or where line numbers are segregated by invoice, associate with each invoice) in column 28 prefixed with an "E".

14. **EXPORT DATE**

For merchandise exported by vessel, record the month, day, and year on which the carrier departed the last port in the exporting country (format: MMDDYY).

For merchandise exported by air, record the month, day, and year in which the aircraft departed the last airport in the exporting country (format: MMDDYY).

For overland shipments from Canada or Mexico and shipments where the port of lading is located outside the exporting country (e.g., goods are exported from Switzerland but laden and shipped from Hamburg, West Germany), record the month, day, and year in which the goods crossed the border of the exporting country (Switzerland in this example; format: (MMDDYY).

For mail shipment, record the date of export as noted on the Customs Form 3509, Notice to Addressee (format: MMDDYY).

For goods entering the U.S. Customs territory from a U.S. Foreign Trade Zone, leave blank.

For multiple dates of export, record the word "MULTI" in this block, and associate the date of export with each line number (or where line items are segregated by invoice, associate with each invoice) in column 28.

For textile merchandise, refer to the additional requirements in paragraph #34D (Visa Number).

15. <u>COUNTRY OF ORIGIN</u>

Record the country of origin utilizing the ISO country codes specified in International Standard ISO 3166 (listed as Appendix C in this issuance).

The country of origin is the country of manufacture, production, or growth of any article. **If the article consists of material produced or derived from, or processed in, more than one foreign territory or country, or insular possession of the U.S., it shall be considered a product of that foreign territory or country, or insular possession where it last underwent a substantial transformation. For purposes of reporting on the CF 7501 <u>only</u>, whenever merchandise has been returned to the U.S. after undergoing**

either repair, alteration, or assembly under HTS heading 9802, the country of origin should be shown as the country in which the repair, alteration, or assembly was performed.

When merchandise is invoiced in or exported from a country other then than in which it originated, the actual country of origin shall be specified rather than the country of invoice or exportation.

When a single entry summary covers merchandise from more than one country of origin, record the word "MULTI" in this block and in column 28, directly below the line number, and prefixed with the letter "O", indicate a separate ISO code for the country of origin corresponding to each line number.

16. <u>**MISSING DOCUMENTS**</u>

Record the appropriate document code number(s) to indicate one or two documents not available at the time of filing the entry summary. The bond charge should be made on the entry summary <u>only</u> for those documents that are required to be filed with the entry summary. For specific instructions concerning missing document policy, consult Customs Directive No. 3550-27, "Entry Simplification - Missing Documents", dated September 8, 1987.

The following codes shall be used:

01. - Commercial Invoice
02.to 09. - Reserved
10. - CF 5523 (19 CFR 141.89)
11.to 13 - Reserved
14. - Lease Statement [19 CFR 10.108]
15. - Re-Melting Certificate [19 CFR 54.6(a)]
16. - Corrected Commercial Invoice (19 CFR 141.89, et al)
17. - Other Agency Forms (19 CFR Part 12)
18. - Duty Free Entry Certificate (19 CFR 10.102; 9808.00.30009 HTS)
19. - Scale weight (19 CFR 151, Subpart B)
20. - End Use Certificate (19 CFR 10.138)
21. - Coffee Form O
22. - Chemical Analysis
23. - Outturn Report (19 CFR 151, Subpart C)
24.to 25. - Reserved
26. - Packing List [19 CFR 141.86(e)]
27.to 97. - Reserved
98. - Not Specified Above
99. - If three or more documents are missing, record the code number for the first document and insert code "99" for any additional documents.

Exception: Duty Free Certificate (#18), and End Use

Certificate (#20) are excepted from the requirement that Customs specifically request the document from an importer or broker. These forms cannot be waived and importers or brokers shall be obligated to file the forms within the appropriate time limits.

If a document has been waived prior to entry summary filing or is not required at time of entry summary do not record that document as a missing document.

17. **I.T. NUMBER**

Record the In-bond Entry Number obtained from the CF 7512C or, if applicable, the air waybill number. If multiple, place additional I.T. numbers across lines 30 to 32 or list on a separate attachment. If AMS Master in-bond movement (MIB), record the 11 digit in bond number obtained from the AMS carrier. Neither the CF 7512 or CF7512C are used for the AMS master in-bond program.

If merchandise moves on an I.T. into a Foreign Trade Zone, do not record that number on the CF 7501 when the merchandise is removed from the zone.

18. **I.T. DATE**

Record the date (format MMDDYY) of the In Bond Entry Number (CF 7512) or if applicable, the Transit Air Cargo Manifest (TACM), or the AMS Master in-bond movement. If multiple, place additional dates across lines 30 to 32 associated with each additional I.T. number to which it is applicable. Note: I.T. date cannot be prior to import date.

19. **BILL OF LADING OR AIR WAYBILL NUMBER**

Record the number assigned on the manifest by the international ocean or air carrier delivering the goods to the United States. Completion of this field is not required for modes of transport other than sea or air.

Effective March 31, 1989, and pursuant to Treasury Decision #88-69, each bill of lading for vessel shipment will be required to conform to a new unique number format. This unique bill of lading number format will change the current master bill of lading number format from 12 to 16 maximum characters in length and will be comprised of 2 elements. The first element is the first four characters of the unique bill number consisting of the SCAC code of the issuer of the bill. The second element may be any length up to a maximum

12 characters and may be alpha and/or numeric. The format of the unique bill of lading number that must be shown on the CF 7501 is as follows:

ABCD1234567

If multiple, list additional B/L or AWB's across the top of columns 30 to 32 or list on a separate attachment.

20. **MODE OF TRANSPORTATION**

Record the method of transportation by which the imported merchandise entered the U.S. port of arrival from the last foreign country utilizing the following two digit numeric codes:

10 - Vessel, non-container (including all cargo at first U.S. port of unlading aboard a vessel regardless of later disposition. Lightered, land bridge and LASH all included). If container status unknown but goods did arrive by vessel, use this code.
11 - Vessel, container
12 - Border, Waterborne (used in cases where vessels are used exclusively to ferry automobiles, trucks, and/or rail cars, carrying passengers and baggage and/or cargo and merchandise, between the U.S. and a contiguous country).
20 - Rail, **non-container**
21 - Rail, container
30 - Truck, **non-container**
31 - Truck, container
32 - Auto
33 - Pedestrian
34 - Road, other
40 - Air, **non-container**
41 - Air, container
50 - Mail
60 - Passenger, hand carried
70 - Fixed transport installation (includes pipelines, powerhouse, etc.)
80 - Not used at this time

For merchandise arriving in the U.S. Customs territory from a U.S. Foreign Trade Zone, leave blank

21. **MANUFACTURER I.D.**

This block is provided to accommodate the manufacturer/shipper identification number. This identifies, by a constructed code, the manufacturer/shipper of the merchandise. For the purposes of this number, the manufacturer should be construed to refer to the invoicing party or parties (manufacturers or other direct suppliers). The name and address of the invoicing party, whose invoice accompanies the Customs entry, should be used to construct the I.D. The method for deriving this number as contained in Customs Directive 3500-13, November 24, 1986, entitled "Instructions for Deriving Manufacturer/Shipper Identification Code", is included in this issuance as Appendix B. **The manufacturer/shipper identification number is required for <u>all</u> entry summaries and entry/entry summaries, including informal entries, filed on the CF 7501.** When merchandise is imported from Canada and produced by a Canadian Vendor, the ISO Code for Canada (CA) will be replaced by the appropriate two letter Province Code listed below.

<u>PROVINCE/TERRITORY</u>	<u>CODE</u>
ALBERTA	XA
BRITISH COLUMBIA	XC
MANITOBA	XM
NEW BRUNSWICK	XB
NEWFOUNDLAND (INCL. LABRADOR)	XW
NORTHWEST TERRITORIES	XT
NOVA SCOTIA	XN
ONTARIO	XO
PRINCE EDWARD ISLAND	XP
QUEBEC	XQ
SASKATCHEWAN	XS
YUKON TERRITORY	XY

When a single entry summary has more than one manufacturer, record the word "MULTI" in this block and, in block #30 indicate for each line item the manufacturer I.D. Code applicable to the particular Harmonized Tariff Schedules of the United States. <u>The Harmonized Tariff Schedules of the United States will hereinafter be referred to as the "HTS"</u>. Additionally, if there is more than one vendor for a particular HTS number, separate line items will be required for each.

22. **<u>REFERENCE NUMBER</u>**

Record the IRS, Social Security, or Customs assigned number of the individual or firm to whom refunds, bills or notices of extension or suspension of liquidation are to be sent (if other than the importer of record and if the CF 4811 is on file). For correct format of number, see instructions under "Consignee Number". Do not use this block to record any other information.

23. **IMPORTING CARRIER**

For merchandise arriving in the U.S. by vessel, record the name of the vessel which transported the merchandise from the foreign port of lading to the first U.S. port of unlading. Do not record the vessel identifier code in lieu of the vessel name. Pursuant to General Statistical Note 1 (a) (ii) of the HTS, the vessel flag is not required to be reported. For merchandise arriving in the U.S. by air, record the IATA code corresponding to the name of the airline which transported the merchandise from the last airport of foreign lading to the first U.S. airport of unlading. Use the IATA two digit alpha code for each airline. A copy of this listing is included in this issuance as Appendix D.

If the carrier file does not contain a specific air carrier's code, write the Designation "*C" for Canadian airlines,, "*F" for other foreign airlines, and "*U" for U.S. airlines.

These designations should be used only for unknown charter and private aircraft. When a private aircraft (HTS 8801.90.0000, 8802.20.0040, 8802.20.0050, 8802.20.0060, 8802.20.0080, 8802.30.0030, 8802.30.0040, 8802.30.0050, 8802.30.0060, 8802.30.0080, 8802.40.0040, 8802.40.0060, 8802.40.0070, and 8802.40.0090) is being entered under its own power (ferried), the designation "**" will be used.

For merchandise arriving in the U.S. by means of transportation other than vessel or air, leave blank.

Do not record the name of a domestic carrier transporting merchandise after initial lading in the U.S.

For merchandise arriving in the U.S. Customs territory from a U.S. Foreign Trade Zone, insert "FTZ" followed by the FTZ number. The following format should be used:

FTZ NNNN

24. **FOREIGN PORT OF LADING**

For merchandise arriving in the U.S. by vessel, record the five digit numeric code listed in the Department of Commerce Schedule K for the foreign port at which the merchandise was actually laden on the vessel that carried the merchandise to the U.S. **(NOTE: A January 1, 1991 edition of the Schedule K listing is included in this issuance as Appendix E).** If the foreign port of lading is not provided for by name in the

Schedule K, use the code for "all other ports" for the port of foreign lading for the country.

For merchandise entering the U.S. Custom territory from a U.S. Foreign Trade Zone, leave blank.

When a single entry summary covers merchandise laden at more than one foreign port, place the word "MULTI" in this block and record the foreign port of lading separately in column #28 directly below the line number of each line item (or group of line items if segregated by invoice) for the merchandise laden at each foreign port (where there are multiple ports of lading and also multiple countries of origin, see instructions under block 15). If both code numbers will be required for one line number, place the country of origin code directly below the line number and place the port of lading code directly under the country of origin code.

If merchandise is transported by a mode of transportation other than vessel, leave blank.

25. <u>**LOCATION OF GOODS/G.O. NUMBER**</u>

Where the entry summary serves as entry/entry summary, record the pier or site where the goods are available for examination. For air shipments, record the flight number. Where FIRMS codes are available, they may be used in lieu of pier/site.

In the case of merchandise placed in general order, record the number assigned by Customs in the following format:

G.O. NNNNNNNNNNN

In the case of goods placed in a bonded warehouse, record the name of the bonded warehouse where the goods will be delivered (or record the Customs assigned number for the bonded warehouse in this block when available).

In the case where the entry summary serves as a warehouse entry/entry summary, record the pier or site where the goods are available for examination followed by the name of the bonded warehouse where the goods will be delivered (or the Customs assigned number). **The use of the Facilities Information and Resources Management System (FIRMS) code in lieu of the pier/site/name of location is acceptable.**

26. <u>**U.S. PORT OF UNLADING**</u>

For merchandise imported by vessel or air, record the <u>four digit numeric</u> Schedule D code which <u>identifies the U.S. port</u>

<u>at which the merchandise was unladen from the importing vessel or aircraft</u> (NOTE: A list of the Schedule D port codes is included in the HTS as Annex A). Do not show the name of the port of unlading instead of the numeric code.

For merchandise arriving in the U.S. by means of transportation other than vessel or air, leave blank.

For merchandise arriving in the U.S. Customs territory from a U.S. Foreign Trade Zone, leave blank.

27. **<u>IMPORT DATE</u>**

For merchandise arriving in the U.S. by vessel, record the month, day, year (MMDDYY) on which the importing vessel transporting the merchandise from the foreign country arrived within the limits of the U.S. port with the intent to unlade.

For merchandise arriving in the U.S. other than by vessel, record the month, day, and year (MMDDYY) in which the merchandise arrived within the limits of the U.S.

For merchandise moving from a Foreign Trade Zone to a bonded warehouse in the U.S. Customs territory, report the date of importation. For merchandise entering the U.S. Customs territory for consumption from a Foreign Trade Zone, leave blank.

28. **<u>LINE NUMBER</u>**

Record the appropriate line number, in sequence, beginning with the number 001.

A "line number" refers to a commodity from one country, covered by a line which includes a net quantity, entered value, HTS number, charges, and rate of duty and tax. However, some line numbers may actually include more than one HTS number and value. For example, many items found in Chapter 98, of the HTS require a dual HTS number. Articles assembled abroad with American components require the HTS number 9802.00.80 along with the appropriate reporting number of the provision in chapters 1 through 97. Also, many items in chapter 91 of the HTS require as many as four HTS numbers. Watches classifiable under subheading 9101.11.40, for example, require that the appropriate reporting number and duty rate be shown separately for the movement, case, strap, band or bracelet and the battery. **A separate line number is required for each commodity which is**

the subject of a Customs binding ruling. For formatting, see the instructions in item #30A of this directive.

For multiple elements in blocks 13, 14, 15, and 24, see specific instructions for those items.

29. **DESCRIPTION OF MERCHANDISE**

A description of the articles in sufficient detail to permit the classification thereof under the proper statistical reporting number in the HTS should be reported across the top of block 30 to 32. The standard definitions from HTS tape extracts from the Customs HTS data base are acceptable for this requirement.

30. **A. HTS NUMBER**

Record the appropriate HTS 10-digit duty/statistical reporting number along with the check digit if one is used (check digits are required on all 10-digit numbers; 8-digit numbers, such as those in Chapter 99 of the HTS, do not require check digits). This number should be left justified. Decimals are to be used in the 10-digit duty/statistical reporting number exactly as they appear in the HTS. The check digit is not to be separated by a dash or decimal. An example of the correct presentation of the duty/statistical reporting number would be as follows:

4012.10.20002

If more than one HTS number is required, follow the reporting instructions in the statistical headnote in the appropriate HTS section or chapter.

Where a reporting number is preceded by an alpha character designating a special program (i.e., GSP="A", CBI="E", Folklore="F", etc.), that indicator is to be placed in column 28, directly below the line number. The special program indicator (SPI) should be right justified, immediately preceding, and on the same line as the HTS number to which it applies. If more than one HTS number is required for that line item, the special program indicator is to be placed on the same line as the HTS number upon which the rate of duty is based. If more than one special program indicator is used, the primary indicator, that is, the one establishing the rate of duty, will be shown first, followed by a period and the secondary special programs indicator immediately following: (e.g., CA.F). If "MULTI" was recorded in block 13, 14 and/or 15, the appropriate exporting country, export date and/or country of origin data is to be shown in column 28 below the special program indicator.

For each item covered by a binding tariff classification ruling, report the ruling number (provided in the applicable ruling letter) directly below the HTS number of the appropriate line item. Precede the binding tariff classification ruling number with the abbreviation "RLNG". For an item(s) classified under the same tariff classification number, but not specifically covered by the binding tariff classification ruling, provide a separate line item breakout for those item(s).

For an item(s) covered by a tariff classification pre-approval authorization (obtained via participation in the Pre-Importation Review Program), report the pre-approval indicator (provided in the pre-approval letter) in column 30 directly below the HTS number of the appropriate line item. The pre-approval indicator should be left justified in column 30 and, if necessary, may extend into column 31. Precede the pre-approval indicator with the abbreviation "INDCTR". For multi-line entry summaries, where the pre-approval indicator applies to all line items on the CF 7501, report the pre-approval indicator on the first line only.

For those line items that require the reporting of more than one data element (i.e. category number and/or manufacturer identification number) in this same area, the hierarchy should be as follows:

> **Category Number**
> **Manufacturer Identification Number**
> **Binding Tariff Classification Ruling Number <u>or</u> Ruling Number**

The correct format for reporting a binding tariff classification ruling number or pre-approval indicator are listed below, respectively:

> **RLNG 654321**
> **INDCTR 356780**

For <u>sets</u> which are classifiable in accordance with General Rules of Interpretation (GRI) 3(b) or 3(c) of the Harmonized Tariff Schedule, report in column 30 the HTS number from which the rate of duty for the set is derived. Precede this number with an SPI of "X". Report with that part of the shipment so classified, the total value, quantity and charges associated with the shipment as well as all applicable duties, taxes, and fees in the appropriate columns of the CF 7501. In addition, each

article in the set (including the article designated with a prefix of "X") should be reported on a separate line as if it were separately classified. Precede these HTS numbers with an SPI of "V". Report the quantity and value attributed to each article associated with the "V" SPI. Also, all other reporting requirements including, but not limited to, quota, visa, licensing, and other government agency requirements, should be repor along with the appropriate HTS number preceded with an SPI of "V". Both the "X" and "V" should be right justified in column 28, immediately preceding, and on the same line as the HTS number to which it applies. Attached are two CF 7501 samples indicating the correct format to be used for entry summaries of sets classifiable in accordance with GRI 3(b) or 3(c).

B. <u>ANTIDUMPING/COUNTERVAILING DUTY CASE NUMBER</u>

Record, directly below the HTS number, the appropriate antidumping/countervailing duty case number(s) as assigned by the Department of Commerce, International Trade Administration. The following format shall be used:

A000-000-000 -or- A-000-000-000 **(AD)**
C000-000-000 -or- C-000-000-000 (CVD)

When bonding is permitted and used, record the phrase "Surety Code" and the surety number [e.g., (SURETY # ____ ________)]. If cash **or government securities are deposited** in lieu of surety, record "Surety #998".

Do not record the column 30 heading letters "A" (TSUSA No.) or "B" (CVD/ADD Case No.) before the HTS number or antidumping/countervailing duty case number.

C. <u>CATEGORY NUMBER</u>

Record, in block 30 directly below the HTS number, the textile category for each separate line as indicated in the HTS for which a textile category number is shown in the following format:

"C NNN" -or- "CAT NNN"

31. **A.** <u>GROSS WEIGHT</u>

Record the gross shipping weight in kilograms for articles imported by <u>ALL</u> modes of transportation. Reporting of the gross shipping weight for articles imported by all modes of transportation was required as of July 1, 1989, as a direct result of an agreement reached between the United States and Canada to exchange import data. The gross weight must be reported on the same line with the entered value. In cases where more than one value is shown on a line item, record the gross weight on the same line as the first tariff number for the line item. Supply separate gross weight information for each line number. If the gross weight is not available for each number, the approximate shipping weight for each item shall be estimated and reported. The total of these estimated weights should equal the actual gross shipping weight. For multi-line summaries, the grand total gross weight need not be shown. In the case of containerized cargo carried in lift vans, cargo vans, or similar substantial outer containers, the weight of such container should not be included in the gross weight of the merchandise covered by each line item.

B. <u>MANIFEST QUANTITY</u>

When the CF 7501 is used in lieu of a CF 3461, insert the manifest quantity covered by the informal entry by Bill of Lading/AWB number, using the smallest exterior package unit. Insert the total quantities being entered without regard to package type. For example, if the entry covers 10 cartons and 10 bales on 1 bill of lading, insert the number "20" in column 31. If there are multiple bills, insert the quantity adjacent to the B/L or AWB number across the top of column 30 to 32 or on a separate attachment.

Do not record the letter "A" or "B" shown in block 31 before the gross shipping weight or manifest quantity

32. <u>NET QUANTITY IN HTS UNITS</u>

When a unit of quantity is specified in the HTS for the item number, report the net quantity in the specified unit, and show the unit after the net quantity figure.

Record quantities in <u>whole numbers</u> for statistical purposes unless fractions of units are required for other Customs purposes. When expressing fractions, decimals only shall be used.

If no unit of quantity is specified in the HTS for the item number, leave blank.

If two units of quantity are shown for the item number in the HTS, report the net quantity for both with the unit of quantity indicated in each case. Insert the quantity in terms of the unit marked in the HTS with a superior "v" on the line with the entered value. Show the quantity in terms of any other unit below the first quantity. Example: Shipment consists of 50 dozen all white T-Shirts, weighing 1 kilo per dozen and valued at $10 per dozen. Report as follows:

****

BLOCK 30	BLOCK 32	BLOCK 33
6205.20.20654	50 doz. 50 kgs.	500

****

33. A. <u>ENTERED VALUE</u>

Record the U.S. dollar value in accordance with the definition in Section 402, Tariff Act of 1930, as amended (19 U.S.C. 1401a) for all merchandise.

This value shall be shown for each HTS item number on the same line with the item number where a value is required.

If the value required for assessment of antidumping or countervailing duties is different from the Entered Value, record in parentheses the amount in this column, on the same line as the antidumping or countervailing duty case number and rate.

Report the value in whole dollars rounded off to the nearest whole dollar (if the total entered value for a line item is less than $.50, report as "0"). Dollar signs shall be omitted.

Effective November 1, 1990, report the total entered value for all line items at the bottom of the first page of the CF 7501 in column #33. This information is required to be reported on all entry summaries, Non-ABI as well as ABI. A CF 7501 sample format showing the proper placement of the entered value is attached.

B. **<u>CHARGES (CHGS)</u>**

In accordance with HTS General Statistical Note 1 (a)(XIV), record the aggregate cost (not including U.S. import duty, if any) in U.S. dollars of freight, insurance and all other costs, charges and expenses incurred in bringing the merchandise from alongside the carrier at the foreign port of exportation in the country of exportation and placing it alongside the carrier at the first U.S. Port of entry. Effective July 1, 1989, record charges for shipments arriving in the U.S. by ALL modes of transportation. For overland shipments from Canada or Mexico, foreign inland freight will be reported as charges.

This value shall be shown in whole numbers for each HTS item number beneath the entered value and identified with the letter "C" (e.g. C550). Dollar signs should be omitted.

Charges are required for each line item valued over **$1250**, and in certain special cases for each line item valued over $250. The HTS provisions which require charges be shown for each line item valued over $250 are included in this issuance as Appendix G.

Charges are not required to be reported for merchandise entered by mode of transportation #60 (passenger, hand carried).

C. **RELATIONSHIP**

Record whether the transaction was between related parties as defined in Section 402(g)(1) of the Tariff Act of 1930, as amended, by placing a "Y" in the column for related and an "N" for not related (the words "related" and "not related" may be used in lieu of "Y" or "N"). "Y" or "N" may be recorded once, at the top of column 33, when applicable to the entire transaction or may be recorded with each line item below entered value and charges. "Y" or "N" must be recorded with each line item when the relationship differs for line items.

Do not record the letter "A", "B", or "C" shown in block 33 before the entered value, charges, or relationship.

34. A. **HTS RATE**

Record the rate(s) of duty for the classified item as designated in the HTS: free, ad valorem, specific, or compound.

B. **ANTIDUMPING/COUNTERVAILING DUTY RATE**

Record the antidumping and/or countervailing duty rate(s) as designated by the Department of Commerce, International Trade Administration, directly opposite the respective **AD/CVD** case number(s) shown in column 30.

When bonding is permitted and used, follow the instructions shown in item #30(B) of this directive.

C. <u>I.R.C. RATE</u>

Record the tax rate(s) for the classified item as designated in the HTS, or record the Customs approved metric conversion tax rate.

If I.R. tax is deferred, precede I.R.C. rate with "DEF". Show the amount in column 35 and in block 38 but do not include in the "Total" in blk 40.

Deferred I.R. tax under 26 U.S.C. 5232(a) should be identified as "IRS DEF, 5232(a)", at the bottom of columns 33 and 34 on the first page of the CF 7501. The deferred IR tax amount should <u>not</u> be shown in column 35, block 38, or block 40.

D. <u>VISA NUMBER</u>

Record the letter "V" followed by the visa number for each line of merchandise as it appears on the document with the visa if the products are exported from a country with a textile visa system as noted in the Customs Service "Status Reported on Current Import Quotas (Restraint Levels)." Certain countries, as designated in the "Visa Footnotes" section of the report, use standardized visa numbers.

The standardized number consists of nine alpha/numeric characters in the following format: NXXNNNNNN. The first character is the last digit of the year of exportation of the merchandise from the country of origin. The second and third characters are the two letter ISO code of the country of origin (Appendix C). The last six characters are the six digit visa number as shown on the visa document. For example, for merchandise exported from the Peoples Republic of China (the PRC or, as shown in Appendix C, China (Mainland)), exported in 1991 from the PRC, with visa number 123456, the standardized visa number would be 1CN123456. In this example, the standardized visa number would begin with "1" even though the merchandise was subsequently shipped through Hong Kong but not exported from Hong Kong until 1992.

Only one Visa number may apply to a single line. If a line **has** merchandise covered by more than one visa, then separate lines must be provided for each Visa number.

When textile merchandise is subject to quota, the date of exportation from the origin country must be reported in addition to the date of exportation from the country of exportation (in accordance with the textile regulations, 19 C.F.R.12.130-1). It will be reported in column 34, under the visa number, if applicable, for each line number affected. Date of exportation from the exporting country will continue to be reported in block 14.

E. <u>OTHER FEES</u>

In the event there is any other fee, charge or exaction not enumerated above, record the rate in this column and identify each fee, charge or exaction across columns 30, 31, and 32 and on the same line as such rate. Examples include the beef fee, honey fee, pork fee, cotton fee, harbor maintenance fee (HMF), sugar fee, and merchandise processing fee (MPF). All fees, with the exception of the HMF, are to be reported at the line item level. The HMF may be shown either at the line item level or once at the bottom of the summary on the same line as the total entered value.

There is no de minimis collection for the MPF. A minimum of $21 and a maximum of $400 is due on each formal entry, release or withdrawal from warehouse for consumption. Report the total amount of actual MPF due in the block 39 summary. However, if this actual amount due is less than $21, report the MPF in the block 39 summary as $21. If the actual amount of MPF due is more than $400, report the MPF in the block 39 summary as $400. There is a de minimis on the <u>HMF</u> if this is the only payment due on the entry summary <u>and</u> the total amount of HMF is $3 or less. When this is the case, the grand total user fee in the block 39 summary should be reported as the total fee amount of all line items, but the amount in box 39 itself should be reported as $0.00.

Pursuant to Article 403 of the United States-Canada Free Trade Agreement (CFTA), the Merchandise Processing Fee (MPF) assessment shall be reduced 20 percent per year, until it is zero, on goods originating in the territory of Canada. This reduced MPF will be available only to those goods which meet the rules of origin criteria outlined in chapter three of the CFTA. To obtain the reduced MPF, the importer must claim it on the CF 7501. If the HTS number has the symbol "CA" indicated in the special duty rate column and the importer claims "CA" as a SPI, then the reduced MPF and the special duty rate

are applicable. The reduced user fee also applies to those HTS numbers for which "CA" is not shown as an SPI, provided the merchandise meets the rules or origin criteria of the CFTA. In order to obtain the reduced user fee in those instances, prefix the HTS number with the symbol "CA". If the special duty rate column contains a "B" or both a "B" and "CA" and the importer wishes to claim the benefits of the "B" and the reduced MPF, precede the HTS number with the symbol "B#". If the special duty rate column contains a "C" or both a "C" and "CA" and the importer wishes to claim the benefits of the "C" and the reduced user fee, precede the HTS number with the symbol "C#". The schedule for the reduced MPF rate to be shown in column 34 of the CF 7501 is as follows:

Calender Year 1990 - .136% (80% of MPF)
Calender Year 1991 - .102% (60% of MPF)
Calender Year 1992 - .068% (40% of MPF)
Calender Year 1993 - .034% (20% of MPF)

Note: The instructions in item #30A of this directive regarding the placement and formatting of SPI's apply to the above as well.

Do not record the letter "A", "B", "C", or "D" shown in block 34 before the HTS rate, antidumping/countervailing duty rate, I.R.C. rate, or visa number.

F. AGRICULTURE LICENSE NUMBER

For merchandise subject to agriculture licensing, report the license number in column 34 directly below the tariff rate for that line item.

The license number will consist of a ten space field. The two acceptable formats are as follows:

(1) N-AA-NNN-N (1-cc-234-5) or (2) N-AB-NNN-N (1-c -234-5)

The letters N and A represent numeric and alphabetic characters respectively. The letter B represents a blank space. For format #1, the first position is the license type. The third and fourth positions are the commodity type code. Positions six through eight represent the license serial number. The tenth position is the license year. Positions two, five and nine are hyphens. Format #2 is identical to the above except position four is blank.

35. **DUTY AND I.R. TAX**

Record the estimated HTS duty, antidumping duty, countervailing duty, I.R. tax, and any other fees or charges calculated by applying the rate times the dutiable value or quantity. The amount shown in this column must be directly opposite the appropriate HTS rate(s), antidumping duty rate, countervailing duty rate, I.R. rate and other fees or charges. This includes those instances where bonding is permitted for antidumping and countervailing duty. Where bonding is accomplished, enclose the CVD/ADD amounts in parentheses. Where I.R. tax is deferred under 26 U.S.C. 5232(a), leave blank. (See instructions under 34 C.) Dollar signs shall be omitted.

36. **DECLARATION**

Self-explanatory

Block 37 through 40 must be completed on the first page, if the entry summary consists of more than one page.

37. **DUTY**

Record the total estimated duty paid (excluding antidumping or countervailing duty).

38. **TAX**

Record the total estimated tax paid, including any amount deferred [except tax deferred under 26 U.S.C. 5232(a)].

39. **OTHER**

Record the total estimated antidumping or countervailing duties or other fees, charges or exactions paid. Do not show antidumping or countervailing duty amounts that were bonded for. **The amounts shown in block 39 of the summary should reflect the amounts actually being paid.**

For entries subject to payment of antidumping duties, countervailing duties and/or any of the various fees, each applicable fee must be indicated in the area encompassed by block 30 through 32, which will serve as the "Block 39 Summary", and the individual amount of each fee must be shown on the corresponding line in block 32. Countervailing and/or Antidumping duty amounts are to be included in the summary only when they are actually deposited. Bonded amounts should not be included. The Block 39 Summary must be on the first page if the entry summary consists of more than one page.

The applicable collection code must be indicated on the same line as the fee or other charge or exaction. Report the fees in the format below:

****

BLOCK 30 through 32

****

Block 39 Summary

Antidumping Duty. 012
Countervailing Duty 013
Tea Fee 038
MPF Interest (Monthly Entry Summaries . . . 044
Beef Fee. 053
Pork Fee. 054
Honey Fee 055
Cotton Fee. 056
Sugar Fee 079
Informal Entry MPF. 311
Dutiable Mail Fee 496
Merchandise Processing Fee. 499
Manual Surcharge. 500
Harbor Maintenance Fee. 501

40. **TOTAL**

Record the sum of blocks 37, 38, 39. Do not include any Internal Revenue deferred tax shown in column 35 and block 38. Do not include any antidumping or countervailing duty which has been bonded for.

If no duty, tax, or other charges apply to the transaction, record "0" in this block.

[37. through 40.], Warehouse Entries

For warehouse entry summaries, show the extensions for all duties, taxes and fees in block 37, 38, and 39. The Harbor Maintenance Fee is required to be paid on all warehouse entry summaries.

41. **SIGNATURE OF DECLARANT, TITLE, AND DATE**

Record the signature of the declarant, the job title of the owner, purchaser or agent who signs the declaration, and the month, day and year when the declaration is signed.

When the entry summary consists of more than one page, the signature of the declarant, title, and date must be recorded on the first page. Facsimile signatures are acceptable when prior approval has been obtained in writing from Customs.

SUMMARY OF ENTERED VALUE/CURRENCY CONVERSION

The summary of entered value and currency conversion (if appropriate) may be shown on a worksheet attached to the entry summary or across columns 30 and 31 just above block 36. On a multi-page entry summary, show the summary of entered values on the last page following the last line item.

If an importer/broker prepares his line items by invoice (i.e., groups line items by invoice), he may prepare his summary of values for each invoice in lieu of a grand summation at the end of the entry summary.

INFORMAL ENTRY

Informal entries may be made on the CF 7501. The following blocks are to be completed for informal entries where applicable: 1, 2, 5, 11, 12, 13, 15, 17, 18, 19, **21**, 23, 27, 28, 29, 30A, 31A, 31B, 32, 33A, 34A, 34C, 35, 36, 37, 38, 39, 40, and 41. **If an informal entry is filed on the CF 7501, the entry number must always be shown in block #1.**

However, when the CF 7501 is used as an informal entry, the importer number, block 12, need not be provided even though the block number is circled on the form. For ABI transmissions, the date of export, mode of transportation and U.S. port of unlading will continue to be required.

When goods are released on a CF 3461 and subsequently followed up by an informal entry summary (CF 7501), the entry date (date of release) must be shown in block 4 on the CF 7501.

Block 25, Location of Goods, will be filled in only if merchandise has been placed in a general order warehouse.

No statistical copy of the CF 7501 will be presented when the form is used as an informal entry.

DRAWBACK

When filing a drawback claim on a form other than the revised CF 331, Manufacturing Drawback Entry and/or Certificate Form, or the CF 7539J, Drawback Entry Covering

Same Condition Merchandise, or the CF 7539C, Drawback Entry Covering Rejected Merchandise, submit 2 copies of the CF 7501 with the following data elements completed:

Block 1, Entry Number
Block 2, Entry Type Code
Block 3, Entry Summary Date (to be date stamped upon submission
Block 5, Port Code
Block 6, Bond Number (Show Surety Code only for accelerated payment Claims
Block 7, Bond Type (only for accelerated payment claims)
Block 10, Ultimate Claimant Number in place of Consignee Number
Block 11, Ultimate Claimant Name and Address in place of Consignee Name and Address
Block 12, Importer Number (show claimant's importer number)
Block 13, Importer Name and Address (show claimant's)
Block 29, Description of Goods
Block 37, Duty (only for accelerated payment claims)
Block 38, I.R. Tax (only for accelerated payment claims)
Block 40, Total (only for accelerated payment claims)

APPRAISEMENT ENTRY

When the CF 7501 is used as an appraisement entry as defined in 19 CFR sections 143.11 through 143.16, the following declaration, requesting appraisement under Section 498(a) of the Tariff Act of 1930, as amended, should be added to the body of the CF 7501 or stapled on top of it in the left margin as follows:

I hereby request appraisement under Section 498(a), Tariff Act of 1930, as amended. I declare, to the best of my knowledge and belief, that this entry and the documents presented therewith set forth all the information in my possession, or in the possession of the owner of the merchandise described herein, as to the cost of such merchandise; that I am unable to obtain any further information as to the value of the said merchandise or to determine its value for the purpose of making formal entry thereof; that the information contained in this entry and in the accompanying documents is true and correct; and that the person(s) named above is the owner of the same merchandise.

Signature ____

Title ____

To the District Director: The merchandise described above has been examined and the contents and values are noted above.

Examiner ______________________________

Date ______________________________

Customs Officer ______________________________

Date ______________________________

DELIMITERS FOR LINE ITEMS

Each line item on the CF 7501 and continuation sheet must be separated by a solid line, broken line, or a space to facilitate the processing of the entry summary.

ADDITIONAL DATA ELEMENTS

Filers of the CF 7501 may, on their own initiative, provide additional or clarifying information on the form provided such additional information does not interfere with the reporting of those required data elements. Such additional or clarifying information may be placed in any location on the form solely at the discretion of the filer provided it does not interfere with any required data element. In this case, the Customs Service will not mandate either what additional information may be on the form or where it is to be placed.

Invoices may be separately identified in the body of the CF 7501 and the continuation sheet across columns 30 to 35 followed by the line items appropriate to that invoice.

Additional Requirements for Warehouse Entry Documentation

1. Designated Warehouse

   For warehouse entries the name of the designated Customs bonded warehouse and the Customs assigned **number** shall be indicated on all copies of the CF 7501 in block 25 entitled "Location of Goods". (In addition, if a warehouse entry/entry summary is filed, this information is to be indicated in addition to the name of the site where the merchandise is available for examination.)

2. Designated Customhouse Licensed Cartman

   This information shall be designated on the 4 copies of the CF 7501 that shall serve as the Permit, Warehouse Proprietor, Customhouse Licensed Cartman (CHL) and Manifest copies. The designation shall be made in the upper portion of the reverse of the CF 7501.

3. Place of Examination - Customs Inspectors Signatures

   The signatures of Customs officers located at the place of examination shall be found on the face of the four copies (cited above) of the CF 7501 above the box entitled "U.S. Customs Use".

4. Delivery Authorization

   The "delivery authorization" signatures of the Customs Inspector countersigned by the receiving CHL Cartman will be indicated in the upper portion of the reverse of the four copies of the CF 7501 listed above.

5. Quantity Control Annotations

   All annotations related to the quantity and condition of merchandise deposited in the Customs bonded warehouse shall be indicated in the lower portion of the reverse of the CHL Cartman and Warehouse Proprietor copies of the CF 7501. This includes such signatures as "joint determinations", "seal concurrences", shortages, damaged, etc. This instruction does not replace the requirements to file a CF 5931 or other applicable document.

Rewarehouse Entry

Where the CF 7501 is filed as a rewarehouse entry, blocks 19, 23, 24, and 26 need not be filled in.

Consolidated Entry Summary

Where the CF 7501 entry summary covers more than one release, report each entry or release number separately, followed by the associated line item number and information. A CF 7501 sample format is attached.

Temporary Importation Entry (TIB)

Effective January 2, 1991, approved TIB Entry Summaries (type 23) can be processed in ACS. The data required to be reported on a temporary importation bond entry summary are the same as those usually reported on a regular consumption entry. Also, Customs Regulations 10.31(a)(3) identifies additional information that is required to be shown on a TIB entry summary. Attached is an example of how the TIB
merchandise that is normally subject to quota, either on consumption entries or on withdrawals from warehouse for consumption, is also subject to quota when entered on a TIB.

Appendix I

Rules for Constructing Manufacturer/Shipper Identification Code

RULES FOR CONSTRUCTING THE MANUFACTURE CODE

These instructions provide for the construction of an identifying code for a manufacturer or shipper from his name and address. The code can be up to 15 characters in length, with no inserted spaces. However it may be thought of as five "pieces" as follows:

COUNTRY (Piece 1: 2 characters)

Use the ISO code for the country, such as "PE" for Peru. The exception to this rule is Canada. "CA" is NOT a valid country for the manufacturer code; instead, show as appropriate one of 12 province codes (XA, XC, XM, XB, XW, XT, XN, XO, XP, XQ, XS, or XY).

MANUFACTURER NAME (Piece 2 and 3: up to 3 characters each)

Use the first three characters, alphabetic or numeric, from each of the first two "words" of the name. There will be no third piece if the name is one word. Amalgamated Plastics Corp. would give "AMAPLA"; Bergstrom would give "BER".

If there are two or more initials together, treat them as a single word. For example, A.B.C. Company or A B C Company would yield "ABCCOM". O.A.S.I.S. Corp. would give "OASCOR". Dr. S.A. Smith yields "DRSA", whereas Dr. S. Smith gives "DRSMI". Shavings B L Inc. gives "SHABL".

In the manufacturer name, ignore the english words "a", "an", "and", "of", "the." For example, The Embassy of Spain would give "EMBSPA".

Portions of a name separated by a hyphen are to be treated as a single word. For example, Rawles - Aden Corp. or Rawles-Aden Corp. would both yield "RAWCOR," H-Cubed Equipment would give "HCUEQU".

Some names include numerics: 20th Century Fox would give "20TCEN", Concept 2000 gives "CON200".

ADDRESS LINE WITH STREET NAME and/or BOX NUMBER (Piece 4: up to 4 characters)

Find the largest number on this line and use up to the first four digits. For example, 11455 Main Street Suite 9999 would yield "1145". A suite number or a post office box should be used if it contains the largest number. However, use no number in the case of One Hundred Century Plaza. There will be no fourth piece if there is no numeric on the address line.

When numbers are separated by commas or hyphens, ignore all punctuation and use the number that remains. For example, either "12,34,56 Alaska Road" or "12-34-56 Alaska Road" would yield "1234". When numbers are separated by a space, the space is a delimiter and the largest of the two numbers should be selected; for example, Apt.509 2727 Cleveland St. gives "2727".

CITY (Piece 5: up to 3 characters)

Use the first three alphabetic characters from the city name. Tokyo would be "TOK", St. Michel would be "STM", 18-Mile High would be "MIL", The Hague would be "THE". Notice that numerics in the city line are to be ignored.

Apply these general rules to construct a manufacturer code:

1) Ignore all punctuation, such as commas, periods, ampersands.
2) Ignore all single character initials, such as the "S" in the Thomas S. Delvaux Company.
3) Ignore leading spaces in front of any name/address element.

Listed below are examples of manufacturer names and addresses and their codes:

LA VIE DE FRANCE 243 Rue de la Payees 62591 Bremond, France	FRLAVIE243BRE
20TH CENTURY TECHNOLOGIES 5 Ricardo Munoz, Suite 5880 Caracas, Venezuela	VE20TCEN5880CAR
THE E.K. RODGERS COMPANIES One World Trade Center London, England SW1Y5HO	GBEKRODLON
THE GREENHOUSE 45 Royal Crescent Birmingham, Alabama 35204	USGRE45BIR
CARDUCCIO AND JONES 88 Canburra Avenue Sydney, Australia	AUCARJON88SID
N. MINAMI & CO., LTD. 2-6, 8-Chome Isogami-Dori, Fukiai-Ku Kobe, Japan	JPMINCO268KOB
BOCCHACCIO S.P.A Via Mendotti, 61 8320 Verona, Italy	ITBOCSPA61VER

(continues)

MURLA-PRAXITELES INC. Athens, Greece	GRMURINCATH
SIGMA COY E.X.T. 4000 Smyrna, Italy 1640 Delgado	ITSIGCOY1640SMY

Appendix I

DEPARTMENT OF THE TREASURY

U.S. CUSTOMS SERVICE

No:89-32

August 24, 1989 xINS

CHICAGO DISTRICT PIPELINE

TO: Customhouse Brokers, Importers, Carriers, and Other Concerned Parties

SUBJ: Supplemental Instructions for Manufacturer/Shipper Identification Code

The purpose of this pipeline is to provide instructions for deriving the identification code for Canadian manufacturers and shippers. These instructions apply to the manufacturer identification code as presented on the CF 7501, and CF 3461 where required.

On July 29, 1987, the United States and Canada signed a Memorandum of Understanding (MOU) on the Exchange of Import Data between the United States and Canada.

One vital factor in facilitating this exchange is uniformity of classification, which should be achieved with the implementation of the Harmonized System. Another factor is the collection of all the export data elements required by each country. Identification of the province of origin for Canadian exports is required by Statistics Canada.

Customs Pipeline 86-100 of December 18, 1986 and Customs Directive 3500-13 of November 24, 1986, "Instructions for Deriving Manufacturer/Shipper Identification Code" is still in effect. The only change is for merchandise imported from Canada and produced by a Canadian vendor. For these shipments, the appropriate Canadian province code should be used in place of the ISO code for Canada (CA) in the first two positions of the manufacturer identification code. All other established instructions for composing the manufacturer identification algorithm remain the same.

The Canadian province codes to be used in constructing the manufacturer identification code are listed below:

PROVINCE/TERRITORY	CODE
ALBERTA	XA
BRITISH COLUMBIA	XC
MANITOBA	XM
NEW BRUNSWICK	XB
NEWFOUNDLAND	XW
NORTHWEST TERRITORIES	XT
NOVA SCOTIA	XN

PROVINCE/TERRITORY	CODE
ONTARIO	XO
PRINCE EDWARD ISLAND	XP
QUEBEC	XQ
SASKATCHEWAN	XS
YUKON TERRITORY	XY

NOTE: These codes are to be used only in the construction of the manufacturer identification code and do not replace the two letter ISO code for Canada (CA) used to identify the exporting country or country of origin.

This Change is effective immediately.

/s/ Robert J. Parsons
Assistant District Director
Commercial Operation

Appendix J
Customs Audit Questionnaires

U.S. Customs Service
Office of Strategic Trade
Regulatory Audit Division

Internal Control Questionnaire for Focused Assessments

Introduction

The purpose of the Internal Control Questionnaire for Focused Assessments (FAs) is to obtain information about the company's organizational structure and internal controls related to Customs transactions. The questionnaire is designed to give the audit team a general understanding of the company's import operations and internal control structure as well as to inform the audit candidates of the areas on which the assessment may focus. As each company's operations are unique, this questionnaire may have been modified to fit the circumstances of each audit candidate.

Review Scope

When the importer responds to the questionnaire completely and comprehensively, the Pre-Assessment Survey (PAS) team can plan its approach to the Focused Assessment. The results of the questionnaire, interviews with company officials and Customs personnel, survey of company procedures, and limited testing will be used to determine the effectiveness of the company's internal control system. A PAS of the company's importing operations and internal controls will be used to determine whether more extensive testing is necessary. Any additional testing will be done in the Assessment Compliance Testing (ACT) phase of the Focused Assessment.

Answering the questionnaire affords the company the opportunity to evaluate its own internal controls and operations pertaining to Customs activities. The company will also be more prepared for the Focused Assessment.

General

1. Provide the name, title, and telephone number of the official(s) preparing information for this questionnaire.
2. Provide the name, title, and telephone number of the person who will be the contact for Customs during the Focused Assessment.

I. Control Environment

A. Organizational Structure, Policy and Procedures, Assignment of Responsibilities
1. Provide a copy of the company's organizational chart and related department descriptions. Include the detail to show the location of the Import Department identified and any structure descriptions that are relevant.
2. Identify the key individuals in each office responsible for Customs compliance (may be included on the organization chart).
3. Provide the names and addresses of any related foreign and/or domestic companies, such as the company's parent, sister, subsidiaries, or joint ventures.

4. If the company has operating policies and procedures manuals for Customs operations, provide a copy of the manuals (preferably in electronic format).
5. If the policies and procedures have the support and approval of management, identify the individuals who approve the procedures.

B. Employee Awareness Training
1. What specialized Customs training is required for key personnel working in the Import Department? If available, provide copies of training logs or other records supporting training.
2. What Customs experience have key personnel involved in Customs-related activities had?
3. Who in other departments is responsible for reporting Customs-related activities to the Import Department?
4. What training is provided to personnel in other departments responsible for reporting Customs-related activities to the Import Department?
5. How does the company obtain current information on Customs requirements?
6. Does the company use the Customs Web site (www.customs.treas.gov)?
7. Does the company request and disseminate binding rulings?

II. Risk Assessment

A. How does the company identify, analyze, and manage risks related to Customs activities?

B. What risks related to Customs activities has the company identified, and what control mechanisms has it implemented?

III. Control Procedures

A. Using source records for support, provide a description and/or flowchart of the company's activities, including general ledger account numbers for recording the acquisition of foreign merchandise in the following areas:
- Purchase of foreign merchandise
- Receipt of foreign merchandise
- Recording in inventory
- Payments made to foreign vendor
- Distribution to customers (e.g., drop shipments)
- Export of merchandise (e.g., assists, Chapter 98)

B. For each aspect of value listed below, respond to the following. Where procedures are documented, reference the applicable sections.
1. What internal control procedures are used to assure accurate reporting to Customs?
2. Who is the person assigned responsibility for accurate reporting?
3. What records are maintained?
   - ❑ Basis of Appraisement (19 CFR 152.101)
   - ❑ Price Paid or Payable
   - ❑ Packing
   - ❑ Selling Commissions
   - ❑ Assists (e.g., Materials/Component Parts, Tools, Dies, Molds, Merchandise Consumed, Engineering, Development, Art Work, Design Work, Plans)
   - ❑ Royalties and License Fees
   - ❑ Proceeds of Subsequent Resale

- ❑ Transportation Costs (e.g., International Freight, Foreign Inland Freight, Transportation Rebates, Insurance)
- ❑ Retroactive Price Adjustments
- ❑ Price Increases
- ❑ Rebates
- ❑ Allowances
- ❑ Indirect Payments
- ❑ Payment of Seller's Debt by Buyer (e.g., Quota)
- ❑ Price Reductions to Buyer to Settle Debts (e.g., Reductions for Defective Merchandise)
- ❑ Purchases on Consignment
- ❑ Quota/Visa
- ❑ Currency Exchange Adjustments

C. For each of the following Customs-related activities, respond to the following. Where procedures are documented, reference the applicable sections.

1. What internal control procedures are used to assure accurate reporting to Customs?
2. Who is the person assigned responsibility for accurate reporting?
3. What records are maintained?
   - ❑ Classification
   - ❑ Quantity
   - ❑ Reconciliation
   - ❑ Trade Agreements
     - (1) Generalized System of Preferences (GSP)
     - (2) Caribbean Basin Initiative (CBI) and Special Access Provision (SAP)
     - (3) Israel Free Trade
     - (4) Insular Possessions
     - (5) Andean Trade Preference Act
     - (6) Trade Development Act of 2000
       - i. African Growth and Opportunity Act (AGOA)
       - ii. Caribbean Basin Trade Partnership Act (CBTPA)
   - ❑ Special Duty Provisions
     - (1) 9801.00.10
     - (2) 9802.00.40
     - (3) 9802.00.50
     - (4) 9802.00.60
     - (5) 9802.00.80
     - (6) 9802.00.90
   - ❑ Antidumping/Countervailing Duties

IV. Information and Communication

1. Describe the procedures for the Import Department to disseminate relevant Customs information to other departments.
2. Describe the procedures for other departments to communicate with the Import Department on matters affecting imported merchandise.
3. Describe the procedures for the Import Department to participate in major planning processes involving importation activities.

V. Monitoring

1. What methods of oversight and monitoring does the Import Department management use to ensure compliance with Customs requirements?
2. Provide information and/or reports on the review and evaluation of compliance with Customs requirements by other internal and external entities (e.g., internal audit department, financial statement auditors).
3. What level of management are these self-reviews reported to for action?

VI. Miscellaneous

A. Provide a copy of your general ledger and post-closing trial balance.

B. Identify the account numbers in which costs for imported merchandise are recorded.

U.S. Customs Service
Office of Strategic Trade
Regulatory Audit Division

Electronic Data Processing (EDP) Questionnaire for Focused Assessments

An important factor in conducting Focused Assessments (FAs) in a timely manner may include obtaining electronic data files needed to facilitate comparisons between the company's data and Customs data, sampling, and transactional testing. Generally, two or more data universes are identified. The first universe consists of a fiscal year's imports. The sampling unit may be entry line items unless a more efficient sampling unit, such as invoice line items or the equivalent, is available from the company. Other universes of financial transactions are used to test for possible unreported dutiable expenses. These universes and sampling items will be determined after the team has an understanding of your system and Customs procedures.

Typically, files useful for the FA program may include, but not be limited to: Customs entry log, purchase orders, vendor master, general ledger (GL), invoice line detail, chart of accounts, foreign purchases journal, AP (Payment History File) or GL expense file for imported merchandise, accounts payable with GL reference, cash disbursements, wire transfers, letters of credit, and inventory records.

Please return a hard copy and a *disk copy* of the completed questionnaire to

U.S. Customs Service

Regulatory Audit Division

Attention:

[address]

Email:

Phone:

Fax:

1. List the files, or an equivalent of the same information, that are maintained on each of your computer systems, and describe how each system communicates or links with other systems. For each system, identify the contact person responsible for maintaining that system or information. Identify which information is maintained manually. The following format may be used:

Record	System	Link to Other System	Contact Person	Title	Division
Customs entry (CF 7501)					
Special duty provision					
Payment history					
Accounts Payable					
Purchase order					
Invoice line detail					
Inventory and receiving					
Shipping, freight, insurance, and bill of lading					
Vendor codes and addresses					
Finished product specifications					
Country of origin certification					
Imported product					
Cost data					
Letters of credit					
Wire transfers					
Cash disbursement					

2. Provide flowcharts and/or narrative description of the data flow between systems.

3. Are your computer systems IBM Compatible? Yes/No

4. What types of electronic media do you use to transport data? [C-Tape, E-Tape, CD-ROM, Zip Cartridge]

5. Specify the capacity for your electronic media.

6. List data center location(s).

7. Specify the EDP Department contact person and phone number.

Appendix K

List of Export/Import-Related Web Sites

EXPORT/IMPORT WEB SITES

EXPORTS	
Bureau of Export Administration, Department of Commerce	www.bxa.doc.gov
-Export Enforcement	
-Licensing	
-Antiboycott Compliance	
-Embargoed Exports	
-Denied Persons List	
Office of Foreign Assets Control, Department of Treasury	www.treas.gov/ofac/
-Embargoed Countries	
-Specially Designated Nationals/Terrorists List	
Census Bureau	www.census.gov
-Shippers Export Declarations	
-Schedule B Numbers	
Automated Export System (electronic SEDs)	www.aesdirect.gov
Defense Trade Controls, Department of State	www.pmdtc.org
U.S. Customs Export Enforcement	www.customs.treas.gov

IMPORTS	
U.S. Customs	www.customs.treas.gov
-Informed Compliance Publications	
-Regulations	
-Rulings	
-Traveler Information	
-Drawback	
-Customs Forms	
-Customs Publications	
-Reconciliation	
Office of Foreign Assets Control, Department of Treasury	www.treas.gov/ofac/
-Embargoed imports	
International Trade Administration Department of Commerce	www.ita.doc.gov
-Antidumping/Countervailing duties	
International Trade Commission	www.usitc.gov

-Antidumping/Countervailing duties	
-Harmonized Tariff Schedules	
Office of Textiles & Apparel	www.otexa.ita.doc.gov

Other U.S. Government Agencies Regulating Imports/Exports	
Consumer Products Safety Commission	www.cpsc.gov
Department of Agriculture	www.usda.gov
Department of Commerce	www.doc.gov
Department of Transportation	www.dot.gov
Environmental Protection Agency	www.epa.gov
Federal Maritime Commission	www.fmc.gov
Federal Trade Commission	www.ftc.gov
Fish & Wildlife Service	www.fws.gov
Food & Drug Administration	www.fda.gov
Foreign Agricultural Service	www.fas.usda.gov
Hazardous Materials	www.hazmat.dot.gov
Office of the U.S. Trade Representative	www.ustr.gov

Other U.S. Government Resources	
Agricultural Exporter Assistance	www.fas.usda.gov/agexport/exporter.html
Code of Federal Regulations	www.access.gpo.gov/su_docs/aces/aces140.html
Congressional Information	www.access.gpo.gov/su_docs/aces/aces140.html
Federal Register	www.access.gpo.gov/su_docs/aces/aces140.html
NAFTA Facts	www.mac.doc.gov/nafta/menu1.htm
National Trade Data Bank & Stat USA	www.stat-usa.gov
Public Laws	www.access.gpo.gov/su_docs/aces/aces140.html
Small Business Association	www.sba.gov
U.S. Business Advisor	www.business.gov
U.S. Export Assistance Centers	www.sbaonline.sba.gov/oit/txt/export/useac.html

Financial	
Asian Development Bank	www.asiandevbank.org

Export-Import Bank of the United States	www.exim.gov
Inter-American Development Bank	www.iadb.org
International Monetary Fund	www.imf.org
Overseas Private Investment Corporation	www.opic.gov
World Bank	www.worldbank.org

Trade Associations	
American Association of Exporters and Importers	www.aaei.org
American Association of Port Authorities	www.seaportsinfo.com
Federation of International Trade Associations	www.fita.org
International Chamber of Commerce	www.iccwbo.org
National Council on International Trade Development	www.ncitd.org
National Customs Brokers & Forwarders Association of America	www.ncbfaa.org
National Industrial Transportation League	www.nitl.org
National Foreign Trade Council	www.nftc.org
World Chambers of Commerce	www.ceemail.com/chamgers.html

Foreign Customs Services and Tariffs	
European Union	www.eurunion.org/infores/euindex.htm
European Union Tariff	http://europa.eu.int/comm/taxation_customs/dds/en/home.htm
Embassies	www.embassies.org
Latin American Trade and Information Network	www.latinet.com
Multiple Foreign Country Tax & Customs Web Sites	www.taxman.nl
Trade Information Center	www.ita.doc.gov/td/tic
World Trade Organization	www.wto.org

Australian Customs & Excise	www.customs.gov.au
Canada Customs	www.ccra--adrc.gc.ca/customs/
French Customs & Excise	http://www.info-france-usa.org/america/embassy/customs/adm.htm
Hong Kong Customs & Excise	info.gov.hk.info/customs/content
India Customs	http://www.cbec.gov.in/cae/customs/cs-mainpg.htm
Ireland Customs	www.revenue.ie
Lithuanian Customs	http://www.cust.lt/eng/
Malaysian Royal Customs & Excise	www.customs.gov.my/index2.htm

Mexico - Secretaria de Hacienda (Spanish only)	www.sat.gob.mx
Peru Customs (Spanish only)	http://www.aduanet.gob.pe/
Russian Federation Customs (Russian only)	www.customs.ru
Singapore Customs & Excise	www.gov.sg/customs/index.html
South African Customs	http://www.sars.gov.za/
United Kingdom Customs & Excise	www.hmce.gov.uk

Miscellaneous Trade/Legal Information	
American National Standards Institute	www.ansi.org
Carnets	www.uscib.org
CIA's World Fact Book	http://www.odci.gov/cia/publications/factbook/index.html
Currency Converter	http://xe.com/cc/
Export Documents	http://tradeport.org/ts/transport/expdocs.html
Federal Reserve Board Foreign Exchange Rates	www.federalreserve.gov/releases/H10/hist/
Foreign Trade Statistics	www.census.gov/foreign-trade/www/
Incoterms	www.iccwbo.org/index_incoterms.asp
International Organization for Standardization	www.iso.ch/iso/en/ISOOnline.frontpage
International Trade Library	www.intl-trade.com/library.html
International Trademark Organization	www.inta.org/inta/
Office of Trade & Economic Analysis	www.trade.gov/tradestats
United Nations	www.un.org
USITC Trade Data Web	http://dataweb.usitc.gov
World Bank Country Data	http://www.worldbank.org/data/countrydata/countrydata.html
World Maps	www.lib.utexas.edu/maps/cia98.html
World Trade Organization Global Statistics	http://www.wto.org/english/res_e/statis_e/statis_e.htm

Marketing	
Commerce Business Daily	http://cbd.cos.com
ExportIT	www.exportit.ita.doc.gov
Global Trade Point Network	www.wtpfed.org
Import/Export Trade Leads	www.importleads.com
Trade Information Center	www.ita.doc.gov/tdtic
Trade Opportunity Program	www.usatrade.gov
U.S. Agency for International Development	www.info.usaid.gov
World Trade Centers	www.wtca.org

Glossary of International Trade Terms

Absolute Quota: A fixed limit on the quantity of goods which can be imported into a country during the quota period, usually one year.

Acceptance: A drawee's signed agreement to pay a draft as presented. It must be written on the draft and may consist of the drawee's signature alone. In documentary collections where the exporter (seller) draws a draft on the purchaser, the purchaser does not become liable legally to make payment until he receives the draft and accepts it. Then, at the maturity date of the draft, the drawee should pay. However, if the drawee fails to pay, there is no bank guarantee of payment even if the presentation of the draft was made to the purchaser through banking channels.

Acceptor, Accepter: A drawee who has accepted a draft.

Adjustment Assistance: Financial, training, and re-employment technical assistance to workers and technical assistance to firms and industries to help them cope with difficulties arising from increased import competition. The objective of the assistance is usually to help an industry to become more competitive in the same line of production, or to move into other economic activities. The aid to workers can take the form of training (to qualify the affected individuals for employment in new or expanding industries), relocation allowances (to help them move from areas characterized by high unemployment to areas where employment may be available), or unemployment compensation (while they are searching for new jobs).

Ad Valorem Tariff: A tariff calculated as a percentage of the value of goods; for example, "15 percent ad valorem" means 15 percent of the value. Usually, but not always, the value is the sales price between the exporter (seller) and importer (buyer).

Advising Bank: A bank located in the exporter's (seller's) country notifying the exporter that the purchaser has opened a letter of credit in favor of the exporter through another (issuing) bank.

Affreightment, Contract of: An agreement by a steamship line to provide cargo space on a vessel at a specified time and for a specified price for an exporter or importer. See "Booking Cargo."

Agent: In a general sense, a person who acts on behalf of another person. This may include selling agents or buying agents. Sales agents are sometimes called sales representatives or manufacturer's representatives. Their role is to perform services for their principal, such as obtaining orders, and they are usually paid a commission for their services.

Air Waybill: A bill of lading for air transportation. Air waybills specify the terms under which the air carrier is agreeing to transport the goods and contain limitations of liability. They are not negotiable.

All Risk Clause: An insurance provision that all loss or damage to goods is insured except that of inherent vice (self-caused). This clause affords one of the broadest obtainable protections; however, it excludes war risks and strikes, riots, and civil commotion unless added by special endorsement for an additional premium.

Anti-Dumping Duties: See "Dumping."

Applicant: The person at whose request or for whose account a letter of credit is issued—for example, the purchaser in a sale transaction opening a letter of credit with the purchaser's bank to pay the exporter (seller).

Appraisement: The process of determination by a customs official of the dutiable value of imported merchandise. This is usually the price paid by the importer for the goods unless Customs believes the price does not reflect a reasonable value, in which case Customs calculates its own value for the assessment of duties using the methods specified in the customs law.

Arbitrage: The business of making profits by buying and selling currencies differing in value due to fluctuating exchange rates in world currency markets. Sometimes used to describe the existence of a difference in value from one currency to another and the decision to buy or sell in a particular currency because of the belief that a particular currency is stronger or will strengthen in the future.

Arms Export Control Act: A U.S. law regulating the export (and in some cases import) of defense articles and services listed on the U.S. Munitions List. The International Traffic in Arms Regulations (ITAR) are issued under the law. It is administered by the Department of State, Office of Defense Trade Controls.

Arrival Draft: A modified sight draft which does not require payment until after arrival of the goods at the port of destination. Similar to "cash on delivery."

Arrival Notice: A notification by the steamship, railroad, or over-the-road trucker. It informs the consignee of the arrival of the goods and usually indicates the pickup location and the allowed free time before storage charges begin.

ASEAN: A free trade area established by the Association of Southeast Asian Nations.

Assist: The situation in which an importer, directly or indirectly, is furnishing to a foreign manufacturer raw materials, tools, dies, molds, manufacturing equipment, certain types of research and development know-how or design work, or other things without receiving payment for such items (or receiving payment for less than their full value) in order that the importer can purchase a product manufactured by the foreign manufacturer at a lower price. An assist must be disclosed to the importing country's customs administration and customs duties paid as an addition to the purchase price for the goods.

Assured: The beneficiary of an insurance policy, for example, due to damage or casualty to cargo or goods during transport.

ATA Carnet: An international customs document that may be used in lieu of national customs entry documents and as security for import duties and taxes to cover the temporary admission and transit of goods.

At Sight: A draft drawn by a seller (exporter) for payment for the goods. It must be paid at the time the draft is presented to the buyer (importer) by the seller's agent, such as a freight forwarder or bank.

Audit: A procedure whereby the customs authorities visit the premises of an importer or exporter and inspect documents and records and interview personnel to determine if importations and/or exportations are being conducted in accordance with applicable law and regulations.

Authority to Pay: Advice from a buyer, addressed through the buyer's bank to the seller, by way of the correspondent of the buyer's bank in the seller's country, authorizing the correspondent bank to pay the seller's drafts for a stipulated amount. The seller has no recourse against cancellation or modification of the Authority to Pay before the drafts are presented, but, once the *drafts drawn on the correspondent bank* are paid by it, the seller is no longer liable as drawer. An Authority to Pay is usually not confirmed by the seller's bank. It is not as safe for a seller as a letter of credit because it is not a promise or guarantee of payment by a bank.

Authority to Purchase: A document similar to an Authority to Pay but differing in that under an Authority to Purchase the *drafts are drawn directly on the buyer* rather than on the seller's bank. They are purchased by the correspondent bank with or without recourse against the drawer. The Authority to Pay is usually not confirmed by the seller's bank.

Automated Commercial System: The electronic data transmission system used by the U.S. Customs Service, customs brokers, and importers to complete import transactions. It contains various modules such as Automated Broker Interface, Automated Manifest System, the Cargo Selectivity System, and Entry Summary System.

Average: See "General Average" and "Particular Average."

Average Adjuster: When a steamship line transporting goods encounters a condition covered by general average or particular average, an independent average adjuster will determine the contribution that each owner of goods being transported on the steamship will have to pay to make the steamship line and the other owners of goods whole.

BAF: Bunker Adjustment Factor: A charge added by ocean carriers to compensate for fluctuating fuel costs.

Bank Draft: A check, drawn by a bank on another bank, customarily used where it is necessary for the customer to provide funds which are payable at a bank in some distant location.

Banker's Acceptance: A time draft where a bank is drawee and acceptor.

Barter: The direct exchange of goods for other goods, without the use of money as a medium of exchange and without the involvement of a third party. For customs purposes the values still need to be determined and proper duties paid if the exchange involves an importation. See "Countertrade."

Beneficiary: (1) Under a letter of credit, the person who is entitled to receive payment, usually the seller (exporter) of the goods. (2) Under an insurance policy, the assured, or person who is to receive payment in case of loss or damage to the goods.

Bill of Exchange: An unconditional order in writing addressed by one person to another, signed by the person issuing it and requiring the addressee to pay at a fixed or determinable future time a certain sum of money to the order of a specified party. In export transactions, it is drawn by the seller (exporter) on the purchaser (importer) or bank specified in a letter of credit or specified by the purchaser. See "Draft."

Bill of Lading (B/L): A document issued by a carrier (railroad, steamship, or trucking company) which serves as a receipt for the goods to be delivered to a designated person or to her order. The bill of lading describes the conditions under which the goods are accepted by the carrier and details the nature and quantity of the goods, name of vessel (if shipped by sea), identifying marks and numbers, destination, etc. The person sending the goods is the "shipper" or "consignor," the company or agent transporting the goods is the "carrier," and the person for whom the goods are destined is the "consignee." Bills of lading may be negotiable or non-negotiable. If negotiable, that is, payable to the shipper's order and properly endorsed, title to the goods passes upon delivery of the bill of lading.

Blank Endorsement: The signature, usually on the reverse of a draft (bill of exchange), bill of lading, or insurance certificate, without any qualification, which then becomes payable or consigned to the person to whom the document is delivered.

Bond: A guaranty issued by an insurance or surety company in favor of an importer's government to ensure payment of customs duties in case the importer fails to pay, for example, due to bankruptcy.

Bonded Warehouse: A warehouse in which goods subject to excise taxes or customs duties are temporarily stored without the taxes or duties being assessed. A bond or security is given for the payment of all taxes and duties that may eventually become due. Operations in the warehouse may include assembly, manipulation, or storage, but usually not manufacturing.

Booking Cargo: The reservation of space on a specified vessel for a scheduled sailing, by or on behalf of a shipper. Technically, it may be effected in two ways, either: (1) by signing a contract of affreightment, a procedure which applies only to bulk commodities, raw materials, or a large movement of special cargo, such as the transfer of a whole manufacturing plant, or to particular types of goods requiring special stowage, like unboxed cars or trucks; or (2) by informal request (verbal) for general cargo.

Booking Number: A number assigned to a cargo booking by the steamship line used as an identifying reference on bills and correspondence.

Boycott: A refusal to deal commercially or otherwise with a person, firm, or country.

Buying Commission: A commission paid by a purchaser to an agent or person under the purchaser's control who identifies suppliers, assists with shipments, and provides other services for the purchaser. Under the GATT Valuation Code, amounts separately paid for such services are not dutiable as part of the purchase price of the goods.

Buy National Policy: A price preference, usually of a governmental purchaser, to purchase goods produced in the same country as the purchaser's or an absolute prohibition against purchasing foreign goods.

Cabotage: Shipping, navigation, and trading along the coast of a country. In the United States these services include traffic between any parts of the continental United States, or between Hawaii, Alaska, and Puerto Rico and is reserved to U.S. flag ships.

CAF: Currency Adjustment Factor: A charge added by ocean carriers to offset currency exchange fluctuations.

Carnet: See "ATA Carnet."

Cash Against Documents (C.A.D.): A method of payment for goods in which documents transferring title—for example, a negotiable bill of lading and a draft—are transferred to the buyer upon payment of cash to an intermediary acting for the seller (usually a bank or freight forwarder).

Cash in Advance (C.I.A.): A method of payment for goods in which the buyer pays the seller in advance of the shipment of the goods. A C.I.A. is usually employed when the goods are built to order, such as specialized machinery.

Cash With Order (C.W.O.): A method of payment for goods in which cash is paid at the time of the order.

Casualty Loss: Damage to goods incurred during transportation, loading, or unloading.

CE Mark: A mark required on certain products imported to the European Community certifying that the product has been tested by an authorized certification agency and meets applicable standards, usually of safety.

Certificate of Inspection: A document issued by an inspection company or other person independent of the seller and buyer that has inspected the goods for quality and/or value. It may be required for payment under the terms of the sales agreement or a letter of credit.

Certificate of Insurance: A document containing certain terms of a full-length insurance policy. A one-page document, it is evidence that there is insurance coverage for a shipment. Beneficiaries of open cargo or blanket insurance policies are authorized to issue their own certificates of insurance.

Certificate of Origin: A document in which the exporter certifies the place of origin (manufacture) of the merchandise being exported. Sometimes these certificates must be legalized by the consul of the country of destination, but more often they may be legalized by a commercial organization, such as a chamber of commerce, in the country of manufacture. Such information is needed primarily to comply with tariff laws which may extend more favorable treatment to products of certain countries. More recently, certain types of certificates of origin, for example, NAFTA Certificates of Origin, require significant analysis of the origin of the raw materials used in production of the product to determine the country of origin.

Certificate of Weight and Measurement: A certificate issued by a company or person independent of the seller and buyer certifying the quantity and dimensions of goods. In some cases, the buyer or buyer's government will allow the seller to make a self-certification.

Charter Party: The contract between the owner of a vessel and a shipper to lease the vessel or a part thereof to transport, usually bulk, goods.

Clean Bill of Lading: One in which the goods are described as having been received in "apparent good order and condition" and without damage. May be required for payment under the sales agreement or letter of credit. See "Foul Bill of Lading."

Collecting Bank: A bank requested by an exporter (seller) to obtain payment from the purchaser. Ordinarily the exporter (seller) will draw a draft on the purchaser and deliver to the collecting bank with a negotiable bill of lading. The bank will transmit it overseas to its correspondent bank (which is also a collecting bank in the chain). If the draft drawn is a sight draft, the bank will deliver the negotiable bill of lading to the purchaser in return for payment. If it is a time draft, the bank will release the bill of lading, thereby permitting the purchaser to obtain the goods upon acceptance of the draft by the purchaser. At the time of maturity of the draft, the purchaser will make payment and the collecting banks will remit the proceeds to the exporter (seller). See "Uniform Rules for Collections."

Combined Transport Bill of Lading: See "Through Bill of Lading."

Commercial Invoice: A document prepared by the exporter (seller) describing the goods being sold, the sales price for the goods, and other charges being billed to the purchaser. Because a commercial invoice is commonly required in order to enable the purchaser to clear the goods through customs, it is necessary to include all information required by the purchaser's country. This may include legalization of the commercial invoice by the purchaser's country's embassy or consulate in the exporter's country, certification by a chamber of commerce in the exporter's country, or particular statements, certifications, or information in the invoice.

Commingling: A condition in which goods subject to different rates of customs duty are packed together. This may result in all goods being assessed the highest duty rate applicable to any of the items.

Commission Agent: See "Agent."

Common Carrier: A transportation carrier such as a steamship line, trucking company, or railroad which accepts shipments from the public. Private carriers are those which are under contract for or owned by particular shippers. Common carriers are usually subject to government regulation, including the filing of tariffs (transportation rates) in some countries so that shippers all pay a uniform charge. Laws in some countries permit exceptions to this so that large-volume shippers may obtain discounts in certain circumstances.

Common Market: An agreement between two or more countries to permit importation or exportation of goods between those countries without the payment of customs duties and to permit freedom of travel and employment and freedom of investment. Goods imported from outside the common market will be subject to a common duty rate.

Compound Duty: A tax imposed on imported merchandise based on a percentage of value and also on the net weight or quantity.

Conference Tariff: Two or more steamship lines which have agreed to set the same price for transporting goods in the same ocean lane which they serve. Generally, such agreements are valid if properly registered with the governmental authorities of the countries served.

Confirming Bank: A bank in the exporter's (seller's) country that also adds its own guarantee of payment to a letter of credit issued by the purchaser's bank in the purchaser's country.

Consignment: 1. The shipment or delivery of goods to a person without making a sale. Under consignment arrangements, the consignee will usually have an agreement that when the consignee is able to sell the goods to a purchaser, the consignee will simultaneously purchase the goods from the consignor and make payment. 2. In some international trade documentation—for example, bills of lading—a transportation carrier may not know whether the transportation which it is effecting is pursuant to a sale or not; therefore, the person to whom the goods are to be delivered is referred to as the consignee and the delivery transaction loosely referred to as a consignment.

Consular Invoice: A document required by some foreign countries showing information as to consignor, consignee, value, and description of the shipment. It is usually sold or legalized by the embassy or consulate of the purchaser's country located in the seller's country.

Consulate: An office of a foreign government in the exporter (seller's) country. The main office is usually the embassy located in the capital city of the exporter's country, and other offices in different cities in the exporter's country are consulates.

Contract of Affreightment: See "Affreightment, Contract of."

Convention on International Sale of Goods: An international treaty describing the obligations and rights of sellers and buyers in international sales. The Convention automatically applies to international sales where seller and buyer are located in countries which are parties to the Convention unless the buyer and seller have agreed specifically in their sales documentation to exclude applicability of the Convention. The United States and many other countries are parties to the Convention.

Countertrade: A reciprocal trading arrangement. Countertrade transactions include:

A. *Counterpurchase transactions,* which obligate the seller to purchase from the buyer goods and services unrelated to the goods and services sold (usually within a one- to five-year period).
B. *Reverse countertrade contracts,* which require the importer to export goods equivalent in value to a specified percentage of the value of the imported goods—an obligation that can be sold to an exporter in a third country.
C. *Buyback transactions,* which obligate the seller of plant, machinery, or technology to buy from the importer a portion of the resultant production during a five- to twenty-five-year period.
D. *Clearing agreements* between two countries that agree to purchase specific amounts of each other's products over a specified period of time, using a designated "clearing currency" in the transactions.
E. *Switch transactions,* which permit the sale of unpaid balances in a clearing account to be sold to a third party, usually at a discount, that may be used for producing goods in the country holding the balance.
F. *Swap transactions,* through which products from different locations are traded to save transportation costs (for example, Soviet oil may be "swapped"

for oil from a Latin American producer, so the Soviet oil is shipped to a country in South Asia, while the Latin American oil is shipped to Cuba).

G. *Barter transactions,* through which two parties directly exchange goods deemed to be of approximately equivalent value without any exchange of money taking place.

Countervailing Duty: Considered a form of unfair competition under the GATT Subsidies Code, an additional duty imposed by the importer's government in order to offset export grants, bounties, or subsidies paid to foreign exporters or manufacturers in certain countries by the government of that country for the purpose of promoting export.

Customs Broker: A person or firm licensed by an importer's government and engaged in entering and clearing goods through customs. The responsibilities of a broker include preparing the entry form and filing it; advising the importer on duties to be paid; advancing duties and other costs; and arranging for delivery to the importer.

Customs Classification: The particular category in a tariff nomenclature (usually the Harmonized System) in which a product is classified for tariff purposes, or the procedure for determining the appropriate tariff category in a country's nomenclature used for the classification, coding, and description of internationally traded goods. Classification is necessary in order to determine the duty rate applicable to the imported goods.

Customs Union: An agreement between two or more countries to eliminate tariffs and other import restrictions on each other's goods and establish a common tariff for goods imported from other countries.

Cut-Off Time: The latest time a container may be delivered to a terminal for loading on a departing ship or train.

Date Draft: A draft maturing a stipulated number of days after its date, regardless of the time of its acceptance. Unless otherwise agreed upon in the contract of sale, the date of the draft should not be prior to that of the ocean bill of lading or of the corresponding document on shipments by other means.

DDC: Destination Delivery Charge: A charge added by ocean carriers to compensate for crane lifts off the vessel, drayage of the container within the terminal, and gate fees at the terminal.

Del Credere Agent: One who guarantees payments; a sales agent who, for a certain percentage in addition to her sales commission, will guarantee payment by the purchasers of goods.

Delivery Order: An order addressed to the holder of goods and issued by anyone who has authority to do so, that is, one who has the legal right to order delivery of merchandise. It is not considered a title document like a negotiable bill of lading. It is addressed and forwarded, together with the dock receipt, if any, to the transportation company effecting the transfer from the pick-up location to shipside pier.

Demurrage: Excess time taken for loading or unloading of a vessel not caused by the vessel operator but due to the acts of a charterer or shipper. A charge is made for such delay. See "Lay Days."

Destination Control Statement: Specific words (legend) inserted in a commercial invoice and bill of lading prohibiting diversion of destination for exported goods subject to U.S. export control laws.

Devaluation: An official lowering of the value of a country's currency in relation to other currencies by direct government decision to reduce gold content or to establish a new ratio to another agreed standard, such as the U.S. dollar. Devaluation tends to reduce domestic demand for imports in a country by raising their prices in terms of the devalued currency and to raise foreign demand for the country's exports by reducing their prices in terms of foreign currencies. Devaluation can therefore help to correct a balance of payments deficit and sometimes provide a short-term basis for economic adjustment of a national economy. See "Revaluation."

Discrepancy: The failure of a beneficiary of a letter of credit to tender to the advising bank the exact documents required by the letter of credit to obtain payment.

Distributor: A person who purchases goods for the purpose of reselling such goods. The distributor is distinguished from an agent because it takes title to the goods, assumes the risk of loss or damage to the goods, and is compensated by marking up the goods on resale.

Dock Receipt: A receipt given for a shipment received or delivered at a steamship pier. A dock receipt is usually a form supplied by the steamship and prepared by the shipper or its freight forwarder. When delivery of a shipment is completed, the dock receipt is surrendered to the vessel operator or his agent and serves as the basis for preparation of the ocean bill of lading.

Documentary Bill: A draft (bill of exchange) accompanied by other documents required by the buyer for payment, for example, bill of lading, inspection certificate.

Documents Against Acceptance (D/A): Instructions given by an exporter to a bank or freight forwarder that the documents (usually a negotiable bill of lading) attached to a draft for collection are deliverable to the drawee (importer-purchaser) only against her acceptance of the draft. The actual payment will be made by the purchaser at some agreed-upon time or date specified in the draft after acceptance. See "Uniform Rules for Collections."

Documents Against Payment (D/P): A type of payment for goods in which the documents transferring title to the goods (negotiable bill of lading) are not given to the purchaser until he has paid the value of a draft drawn on him. Collection may be made through a bank, freight forwarder, or other agent. See "Uniform Rules for Collections."

Draft: A negotiable instrument wherein a drawer orders a drawee to pay a fixed amount of money (with or without interest or other charges) described in the draft, payable on demand or other definite time. It must be payable "to order" or bearer and it must not contain any other instructions, conditions, or orders except an order to pay money. A draft is commonly drawn by an exporter (seller) on the purchaser (drawee) and delivered to a collecting bank or freight forwarder for presentation to the purchaser. See "Bill of Exchange."

Drawback: Import duties or taxes refunded by a government, in whole or in part, when the imported goods are re-exported or used in the manufacture of exported goods.

Drawee: A person (usually the purchaser of goods) ordered in a draft to make payment.

Drawer: A person who makes, creates, or issues a draft and instructs a drawee to make payment to the drawer or another person ("pay to the order of").

Drayage: A charge for delivery of goods or pick-up of goods from docks or other port terminals.

Dumping: Under the GATT Antidumping Code (to which the United States is a party), the export sale of a commodity at "less than normal value," usually considered to be a price lower than that at which it is sold within the exporting country or to third countries. Dumping is generally recognized as an unfair trade practice that can disrupt markets and injure producers of competitive products in the importing country. Article VI of GATT permits the imposition of special antidumping duties against "dumped" goods equal to the difference between their export price and their normal value in the exporting country.

Dunnage: Packing material consisting mainly of rough pine board used as flooring for the ship's hold before loading is begun.

Duty: The tax imposed by a customs authority on imported merchandise.

Embargo: A prohibition upon exports or imports, either with respect to specific products or specific countries. Historically, embargoes have been ordered most frequently in time of war, but they may also be applied for political, economic, or sanitary purposes. Embargoes imposed against an individual country by the United Nations—or a group of nations—in an effort to influence that country's conduct or its policies, are sometimes called "sanctions."

Embassy: The chief diplomatic office of a foreign government in the exporter's country, usually located at the capital city of the exporter's country.

Entry: The formal process by which goods are imported into a country, consisting of filing of documents with the importing country's customs service and the payment of customs duties. Various types of entries are used in different circumstances such as consumption entries, warehouse entries, immediate transportation entries, and transportation and exportation entries.

Escape Clause: A provision in a bilateral or multilateral trade agreement permitting a signatory nation to suspend tariff or other duty reductions when imports threaten serious harm to the producers of competitive domestic goods. Such agreements as the North American Free Trade Agreement contain such "safeguard" provisions to help firms and workers adversely affected by a relatively sudden surge of imports adjust to the rising level of import competition.

European Union: The agreement of the twelve European common market countries entered into in 1992 in Maastricht, Netherlands, to create a monetary and political union.

Examination: The process by which the customs authorities of an importing country inspect the goods identified in the customs entry documents and confirm whether the goods are the same as described in the documents and whether the goods are eligible for entry.

Exchange Controls: Government regulation to ration foreign currencies, bank drafts, and other instruments for settling international financial obligations by countries seeking to ameliorate acute balance of payments difficulties. When such measures are imposed, importers must apply for prior authorization from the government to obtain the foreign currency required to bring in designated amounts and types of goods. Since such measures have the effect of restricting imports, they are considered non-tariff barriers to trade.

Exchange Rate Risk: The possibility that an exporter (seller) will receive less value (for example, U.S. dollars) than it is expecting in a sales transaction. This arises because exchange rates are generally floating rates and if the exporter (seller) agrees to accept payment in the purchaser's currency (for example, yen) and the value of the yen vis-à-vis the U.S. dollar fluctuates between the time of price quotation and the date of payment, the exporter (seller) may receive more or less in U.S. dollars than anticipated at the time that it quoted its price and accepted the purchase order. Sellers and purchasers may agree to share the exchange rate risk in their sales agreement.

Exchange Rates: The price at which banks or other currency traders are willing to buy or sell various currencies which a buyer may need in order to make payment. For example, if a contract for sale is in U.S. dollars a purchaser in a foreign country will need to purchase U.S. dollars from a bank or currency trader in order to make proper payment. Usually, the exchange rate floats or fluctuates based on supply or demand but it may also be fixed by government regulation.

Export License: A permit required to engage in the export of certain commodities to certain destinations. In the United States such controls are usually determined by the Department of Commerce, Bureau of Export Administration; the Department of State, Office of Defense Trade Controls; or Department of Treasury, Office of Foreign Assets Control. Controls are imposed to implement U.S. foreign policy, ensure U.S. national security, prevent proliferation, or protect against short supply.

Export Quotas: Specific restriction or ceilings imposed by an exporting country on the value or volume of certain exports, designed to protect domestic consumers from temporary shortages of the goods, to bolster their prices in world markets, or to reduce injury to producers in importing countries. Some International Commodity Agreements explicitly indicate when producers should apply such restraints. Export quotas are also often applied in Orderly Marketing Agreements and Voluntary Restraint Agreements, and to promote domestic processing of raw materials in countries that produce them.

Export Trading Company: A corporation or other business unit organized and operated principally for the purpose of exporting goods and services, or for providing export-related services to other companies. The Export Trading Company Act of 1982 exempts authorized trading companies from certain provisions of the U.S. antitrust laws and authorizes banks to own and operate trading companies.

Factoring: A procedure whereby an exporter (seller) that is selling on open account or time drafts may sell its accounts receivable or drafts to a factoring company which will make immediate payment of the face value of the accounts receivable less some discount amount and will then collect the amounts owing from the purchasers at the due date for payment.

FEU: Forty-foot Equivalent Unit: A measurement of container capacity.

Fixed Exchange Rate: The establishment of a price at which two currencies can be purchased or sold set either by government regulation or in a sales agreement between a seller and a buyer. In such cases there is no exchange risk because there is no exchange rate fluctuation between the date of price quotation and the date of payment.

Floating Exchange Rate: A condition where the governments issuing two different currencies do not legally regulate the price at which either currency can be bought or sold. See "Exchange Rate Risk."

Force Majeure: The title of a standard clause often found in contracts for sale of goods or transportation exempting the parties from liability for non-fulfillment of their obligations by reason of certain acts beyond their control, such as natural disasters or war.

Foreign Assembler's Declaration: Under U.S. Harmonized Tariff Section 9802.00.80 an importer may pay reduced customs duties when importing a product which has been assembled abroad from U.S.-origin components. The foreign assembler must provide a declaration which is endorsed by the importer certifying that the assembly operation meets the regulatory requirements. If Customs agrees, the U.S. importer pays duty only on the foreign origin materials, labor, and value added after deducting the U.S.-origin materials exported for assembly.

Foreign Corrupt Practices Act: A U.S. law prohibiting the payment of anything of value to a foreign government employee in order to obtain or retain business. The law also prohibits the maintenance of "slush funds" for such payments.

Foreign Sales Corporation (FSC): A company incorporated in Guam, the U.S. Virgin Islands, the Commonwealth of the Northern Mariana Islands, American Samoa, or any foreign country that has a satisfactory exchange-of-information agreement with the United States and is utilized in an export transaction. Use of an FSC in export sales transactions permits a U.S. exporter to exempt a portion of its export profits from U.S. income taxation.

Foreign Trade Zone: An area where goods may be received, stored, manipulated, and manufactured without entering a country's customs jurisdiction and hence without payment of duty. Outside the United States it is usually called a "free trade zone."

Forward Exchange: A market offering various currencies for sale where the sales price of a currency is quoted and sold based on delivery of the currency to the purchaser at some date in the future, for example, the due date when purchaser must make payment of a time draft. Purchasing currency in forward contract is one method to eliminate exchange rate risk.

Foul Bill of Lading: A bill of lading issued by a carrier bearing a notation that the outward containers or the goods have been damaged. A foul bill of lading may not be acceptable for payment under a letter of credit.

Free In and Out (F.I.O.): The cost of loading and unloading of a vessel that is borne by the charterer.

Free of Capture and Seizure (F.C.&S.): An insurance clause providing that loss is not insured if due to capture, seizure, confiscation, and like actions, whether legal or not, or from such acts as piracy, civil war, rebellion, and civil strife.

Free of Particular Average (F.P.A.): The phrase means that the insurance company will not cover partial losses resulting from perils of the sea except when caused by stranding, sinking, burning, or collision. American conditions (F.P.A.A.C.)—partial loss is not insured unless caused by the vessel being sunk, stranded, burned, on fire, or in collision. English conditions (F.P.A.E.C.)—partial loss is not insured unless a result of the vessel being sunk, stranded, burned, on fire, or in collision.

Free Out (F.O.): The cost of unloading a vessel that is borne by the charterer.

Free Port: An ocean port and its adjacent area where imported goods may be temporarily stored and sometimes repackaged; manipulated; or, under the laws of some countries, further processed or manufactured without payment of customs duties until the merchandise is sold in the country or the time period for exportation expires.

Free Trade: A theoretical concept that assumes international trade unhampered by government measures such as tariffs or non-tariff barriers. The objective of trade liberalization is to achieve "freer trade" rather than "free trade," it being generally recognized among trade policy officials that some restrictions on trade are likely to remain.

Free Trade Area: An arrangement between two or more countries for free trade among themselves while each nation maintains its own independent tariffs toward nonmember nations.

Free Trade Zone: See "Foreign Trade Zone."

Freight All Kinds (FAK): The general transportation rate for a shipment of multiple types of merchandise.

Freight Collect: The shipment of goods by an exporter (seller) where the purchaser has agreed to pay the transportation costs and the transportation carrier has agreed to transport the goods on the condition that the goods will not be released unless the purchaser makes payment for the transportation charges.

Freight Forwarder: A person who dispatches shipments via common carriers and books or otherwise arranges space for those shipments on behalf of shippers and processes the documentation or performs related activities incident to those shipments.

Freight Prepaid: An agreement between the seller and a buyer that the seller will pay for the transportation charges before delivery to the transportation carrier.

Full Set: Generally used in reference to bills of lading. Where a steamship line undertakes to transport goods it issues a sole original or full set (generally three copies, which are all originals) of the bill of lading. Where the bill of lading is negotiable the steamship line is authorized to make delivery as soon as any person presents one original bill of lading at the destination.

GATT: The General Agreement on Tariffs and Trade. This is an international treaty which has now been superseded by the World Trade Organization. A number of agreements negotiated under GATT continue in force, such as the Valuation Code, the Antidumping Code, and the Subsidies Code. See "World Trade Organization."

General Average: A deliberate loss or damage to goods in the face of a peril such as dumping overboard, which sacrifice is made for the preservation of the vessel and other goods. The cost of the loss is shared by the owners of the saved goods.

Generalized System of Preferences (GSP): The United Nations program adopted by the United States and many other countries and designed to benefit less developed countries by extending duty-free treatment to imports from such countries. Sometimes certain countries or products are "graduated" and are no longer eligible to receive GSP benefits.

General Order: Merchandise for which proper customs entry has not been made within five working days after arrival is sent to a General Order warehouse. All costs of storage are at the expense of the importer.

Gray Market Goods: Products which have been manufactured and sold by the inventor or duly authorized licensee which are being resold by purchasers into geographical areas not intended or authorized by the original seller. Depending upon the laws of the countries involved, gray marketing may be illegal, encouraged, or regulated. Sometimes economic incentives for gray marketing occur as a result of a manufacturer selling the products to different trade channels at different prices or due to fluctuating exchange rates.

Harmonized Tariff System (Codes): The system adopted by most of the commercial countries of the world in 1989, classifying products manufactured and sold in world commerce according to an agreed-upon numerical system. Common international classifications facilitate balance of trade statistics collection, customs classification, and country of origin determination.

In Bond: The transportation or storage of goods in a condition or location which is exempt under the customs laws from the payment of customs duties for the time period which is allowed by law for transportation or storage. Transportation or storage in bond may be effected by transportation carriers or warehouses that have posted a bond with the customs authorities guaranteeing payment of all customs duties in the event that the goods are improperly released without the payment of customs duties by the owner of the goods.

Inchmaree Clause: A provision in an ocean casualty insurance policy covering the assured against damage to the owner's goods as a result of negligence or mismanagement by the captain or the crew in navigation of the ship or damage due to latent defects in the ship.

Incoterms: A set of sales and delivery terms issued by the International Chamber of Commerce and widely used in international trade. These terms, such as "ex-works," "CIF," and "Delivered Duty Paid," set out in detail the responsibilities and rights of the seller and purchaser in an international sale transaction. See also "Convention on International Sale of Goods" and "Uniform Commercial Code."

Indent Merchant: One who assembles a number of orders from merchants in his locality, such orders being placed with foreign manufacturers by the indent merchant for his own account. He assumes the full credit risk and obtains his commission from those for whom he orders.

Insurable Interest: The legal interest which a person must have in goods in order to be covered by insurance. For example, in an international sale under the Incoterm "ex-works," delivery and risk of loss for damage to the goods passes to the purchaser when the goods are loaded on and leave the seller's factory or warehouse. If the seller has already been paid for the goods at that time, the seller no longer has any legal interest in ownership or payment and cannot receive payment under any insurance coverage that the seller may have, such as a blanket insurance policy covering all sales.

Intellectual Property: Ownership conferring the right to possess, use, or dispose of products created by human ingenuity, including patents, trademarks, and copyrights. These rights are protected when properly registered, but registration in one country does not create rights in another country.

Invisible Trade: Items such as freight, insurance, and financial services that are included in a country's balance of payments accounts (in the "current" account), even though they are not recorded as physically visible exports and imports.

Invoice: See "Commercial Invoice" and "Consular Invoice."

Irrevocable Credit: A letter of credit issued by the purchaser's bank in favor of the seller which cannot be revoked without the consent of the seller (who is the beneficiary of the letter of credit). Under the Uniform Customs and Practice for Documentary Credits (No. 500), all letters of credit are irrevocable unless specifically stated otherwise on their face. This protects the seller against the risk of non-payment due to revocation after release of the goods to the buyer or the buyer's agent.

ISO 9000: A series of quality control standards promulgated by the International Standards Organization.

ITAR: See "Arms Export Control Act."

Jettison: The act of throwing the goods off a steamship into the ocean to lighten the ship in time of peril. It may occur as a way to save a sinking ship or by illegal or improper action by steamship employees. Certain jettisons are covered by insurance or general average but others are not.

Lay Days: The dates between which a chartered vessel is to be available in a port for loading of cargo.

LCL: Less than a full container load.

Legalization: A procedure whereby an embassy or consular employee of the purchaser's country located in the exporter (seller's) country signs or stamps an export document, for example, a commercial invoice, in order to enable the goods to be admitted upon arrival at the purchaser's country.

Letter of Credit (L/C): A formal letter issued by a bank which authorizes the drawing of drafts on the bank up to a fixed limit and under terms specified in the letter. Through the issuance of such letters, a bank guarantees payment on behalf of its customers (purchasers of goods) and thereby facilitates the transaction of business between parties who may not be otherwise acquainted with each other. The letter of credit may be sent directly by the issuing bank or its customer to the beneficiary (sellers of goods), or the terms of the credit may be transmitted through a correspondent bank. In the latter event the correspondent may add its guarantee (confirmation) to that of the issuing bank, depending on the arrangements made between the seller and the purchaser. Letters of credit may be revocable or irrevocable depending on whether the issuing bank reserves the right to cancel the credit prior to its expiration date.

Letter of Indemnity/Guaranty: 1. A document issued by a shipper to a steamship line instructing the steamship line to issue a clean bill of lading even though the goods are damaged, and agreeing to hold the steamship line harmless from any claims. 2. An agreement by a beneficiary of a letter of credit to hold a bank harmless for making payment to the beneficiary even though there are some discrepancies between the documents required by the letter of credit and those presented by the beneficiary. 3. An agreement by an exporter and/or importer to hold a steamship line harmless from any claims that may arise as a result of the steamship releasing goods where a negotiable bill of lading covering the goods has been lost or destroyed.

Lighterage: The cost for conveying the goods by lighters or barges between ships and shore and vice versa, including the loading into, and discharging out of, lighters.

Liner Service: Regularly scheduled departures of steamships to specific destinations (trade lanes).

Liquidation: A U.S. Customs term of art describing the official final determination by the customs authorities of the classification and value of the imported merchandise. For example, any importers, by posting a customs bond, may obtain immediate delivery of merchandise by classifying the imported product and paying customs duties at that time. The importer's classification and value, however, is not binding on the U.S. Customs Service, and within an additional period of time, for example, three to six months, the Service will make its own analysis of the goods and determine whether or not it agrees with the classification, value, and duties paid.

Long Ton: 2,240 pounds.

LTL: A shipment of less than a full truckload.

Manifest: A listing of the cargo being transported by the transportation carrier.

Marine Extension Clause: A provision in an ocean casualty insurance policy extending the ordinary coverage to include time periods where goods are received for shipment but not yet loaded on a steamship, and loaded off the steamship but not yet delivered to the buyer and periods where the ship deviates from its intended course or the goods are transshipped.

Marine Insurance: Insurance which will compensate the owner of goods transported overseas in the event of loss or damage. Some "marine" insurance policies also cover air shipments.

Marine Surveyor: A company or individual which assesses the extent of damage to cargo incurred during ocean transportation. Such survey reports are necessary in order for insurance companies to make payment to the beneficiary of the insurance policy.

Marking Laws: Laws requiring articles of foreign origin and/or their containers, imported into a country to be marked in a specified manner which would indicate to the purchaser the country of origin of the article.

Mate's Receipt: Commonly used in Europe, a document similar to a dock receipt. A mate's receipt is issued by an employee of a steamship line, usually at the wharf or pier where the goods are received from the transportation carrier delivering the goods to the port. It evidences that delivery was made by the ground carrier. The steamship line will prepare the bill of lading based on the information in the mate's receipt.

Maturity: The date on which a time draft must be paid.

Measurement Ton: An alternative way of calculating the transportation charge for articles which may be unusually bulky or light. The steamship line ordinarily will charge the higher of the actual weight or a calculated or constructed weight based upon the dimensions of the goods being transported.

MERCOSUR: A common market established by Argentina, Brazil, Paraguay, and Uruguay.

Metric Ton: 2,200 pounds.

Minimum Freight: The minimum charge that a transportation carrier will charge for transportation. Because such minimum charges exist, freight consolidators provide the service of aggregating small shipments so that lower freight rates can be obtained which are then partially passed back to the shippers.

Most Favored Nation: An agreement in a treaty or in a sales contract whereby one party promises to give to the other party benefits at least equal to the benefits that party has extended to any other country or customer.

Negotiable Instrument: A document containing an unconditional promise or order to pay a fixed amount of money with or without interest or other charges described in the promise or order if it is payable to bearer or order at the time it is issued, is payable on demand or at a definite time, and does not state any other undertaking or instructions in addition to the payment of money. Examples of negotiable instruments include checks and drafts.

Negotiation: A transfer of possession, whether voluntary or involuntary, for value received of a negotiable instrument by a person to another person who thereby becomes its holder.

Non-Negotiable: A document which is incapable of transferring legal ownership or rights to possession of the goods by transfer or endorsement of the document, for example, a railroad, sea, or air waybill.

Non-Tariff Barriers: Obstacles to selling or importing activities other than the customs duties assessed on imported goods, for example, inspections which delay importation, foreign exchange controls which make payment difficult, foreign language labeling regulations, buy national policies, product standards, and quotas.

Non-Vessel Operating Common Carrier (NVOCC): A cargo consolidator of small shipments in ocean trade, generally soliciting business and arranging for or performing containerization functions at the port. The NVOCC is recognized by the Federal Maritime Commission as a common carrier which does not own or operate steamships but publishes tariffs after having filed them with the Commission and becomes the shipper of the goods.

Notify Party: The person listed on a bill of lading or other document that the transportation carrier is supposed to notify upon arrival. A notify party may be the purchaser of the goods, a foreign freight forwarder or customs broker, or a bank or other party, depending upon the terms of the sales agreement and the agreement relating to payment for the goods.

On Board Notation, On Board Endorsement: A legend, stamp, or handwritten statement on the face of a bill of lading issued by a steamship certifying that the goods have actually been loaded on the ship. Often letters of credit will specify that the goods must be on board before the expiration date of the letter of credit in order for the exporter (seller) to receive payment under the letter of credit. See "Received Bill of Lading."

Open Account (O/A): A sale payable when specified, that is, R/M: return mail; E.O.M: end of month; 30 days: thirty days from date of invoice; 2/10/60: 2 percent discount for payment in ten days, net if paid sixty days from date of invoice. Unlike a letter of credit, there is no security or bank guaranty of payment.

Order Bill of Lading: Usually, "To Order" bills of lading are made to the order of the shipper and endorsed in blank, thereby giving the holder of the bill of lading title to the goods being shipped. They may also be to the order of the consignee or bank financing the transaction. Order bills of lading are negotiable (whereas straight bills of lading are not).

Orderly Marketing Agreements (OMAs): International agreements negotiated between two or more governments, in which the trading partners agree to restrain the growth of trade in specified "sensitive" products, usually through the imposition of export or import quotas. Orderly Marketing Agreements are intended to ensure that future trade increases will not disrupt, threaten, or impair competitive industries or their workers in importing countries.

OSD: A notation on a carrier receipt or bill of lading signifying "Over, Short or Damaged."

Packing List: A document describing the contents of a shipment. It includes more detail than is contained in a commercial invoice but does not contain prices or values. It is used for insurance claims as well as by the foreign customs authorities when examining goods to verify proper customs entry.

Particular Average (P.A.): A partial loss or damage to cargo which solely affects "particular" interests. These damages or partial losses are not shared by other interests but are excepted in the ocean carrier's bill of lading. Therefore, except if negligence is involved, claims under particular average cannot be directed against the steamship line.

Passport: An official document issued by a country authorizing one of its citizens or legal residents to leave the country and to be readmitted to the country upon return. See "Visa."

Performance Bond: A guarantee issued by an insurance company, surety company, or other person acceptable to the beneficiary guaranteeing that the applicant (for example, a seller of goods) will manufacture and deliver the goods to the purchaser in accordance with the specifications and delivery schedule.

Perils of the Seas: Conditions covered by marine insurance including heavy weather, stranding, collision, lightning, and seawater damage.

Permanent Establishment: An office, warehouse, or place of business in a foreign country which may cause its owner or lessor to be subject to income taxes in that country. Under the common international tax treaties negotiated between countries of the world, profits made by a seller are not taxable in the buyer's country unless the seller also has a permanent establishment in the buyer's country which has played some part in arranging the sale transaction.

Pick-Up Order: A document used when city or suburban export cargo has to be delivered to a dock, or for pick-up of goods from storage places.

Power of Attorney: A legal document wherein a person authorizes another person to act on the first person's behalf. It may be issued to an attorney-at-law or to any person and authorizes that person to act as an agent for the issuer of the power of attorney for general or limited purposes.

Pre-Shipment Inspections: A procedure whereby a buyer through an independent agent such as an inspection company, will examine the goods being purchased prior to exportation by the foreign seller. These examinations may be for quality alone or, in some cases where the buyer's government requires it, the inspection company may require information on the value of the goods.

Product Liability: The responsibility of a manufacturer, and, in some cases, a seller for defects in goods which cause injury to a purchaser, user, or consumer of the goods or cause damage to the purchaser's business.

Pro Forma Invoice: An abbreviated invoice sent at the beginning of a sale transaction, usually to enable the buyer to obtain an import permit or a foreign exchange permit or both. The pro forma invoice gives a close approximation of the weights and values of a shipment that is to be made.

Provisional Insurance: Temporary insurance issued by an agent of an insurance company covering a temporary time period until the actual insurance application can be reviewed by the insurance company and the insurance policy issued.

Quota: A limitation or restriction on the quantity or duty rate payable on imported goods. See "Absolute Quota" and "Tariff Rate Quota."

Received Bill of Lading: A document issued by a steamship company acknowledging that it has received delivery of goods to be transported at some later time, usually on the first available steamship going to the destination specified by the shipper. Since the goods are not yet loaded on board, there is no guarantee that the goods will be shipped in the near future and, therefore, such bills of lading are generally not acceptable if presented by a seller for payment under a letter of credit which is about to expire.

Recourse: The right to claim a refund for amounts paid to a payee. For example, a factoring company may purchase accounts receivable from an exporter (seller), pay the exporter a discounted amount, and collect the accounts receivable as they become due from the purchasers of the goods. If the purchase of the accounts receivable by the factor is with recourse, if any of the purchasers fails to pay, the factor has the option of pursuing the purchaser or claiming a refund for that amount from the exporter (seller) from whom the accounts receivable were purchased.

Remittance: A payment, usually from one collecting bank to another, for example, under a documentary collection. However, a remittance may also include payments directly by the purchaser to the seller.

Revaluation: A government action whereby its currency is valued upward in relationship to another currency. See "Devaluation."

Revocable Credit: A letter of credit issued by a bank which is subject to revocation by the applicant (purchaser of the goods) at any time. Under the new Uniform Customs and Practice for Documentary Credits, No. 500, letters of credit are irrevocable unless expressly stated to be revocable.

Revolving Credit: An agreement of a bank issuing a letter of credit with the applicant (purchaser of goods) that as soon as the purchaser makes payment for a particular shipment or amount of goods to the seller the bank will automatically issue a new letter of credit covering the next shipment or amount agreed upon between the applicant and the bank.

Royalty: An amount paid by a licensee to acquire certain rights, for example, a lump sum or an ongoing amount to manufacture or sell goods in accordance with the licensed patent, trademark, copyright, or trade secrets. In some situations, royalties paid by the purchaser of goods to the seller of goods must be included in the dutiable value of the goods.

Sales Agreement or Contract: The agreement, oral or written, between the exporter (seller) and the importer (purchaser) describing the terms and conditions upon which the seller and purchaser will execute the sale and describing the rights and responsibilities of each party.

Schedule B: A classification system based on the Harmonized Tariff System applicable to U.S. exports.

Section 301 (of the Trade Act of 1974): A provision of U.S. law that enables the President to withdraw duty reductions or restrict imports from countries that discriminate against U.S. exports, subsidize their own exports to the United States, or engage in other unjustifiable or unreasonable practices that burden or discriminate against U.S. trade.

Selling Commission: Money or compensation paid by the seller of goods to the seller's agent for services performed by that agent, such as identifying prospective purchasers and assisting with export of the goods. If the amount of the selling commission is charged to the purchaser of the goods it will usually become subject to customs duties in the country of importation.

Service Contract: A contract between an ocean carrier and a shipper or a shipper's association, in which the shipper commits to a minimum quantity of freight for transport within a fixed period of time and the carrier discounts its usual transportation charges and guarantees levels of service, such as assured space and transit time.

Shipper's Association: A group of exporters who negotiate with transportation carriers for lower freight rates by committing their aggregate volume of cargo.

Shipper's Export Declaration: A form required by the Treasury Department for shipments over $2,500 ($500 for mail shipments) to all countries except Canada. It is completed by a shipper or its freight forwarder showing the value, weight, consignee, designation, Schedule B number, etc., for the export shipment.

Shipper's Letter of Instructions: A document issued by an exporter or importer instructing the freight forwarder to effect transportation and exportation in accordance with the terms specified in the letter of instructions.

Shipping Conference: Steamship lines establishing regularly scheduled service and common transportation rates in the same trade lanes.

Shipping Permit: Sometimes called delivery permit, a document issued by the traffic department of an ocean carrier after the booking of cargo has been made. It directs the receiving clerk at the pier at which the vessel will load to receive from a named party (exporter or forwarder) on a specified day or time the goods for loading and ocean shipment measurement.

Ship's Manifest: A document containing a list of the shipments comprising the cargo of a vessel.

Short Ton: 2,000 pounds.

Sight Draft (S/D): Similar to cash-on-delivery, a draft so drawn by the seller as to be payable on presentation to the drawee (importer) or within a brief period thereafter known as days of grace. Also referred to as a demand draft, a sight draft is used when the seller wishes to retain control of the shipment until payment.

Single Administrative Document: The document now used throughout the European Union to effect exports and customs clearance among member nations and external countries.

SL&C: (Shipper's Load and Count) Shipments loaded and sealed by shipping and not checked or verified by the carrier.

Special Endorsement: A direction by the payee of a draft specifying the name of an alternative payee to whom the drawee is authorized to make payment after delivery of the draft to the alternative payee.

Specific Duty: A tax imposed on imported merchandise without regard to value. It is usually based on the net weight or number of pieces.

Spot Exchange: The exchange rate that exists between two currencies for immediate purchase and sale.

Stale Bill of Lading: A bill of lading which has not been presented under a letter of credit to the issuing or confirming bank within a reasonable time (usually twenty-one days) after its date, thus precluding its arrival at the port of discharge by the time the vessel carrying the shipment has arrived.

Standby Credit: A letter of credit issued by a bank which is payable upon a simple certification by the beneficiary of the letter of credit that a particular condition or duty has not been performed by the applicant for the letter of credit. For example, an exporter (seller) may have to apply for and obtain a standby letter of credit issued in favor of the purchaser when the purchaser is a foreign government to guarantee that the exporter (seller) will perform the sales agreement and deliver the goods in accordance with the delivery schedule. This is to be distinguished from a documentary letter of credit, where the purchaser is the applicant and payment is made by the bank issuing the letter of credit upon presentation to the bank of certain specified documents, such as bills of lading, insurance certificates, inspection certificates, and weight certificates.

Stevedoring: A charge, generally so much per ton, agreed upon between the ocean carrier and a stevedoring, or terminal, operator covering the allocation of men (longshoremen), gear, and all other equipment for working the cargo in or out of the vessel, under the supervision and control of the ship's master.

Stowage: The placing of cargo into a vessel.

Straight Bill of Lading: A bill of lading in which the goods are consigned directly to a named consignee and not to the seller's or buyer's "order." Delivery can be made only to the named person; such a bill of lading is non-negotiable.

Strikes, Riots and Civil Commotions (S.R.&C.C.): A term referring to an insurance clause excluding insurance or loss caused by labor disturbances, riots, and civil commotions or any person engaged in such actions.

Stripping: Unloading (devanning) a container.

Stuffing: Loading a container.

Subrogation: The right which one person, usually an insurance or surety company, has, after payment to the beneficiary of the insurance policy, for example, for damage to goods, to pursue any third party against whom the beneficiary would have had a claim, such as the person causing the damage to the goods.

Sue & Labor Clause: A provision in a marine insurance policy obligating the assured to do those things necessary after a loss to prevent further loss and to cooperate with, and act in the best interests of, the insurer.

Surveyor: A company or individual which assesses the extent of damages to cargo incurred during ocean transportation. Such survey reports are necessary in order for insurance companies to make payment to the beneficiary of the insurance policy.

Tariff: A duty (or tax) levied upon goods transported from one customs area to another. Tariffs raise the prices of imported goods, thus making them less competitive within the market of the importing country.

Tariff Rate Quota: An increase in the tariff duty rate imposed upon goods imported to a country after the quantity of the goods imported within the quota period reaches a certain pre-established level.

Tax Haven: A country which imposes a low or no income tax on business transactions conducted by its nationals.

Tender: A solicitation or request for quotations or bids issued by a prospective purchaser, usually a government entity, to select the supplier or seller for a procurement or project.

Tenor: The term fixed for the payment of a draft.

TEU: Twenty-foot Equivalent Unit. A measurement of container capacity.

Theft, Pilferage &/or Non-Delivery: A type of risk that may be covered under a transportation insurance policy either within the terms of the main coverage or by special endorsement and payment of the corresponding premium.

Through Bill of Lading: Also called a combined transport bill of lading or intermodal bill of lading, a document issued by the transportation carrier which thereby agrees to effect delivery to the required destination by utilizing various means of transportation, such as truck, railroad, and/or steamship line.

Time Draft: A draft maturing at a certain fixed time after presentation or acceptance. This may be a given number of days after sight (acceptance) or a given number of days after the date of the draft.

TL: A truckload shipment.

Total Loss: A situation where damaged goods covered by an insurance policy are adjudged to have no commercial value and their full value will be paid under the insurance policy.

Trademark: A brand name, word, or symbol placed on a product to distinguish that product from other similar types of products. The right to sell products under a trademark is regulated by the laws and regulations applicable in each country of sale.

Tramp: A steamship or steamship line which does not adhere to a shipping conference and, therefore, is free to charge whatever transportation rates and to sail in any ocean lane it desires.

Transferable Credit: A letter of credit in which the applicant (purchaser of goods) has authorized the beneficiary of the letter of credit (exporting seller of the goods) to transfer its right to payment to a third party, for example, the manufacturer of the goods being sold by the exporter to the purchaser.

Transfer Pricing: Sales of goods between sellers and buyers that are affiliated, for example, by common stock ownership. In such cases, the price may be artificially increased or decreased to vary from the price charged in an arms-length transaction. As a result income tax and customs authorities may readjust the price.

Trust Receipt: A document signed by a buyer, based on which a bank holding title to goods releases possession of the goods to the buyer for the purpose of sale. The buyer obligates himself to maintain the identity of the goods or the proceeds thereof distinct from the rest of his assets and to hold them subject to repossession by the bank. Trust Receipts are used extensively in the Far East, where it is customary to sell on terms of sixty or ninety days, documents against acceptance. The collecting bank permits buyers of good standing to obtain the goods, under a trust receipt contract, before the maturity date of the draft. In some countries, warrants serve the same purpose.

Unconfirmed Credit: A letter of credit issued by the applicant's (purchaser of goods') bank, usually in the purchaser's own country. See also "Confirming Bank."

Uniform Commercial Code: A series of laws applicable in the United States governing commercial transactions, such as sales, leasing, negotiable instruments, bank collections, warehousing, bills of lading, investment securities, and security interests. See also "Convention on International Sale of Goods" and "Incoterms."

Uniform Customs and Practice for Documentary Credits (UCP): A set of international rules and standards agreed upon and applied by many banks in the issuance of letters of credit. The most recent edition (No. 500) went into effect on January 1, 1994.

Uniform Rules for Collections (URC): A set of international rules and standards agreed upon and applied by many banks when acting as a collecting bank in a documentary collection. The most recent edition (No. 522), published by the International Chamber of Commerce, went into effect on January 1, 1996. See "Collecting Bank."

Unitization: The consolidation of a quantity of individual items into one large shipping unit for easier handling.

Usance: The time period during which credit is being extended and which the purchaser of goods or borrower of monies must pay interest.

Valuation: The appraisal of the value of imported goods by customs officials for the purpose of determining the amount of ad valorem duty payable in the importing country. The GATT Customs Valuation Code obligates governments that are party to it to use the "transaction value" of imported goods—usually the price actually paid or payable for the goods—as the principal basis for valuing the goods for customs purposes.

Value-Added Tax (VAT): An indirect tax on consumption that is levied at each discrete point in the chain of production and distribution, from the raw material stage to final consumption. Each processor or merchant pays a tax proportional to the amount by which he increases the value or marks up the goods he purchases for resale.

Visa: 1. A stamp put into a traveler's passport by officials of an embassy or consul authorizing a traveler to enter a foreign country. 2. The document issued by an exporting country allowing export of products subject to an export quota in effect in the exporting country.

Voluntary Restraint Agreements (VRAs): Informal arrangements through which exporters voluntarily restrain certain exports, usually through export quotas, to avoid economic dislocation in an importing country, and to avert the possible imposition of mandatory import restrictions.

Warehouse Receipt: A receipt given by a warehouseman for goods received by him for storage. A warehouse receipt in which it is stated that the commodities referred to therein will be delivered to the depositor or to any other specified person or company is a negotiable warehouse receipt. Endorsement and delivery of a negotiable warehouse receipt serves to transfer ownership of the property covered by the receipt.

Warehouse to Warehouse Clause: A provision in a transportation insurance policy extending coverage from the time of transport from the seller's place of business to the purchaser's place of business.

War Risk Insurance: Separate insurance coverage for loss of goods which results from any act of war. This insurance is necessary during peacetime due to objects, such as floating mines, left over from previous wars.

Wharfage: A charge assessed by a pier or dock owner against freight moving over the pier or dock or against carriers using the pier or dock.

With Average (W.A.): An insurance coverage broader than F.P.A. and representing protection for partial damage caused by the perils of the sea. Additional named perils, such as theft, pilferage, non-delivery, and freshwater damage can be added to a W.A. Clause. Generally, however, damage must be caused by seawater. A minimum percentage of damage may be required before payment is made.

World Trade Organization (WTO): The World Trade Organization consists of 123 signatory countries. The Uruguay Round of negotiations resulted in the formation of the WTO and in numerous agreements relating to the reduction of tariffs and non-tariff barriers to trade. The WTO supersedes GATT, but a number of agreements reached under GATT, such as the Valuation Code, the Antidumping Code, the Subsidies Code, and the Agreement on Government Procurement, continue in revised form under the WTO.

York Antwerp Rules of General Average: An international treaty prescribing the conditions and rules under which damage to a steamship or to goods will be shared by the other owners of goods on the steamship.

Index

(Page numbers in *italics* refer to figures)

absolute quota, 547
acceptances, 70, 73, *77–81*, 284–285, 547, 549
acceptor (accepter), 547
acknowledgment (purchase orders), 70, 73, 284–285
adjustment assistance, 547
administrative summons, 345, *346–347*
ad valorem tariff, 547
advising bank, 547
AES, *see* Automated Export System
AES Direct, 195, 446–448
affiliated companies, 89, 257, 290–291
affreightment, contract of, 547
Afghanistan, 203, 234
Africa, 96
African Development Bank, 45
African Growth and Opportunity Act, 240–241, 258, 322
Agency for International Development, 45
agents, 547–548, 554, *see also* sales agent(s)
agricultural products, *329–330*
air carriers, 32
air freight forwarders, 32
air insurance, 120, 129, 133
  for exports, 37–38
  for imports, 267
air waybill, *126–129*, 548
Albania, 203
allowances, price, 88–89
all risk clause, 548
"all risks" insurance coverage, 37–38, 267
American Arbitration Association, 100, 298
American Foreign Trade Definitions, 33
American National Standards Institute, 20
Andean Trade Preference Act, 258, 322
Angola, 120, 203, 241
animal export certificates, 169, *174*, 175
antiboycott compliance, 24, *25–27*
Anti-Counterfeiting Consumer Protection Act of 1996, 268
antidumping duties, 35, 255, 265
Antiterrorism Act, 241
antitrust laws, 88
  and international purchase agreements, 289–290
  and international sales agreements, 87
  reselling restrictions under, 101–102
applicant, 548
Application for Foreign Trade Zone Activity Permit, 317, *321*
Application for Foreign Trade Zone Admission, 317, *320*
appraisement, 548
arbitrage, 548
arbitration (for dispute resolution), 100, 298–299
Argentina, 98, 120, 213, 297
Armenia, 203, 234
Arms Export Control Act, 197, 232, 235, 548
arms exports, 232, 234–235
arrival draft, 548
arrival notices, 309, *310*, 548
ASEAN, 548
Asian Development Bank, 45
Asian economic crisis, xix
assembly and processing operations, foreign, 382, *383–384*, 385
assists, 21, 260, 262, 548
assured (term), 548
ATA Carnet, 28, *29–31*, 549
Atomic Energy Act of 1954, 197
at sight (term), 549
audits, 353, 362, 535–540, 549
Australia, 98, 213, 297
Austria, 98, 213, 297
authority
  to pay, 549
  to purchase, 549
automated commercial system, 549
Automated Export System (AES), 13, 195, 439–445, 449–453
average adjuster, 549
average(s)
  general, 559, 570
  particular, 564
Azerbaijan, 203, 234

BAF (bunker adjustment factor), 549
Bahamas, 215
Bahrain, 24, 116
bank draft, 549
banker's acceptance, 549
bank(s)
  advising, 547
  collecting, 552
  confirming, 553
Barbados, 215
barriers, non-tariff, 563
barter transactions, 387, 549
Belarus, 21, 98, 203, 234, 297
Belgium, 98, 213, 297
Belize, 215
beneficiary, 550
Bermuda, 215
bill of exchange, 550
bill of lading (B/L), 118–120, 305, 307, 550
  clean, 119, 552
  foul, 558
  inland, *121–123*
  ocean, *124–125*
  order, 564
  received, 565
  stale, 567
  straight, 119, 568
  through, 568
blank endorsement, 550
blanket agreements, 85–86
blanket insurance policies, 37
BNA, 18
Bolivia, 120, 133, 215, 258
bonded warehouse, 258–259, 550
bond(s), 550
  exportation of articles under special, *261*
  importation, 244, *247–249*
  performance, 564
booking cargo, 550
booking confirmation, 44
booking number, 550
Bosnia-Herzegovina, 98, 297
boycotts, 24, 550
Brazil, 116, 215

Index

bribery, 112–113
British Columbia International Arbitration Centre, 100, 298
brokers, customs, *see* customs brokers
Bulgaria, 98, 203, 213, 215, 297
bunker adjustment factor (BAF), 549
Bureau of Export Administration, 8
Burkina Faso, 120
Burma, 234
Burundi, 98, 120, 297
Buy American policies, 264
buying commission, 550
buy national policy, 550
buy-sell export structure, 86–87

cabotage, 551
C.A.D. (cash against documents), 551
CAF (currency adjustment factor), 551
California, 45
Cambodia, 21, 120, 203, 213
Cameroon, 120
Canada, 215, 311
  duty-free imports from, 258
  duty on exports to, 259
  as party to Convention on Contracts for the International Sale of Goods, 98, 297
  tariff-rate quotas on imports from, 254
  temporary importation from, 259
  see also North American Free Trade Agreement
Caribbean Basin, 258
Caribbean Basin Economic Recovery Act, 240, 322
carnets, 28, *29–31*
Carriage of Goods by Sea Act, 32, 37, 133
cash against documents (C.A.D.), 551
cash in advance (C.I.A.), 551
cash payments, 92, *94,* 293
cash with order (C.W.O.), 551
casualty insurance, 120, 129, 133, 267
casualty loss, 551
"CE" mark, 20, 551
Central African Republic, 120
certificate(s)
  of free sale, 162, *165*
  of inspection, 120, *131–132,* 309, 551
  of insurance, 551
  of origin, 133, 152, *161,* 162, *163–164,* 322, 324, 551
  for Products for Export, 162, *165*
  of weight and measurement, 551
charter party, 551
chemical exports, precursor/essential, 169, *172–173*
Chile, 98, 215, 297
China (People's Republic), 213, 215, 234
  import violation penalties in, 21
  international boycotts in, 24
  as party to Convention on Contracts for the International Sale of Goods, 98, 297
C.I.A. (cash in advance), 551
classification, customs, 256, 262, 554
clean bill of lading, 119, 552
"click-wrap" agreements, 278
COCOM export controls, 242
C.O.D. payments, *94*
collecting bank, 552
collection function (export order processing), *9*
collections, uniform rules for, 569
Colombia, 116, 215, 258
Commerce Business Daily, 19
Commerce Control List, 198–200, *201–202,* 203
commercial invoices, 81, *83,* 116, 118, *118,* 285, 307, 552
commercial letters of credit, 270
Commercial News U.S.A., 19
commingling, 552
commission agent export structure, 86
commission(s)
  buying, 550
  sales agent agreement provisions for, 109, 303
  selling, 566
common carriers, 552, 563
common market, 552
Communist countries, quotas/duties on imports from, 258
competing products, distributor handling of, 107, 301–302
compound duty, 552
Comprehensive Anti-Apartheid Act, 197
compromise, offers of, 365
conduct
  purchase agreements formed by, 282
  sales agreements formed by, 63
conference tariff, 552
confidentiality and non-disclosure agreements, 23–24, 59, 269
confirmations, sales, 74
confirmed irrevocable letters of credit, *94*
confirming bank, 553
conflicting provisions
  in purchase documentation, 285–286
  in sales documentation, 81–84
Consent to Forfeiture, *359*
consignment, 553
  export, 36, *93*
  import, 266–267
Constitution of the United States, 14
consular invoices, 133, *160,* 553
consulate, 553
continuous bonds, 244
contract(s)
  of affreightment, 547
  sales, *see* sales agreements
  service, 566
controlled commodities, documentation for, 242
controls
  exchange, 556–557
  export, *see* Export Administration Regulations
Convention on Contracts for the International Sale of Goods, 98–99, 265, 297, 553
  intellectual property rights infringements under, 268
  oral sales agreements under, 60, 280
  packaging warranties under, 32, 295
  passage of title under, 95, 294–295
  title and delivery transfer under, 34, 35
copyrights, 23, 268–269
  export distributor agreement provisions for, 108
  import distributor agreement provisions for, 302
Correct Way to Complete the Shipper's Export Declaration, 186, 419–436
corrupt practices, 112–113
Costa Rica, 215
costing sheets, 65, *66*
Côte d'Ivoire, 116
counterfeit goods, 268
countertrade, 553–554
countertrade transactions, 92, 387
countervailing duties, 255, 554
Country Limitation Schedule, 18
country of origin
  determination of, 260
  marking of, 45, 260
country sourcing (imports), 240–241
Court of International Trade, 353, 365
  information statement for, *369–370*
  summons from, *366–368*
  transmittal to, *371*
credit card payments, 58, 59
credit notification, 270
credit reports, 19, 241
credit(s)
  in international sales, 90
  irrevocable, 561
  letters of, *see* letter(s) of credit
  revocable, 565–566
  revolving, 566
  standby, 567
  transferable, 569
  unconfirmed, 569
Croatia, 98, 297

Index

Cuba, 203, 211, 234
  duties on imports from, 258
  importation from, 241
  prohibited imports from, 258
currency
  exchange control for, 22
  export distributor agreements and fluctuations in, 106–107
  international purchase agreements and fluctuations in, 291–292
  quoted prices and fluctuations in, 90, 301
currency adjustment factor (CAF), 551
customers, 18–19, 210, *211*
Customized Sales Survey, 19
customs bonds, 244, *247–249*
customs brokers, 554
  foreign, 28, 30
  for imports, 243–244, *245–246*
  letters of instruction for, 244, *246*
  power of attorney for, *245*
customs classification, 256, 262, 554
Customs Cooperation Council, 28
Customs Export Enforcement Subpoena, 232, *233–234*
Customs Modernization Act
  and audits, 353, 362
  electronic filing of customs entries under, 9, 13
  liability under, 250
  manuals required by, 8
  reasonable care provisions in, 256
  record-keeping requirements under, 13
Customs rulings, 262
customs union, 554
cut-off time, 554
C.W.O. (cash with order), 551
Czech Republic, 98, 213, 215, 297

D/A, *see* documents against acceptance
dangerous goods, shipper's declarations for, 169, *170–171*
date draft, *93,* 554
DDC (destination delivery charge), 554
DEA (Drug Enforcement Administration), 169
declaration(s)
  foreign assembler's, 558
  shipper's export, 566
deferred duty programs, 258–259
del credere agent, 554
delivered duty paid terms of sale, 58, 278
delivery
  of electronic commerce goods, 58, 278
  non-, 568
delivery instructions, 162, *166*
delivery (pick-up) orders, 162, *167,* 309, 311, *312,* 554, 565
"Delivery Verification" certificate, 225, *226*
Democratic Republic of Congo, 120
demurrage, 554
Denied Persons List, 210
Denmark, 98, 213, 297
department(s)
  combined export/import, 4
  export, 3–4, *5*
  import, 4
destination control statement, 555
destination delivery charge (DDC), 554
detention, 324, *333,* 334
Deutshes Institut for Normung (DIN), 20
devaluation, 555
diamonds, importation of, 241
DIN (Deutshes Institut for Normung), 20
Direction of Trade Statistics Yearbook (International Monetary Fund), 18
disclosure, prior, 362, 365
discounts, 88–89
discrepancy, 555
discrimination, price, 88
dispute resolution
  international sales agreement provisions for, 99–100
  international sales purchase provisions for, 298–299
distributor agreements
  for ongoing purchase transactions, 286–287
  for ongoing sales transactions, 85
distributor(s)
  definition of, 101, 300, 555
  importer as, 241
  sales agents vs., 102–103, 300
  subdistributor appointment by, 107–108, 302
dock receipts, 133, *158–159,* 555
documentary bill, 555
documentary credits, 569
documentation
  EAR requirements for, 223, 225
  export, *see* export documentation
  import, *see* import documentation
  manuals of procedures and, 8, 9, *11,* 11–12, *12*
documents, single administrative, 567
documents against acceptance (D/A), 91, *93,* 175, 555
documents against payment (D/P), 91, *94,* 175, 555
Domestic International Sales Corporation program, 46
Dominican Republic, 116, 133, 215
D/P, *see* documents against payment
draft(s), 555
  arrival, 548
  bank, 549
  date, 554
  for payment, 175, *176–177,* 309
  sight, 567
  time, 568
drawback, 375–376, *377–381,* 382, 555
drawee, 556
drawer, 556
drayage, 556
Drug Enforcement Administration (DEA), 169
dumping, 88, 289, 556
dumping duties, 35
Dun & Bradstreet, 18, 19, 241
dunnage, 556
duty-free/reduced duty programs, 257–258
duty(-ies), 21, 556
  antidumping, 255
  compound, 552
  on consignments, 36, 267
  countervailing, 255, 554
  deferment of, 258–259
  importer's liability for, 265
  on imports from Communist countries, 258
  on lease transactions, 36
  specific, 567
  and terms of purchase, 265–266
  and terms of sale, 35

EAR, *see* Export Administration Regulations
ECCN, *see* Export Control Classification Number
Ecuador, 98, 120, 215, 258, 297
EEC, *see* European Economic Community
effective date, 107
Egypt, 98, 116, 297
EIN (Employer Identification Number), 194
electronic commerce, 276, 278–279
  export considerations with, 57–59
  validity/enforceability of sales contracts for, 278
electronic filing (of customs entries), 9, 13
electronic products, *325–328*
El Salvador, 215
embargo, 556
embassy, 556
EMCs, *see* export management companies
Employer Identification Number (EIN), 194
endorsement(s)
  blank, 550
  on board, 563–564
  special, 567
end uses and users, 18–19, 210, *211*
entry, 556
Entry/Immediate Delivery form, 311, *313*

Index

Entry Summary, 311, *314–316,* 317
  rules for completion of, 493–523
Environmental Protection Agency, 262
escalation clauses (price), 88, 89
escape clause, 556
"essential" chemicals, 169
Estonia, 98, 203, 297
ETCs, *see* export trading companies
Ethiopia, 21, 120
European Economic Community (EEC), 20, 89
European Union, 32, 556
examination, 324, 556
exchange
  forward, 558
  spot, 567
exchange controls, 22, 556–557
exchange rate risk, 557
exchange rate(s), 557
  fixed, 558
  floating, 558
exclusivity
  export distributor agreement provisions for, 103, 106
  import distributor agreement provisions for, 300–301
ex-factory (ex-works) sales, 35, 266
EXIM, *see* U.S. Export-Import Bank
Export Administration Act, 13
Export Administration Regulations (EAR), 197–235
  and Commerce Control List, 198–200, *201–202,* 203
  country group A in, *204*
  country group B in, *205*
  country group D in, *206–207*
  country group E in, *208*
  and "Delivery Verification" certificate, 225, *226*
  and destination, 203, *204–209*
  documentation/record-keeping requirements of, 223, 225, *226*
  and end uses/users, 210, *211*
  exceptions to, 212–213
  "General Prohibitions" in, 210–212
  license applications/procedures under, 213, *214,* 215, *216–222,* 223, *224*
  munitions/arms exports under, 232–235
  re-export transactions under, 223
  scope of, 198
  Special Comprehensive License under, 225, 227, *228–229,* 230
  technology/software exports under, 230–232
  violations of, 232, *233–234*
Export and Import Trade Data Base (Bureau of Census), 18
Export Contact List Service, 19
Export Control Classification Number (ECCN), 195, 200
export controls and licenses, 22–23
export declaration, shipper's, 566
export department, 3–4, *5*
export distributor agreements, 101–109
  appointment of subdistributors provision in, 107–108
  effective date of, 107
  government review of, 107
  handling of competing products provisions in, 107
  intellectual property provisions in, 108
  minimum purchase quantities provisions in, 107
  negotiation issues checklist in, *104–106*
  pricing in, 106–107
  sales agent agreements vs., 101–103
  termination of, 101
  territory/exclusivity provisions in, 103, 106
  warranties and product liability provisions in, 108–109
export documentation, 114–196
  animal/plant/food export certificates as, 169, *174,* 175, *176*
  bills of lading as, 118–120, *121–129*
  casualty insurance policies/certificates as, 120, 129, 133, *134–157*
  certificates of free sale as, 162, *165*
  certificates of origin as, 133, 152, *161,* 162, *163–164*
  commercial invoices as, 116, 118, *118*
  consular invoices as, 133, *160*
  delivery instructions as, 162, *166*
  delivery orders as, 162, *167*
  dock receipts as, 133
  drafts for payment as, 175, *177–178*
  freight forwarder's invoices as, 195, *196*
  freight forwarder's powers of attorney as, 114, *115*
  inspection certificates as, 120, *131–132*
  letters of credit as, 175, 178, *179–191,* 180
  packing lists as, 120, *130*
  precursor/essential chemical exports declaration as, 169, *172–173*
  for sales, *see* sales documentation
  shipper's declarations for dangerous goods as, 169, *170–171*
  Shipper's Export Declaration as, 181, 186, *192–193,* 194–195
  shipper's letters of instructions as, 114, 116, *117*
  special customs invoices as, 162–169, *168*
  warehouse receipts as, 133, *158–159*
  See also sales documentation
Exporters Encyclopedia (Dun & Bradstreet), 18
Export-Import Bank of the United States, 18
exporting, 17–59
  and antiboycott compliance, 24, *25–27*
  and compliance with foreign law, 19–22
  and confidentiality/non-disclosure agreements, 23–24
  and consignment transactions, 36
  controls and licenses for, *see* export controls and licenses
  country of origin marking for, 45
  and electronic commerce, 57–59
  financing/payment insurance for, 45–46, *47–49*
  and foreign branch operations, 57
  and foreign immigration/customs compliance, 24, 28, *29–31*
  and foreign warehousing, 45
  and free trade zones, 45
  and identification of customers, 18–19
  and intellectual property rights, 23
  and lease transactions, 36
  marine/air insurance for, *37,* 37–38
  market/product research for, 18
  packing and labeling considerations in, 30, 32
  product considerations in, 17
  specialized, 375–387
  tax incentives for, 46
  and terms of sale, 32–363, *33, 34*
  translation considerations in, 57
  transportation considerations in, 38, *40–44,* 44
  and use of freight forwarders/foreign customs brokers, 28, 30
  volume considerations in, 18
  see also specific headings
export license, 557
export management companies (EMCs), 46, 57
export manuals, *11*
export order processing
  collection function in, *9*
  order entry function in, *7*
  quotation function in, *6*
  shipment function in, *8*
export quotas, 557
Export Reference Manual (BNA), 18
exports
  duty on, under NAFTA, 259
  quotas on, 243
export sales agent agreements, 109–112
  commissions in, 109
  foreign sales representative appointment checklist for, *110–111*
  pricing in, 109

Index

relationship of parties provision in, 112
shipment provisions in, 112
warranties provisions in, 112
export sales agreements, terms of sale in, 32–36, *33, 34*
export trade certificates of review, 46, *50–56*
export trading companies (ETCs), 46, 57, 557
Export Trading Company Act of 1982, 46
export visas, 243

facsimile orders, 61, 281
facsimile purchase transactions, 281
factoring, 92, 294, 557
F.A.K. (freight all kinds), 559
FCPA, *see* Foreign Corrupt Practices Act
F.C.&S. (free of capture and seizure), 558
FDA (Food and Drug Administration), 324
Federal Communications regulations, 262
FEU (forty-foot equivalent unit), 558
financing
for exporters, 45–46
for imports, 268, 294
through U.S. Export-Import Bank, 45–46, *47–49*
fines, *see* penalties
Finland, 98, 213, 297
F.I.O. (free in and out), 558
fixed exchange rate, 558
floating exchange rate, 558
F.O. (free out), 559
Food, Drug and Cosmetics Act, 162, 197, 262
Food and Drug Administration (FDA), 324
food export certificates, 169, 175, *176*
force majeure, 558
Foreign Agricultural Service, 20
foreign assembler's declaration, 558
foreign branch operations
exporting to, 57
importing from, 270, 276
Foreign Corrupt Practices Act (FCPA), 112–113, 558
Foreign Credit Insurance Association, 46
foreign customs brokers, 28, 30
foreign customs treatment, and buyer/seller relationships, 87
foreign government filings, international sales agreement provisions for, 97
foreign law(s), 14
and customs requirements, 20–21
and exchange controls, 22
exporting and compliance with, 19–22
and government contracting, 21
importing and compliance with, 242–243
and import licenses, 22
and industry standards, 20
and preferential treatment, 21–22
specialized, 22
and value-added taxes, 22
foreign processing and assembly operations, 382, *383–384,* 385
foreign sales corporation (FSC), 558
Foreign Sales Corporation program, 46
Foreign Trade Statistics Regulations, 13
foreign trade zones, 259, 558
foreign warehousing, 45
Forfeiture, Consent to, *359*
forty-foot equivalent unit (FEU), 558
forwarder, freight, 559
forward exchange, 558
foul bill of lading, 558
F.P.A., *see* free of particular average
France, 21, 98, 213, 297
free domicile delivery, 35, 265
free house delivery, 35, 265
free in and out (F.I.O.), 558
free of capture and seizure (F.C.& S.), 558
free of particular average (F.P.A), 559
free out (F.O.), 559
free port, 559
free sale, certificates of, 162, *165*
free trade, 559
free trade area, 559
free trade zones, 45
freight, minimum, 563
freight all kinds (FAK), 559
freight collect, 559
freight forwarder(s), 28, 30, 559
air, 32
contracts with, 114
power of attorney for, 114, *115*
freight forwarder's invoices, 195, *196*
freight prepaid, 559
freight rates, 38, 44
French Guiana, 215
French West Indies, 215
FSC (foreign sales corporation), 558
full set, 559

GATT, *see* General Agreement on Tariffs and Trade
General Agreement on Tariffs and Trade (GATT), 21, 559
Antidumping Code of, 88
duty rates on imports from member countries of, 258
tariff-rate quotas under, 254–255
general average, 559, 570
Generalized System of Preferences (GSP), 240, 257–258, 322, *323,* 560
general order, 560
"General Prohibitions," 210–212
Georgia, 98, 203, 297
Germany, 98, 213, 297
Gold Key Service, 19
governing law
and Convention on Contracts for the International Sale of Goods, 98–99
international purchase agreement provisions for, 296–298
international sales agreement provisions for, 97–99
for purchase agreements, 282
for sales agreements, 62–63
government review, 107
government(s)
Buy American policies and sales to, 264
contracting with, 21
grand jury subpoenas, 350, *351–352*
Graydon America, 19, 241
gray market goods, 89, 291, 560
gray market imports, 269
Greece, 98, 213, 297
Greenland, 215
GSP, *see* Generalized System of Preferences
GSP Declaration, 322, *323*
guaranty, letter of, *186,* 561–562
Guatemala, 116, 215
Guinea, 98, 120, 297
Guyana, 215

Haiti, 133, 215, 234
Harmonized Tariff Schedules, 322
text of, 467–482
Harmonized Tariff System (HTS), 194, 256, 258, 560
hazardous materials, 169
labeling of, 32
packing of, 32
Hazardous Materials Transportation Act, 169
Honduras, 133, 215
Hong Kong, 213
HTS, *see* Harmonized Tariff System
Hungary, 98, 213, 215, 297

identification
of customers, 18–19
of customs classification, 256
of suppliers, 241
Illinois, 45
IMF (International Monetary Fund), 18
immigration compliance, 24, 28
importation bonds, 244, *247–249*
Import Certificates, 242
import department, 4
import distributor agreements
appointment of subdistributors provision in, 302
handling of competing products provision in, 301–302

import distributor agreements (*continued*)
intellectual property provisions in, 302
minimum purchase quantities provision in, 301
pricing in, 301
territory/exclusivity provisions in, 300–301
warranties and product liability provisions in, 302–303
import documentation, 305–372
administrative summons as, 345, *346–347*
Application for Foreign Trade Zone Activity Permit as, 317, *321*
Application for Foreign Trade Zone Admission as, 317, *320*
arrival notices as, 309, *310*
bills of lading as, *124–129,* 305, 307
certificates of origin as, 322, 324
commercial invoices as, *118,* 307
and Court of International Trade, 365, *366–371*
and Customs audits, 353, 362
delivery orders as, 309, 311, *312*
for detention of merchandise, 324, *333,* 334
drafts for payment as, *178,* 309
Entry/Immediate Delivery form as, 311, *313*
Entry Summary as, 311, *314–316,* 317
for examination of merchandise, 324
grand jury subpoenas as, 350, *351–352*
GSP Declaration as, 322, *323*
inspection certificates as, *132,* 309
ITC and Commerce questionnaires as, 372
liquidation notices as, 334, *335–336*
NAFTA certificate of origin as, *163–164,* 322, 324
Notice of Action as, 339, *342*
Notice of Redelivery as, 334, *337–338*
and offers of compromise, 365
packing lists as, *130,* 307, 309
penalty notices as, 353, *363–364*
prepenalty notices as, 353, *361–362*
and prior disclosure, 362, 365
pro forma invoices as, 307, *308*
Protest and Instructions form as, 339, *343–344,* 345
reconciliation as, 322
Request for Information as, 339, *340–341*
Request for Reliquidation as, 334
search warrants as, 345, *348–350*
seizure notices as, 350, 353, *354–360*
for specialized products, 324, *325–332*
Transportation Entry form as, 317, *318–319*
and U.S. Court of Appeals, 365
see also purchase documentation
importer's number, application for, 250, *252–253*
importing, 239–279
and antidumping/countervailing duties, 255
and assists, 260, 262
bonds for, 246, *247–249*
from branches/subsidiaries, 270–276
and Buy American policies, 264
casualty insurance for, 267
commercial considerations in, 263–264
and compliance with foreign law, 242–243
and confidentiality/non-disclosure, 269
and consignment transactions, 266–267
and country of origin, 260
country sourcing for, 240–241
customs classification for, 256, 262
and customs rulings, 262
and deferred duty programs, 258–259
and duty-free/reduced duty programs, 257–258
and electronic commerce, 276, 278–279
financing considerations with, 268
and HTS classification, 258
and identification of suppliers, 241
and intellectual property rights, 268–269
and lease transactions, 267
liability considerations for, 250, *251*
and method/booking of transportation, 268
packaging/labeling considerations in, 262–263
payment considerations with, 269–270, *271–277*
ports of entry for, 250, 254
product considerations in, 239–240
and quotas, 254–255
record-keeping requirements for, 262
specialized, 375–387
of specialized products, 262
and temporary importations, 259–260, *261*
and terms of purchase, 264–266
and translation of foreign documents, 270
use of customs brokers for, 243–244, *245–246*
valuation considerations in, 256–257
volume considerations in, 240
see also specific headings
import licenses, 22
import manuals, *12*
imports
parallel, 89
special restrictions on, 239–240
temporary, 24, 28
import sales agent agreements, 303–304
in bond, 560
inchmaree clause, 560
INCO, *see* International Chamber of Commerce
Incoterms, 33, *33, 34,* 264, 265, 560
indefinite agreements, 101
indemnity/guaranty, letter of, *186,* 561–562
indent merchant, 560
India, 21, 213, 215
industry standards, 20, 264
Information, Request for, 339, *340–341*
information security (Internet), 59, 279
inland bill of lading, 118–120, *121–123*
inspection(s)
certificate of, 120, *131–132,* 309, 551
pre-shipment, 96–97, 295–296, 565
instructions
delivery, 162, *166*
shipper's letter of, 566
insurable interest, 560–561
insurance
air, 37–38, 267
blanket policies for, 37
casualty, 120, 129, 133, 267
certificate of, 551
export, 37–38
import, 267
marine, 37–38, *39, 134–154,* 267, 562
payment, 46
provisional, 565
war risk, 570
insurance claims
request for information for, *157*
standard form for presentation of, *155–156*
intellectual property rights, 561
export distributor agreement provisions for, 108
in foreign countries, 23
import distributor agreement provisions for, 302
with imports, 268–269
infringement of, 23

Index

Inter-American Commercial Arbitration Commission, 100, 298
Inter-American Development Bank, 45
interest, insurable, 560–561
Intermodal Safe Container Transportation Act, 32
International Air Transport Association Dangerous Goods Regulations, 169
International Bank of Reconstruction and Development (World Bank), 45
International Chamber of Commerce (INCO)
  ATA carnet administered by, 28
  Incoterms of, 33, *33, 34*
  international dispute arbitration by, 100, 298
International Company Profiles, 19, 241
International Data Base (Bureau of Census), 18
International Development Cooperation Agency, 45
International Emergency Economic Powers Act, 197
international law, 14
International Maritime Dangerous Goods Code, 169
International Monetary Fund (IMF), 18
International Partner Search, 19
international purchase agreement(s), 286, 288–299
  and currency fluctuations, 291–292
  dispute resolution provisions in, 298–299
  example of, 485–489
  export license provisions in, 296
  governing law provisions in, 296–298
  import financing provisions in, 294
  passage of title provisions in, 294–295
  payment methods in, *93–94*, 292–294
  pre-shipment inspection clauses in, 295–296
  pricing in, 289–291
  purchasing and selling entities in, 288
  quantity term in, 288–289
  security interest provisions in, 294
  termination clauses in, 299
  warranties in, 295
international sales agreement(s), 86–101
  and currency fluctuations, 90
  dispute resolution provisions in, 99–100
  example of, 410–415
  export financing provisions in, 92, 95
  export license provisions in, 97
  foreign government filing provisions in, 97
  governing law provisions in, 97–99
  import license provisions in, 97
  for ongoing sales transactions, 85
  passage of title provisions in, 95
  payment methods in, 90–92, *93–94*
  pre-shipment inspection clauses in, 96–97
  pricing in, 87–90
  product defect clauses in, 96
  quantity term in, 87
  security interest provisions in, 95
  selling and purchasing entities in, 86–87
  termination clauses in, 101
  terms of sale in, 32–36, *33, 34*
  title transfer in, 35
  warranties in, 95–96
International Trade Administration, 19
International Trade Commission (ITC), 372
International Trade Statistics Yearbook, 18, 240
International Traffic in Arms Regulations, 232
Internet, 57, 276, *see also* electronic commerce
invisible trade, 561
invoice(s), 561
  commercial, *see* commercial invoices
  consular, 133, *160*, 553
  freight forwarder's, 195, *196*
  pro forma, 73, 81, *82*, 307, *308*, 565
  special customs, 162, *168*, 169
Iran, 120, 203, 234, 241, 258
Iraq, 203, 234
  importation from, 241
  and international boycott, 24
  as party to Convention on Contracts for the International Sale of Goods, 98, 297
  prohibited imports from, 258
Ireland, 213
irrevocable credit, 561
irrevocable letters of credit, *94, 187–188*
ISO 9000, 561
isolated purchase transactions, 280–286
  commercial invoices for, *83*, 285
  conflicting seller/buyer documentation in, 285–286
  definition of, 280
  importance of written agreements for, 280–281
  offers to purchase in, 283
  price lists for, 283
  purchase agreements for, 281–283
  purchase order acknowledgments/acceptances for, *77–81*, 284–285
  purchase orders for, *74–76*, 284
  quotations for, *66–73*, 283–284
  requests for quotations for, *64*, 283
  side agreements with, 286
  by telex/facsimile, 281
isolated sales transactions
  commercial invoices for, 81, *83*
  and conflicting provisions in seller and buyer documents, 81, 84
  costing sheets for, 65, *66*
  definition of, 60
  documentation for, 60–84
  formation of sales agreements for, 61–63, *62*
  and importance of written agreements, 60–61
  price lists for, 63
  pro forma invoices for, 73, 81, *82*
  purchase order acknowledgments/acceptances for, 70, 73, *77–81*
  purchase orders for, 65, 70, *74–76*
  quotations for, 65, *66–73*
  requests for quotations in, 63, *64*, 65
  sales confirmations for, 73
  side agreements with, 84
  telex/facsimile orders for, 61
ISO 9000 quality standards, 20
Israel, 24, 258
Israel Free Trade Agreement, 258
Italy, 98, 213, 297
ITC (International Trade Commission), 372

Jamaica, 215
Japan, 89, 213
jettison, 561
joint ventures with foreign companies, 57, 270, 276
Justitia International, 19, 241

Kazakhstan, 21, 203
Korea, *see* North Korea; South Korea
Kuwait, 24
Kyrgyzstan, 98, 203, 297

labeling
  for export, 32
  of imports, 263
languages, translation of, 57
Laos, 203, 213, 258
Latvia, 98, 203, 297
law, *see* legal issues
lay days, 561
L/C, *see* letter(s) of credit
LCL, 561
lease transactions
  export, 36
  import, 267

Index

Lebanon, 21, 24
Leeward and Windward Islands, 215
legal issues, 14
  Customs rulings, 262
  with distributors vs. agents, *102*
  dumping, 88, 289
  with warranties, 96
  see also dispute resolution
legalization, 561
Lesotho, 98, 297
letter agreements, 84
letter(s) of credit (L/C), *94,* 175, 178, 180, 270, 561
  advice of irrevocable, *187–188*
  application for, *271–274*
  checklist for, *275–276*
  checklist for beneficiary of, *182–185*
  discrepancies in, 178, 180, *181*
  example of, *189–190*
  instructions for, *179–180*
  for international purchases, 292, 293
  for international sales, 90–91
  standby, 92
  SWIFT codes for, 180, *191*
letters of indemnity/guaranty, *186,* 561–562
letters of instruction, 114, 116, *117,* 244, *246,* 566
liability(-ies)
  under Customs Modernization Act, 250
  for duties, 265
  in export distributor agreements, 108–109
  in import distributor agreements, 302–303
  product, 565
Liberia, 21, 234, 241
Libya, 203, 211, 234
  importation from, 241
  international boycotts in, 24
  prohibited imports from, 258
license(s), 22–23
  exchange control, 242–243
  export, 296, 557
  import, 97
  importing, 270, 276
  international sales agreement provisions for, 97
  and sales to affiliated companies, 57
  for tariff-rate quota imports, 254
  see also Export Administration Regulations
Liechtenstein, 213
lighterage, 562
liner service, 562
liquidation, 562
liquidation notices, 334, *335–336*
Lithuania, 98, 203, 297
litigation, 99–100, 298
London Court of International Arbitration, 100, 298
long-term agreements, 101
long ton, 562
loss, risk of, 95, 294–295
loss(es)
  casualty, 551
  total, 569
LTL, 562
Luxembourg, 98, 213, 297

machine tools, 243
Magnuson-Moss Warranty Act, 96, 295
Malawi, 120
Mali, 120
manifest, 562, 567
manuals of procedures and documentation, 8, 9, *11–12*
Manufacturer/Shipper Identification Code, rules for constructing, 527–531
maquiladora operations, 385
marine extension clause, 562
marine insurance, 120, 129, 133, *134–154,* 562
  for exports, 37–38, *39*
  for imports, 267
marine surveyor, 562
market, common, 552
marketing agreements, orderly, 564
market price, 263–264
market research, 18
marking laws, 562
marking requirements (country of origin), 260
mate's receipt, 562
maturity, 562
Mauritania, 120
measurement ton, 562–563
MERCOSUR, 563
metric ton, 563
Mexico, 120, 215, 311
  duty-free imports from, 258
  duty on exports to, 259
  as party to Convention on Contracts for the International Sale of Goods, 98, 297
  tariff-rate quotas on imports from, 254
  temporary importation from, 259
  see also North American Free Trade Agreement
Middle East, antiboycott compliance and exports to, 24
minimum freight, 563
minimum purchase quantities, 87
  export distributor agreement provisions for, 107
  import distributor agreement provisions for, 301
Miquelon and Saint Pierre Islands, 215
Moldova, 98, 120, 297
Mongolia, 98, 203, 234, 297
most favored nation, 563
munitions, 232, 234–235
Munitions Act, 197
Myanmar, 116

NAFTA, *see* North American Free Trade Agreement
NAFTA Certificate of Origin, 152, 162, *163–164,* 322, 324
National Association of State Development Agencies, 45
National Center for Standards and Certification Information, 20
National Customs Brokers and Freight Forwarders Association of America, 28
National Technical Information Service, 20
National Trade Data Bank, 19
negotiable instrument, 563
negotiation, 563
  for foreign distributor appointments, *104–106*
  for foreign sales agent appointments, *110–111*
Netherlands, 98, 213, 297
Netherlands Antilles, 215
New York Convention, 100, 299
New Zealand, 98, 213, 297
Nicaragua, 215
Nigeria, 24, 120
non-delivery, 568
non-disclosure agreements, *see* confidentiality and non-disclosure agreements
non-negotiable, 563
non-tariff barriers, 563
non-vessel operating common carrier (NVOCC), 563
North American Free Trade Agreement (NAFTA), 13, 152, 162
  and drawback, 375
  as duty-free/reduced duty program, 258
  duty on exports under, 259
  duty treatment under, 240
  and reconciliation, 322
  tariff-rate quotas under, 254
  temporary importations under, 259
North Korea, 203, 211, 213, 234
  duties on imports from, 258
  importation from, 241
  prohibited imports from, 258
Norway, 98, 213, 297
Notice of Action, 339, *342*
Notice of Redelivery, 334, *337–338*
notice(s)
  arrival, 309, *310,* 548
  liquidation, 334, *335–336*
  penalty, 353, *363–364*
  prepenalty, 353, *361–362*
  of seizure, 350, 353, *354–358*
notify party, 563
NVOCC (non-vessel operating common carrier), 563

O/A, *see* open account
ocean bill of lading, 118–120, *124–125*

Index

ODTC, *see* Office of Defense Trade Controls
offer and acceptance, process of, 61
offers
  of compromise, 365
  to purchase, 283
Office of Defense Trade Controls (ODTC), 232, 234–235
Oman, 24
OMAs (orderly marketing agreements), 564
on board notation (on board endorsement), 563–564
ongoing purchase transactions, 286–299
  agreements used in, 286–287, *see also* international purchase agreements
  documentation for, 287–288
  reasons for entering into, 286
ongoing sales transactions, 84–86
  agreements used in, 85, *see also* international sales agreements
  documentation for, 85–86
  reasons for entering into, 84–85
open account (O/A), 564
  buying on, 292
  selling on, 91–92, *93*
order bill of lading, 564
order entry function (export order processing), *7*
orderly marketing agreements (OMAs), 564
order(s)
  delivery, 162, *167,* 554
  general, 560
  pick-up, 565
Organization of Economic Cooperation and Developoment Anti-Bribery Convention, 113
OSD, 564
outside service providers, interrelationships with, *10*
Owens Online, 19, 241
Owner's Declaration, 250, *251*

P.A., *see* particular average
packing
  for export, 30, 32
  of imports, 262–263
packing lists, 120, *130,* 307, 309, 564
Pakistan, 24, 213
Panama, 133, 215
Paraguay, 215
parallel imports, 89, 291
particular average (P.A.), 559, 564
passage of title, 95
passport, 564
patents, 23, 268–269
pay, authority to, 549
payment insurance, 46
payment(s)
  of commissions, 109
  drafts for, 175, *176–177,* 309
  exchange control licenses for, 242–243
  for imports, 269–270, *271–277*
  for Internet sales, 58, 278–279
  made in third countries, 92
  methods of international, 90–92, *93–94,* 290, 292–294
penalties
  for country or origin marking removal, 260
  under Export Administration Act, 232
  for failing to provide documents, 13
  for import violations in foreign countries, 21
  for import violations in U.S., 250
penalty notices, 353, *363–364*
performance bond, 564
perils of the seas, 564
permanent establishment, 564
perpetual agreements, 101
Peru, 98, 120, 215, 258, 297
Petition for Remission or Mitigation, *360*
pick-up (delivery) orders, 162, *167,* 309, 311, *312,* 554, 565
pilferage, 568
plant construction contracts, 385, 387
plant export certificates, 169, 175
Poland, 98, 213, 215, 297
ports
  of entry, 250, 254
  free, 559
Portugal, 213
power of attorney, 565
  for customs brokers, 244, *245*
  for freight forwarders, 114, *115*
"precursor" chemicals, 169
predatory pricing, 88
preferential treatment laws, 21–22
prepenalty notices, 353, *361–362*
pre-shipment inspection clauses
  in international purchase agreements, 295–296
  in international sales agreements, 96–97
pre-shipment inspections, 565
prevailing market price, 263–264
price discounts
  in ongoing sales transactions, 85
  for quantity, 87
price lists
  for isolated purchase transactions, 283
  sales agreements vs., 63
prices/pricing
  discrimination in, 88, 289–290
  and dumping, 88, 289
  export distributor agreement provisions on, 106–107
  import distributor agreement provisions on, 301
  in international purchase agreements, 289–291
  in international sales agreements, 87–90
  prevailing market, 263–264
  rebates/discounts/allowances, and price escalation clauses in, 88, 290
  sales agent agreement provisions for, 109, 303
  transfer, 569
  in umbrella agreements, 86
  Web site quotations of, 58, 278
prior disclosure, 362, 365
processing and assembly operations, foreign, 382, *383–384,* 385
product competitiveness research, 18
product defect clauses
  in international purchase agreements, 295
  in international sales agreements, 95–96
product liability, 565
  export distributor agreement provisions for, 108–109
  import distributor agreement provisions for, 302–303
products
  customs classification of, 256, 262
  distributors' handling of competing, 107, 301–302
  export considerations with, 17
  import considerations with, 239–240
  with special import restrictions, 239–240
  warranties of, 95–96, 295
pro forma invoices, 73, 81, *82,* 307, *308,* 565
Protest and Instructions form, 339, *343–344,* 345
provisional insurance, 565
purchase, authority to, 549
purchase agreement(s), 281–283
  common forms for, 283–286
  formation of, 281–282
  formed by conduct, 282
  as most important import document, 280
  in multiple documents, 282
  in single documents, 281–282
purchase documentation, 280–304
  commercial invoices as, *83,* 285
  conflicting provisions in seller and buyer, 285–286
  and formation of purchase agreements, 281–283
  and importance of written agreements, 280–281
  international purchase agreements as, 288–299
  for isolated transactions, 280–286
  offers to purchase as, 283
  for ongoing transactions, 286–299
  price lists as, 283

purchase documentation (*continued*)
purchase order acknowledgments/acceptances as, *77–81,* 284–285
purchase orders as, *74–76,* 284
quotations as, *66–73,* 283–284
requests for quotations as, *64,* 283
and side agreements, 286
for telex/facsimile orders, 281
purchase orders, 65, 70, *74–76,* 284
acceptance of, 70, 73, *77–81,* 284–285
acknowledgment of, 70, 73, 284–285
purchase quantities, minimum
export distributor agreement provisions for, 107
import distributor agreement provisions for, 301
purchasing entities
in international purchase agreements, 288
in international sales agreements, 86–87

Qatar, 24
quantities, minimum
export distributor agreement provisions for, 107
import distributor agreement provisions for, 301
quantity terms
in international purchase agreements, 288–289
in international sales agreements, 87
quota(s), 20, 565
absolute, 547
export, 243, 557
import, 254–255
on imports from Communist countries, 258
tariff-rate, 254–255, 568
quotation function (export order processing), *6*
quotations, 65, *66–73*
example of, *68–70*
for export transactions, 65, *66*
form for, *67*
for purchase transactions, 283–284
request for, *64*

reasonable care, 256, 456–463
rebates, 88–89
receipt(s)
dock, 133, *158–159,* 555
mate's, 562
trust, 569
warehouse, 133, 570
received bill of lading, 565
reconciliation, 322
Recordkeeping Compliance Handbook, 13
record-keeping requirements, 9, 13
EAR, 223, 225
for imports, 262
recourse, 565
Redelivery, Notice of, 334, *337–338*
reduced duty programs, 257–258
re-export transactions, 223
relationship of parties, 112
Reliquidation, Request for, 334
remittance, 565
Request for Information, 339, *340–341*
Request for Reliquidation, 334
Request for Restrictive Trade Practice or Boycott
for multiple transactions, *26–27*
for single transaction, *25*
requests for quotations (RFQs), 63, *64,* 65, 283
resale, purchase for, 264
reselling, restriction of, 101–102
restricted imports, 239–240
revaluation, 565
Revised American Foreign Trade Definitions, 33, 264
revocable credit, 565–566
revolving credit, 566
RFQs, *see* requests for quotations
risk of loss, 95, 294–295
Robinson-Patman Act, 88
Romania, 98, 213, 215, 297
"routed" forwarders, 28, 30
royalties, 566
Russian Federation, 98, 203, 297
Rwanda, 120, 234

safety standards, 20
sale on open account, 91–92
sales agent (representative) agreements, 303–304
export distributor agreements vs., 101–103
for ongoing purchase transactions, 287
for ongoing sales transactions, 85
termination of, 101
sales agent(s)
distributors vs., 102–103, 300
functions/authority of, 102, 300
importer as, 241
import suppliers as, 241
sales agreements, 566
formation of, 61–63, *62*
formed by conduct, 63
governing law for, 62–63
as most important export document, 60
in multiple documents, 62
single-document, 61–62
validity of electronic, 58
sales confirmations, 74
sales documentation, 60–113
commercial invoices as, 81, *83*
conflicting provisions in seller and buyer, 81, 84
costing sheets as, 65, *66*
export distributor agreements as, 103–109
export sales agent agreements as, 109–112
and Foreign Corrupt Practices Act, 112–113
and formation of sales agreements, 61–63, *62*
and importance of written agreements, 60–61
international sales agreements as, 86–101
for isolated sales transactions, 60–84
nomenclature for terms of sale in, 33, 34
for ongoing sales transactions, 84–101
price lists as, 63
pro forma invoices as, 73, 81, *82*
purchase order acknowledgments/acceptances as, 70, 73, *77–81*
purchase orders as, 65, 70, *74–76*
quotations as, 65, *66–73*
requests for quotations as, 63, *64,* 65
sales confirmations as, 73
and side agreements, 84
for telex/facsimile orders, 61
sales visits to foreign countries, 24, 28
Saudi Arabia, 21, 24
Schedule B, 566
SCM (supply chain management) software, 14
S/D, *see* sight draft
search warrants, 345, *348–350*
security, Internet, 59, 279
security interest, 95, 294
SED, *see* Shipper's Export Declaration
seizure notices, 350, 353, *354–358*
selling commission, 566
selling entities
in international purchase agreements, 288
in international sales agreements, 86–87
Senegal, 116
September 11 terrorist attacks, xix
service contract, 566
shipment, sales agent agreement provisions for, 112, 303
shipment function (export order processing), *8*
shipper's association, 566
shipper's declarations (dangerous goods), 169, *170–171*
shipper's export declaration, 566
Shipper's Export Declaration (SED), 181, 186, *192–193,* 194–195, 223, 225
correct completion of (text), 419–436
price declaration on, 88

shipper's letter of instructions, 114, 116, *117,* 566
shipper's load and count (SL&C), 567
"Shippers Security Endorsement," 32
Shipping Act of 1984, 38, 44
shipping conference, 566
shipping permit, 567
ship's manifest, 567
short ton, 567
side agreements, 84, 286
Sierra Leone, 241
sight draft (S/D), 91, *94,* 270, 293, 567
SIL (Supplemental Information Letter), 345
Singapore, 98, 213, 297
single administrative document, 567
single transaction bonds, 244
SL&C (shipper's load and count), 567
Slovak Republic, 98, 213, 215, 297
Slovenia, 98, 297
Small Business Administration, 45
software programs, 13–14, 211, 230–232
Somalia, 234
sourcing (imports), 240–241
South America, 96
South Korea, 213
Spain, 98, 213, 297
special bond, exportation of articles under, *261*
Special Comprehensive Licenses, 225, 227, *228–230,* 230
special customs invoices, 162, *168,* 169
special endorsement, 567
specialized products Customs entry form(s), 324
  for agricultural products, *329–330*
  for electronic products, *325–328*
  for textiles, *331–332*
Specially Designated Nationalists and Terrorists List, 210
specific duty, 567
spot exchange, 567
S.R.&C.C. (strikes, riots and civil commotions), 568
Sri Lanka, 116
stale bill of lading, 567
Standards Council (Canada), 20
standby credit, 567
standby letters of credit, 92
state laws, 14
states, export financing programs through, 45
steamship tariff, *40–43*
steel, 243
stevedoring, 567
Stockholm Chamber of Commerce Arbitration Institute, 100, 298
stowage, 568
straight bill of lading, 119, 568
strikes, riots and civil commotions (S.R.&C.C.), 568
stripping, 568
stuffing, 568
subdistributors, appointment of, 107–108, 302
subpoenas, grand jury, 350, *351–352*
subrogation, 568
subsidiaries
  export to, 57
  importing from, 270, 276
  pricing considerations with, 89, 290–291
Sudan, 203, 234, 241
sue & labor clause, 568
summons, administrative, 345, *346–347*
Supplemental Information Letter (SIL), 345
suppliers, identification of, 241
supply chain management (SCM) software, 14
Surinam, 215
surveyors, 562, 568
Sweden, 98, 213, 297
Switzerland, 98, 213, 297
Syria, 203, 234
  importation from, 241
  international boycotts in, 24
  as party to Convention on Contracts for the International Sale of Goods, 98, 297

Taiwan, 213
Tajikistan, 203, 234
target quantities, 87
Tariff Act of 1930, 260
tariff-rate quotas, 254–255, 568
tariff(s), 20–21, 38, *40–43,* 568
  ad valorem, 547
  conference, 552
taxes/taxation
  and affiliated company buying prices, 290–291
  and affiliated company selling prices, 89
  on consignments, 36, 267
  of electronic commerce transactions, 59, 279
  and title transfer, 35, 36
  value-added, 22, 570
tax havens, 568
tax incentives, 86–87
tax reduction programs, 46
technology, 211, 230–232
Teikoku Data Bank American, Inc., 19, 241
telex orders, 61, 281
telex purchase transactions, 281
Temporary Importation Bond (TIB), 259–260
temporary importations, 24, 28, 259–260, *261*
tender, 568
tenor, 568
termination clauses
  in international purchase agreements, 299
  in international sales agreements, 101
terms and conditions of purchase, 264–266
  abbreviations used in, 264–265
  documentation to prevent conflict in, 84
  on requests for quotations, 65
terms and conditions of sale
  on commercial invoices, 81
  documentation to prevent conflict in, 84
  for electronic commerce, 58
  in export sales agreements, 32–36, *33, 34*
  in international sales agreements, 32–36, *33, 34*
  on pro forma invoices, 81
  in telex/facsimile orders, 61
territory
  export distributor agreement provisions for, 103, 106
  import distributor agreement provisions for, 300–301
TEU (twenty-foot equivalent unit), 568
textiles, *331–332*
  import quotas for, 255
  visas required for, 243
theft, pilferage &/or non-delivery, 568
through bill of lading, 568
TIB, *see* Temporary Importation Bond
TIC, *see* Trade Information Center
time drafts, 91, *93,* 270, 292–293, 568
titles
  passage of, 35, 36, 95, 294–295
TL, 569
ton(s)
  long, 562
  measurement, 562–563
  metric, 563
  short, 567
total loss, 569
trade
  free, 559
  invisible, 561
Trade Act of 1974, 258, 372
trade fairs, foreign, 24
Trade Information Center (TIC), 18
  Export Programs Guide of (text), 393–408
  software list of, 13–14
trademarks, 23, 268–269, 569
  export distributor agreement provisions for, 108
  import distributor agreement provisions for, 302
trade names
  export distributor agreement provisions for, 108

trade names (*continued*)
  import distributor agreement provisions for, 302
Trade Opportunities Program, 19
trade usages, 63
trade zones, foreign, 558
Trading with the Enemy Act, 197
tramp, 569
transaction value, 256–257, 267
transferable credit, 569
transfer pricing, 569
translation, 57, 270
transportation
  of electronic sales products, 278
  with ex-factory sales, 266
  for exports, 38, 44
  for imports, 268
Transportation Entry, 317, *318–319*
trial marketing agreements, 85
Trinidad and Tobago, 215
trust receipt, 569
Turkey, 213
Turkmenistan, 203
twenty-foot equivalent unit (TEU), 568

UCP (uniform customs and practice for documentary credits), 569
Uganda, 98, 297
Ukraine, 21, 98, 203, 297
umbrella agreements, 85–86
unconfirmed credit, 569
Uniform Commercial Code, 305, 569
  abbreviations in, 265
  and bills of lading, 119
  enforceable purchase agreements under, 281
  enforceable sales agreements under, 60–61
  packaging warranties under, 32
  terms of sale in, 33
uniform customs and practice for documentary credits (UCP), 569
uniform rules for collections (URC), 569
United Arab Emirates, 24
United Kingdom, 213
United Nations, 32, 240
unitization, 569
Untied Nations, 18
URC (uniform rules for collections), 569
Uruguay, 98, 215, 297
Uruguay Round (GATT), 254
U.S. Bureau of Census, 18
U.S. Congress, 14, 372
U.S. Council of International Business, 28
U.S. Court of Appeals, 365
U.S. Customs Service
  customs audit questionnaires of (text), 535–540
  electronic interfaces with, 244
  record-keeping requirements of, 9, 13
U.S. Department of Agriculture, 169, 175
  export financing available through, 45
  food import regulations of, 262
  tariff-rate quotas under, 254
U.S. Department of Justice, 353
U.S. Department of Transportation, 262
U.S. dollar, xix
U.S. Export-Import (EXIM) Bank
  financing available through, 45–46, *47–49*
  payment insurance through, 46
U.S. Foreign Assets Control Regulations, 241
U.S. Foreign Trade Zones Board, 259
U.S. Munitions List, 232
U.S. Supreme Court, 365
usance, 569
Uzbekistan, 98, 120, 203, 297

valuation, 21, 570
  of consignments, 267
  of imports, 256–257
  of lease transactions, 36, 267
  true prices in, 88–89
value-added tax (VAT), 22, 570
Venezuela, 98, 215, 297
Vietnam, 203, 234
visa, 570
visas, 24, 243
volume
  of exported product, 18
  of imported products, 240
  Voluntary Restraint Agreements (VRAs), 243, 570

W.A. (with average), 570
warehouse receipts, 133, 570
warehouses, bonded, 550
warehouse to warehouse clause, 267, 570
warehousing, foreign, 45
warranties
  export distributor agreement provisions for, 108–109
  import distributor agreement provisions for, 302–303
  in international purchase agreements, 295
  in international sales agreements, 95–96
  sales agent agreement provisions for, 112
war risk insurance, 570
Warsaw Terms, 33, 264
Wassenaar arrangement, 242
Web sites, export/import-related, 543–546
weight, certificate of, 551
wharfage, 570
wire transfers, 92, 293
with average (W.A.), 570
World Bank, 45
World Trade and Customs Directory, 21
World Trade Organization (WTO), 46, 570
written agreements
  for exports, 60–61
  for imports, 280–281
  for isolated purchase transactions, 280–281

Yemen, 24
York Antwerp Rules of General Average, 570
Yugoslavia, 21, 98, 234, 297

Zaire, 234
Zambia, 98, 297
Zanzibar, 120

About the Author

Thomas E. Johnson is a partner in the Chicago office of the international law firm of Sandler, Travis & Rosenberg, P.A. Sandler, Travis & Rosenberg, P.A. concentrates its practice in export, import, trade, and international business transactions.

Mr. Johnson received his B.S. degree in economics and international relations from the University of Utah. Thereafter, he lived in Japan, where he learned to speak and read Japanese. Upon returning from Japan, he completed his J.D. cum laude at Northwestern University Law School in Chicago.

Mr. Johnson was with the law firm of Baker & McKenzie for twenty-three years before joining Sandler, Travis & Rosenberg's Chicago office. He is a member of the Illinois and Washington, D.C. bars and is admitted to practice before the Court of International Trade. He is a member of the American Bar Association, Sections of International and Business Law, and the Illinois State and Chicago Bar Associations, Committees on Customs and International Trade.

Mr. Johnson was selected for inclusion in the sixth, seventh, eighth, and ninth editions of *Who's Who in American Law* and the current edition of *Who's Who in Emerging Leaders in America.*

Appointed five times by the U.S. Secretary of Commerce to serve on the Illinois District Export Council, Mr. Johnson is also a member of the Illinois World Trade Center Development Board. In addition, he is past president of the International Trade Club of Chicago and a member of the American Association of Exporters and Importers, the Japan America Society of Chicago, and the American Marketing Association.

Mr. Johnson has lectured on the law of international business transactions for the American Management Association, the Department of State, the Department of Commerce, the World Trade Institute, numerous district export councils, economic development associations and international trade groups, and at world trade conferences and continuing legal education seminars. He has contributed chapters to two books on international business and has published numerous articles on international business in professional and trade journals and magazines.

Mr. Johnson may be contacted at TJohnson@strtrade.com, telephone number (312) 236-6555, fax number (312) 236-6568.